Fast & Easy ECGs

A Self-Paced Learning Program

Second Edition

Bruce Shade
EMT-P, EMS-I, AAS

Connect
Learn
Succeed™

6 7 8 9 LWI 21 20 19 18 17

ISBN 978-0-07-351975-3
MHID 0-07-351975-8

Freelance sponsoring editor: *Kelly H. Lowery, Collaboratellc*
Director, digital products: *Crystal Szewczyk*
Freelance development editor: *Laura Horowitz*
Digital development editor: *Kevin White*
Director, Editing/Design/Production: *Jess Ann Kosic*
Lead project manager: *Rick Hecker*
Senior buyer: *Kara Kudronowicz*
Senior designer: *Srdjan Savanovic*
Senior photo research coordinator: *John C. Leland*
Manager, digital production: *Janean A. Utley*
Media project manager: *Brent dela Cruz*
Interior design: *Pam Verros*
Typeface: *11/13 Minion Pr*
Compositor: *Laserwords Private Limited*
Printer: *LSC Communications*
Credits: The credits section for this book begins on page 696 and is considered an extension of the copyright page.

Library of Congress Cataloging-in-Publication Data

Shade, Bruce R.
    Fast & easy ECGs : a self-paced learning program / Bruce Shade. — 2nd ed.
    p. ; cm.
    Fast and easy ECGs
    Includes index.
    ISBN 978-0-07-351975-3 (alk. paper) — ISBN 0-07-351975-8 (alk. paper)
    I. Title. II. Title: Fast and easy ECGs.
    [DNLM: 1. Electrocardiography—methods—Case Reports. WG 140]

    616.1'207547—dc23   2012004702

The Internet addresses listed in the text were accurate at the time of publication. The inclusion of a Web site
does not indicate an endorsement by the authors or McGraw-Hill, and McGraw-Hill does not guarantee the
accuracy of the information presented at these sites.

www.mhhe.com

About the Author

Bruce Shade is currently employed as the Director of Fleet, Facilities and Support Services for Operations at Community Care Ambulance in Northeast Ohio. He is also a part-time paramedic/firefighter for the City of Willoughby, Ohio, and a paramedic instructor at Cuyahoga Community College (Tri-C) in Cleveland. Bruce is also a member of the Ohio Emergency Medical Services Board.

Bruce has been involved in emergency services since 1972. He started as a volunteer firefighter/EMT and has served as paramedic, educational supervisor, paramedic training program director, and commissioner for the City of Cleveland's Division of Emergency Medical Service. He also served as executive administrator, Disaster and Emergency Coordinator, and Assistant Public Safety Director for the city before retiring in 2006.

Bruce is past President, Vice President, and Treasurer of the National Association of EMTs and chairperson of the Instructor Coordinator Society. He has served as president of several local associations and chairperson of many committees and task forces. Bruce has authored several EMS textbooks and written many EMS-related articles. He has lectured extensively at local, regional, state, and national EMS conferences.

Dedication

This book is dedicated to my wife Cheri, my children Chris and Katie, my son-in-law Mike Tousignant, and my father Elmer Shade, Jr., for all their love and support.

I also want to dedicate this book to several people who made an indelible impression on my life including Claire Merrick (first editor on this textbook), Mitchell J. Brown (public safety director, City of Columbus, Ohio) and Mary Ann Talley (former director of University of South Alabama paramedic training program).

Contents

Preface   xx
Features to Help You Study and Learn   xxii
Acknowledgments   xxv

Section 1: Preparatory

Chapter 1	Anatomy and Electrophysiology of the Heart	2

The Electrocardiogram   4

How Does the Electrocardiogram Work?   5

Structure of the Heart   6
Shape and Position of the Heart   7
The Pericardial Sac   7
The Heart Wall   9
The Internal Heart   10

Cells of the Heart   12
Myocyctes   12
Pacemaker and Electrical Conducting Cells   14

Nerve Impulse Generation and Muscle Contraction   15
Polarized State   15
Depolarization   16
Repolarization   17
Refractory Periods   17

The Heart's Conductive Pathway   18
SA Node   18
AV Node   20
Bundle of His and Right and Left Bundle Branches   20
Purkinje Fibers   20
Alternate Pacemaker Sites   21

The Circulatory System   21
The Heart's Blood Supply   22

How Blood Is Circulated   23
The Cardiac Cycle   23
Cardiac Output   24
Blood Pressure   25

Putting It All Together   25

  Blood Flow through the Atria   25

  Initiation of Impulse in the SA Node   26

  Atrial Depolarization and Contraction   26

  Conduction through the AV Node   27

  Conduction through the His-Purkinje System   28

  Ventricular Depolarization and Contraction   29

  Atrial and Ventricular Repolarization   30

**Influences on the Heart
and Circulatory System**   30

  The Autonomic Nervous System   31

  Sympathetic Nervous System   32

  Parasympathetic Nervous System   33

Chapter 2   **The Electrocardiogram   42**

The Electrocardiogram   44

ECG Machines   44

The Input   47

  Lead Wires and Cables   47

  Electrocardiogram Electrodes   49

  ECG Leads   51

  Lead II   56

The Output   57

  Displays and Printouts   58

  Reading Printouts   59

Calibrating the ECG   61

Artifact   62

Section 2: The Nine-Step Process

Chapter 3   **Analyzing the Electrocardiogram   70**

Characteristics of the Normal ECG   72

Analyzing the Electrocardiogram   72

The Nine-Step Process   73

  Step 1: Heart Rate   73

  Step 2: Regularity   73

  Step 3: P Waves   74

Step 4: QRS Complexes   75
Step 5: PR Intervals   75
Step 6: ST Segments   77
Step 7: Waves   77
Step 8: QT Intervals   78
Step 9: U Waves   79

Flexibility in the Nine-Step Process   79

Dysrhythmia and Cardiac Condition Characteristics   80

Analyzing the ECG on the Monitor Screen   82

Analyzing the Rhythm Strip   83

Analyzing the 12-Lead Tracing   84

Chapter 4   Heart Rate   92

Importance of Determining the Heart Rate   94

Quick Check of the Heart Rate   94

Heart Rates Seen with Various Dysrhythmias   95

Methods of Determining Heart Rate   95
6-Second Interval × 10 Method   96
300, 150, 100, 75, 60, 50 Method   98
1500 Method   101
Rate Calculators   103

**Counting Both the Atrial
and Ventricular Rates   103**

Normal, Slow, and Fast Rates   104
Slow Rates—Bradycardia   104
Fast Rates—Tachycardia   104

Chapter 5   Regularity   108

Importance of Determining Regularity   110

Quick Check of Regularity   110

Methods of Determining Regularity   111
Paper and Pen Method   112
Caliper Method   114
Counting the Small Squares Method   115
Using a Rate Calculator   115

Types of Irregularity   116
Occasionally or Very Irregular   116

Slightly Irregular   119
Irregularity Caused by Sudden Changes
   in the Heart Rate   120
Irregularly (Totally) Irregular   121
Patterned Irregularity   122
Irregularity Caused by Varying Conduction Ratios   125

Chapter 6   P Waves   130

Importance of Determining the P Waves   132
Quick Check of the P Waves   132
Examining the P Waves   133
P Waves Having a Different Appearance   134
Atrial P Waves   135
Varying Atrial P Waves   136
Flutter and Fibrillatory Waves   138
Inverted and Absent P Waves   140
More P Waves than QRS Complexes   142

Chapter 7   QRS Complexes   150

Importance of Determining the QRS Complexes   152
Quick Check of the QRS Complexes   152
Examining the QRS Complexes   153
Measuring QRS Complexes   154
Variations in the QRS Configuration   155
QRS Complexes in Different Leads   156
Where We See Normal QRS Complexes   157
Abnormal QRS Complexes   158
Tall and Low Amplitude QRS Complexes   159
Wide QRS Complexes of Supraventricular Origin   159
Wide, Bizarre-Looking QRS Complexes of Ventricular Origin   163
Absent QRS Complexes   169

Chapter 8   PR Intervals   178

Importance of Determining the PR Intervals   180
Quick Check of the PR Intervals   180
Characteristics of Normal PR Intervals   180
Measuring the PR Intervals   181

PR Intervals That Are Different   181

    Shorter PR Intervals   182
    Longer PR Intervals   184
    Varying PR Intervals   187
    Absent or Not Measurable PR Intervals   188
    Constant PR Intervals Seen with More P Waves   192

Chapter 9   ST Segments, T Waves, QT Intervals, and U Waves   198

Analyzing the Electrocardiogram   200

ST Segments   200

    Normal Characteristics   200
    Measuring the ST Segments   201
    Abnormal ST Segments   202

T Waves   203

    Normal Characteristics   203
    Measuring the T Waves   204
    Abnormal T Waves   205

QT Intervals   206

    Normal Characteristics   206
    Measuring the QT Interval   206
    Abnormal QT Intervals   208

U Waves   209

    Normal Characteristics   209
    Abnormal U Waves   210

Section 2 Practice Makes Perfect   215

Section 3: Origin and Clinical Aspects of Dysrhythmias

Chapter 10   Overview of Dysrhythmias   220

The Heart's Normal Electrical Activity   222

    Nerve Impulse Generation in the Heart   222
    Impulse Generation of the SA Node   223
    Depolarization and Repolarization of the Myocytes   224
    Refractory Periods   228

Dysrhythmias   229

The Effects of Dysrhythmias   229

Characterizing Dysrhythmias   231

    Types of Dysrhythmias   231
    Causes and Mechanisms of Dysrhythmias   235

Site of Origin   239
Sinus Dysrhythmias   239
Atrial Dysrhythmias   239
Junctional Dysrhythmias   240
Ventricular Dysrhythmias   240
AV Heart Block   240

Leads Used to Identify Dysrhythmias   240

How to Spot Dysrhythmias   241

Treatment of Dysrhythmias   241
Physical Maneuvers   243
Electrical Therapy   243
Medications   244

Chapter 11   **Sinus Dysrhythmias   252**

Rhythms Originating from the Sinus Node   254
Appearance of Sinus Rhythms   254
Normal Sinus Rhythm   256

Sinus Bradycardia   257
Description   257
Causes   257
Effects   258
Appearance   259
Treatment   259

Sinus Tachycardia   259
Description   259
Causes   259
Effects   260
Appearance   261
Treatment   261

Sinus Dysrhythmia   261
Description   261
Causes   262
Appearance   263
Treatment   263

Sinus Arrest   263
Description   263
Causes   263
Effects   264
Appearance   265
Treatment   265

Sinoatrial Exit Block 265
   Description 265
   Causes 266
   Effects 266
   Appearance 266
   Treatment 267

Sick Sinus Syndrome 267
   Description 267
   Causes 267
   Effects 268
   Appearance 268
   Treatment 269

Sinus Rhythm as the Underlying Rhythm 269

Practice Makes Perfect 270

Chapter 12   Atrial Dysrhythmias 290

Rhythms Originating in the Atria 292
   P Wave Appearance 292
   QRS Complex Appearance 292
   Effects of Atrial Dysrhythmias 293

Premature Atrial Complexes 293
   Description 293
   Causes 293
   Effects 295
   Appearance 295
   Differentiating Blocked PACs from Sinus Arrest 299
   Treatment 299

Wandering Atrial Pacemaker 300
   Description 300
   Causes 300
   Effects 300
   Appearance 300
   Treatment 301

Atrial Tachycardia 301
   Description 301
   Causes 302
   Effects 302
   Appearance 303
   Treatment 304

Multifocal Atrial Tachycardia   305
  Description   305
  Causes   305
  Effects   306
  Appearance   306
  Treatment   306

Supraventricular Tachycardia   306
Atrial Flutter   307
  Description   307
  Causes   307
  Effects   307
  Appearance   308
  Treatment   309

Atrial Fibrillation   309
  Description   309
  Causes   309
  Effects   309
  Appearance   311
  Treatment   311

Practice Makes Perfect   312

Chapter 13   Junctional Dysrhythmias   332

Dysrhythmias Originating in the Atrioventricular Junction   334
  P Wave Appearance   334
  QRS Complex Appearance   335
  Effects   335

Premature Junctional Complex   335
  Description   335
  Causes   335
  Effects   337
  Appearance   337
  Treatment   338

Junctional Escape Rhythm   338
  Description   338
  Causes   338
  Effects   339
  Appearance   339
  Treatment   340

Accelerated Junctional Rhythm   340
  Description   340

Causes   340
Effects   341
Appearance   341
Treatment   342

Junctional Tachycardia   342
Description   342
Causes   343
Effects   343
Appearance   343

Atrioventricular Nodal Reentrant Tachycardia   344
Description   344
Appearance   345
Effects   346

Preexcitation   346
Wolff-Parkinson-White Syndrome   347
Lown-Ganong-Levine Syndrome   347

Atrioventricular Reentrant Tachycardia   348
Description   348
Appearance   349
Effects   350

Treatment of Supraventricular Tachycardia   350
Practice Makes Perfect   352

Chapter 14   Ventricular Dysrhythmias   370

Dysrhythmias Originating in the Ventricles   372
P Wave Appearance   372
QRS Complex Appearance   373
Effects   373

Premature Ventricular Complexes   373
Description   373
Causes   374
Effects   376
Appearance   376
Treatment   381

Ventricular Escape Beats   381
Description   381
Causes   382
Effects   382
Appearance   382
Treatment   383

Idioventricular Rhythm   384

Description   384
Causes   385
Effects   385
Appearance   385
Treatment   386

Accelerated Idioventricular Rhythm   386

Description   386
Causes   386
Effects   386
Appearance   386
Treatment   386

Ventricular Tachycardia   387

Description   387
Causes   388
Effects   389
Appearance   389
Treatment   389

Polymorphic Ventricular Tachycardia   389

Description   389
Causes   390
Effects   391
Appearance   391
Treatment   391

Ventricular Fibrillation   391

Description   391
Causes   391
Effects   392
Appearance   392
Treatment   392

Asystole   393

Description   393
Causes   393
Effects   394
Appearance   395
Treatment   395

Pulseless Electrical Activity   395

Description   395
Causes   395

Effects   396
Appearance   396
Treatment   396

Practice Makes Perfect   397

Chapter 15   AV Heart Blocks   416

Block of the Atrioventricular Node   418

1st-Degree Atrioventricular Heart Block   419
Description   419
Causes   419
Effects   420
Appearance   420
Treatment   421

2nd-Degree Atrioventricular Heart Block, Type I   421
Description   421
Causes   422
Effects   422
Appearance   422
Treatment   423

2nd-Degree Atrioventricular Heart Block, Type II   423
Description   423
Causes   423
Effects   424
Appearance   424
Treatment   425

3rd-Degree Atrioventricular Heart Block   425
Description   425
Causes   426
Effects   426
Appearance   426
Treatment   427

Atrioventricular Dissociation   427
Description   427
Causes   428
Effects   429
Appearance   429
Treatment   429

Practice Makes Perfect   430

Chapter 16   Pacemakers and Implantable
             Cardioverter-Defibrillators   448

     Pacemakers and Implantable Defibrillators   450
     Temporary Pacemakers   450
        Epicardial Pacing   450
        Transvenous Pacing   450
     Permanent Pacemakers   450
        Uses   451
        Generator   451
        Lead Wire(s)   453
        Function   453
        Cardiac Resynchronization Therapy   456
     Appearance of the Paced ECG   456
        Unipolar vs. Bipolar Systems   458
     Pacemaker Failure   458
        Failure to Capture   458
        Failure to Pace   459
        Failure to Sense   460
        Oversensing   461
        Pacemaker-Mediated Tachycardia   461
     Complications of Pacemakers   462
        Infection   462
        Pacemaker Syndrome   462
     Implantable Cardioverter-Defibrillators   462
        Pulse Generator   463
        Electrode Wires   464
        Recognition of Ventricular Dysrhythmias   464
        Therapies Provided by the ICD   465
        Provider Safety   466
     Practice Makes Perfect   467

Section 4: 12-Lead ECGs

Chapter 17   Overview of 12-Lead ECGs and Electrical Axis   478

     Heart's Normal Electrical Activity   480
     The 12-Lead ECG   480
        Views   480
     Planes of the Heart   481
        Frontal Plane   481

Horizontal Plane   487

Putting the Views Together   499
   Specific Leads and Associated Views   499
   Contiguous Leads   500

15- and 18-Lead ECGs   500

Analyzing the 12-Lead ECG   502

Electrical Axis and the ECG   504
   Vectors   504
   Mean Instantaneous Vector   505
   Waveform Direction   505
   Ventricular Depolarization and Mean QRS Axis   505

Calculating the Electrical Axis   508
   Hexaxial Reference System   508

Altered QRS Axis   515

Practice Makes Perfect   520

Chapter 18   Atrial Enlargement and Ventricular Hypertrophy   532

Hypertrophy and Enlargement   534
   Changes on the ECG   535

Atrial Enlargement   535
   Right Atrial Enlargement   537
   Left Atrial Enlargement   538

Ventricular Hypertrophy   539
   Right Ventricular Hypertrophy   539
   Left Ventricular Hypertrophy   541
   ST Segment and T Wave Changes   543

Practice Makes Perfect   544

Chapter 19   Bundle Branch Block   550

Ventricular Conduction Disturbances   552

The Bundle Branches   552

Bundle Branch Block   554
   Right Bundle Branch Block   556
   Left Bundle Branch Block   558
   Bundle Branch Block and Repolarization   560
   Incomplete Bundle Branch Block   560
   Hemiblock   560

Bifascicular and Trifascicular Blocks   562
Treatments of Bundle Branch Block   564

Practice Makes Perfect   565

Chapter 20   Myocardial Ischemia, Injury, and Infarction   570

Coronary Circulation   572
Right Main Coronary Artery   572
Left Main Coronary Artery   572
Coronary Veins   573
Increased Oxygen Needs   573

The ECG Waveforms   574
Q Waves   574
Normal ST Segments   575
Normal T Waves   576

Coronary Artery Disease   577
Myocardial Ischemia   577
Myocardial Injury   579
Myocardial Infarction   579

ECG Indicators of Ischemia, Injury, and Infarction   580
T Wave Changes   581
ST Segment Changes   584
Q Wave Changes   588
Bundle Branch Block   589
Reciprocal Changes   590
ECG Evolution during Myocardial Infarction   591

Criteria for Diagnosing Myocardial Infarction   593
Clinical History   593
Serum Cardiac Markers   593
ECG Findings   593

Identifying the Myocardial Infarction Location   594
Septal Wall Infarction   594
Anterior Wall Infarction   594
Lateral Wall Infarction   594
Anterolateral Wall Infarction   594
Extensive Anterior Wall Infarction   595
Inferior Infarction   595
Posterior Wall Infarction   596
Right Ventricular Infarction   600

Treatment of Myocardial Infarction   601
   Right Ventricular Infarction Treatment   602
Practice Makes Perfect   603

Chapter 21   Other Cardiac Conditions and the ECG   612

Pericarditis   614
   ECG Changes   614
Pericardial Effusion   615
   ECG Changes   617
Pulmonary Embolism   618
   ECG Changes   618
Electrolyte Imbalance   620
   Hyperkalemia   620
   Hypokalemia   622
   Calcium Disorders   623
Drug Effects and Toxicity   623
   Digoxin   623
   Other Medications   625
Practice Makes Perfect   627

Section 5: Review and Assessment

Chapter 22   Putting It All Together   636

Using the Nine-Step Process and Deductive Analysis   638
Step 1: Heart Rate   638
   Slow Rate   638
   Normal Rate   639
   Fast Rate   639
Step 2: Regularity   639
   Regular Rhythms   640
   Irregular Rhythms   640
Step 3: P Waves   641
   Normal P Waves   641
   Abnormal P Waves   641
Step 4: QRS Complexes   643
   Normal QRS Complexes   643
   Abnormal QRS Complexes   643

Step 5: PR Intervals   645

Normal PR Intervals   645

Abnormal PR Intervals   646

Step 6: ST Segments   646

Normal ST Segments   646

Abnormal ST Segments   646

Step 7: T Waves   648

Normal T Waves   648

Abnormal T Waves   648

Step 8: QT Intervals   650

Normal QT Intervals   650

Abnormal QT Intervals   650

Step 9: U Waves   650

So Why Do It?   652

Practice Ruling Out Dysrhythmias and Conditions   653

Practice Makes Perfect   666

Appendix A   677

Glossary   689

Credits   696

Index   697

Preface

This book is designed to dynamically teach healthcare professionals how to interpret electrocardiograms (ECGs). It presents the information similar to how an instructor might deliver it in the classroom, with lots of illustrations, solid practical content, questions to prompt critical thinking, case presentations, and plentiful practice ECG tracings to promote the application of skills.

One of the first things readers will notice about this text is it is more of a "how-to book" than a "theoretical book." Although there is plenty of detail, the coverage is to the point, telling you and then showing you what you need to know. The breadth of information ranges from simple to complex, but regardless of how advanced the material, the explanations and visuals make the concepts easy to understand. Another aspect of the second edition is that it truly covers both dysrhythmia and 12-lead analysis and interpretation. It reinforces those core concepts from the beginning to the end. This book includes plentiful pictures and figures to help readers see what is being discussed in actual use. We have also included coverage of the treatments used to manage the various dysrhythmias and cardiac conditions to give readers a broader perspective and better prepare them for applying what they have learned.

Structure of the Second Edition

The second edition is divided into five sections:

- **Section 1, Preparatory,** looks at the underlying concepts of the anatomy and electrophysiology of the heart and the electrocardiogram itself.
- **Section 2, The Nine-Step Process,** comprises Chapters 3 through 9 and presents the nine-step process of ECG interpretation. Each chapter provides an in-depth look at one of the steps and introduces the reader to the variances seen with that step.
- **Section 3, Origin and Clinical Aspects of Dysrhythmias,** comprises Chapters 10 through 16 and leads readers through a thorough discussion regarding dysrhythmias. The section covers the origin of dysrhythmias, including the sinus node, the atria, the atrioventricular junction, the ventricles, atrioventricular heart blocks, and pacemakers. And it covers the clinical aspects of each dysrhythmia.
- **Section 4, 12-Lead ECGs,** introduces the concept of 12-lead ECGs in Chapter 17. Then Chapters 18 through 21 cover interpretation and recognition of atrial enlargement and ventricular hypertrophy, bundle branch block, myocardial injury, ischemia and infarction, and a host of other cardiac conditions and their effect on the ECG.
- **Section 5, Review and Assessment,** wraps it all up with the chapter "Putting It All Together" and more practice tracings.

Changes to the Second Edition

The second edition of *Fast & Easy ECGs: A Self-Paced Learning Program* by Bruce Shade is thorough, innovative, and greatly enhanced.

Whereas the first edition had 16 chapters, the second edition is expanded and includes 22 chapters. The following chapters are brand new to this edition:

- **Chapter 3, Analyzing the Electrocardiogram,** gives an overview of the analysis process and introduces the nine-step process for reading ECGs that is used throughout the book.

- **Chapter 9, ST Segments, T Waves, QT Intervals, and U Waves,** is devoted to topics that were included only as subsections in the first edition.

- **Chapter 10, Overview of Dysrhythmias,** gives an overview of all dysrhythmias, including how they are characterized and treatments for them. Coverage of sinoatrial block, sick sinus syndrome, atrioventricular reentrant tachycardia (AVRT), atrioventricular nodal reentrant tachycardia (AVNRT) and ventricular escape have been added. Broader coverage of the electrophysiology of the heart's conduction system and muscle is also included.

- **Chapter 16, Pacemakers and Implanted Cardioverter-Defibrillators,** was previously a subsection but is now expanded to fill an entire chapter.

- **Chapters 17–21** are new to this edition and offer full coverage of 12-lead ECGs and introduces the reader to 15- and 18-lead ECGs.

- **Chapter 22, Putting It All Together,** recaps the entire book and the nine-step process outlined in Chapters 3–9 and used throughout the book.

In addition to the expanded content, *Fast & Easy ECGs* has more than 300 figures and over 400 practice strips. This book also introduces the reader to the treatment modalities for the various dysrhythmias and medical conditions.

We hope the second edition of *Fast & Easy ECGs* is beneficial to both students and instructors. Greater understanding of ECG interpretation will lead to better patient care everywhere.

Features to Help You Study and Learn

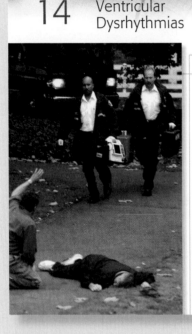

14 Ventricular Dysrhythmias

Chapter Outline

Dysrhythmias Originating in the Ventricles
Premature Ventricular Complexes
Ventricular Escape Beats
Idioventricular Rhythm
Accelerated Idioventricular Rhythm
Ventricular Tachycardia
Polymorphic Ventricular Tachycardia
Ventricular Fibrillation
Asystole
Pulseless Electrical Activity

Preview the Chapter Content

Study the Chapter Outline to get an overview of the subjects to be covered in the chapter.

Learning Objectives

LO 14.1 Describe the origin of ventricular dysrhythmias.

LO 14.2 Describe the key features of dysrhythmias originating from the ventricles.

LO 14.3 Identify the causes, effects, and appearance of premature ventricular complexes.

LO 14.4 Identify the causes, effects, and appearance of ventricular escape beats.

LO 14.5 Identify the causes, effects, and appearance of idioventricular rhythm.

LO 14.6 Identify the causes, effects, and appearance of accelerated idioventricular rhythm.

LO 14.7 Identify the causes, effects, and appearance of ventricular tachycardia.

LO 14.8 Identify the causes, effects, and appearance of polymorphic ventricular tachycardia.

LO 14.9 Identify the causes, effects, and appearance of ventricular fibrillation.

LO 14.10 Identify the causes, effects, and appearance of asystole.

LO 14.11 Identify the causes, effects, and appearance of pulseless electrical activity.

Review the Learning Objectives to see what you will learn. Note that the Learning Objectives numbers are keyed to the text.

LO 14.8 Identify the causes, effects, and appearance of polymorphic ventricular tachycardia.

LO 14.9 Identify the causes, effects, and appearance of ventricular fibrillation.

LO 14.10 Identify the causes, effects, and appearance of asystole.

LO 14.11 Identify the causes, effects, and appearance of pulseless electrical activity.

Case History

It's two o'clock P.M. when pagers go off, alerting your EMS crew of a male who collapsed outside his home.

Upon arrival you find the patient lying next to the sidewalk. You immediately determine an absence of a pulse and initiate chest compressions. Your partner verifies he can feel a carotid pulse with compressions. She then begins ventilating the patient with a bag-valve-mask (BVM) and 100% oxygen. Shortly afterward a fire department first responder unit arrives on scene to help.

Read the Case History for a real-world scenario that features the type of dysrhythmia covered in the chapter.

371

Visualize the Content

300 Full-Color Figures show you in detail where each dysrhythmia originates and teaches you step by step how to read the ECGs that demonstrate each dysrhythmia. In addition, algorithms and tables present content visually to help you memorize the most important elements of each type of dysrhythmia and condition.

Utilize the Sidebar Elements

Sidebar Elements offer a wealth of information.

- **Key Concepts** reiterate the most important content.

- **Reminders** help you remember pertinent content from earlier chapters or the chapter currently being read.

- **Questions** help you recall important information. Answers to the sidebar questions are included at the end of each chapter.

- **Want More Information?** directs you to the Shade website for more information on the topic.

Review the Content

Practice Makes Perfect strips at the end of chapters and sections give you over 400 opportunities to interpret ECG strips using your new knowledge.

Practice Makes Perfect

For each of the 57 ECG tracings on the following pages, practice the Nine-Step Process for analyzing ECGs. To achieve the greatest learning, you should practice assessing and interpreting the ECGs immediately after reading this chapter. Below are questions you should consider as you assess each tracing. Your answers can be written into the area above each ECG marked "ECG Findings". Your findings can then be compared to the answers provided in Appendix A.

1. Determine the heart rate. Is it slow? Normal? Fast? What is the ventricular rate? What is the atrial rate?
2. Determine if the rhythm is regular or irregular. If it is irregular, what type of irregularity is it? Occasional or Irregular? Slight? Sudden acceleration or slowing in heart rate? Total? Patterned? Does it have a variable conduction ratio?
3. Determine if P waves are present. If so, how do they appear? Do they have normal height and duration? Are they tall? Notched? Wide? Biphasic? Of differing morphology? Inverted? One for each QRS complex? More than one preceding some or all the QRS complexes? Do they have a sawtooth appearance? An indiscernible chaotic baseline?
4. Determine if QRS complexes are present. If so, how do they appear? Narrow with proper amplitude? Tall? Low amplitude? Delta wave? Notched? Wide? Bizarre? With chaotic waveforms?
5. Determine the presence of PR intervals. If present, how do they appear? Constant? Of normal duration? Shortened? Lengthened? Progressively longer? Varying?
6. Evaluate the ST segments. Do they have normal duration and position? Are they elevated? (If so, are they flat, concave, convex, arched?) Depressed? (If so, are they normal, flat, downsloping or upsloping?)
7. Determine if T waves are present. If so, how do they appear? Of normal height and duration? Tall? Wide? Notched? Inverted?
8. Determine the presence of QT intervals. If present, what is their duration? Normal? Shortened? Prolonged?
9. Determine if U waves are present. If present, how do they appear? Of normal height and duration? Inverted?
10. Identify the rhythm or dysrhythmia.

1.

ECG Findings:

Key Points cover all of the pertinent content in the chapter.

Key Points 🔑

- Ventricular dysrhythmias occur when the atria, AV junction, or both are unable to initiate an electrical impulse or when there is enhanced automaticity of the ventricular myocardium.
- A key feature of ventricular dysrhythmias are wide (greater than 0.12 seconds in duration), bizarre-looking QRS complexes that have T waves in the opposite direction of the R wave and an absence of P waves.
- Ventricular dysrhythmias include PVC, ventricular escape complexes or rhythm, VT, VF, and asystole.
- PVCs are early ectopic beats that interrupt the normal rhythm and originate from an irritable focus in the ventricular conduction system or muscle tissue.
- PVCs that look the same are called *uniform (unifocal)*, whereas PVCs that look different from each other are called *multiform (multifocal)*.
- PVCs occurring every other beat are called *bigeminal PVCs*, whereas PVCs occurring every third beat are called *trigeminal PVCs* and a PVC seen every fourth beat is called *ventricular quadrigeminy*.
- Two PVCs in a row are called a *couplet* and indicate extremely irritable ventricles.
- An interpolated PVC occurs but does not disrupt the normal cardiac cycle. It appears as a PVC squeezed between two regular complexes.
- Ventricular escape beats occur when there is temporary cessation of the heartbeat, such as with sinus arrest or when the rate of the underlying rhythm falls to less than that the inherent rate of the ventricles. They are compensatory in nature.
- Idioventricular rhythm is a slow dysrhythmia with wide QRS complexes that arise from the ventricles at a rate of 20 to 40 beats per minute.
- VT is a fast dysrhythmia, between 100 and 250 beats per minute, that arise from the ventricles. It is said to be present when there are three or more PVCs in a row. It may come in bursts of 6 to 10 complexes or may persist (sustained VT).
- VT can occur with or without pulses, and the patient may be stable or unstable with this rhythm.
- VT may be monomorphic, where the appearance of each QRS complex is similar, or polymorphic, where the appearance varies considerably from complex to complex.
- Torsades de pointes, which means twisting about the points, is form of VT that exhibits distinct characteristics on the ECG.
- VF results from chaotic firing of multiple sites in the ventricles. This causes the heart muscle to quiver rather than contract efficiently, producing no effective muscular contraction and an absence of cardiac output.
- On the cardiac monitor, VF appears like a wavy line, totally chaotic, without any logic.

- Asystole is the absence of any cardiac activity. It appears as a flat (or nearly flat) line on the monitor screen and produces a complete cessation of cardiac output.
- The presence of asystole should always be verified in two leads.
- PEA is a condition in which there is an organized electrical rhythm on the ECG monitor (which should produce a pulse) but the patient is pulseless and apneic. Sinus rhythm, sinus tachycardia, idioventricular rhythm, or any rhythm that is generally expected to generate a pulse may be the electrical activity seen with PEA.

Assess Your Understanding

The following questions give you a chance to assess your understanding of the material discussed in this chapter. The answers can be found in Appendix A.

1. Ventricular dysrhythmias
   a. originate above the bundle of His.
   b. are seldom life threatening.
   c. have QRS complexes greater than 0.12 seconds in duration.
   d. have notched P waves that precede each QRS complex.

2. The presence of PVCs is an indication of which of the following?
   a. Irritability of the myocardium
   b. Possible hypoxia
   c. Drug toxicity
   d. All of the above

3. Premature ventricular complexes (PVCs)
   a. arise from the AV node.
   b. have a QRS complex that appears narrow and normal in configuration.
   c. have T waves in the same direction as the R waves of complexes.
   d. are followed by a compensatory pause.

4. Match the following types of PVCs with the correct description.

Descriptions		Types of PVCs
a. PVCs that occur every other beat	____	R-on-T phenomenon
b. PVCs that appear different from one another	____	Multiform
c. Occur when the PVC wave falls on the T wave	____	Bigeminal
d. PVCs that occur every 4th beat	____	Quadrigeminal

5. Two PVCs in a row are called
   a. a run of PVCs.
   b. polymorphic.
   c. a couplet.
   d. interpolated.

Assess Your Understanding quizzes, with answers in Appendix A, help you recall the material and test your knowledge.

Referring to the scenario at the beginning of this chapter answer the following questions.

13. There is no pulse with VF because the
    a. heart is contracting too fast.
    b. heart is contracting too slow.
    c. heart is not contracting at all.
    d. stroke volume is too high.

14. The flat line rhythm that occurred after defibrillation is called
    a. asystole.
    b. sinus arrest.
    c. ventricular arrest.
    d. agonal.

15. The goal of defibrillation is to create _____ and hope that a pacemaker will awaken and stimulate ventricular contraction.
    a. sinus rhythm
    b. sinus tachycardia
    c. asystole
    d. VT

Answers to Sidebar Questions ❓

1. PVCs produce occasional irregularity unless there are many PVCs. **p. 376**
2. Noncompensatory pauses are seen with premature atrial complexes and premature junctional complexes. **p. 377**
3. Bigeminal, trigeminal, or quadrigeminal PVCs produce regularly or patterned irregularity. This is where the irregularity repeats over and over in a cycle. **p. 378**

What's Online 📱

Go to www.mhhe.com/shadeECG2e to find:
- Presentations on chapter content
- Types of PVCs exercise
- Crossword puzzle exercises
- Additional ECG tracings for practicing analyzing ventricular dysrhythmias
- Chapter quiz
- Flashcards
- Fill-in-the-blank exercises and answers
- In-depth answers to Practice Makes Perfect ECG tracings and Assess Your Understanding questions

What's Online lists additional content on the Fast & Easy ECG Website for enrichment and review.

Acknowledgments

First, I would like to thank Claire Merrick, the editor on the first edition of this textbook. It was her vision for the project that led to the original signing and publishing of *Fast & Easy ECGs.* Next, I would like to thank Laura Horowitz, the Development Editor of the second edition. Laura pushed past huge challenges that nearly derailed the project on several occasions, including an author who just kept adding days to the project in order to "expound on a concept or create another figure." Even with these obstacles, she displayed incredible patience and guided completion of the book. Further, her work helped to shape the magnificent look of the book as well as ensuring the accuracy of the content. Then there is Gretchen Miller, Editorial Assistant to Laura, who worked tirelessly to organize the figure list and table of contents and perform many other tasks needed to reach publication. Her efforts took a great deal of pressure off my shoulders, allowing me to direct more time and energy to crafting the words of the book and preparing new figures.

Many thanks go to our lead project manager, Rick Hecker. He was the mainstay of the project, continually pushing it along even when it looked like it would fall into the abyss of book publication. Because of the dynamic, visual approach used in this book, it required tremendous talent to meld it all altogether. He was there with us through thick and thin, no matter how many changes and additions were requested. His efforts created a warm, stimulating tapestry that surrounds the words and dynamic pictures.

Bruce Shade

Reviewers

Rhonda Mardel Asher, BSMT (ASCP), CMA (AAMA)
Instructor
Department of Medical Assisting
Pitt Community College
Greenville, NC

Louann B. Bailey, MSN, RN, NP
Lecturer
College of Nursing
Kent State University
Kent, OH

Kevin D. Barnard, MS, CCEMT-P, MREMT-P, EMSI
Assistant Professor
Emergency Medical Technology

Cuyahoga Community College
Cleveland, OH

Leaugeay Barnes, BS, NREMT-P, CCEMT-P
Program Director, Emergency Medical Sciences
Division of Health Professions
Oklahoma City Community College
Oklahoma City, OK

Brandon R. Beck, BS, EMT-P
Program Instructor
EMS Program
Flight Paramedic, LifeSaver
Gadsden State Community College
Gadsden, AL

Daniel R. Beil, BA, EMT-P, EMSI
Program Manager
Emergency Medical Technology
Cuyahoga Community College
Cleveland, OH

Lauri L. Beechler, RN, BSN, CEN, PHRN, NREMT-B
Paramedic Program Director
Loyola University Medical Center
Maywood, IL

Ilene M. Borze, RN, MS, CEN
Director of Nursing Continuing Education
Gateway Community College
Phoenix, AZ

Travis Bott, EMT-P
Instructor, EMS/Fire Science
Columbus State Community College
Columbus, OH

Timothy S. Brisbin, BSN, RN, NCEE, NREMT-P
Nurse Manager/Team Leader
MedCenter Air, Carolinas Medical Center
Charlotte, NC

Jeffrey S. Clayton
Emergency Medical Services
Lanier Technical College
Oakwood, GA

Jesse A. Coale , PA-C
Assistant Professor
Philadelphia University
Philadelphia, PA

Harvey Conner, AS, NREMT-P
Professor, EMS Program
Division of Health Professions
Oklahoma City Community College
Oklahoma City, OK

Martha Driscoll, AS, EMS, AA, NREMT-P
Clinical Coordinator, EMS Programs
Assistant Professor

School of Emergency Services
Daytona State College
Daytona, FL

Diane Fey, Registered Medical Assistant
Education Supervisor
Instructor, Allied Health Department
Lincoln Technical Institute
Philadelphia, PA

Janis R. Guilbeau
University of Louisana
Lafayette College of Nursing and Allied Health Profession
Lafayette, LA

Jeffrey F. Harkcom, EMT
Program Coordinator/Adjunct Instructor
EMS Department
Indian River State College
Ft. Pierce, FL

Peter L. Hauter, EMT-P/IC
Battalion Chief
Lansing Fire Department
Lead Faculty, Paramedic Program
Lansing Community College
Lansing, MI

Deanna B. Head, LPN
CEO
Unitech Training Academy
Lafayette, LA

Janet Hinton, AS, BS, MHS
Assistant Professor
Patsy H. Haslam School of Health Sciences
Mountain State University
Hinton, WV

Joe Jones, AS
Senior Professor
Emergency Medical Services Department
Center for Health Science
Broward College
Fort Lauderdale, FL

section 1

Preparatory

Chapter 1:   Anatomy and Electrophysiology of the Heart

Chapter 2:   The Electrocardiogram

1 Anatomy and Electrophysiology of the Heart

Chapter Outline

The Electrocardiogram

How Does the Electrocardiogram Work?

Structure of the Heart

Cells of the Heart

Nerve Impulse Generation and Muscle Contraction

The Heart's Conductive Pathway

The Circulatory System

How Blood Is Circulated

Putting It All Together

Influences on the Heart and Circulatory System

Learning Objectives

LO 1.1   Define the term *electrocardiogram* and list its uses.

LO 1.2   Describe how the electrocardiograph works.

LO 1.3   Identify the direction an electrocardiogram waveform takes when the impulse moves toward and away from a positive electrode.

LO 1.4   Recall the role of the heart in circulating blood throughout the body.

LO 1.5   Describe the location and position of the heart.

LO 1.6   Define the term *pericardial sac* and describe its function.

LO 1.7   List the three layers of the heart wall.

LO 1.8   Recall the name and describe the function of each of the key structures of the internal heart.

LO 1.9   Identify two important functions of the skeleton of the heart.

LO 1.10 Identify and contrast the structure and function of the different types of heart cells.

LO 1.11 Define the four key properties of the heart cells.

LO 1.12 Recall how nerve impulses are generated and muscles contract in the heart.

LO 1.13 Identify the structures of the heart's conduction system and describe what each does.

LO 1.14 Describe how alternate pacemaker sites can sustain the heartbeat if the SA node fails.

LO 1.15 List the components of the circulatory system.

LO 1.16 Identify how the heart receives most of its blood supply.

LO 1.17 Define the terms *cardiac cycle, cardiac output,* and *blood pressure.*

LO 1.18 List all the elements required for the heart to receive and pump blood to the body.

LO 1.19 Describe the influence of the autonomic nervous system on the heart and circulatory system.

Case History

Emergency medical services responds to the home of a 65-year-old man complaining of a dull ache in his chest for the past two hours which came on while mowing his lawn. He also complains of a "fluttering" in his chest and "shortness of breath." He has a history of hypertension, elevated cholesterol, and a one-pack-a-day smoking habit.

After introducing themselves, the paramedics begin their assessment, finding the patient's blood pressure to be 160/110, pulse 120 and irregular, respirations 20, and oxygen saturation 92% on room air. The patient is awake and alert, his airway is open, his breathing is slightly labored, and his pulses are strong.

The paramedics apply oxygen by nasal cannula and attach the patient to a cardiac monitor by applying electrodes to his chest. The monitor shows a fast, narrow complex rhythm with frequent wide and bizarre-appearing extra complexes. On the basis of what they observe, the paramedics obtain a 12-lead electrocardiogram (ECG) to determine if signs of a heart attack are present. The 12-lead ECG confirms their suspicions. The patient is having a myocardial infarction.

The paramedics then administer aspirin, nitroglycerin, and morphine to the patient and transport him to the nearest appropriate facility. En route to the hospital, the patient states his pain is less and the paramedics notice that the extra complexes are gone from his heart rhythm.

LO 1.1

KEY CONCEPT
The electrocardiogram tells us about the heart's electrical activity.

The Electrocardiogram

The **electrocardiogram,** often referred to as an ECG or EKG, is a tracing or graphic representation of the heart's electrical activity over time. The device that detects, measures, and records the ECG is called an **electrocardiograph.** The name electrocardiogram is derived of different parts: electro, because it's related to electronics, cardio, a Greek word for heart, and gram, a Greek root meaning "to write."

The ECG provides healthcare professionals with valuable information (Figure 1-1). It is used to identify irregularities in the heart rhythm (called **dysrhythmias**); detect electrolyte disturbances and conduction abnormalities; and reveal the presence of, injury, death, or other physical changes in the heart muscle. It is also used as a screening tool for ischemic heart disease

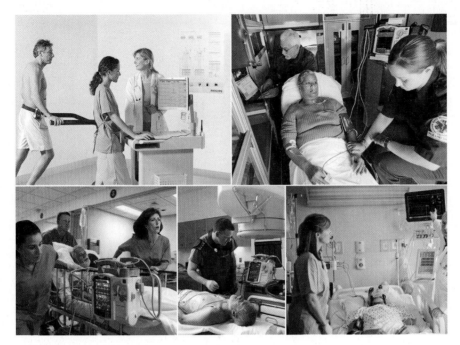

Figure 1-1
The electrocardiogram provides valuable information in a host of clinical settings.

during a cardiac stress test. It is occasionally helpful with diagnosing noncardiac conditions such as pulmonary embolism or hypothermia.

The ECG is used in the prehospital, hospital, and other clinical settings as both an assessment and diagnostic tool. It can also provide continuous monitoring of the heart's electrical activity, for instance, during transport to the hospital or in the coronary care unit. The ECG does not, however, tell us how well the heart is pumping. The presence of electrical activity on the cardiac monitor does not guarantee that the heart is contracting or producing a blood pressure. To determine that, we must assess the patient's pulse and blood pressure, as well as perform an appropriate physical examination.

KEY CONCEPT
The electrocardiogram can identify irregularities in the heart rhythm; detect electrolyte disturbances and conduction abnormalities; and reveal the presence of injury, death, or other physical changes in the heart muscle.

How Does the Electrocardiogram Work?

LO 1.2 and LO 1.3

In simple terms, the electrocardiograph, or ECG machine, detects the electrical current activity occurring in the heart (Figure 1-2). It does this through electrodes placed on the patient's skin. The ECG electrode must be in good contact with the skin to properly detect the heart's electrical currents. Tips for achieving effective contact will be discussed further in Chapter 2. These impulses, which appear as a series of upward (positive) and downward (negative) deflections (waveforms), are then transferred to the ECG machine and displayed on a screen (called the **oscilloscope** or monitor), or they are printed onto graph paper (often referred to as an ECG tracing or strip).

KEY CONCEPT
Electrodes placed on the patient's skin allow the ECG machine to detect the electrical current activity occurring in the heart.

Figure 1-2
The ECG detects electrical
activity in the heart.

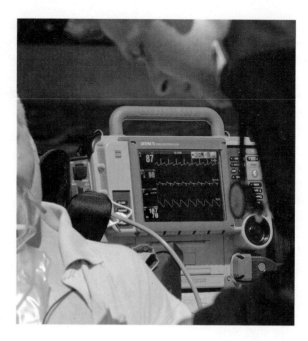

Figure 1-2
The ECG detects electrical
activity in the heart.

KEY CONCEPT

When an impulse occur-
ring in the heart moves
toward a positive electrode
of the ECG, it produces a
positive waveform. When
it moves away from
the positive electrode
or toward a negative
electrode, it produces a
negative waveform.

As the impulse moves toward a positive electrode of the ECG, it produces a positive waveform (upright deflection). Refer to Figure 1-2. In this ECG tracing, all the waveforms (P, QRS, and T) are positive, meaning the impulses are traveling toward a positive electrode. When it moves away from a posi-tive electrode or toward a negative electrode, it produces a negative waveform (downward deflection). The sites for the placement of the electrodes vary depending on which view of the heart's activity is being monitored. Different sites provide different views. We discuss this information in more depth in the next chapters.

This book is designed to teach you how to interpret what you see on an ECG. To do this, it is important for you to understand the anatomy and physiology of the heart. We begin by discussing the location and structure of the heart. Then we talk about how the generation and conduction of nerve impulses leads to contraction of the heart chambers, which then pump blood through-out the body. Finally, we discuss the influence of the autonomic nervous sys-tem on the heart.

LO 1.4

Structure of the Heart

Let's begin by reviewing the structure of the heart. The heart is an amaz-ing organ. It is the pump of the circulatory system. Each time it contracts, it pushes blood throughout the body. The typical adult heart beats an average of 75 times a minute, 24 hours a day, 365 days a year, never stopping to take a rest. In an average day it pumps between 7000 and 9000 liters (L) of blood! This circulates enough blood to deliver needed oxygen and nutrients to the tissues and to remove waste products. Depending on the requirements of the body, the heartbeat can either be sped up (during exercise) or slowed down (while resting or sleeping). Try this experiment: count your pulse rate while sitting or lying comfortably reading this book. Then, if you are physically able, go for a brisk walk (or perhaps run) and then recheck your pulse rate. Your heart should be beating faster; you may even feel the sensation of it pounding in your chest. Your body increases the heart rate and strength of contractions to circulate more blood (and oxygen and nutrients) to your cells and to remove the waste products that have been produced by those working cells.

The term *perfusion* describes the circulatory system's delivery of oxygen and nutrients to the tissues and the removal of waste products. Perfusion is necessary for the body's cells to function and survive. The body's cells die if there is insufficient blood supply to meet their needs.

KEY CONCEPT
The heart is the pump of the circulatory system. It continually circulates enough blood to deliver needed oxygen and nutrients to the tissues and to remove waste products.

Shape and Position of the Heart

LO 1.5

Make a fist. Your heart is about the same size as your closed fist (Figure 1-3A). It is shaped like an inverted blunt cone. Its top (called the *base*) is the larger, flat part whereas its inferior end (called the *apex*) tapers to a blunt, rounded point. The heart is located between the lungs in the **mediastinum** behind the sternum (Figure 1-3B). It lies on the diaphragm in front of the trachea, esophagus, and thoracic vertebrae. About two-thirds of the heart is situated in the left side of the chest cavity. Its base is directed posteriorly and slightly superiorly at the level of the second intercostal space. Its **apex** is directed anteriorly and slightly inferiorly at the level of the fifth intercostal space in the left midclavicular line. This gives it a front-to-back (anterior-posterior) orientation. In this position the right ventricle is closer to the front of the left chest whereas the left ventricle is closer to the side of the left chest (Figure 1-3C). This information will be particularly useful to you when we discuss placement of the various leads in later chapters.

QUESTION
1. **How would you describe the shape of the heart?** *Note:* Answers to the sidebar questions can be found at the end of the chapter.

KEY CONCEPT
The heart is located between the lungs in the mediastinum behind the sternum and rests on the diaphragm with a front-to-back (anterior-posterior) orientation.

Knowing the position and orientation of the heart will help you to understand why certain ECG waveforms appear as they do when the electrical impulse moves toward a positive or negative electrode. The location of the various ECG leads permits us to look at the heart from several different directions.

LO 1.6

The Pericardial Sac

The heart is surrounded by the pericardial sac (also called the **pericardium**), a double-walled closed sac (Figures 1-4 and 1-5). The tough, fibrous, outer

Figure 1-3
(A) The heart is about the size of a closed fist. (B) The position of the heart in the chest. (C) Cross section of the thorax at the level of the heart.

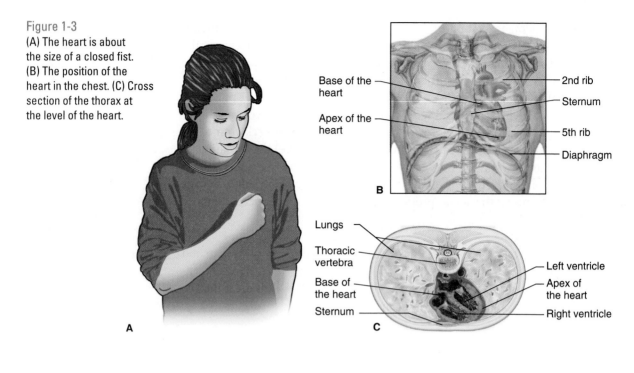

Base of the heart
Apex of the heart
2nd rib
Sternum
5th rib
Diaphragm
B

Lungs
Thoracic vertebra
Base of the heart
Sternum
Left ventricle
Apex of the heart
Right ventricle
C

A

Figure 1-4
The pericardium is the protective sac that surrounds the heart.

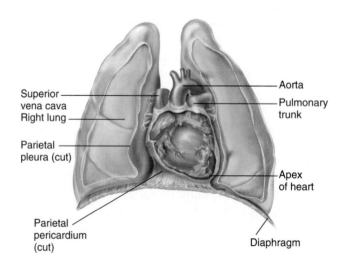

Superior vena cava
Right lung
Parietal pleura (cut)
Aorta
Pulmonary trunk
Apex of heart
Parietal pericardium (cut)
Diaphragm

WANT MORE INFORMATION?
Visit the Fast & Easy ECGs Website at www.mhhe.com/shadeECG2e.

layer is called the *fibrous pericardium* whereas the inner, thin, transparent lining is called the *serous pericardium*. Above the heart, the fibrous pericardium is continuous with the connective tissue coverings of the great vessels, and below, the heart is attached to the surface of the diaphragm. This anchors the heart within the mediastinum. The serous pericardium has two parts: the parietal pericardium, which lines the fibrous pericardium; and the visceral pericardium, which covers the surface of the heart. The pericardial cavity, located between the parietal pericardium and the visceral pericardium, holds

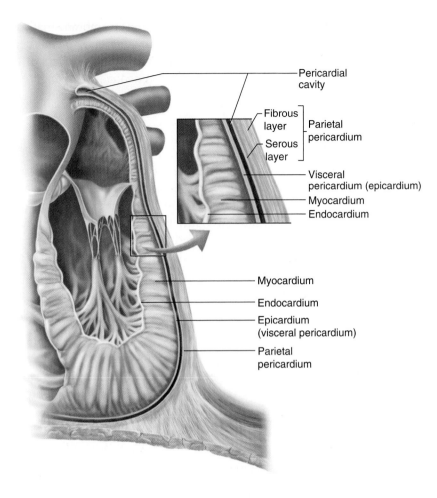

Figure 1-5
This cross section shows the structure of the heart. The enlarged section shows that the wall of the heart has three distinct layers of tissue: the endocardium, myocardium, and epicardium. Also note its relationship to the pericardium.

a small amount of clear lubricating fluid that allows the heart to contract and expand within the chest cavity with minimal friction.

The accumulation of additional fluid in the pericardial space can restrict the heart's ability to contract. This leads to a condition called *pericardial tamponade*. Pericardial tamponade can be life-threatening.

The Heart Wall

The heart wall is comprised of three layers (see Figure 1-5). The middle layer, the muscular layer, is called the **myocardium.** *Myo* means muscle whereas *cardia* means heart. It is the thickest of the three layers and is composed of cylindrical cells that look similar to skeletal muscle.

The innermost layer of the heart wall is called the *endocardium.* The endocardium is a serous membrane that lines the four chambers of the heart and its valves. It has a smooth surface and is continuous with the lining of the arteries and veins. It is watertight to prevent leakage of blood into the other layers.

KEY CONCEPT
The heart is surrounded by a double-walled closed sac called the pericardium. It allows the heart to contract and expand within the chest cavity with minimal friction.

LO 1.7

The outermost layer is the epicardium. It is a thin serous membrane that constitutes the smooth outer surface of the heart. The outer layer of the heart wall is called the *epicardium* when someone is referring to the layers of the heart but is called the *visceral pericardium* when someone is referring to the pericardium.

 LO 1.8

The Internal Heart

The heart is a muscular, hollow organ (Figure 1-6). It has two upper chambers, the **atria,** and two lower chambers, the **ventricles.** The thin-walled atria serve as low-pressure containers that collect blood from the systemic and pulmonary circulation and deliver it to the ventricles. The larger, more muscular ventricles pump blood to the pulmonary and systemic circulation. The left ventricle is thicker and more muscular because it pumps blood through the larger, higher-pressure systemic circulation. The left ventricle is frequently referred to as the workhorse of the heart.

Two Functional Pumps

The heart is separated into two functional units by the **septum** (see Figure 1-6). The word *septum* comes from the Latin word *saeptum,* meaning a "dividing wall or enclosure." The interatrial septum is a thin membranous wall that separates the two atria whereas the more muscular wall, the interventricular septum, separates the two ventricles. For this reason the heart is referred to as a *double pump.* The ventricular septum consists of an inferior

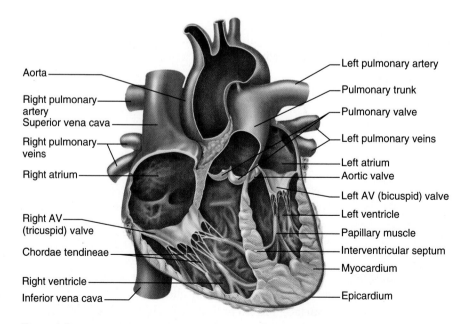

Figure 1-6
Internal anatomy of the heart.

muscular and superior membranous portion and is extensively innervated with heart cells capable of conducting nerve impulses. The septum also provides strength to the walls of the heart.

Heart Valves

Two atrioventricular (AV) valves are located between the atria and ventricles whereas two semilunar valves are located between the ventricles and major arteries (Figure 1-7). The two AV valves include the **tricuspid valve,** situated between the right atrium and right ventricle, and the **bicuspid (or mitral)** valve, located between the left atrium and left ventricle. These valves prevent blood from flowing backward into the atria when the ventricles contract, resulting in the ejection of blood forward from the ventricles and into the pulmonary and systemic circulation. The mitral valve has two cusps whereas the tricuspid valve has three. The cusps are connected to **papillary muscles** in the floor of the ventricle by thin, strong strings of connective tissue called **chordae tendineae.** These cords prevent the cusps from bulging (prolapsing) backward into the atria during ventricular contraction.

The two semilunar valves include the **pulmonic valve,** found at the base of the pulmonary artery, and the **aortic valve,** situated at the base of the aorta, just as they arise from the right and left ventricles, respectively. They prevent the backward flow of blood after the ventricles have contracted and propelled blood into the pulmonary arteries and aorta. Each valve has three cusps that look somewhat like shirt pockets.

Skeleton of the Heart

Between the atria and ventricles is a plate of fibrous connective tissue called the *skeleton of the heart* (Figure 1-8). This plate forms fibrous rings around the AV and semilunar valves, providing firm support. It also acts to separate the atria from the ventricles, functioning in two important ways.

QUESTION
2. **Which side of the heart pumps blood to the systemic circulation?**

KEY CONCEPT
The four heart valves permit blood to flow through the heart in only one direction.

REMINDER
You can also think of the heart as having two upper pumps (the atria) and two lower pumps (the ventricles).

LO 1.9

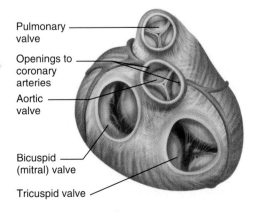

Pulmonary valve

Openings to coronary arteries

Aortic valve

Bicuspid (mitral) valve

Tricuspid valve

Figure 1-7
Superior view of the heart with the atria removed and four heart valves exposed. In the superior view, the top of the heart represents the anterior aspect whereas the bottom of the heart represents the posterior aspect.

The skeleton of the heart consists of fibrous connective tissue rings that surround the heart valves and separate the atria from the ventricles. Cardiac muscle tissue attaches to the fibrous connective tissue.

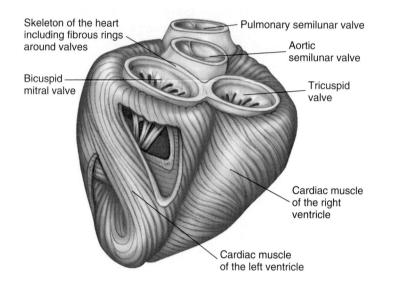

Skeleton of the heart including fibrous rings around valves

Pulmonary semilunar valve

Aortic semilunar valve

Bicuspid mitral valve

Tricuspid valve

Cardiac muscle of the right ventricle

Cardiac muscle of the left ventricle

KEY CONCEPT

The skeleton of the heart provides firm support for the AV and semilunar valves and acts to separate and insulate the atria from the ventricles.

REMINDER

The AV valves prevent blood from flowing backward into the atria when the ventricles contract. The semilunar valves prevent blood from flowing backward into the ventricles.

LO 1.10

First, it allows the top and bottom parts of the heart to act as separate, sequential pumps. Second, it electrically insulates the atria from the ventricles. This insulation allows the atria to be depolarized without depolarizing the ventricles and allows the ventricles to be depolarized without depolarizing the atria.

The cardiac muscles are attached to the fibrous connective tissue and arranged in such a way that, when the ventricles contract, they do so in a wringing motion, which shortens the distance between the base and the apex of the heart. This results in the most efficient ejection of blood out of the ventricles.

Cells of the Heart

There are two basic types of cells in the heart—the myocardial cells (also referred to as the working cells), which contract to propel blood out of the heart's chambers, and the specialized cells of the electrical conduction system, which initiate and carry impulses throughout the heart.

Myocyctes

Structurally, **myocytes** (the working cells) are cylindrical branching cells that usually contain only one centrally located nucleus (Figure 1-9). They are enclosed in a plasma membrane called a **sarcolemma.** The individual myocytes are made up of a small latticework of intricate strands composed of two protein filaments referred to as **actin** and **myosin.** These filaments lie side by side and are connected by crossbridges. These contractile elements permit the muscle fiber to shorten itself and then return to its original length. Their organization gives cardiac muscle a striated (banded) appearance when viewed under a microscope. The process of contraction requires a

Figure 1-9
Myocardial cells.
(A) Cells seen through a light microscope. (B) Myocytes and intercalated discs. (C) Actin and myosin filaments.

plentiful supply of energy. This is supplied by the mitochondria, interspersed within the cell.

The myocytes are bound together with adjoining cells both end to end and laterally, forming a branching and anastomosing network of cells called a **syncytium.** The heart consists of two syncytia, the atrial syncytium and the ventricular syncytium. The atrial syncytium consists of the walls of the right and left atria whereas the ventricular syncytium consists of the walls of the right and left ventricles.

REMINDER

The structure of the myocardial cells permits the rapid conduction of electrical impulses from one cell to another. This results in the cardiac muscle cells acting as a single unit, permitting coordinated contraction of a whole group of cells.

Specialized cellular contacts called **intercalated discs** are located where the branches join. The intercalated disks fit together to form electrical connections. **Gap junctions** permit the rapid conduction of electrical impulses from one cell to another. This results in the myocytes acting as a single unit, permitting coordinated contraction of a whole group of cells. This characteristic allows the walls of the myocardium to contract almost simultaneously when stimulated by an electrical impulse. The highly coordinated contractions of the heart depend on this characteristic. Specialized structures in the cellular membrane called **desmosomes** hold the myocytes together to prevent them from pulling apart when the heart contracts.

The cells of the heart have four key properties: contractility, automaticity, excitability, and conductivity. The working cells possess the property of **contractility.** This is the ability to contract when stimulated by an electrical impulse (see Figure 1-10).

Pacemaker and Electrical Conducting Cells

In order for the heart muscles to contact, they must first be electrically stimulated. The specialized cells responsible for generating and carrying impulses throughout the heart are called *pacemaker cells* and *electrical conducting cells.* These cells differ from the working cells as they lack myofibrils and cannot contract. Also, these cells contain more gap junctions than do the working cells. This allows them to conduct electrical impulses extremely fast.

The pacemaker cells generate electrical impulses by spontaneously depolarizing over and over at a particular rate. This means they produce an electrical impulse without the need for outside nerve stimulation. This is referred to as the property of **automaticity** (see Figure 1-10). The heart is unique in this property. All other muscles in the body require stimulation from nerve impulses supplied by the nervous system. If nerves supplying the voluntary muscles are cut, these muscles cease to function; in other words, they are paralyzed. In contrast, if the nerves supplying the heart are severed, the heart will continue to beat.

The electrical conducting cells, through the properties of **excitability** and **conductivity** (see Figure 1-10), carry the impulses throughout the heart.

KEY CONCEPT
The working cells contract to propel blood out of the heart's chambers.

LO 1.11

QUESTION
3. **What device detects, measures, and records the heart's electrical activity?**

KEY CONCEPT
In order for heart muscles to contact, they must first be electrically stimulated. The specialized cells responsible for generating and carrying impulses throughout the heart are called pacemaker cells and electrical conducting cells.

Automaticity—ability of the myocardial cells to spontaneously initiate an electrical impulse without being stimulated from another source.

Excitability—ability of myocardial cells to respond to impulses generated by other myocardial cells.

Conductivity—ability of myocardial cells to receive an electrical impulse and transmit it to another myocardial cell.

Contractility—ability of myocardial cells to shorten, causing myocardial contraction in response to an electrical stimulus.

Figure 1-10
The key properties of myocardial cells are automaticity, excitability, conductivity, and contractility.

Excitability is the ability to respond to an electrical stimulus whereas conductivity is the ability to transmit an electrical stimulus from cell to cell. Normally, the electrical conducting (nonpacemaker) cells do not possess the property of automaticity but under certain conditions (as will be discussed later in this textbook) can acquire it.

Nerve Impulse Generation and Muscle Contraction

To better understand how nerve impulses are generated and conducted and how they cause muscles to contract, let's review some basic concepts.

Polarized State

As previously stated, for any muscle to contract, it must first be electrically stimulated. Myocardial cells, like all other cells in the body, are bathed in electrolyte solution. The primary electrolytes responsible for initiating electrical charges are sodium (Na+), potassium (K+), and calcium (Ca++).

In the resting, or **polarized,** state (meaning no electrical activity takes place) the cells have a high concentration of negatively charged ions, proteins, and organelles on the inside of the cell. On the outside, there is a high concentration of positively charged ions (Figure 1-11). This difference in electrical charge between the inside and the outside of the cell creates a **resting membrane potential (RMP).** In the polarized state the RMP is negative, indicating that the cell is ready to fire or discharge. This negative RMP is

REMINDER

Automaticity, excitability, conductivity, and contractility are the four key properties that allow the myocardial cell to generate impulses, respond to them, and conduct them throughout the heart, resulting in contraction of the muscle.

LO 1.12

REMINDER

Electrical activity causes the heart muscle to contract and pump blood. However, the presence of electrical activity does not guarantee muscle contraction.

Figure 1-11
In the polarized or resting state, the outside of the cell has a high concentration of positively charged ions while the inside of the cell has a high concentration of negatively charged ions. Under these conditions a negative electrical potential exists across the cell membrane.

sustained by the cell membrane's ability to prevent positively charged ions, such as sodium, from entering the cell and the negatively charged ions from leaving the cell.

Even though there are positively charged ions on the inside of the cell, such as potassium (a key ion that facilitates repolarization as discussed below), there are also an abundance of negatively charged ions, proteins, and organelles needed to sustain the cell. This keeps the inside of the cell negatively charged (in relationship to the outside of the cell) during the polarized state.

Depolarization

Impulses are generated and subsequently transmitted when positively charged ions, such as sodium, rapidly move inside the cells, causing the interior to become positively charged (Figure 1-12). This is called **depolarization.** Calcium, another positively charged ion, also enters the cell but more slowly. This rapid change in electrical charge (going from a negative to positive charge) is referred to as the **action potential** of the cell and reflects its ability to depolarize. The action potential is measured in millivolts (mV). Depolarization of myocardial cells causes calcium to be released and come into close proximity with the actin and myosin filaments of the muscle fibers. The filaments then slide together, one upon another, producing a shortening of the muscle fibers and subsequent myocardial contraction.

Different cells in the heart have different action potentials depending on what function they play in the generation and/or conduction of nerve impulses. The way this process occurs differs between the pacemaker cells of the

Figure 1-12
Myocyte depolarization begins when an electrical stimulus causes the cell membrane to become permeable to positively charged sodium ions. Sodium rushes into the cell, followed by a slower influx of positively charged calcium ions. This causes the inside of the cell and the cell membrane potential to rapidly become positive.

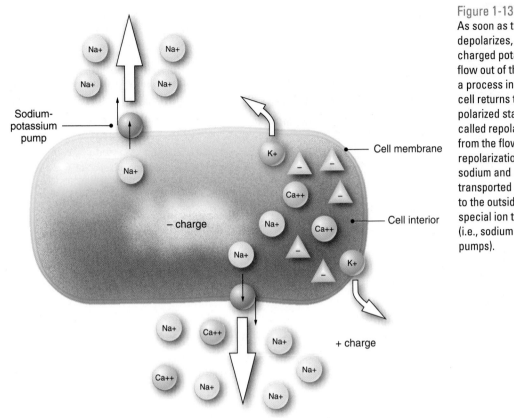

Figure 1-13
As soon as the cell depolarizes, positively charged potassium ions flow out of the cell, initiating a process in which the cell returns to its original, polarized state. This is called repolarization. Aside from the flow of potassium, repolarization involves sodium and calcium being transported from the inside to the outside of the cell by special ion transport systems (i.e., sodium potassium pumps).

sinoatrial (SA) node, the AV node, and the nonpacemaker cells. The positively charged ions move through the cell membrane by way of voltage-gated channels. These channels open and close on the basis of the voltage changes in the cell membrane.

Repolarization

Depolarization is followed by positively charged ions, such as potassium, leaving the cell, causing the positive charge to lower. Then the other positively charged ions, such as sodium, are removed by special transport systems, such as the sodium-potassium pumps, until the electrical potential inside the cell reaches its original negative charge. This is called **repolarization** (Figure 1-13).

Refractory Periods

Following depolarization and during the **absolute refractory period** (Figure 1-14), no stimulus, no matter how strong, will depolarize the cell. This prevents spasm-producing (tetanic) contractions in the cardiac muscle. During the later phase of repolarization, the **relative refractory period,** a sufficiently strong stimulus *will* depolarize the myocardium.

KEY CONCEPT
Repolarization occurs when positively charged ions, such as potassium, leave the cell and sodium and calcium are transported out of the cell.

REMINDER
Repolarization is the process of restoring the cell to its pre-depolarization state.

QUESTION
4. How soon can the cell respond to its next electrical stimulus?

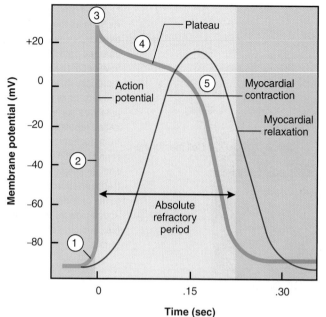

1. Voltage-gated sodium channels open.

2. Na⁺ inflow depolarizes the membrane and triggers the opening of still more Na⁺ channels, creating a positive feedback cycle and a rapidly rising membrane voltage.

3. Na⁺ channels close when the cell depolarizes, and the voltage peaks at nearly +30 mV.

4. Ca²⁺ entering through slow calcium channels prolongs depolarization of membrane, creating a plateau. Plateau falls slightly because of some K⁺ leakage, but most K⁺ channels remain closed until end of plateau.

5. Ca²⁺ channels close and Ca²⁺ is transported out of the cell. K⁺ channels open, and rapid K⁺ outflow returns the membrane to its resting potential.

Figure 1-14
During the absolute refractory period, no stimulus will depolarize the cell. This figure represents the absolute and relative refractory periods to the movement of electrolytes during depolarization and repolarization.

LO 1.13

REMINDER

The wave of depolarization is carried throughout the heart via the heart's conduction system. The conduction system is a grouping of specialized tissues that form a network of connections, much like an electrical circuit.

QUESTION
5. **What does the term intrinsic mean?**

KEY CONCEPT
The SA node serves as the heart's primary pacemaker.

The Heart's Conductive Pathway

The specialized cells responsible for generating and carrying impulses throughout the heart form the **conductive pathway** (Figure 1-15). The conductive pathway has two types of cells—the pacemaker cells and the electrical conducting cells.

SA Node

The electrical event that normally initiates the heartbeat is produced by a group of specialized electrical tissues called the **sinoatrial (SA) node.** The SA node is located high on the posterior wall of the right atrium (see Figure 1-15), just below the opening of the superior vena cava and just under the epicardium. The term *node* means a knot or lump.

The event or impulse is generated automatically. The cells that possess the property of automaticity are called *pacemaker cells.* The SA node serves as the heart's primary pacemaker and has an intrinsic rate of 60 to 100 beats per minute.

It is thought that, once the impulse is generated, it is carried across the interatrial septum and to the left atrium by way of the intraatrial conductive pathway (Bachmann's Bundle) and through the right atrium by way of the anterior,

1. Electrical impulses originate in the SA node and travel across the wall of the atrium (*arrows*) from the SA node to the AV node.

2. Electrical impulses pass through the AV node and along the bundle of His, which extends from the AV node, through the fibrous skeleton, into the interventricular septum.

3. The bundle of His divides into right and left bundle branches, and electrical impulses descend to the apex of each ventricle along the bundle branches.

4. Electrical impulses are carried by the Purkinje fibers from the bundle branches to the ventricular walls.

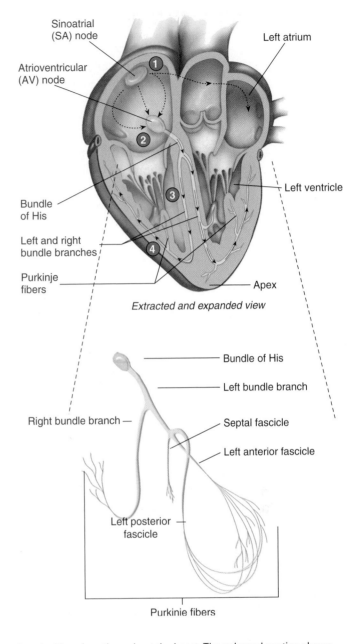

Extracted and expanded view

Figure 1-15
The heart's conduction system generates and carries electrical impulses throughout the heart. The enlarged section shows the His-Purkinje system.

middle, and posterior internodal tracts. These conductive pathways do not normally possess the property of automaticity; instead they just respond to and carry impulses generated by the SA node. The presence of the intraatrial and internodal tracts has not been conclusively proven as they cannot be distinguished structurally from the rest of the atrium. However, the rapid speed at which the impulse moves through the atria strongly supports the belief that these conductive pathways exist.

AV Node

Following their path through the right and left atria, the impulses reach the **atrioventricular (AV) node.** The AV node lies on the floor of the right atrium just medial to the mitral valve and just above the ventricle (see Figure 1-15). It is the only pathway (unless there are accessory pathways as described later in this text) for impulses to move from the atria to the ventricles. Conduction through the AV node is slower, allowing time for the atria to contract and finish filling the ventricles with blood. You can think of the AV node as being a gatekeeper. The impulse travels through the AV node more slowly because the myocytes are thinner in this area, but, more importantly, they have fewer gap junctions over which the impulse can be conducted.

The AV node is anatomically less well-defined than the SA node. It is composed of three layers: the upper, middle, and lower, which have unique conduction characteristics.

Like the SA node, the upper and lower AV nodal tissue has pacemaker cells that allow it to initiate the heartbeat if conditions warrant. The AV node has an intrinsic heart rate of 40 to 60 beats per minute. The nodal tissue in the middle lacks automaticity and is slow to depolarize, giving the ventricles time to fill as described previously. The AV node, its atrial pathways, and the bundle of His make up the conductive tissue of the AV junction.

Bundle of His and Right and Left Bundle Branches

The AV node gives rise to a conducting bundle to the heart, the **bundle of His.** It is also called the *AV bundle* (see Figure 1-15). This bundle passes from the walls of the right atrium through a small opening in the fibrous skeleton to reach the interventricular septum.

In the interventricular septum the bundle divides into the left and right bundle branches. The bundle branches extend beneath the endocardium on either side of the interventricular septum to the apex of each ventricle. The right bundle branch goes to the right ventricle. The left bundle branch goes to the left ventricle.

The left bundle branch divides further into three divisions: the septal fascicle, the anterior fascicle, and the posterior fascicle (see Figure 1-15). The septal fascicle carries the impulse to the interventricular septum in a right-to-left direction. The anterior and posterior fibers spread to their respective sides of the heart.

The bundle of His, bundle branches, and Purkinje fibers are referred to as the His-Purkinje system.

Purkinje Fibers

The right and left bundle branches terminate in the **Purkinje fibers.** The Purkinje fibers consist of countless tiny fibers that spread out widely like the twigs of a tree branch. They extend just underneath the endocardium and

KEY CONCEPT

The AV node is the normal only pathway for impulses to move from the atria to the ventricles.

REMINDER

The fibrous skeleton acts as an insulator to prevent electrical impulses from getting to the ventricles by any other route than that described.

REMINDER

The effect of the skeleton of the heart might be compared with how insulation in the walls of a house help keep noise from being heard from one room to the next.

KEY CONCEPT

The bundle of His and right and left bundle branches carry impulses from the AV node to the ventricles.

KEY CONCEPT

The Purkinje fibers extend just underneath the endocardium and terminate in the endocardial cells. The ventricular tissue can be called upon to act as the pacemaker.

The heart's pacemakers

SA node
60–100

AV node
40–60

Purkinje
fibers
20–40

Figure 1-16
Intrinsic rates of pacemaker sites in the heart's conduction system.

terminate in the endocardial cells. These fibers conduct impulses rapidly through the muscle to assist in its depolarization and contraction, resulting in ventricular depolarization starting in the endocardium and proceeding outward to the epicardium.

Like the SA node and AV junction, the ventricles, including the bundle branches and Purkinje fibers, can also serve as the heart's pacemaker, discharging impulses at a rate of 20 to 40 beats per minute. If the SA node or AV junction fail to initiate a heartbeat or there is a blockage of conduction through the AV node or bundle of His, the Purkinje fibers will fire as the last resort.

Alternate Pacemaker Sites

Normal depolarization of the myocardium progresses from the atria to the ventricles in an orderly fashion (Figure 1-16). Pacemaker cells in the lower areas of the heart, such as the junctional tissue and Purkinje fibers, do not normally initiate the heartbeat because they receive impulses from the SA node. However, other sites in the heart can assume control by discharging impulses faster than the SA node. They can also passively take over, either because the SA node has failed or it is generating impulses too slowly. Normally, the farther from the SA node, the slower will be the pacemaker's intrinsic rate.

The Circulatory System

In order to achieve and maintain homeostasis in the body, the circulatory system performs a number of vital functions: It carries nutrients, gases, and wastes to and from the body cells; helps fight diseases; and helps stabilize the body temperature and pH. The chief elements of the circulatory system are the heart, blood, and blood vessels (Figure 1-17).

KEY CONCEPT
The key structures of the heart's conduction system are the SA node, intraatrial conductive pathway, internodal pathways, AV node, bundle of His, right and left bundle branches, and Purkinje fibers.

■ **LO 1.14**

KEY CONCEPT
If the primary pacemaker site were to fail, one of the other pacemaker sites can initiate the heart's electrical impulses.

■ **LO 1.15**

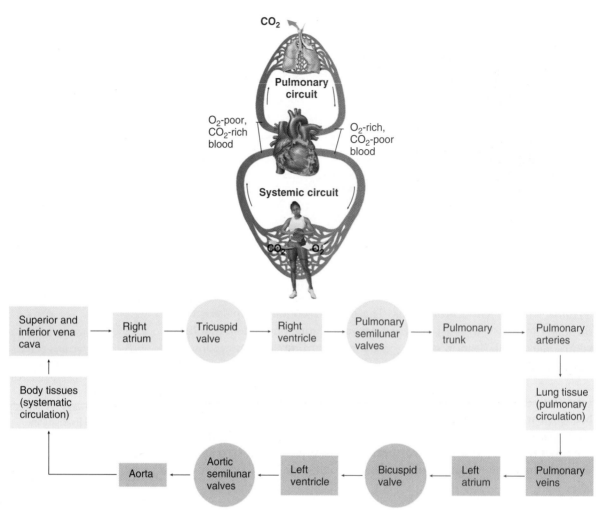

Figure 1-17
Blood flow through the heart and systemic and pulmonary circulations.

KEY CONCEPT

The heart, blood, and blood vessels are the chief components of the circulatory system.

QUESTION

6. What one word best describes the role of the heart in circulating blood?

LO 1.16

The circulatory system includes the pulmonary circulation, a "loop" through the lungs, and the systemic circulation, a "loop" through the rest of the body to provide oxygenated blood to the body cells. The arteries of the systemic circulation carry oxygenated blood whereas the veins carry deoxygenated blood. The reverse is true in the pulmonic circulation, where the pulmonary artery carries deoxygenated blood to the lungs and the pulmonary veins carry oxygenated blood back to the heart. The circulatory system of an average adult contains roughly 4.7 to 5.7 L of blood, which consists of plasma that contains red blood cells, white blood cells, and platelets.

The Heart's Blood Supply

The heart receives most of its blood supply via the **coronary arteries** (Figure 1-18). These arteries originate from the base of the ascending aorta immediately above the leaflets or cusps of the aortic valve. The two major

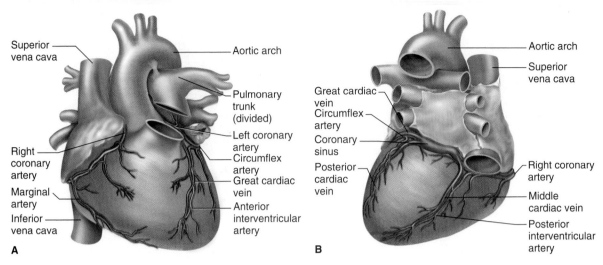

Figure 1-18
The coronary blood vessels supply the heart with oxygen and nutrients and remove waste products. (A) Anterior aspect.
(B) Posterior aspect.

coronary arteries are the right main coronary artery and the left main coronary artery. After passing through the capillaries in the myocardium, blood flows into the **coronary veins.** It then empties into the coronary venous sinus, which in turn drains into the right atrium. If the flow of blood in the coronary arteries is diminished, myocardial ischemia may result. When severe ischemia occurs, necrosis or death of muscle tissue can occur.

The heart has a protective mechanism. Interconnections, or anastamoses, between the coronary arteries, called *coronary collateral vessels,* can act to protect the heart by enlarging to provide blood flow to regions of the heart where blood supply is decreased as a result of occlusion of any of the coronary arteries.

How Blood Is Circulated

Now let's apply what we have learned so far to the pumping action of the heart as it works to circulate blood throughout the body.

The Cardiac Cycle

The **cardiac cycle** is the repetitive process of pumping blood that starts with the beginning of cardiac muscle contraction and ends with the start of the next contraction. Pressure changes within the cardiac chambers are produced by myocardial contraction. This causes movement of blood from areas of higher pressure to areas of lower pressure.

There are two phases of the cardiac cycle: **diastole** and **systole** (Figure 1-19). Diastole is the relaxation and filling of both the atria and ventricles. However,

QUESTION
7. Where is the aortic valve located?

QUESTION
8. Why are the blood vessels that supply the heart muscle called the coronary arteries?

KEY CONCEPT
The coronary arteries provide the heart muscle with most of its blood supply.

 LO 1.17

A Diastole — relaxation and filling of the heart

B Systole — contraction of the heart

Figure 1-19
The two phases of the cardiac cycle are (A) diastole, the relaxation and filling of both the atria and ventricles and (B) systole, contraction of the atria and ventricles.

KEY CONCEPT
The cardiac cycle refers to all or any of the events related to the flow of blood that occur from the beginning of one heartbeat to the beginning of the next.

clinically it is most often used to describe ventricular relaxation and filling. It is during this time that the heart receives most of its blood supply from the coronary arteries, as during systole the myocardium compresses the coronary arteries and restricts blood flow. Thus, in addition to the diastolic blood pressure's reflecting the pressure in the heart during the relaxation phase, it also tells us about the perfusion of the heart.

Contraction of the atria and ventricles is referred to as systole. Again, clinically it is most often used to describe ventricular systole. The systolic blood pressure is the pressure within the systemic arteries during ventricular contraction.

Cardiac Output

Contraction of the ventricles normally results in 60 to 100 mL of blood being ejected into both the pulmonary and systemic circulation. The amount of blood ejected from the ventricles is referred to as the **stroke volume.** It is dependent on **preload** (stretching force exerted on the ventricular muscle at end diastole), contractile force of the myocardium, and **afterload** (workload against which the heart must pump).

The amount of blood pumped from the heart in one minute is called the **cardiac output** (Figure 1-20). It is expressed in liters per minute. The cardiac output is the equivalent of the heart rate multiplied by the stroke volume:

$$\text{Heart Rate} \times \text{Stroke Volume} = \text{Cardiac Output}$$

KEY CONCEPT
Cardiac output is the amount of blood pumped from the heart in one minute.

Cardiac output for the right and left ventricles is normally equal. Decreases in either the heart rate or stroke volume result in decreased cardiac output whereas increases in either result in increased cardiac output. Factors that influence the heart rate, the stroke volume, or both will influence cardiac output and, thus, tissue perfusion.

Figure 1-20
Cardiac output is the amount of blood pumped from the heart in one minute.

Blood Pressure

The **blood pressure** is the force that blood exerts against the walls of the blood vessels as it passes through them. The term blood pressure generally refers to arterial pressure, i.e., the pressure in the larger arteries. This pressure causes blood to flow. The blood pressure is the equivalent of the cardiac output multiplied by the peripheral vascular resistance:

Cardiac Output × Peripheral Vascular Resistance = Blood Pressure

A decrease in cardiac output or peripheral vascular resistance results in a decrease in the blood pressure whereas increases in either result in increased blood pressure.

Blood pressure is most commonly measured by using a sphygmomanometer, which historically used the height of a column of mercury to reflect the circulating pressure. Today, blood pressure values are still reported in millimeters of mercury (mm Hg), though modern aneroid and electronic devices do not use mercury.

KEY CONCEPT
Blood pressure is the force exerted by circulating blood on the walls of blood vessels.

Putting It All Together

LO 1.18

It is now time to talk about how the heart receives blood from the systemic and pulmonary circulations, is stimulated to contract, and then pumps blood throughout the body.

Blood Flow through the Atria

At the beginning of the cardiac cycle, the right and left atria receive blood from the systemic and pulmonary circulation and deliver it to the ventricles. Deoxygenated blood returned from the body via the superior and inferior vena cava, the largest veins in the body, is delivered to the right atrium. The superior vena cava and the inferior vena cava are sometimes called the great veins. The left atrium receives blood oxygenated in the lungs and returned via the pulmonary veins. As the atria fill with blood, the pressure within the atria rises, forcing the tricuspid and mitral valves open and allowing blood to

QUESTION
9. What stimulates the heart muscle to contract?

Figure 1-21
At the beginning of the cardiac cycle, blood flows into the right and left atria, forcing the AV valves open and allowing blood to flow into the right and left ventricles.

Figure 1-22
Normally, the electrical activity that initiates the heartbeat originates from the SA node.

flow into the right and left ventricles (Figure 1-21). Approximately 70% of the blood coming into the chambers flows passively through the atria and into the ventricles before the atria contract.

Initiation of Impulse in the SA Node

The SA node initiates the electrical event that normally causes the heartbeat (Figure 1-22). As described earlier, the ability of certain myocardial cells to discharge electrically (action potential) without the need for external stimulus is called *automaticity*.

Atrial Depolarization and Contraction

From the SA node, the electrical impulse spreads from cell to cell in a wave-like manner across the atrial muscle, depolarizing the right atrium, the inter-atrial septum, and then the left atrium (Figure 1-23). This electrical current

QUESTION
10. What is the intrinsic rate of the SA node?

REMINDER
The other myocytes, under certain circumstances, also have the property of automaticity.

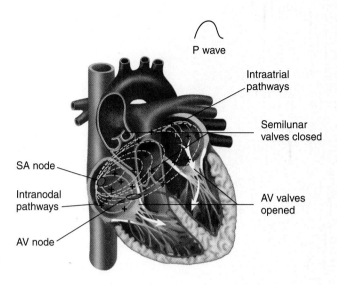

P wave

Intraatrial pathways

Semilunar valves closed

SA node

Intranodal pathways

AV node

AV valves opened

Figure 1-23
From the SA node, the electrical impulse moves in a wavelike manner across the atria. This causes the atria to contract, pushing the remaining atrial blood into the ventricles.

produces a waveform called the **P wave.** Remember, the structure of the cardiac muscles (which forms the atrial and ventricular syncytium) permits the rapid conduction of electrical impulses from one cell to another, making it possible for impulses to move quickly throughout the heart. The two key properties of the myocardial cells responsible for moving the impulses from cell to cell are excitability and conductivity. This brings about nearly simultaneous contraction of the right and left atria, squeezing the blood in the chambers and forcing it forward into the ventricles. Contraction of the atria pushes the remaining 30% of the blood into the ventricles (remember, up to 70% of the blood flows passively through the atria).

Following contraction of the atria, the pressure in the atria and ventricles equalizes, and the tricuspid and mitral valves close. At the same time, the impulse is carried through the atria by the intranodal pathways to the AV node.

Conduction through the AV Node

The internodal pathways carry impulses through the atria to the AV node (Figure 1-24). It is the only pathway (unless there are accessory pathways as described later in this text) for impulses to move from the atria to the ventricles. The impulse travels slowly through the AV node, creating a slight delay that allows the atria to finish pushing any remaining blood into the ventricles. This is referred to as the atrial kick. It also allows the ventricular muscle to stretch to its fullest for peak cardiac output.

On the ECG this electrical stimulation occurs during the P wave. As discussed earlier, the heart skeleton (the plate of fibrous connective tissue) that lies between the atria and the ventricles and includes the heart valves insulates the atrial myocardium from the ventricular myocardium. This allows the electrical stimulus to stimulate the atria as it travels through the upper portion of the heart, permitting the upper chambers of the heart to contract as a unit, pumping blood to the ventricles. Likewise, once the impulse travels

KEY CONCEPT
The impulse arising from the SA node and traveling through the atria generates a positive waveform on the ECG and contraction of the atria.

QUESTION
11. What do the terms excitability and conductivity mean?

QUESTION
12. What is the intrinsic rate of the AV node?

KEY CONCEPT
The delay of the impulse traveling through the AV node allows the ventricles to finish filling.

Figure 1-24
The wave of depolarization slows as it passes through the AV node. This allows the atrial contraction to finish filling the ventricles. This electrical activity occurs simultaneously with the P wave.

Figure 1-25
After slowly passing through the AV node, depolarization rapidly shoots through and activates the His-Purkinje system. This is represented on the ECG as a flat line called the *PR segment.*

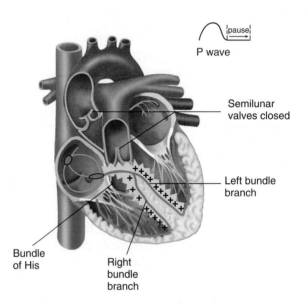

KEY CONCEPT
The impulse traveling through the bundle of His, left and right bundle branches, and the terminal Purkinje fibers is seen as a flat line on the ECG.

QUESTION
13. What is the intrinsic rate of the ventricles?

through the ventricles, it causes them to contract as a unit, pumping blood to the lungs and to the body.

Conduction through the His-Purkinje System

After slowly moving through the AV node, the impulse then rapidly shoots through the bundle of His, the left and right bundle branches, and the terminal Purkinje fibers (the His-Purkinje system) (Figure 1-25). On the ECG this produces a flat line that follows the P wave. This is because the electrical currents are so small they are not seen on the ECG. This part of the ECG is called the **PR segment.** The His-Purkinje system is responsible for initiating the contraction of the ventricles.

Ventricular Depolarization and Contraction

Depolarization of the whole ventricular myocardium produces contraction of the ventricles and a waveform called the **QRS complex** on the ECG. The sizes of the P wave and the QRS complex are considerably different because of how much thicker the ventricles are compared with the atria. The ventricles, a much bigger mass, produce a bigger waveform. Ventricular depolarization initiates vigorous contraction of the ventricles, causing the ventricular pressure to rise sharply, up to about 120 mm Hg in the left ventricle and 26 mm Hg in the right ventricle (Figure 1-26).

When the ventricular pressure exceeds the pressure in the aorta and pulmonary artery, the tricuspid and mitral valves close completely, and the pulmonic and aortic valves snap open. This allows the blood to be forcefully ejected from the right ventricle into the pulmonary artery, from which it is carried to the lungs. The blood from the left ventricle is ejected into the aorta, from which it is circulated to the tissues of the body.

At the end of the contraction, the ventricles relax, and back pressure in the aorta and pulmonary artery causes the aortic and pulmonic valves to close.

The difference we see in how the atria and ventricles move blood is important as we talk about various cardiac dysrhythmias. Dysrhythmias originating from the atria are generally not life threatening whereas dysrhythmias that rise from the ventricles can be. This is because the ventricles are responsible for pushing blood throughout the body; if they fail, blood circulation throughout the body is compromised.

KEY CONCEPT
The impulse traveling through the His-Purkinje system generates a positive waveform on the ECG and contraction of the ventricles. The muscle contraction causes the ventricles to push the blood into the pulmonary and systemic circulation.

QUESTION
14. How can both ventricles contract simultaneously when the left ventricle has more mass than the right?

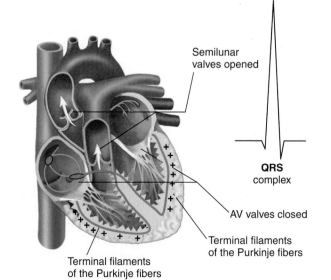

Semilunar valves opened

QRS complex

AV valves closed

Terminal filaments of the Purkinje fibers

Terminal filaments of the Purkinje fibers

Figure 1-26
The wave of depolarization passing through the whole ventricular myocardium produces contraction of the ventricles and a QRS complex on the ECG.

Figure 1-27
Repolarization of the ventricles is represented on the ECG by the ST segment and T wave.

Atrial and Ventricular Repolarization

Repolarization of the ventricles, which occurs following the conclusion of depolarization, is represented on the ECG by the **ST segment** and the **T wave** (Figure 1-27). Atrial repolarization occurs during ventricular depolarization and is therefore hidden, or obscured, by the QRS complex.

Normal depolarization of the myocardium progresses from the atria to the ventricles in an orderly fashion. The electrical stimulus causes the heart muscle to contract. The ECG shows the electrical stimuli as it travels through the heart. The heart performs its pumping action over and over in a rhythmic sequence circulating blood through the pulmonary and systemic circulation.

QUESTION
15. Which pacemaker site in the heart is the primary pacemaker?

Influences on the Heart and Circulatory System

You should be familiar with the terms chronotropic, dromotropic, and inotropic. Chronotropic refers to the heart rate. Dromotropic refers to the rate of impulse conduction through the heart's conduction system. Inotropic refers to the contractility of the heart.

Regulation of the heart rate, speed of electrical conduction, and strength of contraction are influenced by the brain (via the autonomic nervous system), hormones of the endocrine system, and the heart tissue (Figure 1-28). Receptors in the blood vessels, kidneys, brain, and heart constantly monitor the adequacy of the cardiac output. **Baroreceptors** detect changes in pressure, usually within the heart or the main arteries. **Chemoreceptors** have the job of sensing changes in the chemical composition of the blood. If abnormalities are identified, nerve signals are sent to the appropriate target organs, generating the release of hormones or **neurotransmitters** to fix the situation. Once conditions are normal, the receptors stop firing and the signals cease.

QUESTION
16. What is the average heart rate in the adult?

1. Baroreceptors are responsible for detecting changes in pressure, usually within the heart or the main arteries.
   Chemoreceptors sense changes in the chemical composition of the blood. This information is transmitted to the cardioregulatory center in the medulla oblongata.

2. When the blood pressure is elevated, the cardiorespiratory center may activate the parasympathetic nervous system, which acts to slow the heart rate and lower the blood pressure.

3. If the blood pressure is low the cardiorespiratory center will activate the sympathetic nervous system, which acts to increase the heart rate and contractility. This increases cardiac output and raises the blood pressure.

4. The cardioregulatory center causes the release of epinephrine and some norepinephrine from the adrenal medulla into the general circulation. Epinephrine and norepinephrine increase the heart rate and stroke volume.

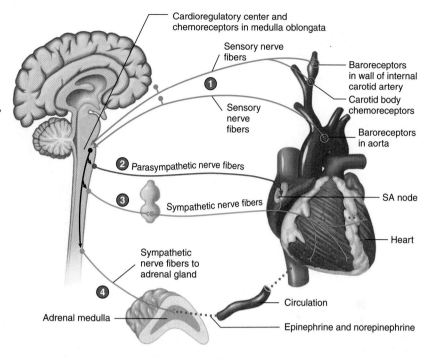

Figure 1-28

Baroreceptor and chemoreceptor reflexes. Sensory (green) nerves carry information from sensory receptors to the medulla oblongata and extend to the heart to regulate its function. Epinephrine and norepinephrine from the adrenal gland also help regulate the heart's action.

The Autonomic Nervous System

LO 1.19

Whereas the myocardial cells can generate electrical impulses on their own, the autonomic nervous system can influence the rate and strength of myocardial contractions (Figure 1-29). This is needed because the cardiovascular system must continually adjust the blood supply to meet demands at the cellular level.

Nervous control of the heart originates from two separate nerve centers located in the medulla oblongata, a part of the brainstem. One of these centers, the cardioaccelerator, is part of the sympathetic nervous system whereas the other, the cardioinhibitor, is part of the parasympathetic nervous system. Both systems exert their effects via neurotransmitters that bind to specific receptors. Impulses from the cardioaccelerator center are transmitted to the heart by way of the sympathetic nerves. Impulses from the cardioinhibitor center are transmitted to the heart by way of the vagus nerve.

The sympathetic and parasympathetic nervous systems work in opposition to one other. The parasympathetic branch dominates during custodial or basal functions whereas the sympathetic system dominates during stress. For example, during physical exertion the sympathetic system causes the heart to beat faster whereas during rest the heart beats slower.

KEY CONCEPT
The autonomic nervous system can influence the rate and strength of myocardial contractions.

Cardioaccelerator

Sinoatrial node

Vagus nerve

Cardioinhibitor

Sympathetic nerves

Descending
nerve pathway
from brain

Medulla
The medulla is an area of the brain
involved in vital body functions
such as heart rate and breathing.

Atrioventricular
node

Figure 1-29
Parasympathetic and sympathetic innervation of the heart.

Sympathetic Nervous System

The sympathetic branch of the autonomic nervous system is carried through nerves in the thoracic and lumbar ganglia, causing the release of the neurotransmitter **norepinephrine** (Figure 1-30). **Epinephrine (adrenalin),** released from the adrenal glands, also functions as a sympathetic branch neurotransmitter. For this reason, the sympathetic branch is called the **adrenergic** system. Stimulation of the sympathetic nervous system produces what we describe as the "fight-or-flight" response—constriction of blood vessels, enhancement of myocardial cell excitability, increased rate of pacemaker firing, increased conduction speed, increased contractility, coronary vasodilation, and a feeling of nervousness.

> **KEY CONCEPT**
> In the heart, stimulation of the sympathetic nervous system produces enhancement of myocardial cell excitability, increased rate of pacemaker firing, increased conduction speed, increased contractility, and coronary vasodilation.

Sympathetic fibers exert their effect by stimulating special receptors. These receptors are divided into categories depending on their response. The two major categories are alpha and beta receptors. The primary sympathetic receptors in the heart are beta receptors—they affect all areas of the heart.

Sympathetic system
Activates beta receptors

Cardioaccelerator
effects

↑ Rate of pacemaker firing

↑ Spead of impulse conduction
through heart

↑ Force of contraction

Coronary vasodilation

Figure 1-30
Activation of the sympathetic
nervous system stimulates
the heart to beat faster and
stronger.

Parasympathetic system
Activates cholinergic receptors

Vagus nerve

Stimulates

Cardioinhibitor
effects

↓ Rate of SA node pacing

↓ Speed of AV conduction

Inhibits

Figure 1-31
Activation of the
parasympathetic nervous
system causes the heart to
beat slower.

Parasympathetic Nervous System

The parasympathetic branch of the autonomic nervous system is carried
through the vagus nerve and releases the neurotransmitter acetylcholine (Figure 1-31). It is therefore referred to as the **cholinergic** system. The

parasympathetic nervous system works just the opposite of the sympathetic branch, causing a slowing of the heart rate and AV conduction. It also controls intestinal activity and affects papillary responses. The areas of the heart most affected by the parasympathetic fibers are the SA node; atria; AV junction; and to a small extent, the ventricles.

The parasympathetic nervous system may also have a modest effect on myocardial contractility by slowing the rate of contraction. In extreme instances, excess stimulation of the parasympathetic nervous system can lead to cardiac arrest.

Key Points

- The electrocardiogram is a graphic representation of the heart's electrical activity. It is used to identify irregularities in the heart rhythm and to reveal the presence of injury, death, or other physical changes in the heart muscle.

- The electrocardiograph detects the electrical activity occurring in the heart through electrodes attached to the patient's skin.

- Nerve impulses stimulate cardiac muscles to contract. Without electrical stimulation the muscles will not contract.

- The heart is the pump of the circulatory system.

- The heart is located between the lungs in the mediastinum behind the sternum and rests on the diaphragm with a front-to-back (anterior-posterior) orientation.

- The heart is surrounded by a double-walled closed sac called the *pericardium*. It allows the heart to contract and expand within the chest cavity with minimal friction.

- The heart wall consists of three layers: the myocardium, endocardium, and epicardium.

- The heart consists of two upper chambers, the atria, and two lower chambers, the ventricles.

- A muscular wall, the septum, separates the right side from the left side of the heart.

- The skeleton of the heart provides firm support for the AV and semilunar valves and acts to separate and insulate the atria from the ventricles.

- There are two basic types of cells in the heart: the myocardial cells (also referred to as the working cells), which contract to propel blood out of the heart's chambers, and the specialized cells of the electrical conduction system, which initiate and carry impulses throughout the heart.

- Automaticity, excitability, conductivity, and contractility are the four key properties of myocardial cells.

- Sodium, calcium, and potassium are the key electrolytes responsible for initiating electrical activity.

- Depolarization of the cells occurs when positive electrolytes move from outside to inside the cell. This causes the inside of the cell to become more positively charged. Depolarization of myocardial cells causes calcium to be released and come into close proximity with the actin and myosin filaments of the muscle fibers. The filaments then slide together, one upon another, producing a shortening of the muscle fibers and subsequent myocardial contraction.

- The key structures of the heart's conduction system are the SA node, intraatrial conductive pathway, internodal pathways, AV node, bundle of His, right and left bundle branches, and Purkinje fibers.

- The intrinsic rate of the SA node is 60 to 100 beats per minute. The intrinsic rate of the AV node is 40 to 60 beats per minute, and the intrinsic rate of the Purkinje fibers is 20 to 40 beats per minute.

- The chief elements of the circulatory system are the heart, blood, and blood vessels.

- The coronary arteries perfuse the myocardium during diastole.

- Cardiac output is the amount of blood pumped from the heart in 1 minute. The cardiac output is equal to the heart rate multiplied by the stroke volume.

- The electrical impulse that normally initiates the heartbeat arises from the SA node. From there it travels through the atria, generating a positive waveform (the P wave), which shows on the ECG, leading to contraction of the atria. The atrial muscle contraction pushes the remaining blood from the atria into the ventricles.

- The impulse is slowed as it passes from the atria to the ventricles through the AV node.

- On the ECG, the impulse traveling through the His-Purkinje system is seen as a flat line following the P wave.

- The QRS complex is generated and the ventricles contract as a result of the electrical impulse stimulating the ventricles. Ventricular muscle contraction causes the blood to be pushed into the pulmonary and systemic circulation.

- The ST segment and T wave represent repolarization of the ventricles, which takes place following the conclusion of depolarization. Atrial repolarization occurs but is hidden by the QRS complex.

- Depolarization of the myocardium progresses from the atria to the ventricles in an orderly fashion. The electrical stimulus causes the heart muscle to contract.

- Other sites in the heart can assume control by discharging impulses faster than the SA node.

- They can also passively take over, either because the SA node has failed or is generating impulses too slowly.

- The autonomic nervous system can influence the rate and strength of myocardial contractions.

- The two divisions of the autonomic nervous system are the sympathetic and the parasympathetic nervous systems.

Assess Your Understanding

The following questions give you a chance to assess your understanding of the material discussed in this chapter. The answers can be found in Appendix A.

1. The electrocardiogram measures
   a. pulse strength.
   b. blood pressure.
   c. cardiac output.
   d. the heart's electrical activity.

2. The electrocardiograph can do all of the following EXCEPT
   a. identify irregularities in the heart rhythm.
   b. determine perfusion status of the patient.
   c. reveal the presence of, injury of, death of, or other physical changes in the heart muscle.
   d. diagnose noncardiac diseases such as pulmonary embolism or hypothermia.

3. When an electrical impulse in the heart moves toward a positive electrode, the ECG waveform takes negative deflection.
   a. True
   b. False

4. The heart acts as the _____ of the circulatory system.
   a. pipeline
   b. pump
   c. transportation medium
   d. nervous control center

5. The heart
   a. is located above the lungs.
   b. has a side-to-side orientation.

    c. lies on the diaphragm in front of the trachea, esophagus, and thoracic vertebrae.

    d. lies mostly in the right side of the chest.

6. Which of the following statements regarding the pericardium is accurate?

    a. It is a double-walled, open sac.

    b. The tough, fibrous, outer layer of the pericardium is called the *serous pericardium.*

    c. The parietal pericardium covers the surface of the heart.

    d. The pericardial cavity holds a small amount of clear lubricating fluid.

7. The myocardium is

    a. the thickest of the three layers of the heart.

    b. smooth and is continuous with the lining of the arteries and veins.

    c. watertight to prevent leakage of blood into the other layers of the heart.

    d. the outermost layer of the heart.

8. The upper chambers of the heart are called the

    a. ventricles.

    b. atria.

    c. vena cava.

    d. venules.

9. Functions of the skeleton of the heart include

    a. allowing the top and bottom parts of the heart to act as separate pumps.

    b. enhancing conduction from the atria to the ventricles.

    c. contracting to allow the atria to finish filling ventricles.

    d. allowing the heart to be depolarized all at once.

10. The working cells of the heart initiate and carry impulses throughout the heart.

    a. True

    b. False

11. Automaticity, a property of the heart, is the ability to

    a. carry an impulse.

    b. respond to an electrical stimulus.

    c. contract when stimulated by an electrical impulse.

    d. produce an electrical impulse without the need for outside nerve stimulation.

12. Which of the following is true?
    a. During the polarized state, the inside of the cell is positively charged.
    b. Depolarization occurs when there is a rapid influx of positively charged ions from outside to inside the cell.
    c. Repolarization begins with the removal of sodium from the interior of the cell.
    d. During depolarization, sodium enters the cells through the slow channels.

13. _____ stimulate muscle cells to contract.
    a. Changes in pressure
    b. Nerve impulses
    c. Outside influences
    d. Polarization of the nerve cells

14. The electrical impulse that normally initiates the heartbeat arises from the
    a. SA node.
    b. AV node.
    c. bundle of His.
    d. Purkinje fibers.

15. The impulse traveling through the His-Purkinje system generates a _____ on the ECG.
    a. P wave
    b. T wave
    c. flat line
    d. QRS complex

16. The QRS complex represents
    a. atrial depolarization.
    b. ventricular depolarization.
    c. delay of the impulse as it travels through the AV node.
    d. ventricular repolarization.

17. Depolarization of the heart progresses from the _____ to the _____ in an orderly fashion.
    a. atria, ventricles
    b. ventricles, atria
    c. bundle of His, Purkinje fibers
    d. ventricles, bundle branches

18. The T wave represents
    a. atrial depolarization.
    b. AV node depolarization.
    c. ventricular repolarization.
    d. initiation of the electrical stimulus.

19. Which of the following is accurate regarding the alternate pacemaker sites of the heart?
    a. Unless the SA node fails, no other site can assume control of the heartbeat.
    b. An alternate pacemaker site can initiate the heartbeat if the SA node fails to do so.
    c. The farther it is from the SA node, the faster the pacemaker's intrinsic rate is.
    d. Impulse initiation from an alternate pacemaker site will produce an "extra" P wave.

20. The pacemaker cells of the _____ have an intrinsic rate of 40 to 60 beats per minute.
    a. SA node
    b. AV node
    c. Purkinje fibers
    d. bundle of His

21. Components of the circulatory system include
    a. the pulmonary circulation that carries blood to and from the systemic circulation.
    b. blood that consists mostly of blood cells and little plasma.
    c. the systemic circulation that carries blood to and from the lungs where it is oxygenated.
    d. roughly 4.7 to 5.7 L of blood.

22. The myocardium receives its blood supply via the
    a. vena cava.
    b. coronary arteries.
    c. blood it pumps to the systemic and pulmonary circulation.
    d. pulmonary arteries.

23. Cardiac output is equal to
    a. afterload multiplied by preload.
    b. contractility multiplied by the stroke volume.
    c. heart rate divided by the contractility.
    d. stroke volume multiplied by the heart rate.

24. The sympathetic branch of the autonomic nervous system
    a. is mediated by the neurotransmitter acetylcholine.
    b. is often called the *cholinergic system.*
    c. produces the "fight-or-flight" response.
    d. works the same as the parasympathetic branch.

25. All of the following are true regarding the parasympathetic nervous system EXCEPT
    a. it is mediated through the vagus nerve.
    b. its fibers mostly affect the SA and AV nodes of the heart.
    c. it is sometimes referred to as the adrenergic system.
    d. it works just the opposite of the sympathetic branch.

Referring to the scenario at the beginning of this chapter, answer the following questions.

26. If the flow of blood in the coronary arteries is diminished, what will likely occur?
    a. Myocardial ischemia
    b. Hypertension
    c. Increased cardiac output
    d. Decreased diastole

27. The patient's initial heart rate is fast because of
    a. the effects of nicotine.
    b. sympathetic nervous system stimulation.
    c. hypertension.
    d. parasympathetic nervous system stimulation.

28. Which of the following will likely occur if the patient experiences severe myocardial ischemia and it is not corrected?
    a. Blood flow through the coronary veins increases.
    b. The heart extracts more oxygen from the blood it pumps through its chambers.
    c. The heart beats erratically.
    d. The affected myocardial tissue becomes necrotic.

? Answers to Sidebar Questions

1. It is shaped like an inverted blunt cone. Its top is the larger, flat part while its inferior end tapers to a blunt, rounded point. **p. 7**

2. The left side of the heart pumps blood to the systemic circulation. **p. 11**

3. The device that detects, measures, and records the electrical activity of the heart is an electrocardiograph machine. **p. 14**

4. Once the cell has returned to its polarized state, it can be stimulated again, but during the relative refractory period, a sufficiently strong stimulus will depolarize the myocardium. This aspect of depolarization will become important later when we discuss ventricular ectopy. **p. 17**

5. Intrinsic means the range of impulses the pacemaker site can naturally generate per minute. **p. 18**

6. The heart is the pump of the circulatory system. **p. 22**

7. The aortic valve is situated at the base of the aorta just as it arises from the left ventricle. **p. 23**

8. They are called the coronary arteries because they encircle the heart like a crown. **p. 23**

9. The electrical activity of the heart causes the heart muscle to contract. **p. 25**

10. The intrinsic rate of the SA node is 60 to 100 beats per minute. **p. 26**

11. Excitability is the ability to respond to an electrical stimulus while conductivity is the ability to transmit an electrical stimulus from cell to cell throughout the myocardium. **p. 27**

12. The intrinsic rate of the AV node is 40 to 60 beats per minute. **p. 27**

13. The intrinsic rate of the ventricles is 20 to 40 beats per minute. **p. 28**

14. While the left ventricle is thicker and more muscular, the impulse is quickly carried to the myocardial cells by the three divisions of the left bundle branch: the septal fascicle, anterior fascicle, and posterior fascicle. This helps to depolarize both ventricles at the same time and produce simultaneous contraction. **p. 29**

15. The primary pacemaker of the heart is the SA node. **p. 30**

16. The average heart rate in the adult is 72 beats per minute. **p. 30**

What's Online

Go to www.mhhe.com/shadeECG2e to find:

- Presentations on chapter content
- Animation quizzes
- Crossword puzzle exercises
- Fill-in-the-blank exercises and answers

2 The Electrocardiogram

Chapter Outline

The Electrocardiogram   **The Input**   **Calibrating the ECG**

ECG Machines   **The Output**   **Artifact**

Learning Objectives

LO 2.1   Differentiate between an electrocardiogram and an electrocardiograph.

LO 2.2   List the uses for the electrocardiograph (ECG).

LO 2.3   Identify how an ECG machine obtains electrical signals generated by the heart.

LO 2.4   Recall the purpose and proper use of ECG lead wires and cables.

LO 2.5   Describe what an ECG electrode consists of and recall its proper use and application.

LO 2.6   Recall the direction a waveform takes when the electrical current is moving toward a positive electrode.

LO 2.7   Define the terms *bipolar* and *unipolar leads* and identify which leads are bipolar and which are unipolar.

LO 2.8   Differentiate between the frontal plane and the horizontal plane of the heart.

LO 2.9   Identify the most commonly used ECG lead for continuous cardiac monitoring and describe the position of the ECG electrodes for this lead.

LO 2.10   Describe the benefits and shortcomings of seeing an ECG rhythm on the oscilloscope as well as seeing it on a printout.

LO 2.11   Recall what the horizontal and vertical lines on ECG paper represent and list the values of the boxes they create.

LO 2.12   Define the term *isoelectric line.*

LO 2.13   Describe what is meant by the expression *calibrating the ECG.*

LO 2.14   Define the term *artifact* and give three common examples.

Case History

It is a busy morning in the cardiac rehabilitation unit where patients, after undergoing cardiac bypass surgery, come to exercise under observation of trained therapists. A 72-year-old man is on the stationary bike when he begins to feel lightheaded and then passes out, falling off the bike onto the floor. A therapist rushes to his side to find him slowly regaining consciousness.

The therapist is able to print out a continuous recording of his heart rhythm before, during, and after the incident because the patient was on a cardiac monitor during his exercise routine.

EMS is summoned to transport the patient to the emergency department, and the therapist provides the paramedics with the electrocardiogram (ECG) printout, which shows that the patient was in a slightly fast but otherwise normal heart rhythm before exercise. The rhythm became very slow with pauses up to 10 seconds long during exercise and then returned to normal after he fainted.

LO 2.1

QUESTION
1. How are the electrical impulses of the heart produced and conducted? *Note:* Answers to sidebar questions can be found at the end of the chapter.

LO 2.2

The Electrocardiogram

As discussed in Chapter 1, the ECG is a tracing of the heart's electrical activity. The device that measures and records the ECG is called an electrocardiograph, although you will probably hear it called the "ECG," "EKG," "monitor," or "12 lead." To avoid confusion, we will use ECG machine when referring to the electrocardiograph.

ECG Machines

While many before him contributed to the understanding of heart's electrical activity and how to record it, Dutch physiologist Willem Einthoven, MD, PhD is credited with inventing the first ECG machine in 1903. Initially, it was a cumbersome and costly device, taking five technicians to operate. During the procedure, patients sat with both arms and the left leg in separate buckets of saline solution (Figure 2-1). These buckets acted as electrodes to conduct the current from the skin's surface to the filament of the device. The three points of electrode contact on the limbs produced what is known as **Einthoven's Triangle,** a principle still used in modern day ECG recording. The EKG was so named because Einthoven had the earliest ECG machines manufactured in Germany, and "kardio" is German for heart.

ECG machines have many uses in both the hospital and out-of-hospital settings. Commonly, they are employed to provide continuous monitoring of the heart rhythm. This is done to check for abnormalities in the heart rhythm called dysrhythmias. Dysrhythmias may be seen as a significant increase or decrease in the heart rate, impulses that arise outside the heart's normal pacemaker site (the SA node), and/or delays or blockage in impulse conduction through the atrioventricular (AV) junction.

REMINDER
Dysrhythmias are abnormalities or disturbances in the heart rhythm. Many are insignificant and have no effect on cardiac output whereas others may be life threatening.

Figure 2-1
Picture of the first EGG
machine.

PHOTOGRAPH OF A COMPLETE ELECTROCARDIOGRAPH, SHOWING THE MANNER IN WHICH THE ELECTRODES ARE ATTACHED TO THE PATIENT, IN THIS CASE THE HANDS AND ONE FOOT BEING IMMERSED IN JARS OF SALT SOLUTION

Other uses of the ECG machine are to identify developing or existing cardiac and noncardiac conditions such as myocardial ischemia and/or infarction, inflammation, enlargement and/or hypertrophy of the heart muscle, changes in or blockage of the heart's conduction system, accumulation of fluid in the pericardial sac, or electrical effects of medications and electrolytes and to evaluate the function of artificial implanted pacemakers (devices used to initiate or control the heart rate). The ECG machine is also commonly used to conduct assessments such as stress testing and to obtain a baseline recording before, during, and after medical procedures.

A variety of ECG machines are available for use (Figure 2-2). The type used to provide continuous cardiac monitoring is often referred to as an ECG monitor and is equipped with a display screen (oscilloscope) to view the rhythm. Depending on their use, these devices may view one lead or up to several leads at a time. They may also have the capability to switch between several different leads (Figure 2-2A). This type of ECG machine is often equipped with a defibrillator (a device used to deliver an electrical shock to the heart) and a pacemaker (a device used to stimulate the heart to beat at a desired rate) and may have the capability to obtain and record 12-lead ECGs. Some ECG machines are also equipped with an automatic blood pressure device, pulse oximetry sensor, and/or an end-tidal carbon dioxide (CO_2) detector. Some ECG monitors are portable and used in the prehospital care setting or in the clinical environment where patients are transported from one point to another whereas others are larger and fixed in place, such as those in emergency departments and coronary care and intensive care units (Figure 2-2B).

Figure 2-2
Various types of ECG
machines.

A. Portable

C. 12 lead on cart

B. Stationary

The type of ECG machine used exclusively to perform 12-lead ECGs (Figure 2-2C) may or may not include a display screen or the features described earlier. It is typically kept on a cart so it can be moved to the location where it is needed. Through the recording of 12 different views of the heart, this machine is used to identify the presence of both cardiac and noncardiac conditions and evidence of injury to the heart. It can also be used to identify cardiac dysrhythmias, although this occurs from the static recording and not continuous monitoring. Additionally, some new ECG machines are equipped to record as many as 15 to 18 leads, giving the clinician the ability to view the right lateral and posterior aspects of the heart.

Many of today's ECG devices are equipped to provide a computerized interpretation of the patient's cardiac rhythm and to analyze normal or abnormal ECG findings. To do this, the device records the patient's ECG tracing and examines it against an internal set of criteria and rules of logic. The result is a computerized ECG analysis or "interpretive" 12-lead ECG that is printed on the ECG report.

To more easily understand the ECG machine, we will first talk about how it obtains the information (the input). Then, we will discuss how it displays the information (the output). Learning about ECGs can be intimidating. For this reason we discuss how to interpret dysrhythmias in the next several chapters and then learn how to analyze the other, more complex, aspects of the ECG.

The Input

LO 2.3

The heart's electrical activity is detected by electrodes placed on the patient's skin. Evidence of the activity is then transferred to the ECG machine by wires or cables that are connected to electrodes. The ECG machine then displays the electrical activity on the oscilloscope, or it is printed onto graph paper.

In electrocardiography, the term ECG lead has two meanings: it refers to either the wire that connects an electrode to the ECG machine or (more commonly) to a combination of electrodes that form an imaginary line in the body along which the electrical signals are measured.

Lead Wires and Cables

LO 2.4

There may be 3, 4, or 5 lead wires for monitoring purposes and up to 10 lead wires for 12-lead ECGs. Some lead wire sets have a primary cable that includes four standard leads and a connector to which a cable having an additional six leads can be attached. This allows the ECG machine to be used either for monitoring purposes or to obtain 12-lead ECGs.

The lead wires each have a clip, snap, or pin-type connector on the distal end. This allows attachment to the metal snap or tab on the ECG electrode. The lead wires then feed into a connector or into a cable that attaches to the ECG machine (Figure 2-3).

The lead wires are color-coded to help you remember where each electrode is placed. However, do not rely solely on the color of the wires for proper placement of the electrodes because the colors vary between two different

Figure 2-3
Lead wires with ECG
electrodes.

WANT MORE INFORMATION?

Visit the Fast & Easy ECGs Website at www.mhhe.com/ shadeECG2e.

standard agencies: the American Heart Association (AHA) and the International Electrotechnical Commission (IEC). Instead, use the lettering commonly located on the top of the lead wire connector for each lead. For example, LL stands for left leg, LA stands for left arm, RA stands for right arm, and RL stands for right leg. The leads that are placed across the chest are labeled V_1, V_2, V_3, V_4, V_5, and V_6. Those that are used with an ECG machine capable of viewing 15 or 18 leads and placed across the right side of the chest are labeled V_4R, V_5R, and V_6R while the ones placed across the posterior of the chest are labeled V_7, V_8, and V_9.

Although the lead wires are encased in a plastic or rubberized covering, they are still somewhat fragile, so handle them with care. Bending, stressing, and straining of lead wires during repeated use can cause structural failure, which can result in artifact or prevent transmission of signals.

Another problem with lead wires is that they can easily become tangled with each other or with cables for other sensors, especially during extension and storage. Detangling of the lead wires consumes time, may delay urgently needed medical procedures, and can cause premature failure. For this reason, try to keep the lead wires separated from each other as you put them away or you pull them out (Figure 2-4).

Last, since the lead wires are typically not disposed of following each application, they can become soiled during use by contact with contaminants such

Figure 2-4
Untangling lead wires for proper storing.

as blood, other bodily fluids, and medicinal preparations. For this reason they should be properly cleaned/decontaminated after each use (be sure to follow the manufacturer's recommendations).

Electrocardiogram Electrodes

In the past, electrodes were flat, metal plates held in place with straps that went around the arms and legs and suction cups applied with conductive paste. ECG electrodes in use today are typically disposable and consist of a wet or dry electrolyte gel (which acts to assure good signal pick-up), a metal snap or tab (where the ECG lead wire is attached), and a self-adhesive pad that holds the electrode to the skin. The self-adhesive pad may consist of foam, paper, cloth or other such material. Electrodes come in a variety of shapes and sizes and offer a number of different features. Some have pull tabs for easier placement and removal; others can be used in diaphoretic patients or those with hairy chests. Some are latex free to eliminate the likelihood of an allergic reaction whereas others have a radiotranslucent snap to prevent their being seen on x-rays or magnetic resonance imaging (MRI) taken of the patient. Some ECG electrodes can be repositioned and still effectively adhere to the skin. Electrodes are available for adults as well as pediatric patients.

Preparing the Electrode Sites

To get the best possible signal (noise-free recording), there must good contact between the electrode and the patient's skin (Figure 2-5). Otherwise, the ECG tracing may include artifact (wandering baselines, small complexes, fuzzy tracings, etc.), making analyzing and interpreting the ECG tracing difficult.

Before the electrode is placed, the skin site should be cleaned to remove dead skin cells and oils (Figure 2-5A). Gently abrading the skin by using the small abrasive scrub pad found on the peel-away portion of the electrode or briskly rubbing the site with a piece of dry rough material such as a towel or a piece of gauze can adequately prepare the skin. Use soap and water to remove oil or dirt from the skin. If the surface is wet or moist, use a towel or gauze dressing to dry it. Also, if dense hair is present at the area where the electrodes are to be placed, clip it close to the surface. Avoid shaving hair as it can irritate the skin.

Some references suggest the use of alcohol to clean the electrode site. Others indicate that the use of alcohol actually increases the impedance of the chest, thus interfering with detection of the electrical activity. Follow local protocol and procedure guidelines.

Another hint for assuring a noise-free recording is to eliminate any muscle tension. Place the patient's arms and legs in a comfortable position in which the extremities are resting on a supportive surface. Any self-support of limbs by the patient may introduce fine muscle artifact even though the patient appears not to be moving. If artifact is still present and the patient tolerates it, try laying him or her in a flat position. This often eliminates artifact and allows you to acquire a good tracing.

Figure 2-5
Technique for placing
electrodes and attaching
lead wires.

A   B

C

Placing the Electrodes

When using snap-on lead wires, you should attach the electrode to the lead wire before placing the electrodes onto the patient's skin. This is more comfortable for the patient and preserves the integrity of the electrode gel. When using clip-on type lead wires, apply the gel to the metal snap of the electrode after the electrode has been placed on the skin. Whichever way you use, make sure the leads are connected tightly to the electrodes. Avoid removing the electrodes from their sealed protective envelope before use as the conductive gel may dry. This can decrease the signal detection.

The electrodes can be easily peeled away from the protective backing to expose the gel disc and the sticky surface of the adhesive pad (Figure 2-5B). Make sure the gel is moist (unless it is the dry gel type). If the electrode has become dry, or if it is past its expiration date, discard it and use a new one as a dry electrode decreases electrical contact.

REMINDER

Be sure to check the expiration date on the electrode package. Outdated electrodes should be discarded.

Then, place the electrodes on the patient in the proper positions. Look for a flat surface. While the electrode is flexible enough to keep contact with a surface that is slightly irregular, a flat surface is always preferred. Select sites over soft tissues. Avoid areas where the large bones are near the skin surface as bones are not good conductors and can interfere with detection of the signal. Also, avoid areas where there are thick muscles or skin folds. Those areas can produce ECG artifacts.

Place each electrode onto the patient and, using a circular motion, smooth down the adhesive area (Figure 2-5C). Avoid applying pressure on the gel disc itself as this could result in a decrease in conductivity and adherence. The electrode should lie flat. Repeat the procedure for each electrode. One last point: the lead wires should be positioned so that they do not tug on the electrodes and lift the gel pad away from skin. This will reduce their ability to detect the heart's electrical signals.

ECG Leads

 LO 2.6

The ECG machine shows the changes in the voltage, detectable during the time course of the heartbeat, between pairs of electrodes placed at certain points on the skin. Think of the main electrodes used with the ECG machine as being electrical poles, in other words, representing positive or negative charges. Between the two poles (the positive and negative electrodes) lies an imaginary line representing its view of the direction the electrical current is moving through the heart.

Settings on most ECG machines allow electrodes to be made either positive or negative, depending on the required lead. A lead records the electrical signals of the heart from a particular combination of recording electrodes that are placed at specific points on the patient's body. The direction the electrical current takes, toward a positive or negative electrode, determines the direction a waveform points on an ECG (Figure 2-6). An electrical current traveling more toward a positive electrode produces a waveform that points upward. A current traveling farther away from a positive electrode or toward a negative electrode produces a waveform that points downward. A **biphasic** waveform (one that has both a positive and negative deflection) is recorded when the impulse travels perpendicular to where the electrode is positioned.

REMINDER

Depolarization is the advancing wave of sodium ions.

One Lead or Many Leads?

Positioning the ECG electrodes in various positions on the patient's body gives us different views of the heart. As mentioned earlier, each configuration or positioning of lead wires is referred to as a lead. If all we are doing is identifying the presence or emergence of dysrhythmias, one lead can typically provide us all the information we need. If, on the other hand, we are trying to identify cardiac conditions, then we need to use many leads to view as much of the heart as possible.

REMINDER

A dysrhythmia is an irregularity in the heartbeat.

Impulses traveling away from a positive electrode and/or toward a negative electrode will produce downward deflections.

Impulses traveling perpendicular to the positive electrode may produce a biphasic waveform (one that has both a positive and negative deflection).

Impulses traveling toward a positive electrode produce upward deflections.

Negative electrode

Positive electrode

Figure 2-6
The direction the electrical impulse takes toward or away from a positive electrode causes the waveform to deflect either upward or downward.

KEY CONCEPT
Because the electrodes positioned on the patient's skin detect the heart's electrical activity, placing them in a different location changes the lead or view.

To help understand the concept of ECG leads, think about taking pictures of a house (Figure 2-7). From the front you get one picture and from the side of the house you get another picture. If there is damage on the back of the house, you should be able to see it in pictures taken at the rear of the house. The different ECG leads work in the same way; each provides a view that the other leads do not. The location or sites where the electrodes are placed vary depending on which view of the heart's activity is being assessed.

You might ask, "Why do I need to see different views of the heart?" As an example, suppose your patient is complaining of chest pain. You are attempting to determine if it is due to myocardial infarction. The presence of certain findings in two or more contiguous (anatomically next to each other) leads can indicate the presence of myocardial infarction (as well as ischemia and injury). In other words, multiple views are necessary to determine this condition. Further, depending on which lead we see the findings in, we can determine the location of the myocardial infarction.

In addition to identifying the presence and location of myocardial infarction, we can use the different ECG leads to identify physical changes in the heart muscle, conduction defects, electrical effects of medications and electrolytes, and to evaluate pacemaker function.

Figure 2-7
Think of each lead as being
a different view or picture of
the heart.

As we discuss ECG leads further, we review the concepts of bipolar and uni-polar leads and how ECG leads view the frontal and horizontal planes of the heart. Our goal here is simply to provide you with the fundamental principles. We cover ECG leads in more detail in Chapters 10 and 18.

Bipolar and Unipolar Leads

LO 2.7

ECG leads are either bipolar or unipolar (Figure 2-8). A bipolar lead records the flow of the electrical impulse between the two selected electrodes. Bipolar leads have a third (and often a fourth) electrode called a *ground.* The ground is used to help prevent electrical interference from appearing on the ECG and has zero electrical potential when compared with the positive and negative electrodes.

Unipolar leads use only one positive electrode and a reference point calcu-lated by the ECG machine. The reference point (with zero electrical potential) lies in the center of the heart's electrical field located left of the interventricu-lar septum and below the AV junction.

Planes of the Heart

LO 2.8

Electrodes can be placed at specific spots on the patient's extremities and chest wall to view the heart's electrical activity from two distinct planes (Figure 2-9): the frontal and horizontal. These planes provide a cross-sectional view of the heart.

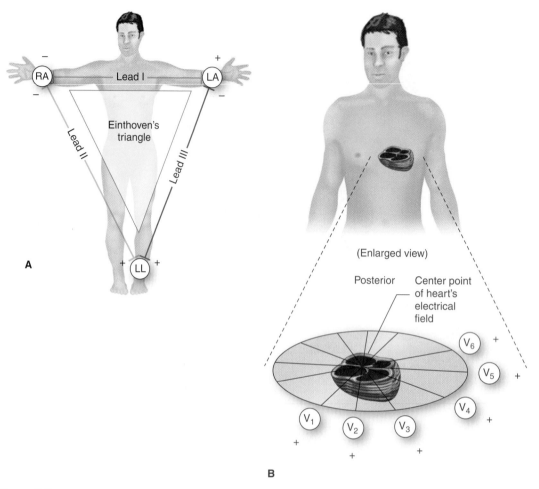

Figure 2-8
Bipolar and unipolar leads. (A) A bipolar lead requires a positive and negative electrode. (B) A unipolar lead has just a positive electrode and a reference point that is calculated by the ECG machine.

Frontal Plane   The frontal plane is a vertical (front and back, also referred to as an anterior and posterior) cut through the middle of the heart. The leads arranged on the frontal plane view the inferior (below), superior (above), and lateral (side) aspects of the heart. The leads that view the heart along the frontal plane are also referred to as *limb leads*.

The limb leads includes four electrodes; they are placed on the arms and legs or on the upper torso at least 10 centimeters (cm) from the heart (Figure 2-10). When the electrodes are positioned on the limbs, they can be located far down on the limbs or close to the hips and shoulders, but they must be even (right vs. left). Placement of the electrodes on the upper torso is often preferred over placement on the arms and legs during continuous monitoring as it maximizes patient comfort and minimizes muscle artifact.

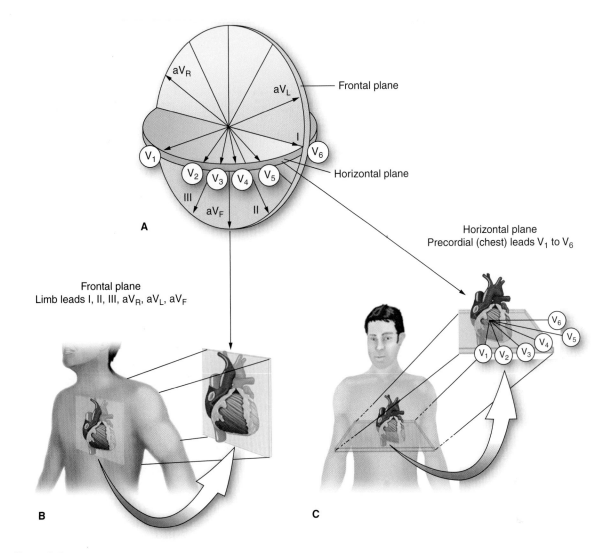

Figure 2-9
Frontal and horizontal planes provide a cross-sectional view of the heart.

Proper positioning of the electrodes for the limb leads is as follows:

- The right arm electrode, labeled RA, is positioned anywhere on the right arm or below the right clavicle in the midclavicular line (middle of the clavicle).
- The left arm electrode, labeled LA, is positioned anywhere on the left arm or below the left clavicle in the midclavicular line.
- The left leg electrode, labeled LL, is positioned anywhere on the left leg or left midclavicular line, below the last palpable rib.
- In four-lead wire systems, the right leg electrode, labeled RL, is positioned on the right leg or right midclavicular line, below the last palpable rib.

Figure 2-10
Position of limb leads. (A) Location of electrodes applied to the extremities and (B) location of electrodes applied to the chest.

QUESTION
2. **What are bipolar leads?**

Horizontal Plane   The horizontal plane is a transverse (top and bottom, also referred to as a *superior* and *inferior*) cut through the middle of the heart. The leads arranged on this plane provide us with anterior, lateral, and posterior (back) views. These leads are called the *precordial leads* (also referred to as *V leads* or *chest leads*). There are six primary precordial leads (Figure 2-11). As mentioned earlier, depending on the capability of the ECG machine as well as the placement of the ECG electrodes, up to six more leads can be obtained. The precordial leads are placed horizontally across the chest.

LO 2.9

Lead II

To give you an example of an actual ECG lead, let's discuss lead II. This is the lead most commonly used to monitor for emerging or existing cardiac dysrhythmias.

Lead II is a combination of a positive lead wire, a negative lead wire, and one or two ground lead wires. Remember from our earlier discussion, because it requires two electrodes of opposite polarity (positive and negative), it is referred to as a bipolar lead.

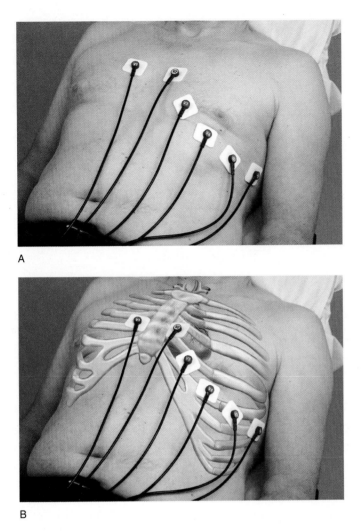

Figure 2-11
Position of precordial leads.
(A) View of leads on surface
of chest; (B) View of leads on
chest with internal anatomy
(ribs and heart shown)

A

B

With lead II, the LL lead is the positive electrode, the RA lead is the negative electrode, and the LA lead is the ground (Figure 2-12). In 4-lead wire systems, the RL lead is another ground.

Lead II detects the dominant electrical activity of the heart as it moves from a right superior to a left inferior direction. The waveforms in lead II are mostly upright because the wave of depolarization is moving toward the positive electrode.

KEY CONCEPT
Lead II is a commonly used lead for providing continuous ECG monitoring.

The Output

LO 2.10

In the first part of the chapter we discussed how the ECG machine obtains the information (the input). Now, let's discuss how it displays it (the output).

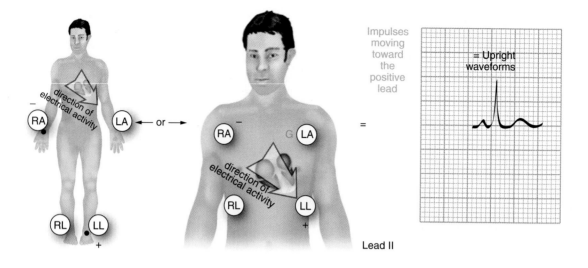

Figure 2-12
Lead locations on extremities or the chest for lead II. In lead II the positive electrode is located on the left foot or left midclavicular line, below the last palpable rib while the negative electrode is positioned just below the right clavicle or on the right arm. The main waveforms seen in lead II are upright.

REMINDER

It is the electrical impulse that depolarizes the heart and causes the muscle to contract. The muscle contraction propels the blood out of its chambers and throughout the body.

QUESTION
3. What ECG waveforms are generated as a result of the heart's electrical activity?

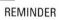

REMINDER

Static ECG tracings are printed on ECG paper, while the dynamic mode is the real-time movement seen across the oscilloscope.

The ECG machine translates the electrical impulses generated in the heart into wave-like signals that are recorded on paper or displayed on a monitor as a series of waveforms, intervals, and segments.

Displays and Printouts

ECG rhythms shown on the oscilloscope are called **dynamic ECGs** and represent real time electrical activity whereas those printed on graph paper are called **ECG tracings** or **static ECGs** (also referred to as *rhythm strips* or *printouts*) and show what has already occurred. Each type has different purposes. It is much easier to analyze a static ECG to determine abnormalities than it is to examine an image moving across a screen. On the other hand, the static ECG tracing is "past news," so it is also necessary to look at the ECG monitor to see what is presently occurring (Figure 2-13). ECG machines are typically capable of producing a tracing, whereas not all are equipped with an oscilloscope.

Another thing to consider is that today's ECG monitors are configured with multiple filters for signal processing. The most common settings are monitor mode and diagnostic mode. The monitor mode ECG display is more filtered than the diagnostic mode. In monitor mode, filtering limits artifact for routine cardiac rhythm monitoring and helps reduce wandering baseline. In diagnostic mode, the filters allow accurate ST segments to be recorded. When we are trying to analyze ST segment changes, a printout must be used as the ECG monitor will not be accurate.

Figure 2-13
Monitor display vs. printouts.

Reading Printouts

LO 2.11

Although looking at the tracing on the monitor screen can reveal important information, to more accurately analyze the tracing requires using a printout. Further, to measure the various waveforms, durations, and intervals, you need to see where each begins and ends as well as the amplitude of each waveform.

Special Paper

A special type of paper is used to record the heart's electrical activity. The paper comes in a variety of sizes depending on its use. ECG machines used to provide continuous monitoring may employ narrow paper that prints out a rhythm strip of a single lead whereas ECG machines that produce a 12-lead ECG use wider paper in order to show all the leads.

Regardless of its size, the paper, made of thermally sensitive material, consists of horizontal and vertical lines that form a grid. The narrow lines that run vertically and horizontally intersect to form squares. There are five of these squares between heavier (thicker) lines (that run vertically and horizontally) (Figure 2-14).

Horizontal Lines

The distance between the lines, or boxes, running horizontally represents time or duration. Each small square running horizontally represents 0.04 seconds in duration. Five of these small squares (making up a larger box) represent 0.20 seconds in duration. Five of these larger boxes represent one second. Fifteen larger boxes equal a three-second interval. Horizontal measurements

Figure 2-14
ECG paper with stylus-generating waveforms. Vertical lines represent amplitude in electrical voltage in millivolts or millimeters while horizontal lines represent time or duration.

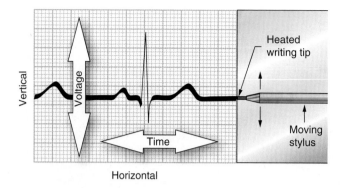

Horizontal

are used to determine the heart rate. You can also use these standardized distances to determine the width or duration of any portion of an ECG complex, segment, or interval.

On the top or bottom (and sometimes both) of the printout there are often vertical slashes or markings to represent three-second intervals (depending on the manufacturer there may be shorter or longer time frames). These markings can help you quickly determine the approximate heart rate. The ECG recorder is set to a standard speed of 25 mm per second so that tracings made from different machines may be uniformly compared (Figure 2-15). Some ECG machines are equipped with a feature that allows you to speed up the printout to pass 50 mm of paper per second. This effect stretches out the tracings, which can make it easier to diagnose fast rhythms when it is difficult to see the P wave.

If the ECG paper does not have vertical lines to allow you to quickly determine the heart rate, count out 15 boxes and place a vertical mark. Then repeat the step to give you two three-second sections or a full six-second section of the tracing.

Vertical Lines

The distance between the lines, or boxes, running vertically represents amplitude in millimeters (mm) or electrical voltage in millivolts (mV). Each small square running vertically represents 1 mm or 0.1 mV. The larger boxes are made up of five small squares and represent 5 mm or 0.5 mV. To determine the amplitude of a wave, segment, or interval, count the number of small boxes from the baseline to its highest or lowest point.

Recording the Tracing

A heated stylus that responds to the electrical stimulus detected through the ECG electrodes moves up and down and produces markings on the paper. When no electrical stimulus is flowing through the electrode (usually representing the polarized state of the cells), or it is too small to detect, the stylus burns a straight line (isoelectric) in the paper. This flat line is also called the **isoelectric line.** We use this line as a baseline or reference point to identify the changing electrical amplitude.

Depending on what you are using the ECG for, you will typically print off either a rhythm strip or a 12-lead tracing. Some ECG machines are capable of

KEY CONCEPT

Each small square represents 0.04 seconds in duration, while one large square represents 0.20 seconds.

KEY CONCEPT

The horizontal axis on the ECG tells us about rate and duration, while the vertical axis tells us about electrical voltage or strength of the impulses.

QUESTION

4. Thirty larger boxes on the ECG paper represent how many seconds?

LO 2.12

Figure 2-15
From right to left: horizontally each small square represents 0.04 seconds in duration. Five of these small squares (making up a larger box) represent 0.20 seconds in duration. Fifteen of these larger squares represent three seconds. Vertically each small square represents 0.1 millivolt (1 mm) while five of these small squares represent 0.5 mV (5 mm).

analyzing certain aspects of the tracing and including that information on the printout. Even if the ECG machine provides an analysis, you should always take time to analyze the tracing to verify the accuracy of the information.

Calibrating the ECG

LO 2.13

Calibration is the process of determining that the settings on the ECG match the proper standards. If the ECG machine is properly calibrated, the height of the P waves, QRS complexes, and T waves can provide you with certain information. For example, small complexes can indicate conditions such as pericardial effusion whereas tall QRS complexes may point to the presence of left ventricular hypertrophy (both these conditions are discussed in later chapters). To help assure the ECG machine is properly calibrated, you can place a registration or calibration mark as a reference point on the ECG tracing. This

Standard signal
of 1.0 mV produces
a registration mark

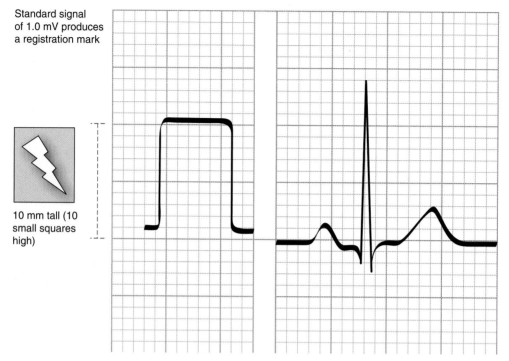

10 mm tall (10
small squares
high)

Figure 2-16
Calibration of the ECG.

is sometimes called *calibrating the ECG machine.* A standard signal of 1.0 mV will produce a registration point 10 mm tall (10 small squares high). On most ECG machines this mark is created automatically whereas with others it is necessary to manually place this registration point. This registration mark should be included on every ECG tracing (Figure 2-16).

LO 2.14

Artifact

Many factors can interfere with the signal being detected and transferred to the ECG machine. We refer to this as **noise** or **artifact** (Figure 2-17). Noise or artifact has no relationship to the electrical activity of the heart and makes it hard to accurately interpret the ECG. Three common types of artifact are muscle artifact, wandering baseline, and electromagnetic interference (EMI).

Muscle artifact appears as a high frequency, low amplitude, relatively irregular distortion of the baseline and QRS complexes. It is often caused by poorly supported or tense muscles in the arms and legs or shivering. It may be mimicked by loose, improperly placed, dried out, or outdated electrodes; a loose lead wire; poor patient cable connection; worn-out lead wires; a malfunctioning ECG machine; poor skin preparation; or vibration from a moving vehicle.

Ways to prevent or minimize muscle artifact include keeping the electrodes in their unopened package until it is time to use them, avoiding the use of

Figure 2-17
Artifact is markings on the ECG caused by such things as: (A) the patient moving; (B) shivering, or experiencing muscle tremors; electrodes that are loose or improperly placed; worn-out lead wires; a malfunctioning ECG machine; or the presence of 60-cycle current interference.

electrodes that are past their expiration date, properly preparing the skin, resting the arms and legs on a supportive surface, ensuring patient comfort and coaching the patient to relax, ensuring good patient/electrode contact, replacing dried out electrodes, securing cable connections, and stopping the vehicle while acquiring the ECG.

Wandering baseline is a low-frequency, high-amplitude artifact. It may be observed during deep inhalations and exhalations, patient movement, or the acceleration and deceleration forces of a moving vehicle. Ways to prevent or minimize wandering baseline include asking the patient to breathe quietly while the ECG is being acquired, preventing patient movement, performing good skin preparation, checking all electrodes for good contact, and stopping the vehicle while acquiring the ECG.

Electromagnetic interference originates outside the patient and is caused by interference from electronic sources such as power cords, insufficiently grounded alternating current (AC) powered equipment, and nearby use of portable radios. This is also called alternating current (AC) or 60-cycle interference. Ways to prevent or minimize electromagnetic interference include moving away from a noisy environment, ensuring power cords are not touching or lying near the ECG cable or lead wires, moving away from or unplugging AC-powered equipment that is causing interference, and checking the lead wires and patient cable for observable damage.

The way you can differentiate artifact from waveforms produced by the heart is that there is usually little consistency to the artifact whereas electrical activity produced by the heart usually looks the same (or at least similar) across the rhythm strip. As you will learn throughout this text, some dysrhythmias produce chaotic-looking waveforms (such as atrial and ventricular fibrillation), but even those waveforms generally repeat themselves. In some cases artifact can mimic life-threatening dysrhythmias. For this reason, always compare your rhythm interpretation with the clinical status of the patient. If the patient is awake and alert but the ECG shows a rhythm inconsistent with life, you know you are dealing with artifact.

Key Points 🔍

- Electrodes placed on the patient's skin detect the heart's electrical activity. The electrical activity is then transferred to the ECG machine by color-coded wires (called *lead wires*) and displayed on a screen (oscilloscope) or printed onto graph paper.
- The graphic record or tracing is called an *electrocardiogram*.
- The ECG machine has many uses in hospital and out-of-hospital settings.
- Abnormalities in the cardiac rate and/or rhythm are called *dysrhythmias*.
- Impulses that travel toward a positive electrode are recorded on the ECG as upward deflections. Impulses traveling away from a positive electrode or toward a negative electrode are recorded as downward deflections.
- Each lead provides a different view of the heart.
- The shape of the waveform is described from the perspective of the positive electrode of the selected lead.
- The limb leads are produced by placing electrodes on the right arm, left arm, left leg, and right leg. They provide a view of the electrical activity along the heart's frontal plane.
- The precordial leads provide information about the electrical activity along the horizontal plane of the heart.
- ECG rhythms shown on the oscilloscope are called *dynamic ECGs* whereas those printed on graph paper are called *ECG tracings* or *static ECGs*.
- The ECG paper used to record the heart's electrical activity consists of horizontal and vertical lines that form a grid. The smallest of the squares represents 0.04 seconds in duration.

- Five of the small boxes represent 0.20 seconds in duration and make up the larger boxes denoted by a heavier line. Fifteen larger boxes equal a three-second interval. You can use the horizontal measurements to determine the heart rate.

- Vertically on the ECG paper, the distance between the lines, or boxes, represents amplitude in mm or electrical voltage in mV. Each small square represents 1 mm or 0.1 mV while the larger boxes, made up of five small squares, represent 5 mm or 0.5 mV.

- The flat line that precedes the electrical impulses is called the *isoelectric line*.

- To help assure the ECG machine is properly calibrated, you should place a registration or calibration mark as a reference point on each ECG tracing.

- Artifact is markings on the ECG tracing that have no relationship to the electrical activity of the heart. They can be caused by such things as the patient's moving, shivering, or experiencing muscle tremors; electrodes that are loose or improperly placed; worn-out lead wires; a malfunctioning ECG machine; or the presence of 60-cycle current interference.

Assess Your Understanding

The following questions give you a chance to assess your understanding of the material discussed in this chapter. The answers can be found in Appendix A.

1. An electrocardiogram is a/an
   a. graphic record of the heart's electrical activity.
   b. device that measures and records the ECG.
   c. irregular rhythm.
   d. device that measures the heart's mechanical activity.

2. The electrocardiograph can be used to do all the following EXCEPT
   a. detect cardiac dysrhythmias.
   b. determine cardiac output.
   c. identify the presence of myocardial ischemia and/or infarction.
   d. evaluate the function of artificial implanted pacemakers.

3. _____ positioned on the patient's skin detect the heart's electrical activity.
   a. Electrodes
   b. Lead wires
   c. Tracings
   d. Leads

4. Impulses that travel toward a positive electrode and away from a negative electrode are recorded on the electrocardiogram as _____ deflections.
   a. downward
   b. perpendicular
   c. neutral
   d. upward

5. The lead most commonly used for continuous cardiac monitoring is lead
   a. I.
   b. MCL_1.
   c. V_1.
   d. II.

6. With lead II, the _____ lead wire is the positive electrode.
   a. LL
   b. RA
   c. LA
   d. RL

7. Bipolar leads
   a. record the flow of the electrical impulse between the three selected electrodes.
   b. are used only in the hospital setting.
   c. require two electrodes of opposite polarity.
   d. use only one positive electrode and a reference point calculated by the ECG machine.

8. The frontal plane gives us a/an _____ view of the heart's electrical activity.
   a. anterior and posterior
   b. superior and inferior
   c. anterior and superior
   d. lateral and inferior

9. The limb leads are obtained by placing electrodes on the
   a. right arm, left arm, left leg, and right leg.
   b. chest and back.
   c. right arm, left leg, and right leg.
   d. left arm and left leg.

10. An ECG printout
    a. is called a "dynamic ECG."
    b. shows the heart's current electrical activity.

c. provides a more accurate picture of the ST segments than does the oscilloscope.

d. is harder to analyze than looking at the ECG monitor.

11. Each small square on the ECG paper running horizontally represents _____ seconds in duration.

a. 0.01

b. 0.04

c. 0.12

d. 0.20

12. The larger box on the ECG paper, made up of five small squares, represents _____ seconds in duration.

a. 0.12

b. 0.15

c. 0.20

d. 0.32

13. On the top or bottom of the ECG paper there may be vertical slashes or markings to represent _____ second intervals.

a. 1

b. 3

c. 5

d. 10

14. Each small square on the ECG paper running vertically represents

a. 0.1 mV.

b. 5 mm.

c. 10 mm.

d. 2.0 mV.

15. The reference point used to identify the changing electrical amplitude on the ECG is called the

a. isoelectric line.

b. ST segment.

c. PR interval.

d. QT interval.

16. A calibration mark serves as a reference point on the ECG tracing from which you can assess the height of the P waves, QRS complexes, and T waves.

a. True

b. False

17. Artifact is

a. a normal part of each ECG tracing.

b. an indication of decreased cardiac output.

c. sometimes caused by muscle tremors.

d. consistently the same across the ECG tracing.

Referring to the scenario at the beginning of this chapter, answer the following questions.

18. Examination of the ECG by EMS and healthcare personnel provides the patient's
   a. pulse rate.
   b. heart rate.
   c. blood pressure.
   d. cardiac output.

19. The patient fainted because
   a. he overexerted himself.
   b. his sympathetic nervous system was overstimulated.
   c. his blood pressure medications are too strong.
   d. his cardiac output dropped too low.

20. Which of the following nerves controls heart rate?
   a. Phrenic
   b. Aortic
   c. Vagus
   d. Diaphragmatic

? Answers to Sidebar Questions

1. Impulses are generated and subsequently conducted through the heart when positively charged ions, such as sodium, rapidly but briefly move inside the cells, causing the interior to become positively charged. This is called depolarization. **p. 44**

2. A bipolar lead requires two electrodes of opposite polarity (positive and negative). **p. 56**

3. Each cycle of depolarization and repolarization of the heart produces a P wave, QRS complex, and T wave. **p. 58**

4. Thirty larger boxes on the ECG paper represent 6 seconds. **p. 60**

What's Online

Go to www.mhhe.com/shadeECG2e to find:

- Presentations on chapter content
- Crossword puzzle exercises
- Chapter quiz
- Flashcards
- Fill-in-the-blank exercises and answers

section 2

The Nine-Step Process

Chapter 3:   Analyzing the Electrocardiogram

Chapter 4:   Heart Rate

Chapter 5:   Regularity

Chapter 6:   P Waves

Chapter 7:   QRS Complexes

Chapter 8:   PR Intervals

Chapter 9:   ST Segments, T Waves, QT Intervals, and U Waves

Section 2:   Practice Makes Perfect

3 Analyzing the Electrocardiogram

Chapter Outline

Characteristics of the Normal Electrocardiogram

Analyzing the Electrocardiogram

The Nine-Step Process

Flexibility in the Nine-Step Process

Dysrhythmia and Cardiac Condition Characteristics

Analyzing the ECG on the Monitor Screen

Analyzing the Rhythm Strip

Analyzing the 12-Lead Tracing

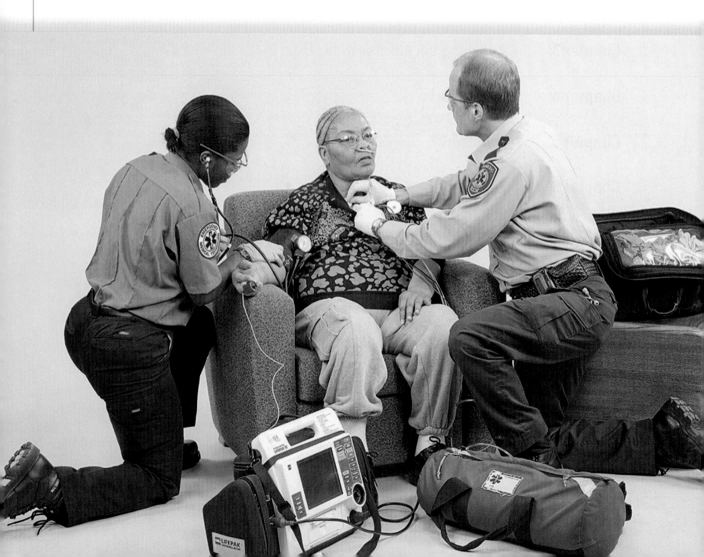

Learning Objectives

LO 3.1 Identify the characteristics of a "normal" ECG.

LO 3.2 Describe the purpose and benefits of an organized approach for analyzing an ECG tracing.

LO 3.3 List and describe the elements of the Nine-Step Process.

LO 3.4 Define the term *morphology*.

LO 3.5 Discuss how identifying characteristics of an ECG can help identify dysrhythmias and cardiac conditions.

LO 3.6 Recall how to assess an ECG rhythm on the ECG monitor.

LO 3.7 Discuss how to assess an ECG rhythm strip.

LO 3.8 Discuss how to assess a 12-lead ECG tracing.

Case History

Your patient is a 67-year-old female whose chief complaint is chest pain. Your assessment of her pulse identifies gross irregularity, prompting you to quickly attach her to your ECG machine. Across the monitor screen, you observe what appears to be a very irregular rhythm that lacks upright P waves but has normal looking QRS complexes. You print out the tracing and show it to your partner who immediately exclaims, "I don't remember seeing anything like that in my ECG book; I don't know what to call that!" You recall what was drilled into your head during your paramedic course: "Use a step-by-step process to analyze your ECG tracings, and don't try to memorize rhythm strips." You then look more closely at the tracing. The rate is approximately 90 beats per minute, the regularity is totally irregular, there is a chaotic-looking baseline in front of each normal-looking QRS complex, and there are no PR intervals. From what you know about ECG dysrhythmias, this has all the characteristics of just one dysrhythmia. You tell your partner, "I bet you lunch this is atrial fibrillation." Later that day, following your free lunch, you call your paramedic instructor to thank her for teaching you how to analyze ECGs using a step-by-step approach.

LO 3.1

Characteristics of the Normal ECG

> **REMINDER**
>
> As we proceed through this section and for the purposes of our discussion, we will refer to how the waveforms should look in lead II. If another lead is used, the appearance of the waveforms may be different. Later in this book, we will discuss how the waveforms should appear in the other leads.

As discussed earlier, depolarization and repolarization of the atria and ventricles are electrical events. The path of the electrical activity through the heart is displayed in a series of waves and complexes, commonly known as the P wave, QRS complex, and T wave. The ECG detects this electrical activity. However, in order to use the information we must first analyze and interpret it. To analyze an ECG, we can directly observe the rhythm on an ECG monitor screen or print a tracing so that the specific waveforms, segments, and intervals can be measured and examined. We then compare our findings against what is considered the normal ECG, commonly referred to as *sinus rhythm* (Figure 3-1). Sinus rhythm consists of the following:

- Waveforms and intervals that appear at regular intervals at a rate of 60 to 100 beats per minute (in the adult).
- Upright and slightly **asymmetrical** P waves, each followed by a QRS complex of normal upright contour, duration, and configuration.
- A PR interval (PRI) of normal duration that precedes each QRS complex.
- A flat ST segment followed by an upright and slightly asymmetrical T wave.
- A normal QT interval (QTI).
- Sometimes the presence of a U wave.

LO 3.2

Analyzing the Electrocardiogram

In this chapter and the next several chapters, we focus on the steps used to analyze the ECG. When looking at an ECG rhythm or tracing, it may appear like just a bunch of scribbles and lines, particularly for those who are new to ECG analysis and interpretation. The key to making sense of what you see is to approach it in a logical and systematic manner. In this book we teach you to use a nine-step process.

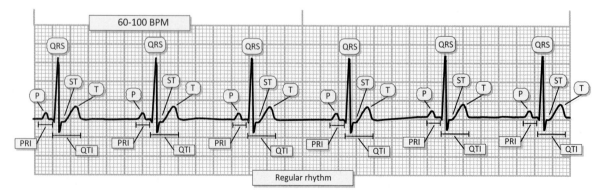

Figure 3-1

Normal sinus rhythm is a repetitive cycle of ECG waveforms, intervals, and segments occurring at a rate of between 60 to 100 beats per minute (BPM).

The Nine-Step Process

LO 3.3

The Nine-Step Process assesses the main elements of the ECG tracing. Once learned, it is an effective tool for analyzing ECG tracings regardless of whether for dysrhythmia recognition or identification of cardiac conditions. It includes the following elements (Figure 3-2):

1. **Heart rate:** Determine the rate. (Is it normal, fast, or slow?)
2. **Regularity:** Determine the regularity. (Is it regular or irregular?)
3. **P waves:** Assess the P waves. (Is there a uniform P wave preceding each QRS complex?)
4. **QRS complexes:** Assess the QRS complexes. (Are the QRS complexes within normal limits? Do they appear normal?)
5. **PR intervals:** Assess the PR intervals. (Are the PR intervals identifiable? Are they within normal limits? Are they constant in duration?)
6. **ST segments:** Assess the ST segment. (Is it a flat line? Is it elevated or depressed?)
7. **T waves:** Assess the T waves. (Are they slightly asymmetrical? Are they of normal height? Is it oriented in the same direction as the preceding QRS complex?)
8. **QT intervals:** Assess the QT intervals. (Are they within normal limits?)
9. **U waves:** Look for U waves. (Are they present?)

Step 1: Heart Rate

The heart rate is one of the first characteristics of an ECG tracing that should be assessed (Figure 3-3). The average heart rate in the adult is 60 to 100 beats per minute. A heart rate that is slower or faster is considered abnormal and may indicate significant problems requiring prompt intervention on your part. For this reason, we need to check it as soon as possible. In Chapter 4, we describe a number of methods that can be used to determine the heart rate.

KEY CONCEPT
The average heart rate in the adult is 60 to 100 beats per minute.

Step 2: Regularity

The regularity of the rhythm is another one of the characteristics of an ECG tracing that should be assessed initially (refer to Figure 3-3). Normally the heart beats in a regular, rhythmic fashion, producing specific waveforms and intervals with each heartbeat. This cycle repeats itself over and over

The Nine-Step Process

| Rate | Rhythm | P waves | QRS complexes | PR intervals | ST segments | T waves | QT intervals | U waves |

Figure 3-2
The Nine-Step Process.

Characteristics of normal heart rate and rhythm:
The normal heart rate is 60 to 100 BPM and beats in a regular fashion.

Heart rate findings in this tracing:
This tracing has a heart rate of 76
beats per minute and a regular rhythm.

Figure 3-3
Determining the heart rate and regularity are important steps in assessing the ECG. Note: This tracing includes three leads: Lead II is in the top position, lead I is in the second position, and lead III is in the third position.

KEY CONCEPT
Normally the heart beats in a regular, rhythmic fashion.

again. The distance between the consecutive P waves should be the same, just as the distance between the consecutive QRS complexes should be the same throughout the tracing. When the distances between the consecutive P waves and/or consecutive QRS complexes differ, the rhythm is irregular. In Chapter 5, we describe several ways to easily identify whether or not the rhythm is regular and describe several types of irregularity that may be seen.

 LO 3.4

Step 3: P Waves

Assessing the P waves (Figure 3-4) can tell us if the impulse that initiated the heart beat arose from the sinoatrial (SA) node and if it is traveling through the atria and atrioventricular (AV) junction in a normal fashion. When assessing the waveforms seen on an ECG tracing, we look at the **morphology** of the complexes. The term *morphology* refers to the appearance of the complexes. The morphology may be normal, wide, short, tall, flat, spiked, jagged, or bizarre (meaning its shape is far from normal). It often yields a great deal of information and can help us identify both dysrhythmias as well as cardiac conditions.

KEY CONCEPT
When referring to the shape of any particular wave form on the ECG, we use the term morphology.

KEY CONCEPT
Normally there is one upright P wave preceding each QRS complex.

Characteristically, the P wave arises from the isoelectric line, appearing as an upright and slightly asymmetrical waveform. There is one P wave preceding each QRS complex. Its amplitude is 0.5 to 2.5 mm and its duration is 0.06 to 0.10 seconds. If the P wave meets all of these characteristics, it has most likely originated from the SA node. P waves that originate from the SA node are referred to as *sinus P waves*.

Characteristics of normal P waves:
Asymmetrical waveform. There is one P wave preceding each QRS complex
Its amplitude is 0.5 to 2.5 mm and its duration is 0.06 to 0.10 seconds.

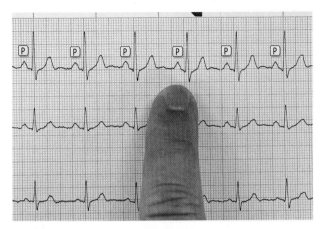

P waves findings in this tracing:
Asymmetrical waveform. There is one P wave preceding each QRS complex. Its amplitude is 2.5 mm and its duration is 0.11 seconds. Further, there appears to be notching of the P wave.

Figure 3-4
Assessing the P waves, the third step, helps to identify if the impulse arose from the SA node and if it traveled through the atria and AV junction in a normal manner.

Step 4: QRS Complexes

Assessing the QRS complexes yields valuable information for both dysrhythmia interpretation and identification of various cardiac conditions (Figure 3-5). In sinus rhythm, the QRS complex follows the P wave and PR segment. It is larger in appearance than the P wave and consists of up to three parts: the Q wave, the R wave, and the S wave.

The waves of the QRS complex are generally narrow and sharply pointed. The Q wave is the first downward deflection from the baseline. Its duration is less than 0.04 seconds (1 mm or one small square) and its amplitude is less than 25% of the R wave in that lead. The Q wave is not always present. The R wave is the first upward deflection after the P wave, and the S wave is the first negative deflection after the R wave that extends below the baseline. The QRS complex is normally 0.06 to 0.10 seconds (one and a half to two and a half small boxes) in duration. The duration is measured from the beginning of the Q wave to the end of the S wave or the beginning of the R wave if the Q is not present. The amplitude of the QRS complex is 5 to 30 mm high (but differs with each lead selected). The QRS complex represents movement of the electrical impulse through the ventricles, causing their contraction.

Step 5: PR Intervals

Another important step in assessing the ECG is measuring the PR intervals (Figure 3-6). The **PR interval** is the distance from the beginning of the P wave to the beginning of the Q wave. The PR interval represents depolarization of the heart from the SA node through the atria, AV node, and His-Purkinje system. The first portion of the PR interval is the P wave (discussed earlier),

QUESTION
1. For what purpose do we use the isoelectric line? *Note:* Answers to sidebar questions can be found at the end of the chapter.

QUESTION
2. The amplitude of the normal P wave is represented by how many small squares? Also, the normal duration of the P wave is represented by how many small squares?

KEY CONCEPT
The waves of the QRS complex are generally narrow and sharply pointed.

REMINDER
The Q wave is not always present.

Characteristics of normal QRS complexes:
There should be one QRS complex following each P wave. The QRS complex is narrow and sharply pointed. It is normally 0.06 to 0.10 seconds in duration and has an amplitude of 5 to 30 mm high (but differs with each lead selected).

QRS complex findings in this tracing:
There is one QRS complex following each P wave. The QRS complex is narrow at 0.08 seconds in duration and 19 mm in amplitude.

Figure 3-5
Assessing the QRS complexes is the fourth step in assessing the ECG.

Characteristics of normal PR intervals:
There should be one PR interval preceding each P wave.
Each PR interval is the same at 0.12 to 0.20 seconds in duration.

PR interval findings in this tracing:
There is one PR interval preceding each QRS complex. The duration is the same for each at 0.12 seconds.

Figure 3-6
Assessing the PR intervals is the fifth step in assessing the ECG.

while the second portion is the PR segment. The **PR segment** represents the impulse traveling through the His-Purkinje system and is seen as a flat (isoelectric) line. The PR segment has this appearance because the electrical currents are so small they are not seen on the ECG. The His-Purkinje system is responsible for carrying the impulse to the ventricles.

A normal PR interval indicates the impulse originated from the SA node and traveled through the atria, the AV node, and the His-Purkinje system in a regular, unobstructed course. A normal PR interval is 0.12 to 0.20 seconds in duration; in other words, it extends across three to five small squares. The PR intervals should be the same duration (constant) across the ECG tracing.

With some conditions we may see a PR interval shorter or longer than normal. This tells us that something abnormal is occurring in or around the AV junction. A short PR interval (less than 0.12 seconds in duration) is seen when the electrical impulse arises close to or in the AV junction. A longer PR interval (greater than 0.20 seconds in duration) indicates an even greater delay in conduction of the impulse through the AV junction. It is often associated with a condition called AV heart block. Both shorter and longer PR intervals will be discussed in later chapters.

Step 6: ST Segments

Following the QRS complex is a pause referred to as the ST segment (Figure 3-7). The ST segment starts at the J point (the point or junction at which the QRS complex meets the ST segment) and ends at the beginning of the T wave. The ST segment therefore connects the QRS complex and the T wave. During this period, the ventricles are preparing to repolarize.

The ST segment appears as a flat or isoelectric line that is on the same horizontal line (or close to it) as the PR segment of the preceding complex and has a duration of 0.08 to 0.12 seconds.

Step 7: Waves

Following the ST segment, we should see the T wave (Figure 3-8). It is larger than the P wave and slightly asymmetrical. The peak of the T wave is closer to the end of the wave than the beginning, and the first half has a more gradual slope than the second half. Normally, the T wave is not more than 5 mm in height in the limb leads or 10 mm in any precordial lead. The T wave is normally oriented in the same direction as the preceding QRS complex. It represents ventricular repolarization (or recovery).

KEY CONCEPT
Normally, the PR intervals are constant and have a duration of 0.12 to 0.20 seconds.

KEY CONCEPT
The ST segment appears as a flat or isoelectric line.

QUESTION
3. What does the T wave represent?

KEY CONCEPT
Normally, the T wave is an asymmetrical upright waveform that is not more than 5 mm in height in the limb leads or 10 mm in any precordial lead.

Characteristics of normal ST segments:
The ST segment is a flat line that starts at the J point and ends at the beginning of the T wave. It has a duration of 0.08 to 0.12 seconds.

ST segment findings in this tracing:
There is an ST segment connecting each QRS complex to the T wave. The duration is 0.08 seconds.

Figure 3-7
Assessing the ST segment, the sixth step, can reveal important information.

Characteristics of normal T waves:

The T wave is larger than the P wave and slightly asymmetrical. Normally, the T wave is not more than 5 mm in height in the limb leads or 10 mm in any precordial lead and is oriented in the same direction as the preceding QRS complex.

T wave findings in this tracing:

In the middle lead the T wave is the same size as the P wave. However, in the top and bottom leads the T wave is larger than the P waves. It is also biphasic. In the top lead the T wave is 5 mm in height and oriented in the same direction as the preceding QRS complex.

Figure 3-8
Assessing the T waves is the seventh step in assessing the ECG.

Characteristics of normal QT intervals:

The QT interval is the distance from the onset of the QRS complex until the end of the T wave and has a normal duration of 0.36 to 0.44 seconds.

QT interval findings in this tracing:
The QT intervals in this tracing have a duration of 0.40 seconds.

Figure 3-9
Assessing the QT intervals (QTI), the eighth step, can help identify certain cardiac conditions.

Step 8: QT Intervals

Another measurement on the ECG rhythm is the **QT interval** (Figure 3-9). This interval is the distance from the onset of the QRS complex until the end of the T wave and has a normal duration of 0.36 to 0.44 seconds. It measures the time of ventricular depolarization and repolarization. It varies according to age, sex, and heart rate—the faster the heart rate, the shorter the QT interval. The QT interval should not be greater than half the distance between consecutive R waves when the rhythm is regular.

KEY CONCEPT

Normal values for the QT interval are between 0.36 and 0.44 seconds.

Characteristics of normal U waves:
There may be a small U wave following the T wave.

U wave findings in this tracing:
There is a small U wave following
each T wave.

Figure 3-10
Assessing the U waves is the ninth step in analyzing ECG tracings.

Step 9: U Waves

In about 50% to 75% of ECGs, a small upright (except in lead aV_L) waveform called the **U wave** is seen following the T wave, but before the next P wave (Figure 3-10). Its voltage is so low, however, that the U wave often goes unnoticed.

REMINDER
The waveform that represents atrial repolarization is usually hidden by the QRS complex and for this reason is not seen.

Flexibility in the Nine-Step Process

Even though we list nine steps, you can sometimes identify dysrhythmias and conditions using just some of these steps. When assessing dysrhythmias, the first five steps (or so) often yield enough information to determine what is occurring on the tracing. Similarly, when evaluating the 12-lead ECG for cardiac conditions, assessment of the ST segment, QRS complex, and T wave usually yields enough information to identify many common conditions. Why then, do you need to memorize them all? Well, the quick answer is, you never know when just a few steps can identify a dysrhythmia or condition and when all nine steps will be needed.

Also, although we list the nine steps of analyzing an ECG tracing in a particular order, there is no requirement to follow that order. For example, determining regularity can be done before identifying the heart rate. Likewise, in some cases the first thing you might notice when looking at an ECG are bizarre-looking QRS complexes suggestive of a dysrhythmia originating from the ventricles. In that case, assessing the QRS complexes may be the first step you use to analyze the tracing. What is important is remembering all the steps and trying to follow the same order so you do not leave out one or two that may help you identify a dysrhythmia or condition.

The information you gather during the Nine-Step Process is referred to as *the characteristics of the tracing.* We compare these findings to what is considered the normal ECG: sinus rhythm.

KEY CONCEPT
The first five steps are better suited for dysrhythmia recognition whereas assessing just the QRS complexes, ST segments, and T waves often provides the needed information to identify many cardiac conditions.

QUESTION
4. The average heart rate in the adult is between _____ and _____ beats per minute.

LO 3.5

Dysrhythmia and Cardiac Condition Characteristics

Each dysrhythmia and cardiac condition has certain characteristics or features. These characteristics are what we use to determine the presence of dysrhythmias and/or cardiac conditions in the ECG tracings.

Over the next three pages, we talk about the characteristics associated with two dysrhythmias. Not to worry, we cover these dysrhythmias more thoroughly in subsequent chapters. Our discussion here is just to make you aware of how characteristics are used in dysrhythmia and cardiac condition analysis and interpretation.

The dysrhythmia sinus bradycardia (Figure 3-11) is a slow rhythm that arises from the SA node and travels through the conduction system in a normal manner. It has the following characteristics:

- Waveforms and intervals that appear at regular intervals at a rate of less than 60 beats per minute (in the adult).
- Upright and slightly asymmetrical P waves, each followed by a QRS complex of normal upright contour, duration, and configuration.

Figure 3-11
When comparing the characteristics of sinus bradycardia to normal sinus rhythm, you can see that the only difference is the heart rate.

- A PR interval of normal duration that precedes each QRS complex.
- A flat ST segment followed by an upright and slightly asymmetrical T wave.
- A normal QT interval.
- Sometimes the presence of a U wave.

You can see that the only difference between sinus bradycardia and sinus rhythm is the heart rate. Thus, the key characteristic of sinus bradycardia is a slow heart rate.

Let's look at another example. Remember our case history at the beginning of this chapter? The dysrhythmia atrial fibrillation (Figure 3-12) occurs when the atria fire chaotically from many different sites. Because the atrial impulses bombard the AV node in such a chaotic manner, not all the impulses get through, producing a totally irregular rhythm. Atrial fibrillation has a number of distinct characteristics including the following:

- Waveforms and intervals appear at totally irregular intervals. The atrial heart rate exceeds 350 beats per minute while the ventricular heart rate depends on how many impulses pass through the AV node.
- There is an absence of P waves; instead there is a chaotic-looking baseline preceding each QRS complex.

Figure 3-12
Comparing the characteristics of atrial fibrillation to normal sinus rhythm.

- The QRS complexes are of normal upright contour, duration, and configuration.
- There are no PR intervals.
- The ST segment and T wave may be indistinguishable or absent.
- The presence of QT intervals depends on whether or not the T waves are identifiable.
- U waves are not seen.

Atrial fibrillation has a number of key characteristics, including a totally irregular rhythm and a chaotic-looking baseline preceding each QRS complex. This is the only dysrhythmia having these characteristics so, when you see them, you know it is likely atrial fibrillation.

If you know the characteristics associated with the various dysrhythmias and conditions, then you can identify what you are seeing. Character recognition is a far better approach for analyzing and interpreting ECG tracings than simply trying to memorize sample ECG tracings you might see in this or any other textbook.

The approach we take in later chapters is to teach you the characteristics of each cardiac dysrhythmia and condition. You can then recall them during your systematic analysis and interpretation of ECG tracings.

LO 3.6

Analyzing the ECG on the Monitor Screen

A quick analysis of an ECG can be done by looking at the tracing as it moves from left to right horizontally across an ECG monitor screen (Figure 3-13). The heart rate; regularity of the rhythm; and morphology of the P waves, QRS complexes, and T waves can all be seen. Many ECG monitor screens also display information such as the approximate heart rate.

Remember, we refer to ECGs seen on the monitor screen as being dynamic; in other words, the tracing demonstrates what is occurring in the heart right now. Seeing what is currently occurring in the heart is the main benefit of observing the ECG tracing on the monitor screen. However, a drawback to the use of monitor screens is the difficulty in analyzing a tracing that is moving across the screen. While it gives us good information, identifying regularity, viewing the waveforms, and measuring intervals and segments is far easier when the tracing is on a piece of paper than when it is moving across a screen.

When analyzing the tracing on the ECG monitor, follow it from left to right, observing the rate, regularity, and presence of P waves and getting a general view of the PR interval, the QRS complexes, and the T waves. If you identify anything abnormal, print a tracing for further analysis.

Then compare your findings against normal sinus rhythm.

Figure 3-13
Analyzing an ECG tracing using the ECG monitor.

Analyzing the Rhythm Strip

LO 3.7

A rhythm strip is a printout of just one or a few leads. It is referred to as a static tracing, representing just what occurred in the heart at the time the tracing was recorded. The size of the paper varies depending on the manufacturer. The rhythm strip usually gives you enough information to identify existing or emerging dysrhythmias. Sometimes, however, it may be necessary to print out several rhythm strips to capture the necessary information.

To analyze rhythm strips we look at the waveforms, intervals, and durations of each from left to right (Figure 3-14). The benefit to analyzing a static tracing is that we can measure the size of the waveforms, durations, and segments, giving us a much more thorough assessment than what we can gain using the ECG monitor.

We then compare our findings against normal sinus rhythm.

Figure 3-14
Analyzing a rhythm strip.

LO 3.8

Analyzing the 12-Lead Tracing

The 12-lead tracing is a printout of 12 views of the heart. Two groups of three views are located on the left side of the report while two groups of three views are located on the right side of the report (Figure 3-15).

Only a small section of each lead is included, making it difficult to use this type of tracing to identify dysrhythmias. However, most ECG machines print out a rhythm strip along the bottom of the tracing. This rhythm strip is usually one lead but may include up to three different leads. This allows you to more easily find dysrhythmias.

Some devices print standard measurements such as the QRS axis and ECG intervals at the top of the report. The intervals are often reported in milliseconds. The report may also include a 1-mV reference pulse, an annotation of the ECG size setting, the frequency response, and the recorder speed. The 12-lead ECG is usually printed in x1.0 size in which 1 mV = 10 mm (two large boxes) on the ECG paper. The standard diagnostic frequency response is 0.05 to 150 Hz. Recorder speed is typically 25 mm/sec. Consistency in the areas of frequency response, ECG size, and recorder speed are important when interpreting a 12-lead ECG and comparing reports.

There are several ways to analyze the 12-lead tracing. We can look at each lead (from left to right), starting at the top and moving to the bottom in the first column, then in the second column, next in the third column, and then lastly, in the fourth column (Figure 3-16A). Alternatively, depending on what we are looking for, we can analyze groups of ECG leads (Figure 3-16B) to reveal certain conditions such as **axis deviation,** myocardial injury or

Figure 3-15
Elements of the 12-lead ECG tracing.

infarction, enlargement or ventricular **hypertrophy, and bundle branch** block. The presence of these conditions can be seen in these leads as they view that area of the heart where the condition is occurring.

Again, we then compare our findings against normal sinus rhythm.

Lastly, if a dysrhythmia or abnormality is identified, compare it to your patient assessment findings. This will help identify the significance of the dysrhythmia or abnormality and assist you in making the appropriate treatment decisions.

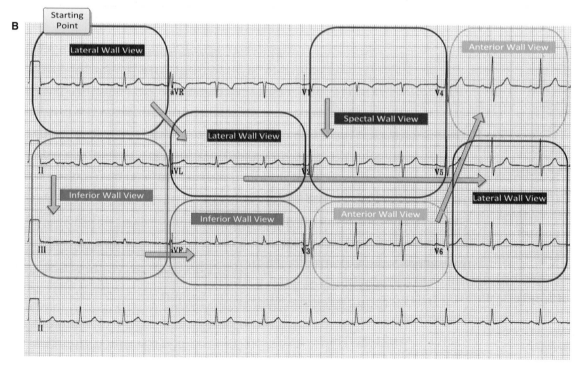

Figure 3-16

Analyzing 12-lead tracings. (A) Tracings can be analyzed from top to bottom. (B) Tracings can be analyzed by looking at groups of ECG leads.

Key Points 🔍

- The key to making sense of what you see on any ECG tracing is to approach it in a logical and systematic manner.

- The Nine-Step Process assesses the main elements of the ECG tracing and includes the following elements: determine the rate (Is it normal, fast, or slow?); determine the regularity (Is it regular or irregular?); assess the P waves (Is there a uniform P wave preceding each QRS complex?); assess the QRS complexes (Are they within normal limits? Do they appear normal?); assess the PR intervals (Are they identifiable? Are they within normal limits? Are they constant in duration?); assess the ST segments (Is it a flat line? Is it elevated or depressed?); assess the T waves (Are they slightly asymmetrical? Are they of normal height? Is it oriented in the same direction as the preceding QRS complex?); look for U waves (Are they present?); assess the QT intervals (Is it within normal limits?).

- The average heart rate in the adult is 60 to 100 beats per minute. A heart rate that is slower or faster is considered abnormal.

- Normally the heart beats in a regular, rhythmic fashion, producing specific waveforms and intervals with each heartbeat. This cycle repeats itself over and over again. An irregular rhythm is abnormal.

- Throughout the ECG tracing, there should be one normal upright P wave preceding each narrow upright QRS complex.

- The PR interval that precedes each QRS complex should be of the same duration and within 0.12 and 0.20 seconds.

- After each QRS complex of the ECG tracing, there should be a flat ST segment, followed by an upright and slightly asymmetrical T wave.

- The QT intervals in an ECG tracing should be between 0.30 and 0.44 seconds in duration.

- U waves may or may not be present in the ECG tracing.

- Although following the exact order of the Nine-Step Process is not required, you should try to employ all the steps where indicated.

- What we identify in the step-by-step analysis of an ECG tracing is compared against the characteristics of normal sinus rhythm.

- Each dysrhythmia and cardiac condition has characteristics that are unique to it, making it identifiable to anyone who knows for what to look for.

- We can analyze an ECG on the monitor screen, on a rhythm strip, or on a 12-lead ECG tracing.

Assess Your Understanding

The following questions give you a chance to assess your understanding of the material discussed in this chapter. The answers can be found in Appendix A.

1. Using an organized approach to analyzing ECG tracings
   a. takes more time but increases your effectiveness.
   b. is only used with complicated dysrhythmias and cardiac conditions.
   c. helps to ensure that you identify all the characteristics seen in the tracing.
   d. can help identify cardiac output.

2. The elements of the Nine-Step Process include all of the following EXCEPT
   a. heart rate.
   b. P waves.
   c. ST segments.
   d. axis.

3. The normal heart rate in the adult is between _____ and _____ beats per minute.
   a. 60, 75
   b. 70, 90
   c. 60, 100
   d. 80, 100

4. During the _____ initiation of the impulse in the SA node, its movement through the atria and activation of the AV node occurs.
   a. P wave
   b. PR interval
   c. QRS complex
   d. ST segment

5. The normal PR interval is _____ seconds in duration.
   a. 0.12 to 0.20
   b. 0.04 to 0.08
   c. 0.36 to 0.44
   d. 0.06 to 0.12

6. The PR interval represents
   a. repolarization of the ventricles.
   b. depolarization of the heart from the SA node through the atria, AV node, and His-Purkinje system.
   c. depolarization of the atria.
   d. movement of the electrical impulse through the ventricles.

7. The Q wave is the first _____ deflection after the PR segment.
   a. biphasic
   b. positive
   c. negative
   d. none of the above

8. Characteristics associated with normal sinus rhythm include
   a. heart rate of 56 beats per minute.
   b. an irregular rhythm.
   c. one upright P wave preceding each QRS complex.
   d. PR intervals that vary in duration.

9. The term we use to describe the appearance of waveforms is
   a. morphology.
   b. deflection.
   c. amplitude.
   d. vector.

10. Characteristics that differ from those seen with normal sinus can help us to identify various dysrhythmias and cardiac conditions.
   a. True
   b. False

11. Using the Nine-Step Process
   a. is required for all ECG tracings.
   b. requires an extensive understanding of ECGs.
   c. allows you to identify the characteristics of the tracings you are analyzing.
   d. is better suited for 12-lead ECGs than it is for dysrhythmia analysis and interpretation.

12. When we analyze an ECG tracing on the ECG monitor,
   a. it shows what is occurring in real time.
   b. it provide us the most accurate picture of what has occurred in the heart.
   c. only the atrial waveforms can be seen.
   d. it is the best way of assessing the regularity of the rhythm.

13. The rhythm strip provides us
   a. all views of the heart.
   b. a good tool for identifying cardiac dysrhythmias.
   c. the information needed to identify cardiac conditions.
   d. a dynamic picture of the heart's electrical activity.

14. A 12-lead ECG tracing
    a. should always be assessed from the left to right and from the top to the bottom of each column.
    b. is the most accurate way of assessing the dynamic electrical activity occurring in the heart.
    c. yields much of the information needed to identify cardiac conditions.
    d. records the heart's electrical activity in four limb leads and six chest leads.

15. You are trying to determine if your patient, who is complaining of chest pain, is experiencing myocardial ischemia. The best way to do this is
    a. view his heart's electrical activity on the ECG monitor screen.
    b. perform a 12-lead ECG.
    c. analyze a recently recorded rhythm strip.
    d. take the patient's blood pressure.

Answers to Sidebar Questions

1. We use the isoelectric line as a baseline or reference point to identify the changing electrical amplitude. **p. 75**

2. The P wave should extend no more than two to three small boxes in height and one and a half to three small boxes in duration. **p. 75**

3. The T wave represents ventricular repolarization (or recovery). **p. 77**

4. The average heart rate in the adult is between 60 and 100 beats per minute. **p. 79**

What's Online

Go to www.mhhe.com/shadeECG2e to find:
- Presentations on chapter content
- Crossword puzzle exercises
- Chapter quiz
- Flashcards
- Fill-in-the-blank exercises and answers

4 Heart Rate

Chapter Outline

Importance of Determining the Heart Rate

Quick Check of the Heart Rate

Heart Rates Seen with Various Dysrhythmias

Methods of Determining Heart Rate

Counting Both the Atrial and Ventricular Rates

Normal, Slow, and Fast Rates

Learning Objectives

LO 4.1 State why it is important to determine the heart rate in an ECG rhythm.

LO 4.2 Identity whether an ECG rhythm has either a slow, normal, or fast heart rate.

LO 4.3 Describe the benefit of using a shortcut method to determine the heart rate.

LO 4.4 Use the 6-second interval $\times$ 10 method to determine the heart rate.

LO 4.5 Use the 300, 150, 100, 75, 60, 50 method to determine the heart rate.

LO 4.6 Use the 1500 method to determine the heart rate.

LO 4.7 Describe how to accurately measure both atrial and ventricular heart rates.

LO 4.8 Define the terms *bradycardia* and *tachycardia*.

Case History

A 36-year-old woman presents to the emergency department complaining of a rapid heartbeat. She was recently diagnosed with hyperthyroidism for which she has begun treatment. She states that, after a heated argument with her husband over finances, she noticed that her heart was "pounding out of her chest." She feels lightheaded but denies chest pain.

The patient is promptly brought back to the major medical room and placed on a cardiac monitor while her vital signs are assessed. Her blood pressure is 105/60, pulse 160, respiratory rate 24, and oxygen saturation 99% on room air. The emergency physician examines the cardiac monitor and observes that the rhythm is fast, with narrow QRS complexes. The heart rate readout on the monitor appears to be malfunctioning, indicating a rate of 320 beats per minute. The physician runs a printout of the rhythm and, using the skills she learned in ECG rhythm recognition, is able to measure the rate using a few rules of thumb. She determines that the patient's heart rate is actually 150 beats per minute.

LO 4.1

Importance of Determining the Heart Rate

Determining the heart rate from ECG tracings yields important information. A rhythm that is either slow or fast is considered abnormal. A variety of conditions can produce slow or fast heart rates. Some of these conditions can be quite serious. Further, some slow or fast rhythms can deteriorate into deadly cardiac dysrhythmias (Figure 4-1). For these reasons, each slow or fast rhythm should be properly investigated.

LO 4.2

Quick Check of the Heart Rate

The first step in analyzing an ECG is to determine the heart rate (Figure 4-2). Begin by quickly checking the ECG monitor or tracing to see if the rate is slow, normal, or fast. For this initial look, do not be concerned about calculating the exact heart rate. Instead, identify which group it fits in—slow, normal, or fast. Some ECG rhythms may be profoundly slow or fast, in which case you should quickly assess the patient for adequate cardiac output. If cardiac output is compromised, immediate treatment is necessary.

A quick assessment of the heart rate can be done by looking at the space between QRS complexes (Figure 4-3). More space indicates a slower heart rate while less space indicates a faster heart rate.

KEY CONCEPT

Before calculating the heart rate, first look to see if the heart rate is slow, normal, or fast.

Figure 4-1
Deterioration of an ECG rhythm into ventricular tachycardia and then ventricular fibrillation.

The Nine-Step Process

Rate | Rhythm | P waves | QRS complexes | PR intervals | ST segments | T waves | QT intervals | U waves

Figure 4-2
The first step to assessing an ECG is to determine the heart rate.

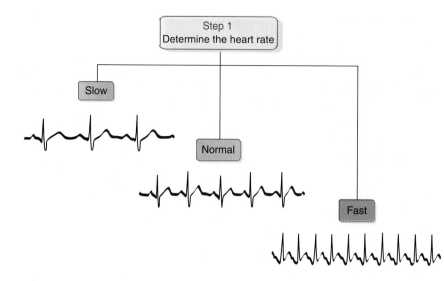

Figure 4-3
The first step in analyzing the heart rate is to determine if the heart rate is slow, normal, or fast.

You can practice determining whether a heart rate is slow, normal, or fast with the *Section 2 Practice Makes Perfect* exercises beginning on page 215. Answers to these exercises can be found in Appendix A.

Many ECG machines (as well as other devices used to assess vital signs) provide a visual display of the patient's heart rate. However, you should not rely on these displays alone. Always confirm the reading by comparing it with the heart rate seen on the ECG tracing and/or by taking a pulse.

The heart rate seen on the ECG tracing should always be compared with the pulse rate (obtained by palpation). The pulse rate should be counted for 15 seconds in regular rhythms and 30 to 60 seconds in irregular rhythms. It is important to palpate a pulse as some impulses may fail to generate contractions of the heart.

Heart Rates Seen with Various Dysrhythmias

Identifying the heart rate of a rhythm can help identify which dysrhythmia we may be facing as certain dysrhythmias are slow or fast whereas others are not. If the rhythm has a normal heart rate, we can automatically exclude those that are characteristically slow or fast. As we discuss this concept further, you will see that excluding a list of dysrhythmias that lacks the features you see in the tracing makes your life a lot easier.

Methods of Determining Heart Rate

Following the quick assessment, analyze the tracing to determine the approximate or actual heart rate. Rather than printing off a whole minute of ECG tracing and counting the number of QRS complexes, you can use a shortcut

QUESTION
1. What is the range of the normal heart rate in the adult? *Note:* Answers to sidebar questions can be found at the end of the chapter.

REMINDER
Remember the discussion in Chapter 1: Heart rate × stroke volume = cardiac output. A very slow or fast heart rate can cause cardiac output to decrease by lowering the rate or decreasing the stroke volume.

QUESTION
2. What single ECG rhythm is considered normal?

LO 4.3

Figure 4-4
Using a shortcut method to
determine the heart rate can
save time.

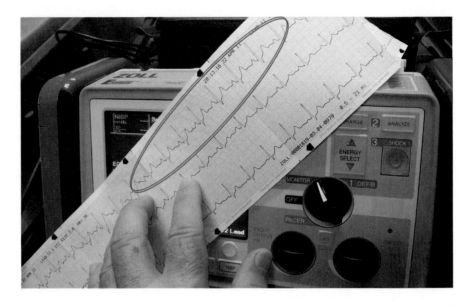

method to determine the heart rate. In this text we describe three commonly used methods:

- 6-second interval × 10 method
- 300, 150, 100, 75, 60, 50 method
- 1500 method

The names we've given to the methods for calculating the heart rate may differ from those found in other references. This was done intentionally to make it easier to remember them as each name is descriptive of the way the methods work.

Each method assesses a section of the tracing to approximate the heart rate (Figure 4-4) and has its advantages and disadvantages.

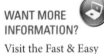

WANT MORE
INFORMATION?
Visit the Fast & Easy
ECGs Website at
www.mhhe.com/
shadeECG2e.

LO 4.4

6-Second Interval × 10 Method

The *6-second interval × 10 method* involves multiplying by 10 the number of QRS complexes found in a 6-second portion of the ECG tracing (Figure 4-5).

Remember that ECG paper typically has markings on the top and/or bottom indicating each 3-second block of time (see Chapter 2). Two of these successive (adjacent to each other) blocks of time equal 6 seconds. When you multiply that amount of time by 10, it represents 60 seconds or 1 minute.

Not all ECG tracing paper is marked in 3-second blocks of time. For example, some are measured in 1-second blocks of time. In that case, six of these successive blocks of time equal 6 seconds.

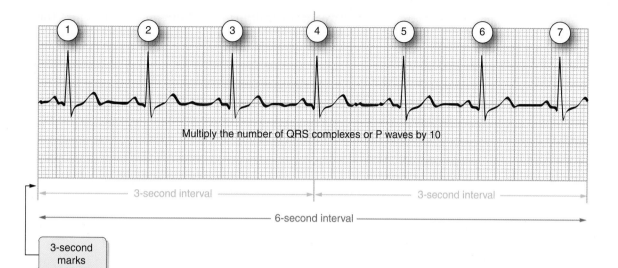

Figure 4-5
To employ the 6-second interval x 10 method, multiply by 10 the number of QRS complexes (for the ventricular rate) or P waves (for the atrial rate) found in a 6-second portion of the ECG tracing. The rate shown in the ECG tracing here is 70.

Therefore to calculate the heart rate

1. Identify two successive 3-second marks.
2. Count the number of QRS complexes in that 6-second section.
3. Multiply that number by 10.

This final number is the approximate heart rate per minute.

Here are some examples of calculating heart rates using this method:

- Eight QRS complexes in the 6-second block—the patient has a heart rate of 80 beats per minute
- Twelve QRS complexes in the 6-second block—the patient has a heart rate of 120 beats per minute
- Four QRS complexes in the 6-second block—the patient has a heart rate of 40 beats per minute.

The 6-second interval × 10 method is an effective means for assessing the rate of an irregular rhythm. This is because the QRS complexes are measured over 6 seconds. Advantages of the 6-second interval × 10 method are that it is quick and easy and it does not require any tools or devices. A disadvantage is that it does not calculate the heart rate as accurately as other methods. In other words, the heart rate might actually be 54 beats a minute instead of 50.

Whereas the 6-second interval × 10 rule is effective for calculating the heart rate in irregular rhythms, there are some dysrhythmias in which the

KEY CONCEPT
You can quickly determine the heart rate by multiplying by 10 the number of QRS complexes found in a 6-second portion of the ECG tracing.

degree of irregularity makes it difficult to find enough consistent tracing to determine an average. For example, you may count eight QRS complexes (and/or P) waves in one 6-second section and 11 QRS complexes (and/or P) waves in another, making it difficult to obtain an accurate heart rate. In these cases, try using a 12-second area of the tracing (4 successive blocks). Count the number of QRS complexes (and/or P waves) and multiply them by 5 (instead of 10).

In addition to determining the ventricular rate, this method can also be used to calculate the atrial rate. Simply multiply by 10 the number of P waves found in a 6-second portion of the ECG tracing.

You can practice determining heart rate using the 6-second interval × 10 method with the *Section 2 Practice Makes Perfect* exercises on page 215.

LO 4.5

300, 150, 100, 75, 60, 50 Method

The *300, 150, 100, 75, 60, 50 method,* also called the *countdown, sequence,* or *triplicate method,* involves locating an R wave on a bold line on the ECG paper (Figure 4-6). Let's refer to that as the "start point." Each bold line to the right of the start point has a value that denotes the heart rate. The first bold line is the 300 line. The bold line after that is the 150 line, the one after that is the 100 line, the next line is 75, the line after that is 60, and the next line is 50. Assume for a minute that you are assessing the heart rate. You have located an R wave that falls on a bold line. If the next R wave falls on the second bold line, the heart rate is 150 beats per minute. Instead, if the next R wave falls on the fourth bold line, then the heart rate is 75 beats per minute.

Figure 4-6
The 300, 150, 100, 75, 60, 50 method involves locating an R wave (or P wave) on a bold line on the ECG paper (the start point). Each bold line to the right of the start point has a value that denotes the heart rate. The end point is where the next R wave (or P wave) is located. The rate shown in this ECG tracing is just under 100 beats per minute.

Therefore, to calculate the heart rate

1. Find an R wave located on a bold line, and then
2. Find the next consecutive R wave. If it is on a bold line, then the heart rate is the value of that line (300, 150, 100, 75, 60, 50).

Note that we use the terms *R* and *QRS complex* interchangeably. This is because when you are trying to line up the waveform to a bold line, it is much easier to use the tallest of the three waveforms (of the QRS complex), the R wave. When we say to look for an R wave, we mean look for the most prominent deflection of the QRS complex. In some cases the S wave may be the most prominent.

Advantages of the 300, 150, 100, 75, 60, 50 method are that it is quick; that it is fairly accurate; and that it requires no special tools, calculations, or rulers. A disadvantage is that this method can be used only if the rhythm is regular.

If the heart rate is less than 50 beats per minute, then the next bold line (following the 50 line) has a value of 43, and the line following that has a value of 37. If the heart rate is slower than 37, then you must use the 6-second interval × 10 method to determine the heart rate.

If the second R wave falls between two bold lines, you can more precisely determine the heart rate if you use identified values for each of the thin lines (Figure 4-7). This set of values is not as easy to remember as the 300, 150, 100, 75, 60, 50 method, so having a cheat sheet or rate calculator is a good idea.

Figure 4-8 shows three examples of calculating the heart rate using the 300, 150, 100, 75, 60, 50 method.

Alternatively, when the second R wave does not fall on a bold line, you can approximate the heart rate (Figure 4-9). For example, if it falls between the third and fourth lines, you can say the heart rate is "between 75 and 100 beats per minute."

This method can also be used to calculate the atrial rate. Begin by finding the peak of a P wave that falls on a bold line. Then locate the next consecutive P wave.

> **KEY CONCEPT**
> You can quickly determine the heart rate by locating an R wave that falls on a bold line on the ECG paper, then locating the next R wave. Each bold line to the right of the start point has a value that denotes the approximate heart rate (300, 150, 100, 75, 60, 50).

Start point

300	150	100	75	60	50	43	38	33
250	136	94	72	58	48	42	37	
214	125	88	68	56	47	41	36	
188	115	84	65	54	45	40	35	
167	107	79	63	52	44	39	34	

Figure 4-7
Using the identified values for each of the thin lines allows you to more precisely determine the heart rate.

In this example, the first and second R waves fall close to the bold lines making determination of the heart rate easier. This rhythm has a heart rate of 100 BPM.

In this example, the first R wave falls close to the bold line but the second R wave is a box off to the right of the bold line. Here, using the values for the smaller lines (shown earlier), you can see this rhythm has a heart rate of 134 BPM.

1a) Either use calipers or mark two lines on a piece of paper to represent the distance between the first two R waves.

1b) Then align the first leg of the caliper or the drawn line with the bold line to the right of the first R wave. Where the second leg of the caliper or drawn line falls represents where the second R wave would fall.

2) Since one of the R waves falls on a bold line you can simply reverse the direction. Go from right to left instead of left to right to align your R waves to the next appropriate line.

In this example, the first R wave does not fall close to a bold line. There are two ways to deal with this problem. Whichever method you use yields a heart rate of 54 BPM.

Figure 4-8
Three examples of calculating the heart rate using the 300, 150, 100, 75, 60, 50 method.

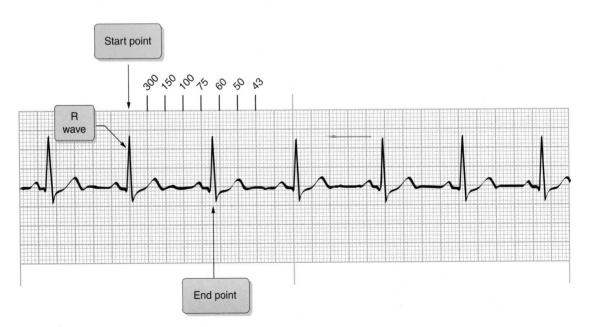

Figure 4-9
When the second R wave does not fall on a bold line, you can approximate the heart rate. The heart rate of this tracing is between 60 and 75 beats per minute.

The values for each bold (and thin) line are the same as previously described.

To determine the heart rate using the 300, 150, 100, 75, 60, 50 method, it is acceptable to move either right or left of the start point. Sometimes you can find better alignments of the R waves and the bold lines looking to the left instead of to the right.

An easy way to determine the rate when the R wave does not fall on a bold line is to place a piece of paper over the ECG tracing, then mark it where the first R falls. Next, mark it where the second R wave falls. Slide the paper to the right or left until the first mark lines up with a bold line. Use the second mark to identify the heart rate.

As you will see from the discussion that follows, the two quickest methods for determining the heart rate are the 6-second interval × 10 method and the 300, 150, 100, 75, 60, 50 method.

You can practice determining heart rate using the 300, 150, 100, 75, 60, 50 method with the *Section 2 Practice Makes Perfect* exercises on page 215.

1500 Method

LO 4.6

Another way to calculate the heart rate is to use the 1500 method, so named because 1500 small squares on the ECG paper are equal to 1 minute (Figure 4-10). To use this method, count the number of small squares between two consecutive R waves and divide 1500 by that number. For example, if you

Figure 4-10
To use the 1500 method, count the number of small squares between two consecutive R waves and divide 1500 by that number.

have 20 small squares (equal to four large boxes) the heart rate is 75 beats per minute (1500 ÷ 20 = 75).

Therefore, to calculate the heart rate

1. Count the number of small squares between two consecutive R waves.
2. Divide 1500 by that number.

KEY CONCEPT
You can determine the heart rate by counting the number of small squares between two consecutive R waves and dividing 1500 by that number.

This can be used to calculate the atrial rate as well by measuring the number of small squares between the peaks of two consecutive P waves.

Advantages of the 1500 method are that it is the most accurate and requires no special tools or rulers. Disadvantages of this method are that it requires you to do math at a time when things may be extremely hectic and that it cannot be used if the rhythm is irregular.

Following (Figure 4-11) are three examples showing calculating the heart rate using the 1500 method.

You can practice determining heart rate using the 1500 method with the *Section 2 Practice Makes Perfect* exercises on page 215.

In this example, there are 15 small boxes between consecutive R waves. Dividing 1500 by 15 yields a heart rate of 100 BPM.

In this example, there are 11 small boxes between consecutive R waves. Dividing 1500 by 11 yields a heart rate of 136 BPM. Comparing that to what we calculated the heart rate to be in Figure 4- (134 BPM) you can see there is a slight difference.

In this example, there are slightly more than 28 small boxes between consecutive R waves. Dividing 1500 by 28 (28.2 to be more accurate) yields a heart rate of 53 BPM. Comparing that to what we calculated the heart rate to be in Figure 4-8 (54 BPM) you can see there is a slight difference.

Figure 4-11
Calculating heart rate using the 1500 method. We are using the same examples show in Figure 4-10 to allow you to see the difference in accuracy between the two methods of calculating heart rate.

Figure 4-12
To use a heart rate calculator, begin by placing the calculator over the ECG tracing. Position the start mark on an R wave, then find the next consecutive R wave. Where that next R wave lines up is the approximate heart rate.

Rate Calculators

Rate calculators are simple paper or plastic devices about the size of a bookmark. They can be overlaid on the ECG tracing to show the heart rate and, in some cases, the duration of the various waveforms, segments, and intervals. They are easy to use (Figure 4-12) and typically have a start mark at one end and numbers indicating the rate along the bottom. To use a rate calculator, begin by placing the calculator over the ECG tracing. Next, position the start mark on an R wave and then find the next consecutive R wave. The approximate heart rate is where the next R wave lines up.

The advantage of these devices is that they allow you to quickly identify the heart rate. The disadvantages are that you must have it available any time you need to calculate a patient's heart rate and that they cannot be used on irregular rhythms.

A heart rate calculator is included on the back cover of this book. You can practice determining heart rate by using the rate calculator with the *Section 2 Practice Makes Perfect* exercises on page 215.

KEY CONCEPT
You count the P waves to determine the atrial rate and the QRS complexes to determine the ventricular rate.

Counting Both the Atrial and Ventricular Rates

LO 4.7

We talk about counting the QRS complexes to determine the ventricular rate, but we also count the P waves to determine the atrial rate (Figure 4-13).

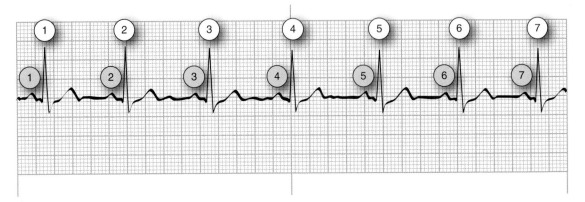

Figure 4-13
When calculating the heart rate, count the number of QRS complexes (for the ventricular rate) and P waves (for the atrial rate). They should be the same. In this 6-second ECG tracing, there are 7 QRS complexes and 7 P waves. Using the 6-second interval x 10 method, the ventricular and atrial rates are 70 beats per minute.

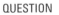

QUESTION
3. What effect may bradycardia have on cardiac output?

In some dysrhythmias, the atrial rate may be less than or greater than the ventricular rate. The rate-calculating methods previously discussed can also be used to identify the atrial rate.

Normal, Slow, and Fast Rates

LO 4.8

QUESTION
4. If the 6-second interval × 10 method is used to determine the heart rate, bradycardia is present if there are fewer than how many QRS complexes?

In the average adult, the normal heart rate is between 60 and 100 beats per minute. Normal sinus rhythm, as well as many dysrhythmias (to be discussed in later chapters), characteristically have a normal rate.

Rates above 100 beats per minute or below 60 beats per minute are considered abnormal. When we say abnormal, we do not necessarily mean that it is a bad thing but rather that it is outside the normal range.

Slow Rates—Bradycardia

LO 4.9

A heart rate less than 60 beats per minute is called **bradycardia** and can occur for many reasons. It may or may not have an adverse affect on cardiac output. In the extreme it can lead to severe reductions in cardiac output and eventually deteriorate into asystole (an absence of heart rhythm).

QUESTION
5. What effect can extremely fast tachycardia have on cardiac output?

Fast Rates—Tachycardia

A heart rate greater than 100 beats per minute is called **tachycardia.** Tachycardia has many causes and leads to increased myocardial oxygen consumption, which can have an adverse effect on patients with coronary artery disease and other medical conditions. Extremely fast rates can have an adverse affect on cardiac output. Also, tachycardia that arises from the ventricles may lead to a chaotic quivering of the ventricles called *ventricular fibrillation.*

KEY CONCEPT
A heart rate less than 60 beats per minute is called bradycardia and one that is greater than 100 is called tachycardia.

Key Points

- Start assessing the heart rate by quickly checking the ECG monitor or tracing to see if the rate is slow, normal, or fast.
- The 6-second interval × 10 method of calculating the heart rate involves multiplying by 10 the number of QRS complexes found in a 6-second portion of the ECG tracing. Because the QRS complexes are measured over 6 seconds, this method is the most effective means for assessing irregular rhythms.
- The 300, 150, 100, 75, 60, 50 method for calculating the heart rate involves locating an R wave on a bold line on the ECG paper, then finding the next consecutive R wave and using the 300, 150, 100, 75, 60, 50 values for subsequent bold lines to determine the rate.
- To use the 1500 method, you count the number of small squares between two consecutive R waves and divide 1500 by that number.
- Rate calculators are easy to use and can effectively determine the heart rate.
- We count the QRS complexes to determine the ventricular rate and count the P waves to determine the atrial rate.
- Rates above or below 60 to 100 beats per minute in the typical adult are considered abnormal.
- A heart rate less than 60 beats per minute is called *bradycardia*.
- A heart rate greater than 100 beats per minute is called *tachycardia*.
- Both extremely slow and fast heart rates can result in decreased cardiac output.

Assess Your Understanding

The following questions give you a chance to assess your understanding of the material discussed in this chapter. The answers can be found in Appendix A.

1. If the QRS complexes are close together the heart rate is
   a. slow.
   b. normal.
   c. profoundly slow.
   d. fast.

2. Determining the heart rate helps you identify abnormal ECG rhythms.
   a. True
   b. False

3. A benefit of using a shortcut method for determining the heart rate is that it
   a. can help identify the regularity of an ECG tracing.
   b. helps determine the patient's actual cardiac output.

    c.   is faster than counting the complexes found on a whole minute's worth of ECG tracing.

    d.   is the most accurate way of identifying the heart rate.

4.   The 6-second interval × 10 method

    a.   can be used to estimate the heart rate in irregular rhythms.

    b.   involves multiplying by 25 the number of QRS complexes found in a 6-second portion of the ECG tracing.

    c.   is the most accurate method of determining the heart rate.

    d.   can be used only to determine the ventricular rate.

5.   The 300, 150, 100, 75, 60, 50 method

    a.   can be used to measure the heart rate in irregular rhythms.

    b.   involves identifying a T wave that falls on a bold line.

    c.   requires the use of a rate calculator to determine the heart rate.

    d.   requires you to identify a start point from which to identify where the next R wave falls.

6.   To use the 1500 method,

    a.   count the number of small squares between two consecutive R waves and divide 1500 by that number.

    b.   find an R wave that falls on a bold line and begin counting the small squares.

    c.   count the number of QRS complexes in a 6-second section of the ECG tracing.

    d.   divide by 1500 the number of QRS complexes in a 3-second section of the ECG tracing.

7.   Which one of the following methods for determining the heart rate in a regular rhythm is the most accurate?

    a.   6-second interval × 10 method

    b.   300, 150, 100, 75, 60, 50 method

    c.   1500 method

    d.   Quick assessment method

8.   The atrial heart rate is always the same as the ventricular heart rate.

    a.   True

    b.   False

9.   The average heart rate in the adult patient is between _____ beats per minute.

    a.   50 and 75

    b.   70 and 90

    c.   65 and 95

    d.   60 and 100

10. Tachycardia
    a. is a dysrhythmia that has a heart rate greater than 80 beats per minute.
    b. leads to decreased myocardial oxygen consumption.
    c. can be produced by stimulation of the parasympathetic nervous system.
    d. may be brought about by exercise or exertion.

Referring to the scenario at the beginning of this chapter, answer the following questions.

11. It is unlikely that the patient's heart rate was actually 320 because
    a. she was awake.
    b. her blood pressure was not low.
    c. she was able to answer questions.
    d. All of the above.

12. The most likely cause of the patient's fast heart rate was
    a. anxiety.
    b. hypoxia.
    c. hyperthyroidism.
    d. amphetamine use.

Answers to Sidebar Questions

1. The normal heart rate range in the adult is 60 to 100 beats per minute. **p. 95**

2. Normal sinus rhythm. **p. 95**

3. Cardiac output is a product of heart rate × stroke volume. If we reduce the heart rate, it may reduce cardiac output. **p. 104**

4. In bradycardia there are fewer than six QRS complexes in the 6-second portion of the ECG tracing. **p. 104**

5. Cardiac output is a product of heart rate × stroke volume. Extremely fast heart rates reduce stroke volume by not allowing enough time between heartbeats for the ventricles (and coronary arteries) to refill with blood. A reduction in stroke volume can lead to decreased cardiac output. **p. 104**

What's Online

Go to www.mhhe.com/shadeECG2e to find:
- Presentations on chapter content
- Crossword puzzle exercises
- ECG tracings for practicing determining the heart rate
- Chapter quiz
- Flashcards
- Fill-in-the-blank exercises and answers

5 Regularity

Chapter Outline

Importance of Determining Regularity

Quick Check of Regularity

Methods of Determining Regularity

Types of Irregularity

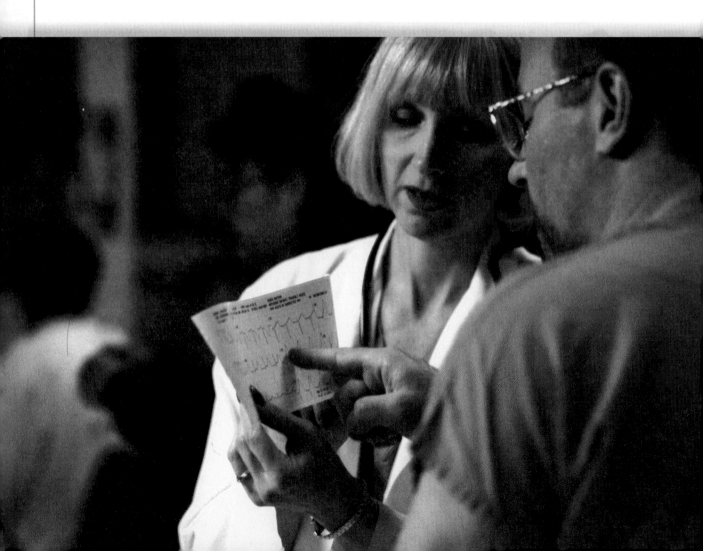

Learning Objectives

LO 5.1 State why it is important to determine the regularity of an ECG rhythm.

LO 5.2 Recall that identifying regularity is one of the steps used to analyze an ECG tracing.

LO 5.3 Recall how P-P and R-R intervals are used to determine the regularity of a rhythm.

LO 5.4 Describe three methods that can be used to determine atrial and ventricular regularity.

LO 5.5 Identify each of the different types of irregularity.

Case History

An 85-year-old woman presents to her family physician's office for her yearly checkup. She has a history of atherosclerotic heart disease and noninsulin-dependent diabetes. She has been careful to follow her doctor's advice and takes her medications regularly. She denies any new complaints.

While taking her vital signs, the nurse notes that the woman's heart rate is irregular. He examines the patient's medical record to see if this condition has been previously recorded. He finds no evidence that the patient has ever had an irregular heart rhythm and calls the physician into the room to examine the patient. A cardiac monitor is attached to the patient, and an ECG tracing is run. The nurse and physician examine the tracing and observe that the rate is within normal limits but is irregularly irregular. Then, they compare it with a previous tracing, noting that there is a difference between the two.

Importance of Determining Regularity

An initial step in analyzing an ECG rhythm is to determine if it is regular or irregular (Figure 5-1). This chapter focuses on why it is important to evaluate the regularity of each tracing, details the steps that can be used to determine regularity, and describes the different types of irregularity. Determining the regularity of ECG tracings provides us with significant information. An irregular rhythm is considered abnormal. A variety of conditions can produce irregular rhythms, some of which can be quite serious. Further, some irregular rhythms can deteriorate into deadly cardiac dysrhythmias (Figure 5-2). For these reasons, each irregular rhythm should be properly assessed.

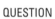
QUESTION
1. What does the term dysrhythmia mean?
Note: Answers to sidebar questions can be found at the end of the chapter.

QUESTION
2. What single rhythm is considered normal?

Quick Check of Regularity

As we discussed in Chapter 2, one of the uses of the ECG is to identify existing or emerging dysrhythmias. We do this by observing the rhythm directly on the ECG monitor screen or by printing an ECG tracing so that the specific waveforms, segments, and intervals can be measured and examined.

As mentioned in Chapter 3, the heart normally beats in a regular, rhythmic fashion, producing a P wave, QRS complex, and T wave with each heartbeat. This cycle repeats itself over and over again. The distance between the consecutive P waves should be the same, just as the distance between the consecutive QRS complexes should be the same throughout the tracing. We call these distances the *P-P interval* and the *R-R interval* (Figure 5-3).

Figure 5-1
Deterioration of an ECG rhythm into ventricular fibrillation.

Figure 5-2
Determining the regularity is an initial step in analyzing an ECG tracing.

Figure 5-3
The distance between consecutive R waves is called the *R-R interval;* the distance between consecutive P waves is called the *P-P interval.*

Identifying the regularity of a rhythm can help classify which dysrhythmia we may be facing, as certain dysrhythmias are regular while others are not. (Note that many dysrhythmias have a regular rhythm; that does not mean they are normal; it just means their rhythm is regular.) If the rhythm is irregular, we can automatically exclude those that are characteristically regular. As we discuss this concept further, you will see that excluding a list of dysrhythmias that lack the features you see in the tracing makes identifying the dysrhythmia easier.

Methods of Determining Regularity

To assess atrial regularity, we analyze the P-P intervals (Figure 5-4). Again, if the distance remains the same between the P-P intervals, then the atrial rhythm is regular. If the distance differs, the atrial rhythm is irregular. Rhythms are considered regular even if there is a slight variance in the R-R or P-P interval. A good rule to follow is one small square (0.04 seconds) difference is still considered normal.

To assess the ventricular regularity, we analyze the R-R intervals. Again, if the distance remains the same between the R-R intervals, then the ventricular rhythm is regular. If the distance differs, the ventricular rhythm is irregular. If an R wave is not present, then you can use either the Q wave or the S wave of consecutive QRS complexes. You should use the uppermost or lowermost (tallest) point of the QRS for consistency in measurement. You should compare the intervals in several cycles. Consistently similar intervals represent a regular rhythm whereas dissimilar intervals indicate an irregular rhythm.

The final step is to compare the P-P interval with the R-R interval to determine whether they are the same and appear to be associated with each other. In other words, determine if there is a P wave before every QRS complex and a QRS complex after every P wave.

REMINDER

Typically, you will know the patient has an irregular rhythm by checking his or her pulse. This may prompt you to order an ECG when the patient's condition might not otherwise call for it.

LO 5.3

REMINDER

As described in Chapter 3, we use the R wave to measure the distance between QRS complexes, as it is typically the tallest waveform of the QRS complex.

KEY CONCEPT

If the distance between the R-R or P-P intervals remains the same, the rhythm is regular. If the distance differs, the rhythm is irregular.

In this rhythm, each R-R and P-P interval is 21 small boxes apart. For this reason it is considered regular.

In this rhythm, the number of small boxes differs between some of the R-R and P-P intervals. For this reason it is considered irregular.

Figure 5-4
The rhythm is regular if the distance between consecutive R waves and P waves is the same. If it changes, the rhythm is irregular.

QUESTION
3. Which method of calculating the heart rate may be used with irregular rhythms?

 LO 5.4

Several methods can be used to determine the regularity of a rhythm, including marking a paper with a pen (or pencil), employing calipers, and counting the number of small squares between each P-P interval and R-R interval.

Paper and Pen Method

Using paper and a pen (or pencil) is simple and quick and requires no special tools (Figure 5-5). To assess the regularity of a rhythm with paper and a pen, do the following:

1. Place the ECG tracing on a flat surface.

2. Place the straight edge of a piece of paper above or over the ECG tracing so that the intervals are still visible.

3. Identify a starting point, the peak of an R wave or P wave, and place a mark on the paper in the corresponding position above it (let's call this mark 1).

Figure 5-5
To employ the paper and pen method, place marks on a paper above two consecutive P waves or R waves. Then move the paper across the tracing, matching the marks on the paper against subsequent consecutive P waves or R waves.

4. Find the peak of the next consecutive R wave or P wave, and place a mark on the paper in the corresponding position above it (let's call this mark 2).
5. Move the paper across the ECG tracing, aligning the two marks with succeeding R-R intervals or P-P intervals.

If the two marks line up with subsequent consecutive P or R waves, the rhythm is regular. If the distance between the intervals differs, the rhythm is irregular. You can tell this when mark 2 falls either before or after the next consecutive P wave or R wave.

An additional method similar to the paper marking method is to use the tip of a pen or pencil to determine regularity. *Lay the pen or pencil flat on the ECG strip with the tip on an R or P wave. Slide your fingernail along the pen to the next R or P wave.* Mark the pen in the spot aligned with the second waveform or keep your fingernail in that position. Now, slide the pen along the ECG strip aligning the tip of the pen with subsequent waveforms. If the rhythm is regular, the mark (you made on the pen) or your fingernail will line up with the next waveforms. If the rhythm is irregular, it will not line up.

KEY CONCEPT
The paper and pen method is a quick and simple way to determine the regularity of an ECG tracing.

WANT MORE INFORMATION?
Visit the Fast & Easy ECGs Website at www.mhhe. com/shadeECG2e.

Caliper Method

The calipers typically used to analyze ECGs are hinged at the top with two legs that extend downward (Figure 5-6). The hinged top allows the legs to be extended away from each other to establish the distance between various waveforms. The legs are pointed at the bottom to allow them to be positioned over even the smallest waveform. To assess the regularity of a rhythm with calipers, do the following:

1. Place the ECG tracing on a flat surface.
2. Place one point of the caliper on a starting point. Most often the starting point is the peak of an R wave or P wave.
3. Open the calipers by pulling the other leg until the point is positioned on the next R wave or P wave.
4. With the calipers open in that position, and keeping the point positioned over the second P wave or R wave, rotate the calipers across to the peak of the next consecutive (the third) P wave or R wave. Alternatively, you can move them so they are lined up on the next consecutive R wave.

Figure 5-6
The opened calipers are moved across the tracing from the point of one R wave or P wave to the next consecutive R wave or P wave (the R-R or P-P interval).

If the R-R interval or P-P interval is the same, the point will be above the next R wave or P wave. If the R-R interval or P-P interval is different, the point will be situated either before or after the identified waveform. Next, either slide or rotate the calipers across to the next R wave or P wave, then the next, and so on. If the rhythm is regular, the distance of each interval should be the same. If the rhythm is irregular, the distances of the intervals will differ.

QUESTION

4. How do you know a heart rhythm is irregular when using either the calipers method or paper and pen method?

Counting the Small Squares Method

Another way to determine the regularity of an ECG is to count the number of small squares on the ECG paper between the peaks of two consecutive R waves (or P waves) and then compare that with the other R-R (or P-P) intervals (Figure 5-7). You can speed up the process by using the larger boxes (made up of five small squares) for all but the last portion.

Using a Rate Calculator

Rate calculators can also be used to determine regularity. Begin by placing the calculator over the ECG tracing. Position the start mark on the peak of an R wave. Then find the next consecutive R wave. Where that next R wave lines up is then noted (this is the heart rate for that ECG). Next, move the calculator over other R-R intervals and compare your findings with what you found in the first R-R interval.

This R-R interval is 21 small boxes in duration.

1 + 5 + 5 + 5 + 5 = 21

21

For this figure, we started counting from the last R wave and moving to the left because it fell on the bold line making counting of the small squares easier.

Figure 5-7
Count the number of small boxes between consecutive R and/or P waves (each R-R and P-P interval) and then compare the numbers with each other. If they are the same, the rhythm is regular; if they differ, the rhythm is irregular.

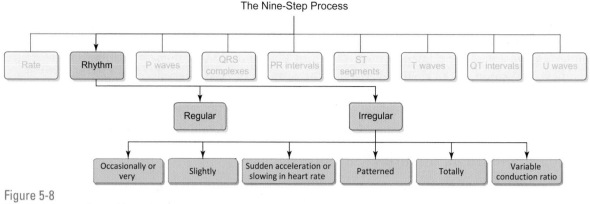

Figure 5-8
Algorithm for regular and irregular rhythms.

LO 5.5

Types of Irregularity

If the rhythm is irregular, we can further analyze it to determine the type of irregularity (Figure 5-8). This can help us identify what dysrhythmia may be present, as certain dysrhythmias have a characteristic type of irregularity. As we discuss each type of irregularity, we also describe, in a general sense, its likely causes. In later chapters, as we discuss the various dysrhythmias, we will identify whether or not an irregular rhythm is one of the characteristics associated with that dysrhythmia and what type of irregularity will be present. Note that the names given here for the types of irregularity may differ from those found in other references. This was done intentionally to make them more descriptive.

An irregularity in the rhythm can range from being occasionally irregular to being totally irregular. It is important to have a general sense of the difference as a very irregular rhythm can be a warning that the heart is extremely irritable and may deteriorate to a worse condition.

Occasionally or Very Irregular

When a rhythm is occasionally irregular, it appears mostly regular, but from time to time you see an area where it is irregular (Figure 5-9). The irregularity may be so infrequent that you might not see it at first.

A rhythm may also look very irregular. We need to be concerned with very irregular rhythms as they suggest the heart is extremely irritable. Looking at the ECG tracing in Figure 5-10, you see areas where the distance of the R-R intervals appears to be the same and areas where the distance differs. The areas that are the same are considered the underlying rhythm. We compare the underlying rhythm with the other R-R intervals.

Occasional or very irregular rhythms occur due to early beats or pauses in or arrest of the impulses arising from the SA node. These are described in the following pages.

Figure 5-9
An occasionally irregular rhythm appears mostly regular, but from time to time it is irregular.

Figure 5-10
A very irregular rhythm has many areas of irregularity.

Early Beats

Occasionally irregular or very irregular rhythms are often caused by impulses that occur earlier than normal (Figure 5-11). These beats fire before the SA node has a chance to initiate the impulse. These **early beats** (also called *premature beats* or *ectopy*) can arise from any of the cells of the heart, including the atria, AV junctional tissue, or ventricles. The R-R interval between the normal complex and the early beat is shorter than the interval between normal complexes. This makes the rhythm irregular. If early beats occur only a

Normally, the SA node initiates impulses, resulting in a repetitive cycle of P, QRS, and T waveforms.

A premature beat occurs when a site in the a) atria, b) AV junction, or c) ventricles fires before the SA node is able to initiate an impulse.

Following the premature beat, the SA node typically reinitiates impulses in the normal manner.

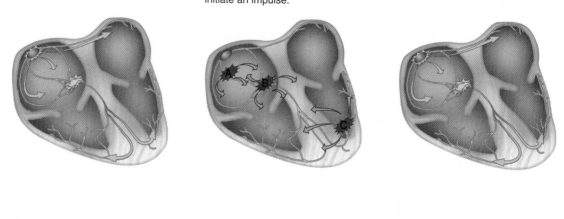

Premature complex results in shortened R-R interval

Figure 5-11
Irregularity can be caused by early beats that arise from the (a) atria, (b) AV tissue, or (c) ventricles.

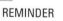

REMINDER
If the R-R interval is shorter than normal, it is typically due to an early beat.

few times a minute, we can describe it as occasionally irregular. If a number are seen, it can be described as very or frequently irregular. Frequent early beats are more likely to progress to very fast atrial, junctional, or ventricular rates (tachycardia). Worse, the rhythm may deteriorate into a quivering of the heart muscle called *ventricular fibrillation*.

Pause or Arrest of the Sinus Node

A rhythm can also appear occasionally or very irregular when the SA node fails to initiate an impulse (Figure 5-12). This is seen as a pause in the ECG rhythm. Typically, the rhythm leading up to the pause looks normal. Then there is suddenly an absence of a P wave, QRS complex, and T wave. This creates a gap or pause. Usually with this condition the SA node recovers and fires another impulse. If the SA node fails to fire, then an escape

Normally, the SA node initiates impulses, resulting in a repetitive cycle of P, QRS, and T waveforms.

When the SA node fails to initiate an impulse, there is a resulting absence of a P wave, QRS complex, and T wave.

Following the skipped beat, the SA node typically reinitiates impulses in the normal manner.

Longer R-R interval
and P-P interval

Figure 5-12
The failure of the sinus node to initiate the heart beat produces an irregular rhythm.

pacemaker from the atria, AV junction, or ventricles initiates an impulse. The prominent characteristic you see is a longer than normal R-R interval that occurs because of the dropped beat. If the SA node frequently fails to fire, there will be many pauses, causing the rhythm to look very or frequently irregular. Frequent pauses in the firing of the sinus node may cause so many dropped beats that the heart rate becomes bradycardic and cardiac output is reduced.

Slightly Irregular

A rhythm may appear to change only slightly as the P-P intervals and R-R intervals vary just a bit (Figure 5-13). It might be so slight that you do not easily see it, but you detect it when you measure the R-R or P-P intervals. The difference between slightly irregular and occasionally irregular rhythms is that slightly irregular rhythms are continuous throughout the ECG tracing; with occasional irregularity, the rhythm is mostly regular but there are areas where it is irregular.

Each heartbeat is
initiated from a
different site in
the atria.

Figure 5-13
A slightly irregular rhythm can occur when, instead of arising from the SA node, the heart's pacemaker shifts from
site to site throughout the atria. The number of small boxes for each R-R and P-P interval varies slightly throughout
the ECG strip.

QUESTION
5. **What is role of the SA
node?**

One cause of a slightly irregular rhythm is when initiation of the heart-beat changes from site to site with each beat; instead of arising from the SA node, the pacemaker site shifts to different locations around the atria. As the site changes, so do the P-P and R-R intervals. Again, these differences can be slight.

Irregularity Caused by Sudden Changes in the Heart Rate

A rhythm may also appear irregular when the heart rate suddenly accelerates (Figure 5-14). We use the term *paroxysmal* to describe a dysrhythmia that has a sudden, rapid onset (and resolution). Because the R-R intervals or P-P intervals go from normal distances to shorter distances, it creates an irregular-looking rhythm. Any of type of tachycardia that arises outside the SA node can occur suddenly. To know this type of irregularity is present, we would have to observe its onset or resolution

The rhythm can also appear irregular when the heart rate suddenly slows down. Because the R-R intervals or P-P intervals go from normal distances to more space between the respective waveforms, it creates an irregular-looking

Normally, the SA node initiates impulses, resulting in a repetitive cycle of P, QRS, and T waveforms.

An ectopic site from above the ventricles fires rapidly and takes over as pacemaker.

Figure 5-14
Irregularity can also result from sudden rapid acceleration of the heart rate.

rhythm. A variety of conditions can lead to an abrupt slowdown of the heart rate. We will describe each in latter chapters. To know this type of irregularity is present, we would have to observe its onset or when the heart began to return to normal.

Irregularly (Totally) Irregular

An irregularly irregular or totally irregular rhythm, also called a *chaotically* or *grossly irregular rhythm*, is one in which there is no consistency to the irregularity. Looking across the tracing, you will find it hard to find an R-R interval that is the same as others (Figure 5-15). This creates the appearance of an irregularly irregular rhythm.

Totally irregular rhythms are typically one condition (which we describe in detail in Chapter 12). Do not worry about knowing the name of the dysrhythmia. Rather, let's just focus on how it produces a totally irregular rhythm. With this dysrhythmia, the atria fire at a rate in excess of 350 beats per minute and from multiple sites. These impulses bombard the AV node so rapidly that it cannot respond to all the impulses, allowing just some to get through to the ventricles. The R-R intervals vary from interval to

REMINDER
Cardiac output is the product of heart rate and stroke volume. If the heart rate is reduced due to an irregular rhythm, it may reduce cardiac output.

In one dysrhythmia ectopic sites in the atria fire at a rate of more than 350 times per minute.

Only some of the atrial impulses are conducted through the AV node.

Not conducted

Conducted

Figure 5-15
An irregularly irregular rhythm is seen as a complete lack of consistency in the space between the R waves.

interval because the impulses are conducted so haphazardly (as many are being generated). This creates the appearance of an irregularly irregular rhythm. Fast rhythms have short R-R intervals, making it difficult to identify the presence of this type of irregularity, so take your time while identifying regularity in fast rates.

Patterned Irregularity

Patterned irregularity, also called *regularly irregular*, is when the irregularity repeats over and over in a cyclic fashion. Early beats occurring at regular intervals, a condition where the heart rate speeds up and slows down in a cyclical way, and one type of conduction blockage that occurs in the AV node, are all characterized as being regularly irregular.

Early beats can be seen in a given pattern, such as those that occur in every other (second) complex (called *bigeminy*), every third complex *(trigeminy)*, or every fourth complex *(quadrigeminy)*, thus producing a patterned irregularity. These early beats can arise from the atria, AV node, or ventricles (Figure 5-16).

We may also see patterned irregularity when the rhythm speeds up and slows down in a rhythmic fashion (Figure 5-17). The speeding up and slowing

Normally, the SA node initiates impulses, resulting in a repetitive cycle of P, QRS, and T waveforms.

Premature beats occur when a site in the atria, AV node, or ventricles fires before the SA node is able to initiate an impulse.

Following the premature beat, the SA node typically reinitiates impulses in the normal manner.

Premature complexes result in shortened R-R intervals.

Figure 5-16
Patterned irregularity can be caused by early beats that occur every other beat, every third beat, or every fourth beat.

down of the heart rate often corresponds with the respiratory cycle and changes in intrathoracic pressure. The heart rate increases during inspiration and decreases during expiration. As a result of the speeding up and slowing down of the heart, you see a narrowing and then a widening of the R-R intervals. This cycle continually repeats.

Patterned irregularity can also occur because of a blockage in the heart's conduction system when the AV node is weakened and tires more and more with each conducted impulse until finally it is so tired that it fails to conduct the impulse through to the ventricles (Figure 5-18). This results in a dropped ventricular beat. This causes the R-R intervals to be longer wherever there is a dropped ventricular beat. With the dropped ventricular beat, the AV node has a chance to rest. The next impulse conducting through the AV node will be carried through faster, but each subsequent impulse will be delayed until finally another ventricular beat is dropped. This cycle repeats over and over, producing a recognizable pattern.

QUESTION
6. What is the role of the AV node?

Figure 5-17
Patterned irregularity can be caused by the cyclic speeding up and slowing down of the heart rate.

Figure 5-18
Patterned irregularity can be caused by a weakened AV node that delays the conduction of the impulse in a cyclic fashion.

Figure 5-19
Where the atrial to ventricular conduction ratio varies, the distance between the R-R intervals changes, producing an irregular rhythm.

Irregularity Caused by Varying Conduction Ratios

Normally, each impulse initiated in the SA node is conducted to the ventricles. This results in one P wave preceding each QRS complex. The number of atrial waveforms (P waves) to ventricular waveforms (QRS complexes) is referred to as the *conduction ratio*. It is normally 1-to-1 (in other words there is one P wave for each QRS complex). The conduction ratio should remain constant throughout the tracing. However, if the conduction ratio changes, the R to R intervals will not be the same distance. For example, the ratio might be 1-to-1 but then change to 3-to-1, thus producing an irregular rhythm (Figure 5-19).

Key Points

- An initial step in analyzing an ECG rhythm is determining its regularity. This yields important information.
- Irregular rhythms are considered abnormal.

- A variety of conditions can produce irregular rhythms. Some of these conditions can be quite serious, so each irregular rhythm should be properly investigated.

- The P-P and R-R intervals can be used to determine whether an ECG rhythm is regular or irregular. If the distance of the R-R intervals or P-P intervals is the same, the rhythm is regular. If the distance differs, the rhythm is irregular.

- Several methods can be used to determine rhythm regularity, including using calipers, marking a paper with a pen, and counting the small squares between each R-R interval.

- Irregularity may be occasionally irregular or very irregular. It may also be slightly irregular. It can also be patterned or irregularly (totally) irregular.

- A pacemaker that changes location from site to site can produce a slightly irregular rhythm.

- A very irregular rhythm is one that has many areas of irregularity. A common cause is frequent early beats.

- A normal rate that suddenly accelerates to a rapid rate or a normal rate that suddenly slows produces irregularity in the rhythm.

- A totally irregular rhythm is one in which there is no consistency to the irregularity.

- Patterned irregularity is where the irregularity repeats over and over in a cyclic fashion.

- Irregularity can also be seen in dysrhythmias that have a varying atrial-to-ventricular conduction ratio.

 ## Assess Your Understanding

The following questions give you a chance to assess your understanding of the material discussed in this chapter. The answers can be found in Appendix A.

1. Normally, the heart beats in a
   a. slightly irregular manner, producing a series of waveforms with each heartbeat.
   b. regularly irregular, rhythmic fashion, producing a P wave, QRS complex, and T wave with each heartbeat.
   c. regular, rhythmic fashion with periods of sudden heart rate acceleration and slowing.
   d. regular, rhythmic fashion, producing a P wave, QRS complex, and T wave with each heartbeat.

2. Determining the regularity of an ECG tracing
   a. is always done first.
   b. should be done only if the health care provider detects an irregular pulse.
   c. is considered an important analysis step.
   d. seldom reveals important information.

3. The distance between two consecutive R waves is called the
   a. R-R interval.
   b. RR segment.
   c. PR interval.
   d. ST segment.

4. An irregular rhythm
   a. is considered normal.
   b. is caused by only a few conditions.
   c. produces a fast heart rate.
   d. should be properly investigated.

5. Calipers can be used to analyze an ECG by
   a. placing one leg on a starting point and extending the second leg four large boxes to the right.
   b. establishing the distance between the first R-R or P-P interval and then adjusting the width of the calipers as you assess each consecutive interval.
   c. placing one leg on a starting point and extending the second leg to the next consecutive waveform being assessed, then comparing this distance across the ECG strip.
   d. moving the calipers across the tracing from each P wave to the next consecutive R wave.

6. The paper and pen method
   a. can be used only to measure regular rhythms.
   b. involves identifying an R wave that falls on a bold line.
   c. requires placing a mark over each R wave on the ECG tracing and then using calipers to determine the distance between them.
   d. involves placing two marks on the paper, the first above one of the R waves on the ECG tracing and the second above the next consecutive R wave.

7. To use the counting the small square method, you
   a. count the number of small squares between the peaks of two consecutive R waves and then compare that to the other R-R intervals.
   b. find an R wave that falls on a bold line and begin counting small squares.

    c.   count the number of small squares in a 6-second section of the ECG tracing.

    d.   divide by 1500 the number of QRS complexes in each 6-second section of the ECG tracing.

8.   Which of the following methods for determining heart rhythm regularity is the easiest one, for which you can use readily available supplies?

    a.   counting small squares method

    b.   caliper method

    c.   paper and pen method

    d.   rate calculator method

9.   A/an _____ irregular rhythm is one that appears mostly regular, but from time to time you see an area where it is irregular.

    a.   occasionally

    b.   patterned

    c.   frequently

    d.   slightly

10.   Early beats

    a.   arise from the atria but not the other areas of the heart.

    b.   cause the R-R intervals between the normal and early beat to be shorter than normal.

    c.   cause the P-P intervals between the normal and early beat to be longer than normal.

    d.   cause the rhythm to be chaotically irregular.

11.   Failure of the SA node to initiate an impulse causes the

    a.   rhythm to be irregularly irregular.

    b.   R-R interval between the normal and the beat following the dropped beat to be shorter than normal.

    c.   rhythm to have patterned irregularity.

    d.   R-R interval that occurs because of the dropped beat to be longer than normal.

12.   A/an _____ irregular rhythm is one where the P-P intervals and R-R intervals vary only a bit.

    a.   slightly

    b.   patterned

    c.   occasionally

    d.   frequently

13.   A patterned irregular rhythm is seen when

    a.   the heart rate suddenly accelerates.

    b.   there are many early beats.

    c.   initiation of the heartbeat changes from site to site with each heartbeat.

    d.   early beats occur every other (second) complex, every third complex, or every fourth complex.

14. With an irregular rhythm caused by a variable conduction ratio
    a. the R-R intervals will occasionally be different durations.
    b. the number of atrial impulses preceding each QRS complex varies.
    c. there is one P wave preceding each QRS complex.
    d. the rhythm is totally irregular.

Referring to the scenario at the beginning of this chapter, answer the following question.

15. The type of irregularity with this patient's ECG tracing means there is
    a. no pattern to the irregularity.
    b. occasional irregularity in the tracing.
    c. an area in the tracing where the heart rate suddenly accelerates.
    d. a mostly regular rhythm, but from time to time you see an area where it is irregular.

Answers to Sidebar Questions

1. A dysrhythmia is any deviation in the heart rate or rhythm from normal. **p. 110**

2. Normal or regular sinus rhythm is the only rhythm considered normal. It is what we measure everything else against. **p. 110**

3. The 6-second interval × 10 method is used to calculate the heart rate in irregular rhythms. Regular rhythms can be assessed using the 300, 150, 100, 75, 60, 50 method; 1500 method; or rate calculators. **p. 112**

4. The distances between the intervals differs; in other words, the distance from the location you identify as the starting point and the location where the second caliper point or pen mark falls is either before or after the second P wave or R wave in one or more P-P intervals or R-R intervals. **p. 115**

5. The SA node is the primary pacemaker of the heart. **p. 120**

6. The AV node is the only pathway for impulses to move from the atria to the ventricles. The impulse travels through the AV node, slowly creating a slight delay that allows the atria to finish pushing any remaining blood into the ventricles. **p. 123**

What's Online

Go to www.mhhe.com/shadeECG2e to find:

- Presentations on chapter content
- Crossword puzzle exercises
- ECG tracings for practicing determining the heart rate
- Chapter quiz
- Flashcards
- Fill-in-the-blank exercises and answers

6 P Waves

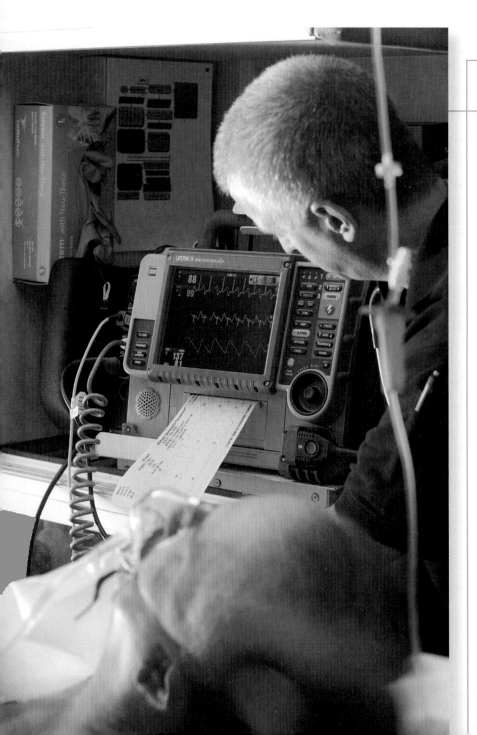

Chapter Outline

Importance of Determining the P Waves

Quick Check of the P Waves

Examining the P Waves

Learning Objectives

LO 6.1 State why it is important to analyze the P waves of an ECG tracing.

LO 6.2 Describe the characteristics of the normal P wave.

LO 6.3 Describe how to analyze the P waves.

LO 6.4 Describe what is meant by the term *abnormal P waves*.

LO 6.5 Identify the causes of peaked, notched, or enlarged sinus P waves.

LO 6.6 Recall the appearance of P waves seen with dysrhythmias that arise from the atria.

LO 6.7 Identify the causes of inverted P waves and absent P waves.

LO 6.8 Describe the conditions in which there will be more P waves than QRS complexes.

Case History

EMS is dispatched for a 75-year-old man residing in a nursing home complaining of "nonspecific weakness." Upon arrival, the paramedics note that the patient is ashen and diaphoretic, lying on the floor next to his bed. After introducing themselves, the paramedics perform an initial assessment and obtain a history of the events leading up to the patient's collapse. They learn that he apparently felt fine when he went to bed, but after rising he went to the bathroom, began to feel weak, and slumped to the floor.

The patient is now awake and alert but feels lightheaded when he tries to sit up. Vital signs show a BP of 140/90, a pulse of 36, and unlabored respirations of 18. His oxygen saturation is 94% on room air. The cardiac monitor is attached and reveals a slow rhythm with a narrow QRS complex. One paramedic examines the strip more closely while her partner establishes an intravenous line. The rhythm strip reveals the absence of normal P waves and instead has saw-toothed waveforms called *F waves*. A QRS complex occurs after every fourth F wave.

The patient is promptly transported to the hospital for definitive treatment.

QUESTION
1. Why do we need to know from where the impulses that are stimulating the heart to beat are originating? *Note:* Answers to the sidebar questions can be found at the end of the chapter.

KEY CONCEPT
The heart normally beats in a regular, rhythmic fashion, producing a P wave, PR interval, QRS complex, ST segment, QT interval, and T wave with each heartbeat.

LO 6.1

Importance of Determining the P Waves

As mentioned previously, the heart normally beats in a regular, rhythmic fashion, producing a P wave, PR interval, QRS complex, ST segment, T wave and QT interval, with each heartbeat. There may also be an U wave. This cycle repeats over and over.

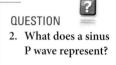

QUESTION

2. **What does a sinus P wave represent?**

The presence or absence of P waves as well as their appearance can help us identify where the impulses that are stimulating the heart to beat are originating. This is another step in analyzing the ECG (Figure 6-1). Obviously, this is important to know. Also, the appearance of the P waves can tell us how well the impulses are being conducted through the atria.

LO 6.2

Quick Check of the P Waves

KEY CONCEPT

One way of analyzing the relationship between the P waves and QRS complexes is to ask: "Is there a P wave preceding each QRS complex?"

The initial assessment for P waves can be done quickly; simply determine whether or not they are present. Questions to ask while analyzing the tracing are, "Is there a uniform P wave preceding each QRS complex (Figure 6-2)?" and "Do the P waves appear normal?" (Alternatively, we can ask, "Is every P wave followed by a QRS complex?" or "Are there any P waves without a QRS complex?")

Figure 6-1
Evaluating the P waves is another important step used to analyze an ECG tracing.

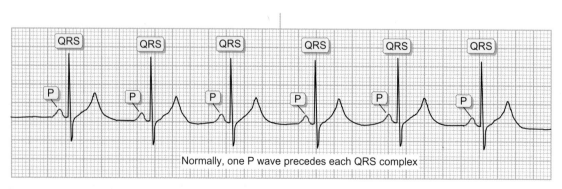

Figure 6-2
When assessing the P waves, look for a normal P wave to precede each QRS complex.

Examining the P Waves

LO 6.3

In Chapter 4 we focused on determining the heart rate whereas in Chapter 5 we addressed identifying regularity. In those two steps, the lead (or view) used does not affect how the ECG tracing is analyzed. With the next steps of analyzing an ECG rhythm, however, lead selection does affect the appearance of the waveforms, so you need to be familiar not only with how normal waveforms look but also with how the waveforms look in the different leads. For our discussion in this chapter, we review only how the P waves appear in lead II. Later in the textbook we discuss how they should appear in other leads. Another point to mention is that our discussion regarding dysrhythmias in this chapter is to give you a sense of the normal P waves and why changes occur. This is not intended to be an in-depth discussion of any dysrhythmia or condition but rather a description of what produces the changes you see in the P waves. Do not worry about learning the names of any of the dysrhythmias at this point.

KEY CONCEPT
Another important step used to analyze an ECG rhythm is the assessment of the P waves.

As discussed earlier, the P wave is the first waveform at the start of the cardiac cycle. It begins with its movement away from the baseline and ends on its return to the baseline. Right atrial depolarization produces the initial portion of the P wave whereas left atrial depolarization produces the terminal portion of the P wave. To examine the P waves, we look closely at their characteristics, especially their deflection, location, and morphology.

REMINDER
The term morphology means the appearance of a waveform.

Characteristics of Normal P Waves

Location	One P wave precedes each QRS complex
Amplitude	0.5 to 2.5 mm
Duration	0.06 to 0.10 seconds
Morphology	A P wave is usually rounded and upright (or inverted or biphasic in certain leads). It has a more abrupt upslope with a gradual downslope, producing an asymmetrical appearance.

As stated earlier, to examine the P waves (Figure 6-3), first look to see if there is a P wave preceding each QRS complex. Then look at each P wave for uniformity. Does each wave look the same? Then measure the wave's duration and amplitude. Identify where it begins and then where it ends. Count the number of small boxes between the beginning and end. Then look at where the P wave first begins to leave the isoelectric line and then where it peaks. Count the number of small boxes between the beginning and the peak.

If the morphology of a P wave is normal—for example, in lead II it is upright and round but slightly asymmetric—and if it precedes each QRS complex, this electrical impulse most likely originated in the SA node and was carried through the atria and AV node in a normal manner. Normal (regular) sinus rhythm is the rhythm with which we compare all others. All dysrhythmias that

WANT MORE INFORMATION?
Visit the Fast & Easy ECGs Website at www.mhhe .com/shadeECG2e.

Figure 6-3
P wave characteristics.

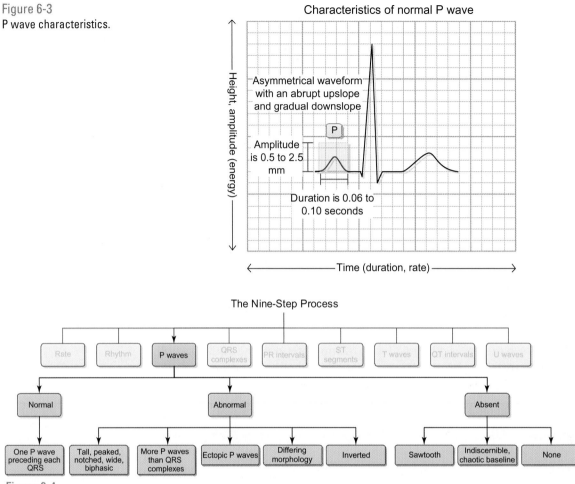

Figure 6-4
Algorithm for normal and abnormal P waves.

originate from the SA node should have normal-looking P waves. However, in faster tachycardias that arise from the SA node, the P wave can sometimes be buried in the T wave of the preceding beat and may have greater amplitude.

LO 6.4

P Waves Having a Different Appearance

Abnormal P waves are those that look different, are inverted, are absent, follow the QRS complex, or are not followed by a QRS complex (Figure 6-4).

A variety of conditions can cause P waves to look different. In some cases, the P wave originates in the SA node, but the atria are altered or damaged, resulting in abnormal conduction of the atrial impulse. In other cases, the P wave appears different because the pacemaker site originates from a site other than the SA node.

QUESTION

3. Which rhythm has a characteristic heart rate of 60 to 100 beats a minute, a regular rhythm, and a P wave preceding each QRS complex?

LO 6.5

Peaked, Notched, or Enlarged Sinus P Waves

Tall (greater than 2.5 mm), narrow, and symmetrically peaked P waves may be seen with increased right atrial pressure and right atrial enlargement

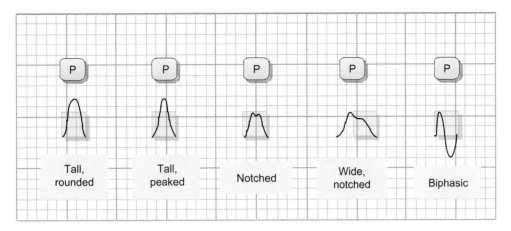

Figure 6-5
Types of abnormal atrial waveforms include tall, peaked, notched, wide, or biphasic sinus P waves.

(Figure 6-5). This is called **P pulmonale.** We may also see abnormally tall P waves in sinus tachycardia (a faster than normal heart rate that originates from the SA node) and **hypokalemia** (a low level of potassium in the blood). Conversely, waves with decreased amplitude can be seen with **hyperkalemia** (a high level of potassium in the blood).

Notched or wide (prolonged—greater than 0.12 seconds in duration) P waves may be seen in increased left atrial pressure and left atrial enlargement. This is called **P mitrale.** These types of P waves may also be seen when there is a delay or block in the movement of electrical impulses through the interatrial conduction tract between the right and left atria, resulting in one atrium depolarizing before the other.

Biphasic P waves are normal in lead V₁. These waves have an initial positive deflection (reflecting right atrial depolarization) followed by a negative deflection (reflecting left atrial depolarization).

KEY CONCEPT
Tall and symmetrically peaked P waves suggest increased right atrial pressure and right atrial enlargement. Notched or wide (prolonged) P waves indicate increased left atrial pressure and left atrial enlargement.

Atrial P Waves

LO 6.6

Some dysrhythmias originate outside the SA node. Those that arise from the atrial tissue or in the internodal pathways are referred to as atrial dysrhythmias. The impulses produce P waves (called *P prime* or *P′*) that look different than the sinus P waves because the impulses arise from outside the SA node.

How the P′ wave looks depends on where it originates and the direction the electrical impulse travels through the atria. As a rule, the closer the site of origin is to the SA node, the more it looks like a normal P wave. If the ectopic pacemaker arises from the upper- or middle-right atrium, depolarization occurs in a normal direction—from right to left and then downward. If it is

KEY CONCEPT

Early atrial beats preceded by a P′ wave have different morphology than the other normal beats.

KEY CONCEPT

Tachycardia that arises from the atria has P′ waves that have a different morphology than normal beats.

QUESTION

4. What type of irregularity is characteristic of a pacemaker that changes from site to site in the atria with each heartbeat?

REMINDER

In tachycardia that arises from the atria, the P waves may be buried in the T wave of the preceding beat.

KEY CONCEPT

Waveforms (such as P waves) that look alike from beat to beat are coming from the same location (foci). Waveforms that look different are coming from a different location(s).

initiated from the upper-right atrium, the P′ wave should be upright in lead II, resembling a normal sinus P wave. A P wave initiated from the middle of the right atrium is less positive than one that originates from the upper-right atrium.

If the impulse arises from the lower-right atrium near the AV node or in the left atrium, depolarization occurs in a **retrograde** direction (meaning the impulse conducts upward [backward] through the heart instead of downward)—from left to right and then upward, resulting in the P′ wave being inverted in lead II.

P′ Waves Seen with Early Beats Arising from the Atria

Early beats that arise from the atria or internodal pathways, before the SA node has a chance to fire, produce P′ waves that have a different morphology (appearance) than the other normal beats (Figure 6-6). How they look depends on where they originate (as described previously). The P′ waves may be obscured or buried in the T wave of the preceding beat (resulting in a short P′-P′ interval as described later in this chapter). This causes the T wave to appear different than those following the other beats. The T wave may look peaked, notched, or larger than normal, suggesting that the P′ is buried in the T wave.

You may see an atrial P′ wave that is not followed by a QRS complex. This is due to a nonconducted or blocked early beat that arises from the atria (Figure 6-7).

P′ Waves Seen with Tachycardia Arising from the Atria

Tachycardia can arise from the atria, resulting in rapid depolarization that overrides the SA node (Figure 6-8). It produces a heart rate of between 150 to 250 beats per minute. The P wave in tachycardia that arises from the atria has a different morphology than normal P waves. The P′ wave is likely to be buried in the T wave of the preceding beat. For this reason, we refer to tachycardias with normal QRS complexes and no discernable P waves as supraventricular tachycardias (meaning that the tachycardia arises from above the ventricles).

Varying Atrial P Waves

P waves coming from one site will look similar. P′ waves that continuously change in appearance indicate that the impulse is arising from different locations in the atria (Figure 6-9). In two dysrhythmias that arise from the atria and are discussed in Chapter 12, the pacemaker site shifts transiently from beat to beat from the SA node to other latent (hidden) pacemaker sites in the atria and AV junction. This produces their most distinguishing characteristic—a change in P′ wave morphology from beat to beat.

Normally, the SA node initiates impulses, resulting in a repetitive cycle of P, QRS, and T waveforms.

Early atrial beats occur when a site in the atria fires before the SA node is able to initiate an impulse.

Following the early beat, the SA node typically reinitiates impulses in the normal manner.

Early atrial beat

Early atrial beat

Figure 6-6

P′ waves seen with early beats arising from the atria differ from sinus P waves and may be buried in the preceding T wave.

Normally, the SA node initiates impulses, resulting in a repetitive cycle of P, QRS, and T waveforms.

Early atrial beats fire and produce a P' wave but the impulse does not reach the ventricles.

Following the early beat, the SA node typically reinitiates impulses in the normal manner.

Nonconducted or blocked early beat

P'

No QRS

Figure 6-7
With a blocked early atrial beat, there is a P' wave but no QRS complex.

Flutter and Fibrillatory Waves

The appearance of the atrial waveforms is very different in two other dysrhythmias that arise from the atria. In one dysrhythmia, the atrial impulses appear as characteristic flutter waveforms whereas in the other there is a characteristic chaotic-looking baseline preceding each QRS complex.

Saw-Toothed Waveforms

In one dysrhythmia that arises from the atria, the atria fire at a rate of between 250 and 350 beats per minute (Figure 6-10). Normal P waves are absent, and instead, we see flutter waves (F waves). They are often described as a saw-toothed pattern.

KEY CONCEPT
Atrial waveforms that appear as a saw-toothed pattern are produced by a rapid firing impulse that arises from the atria.

With this dysrhythmia, the atrial-to-ventricular conduction ratio of impulses is usually 2:1, 3:1, or 4:1. An atrial-to-ventricular conduction ratio of 1:1 is rare because the ventricles are unable to repolarize quickly enough to respond to each of the atrial impulses. The conduction ratios may be constant or variable, meaning that over the course of minutes the conduction ratio changes.

Tachycardia arises from an ectopic site in the atria.

Figure 6-8
If seen, the morphology of the P′ waves associated with tachycardia that arises from the atria is different from normal beats.

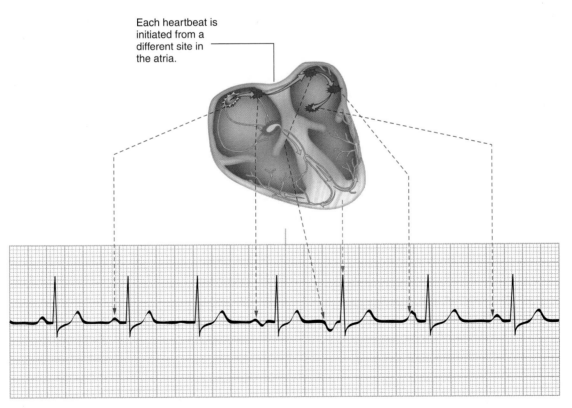

Each heartbeat is initiated from a different site in the atria.

Figure 6-9
Varying P′ waves occur when, instead of arising from the SA node, the heart's pacemaker shifts from site to site throughout the atria.

Ectopic site in the atria fires at a rate of 250 to 350 times per minute.

Not all the atrial impulses are conducted through the AV node. This results in more atrial complexes than QRS complexes.

Not conducted

Conducted

Figure 6-10
A rapid atrial rate of between 250 and 350 beats per minute from one site produces a saw-toothed pattern of F waves.

Chaotic-Looking Baseline

In another dysrhythmia that arises from the atria, the atria fire faster than 350 beats per minute (Figure 6-11). This produces a fibrillatory waveform, reflective of what is occurring with the atrial muscle. This is best described as a chaotic-looking baseline with no discernable P waves (in other words there is an absence of identifiable P waves). Instead of P waves, we see uneven baseline of **f waves,** waves that occur at a rate of greater than 350 times per minute. In some areas along the baseline you may see what looks like a P wave or two but nothing that really appears the same throughout the tracing.

LO 6.7

KEY CONCEPT
Dysrhythmias that arise from the AV junctional tissue have inverted P waves (in lead II) immediately before, during, or after the QRS complex.

Inverted and Absent P Waves

In addition to the inverted P′ waves arising from the lower-right atrium near the AV node or in the left atrium, inverted P′ waves can also arise from the AV junction (Figure 6-12). The inverted P′ wave occurs when the electrical impulse travels upward through the AV junction into the atria, causing retrograde (backward) atrial depolarization. It can occur before, during (buried in QRS), or after the QRS complex. We describe those buried in the QRS complex as absent. This may change the morphology of the QRS complex.

Ectopic sites in the atria fire at a rate greater than 350 times per minute.

Only some of the atrial impulses are conducted through the AV node.

Not conducted

Conducted

Figure 6-11

In one atrial dysrhythmia, the atria fire at a rate in excess of 350 beats per minute from multiple sites, causing a chaotic-looking baseline with no discernable P waves.

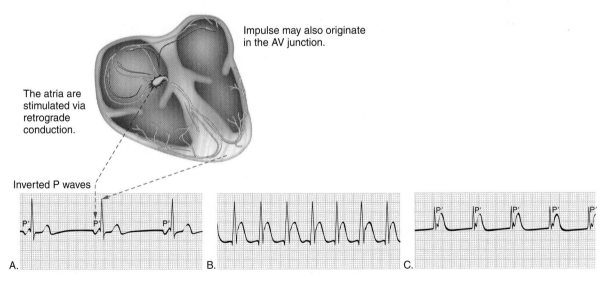

Impulse may also originate in the AV junction.

The atria are stimulated via retrograde conduction.

Inverted P waves

A.   B.   C.

Figure 6-12

Impulses arising from the lower-right atrium near the AV node, in the left atrium, or from the AV junction have inverted P′ waves that can occur before, during (buried in QRS), or after the QRS complex. (A) Inverted P waves preceding the QRS complexes. (B) Absent P waves. (C) P waves that follow the QRS complexes.

P waves are also absent in dysrhythmias that arise from the ventricles. This occurs because the ventricles are below the AV node and do not retrogradedly depolarize the atria.

LO 6.8 More P Waves than QRS Complexes

Normally, there is only one P wave preceding each QRS complex. However, in some dysrhythmias we may see more P waves than QRS complexes. This indicates that the impulse was initiated in the SA node (or other ectopic sites in the atria) but was blocked and did not reach the ventricles. The most common cause for this is a block in the AV node or junction. The term we use to describe this blockage is AV heart block. We can also see this with blocked early beats that arise from the atria as mentioned earlier in this chapter.

P Waves Seen with AV Heart Block

With the most severe cases of AV heart block, only some, or worse yet none, of the electrical impulses initiated by the SA node reach the ventricles (Figure 6-13). This results in the QRS complex being dropped, and there are more P waves than QRS complexes. The P waves should all be normal because the impulses are initiated from the SA node. They just are not all followed by a QRS complex.

Impulse originates in SA node

Blocked

Some of the impulses are blocked as they travel through the AV node.

Figure 6-13
Impulses are initiated in the SA node but do not all reach the ventricles. This results in more P waves than QRS complexes.

Depending on the degree of AV heart block, the atrial-to-ventricular conduction ratio may be constant, usually 2:1, 3:1, or 4:1 (atrial to ventricular beats); they may change (due to changing conduction ratios or start and stop); or the atrial and ventricular impulses may be unrelated.

In the most severe form of AV heart block, the AV node is completely blocked (Figure 6-14). The atria are stimulated to contract by an impulse that originates in the SA node. For this reason, the atrial rate should be within a normal range. The ventricles are stimulated to contract by an escape pacemaker that arises from somewhere below the AV node, resulting in a slower heart rate. There should be more P waves than QRS complexes because the SA node has an inherently faster rate than the AV junction or ventricles. Also, because the pacemaker sites (SA node and ventricles) are firing independently of each other, the P waves seem to "march through" the QRS complexes.

The P waves associated with blocked early beats that arise from the atria (described earlier in this chapter) can be confused with AV heart block. A key difference between the two is that with early beats, the P′-P interval is shorter whereas, with AV heart block, the P-P interval remains constant. With early atrial beats, the P′ wave also looks different than the other P waves whereas, with AV heart block, the P waves look alike.

REMINDER

Remember, heart rate × stroke volume = cardiac output. AV heart blocks, which result in dropped QRS complexes, can cause decreased cardiac output by lowering the heart rate.

KEY CONCEPT

More P waves than QRS complexes indicate that the impulse was initiated in the SA node or another ectopic site in the atria but was blocked and did not reach the ventricles.

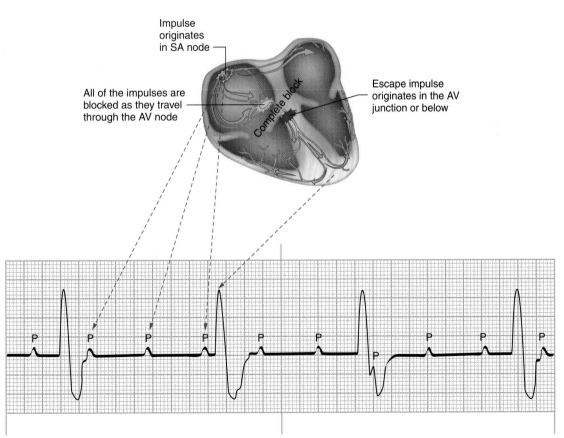

Impulse originates in SA node

All of the impulses are blocked as they travel through the AV node

Complete block

Escape impulse originates in the AV junction or below

Figure 6-14
With the most severe form of AV node blockage, there are more P waves than QRS complexes. Further, the P waves appear to march through the QRS complexes.

Key Points 🔍

- Normally, the heart beats in a regular, rhythmic fashion, producing a P wave, PR interval, QRS complex, ST segment, T wave, and QT interval with each heartbeat. This cycle repeats over and over.

- Another important step used to analyze an ECG rhythm is examining the P waves.

- The P wave is the first deflection from the baseline at the beginning of the cardiac cycle.

- A normal P wave (upright and round in lead II) preceding each QRS complex indicates that the electrical impulse likely originated in the SA node and was carried through the atria in a normal manner.

- The amplitude of a normal P wave is 0.5 to 2.5 mm high, and the duration is 0.06 to 0.10 seconds.

- P waves that originate in the SA node but conduct abnormally through altered, damaged atria will have an altered morphology.

- P waves that result from a pacemaker site outside the SA node will have an altered morphology.

- Tall and symmetrically peaked P waves may be seen with increased right atrial pressure and right atrial enlargement.

- Notched or wide (enlarged) P waves may be seen with increased left atrial pressure and left atrial enlargement.

- Impulses that arise from the atria produce P prime (P′) waves that look different than the sinus P waves.

- P′ waves that arise from the upper-right atrium should be upright in lead II, resembling a normal sinus P wave.

- A P′ wave that arises from the middle of the right atrium is less positive than one that originates from the upper-right atrium.

- A P′ wave that arises from the lower-right atrium near the AV node or in the left atrium results in atrial depolarization occurring in a retrograde direction. This produces an inverted P′ wave in lead II.

- Early beats can arise from the atria or internodal pathways. The P′ wave in these early beats has a different morphology than normal beats.

- Tachycardia that arises from the atria produces a heart rate of between 150 and 250 beats per minute. It has P′ waves, which look different than normal beats. These P′ waves are often buried in the T wave of the preceding beat.

- P waves that continuously change in their appearance indicate that the pacemaker is originating from a different site with each heartbeat.

- In one dysrhythmia that arises from the atria, the atria fire at a rate of between 250 and 350 beats per minute (see Figure 6-12). Normal P waves are absent, and, instead, flutter waves (F waves) are present. These are often described as having a sawtoothed appearance.

- In another dysrhythmia that arises from the atria, there are no discernable P waves. Instead, there is a chaotic-looking baseline of f waves preceding the QRS complexes.

- Impulses that arise from the AV junction produce an inverted P′ wave that may immediately precede, or occur during or following, the QRS complex.

- Normally, there is only one P wave preceding each QRS complex.

- More P waves than QRS complexes indicate that the impulse was initiated in the SA node or atria but was blocked and did not reach the ventricles. The most common causes for this are AV heart block and blocked early beats that arise from the atria.

Assess Your Understanding

The following questions give you a chance to assess your understanding of the material discussed in this chapter. The answers can be found in Appendix A.

1. To analyze the atrial activity of an ECG you should assess the
   a. regularity.
   b. P waves.
   c. PR intervals.
   d. heart rate.

2. The amplitude of the P wave normally does not exceed _____ mm high.
   a. 1.0
   b. 2.5
   c. 3.0
   d. 0.5

3. An upright, round P wave (in lead II) that precedes each QRS complex indicates that the electrical impulse originated in the
   a. AV node and was carried through the atria in a retrograde manner.
   b. ventricles and was carried through the atria in the normal manner.
   c. SA node and was carried through the AV node in a retrograde manner.
   d. SA node and was carried through the atria in a normal manner.

4. The characteristic considered normal (in lead II) is a/an
   a. P wave that follows the QRS complex.
   b. inverted P wave.

    c.   peaked or notched P wave.

    d.   rounded and upright P wave.

5.   Which of the following is best evaluated by choosing the appropriate lead?

    a.   heart rate

    b.   regularity

    c.   P waves

    d.   PR interval

6.   With increased left atrial pressure and left atrial enlargement, the P wave is normally

    a.   inverted.

    b.   notched or wide.

    c.   pointed.

    d.   biphasic.

7.   Which of the following will produce P waves that look different than sinus P waves?

    a.   enlarged or damaged atria

    b.   AV heart block

    c.   tachycardia arising from the sinus node

    d.   all of the above

8.   An impulse that arises closer to the SA node

    a.   has the same appearance as a normal P wave.

    b.   is inverted.

    c.   looks more like a normal P wave.

    d.   is biphasic or notched.

9.   Early beats that arise from the atria

    a.   occur only in the right atrium.

    b.   always have an inverted P wave.

    c.   may have P′ waves buried in the T wave of the preceding beat.

    d.   have P waves that look the same as P waves that arise from the SA node.

10.   With tachycardia that arises from the atria,

    a.   the P′ wave is typically notched or widened.

    b.   the P′ wave looks different than P waves that arise from the SA node.

    c.   the P′ wave is hidden within the QRS complex.

    d.   there are more P′ waves than QRS complexes.

11. An atrial pacemaker site that changes from location to location has
    a. P waves that continually change in appearance.
    b. one pacemaker site from which the impulses arise.
    c. inverted P′ waves.
    d. a chaotic baseline preceding each QRS complex.

12. When the atria fire faster than 350 beats per minute, the P waves
    a. are indiscernible; instead, there is a chaotic-looking baseline.
    b. appear in a saw-tooth pattern.
    c. are inverted (in lead II).
    d. are buried in the T wave of the preceding beat.

13. Dysrhythmias that arise from AV junctional tissue have _____ P′ waves.
    a. upright
    b. inverted
    c. biphasic
    d. peaked

14. With ventricular dysrhythmias, the P′ waves
    a. change in appearance.
    b. have a saw-tooth appearance.
    c. immediately precede the QRS complexes.
    d. are absent.

15. Which of the following has more P waves than QRS complexes?
    a. a dysrhythmia where the pacemaker changes from site to site with each beat
    b. early beats that arise from the atria
    c. AV heart block
    d. dysrhythmias that arise from the AV junction

Referring to the scenario at the beginning of this chapter, answer the following questions.

16. From where did the patient's dysrhythmia originate?
    a. sinus node
    b. AV junctional tissue
    c. ventricles
    d. atria

17. The firing rate of the F waves is _____ beats per minute.
    a. 36
    b. 72
    c. 108
    d. 144

Answer to Sidebar Questions

1. The presence or absence of P waves as well as their appearance can help us identify where the impulses that are stimulating the heart to beat are originating as well as how they are conducting through the atria. **p. 131**

2. The P wave represents initiation of the impulse in the SA node and its transmission through the atria from right to left and downward. The first part of the P wave represents depolarization of the right atrium whereas the second part of the P wave represents depolarization of the left atrium. The impulse traveling through the AV node occurs during the P wave. **p. 132**

3. These features are characteristic of normal sinus rhythm. **p. 134**

4. Typically, the rhythm is slightly irregular when a pacemaker changes from site to site in the atria with each heartbeat. **p. 136**

What's Online

Go to www.mhhe.com/shadeECG2e to find:
- Presentations on chapter content
- Crossword puzzle exercises
- ECG tracings for practicing analyzing P waves
- Chapter quiz
- Flashcards
- Fill-in-the-blank exercises and answers

7 QRS Complexes

Chapter Outline

Importance of Determining the QRS Complexes

Quick Check of the QRS Complexes

Examining the QRS Complexes

Measuring QRS Complexes

Variations in the QRS Configuration

QRS Complexes in Different Leads

Where We See Normal QRS Complexes

Abnormal QRS Complexes

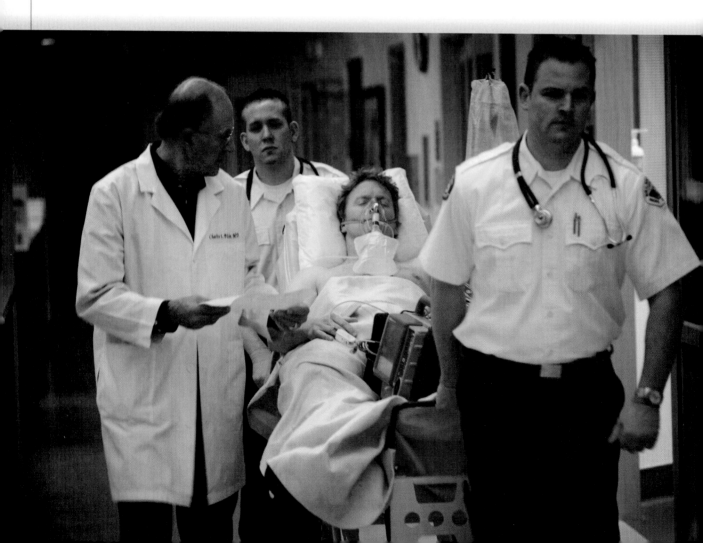

Learning Objectives

LO 7.1 State why it is important to analyze the QRS complexes of an ECG tracing.

LO 7.2 Describe the characteristics of the normal QRS complex.

LO 7.3 Recall how to measure the QRS complex.

LO 7.4 Describe the variations in the QRS configuration.

LO 7.5 Recognize that the appearance of the QRS complexes differs in the various ECG leads.

LO 7.6 Recall when normal QRS complexes are seen.

LO 7.7 Describe what is meant when we say "abnormal QRS complexes."

LO 7.8 Identify when tall and low amplitude QRS complexes are seen.

LO 7.9 Recall the causes of wider than normal QRS complexes.

LO 7.10 Identify the causes of absent QRS complexes.

Case History

EMS is called to the home of a 39-year-old man complaining of chest pain. Upon arrival they find the patient lying on the couch. He is awake and alert. He states that he has a dull ache in his chest. His vital signs are normal, and the ECG leads are quickly attached and show a normal sinus rhythm. The paramedics apply oxygen via nasal cannula to the patient and establish an intravenous line. The patient's chest pain resolves after the application of oxygen and the administration of aspirin and one sublingual nitroglycerin.

En route to the hospital the paramedics notice the occurrence of early beats. They are wide and bizarre in configuration, without associated P waves, and each complex appears different than the others. The patient continues to be pain free, but the early beats appear to be coming more frequently. The paramedics contact medical control at the receiving hospital and describe the rhythm. The physician approves their request to deliver an antidysrhythmic agent and the early beats cease. The patient is delivered to the hospital without further incident.

Importance of Determining the QRS Complexes

As part of analyzing an ECG, we examine and measure the specific wave-forms, segments, and intervals. In this chapter we discuss assessment of the QRS complexes (Figure 7-1).

Assessing the QRS complexes is important because it tells us how well the impulses are traveling through the ventricles or if the impulses are originating from the ventricles. This is important to know as delays or interruption of conduction through the ventricles or impulses that arise from the ventricles can lead to serious or even life-threatening conditions.

Quick Check of the QRS Complexes

The initial assessment for QRS complexes can be done quickly. Questions to ask include, "Are the QRS complexes present and within normal limits? Do they appear normal in their configuration? Do they all look alike?" (Figure 7-2.)

Figure 7-1
Assessing the QRS complexes is another part of The Nine-Step Process algorithm.

Figure 7-2
When assessing the QRS complexes, look for a normal QRS complex to follow each P wave and PR interval.

Examining the QRS Complexes

To examine the QRS complexes, we look closely at their characteristics, especially their location, configuration, and deflection (Figure 7-3).

As discussed, the QRS complex is the waveform immediately following the PR interval. Its starting point is where the first wave of the complex starts to move away (sharply or gradually) from the baseline. The QRS complex ends at the point where the last wave of the complex starts to flatten (sharply or gradually) at, above, or below the baseline. The QRS complex is much bigger than the P wave because depolarization of the ventricles involves considerably larger muscle mass than depolarization of the atria. The QRS complex characteristically looks thinner than the other parts of the ECG because the ventricles depolarize so fast. This minimizes contact time between the stylus and the ECG paper.

Characteristics of Normal QRS Complexes	
Location	A QRS complex follows the PR interval.
Amplitude	5 to 30 mm (but it differs with each lead employed).
Duration	0.06 to 0.10 seconds. The duration is measured from the beginning of the Q wave (or the beginning of the R wave if the Q is not present) to the end of the S wave.
Morphology	The QRS complex includes the Q, R, and S waves.

The elements of the QRS complex are described below:

- **Q wave.** The Q wave is the first negative deflection from the baseline following the P wave. It is always negative. In some cases the Q wave is absent. The normal duration of the Q wave in the limb leads (with the

REMINDER

If the Q wave is absent, the resulting complex is measured from the beginning of the R wave.

Characteristics of normal QRS complex

Sharply pointed, narrow waveform

Amplitude is 5 to 30 mm

R

J point

ST segment

Baseline

Q   S

Duration is 0.06 to 0.10 seconds

Height, amplitude (energy)

Time (duration, rate)

Figure 7-3
The QRS complex consists of the Q wave, R wave, and S wave. The J point is where the S wave connects to the ST segment. The ST segment is the flat line that connects the S wave with the T wave.

exception of leads III and aV_R) is less than 0.04 seconds. The amplitude is normally less than 25% of the amplitude of the R wave in that lead.

- **R wave.** The R wave is the first positive, triangular deflection in the QRS complex. It follows the Q wave (if it is present).

- **S wave.** The S wave is the first negative deflection that *extends below* the baseline in the QRS complex following the R wave.

The point at which the QRS complex meets the ST segment is called the *junction* or *J point.*

The Q wave represents depolarization of the interventricular septum. It is activated from left to right. The R and S waves represent simultaneous depolarization of the right and left ventricles. The QRS complex mostly represents the electrical activity occurring in the left ventricle because of its greater muscle mass.

Generally speaking, men have higher QRS complex amplitude than women, and young people have higher amplitudes than the elderly. The precordial leads have higher amplitude than the limb leads because the electrodes are closer to the heart.

Measuring QRS Complexes

To measure the width (duration) of a QRS complex, first identify the complex with the longest duration and the most distinct beginning and ending (Figure 7-4). Normally, the QRS complex will not extend beyond two and a half small boxes (0.10 seconds in duration). Start by finding the beginning of the QRS complex. This is the point where the first wave of the complex, which will either be the Q wave or the R wave, begins to deviate from the baseline. Then measure to the point where the last wave of the complex transitions into the ST segment. Typically, it is where the S wave or R wave (in the absence of an S wave) begins to level out (flatten) at, above, or below the baseline. This is considered the end of the QRS complex.

To make measuring easier, try to find a QRS complex where the waveform begins on one of the bold or thin lines. Then count the number of small squares (boxes) between the beginning and the end of the complex. If none of the Q or R waves falls squarely on a line, then you can use calipers or the paper and pencil technique. Start by placing the first point at the beginning of the complex; then place the second point at the end of the complex. This establishes the distance from the beginning to the end. Now slide the calipers or paper (with lines you have drawn) horizontally across the tracing so that the first point lines up with a bold or thin line. Now count the number of squares between it and the second point.

Determining where the QRS complex ends can be difficult because you don't always see a clear transition with nice, straight lines (Figure 7-5). Instead,

Figure 7-4
Measure the QRS complex from where the Q or R wave starts to where the S wave ends (J point).

particularly when there is depression or elevation of the ST segment, you need to look for a small notch, slope, or other movement that suggests an alteration of electrical flow. Include in your measurement the entire S wave, but don't let it overlap into the ST segment or the T wave. It is helpful to look for the end of the QRS complex in as many leads as possible as you can sometimes see it in one lead but not another. In some ECG tracings you have to use your best educated guess and common sense to conclude what is the duration of the QRS complex.

Variations in the QRS Configuration

LO 7.4

The QRS complex can take various forms (Figure 7-6). Although we said it consists of positive (upright) deflections called R waves and negative (inverted) deflections called Q and S waves, all three waves are not always seen. Also, the waveforms will look different depending on which lead is used. If the R wave is absent, the complex is called a QS complex. Likewise, if the Q wave is absent, the complex is called an RS complex. Waveforms of normal or greater than normal amplitude are denoted with a large case letter, whereas waveforms less than 5 mm in amplitude are denoted with a small case letter (e.g., "q," "r," "s"). Later, when we discuss myocardial infarction, this will become important as it helps us determine whether a Q wave is significant.

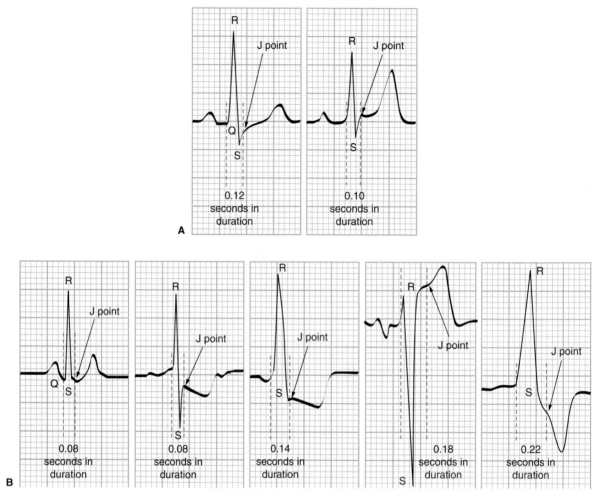

Figure 7-5
Measuring the QRS complex. (A) These two QRS complexes have easy to see J points. (B) These QRS complexes have less-defined transition, making measurement of the QRS complex more challenging.

Although there is only one Q wave, there can be more than one R wave and S wave in the QRS complex. A positive impulse immediately following the R wave is called R prime (R′). A double positive impulse immediately following the R wave is called double R prime (R″). A negative impulse immediately following the S wave is called S prime (S′). A double negative impulse immediately following the S wave is called double S prime (S″). This discussion becomes more significant in Chapter 19 when we discuss bundle branch block.

QUESTION
3. Why does the QRS complex look different in the various ECG leads?

LO 7.5

QRS Complexes in Different Leads

Although we haven't discussed the various ECG leads yet, it important to know that the appearance of the QRS complex differs depending on which ECG lead is viewed. At this point, don't worry about learning how they look in the different leads (Figure 7-7). Instead, just realize the appearance of the QRS complexes differs. In leads I, II, III, aV_F, and V_4 to V_6, the deflection of the QRS

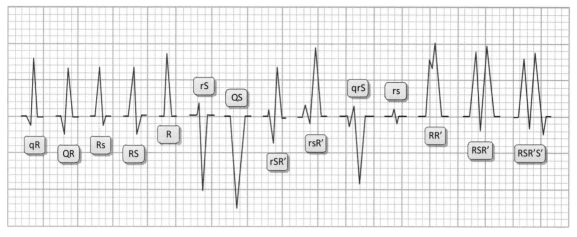

Figure 7-6
Variations in QRS configurations.

Figure 7-7
Direction of QRS waves in various leads.

complex is characteristically positive or upright. In leads aV_R, V_1 and V_2, the QRS complex is largely negative or inverted. In leads V_3 and V_4, the QRS complex is biphasic. In leads III and aV_L the QRS complex may also be biphasic.

Where We See Normal QRS Complexes

LO 7.6

The QRS complexes should appear normal (upright and narrow) if

- The rhythm is initiated from a site above the ventricles—meaning in the SA node, atria, or AV junction.

- Conduction has progressed normally from the bundle of His, through the right and left bundle branches, and through the Purkinje network.

- Normal depolarization of the ventricles has occurred.

KEY CONCEPT
If the rhythm is initiated from the SA node, atria, or AV junction, the QRS complexes should appear normal.

Unless there is a conduction delay through the ventricles, normal sinus rhythm and any dysrhythmia initiated by a pacemaker site above the ventricles can be expected to have normal QRS complexes.

Generally, you can look at the QRS complex and get a sense of whether it is narrow or wide.

LO 7.7

Abnormal QRS Complexes

Abnormal QRS complexes are produced by abnormal depolarization of the ventricles. The pacemaker site in these abnormal QRS complexes can be the SA node or an ectopic pacemaker in the atria, AV junction, bundle branches, Purkinje network, or ventricular myocardium.

The onset and end of an abnormal QRS complex are the same as those of a normal QRS complex. The direction can be mostly positive (upright), mostly negative (inverted), or biphasic. Its duration is often greater than 0.10 seconds. The amplitude of waves in the abnormal QRS complex varies from 1 to 2 mm to 20 mm or more. The morphology of the abnormal QRS complex can vary from being only slightly abnormal to extremely wide, notched, or slurred. We refer to these extremely abnormal configurations as bizarre-looking because they deviate so far from normal (Figure 7-8).

A variety of conditions can cause abnormal QRS complexes including

- Ventricular hypertrophy
- Obesity, hyperthyroidism, pleural effusion
- Bundle branch block
- Intraventricular conduction disturbance

Figure 7-8
Algorithm to evaluate QRS complexes.

- Aberrant ventricular conduction
- Ventricular preexcitation
- An electrical impulse originating in a ventricular ectopic or escape pacemaker
- Ventricular pacing by a cardiac pacemaker

As a point of information, waveforms that look alike from beat to beat (such as QRS complexes) are coming from the same location. Occasionally, frequently, or continuously repeating waveforms that look different are coming from a different location(s) or traveling through the conduction systems differently.

Tall and Low Amplitude QRS Complexes

Very tall QRS complexes are usually caused by **hypertrophy** of one or both ventricles or by an abnormal pacemaker or aberrantly conducted beat (Figure 7-9). Hypertrophied ventricles are larger and, therefore, have more myocardial cells.

Low-voltage or abnormally small QRS complexes may be seen in obese patients, hyperthyroid patients, and patients with pleural effusion.

Wide QRS Complexes of Supraventricular Origin

Any rhythm that originates from above the ventricles (i.e., the SA node or an ectopic pacemaker in the atria or AV junction) is referred to as a supraventricular

LO 7.8

KEY CONCEPT
Tall QRS complexes suggest hypertrophy of one or both ventricles, an abnormal pacemaker, or aberrantly conducted beat.

LO 7.9

Figure 7-9
Examples of tall QRS complexes and low-voltage QRS complexes.

rhythm. Even though a cardiac rhythm originates from a supraventricular site, the subsequent conduction of the impulses through the ventricles can be impaired or can occur differently than normal. This can result in wide, bizarre QRS complexes.

Intraventricular Conduction Defect

One type of abnormal conduction is referred to as an intraventricular conduction defect (Figure 7-10). Intraventricular conduction defect usually occurs as a result of right or left bundle branch block. Bundle branch block takes place when conduction of the electrical impulse is partially or completely blocked in either the right or left bundle branch while conduction continues uninterrupted through the unaffected bundle branch. A block in one bundle branch causes the ventricle on that side to be depolarized later than the other. This results in an abnormal QRS complex. In bundle branch blocks, the QRS complex is greater than 0.12 seconds in duration and appears bizarre (abnormal in size and shape).

Bundle branch block may be either partial or complete. As its name implies, partial, or incomplete, bundle branch block results in only part of the conduction being delayed. This results in less of a delay in ventricular depolarization

Impulse originates in SA node

Block

Figure 7-10
In bundle branch block, wide QRS complexes occur because conduction of the electrical impulse is partially or completely blocked in either the right or left bundle branch while conduction continues uninterrupted through the unaffected bundle branch.

than would be expected in complete bundle branch block. This causes the QRS complex to be greater than 0.10 seconds but not greater than 0.12 seconds in duration. However, the QRS complex has some abnormalities, such as notching, and does not appear completely normal.

Complete and partial bundle branch block may exist with normal sinus rhythm and in any supraventricular dysrhythmia. For this reason the QRS complexes are preceded by a P wave. The appearance of the P waves depends on their site of origin.

Other causes of intraventricular conduction defect include myocardial infarction; fibrosis; hypertrophy; electrolyte imbalance, such as hypokalemia and hyperkalemia; and excessive administration of such cardiac drugs such as quinidine, procainamide, and flecainide (Figure 7-11). The QRS complexes are preceded by a P wave because the pacemaker site is above the ventricles. The appearance of the P waves depends on their site of origin.

QUESTION
4. What does the term supraventricular mean?

Aberrant Conduction

Aberrant conduction is a brief failure of the right or left bundle branch to normally conduct an electrical impulse (Figure 7-12). It can occur when electrical impulses, such as early beats and tachycardias that arise above the ventricles,

Hearbeat is initiated from SA node in normal way

Figure 7-11
The presence of a P wave preceding each QRS complex indicates that the rhythm is arising from the SA node. The wide QRS complexes result from a conduction defect through the ventricles.

Normally, the SA node initiates impulses, resulting in a repetitive cycle of P, QRS, and T waveforms.

Premature impulse travels down one of the bundle branches before the other.

Following the premature beat, the SA node typically reinitiates impulses in the normal manner.

P'

Figure 7-12
In aberrant conduction, the QRS complex appears wider than normal due to the impulse traveling down one unaffected bundle branch while stimulation of the other bundle branch follows.

reach the bundle branch shortly after it has just conducted an impulse. It is refractory and not able to be stimulated. One bundle branch may be less refractory than the other and will conduct the impulse. The refractory bundle branch will then be stimulated following a delay. This produces an abnormal QRS complex. The abnormal QRS complex frequently looks like incomplete or complete bundle branch block and may mimic ventricular dysrhythmias. Aberrant ventricular conduction can occur in many supraventricular dysrhythmias.

Ventricular Preexcitation

Another cause of wider than normal QRS complexes is ventricular preexcitation (Figure 7-13). This is the premature depolarization of the ventricles that occurs when an impulse arises from a site above the ventricles but travels through abnormal accessory conduction pathways to the ventricles. (Ventricular preexcitation will be covered in more detail in Chapter 13.) These abnormal conduction tracts bypass the AV junction, or bundle of His, allowing the electrical impulses to initiate depolarization of the ventricles early. This results in an abnormally wide QRS complex (greater than 0.10 seconds). It also has characteristically abnormal slurring, and sometimes notching, at

Figure 7-13
Ventricular preexcitation is premature depolarization of the ventricles that occurs when an impulse arises from a site above the ventricles but travels through abnormal accessory conduction pathways to the ventricles.

its onset. This is called the **delta wave**. The abnormal shape and width of the QRS complex is the result of the fusion of the abnormal premature depolarization of the ventricle (which produces the delta wave) with the normal depolarization of the rest of the ventricles.

Pacemaker-Induced QRS Complexes

Certain conditions require the insertion of a cardiac pacemaker (Figure 7-14). Cardiac pacemaker–induced QRS complexes are generally 0.12 seconds or greater in width and appear bizarre. Preceding each pacemaker-induced QRS complex is a narrow, often biphasic, deflection called the *pacemaker spike*.

Wide, Bizarre-Looking QRS Complexes of Ventricular Origin

Dysrhythmias that originate from the ventricular tissue are referred to as *ventricular dysrhythmias* (Figure 7-15). The three dysrhythmias we will discuss are early beats, an escape rhythm, and tachycardia, all of which arise from the ventricles. The key characteristic seen with ventricular dysrhythmias is wide

KEY CONCEPT
Wide QRS complexes that arise from above the ventricles are caused by intraventricular conduction defect, bundle branch block, aberrant conduction, or ventricular preexcitation.

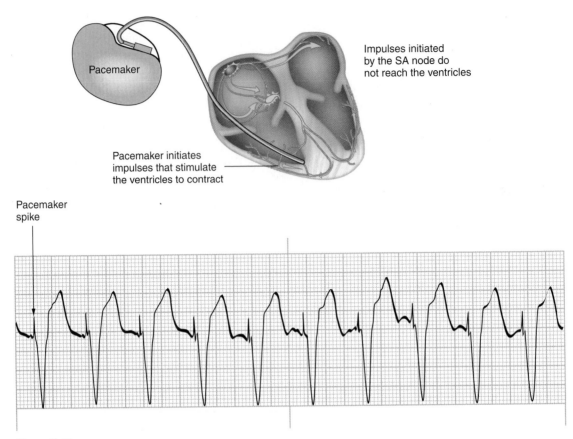

Pacemaker

Impulses initiated by the SA node do not reach the ventricles

Pacemaker initiates impulses that stimulate the ventricles to contract

Pacemaker spike

Figure 7-14
Characteristic features of cardiac pacemakers include wide QRS complexes (greater than 0.10 seconds) and a narrow, often biphasic, deflection called the *pacemaker spike*, which precedes each pacemaker-induced QRS complex.

(greater than 0.12 seconds in duration) QRS complexes. The QRS complexes are usually bizarre-looking. Beats that arise from the ventricles are not preceded by a P wave (if seen, they are dissociated). The T waves of ventricular beats deflect in an opposite direction of the R waves.

Early Beats that Arise from the Ventricles

KEY CONCEPT
Early beats that arise from the ventricles have a wide (greater than 0.12 seconds in duration), large and bizarre-looking QRS complex.

Early beats that arise from the ventricles before the SA node has a chance to fire (Figure 7-16) interrupt the normal rhythm. These impulses arise from below the AV junction, producing QRS complexes that look different from those that arise above or at the AV junction. As described, the QRS complexes associated with these early beats are wide, large, and bizarre-looking. A pause, called a **compensatory pause,** follows the early beat. This will be discussed in more detail in Chapter 14.

KEY CONCEPT
An escape rhythm that arises from the ventricles is slow (20 to 40 beats per minute) and has wide, large, and bizarre-looking QRS complexes.

Escape Rhythm that Arises from the Ventricles

A sustained escape rhythm arises from the ventricles when stimuli from the SA node or AV junction fail to reach the ventricles or their rate falls to less than that of the ventricles (Figure 7-17). The key characteristics of this dysrhythmia are a rate of 20 to 40 beats per minute and QRS complexes that are

Figure 7-15
Different-looking QRS complexes associated with ventricular beats and/or rhythms.

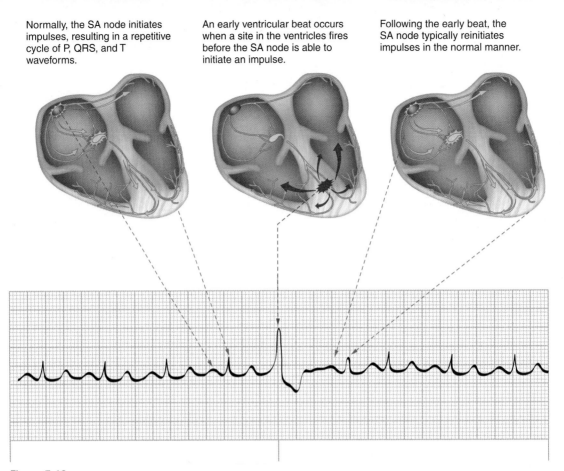

Normally, the SA node initiates impulses, resulting in a repetitive cycle of P, QRS, and T waveforms.

An early ventricular beat occurs when a site in the ventricles fires before the SA node is able to initiate an impulse.

Following the early beat, the SA node typically reinitiates impulses in the normal manner.

Figure 7-16
QRS complexes associated with early beats that arise from the ventricles are wide, large, and bizarre-looking.

Impulses initiated from ventricular escape pacemaker

Figure 7-17
Wide, bizarre-looking QRS complexes firing at a rate of less than 40 beats per minute and an absence of P waves are seen with an escape rhythm that arises from the ventricles.

wide (greater than 0.12 seconds), large, and bizarre-looking. As with PVCs, the T wave typically takes the opposite direction of the R wave. The rhythm arises from one site so it is usually regular. It becomes irregular as the heart dies.

Tachycardia that Arises from the Ventricles

Tachycardia that arises from the ventricles results from rapid depolarization of the ventricles that overrides the SA node (Figure 7-18). It occurs when there are three or more early beats in a row. It may occur in bursts of 6 to 10 early beats or be sustained. In sustained tachycardia that arises from the ventricles, the heart rate is between 100 and 250 beats per minute. The rhythm consists of frequent, wide (greater than 0.12 seconds), and bizarre-looking QRS complexes. The QRS complexes occur regularly, and there is no isoelectric line shown between the cardiac cycles. T waves may or may not be present. If seen, they are typically the opposite direction of the R waves.

Tachycardia that arises from the ventricles has a very fast heart rate that causes cardiac output to decrease by lowering the stroke volume.

The QRS complexes associated with tachycardia that arises from one site in the ventricles should all look alike. On the other hand, when the tachycardia

REMINDER

Remember our discussion in Chapter 1: heart rate × stroke volume = cardiac output. An escape rhythm that arises from the ventricles can lead to decreased cardiac output because of the slower heart rate.

KEY CONCEPT

Tachycardia that arises from the ventricles has a heart rate of between 100 and 250 beats per minute and wide, large, and bizarre-looking QRS complexes.

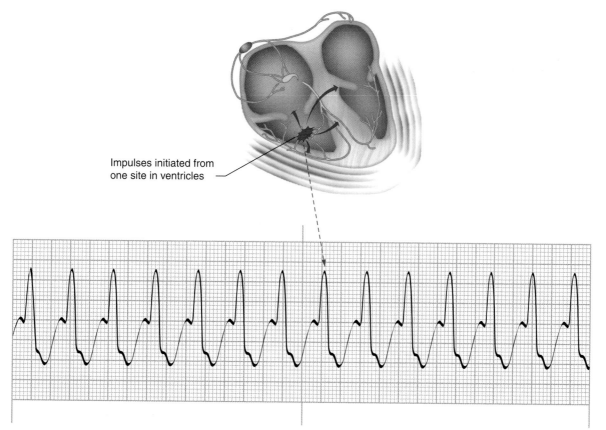

Impulses initiated from one site in ventricles

Figure 7-18

Wide, bizarre-looking QRS complexes firing at a rate of between 100 and 250 beats per minute and an absence of P waves is seen with tachycardia that arises from the ventricles.

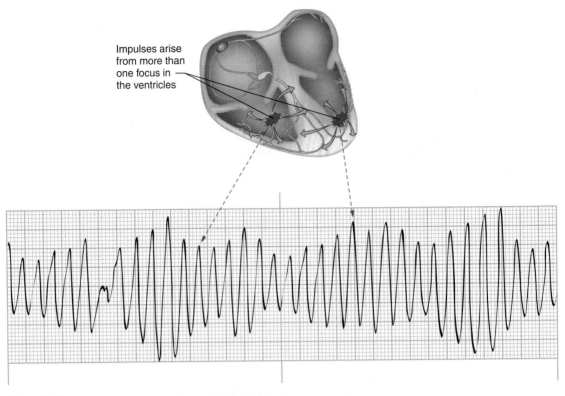

Impulses arise from more than one focus in the ventricles

Figure 7-19
Form of tachycardia arising in the ventricles in which the shape of the ventricular waveforms changes between upright and downward deflections. It appears as a spindle-shaped rhythm.

QUESTION
5. **What type of regularity is characteristic of tachycardia that arises from the ventricles?**

REMINDER
Remember our discussion in Chapter 1: heart rate × stroke volume = cardiac output. AV heart blocks, which result in slower heart rates, can cause decreased cardiac output.

KEY CONCEPT
Wide QRS complexes seen with AV heart block indicate the ventricular pacemaker site is in the ventricles.

arises from more than one site in the ventricles, the shape of the ventricular waveforms can be expected to change (Figure 7-19). In one particular form of tachycardia, the ventricular waveforms appear as a series of QRS complexes that rotate about the baseline (usually gradually) between upright deflections and downward deflections. It is described as a "spindle-shaped rhythm." The rate is 150 to 300 beats per minute (typically 200 to 250 beats per minute), the rhythm is usually irregular, the QRS complexes are wide, and the P waves are usually absent.

AV Heart Block

Another dysrhythmia in which abnormal QRS complexes may occur is in the most severe form of AV heart block (Figure 7-20). Remember, we said that with the most severe form of AV heart block there is complete blockage of the AV node. The atria are stimulated to contract by the impulse that originates from the SA node, whereas the ventricles are stimulated to contract by an escape pacemaker that arises somewhere below the AV node, resulting in a slower heart rate. The location of the ventricular pacemaker site determines the appearance of the QRS complex. Normal (narrow) QRS complexes indicate that the ventricular pacemaker is closer to the AV junction. Wide, large (bizarre-looking) QRS complexes indicate that the ventricles are likely being paced by a ventricular focus.

Figure 7-20
With the most severe form of AV heart block, the ventricles are stimulated by an escape pacemaker site that arises from somewhere in the His-Purkinje system. The more distal the pacemaker site, the wider the QRS complex.

Absent QRS Complexes

LO 7.10

This section describes two dysrhythmias in which the QRS complexes are absent or so bizarre as to indicate that no coordinated depolarization of the ventricles is occurring and therefore the patient is pulseless.

Ventricular Fibrillation

Ventricular fibrillation (VF) is the erratic firing of multiple sites in the ventricles causing the heart muscle to quiver instead of contracting as it normally does (Figure 7-21). On the ECG monitor it looks like a chaotic wavy line, rising and falling without any logic. There are no discernible waveforms. There is no coordinated contraction of the ventricles so the amount of blood pumped by the heart drops to zero. This ultimately causes all life-supporting physiological functions to cease because of a lack of circulating blood flow. VF is immediately life threatening. If the patient is not promptly treated (with CPR/defibrillation), death occurs.

Asystole

Asystole is ventricular or cardiac standstill (Figure 7-22). *Asystole* literally means without contraction of the heart (*a* means without and *systole* means heart contraction). It is essentially the absence of any cardiac activity in the

KEY CONCEPT
Death occurs if ventricular fibrillation is not promptly treated. Defibrillation is considered an essential treatment of ventricular fibrillation. VF is the most common cause of prehospital cardiac arrest in adults.

KEY CONCEPT
Ventricular fibrillation has no discernible waveforms. It looks like a chaotic wavy line, rising and falling without any logic.

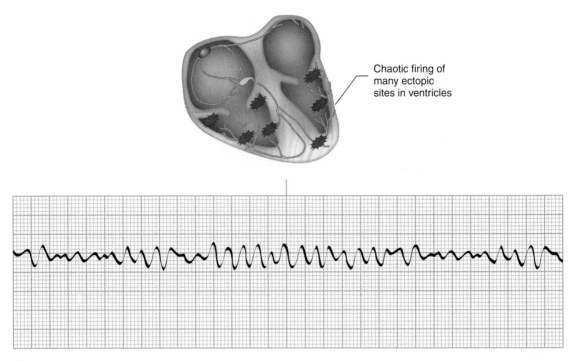

Chaotic firing of
many ectopic
sites in ventricles

Figure 7-21
Ventricular fibrillation results in a chaotic-looking rhythm with no similarity in the waveforms or the distance between them.

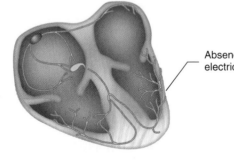

Absence of any
electrical activity

Figure 7-22
Asystole is the absence of any cardiac activity in the heart.

ventricles. Asystole appears as a flat (or nearly flat) line on the ECG. It produces complete cessation of cardiac output. Like ventricular fibrillation, it is immediately life threatening. Sometimes P waves are seen with asystole. This indicates the presence of electrical activity in the atria. They are typically seen only for a short time.

Asystole is a terminal rhythm. Once a person becomes asystolic, the chances of recovery are extremely low. You must always verify the presence of asystole in two leads before initiating treatment. Misplacement of a lead or a loose wire can mimic asystole (or VF) on the ECG.

KEY CONCEPT
Asystole is the absence of any cardiac activity in the ventricles, resulting in the appearance of a flat line on the ECG.

Key Points 🔍

- Another important step of analyzing an ECG rhythm is examining the QRS complexes.

- The starting point of the QRS complex is where the first wave of the complex starts to move away (sharply or gradually) from the baseline. It ends at the point at which the last wave of the complex transitions into the ST segment. This is where it begins to flatten (sharply or gradually) at, above, or below the baseline.

- The QRS complex is larger than the P wave because ventricular depolarization involves a considerably larger muscle mass than atrial depolarization.

- A normal QRS complex indicates that the electrical impulse originated at or above the bundle of His and was carried through the ventricles in a normal manner.

- The amplitude of a normal QRS complex is 5 to 30 mm high, and the duration is 0.06 to 0.10 seconds.

- The Q wave is the first negative deflection from the baseline following the P wave. The R wave is the first positive deflection following the Q wave (the P wave, if the Q wave is absent). The S wave is the first negative deflection that extends below the baseline in the QRS complex following the R wave.

- The ventricles depolarize rapidly; therefore the QRS complex characteristically looks narrower than the other parts of the ECG.

- If the Q wave is absent, we measure the QRS complex from the beginning of the R wave.

- Normal sinus rhythm and dysrhythmias that arise from above the ventricles will usually (unless there is a conduction delay through the ventricles or other type of abnormality as described earlier) have normal QRS complexes.

- Abnormal QRS complexes are produced by abnormal depolarization of the ventricles.

- The pacemaker site in abnormal QRS complexes can be the SA node or an ectopic pacemaker in the atria, AV junction, bundle branches, Purkinje network, or ventricular myocardium.

- The duration of an abnormal QRS complex is greater than 0.12 seconds.

- The shape of an abnormal QRS complex varies widely from one that looks almost normal to one that is wide and bizarre-looking and/or slurred and notched.

- Intraventricular conduction defect is a condition where conduction through the ventricles is impaired.

- Very tall QRS complexes are usually caused by hypertrophy of one or both ventricles or by an abnormal pacemaker or aberrantly conducted beat.

- Low-voltage or abnormally small QRS complexes may be seen in obese patients, hyperthyroid patients, and patients with pleural effusion.

- Wide, bizarre QRS complexes of supraventricular origin are often the result of an intraventricular conduction defect, which usually occurs as a result of right or left bundle branch block. Bundle branch block may be either partial or complete.

- Aberrant conduction occurs when electrical impulses, such as early beats and tachycardias, reach the bundle branch while it is still refractory after conducting a previous electrical impulse.

- Wider than normal QRS complexes may also be due to ventricular preexcitation. This also causes an abnormal slurring, and sometimes notching, at its onset called the *delta wave*.

- Cardiac pacemaker–induced QRS complexes are generally 0.12 seconds or greater in width and appear bizarre-looking. Preceding each pacemaker-induced QRS complex is a pacemaker spike.

- Ventricular dysrhythmias are those dysrhythmias that originate from the ventricular tissue.

- Wide (greater than 0.12 seconds in duration) QRS complexes are the key characteristic seen with ventricular dysrhythmias. Also, the QRS complexes are usually bizarre-looking, and the T waves deflect in an opposite direction to the R waves.

- Early beats can arise from the ventricles before the SA node has a chance to fire.

- An escape rhythm arising from the ventricles typically has a sustained rate of 20 to 40 beats per minute (although it may be slower).

- Tachycardia arising from the ventricles results from rapid depolarization of the ventricles that overrides the SA node. This type of tachycardia is said to be present when there are three or more early beats (arising from the ventricles) in a row or the heart rate is sustained at a rate of between 100 and 250 beats per minute.

- In one form of tachycardia arising from multiple sites in the ventricles, the shape of the ventricular waveforms changes. It appears as a series of QRS complexes that rotate about the baseline between upright deflections and downward deflections.

- The most severe form of AV heart block is another dysrhythmia in which there may be abnormal QRS complexes. Wide, large (bizarre-looking) QRS complexes indicate the ventricles are likely being paced by a ventricular focus.

- Ventricular fibrillation is the erratic firing of multiple sites in the ventricles, causing the heart muscle to quiver instead of contracting and pumping blood throughout the body.

- Defibrillation is considered an essential treatment of ventricular fibrillation and must be delivered promptly.

- Asystole is the lack of any cardiac activity in the ventricles. On the ECG you will see a flat (or nearly flat) line. It produces complete cessation of cardiac output.

Assess Your Understanding

The following questions give you a chance to assess your understanding of the material discussed in this chapter. The answers can be found in Appendix A.

1. The appearance of the _____ is affected by the lead used.
   a. heart rate
   b. QRS complexes
   c. regularity
   d. PR interval

2. In lead II the deflection of the QRS complex is characteristically
   a. inverted.
   b. positive.
   c. pointed.
   d. biphasic.

3. Analyzing the QRS complex helps identify how the electrical impulse is being carried through the
   a. SA node.
   b. atria.
   c. ventricles.
   d. AV node.

4. The normal duration of the QRS complex is _____ second(s).
   a. 0.06 to 0.10
   b. 0.8 to 0.12
   c. 1.0
   d. 0.06 to 0.12

5. An upright (in lead II), narrow QRS complex indicates that the electrical impulse originated
   a. in the AV node and was carried through the atria in a retrograde manner.
   b. in the ventricles and was carried through the atria in a normal manner.
   c. in the SA node and was carried through the AV node in a retrograde manner.
   d. at or above the AV node and was carried through the ventricles in a normal manner.

6. The R wave is the
   a. first positive deflection in the QRS complex.
   b. second negative deflection that extends below the baseline.
   c. first negative deflection from the baseline following the P wave.
   d. flat line that precedes the Q wave.

7. Which of the following will produce normal QRS complexes?
   a. altered, damaged, or abnormal ventricles
   b. tachycardia that arises from the ventricles
   c. early beats that arise from the atria
   d. an escape pacemaker rhythm that originates from the ventricles

8. Which of the following is true regarding the amplitude of QRS complexes?
   a. Women have larger amplitudes than men.
   b. The elderly have higher amplitudes than young people.
   c. Precordial leads have higher amplitudes than the limb leads.
   d. Both a and c.

9. Intraventricular conduction defect
   a. is the result of accelerated conduction through the ventricles.
   b. produces tall QRS complexes.
   c. causes the QRS complexes to appear abnormal.
   d. is usually seen in myocardial infarction, fibrosis, and hypertrophy.

10. Low-voltage or abnormally small QRS complexes are seen in
    a. hypertrophy.
    b. obese patients.
    c. early beats arising from the ventricles.
    d. slow heart rate that arises from the SA node.

11. Which of the following is the most common cause of intraventricular conduction defect?
    a. hypertrophy
    b. accessory pathways
    c. bundle branch block
    d. a cardiac pacemaker

12. Bundle branch blocks
    a. may be partial or complete.
    b. have a delta wave preceding the QRS complex.
    c. have a pacemaker spike.
    d. have QRS complexes not preceded by a P wave or PR interval.

13. Aberrant conduction
    a. occurs when an impulse is late arriving at the bundle branch.
    b. results in narrow, spike-shaped QRS complexes.
    c. mimics supraventricular dysrhythmias.
    d. occurs when the impulse reaches one of the bundle branches while it is still refractory.

14. Early beats that arise from the ventricles
    a. are preceded by a P wave.
    b. always have an inverted QRS complex.
    c. produce QRS complexes that look different than those that arise above or at the AV junction.
    d. have narrow, upright QRS complexes.

15. An escape pacemaker rhythm that arises from the ventricles has
    a. wide, bizarre-looking QRS complexes.
    b. a P wave that precedes each QRS complex.
    c. T waves that take the same direction as the R wave.
    d. a ventricular rate of 40 to 60 beats per minute.

16. Tachycardia that arises from the ventricles has
    a. a pacemaker site in the SA node.
    b. wide and bizarre-looking QRS complexes.
    c. a fast rate that is always sustained.
    d. narrow QRS complexes.

17. With the most severe form of AV block, the QRS complexes
    a. are always wide and bizarre-looking.
    b. are associated with irregular and frequent early beats.
    c. follow each P wave but at a slower rate.
    d. are slower than the P wave rate because there is complete blockage of the AV node.

18. With ventricular fibrillation,
    a. there is adequate cardiac output.
    b. a chaotic wavy line is seen on the ECG.
    c. there is erratic firing from one site in the ventricles.
    d. there is a flat line on the ECG.

19. Asystole
    a. is the erratic firing of multiple sites in the ventricles.
    b. produces an effective electrical rhythm but no contraction of the heart muscle.
    c. usually produces P waves.
    d. is seen as a flat line on the ECG.

Referring to the scenario at the front of this chapter answer the following questions.

20. Where are the extra QRS complexes originating from?
    a. ventricles
    b. SA node
    c. AV node
    d. atria

21. The most likely cause of the patient's extra beats is
    a. anxiety.
    b. pain.
    c. ischemia.
    d. hypertrophy.

? Answers to Sidebar Questions

1. More of the current is moving away from the positive electrode than moving toward it. **p. 154**

2. The normal duration of the QRS complex is 0.06 to 0.10 seconds. **p. 154**

3. The direction the electrical current takes, toward a positive or negative electrode, determines the direction a waveform points on an ECG. The waveforms seen in each lead look different because they reveal another view of the heart. **p. 156**

4. Supraventricular means above the ventricles—this could be the SA node, atria, or AV junction. **p. 161**

5. Tachycardia that arises from one site in the ventricles is regular because the dysrhythmia arises from one pacemaker site. **p. 168**

What's Online

Go to www.mhhe.com/shadeECG2e to find:

- Presentations on chapter content
- Crossword puzzle exercises
- ECG tracings for practicing analyzing QRS complexes
- Chapter quiz
- Flashcards
- Fill-in-the-blank exercises and answers

8 PR Intervals

Chapter Outline

Importance of Determining the PR Intervals

Quick Check of the PR Intervals

Characteristics of Normal PR Intervals

Measuring the PR Intervals

PR Intervals That Are Different

Learning Objectives

LO 8.1   State why it is important to analyze the PR intervals of an ECG tracing.

LO 8.2   Describe the characteristics of the normal PR interval.

LO 8.3   Recall how to examine the PR intervals.

LO 8.4   Describe what is meant when we say, "PR intervals that are different."

LO 8.5   Identify the causes of shorter PR intervals.

LO 8.6   Recall the causes of longer PR intervals.

LO 8.7   Identify the causes of varying PR intervals.

LO 8.8   Recall the causes of absent or not measurable PR intervals.

LO 8.9   List the causes of the constant PR intervals seen with more P waves.

Case History

A 77-year-old woman who had a heart attack three days ago is transferred from the ICU to the medical floor for continued observation. Her heart rhythm is continuously monitored by the telemetry unit. During the patient's morning walk, the nurses receive a call from the telemetry unit informing them that the patient's rhythm has become irregular. After locating the woman, the nurses return her to her bed and obtain the rhythm strips from the telemetry unit. Her attending physician is summoned, and her vital signs obtained and found to be normal except for a regularly irregular pulse.

The patient's physician arrives and examines the rhythm strip with the nurse. He notes that the PR interval increases in length following each P wave until after every third one when the QRS complex is missing entirely. They discuss that this is a common complication after a myocardial infarction. The patient is moved back to the ICU for close observation because of the possibility for further deterioration.

The Nine-Step Process

Figure 8-1
Assessing the PR interval is part of the Nine-Step Process algorithm.

Importance of Determining the PR Intervals

As part of analyzing an ECG we examine and measure the specific waveforms, segments, and intervals. In this chapter we discuss assessment of the PR intervals (Figure 8-1).

The presence or absence of PR intervals as well as their duration can help us identify if and how well the impulses are traveling through the atrioventricular (AV) junction and bundle of His. This is important to know because delays or interruption of conduction through the AV node and/or junction can lead to serious or even life-threatening conditions.

Quick Check of the PR Intervals

The initial assessment for PR intervals waves can be done quickly. Questions to ask include, "Is there a PR interval preceding each QRS complex? Do they appear of normal duration? Are they all the same?"

Characteristics of Normal PR Intervals

As discussed previously, the PR interval is the distance from the beginning of the P wave to the beginning of the Q wave (or R wave if the Q wave is absent). The PR interval denotes depolarization of the heart from the SA node through the atria, AV node, and His-Purkinje system. A normal PR interval (Figure 8-2) indicates the impulse originated from the SA node (or close to it) and traveled through the atria and AV node in a regular and unobstructed course.

Characteristics of Normal PR Intervals	
Location	Starts at the beginning of the P wave and ends at the beginning of the Q wave (or R wave if the Q wave is absent).
Duration	0.12 to 0.20 seconds.
Morphology	P wave and a flat line.

Characteristics of normal PR interval

Includes P wave and flat line that precedes each QRS complex

PRI

Duration is 0.12 to 0.20 seconds and constant

Height, amplitude (energy)

Time (duration, rate)

Figure 8-2
When assessing the PR intervals, look for a normal PR interval to precede each QRS complex.

If a P wave precedes each QRS complex and the duration of the PR interval is normal and constant, you can assume that this electrical impulse originated in the SA node and was carried through the atria, AV junction, and His-Purkinje system in a normal manner. As such, we can say that the PR interval is usually normal, with impulses that arise from the SA node. A PR interval within 0.12 to 0.20 seconds can also be present with some dysrhythmias that arise from the atria, provided that the ectopic site is located in the upper atrial wall. As an example, early beats or tachycardia that arises from the atria can have a normal PR interval if the ectopic site from which they arise is high enough in the atria.

QUESTION
2. How many squares make up the normal PR interval?

Measuring the PR Intervals

LO 8.3

First, determine if the PR intervals are identifiable. If they are, measure from where the P wave begins to where the Q wave begins (Figure 8-3). To make measuring the PR interval easier, find a P wave that begins on a vertical line, and then measure to where the Q or R wave begins. Are the waves within normal limits? The PR interval should extend across between 3 and 5 small boxes (0.12 to 0.20 seconds in duration).

Then compare each PR interval to the others. Are they the same (in other words, are they constant?) or do they differ? Last, determine if there a relationship between the P waves and QRS complexes.

PR Intervals That Are Different

LO 8.4

PR intervals are considered abnormal if they are shorter than 0.12 seconds, longer than 0.20 seconds, or absent or if they vary in duration (Figure 8-4). A variety of conditions can cause abnormal PR intervals.

Figure 8-3
Measuring the PR interval.

Measure from the
beginning of the P
wave to the beginning
of the Q wave

PRI

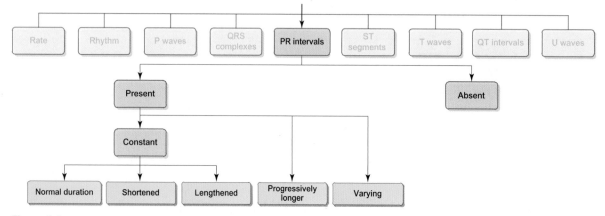

The Nine-Step Process

| Rate | Rhythm | P waves | QRS complexes | PR intervals | ST segments | T waves | QT intervals | U waves |

Present   Absent

Constant

| Normal duration | Shortened | Lengthened | Progressively longer | Varying |

Figure 8-4
Algorithm for normal and abnormal PR intervals.

LO 8.5

Shorter PR Intervals

A shorter than normal PR interval is less than 0.12 seconds in duration. Shorter PR intervals occur when the impulse originates in the lower atria, in the AV junction, or where there is an accessory pathway between the atria and ventricles. The shorter the distance the impulse has to travel, the shorter the duration of the PR interval. If we suspect the P wave is not originating in the SA node, we refer to this shortened PR interval as a P′R (P prime R) interval.

QUESTION
3. What does P′ mean?

Short P′R Intervals Seen with Dysrhythmias Arising from the Atria

Early beats and tachycardia that arise from the atria or internodal pathways before the SA node has a chance to fire can produce P′R intervals that differ from the underlying rhythm. If the early beat arises from a site in the lower right atrium or in the upper part of the AV junction, the P′R interval should be less than 0.12 seconds in duration (Figure 8-5). Also, with atrial

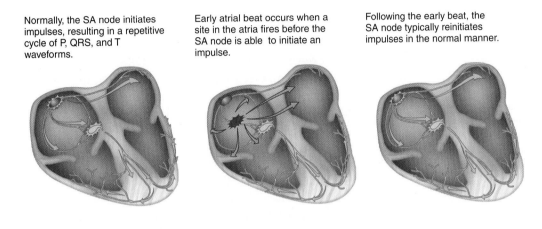

Normally, the SA node initiates impulses, resulting in a repetitive cycle of P, QRS, and T waveforms.

Early atrial beat occurs when a site in the atria fires before the SA node is able to initiate an impulse.

Following the early beat, the SA node typically reinitiates impulses in the normal manner.

A shorter than normal PR interval occurs when the early atrial beat arises closer to the AV junction.

A P′R interval within normal duration occurs when the early atrial beat arises from a site in the upper- or middle-right atrium.

Figure 8-5
Short P′R intervals seen with dysrhythmias that arise from the atria.

tachycardia the P′ waves may be buried in the T wave of the preceding beat, so it may be hard or even impossible to accurately measure the P′R interval.

If an early beat is initiated in the upper or middle right atrium, the P′R interval is generally normal (0.12 to 0.20 seconds in duration). If an early beat arises from a site high in the left atrium, the PR interval may be prolonged.

Short P′R Intervals Seen with Dysrhythmias Arising from the AV Junction

As mentioned in Chapter 6, when impulses arise from the AV junction, an inverted P′ wave may precede the QRS complex (Figure 8-6). The P′ wave may also occur during (and be buried in) the QRS complex or follow it. This causes the electrical impulse to travel upward through the AV junction into the atria, causing retrograde atrial depolarization. The P′R interval will be shorter when the P′ wave appears before the QRS complex.

If the P wave is buried in the QRS complex, the P′R interval will be absent. If the P′ wave follows the QRS complex, it is referred to as the RP′ interval and is usually less than 0.20 seconds.

As we discussed earlier, because the P′ waves seen with early junctional beats and tachycardia arising from the junctional tissue can be buried in the T wave of the preceding beat, it may be hard to determine the P′R interval.

Short P′R Intervals Seen with Accessory Pathways

Another cause of a shorter than normal PR interval is the presence of accessory pathways between the atria and ventricles. These accessory pathways allow the impulse to bypass the AV node and move to the ventricles more quickly (Figure 8-7). This is referred to as *ventricular preexcitation* and will be discussed in more depth in Chapter 13.

LO 8.6

Longer PR Intervals

A longer than normal PR interval is greater than 0.20 seconds in duration. Greater PR intervals occur when the impulse is delayed beyond normal as it passes through the AV junction. The longer it takes the impulse to travel through the AV node, the longer the duration of the PR interval. A variety of conditions can cause the PR interval to be longer than normal.

Blockage of the AV Junction

The most common cause of longer than normal PR intervals is a delay in or blockage in the conduction of the impulse as it passes through the AV junction (Figure 8-8). As mentioned in Chapter 6, we use the term AV heart block to describe these delays or blockage.

In its milder form, there is a delay in impulse conduction through the AV junction. While there is a delay, the impulse is still able to reach the bundle of His, bundle branches, and the ventricles. The key characteristic of this

QUESTION [?]
4. Why would an early beat arising from the atria have a PR interval longer in duration?

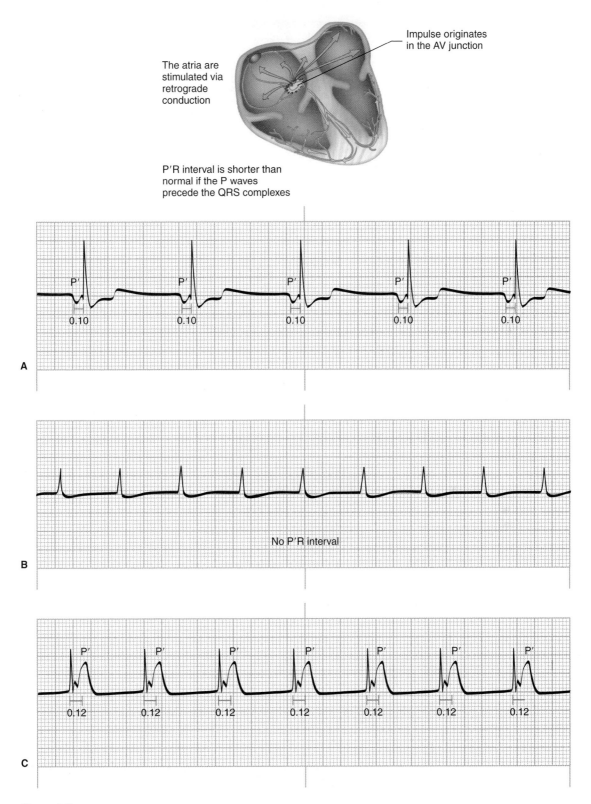

Figure 8-6
P′R intervals seen with dysrhythmias arising from the AV junctional tissue. (A) Shorter than normal P′R intervals are
seen when the P wave precedes the QRS complexes. (B) No P′R intervals are seen when the P waves are buried in the
QRS complexes. (C) The RP′ interval is measured when the P wave follows the QRS complex.

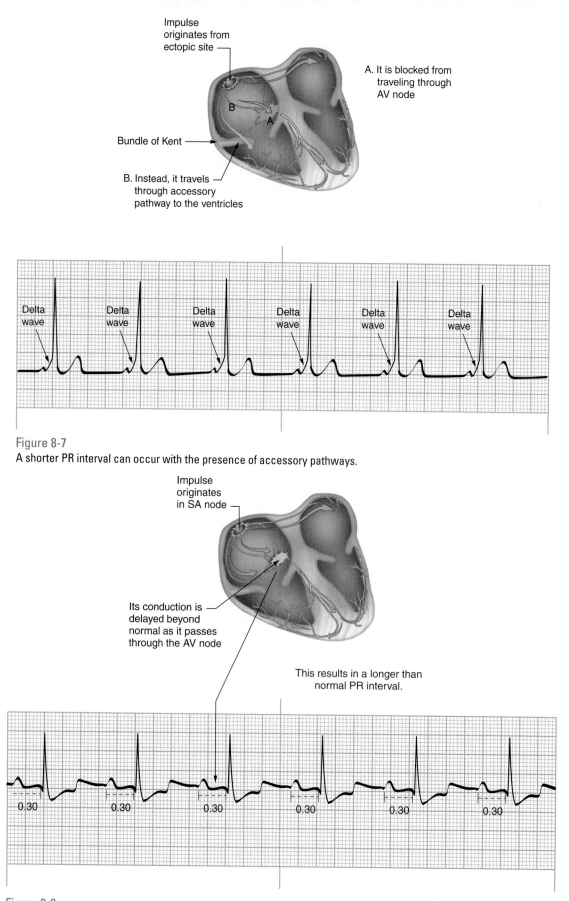

Impulse originates from ectopic site

A. It is blocked from traveling through AV node

Bundle of Kent

B. Instead, it travels through accessory pathway to the ventricles

Delta wave

Figure 8-7
A shorter PR interval can occur with the presence of accessory pathways.

Impulse originates in SA node

Its conduction is delayed beyond normal as it passes through the AV node

This results in a longer than normal PR interval.

0.30

Figure 8-8
A PR interval of greater than 0.20 seconds in duration is due to an abnormal delay in conduction through the AV node.

condition is a PR interval greater than 0.20 seconds that is constant in duration with each beat.

Varying PR Intervals

The PR interval may also be seen to vary or change. This occurs when the pacemaker site in the atria changes from beat to beat and in one form of AV heart block.

Changing Pacemaker Site

When the pacemaker site moves from beat to beat from the sinus node to other latent pacemaker sites in the atria and AV junction (Figure 8-9), the P′ waves appear different and the P′R intervals tend to vary because of the changing pacemaker site.

> **KEY CONCEPT**
> When the pacemaker changes from site to site, the P′R interval varies from beat to beat.

AV Heart Block

The PR interval may also vary in a milder form of AV heart block in which the weakened AV node fatigues more and more with each conducted impulse until finally it is so tired that it fails to conduct an impulse through to the ventricles. This results in a changing PR interval, one that becomes increasingly longer until there is a dropped QRS complex (Figure 8-10). With the dropped ventricular beat, the AV node has a chance to rest. The next impulse

Figure 8-9
When the pacemaker site continually changes, the duration of the P′R interval varies.

Figure 8-10
In a milder type of AV heart block, the PR interval becomes increasingly longer until finally a QRS complex is dropped.
The cycle then starts all over.

conducting through the AV node is carried through faster, but then each subsequent impulse is delayed until another ventricular beat is dropped.

LO 8.8

Absent or Not Measurable PR Intervals

The PR interval will be absent or not measurable in certain dysrhythmias. These dysrhythmias can arise from the atria, AV junction, or ventricles and in the most severe form of AV heart block.

Absent P'R Intervals Seen with Impulses Arising from the Atria

When the atria fire at a rate of between 250 and 350 beats per minute (Figure 8-11) and flutter waves (F waves) are seen instead of the normal P waves, the PR intervals are not measurable.

Also, there are no PR intervals when the atria fire faster than 350 beats per minute (Figure 8-12), producing a chaotic-looking baseline with no discernable P waves.

KEY CONCEPT
Electrical activity that arises from the ventricles lacks measurable PR intervals.

Not all the atrial impulses are conducted through the AV node. This results in more atrial waveforms than QRS complexes.

With one atrial dysrhythmia, an ectopic site in the atria fires at a rate of 250 to 350 times per minute.

Not conducted

Conducted

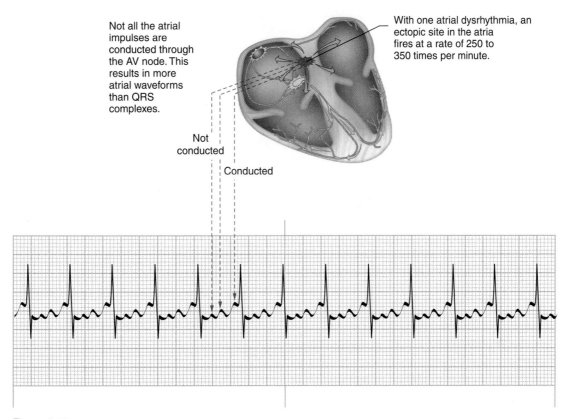

Figure 8-11
When flutter waves are present, the PR intervals cannot be determined.

Only some of the atrial impulses are conducted through the AV node.

One atrial dysrhythmia ectopic sites in the atria fire at a rate of more than 350 times per minute.

Not conducted

Conducted

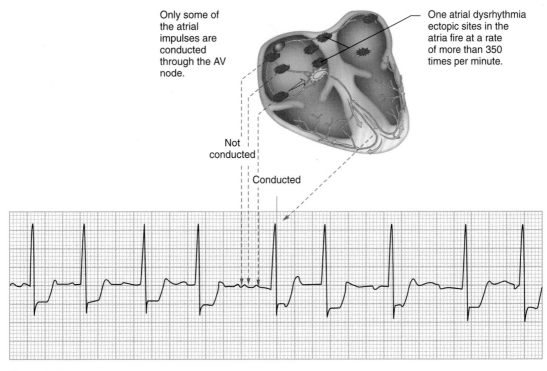

Figure 8-12
With a chaotic atrial baseline, the PR intervals cannot be determined because there are no discernable P waves.

Impulses initiated from ventricles

Wide, bizarre-looking QRS complexes

A

Early beat arising from the ventricle

Early beat arising from the ventricle

Early beat arising from the ventricle

B

C

Figure 8-13
With ventricular dysrhythmias, there is an absence of P waves and no PR intervals. (A) Early beats arising from the ventricles. (B) Escape rhythm arising from the ventricles. (C) Tachycardia arising from the ventricles.

Ventricular Dysrhythmias

Dysrhythmias that originate in the ventricular tissue are referred to as ventricular dysrhythmias (Figure 8-13). The key characteristics seen with ventricular dysrhythmias are wide, bizarre-looking QRS complexes. Beats that arise from the ventricles are not preceded by a P wave (if seen, the P waves are dissociated), and the PR intervals are not measurable.

Atrioventricular Heart Block

In the more severe form of AV heart block, there is complete blockage of the AV node (Figure 8-14). The atria are stimulated to contract by the impulse that originates from the SA node. For this reason the atrial rate should be within a normal range. The ventricles are stimulated to contract by an escape pacemaker that arises from somewhere below the AV node, resulting in a slower rate. The pacemaker sites (SA node and ventricles) fire independently of each other, so the P-P intervals and the R-R intervals appear to be disassociated with one another. For this reason, the PR intervals are not measurable. The P waves will march through the QRS complexes.

KEY CONCEPT

In the most severe form of AV heart block, the PR interval is not measurable due to the atria and ventricles being depolarized from different pacemaker sites.

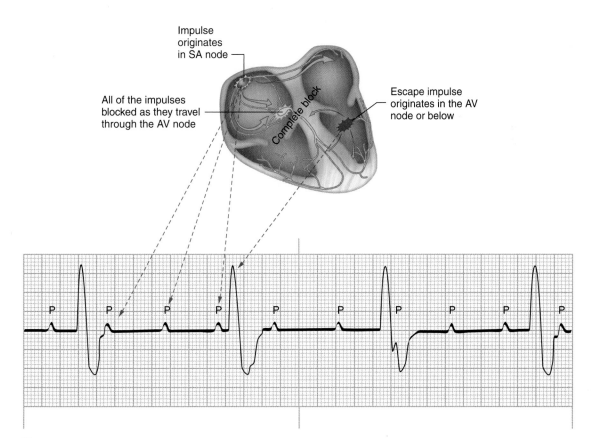

Figure 8-14
With the more severe form of AV heart block, there are no PR intervals as the P waves appear to march through the QRS complexes.

Impulse originates in SA node

Impulse originates in SA node

Some of the impulses are blocked as they travel through the AV node.

There are more P waves than QRS complexes.

Figure 8-15
With one form of AV heart block, the PR intervals of the conducted beats are constant.

LO 8.9

Constant PR Intervals Seen with More P Waves

AV Heart Block

Normally, there is only one P wave preceding each QRS complex. However, in some forms of AV heart block we may see more P waves than QRS complexes. This indicates that the impulse was initiated in the SA node but was blocked and did not reach the ventricles. The atrial-to-ventricular conduction ratio is usually 2:1, 3:1, or 4:1. PR intervals that are constant (of the same duration) for the conducted beats (Figure 8-15) are characteristic of one type of AV heart block. The PR interval can be normal in duration or prolonged.

Key Points 🔍

- Another important step in analyzing an ECG rhythm is examining the PR intervals.

- The PR interval is the distance from the beginning of the P wave to the beginning of the Q wave (or R wave if the Q wave is absent).

- The PR interval denotes depolarization of the heart from the SA node through the atria and AV node.

- A normal PR interval indicates that the impulse originated in the SA node (or close to it) and traveled through the atria and AV node in a regular and unobstructed course.

- The duration of the PR interval is normally 0.12 to 0.20 seconds.

- PR intervals are considered abnormal if they are shorter or longer than normal, absent, or varying in duration.

- Shorter P'R intervals occur when the impulse originates in the atria close to the AV junction or in the AV junction or when there is an accessory pathway between the atria and ventricles.

- A longer than normal PR interval is greater than 0.20 seconds in duration. Greater PR intervals occur when the impulse is delayed beyond normal as it passes through the AV junction.

- When the pacemaker site moves from beat to beat, the P'R intervals will vary.

- With one type of AV heart block, the PR intervals are progressively longer until a QRS complex is dropped, and then the cycle starts over.

- PR intervals are not measurable in the presence of flutter waves, a chaotic atrial baseline, or dysrhythmias that originate from the ventricles.

- In the most severe form of AV heart block, the PR intervals are not measurable.

- With one form of AV heart block, some of the sinus beats are blocked in the AV node and do not reach the ventricles. This leads to more P waves than QRS complexes. The PR intervals associated with the P waves conducted through to the ventricles are constant.

Assess Your Understanding

The following questions give you a chance to assess your understanding of the material discussed in this chapter. The answers can be found in Appendix A.

1. The duration of the PR interval _____ from beat to beat.
   a. may change
   b. is constant
   c. may be progressively longer
   d. increase and decrease

2. PR interval is the distance from the
   a. end of the P wave to the beginning of the Q wave.
   b. beginning of the P wave to the beginning of the Q wave.
   c. beginning of the Q wave to the end of the S wave.
   d. end of the Q wave to the beginning of the R wave.

3. The PR interval denotes depolarization of the heart from the
   a. bundle of His through the ventricles.
   b. SA node through the atria, AV node, and His-Purkinje system.
   c. AV node through the bundle of His.
   d. SA node through the atria and AV node.

4. The normal duration of the PR interval is _____ second(s).
   a. 0.06 to 0.10
   b. 0.8 to 0.12
   c. 1.0
   d. 0.12 to 0.20

5. A shorter than normal PR interval is less than _____ second(s) in duration.
   a. 0.12
   b. 0.08
   c. 0.10
   d. 0.20

6. Which of the following characteristics is considered normal?
   a. a P wave that follows the QRS complex
   b. a PR interval that changes continually
   c. a PR interval that is 0.18 seconds in duration
   d. a P'R interval that is 0.10 seconds in duration

7. Which of the following is characteristic of delayed conduction through the AV node?
   a. varying PR intervals
   b. PR intervals of less than 0.12 seconds
   c. more P waves than QRS complexes
   d. constant PR intervals of greater than 0.20 seconds

8. With a pacemaker site that changes from beat to beat throughout the atria, the P'R intervals
   a. are constant.
   b. vary.
   c. are longer in duration than 0.20 seconds.
   d. become progressively longer.

9. With AV heart block, the PR intervals may be all of the following EXCEPT
    a. constant.
    b. absent.
    c. shorter in duration than 0.12 seconds.
    d. progressively longer.

10. There will be an absence of PR intervals in
    a. early beats that arise from the atria.
    b. the most severe form of AV heart block.
    c. beats that arise from the SA node.
    d. a pacemaker site within the atria that changes from beat to beat.

11. If there is an accessory pathway between the atria and ventricles, the PR intervals may
    a. continually change in duration.
    b. be longer than normal.
    c. be absent.
    d. be less than 0.12 seconds in duration.

12. PR segments are commonly described as
    a. flat.
    b. rounded.
    c. asymmetrical.
    d. biphasic.

Referring to the scenario at the beginning of this chapter, answer the following questions.

13. This patient is most likely experiencing
    a. early beats arising from the atria.
    b. normal sinus rhythm.
    c. AV heart block.
    d. tachycardia that is arising from the atria.

14. The PR intervals that change in duration are considered
    a. normal.
    b. abnormal.
    c. characteristic of specific dysrhythmias.
    d. b and c.

Answers to Sidebar Questions

1. Delays or interruption of conduction through the AV node and/or junction can lead to serious or even life-threatening conditions. For this reason, it is important to assess the PR intervals. **p. 180**

2. The normal PR interval extends across 3 to 5 small squares. **p. 181**

3. P′ means that the P wave arises from an ectopic site. **p. 182**

4. In an early beat arising from the atria, the PR interval can be normal or longer in duration if the beat arises nearer to the SA node or in the upper left atrium. **p. 184**

What's Online

Go to www.mhhe.com/shadeECG2e to find:

- Presentations on chapter content
- Crossword puzzle exercises
- ECG tracings for practicing analyzing QRS complexes
- Chapter quiz
- Flashcards
- Fill-in-the-blank exercises and answers

9 ST Segments, T Waves, QT Intervals, and U Waves

Chapter Outline

Analyzing the Electrocardiogram

ST Segments

T Waves

QT Intervals

U Waves

Learning Objectives

LO 9.1 State why it is important to analyze the ST segments, T waves, QT intervals, and U waves of an ECG tracing.

LO 9.2 Describe the characteristics of the normal ST segment.

LO 9.3 Recall how to measure the ST segment.

LO 9.4 Describe two types of abnormal ST segments.

LO 9.5 Describe the characteristics of the normal T wave.

LO 9.6 Recall how to measure the T wave.

LO 9.7 Describe what is meant when we say "abnormal T waves" and list their causes.

LO 9.8 Identify the characteristics of the normal QT interval.

LO 9.9 Describe how to measure the QT interval.

LO 9.10 Describe two types of abnormal QT intervals and identify their causes.

LO 9.11 Describe the characteristics of the normal U wave.

LO 9.12 List those conditions in which U waves may be seen.

Case History

EMS is called to a local plant for a 53-year-old female who is experiencing shortness of breath. Upon arrival they find the patient sitting on a bench in the locker room. She is awake and able to answer questions. She states she was lifting some heavy boxes when suddenly she couldn't breathe. She denies chest pain but does admit to having pressure "under her breastbone." Except for an elevated blood pressure, her vital signs are normal. The 12-lead ECG leads are quickly attached. It shows a slow sinus rhythm with elevated ST segments and inverted T waves in several leads. The paramedics apply oxygen and establish an intravenous line. The patient's chest discomfort remains despite the application of oxygen and the administration of aspirin and sublingual nitroglycerin.

En route to the hospital the patient continues to experience chest discomfort. The paramedics contact medical control and report their findings. The physician approves their request to deliver an analgesic agent and a second dose of nitro-glycerin. The patient is delivered to the hospital without any improvement in her condition.

LO 9.1

REMINDER

The heart normally beats in a regular, rhythmic fashion.

WANT MORE INFORMATION?

Visit the Fast & Easy ECGs Website at www.mhhe.com/ shadeECG2e.

Analyzing the Electrocardiogram

As we said in previous chapters, the heart normally beats in a regular, rhythmic fashion, producing a P wave, a PR interval, a QRS complex, an ST segment, a T wave, a QT interval, and possibly a U wave with each heartbeat. This cycle repeats over and over.

As part of analyzing an ECG, we examine and measure the specific waveforms, segments, and intervals. In this chapter we discuss assessing the ST segments, T waves, QT intervals and U waves (Figure 9-1).

ST Segments

The ST segment yields important information because it represents the end of ventricular depolarization and the beginning of ventricular repolarization. The ST segment is the isoelectric line that follows the QRS complex and connects it to the T wave (Figure 9-2). Elevation or depression of the ST segment is a hallmark feature of myocardial ischemia and injury.

LO 9.2

QUESTION

1. What direction do the positive electrolytes move during repolarization? *Note:* Answers to sidebar questions can be found at the end of the chapter.

KEY CONCEPT

The ST segment is an isoelectric line that follows the QRS complex and connects it to the T wave.

QUESTION

2. What is the PR segment?

Normal Characteristics

The ST segment begins at the J point. Extending horizontally, it gradually (almost imperceptibly) curves upward to the beginning of the T wave. Under normal circumstances, the ST segment appears as an isoelectric line (neither positive nor negative), although it may vary by 0.5 to 1.0 mm in some leads (precordial). The duration of the normal ST segment is 0.08 to 0.12 seconds or less and dependent on the heart rate. With a faster heart rate, the duration of the ST segment is less compared with longer ST segments that occur with a slower heart rate. The term *ST segment* is used regardless of whether the final wave of the QRS complex is an R or S wave.

Characteristics of a Normal ST Segments	
Location	Follows the QRS complex and connects it to the T wave.
Deflection	Isoelectric line (neither positive or negative). Can vary by 0.5 to 1.0 mm in some precordial leads.

The Nine-Step Process

Figure 9-1
Another important step in assessing the ECG are to assess the ST segment, T wave, QT interval, and U waves (when seen).

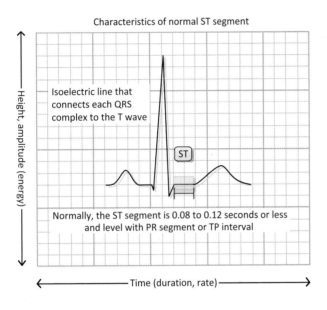

Characteristics of normal ST segment

Isoelectric line that connects each QRS complex to the T wave

ST

Normally, the ST segment is 0.08 to 0.12 seconds or less and level with PR segment or TP interval

Height, amplitude (energy)

←——————— Time (duration, rate) ———————→

Figure 9-2
The ST segment is the line that follows the QRS complex and connects it to the T wave.

Measuring the ST Segments

When assessing the ST segment, the question to ask is, "What is the deflection?" To determine this, we use the PR segment as the baseline from which to evaluate the degree of displacement of the ST segment from the isoelectric line. Draw a straight line (or use a paper) extending from the PR segment out past the J point (Figure 9-3). Some recommend that, instead of using the PR segment to identify the isoelectric line, the TP interval be used. The TP interval is space between the T wave and the P wave of the beat that follows it. For proper measurement, we use a point 0.04 seconds (one small box) after the J point to identify the presence of elevation or depression. Remember from our discussion in Chapter 8 that the J point is the point that marks the end of the QRS complex and the beginning of the ST segment. It isn't always easy to identify the J point. Sometimes you have to look for that small notch, slope, or other movement that suggests an alteration of electrical flow (see Figure 8-4). Further, it may be difficult to determine the J point in patients experiencing rapid heart rate or hyperkalemia.

The ST segment is considered elevated if it is above the baseline and depressed if it is below it. (Remember, it can vary by 0.5 to 1.0 mm in some leads.)

LO 9.3

KEY CONCEPT
ST segment depression or elevation can be evaluated by comparing the ST segment with the PR segment or the ST segment with the TP segment.

WANT MORE INFORMATION?

Want practice? Visit the Fast & Easy ECGs Website at www.mhhe.com/shadeECG2e.

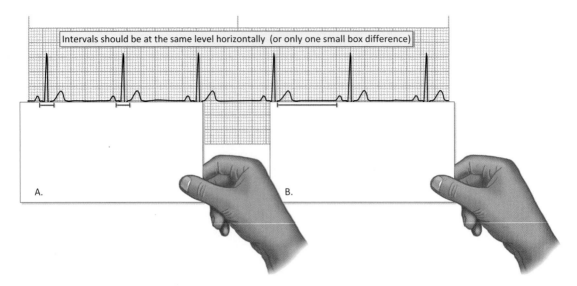

Figure 9-3
Identify the deflection of the ST segment by drawing a straight line (or using a piece of paper) from (A) the PR segment across the QRS complex or from (B) the ST segment to the P wave that follows it.

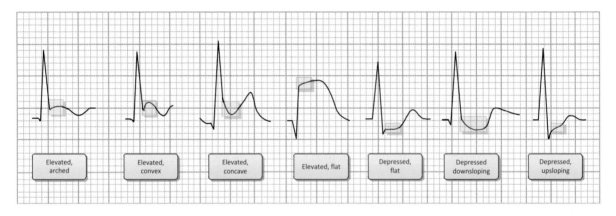

Figure 9-4
Different appearances of ST segment elevation and depression.

LO 9.4

Abnormal ST Segments

Abnormal ST segments are indicative of abnormal ventricular repolarization. Two types are ST segment elevation and ST segment depression.

ST Segment Elevation

An elevated ST segment is one that is 1 mm or more above the baseline. Its presence may indicate marked myocardial injury and be an early indicator of myocardial infarction. Elevated ST segments can appear as flat, concave (curving inward), convex (curving outward), or arched (Figure 9-4). Convex-shaped ST segment elevation is most often due to myocardial injury and infarction. ST segment elevation on the single-lead ECG pattern is usually not as significant as it is on the 12-lead ECG.

Figure 9-5
ST segment algorithm.

Other causes of elevated ST segments include bundle branch block, pericarditis, ventricular hypertrophy, ventricular fibrosis or aneurysm, hyperkalemia, and hypothermia. These will be discussed in more detail in later chapters.

Although we should be concerned whenever we see ST segment elevation, it is important to note that physiological (also called *normal variant*) ST elevation is quite common. This presents as ST segment changes that are usually limited to leads V_1, V_2, and V_3 and an absence of cardiac symptoms. Further, cardiac ultrasound shows no myocardial wall abnormality, and the changes are fixed and do not evolve like those seen with myocardial infarction.

ST Segment Depression

An ST segment is considered depressed when it is more than 1.0 mm below the baseline. A depressed ST segment may indicate myocardial ischemia or reciprocal changes opposite the area of myocardial injury. The depressed ST segment can appear as flat, upsloping, or downsloping (Figure 9-5; also see Figure 9-4).

ST segment depression may also occur with right and left ventricular hypertrophy (strain pattern), right and left bundle branch block, hypokalemia, and hyperventilation, among other conditions. It can also occur with digitalis use.

T Waves

Next, we should see the T wave. Assessing T waves is important as it represents the completion of ventricular repolarization (recovery). The T wave is a wide, broad waveform. Remember, atrial repolarization occurs during the QRS complex and is not visible on the regular ECG.

Normal Characteristics   ▌ LO 9.5

The T wave is larger than the P wave and slightly asymmetrical (Figure 9-6). The peak is closer to the end than to the beginning, and the first half has a

Figure 9-6
The T wave follows the ST segment and represents ventricular repolarization.

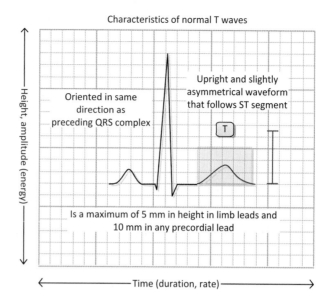

Characteristics of normal T waves

Upright and slightly asymmetrical waveform that follows ST segment

Oriented in same direction as preceding QRS complex

T

Is a maximum of 5 mm in height in limb leads and 10 mm in any precordial lead

Height, amplitude (energy)

Time (duration, rate)

KEY CONCEPT
The T wave is slightly asymmetrical and oriented in the same direction as the preceding QRS complex.

more gradual slope than the second half. Normally, the T wave is not more than 5 mm in height in the limb leads or 10 mm in any precordial lead. Also, it is normally oriented in the same direction as its associated QRS complex. This is because depolarization begins at the endocardial surface and spreads to the epicardium, whereas repolarization begins at the epicardium and spreads to the endocardium.

T waves are normally positive in leads I, II, and V_2 to V_6 and negative in lead aV_R. They can also be positive in aV_L and aV_F but may be negative if the QRS complex is less than 6 mm in height. In leads III and V_1, the T wave may be positive or negative.

QUESTION
3. Why is the direction of the T wave the same as the QRS complex?

Characteristics of a Normal T Wave

Location	Follows the ST segment.
Configuration	Upright and slightly asymmetrical.
Amplitude	Maximum of 5 mm in height in the limb leads and maximum of 10 mm in any precordial lead.
Deflection	Oriented in the same direction as the preceding QRS complex.

LO 9.6

Measuring the T Waves

When evaluating the T wave, the three most important questions to ask are:

1. What is the configuration?
2. What is the amplitude?
3. What is the deflection?

To measure the T wave, identify its starting and ending point, then move to the center of the waveform. Next, count the number of small boxes between the isoelectric line and the top of the waveform (Figure 9-7).

Abnormal T Waves

LO 9.7

Abnormal T waves indicate the presence of abnormal ventricular repolarization. Abnormal T waves include those that are tall, peaked or tented, inverted (in leads where they should be upright), biphasic, flat, wide, and heavily notched and those having bumps (Figure 9-8).

Tall or peaked T waves, also known as *tented T waves*, are seen in myocardial ischemia or hyperkalemia (Figure 9-9). Heavily notched or pointed T waves in an adult may indicate pericarditis. Inverted T waves in leads I, II, and V_3 through V_6 may be seen with myocardial ischemia. Deeply inverted T waves are seen with significant cerebral disease such as subarachnoid hemorrhage.

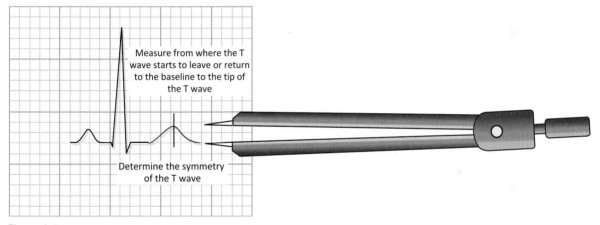

Figure 9-7
Measuring the T wave.

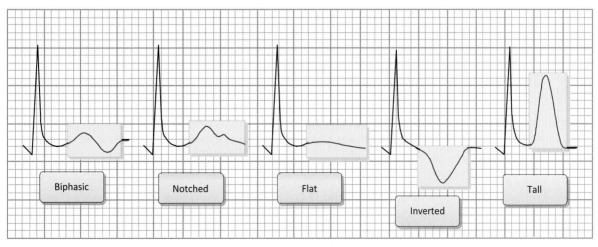

Figure 9-8
Appearance of abnormal T waves.

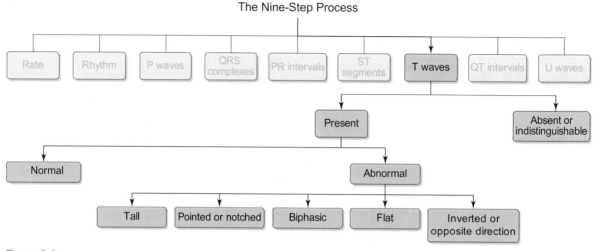

Figure 9-9
T wave algorithm.

Flat T waves are seen with certain electrolyte imbalances. T waves with bumps may be seen when P waves are buried in the T waves. This occurs with early beats that arise from the atria or AV junctional tissue or in certain types of AV heart block.

Also, T waves seen with impulses that arise from the ventricles take a direction opposite of their associated QRS complexes.

QT Intervals

In addition to the other steps used to analyze the ECG, it is also important to assess the QT intervals. The QT interval represents the time needed for ventricular depolarization and repolarization.

 LO 9.8

Normal Characteristics

The QT interval extends from the beginning of the QRS complex to the end of the T wave. Its duration varies according to age and sex, but it is usually between 0.36 and 0.44 seconds (Figure 9-10). The QT interval also changes with the heart rate. The QT interval is shorter with faster rates and longer with slower heart rates. A good rule to follow is that the QT interval should not be greater than half the distance between consecutive R waves when the rhythm is regular.

LO 9.9

Measuring the QT Interval

When assessing the QT interval, focus on its most important characteristics—location and duration. To measure the QT interval, first locate the isoelectric line immediately preceding the Q wave (or R wave if there is no Q wave). Next,

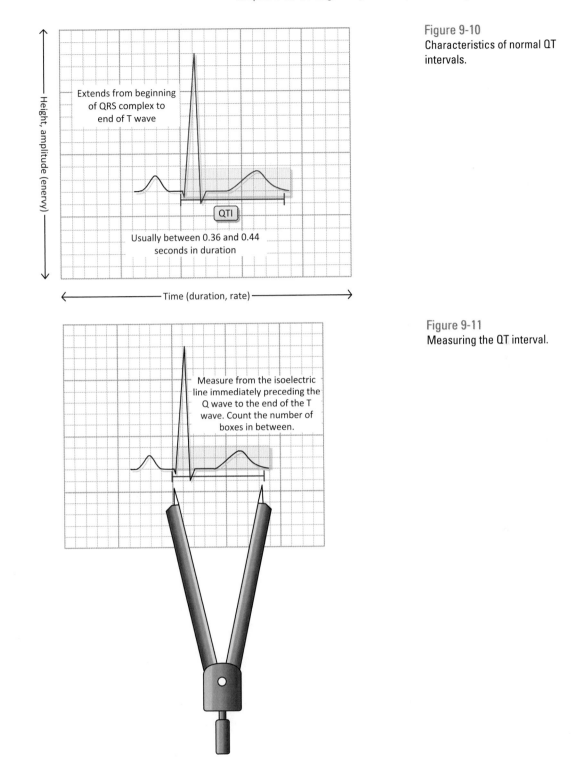

Figure 9-10
Characteristics of normal QT intervals.

Extends from beginning of QRS complex to end of T wave

QTI

Usually between 0.36 and 0.44 seconds in duration

Height, amplitude (energy)

Time (duration, rate)

Figure 9-11
Measuring the QT interval.

Measure from the isoelectric line immediately preceding the Q wave to the end of the T wave. Count the number of boxes in between.

locate the end of the T wave. Count the number of boxes in between these two points (Figure 9-11). Since each small box represents 0.04 seconds, the normal QT interval should extend across at least nine but not more than 11 small boxes. Preferably, you should record three consecutive measurements of the QT interval. Then, calculate the mean. It is best to use lead II to measure the QT interval. If lead II is not suitable, then leads in the sequence of V_5, V_4, V_3, V_2 should be used.

Characteristics of a Normal QT Interval	
Location	Extends from the Q wave (or R wave) to the end of the T wave.
Duration	Usually between 0.36 and 0.44 seconds.

LO 9.10

Abnormal QT Intervals

An abnormal QT interval duration can indicate myocardial irregularity. The two types of abnormal QT intervals are prolonged QT intervals and shortened QT intervals (Figure 9-12).

Prolonged QT Intervals

A prolonged QT interval indicates prolonged ventricular repolarization, which means the relative refractory period is longer. In certain conditions, such as myocardial ischemia or infarction, a prolonged QT interval can predispose the patient to life-threatening ventricular dysrhythmias such as torsades de pointes.

Causes of prolonged QT interval include congenital conduction system defect. Called *prolonged QT interval syndrome,* it is present in certain families. Also, drugs such as haloperidol, methadone, and Class IA antidysrhythmic drugs like amiodarone or sotalol can produce QT interval prolongation.

Shortened QT Intervals

A shortened QT interval can be caused by hypercalcemia or digoxin toxicity.

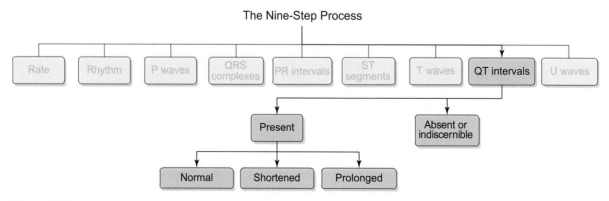

Figure 9-12
QT interval algorithm.

U Waves

The U wave is a small wave that follows the T wave. It is not always seen. The origin of U waves is speculative; however, they are thought to represent repolarization of the papillary muscles or Purkinje fibers. U waves are considered normal in younger persons (less than 35–40 years of age) but not so common in the elderly.

Normal Characteristics

LO 9.11

When present, the U wave is rounded, has the same polarity as the T wave, and is usually less than one-third its amplitude (Figure 9-13). The U wave will sometimes merge with the T wave. U waves are usually best seen in the right precordial leads, especially V_2 and V_3. The normal U wave is asymmetrical, with the beginning portion being more abrupt than the ending portion (just the opposite of the normal T wave).

Characteristics of a Normal U Wave	
Location	When present, follows the T wave.
Configuration	Upright and slightly asymmetrical.
Amplitude	Usually less than one-third the amplitude of the T wave.
Deflection	Oriented in the same direction as the preceding T wave.

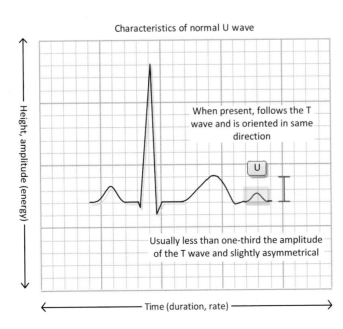

Characteristics of normal U wave

When present, follows the T wave and is oriented in same direction

U

Usually less than one-third the amplitude of the T wave and slightly asymmetrical

Height, amplitude (energy)

Time (duration, rate)

Figure 9-13
Characteristics of U waves.

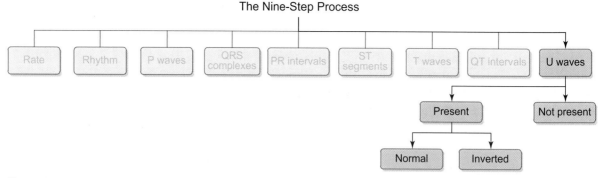

Figure 9-14
U wave algorithm.

 LO 9.12

Abnormal U Waves

Prominent U waves are most often seen in hypokalemia but may be present in hypercalcemia, thyrotoxicosis, digitalis toxicity, epinephrine and Class 1A and 3 antidysrhythmics use, mitral valve prolapse, and left ventricular hypertrophy, as well as in congenital long QT syndrome and in the setting of intracranial hemorrhage.

An inverted U wave may represent myocardial ischemia or left ventricular volume overload (Figure 9-14).

Key Points 🔍

- Assessing the ST segments, T waves, QT intervals, and U waves is a part of analyzing an ECG tracing.

- The ST segment is the isoelectric line that follows the QRS complex and connects it to the T wave. It represents the end of ventricular depolarization and the beginning of ventricular repolarization.

- ST segment depression or elevation can be evaluated by comparing the ST segment with the PR segment. It is considered elevated if it is above the baseline and depressed if it is below it.

- Elevation or depression of the ST segment is a hallmark feature of myocardial ischemia and injury.

- The T wave represents the completion of ventricular repolarization (recovery).

- The T wave is larger than the P wave and slightly asymmetrical. It is oriented in the same direction as the preceding QRS complex.

- When evaluating the T wave, focus on its three most important characteristics: configuration, amplitude, and deflection.

- Abnormal T waves indicate the presence of abnormal ventricular repolarization.
- Tall or peaked and inverted T waves (in certain leads) may be seen in myocardial ischemia.
- The QT interval represents the time needed for ventricular depolarization and repolarization.
- The QT extends from the beginning of the QRS complex to the end of the T wave. Its duration varies according to age, sex, and heart rate, but it is usually between 0.36 and 0.44 seconds.
- In certain conditions, such as myocardial ischemia or infarction, a prolonged QT interval can predispose the patient to life-threatening ventricular dysrhythmias.
- When present, the U wave is a small, rounded wave that follows the T wave. It has the same polarity as the T wave.
- Prominent U waves are most often seen in hypokalemia.

Assess Your Understanding

The following questions give you a chance to assess your understanding of the material discussed in this chapter. The answers can be found in Appendix A.

1. The ST segment represents
   a. atrial repolarization.
   b. ventricular depolarization.
   c. the beginning of ventricular repolarization.
   d. atrial and ventricular repolarization.

2. The ST segment is characteristically
   a. neither positive nor negative.
   b. curved downward.
   c. 1 to 2 mm above the isoelectric line.
   d. biphasic.

3. To measure the ST segment we draw a line from the _____ through the _____.
   a. PR segment, next PR segment
   b. R wave, T wave
   c. P wave, Q wave
   d. PR segment, J point

4. An elevated ST segment is _____ the isoelectric line.
   a. below
   b. horizontal to
   c. vertical to
   d. above

5. Convex-shaped ST segment elevation is most often due to
   a. myocardial injury.
   b. pericarditis.
   c. hyperkalemia.
   d. digitalis use.

6. The T wave represents
   a. ventricular depolarization.
   b. atrial repolarization.
   c. ventricular repolarization.
   d. abnormal electrical activity.

7. Which of the following is characteristic of normal T waves?
   a. It has a symmetrical shape.
   b. It is larger than the P wave.
   c. It has a deflection that is opposite of its associated QRS complex.
   d. Its beginning has a more abrupt slope than the end.

8. The maximum amplitude of T waves in the precordial leads is ____ mm in height.
   a. 5
   b. 8
   c. 10
   d. 15

9. To determine the amplitude of the T wave, you measure from the isoelectric line to the beginning of the waveform.
   a. True
   b. False

10. Inverted T waves may be seen with
    a. hyperkalemia.
    b. pericarditis.
    c. early beats arising from the atria.
    d. myocardial ischemia.

11. The QT interval represents the time needed for ventricular repolarization.
    a. True
    b. False

12. The normal QT interval has a duration of _____ to _____ seconds.
    a. 0.24, 0.48
    b. 0.28, 0.44
    c. 0.36, 0.44
    d. 0.44, 0.56

13. To measure the QT interval, we measure from the beginning of the _____ to the end of the _____.
    a. Q wave, T wave
    b. S wave, T wave
    c. R wave, U wave
    d. P wave, S wave

14. Prolonged QT intervals may be seen with
    a. pericarditis.
    b. digitalis toxicity.
    c. hypercalcemia.
    d. congenital conduction system defect.

15. Which of the following describes U waves?
    a. have sharply pointed waveforms
    b. immediately follow the ST segment
    c. take the same direction as the T wave
    d. always merged with the T wave

16. Prominent U waves are most often seen with
    a. hypokalemia.
    b. bradycardia.
    c. myocardial ischemia.
    d. the use of haloperidol and methadone.

17. Your patient has a QT interval that is 0.48 seconds in duration. This is referred to as a _____ QT interval.
    a. prolonged
    b. normal
    c. shortened
    d. refractory

18. In the presence of myocardial ischemia or infarction, a prolonged QT interval can predispose the patient to
    a. bradycardia.
    b. asystole.
    c. torsades de pointes.
    d. heart failure.

Referring to the case history at the beginning of this chapter, answer the following questions:

19. Elevated ST segments and inverted T waves on the 12-lead ECG suggest the patient is experiencing
    a. pericarditis.
    b. hypercalcemia.
    c. heart failure.
    d. myocardial ischemia and injury.

20. The patient's heart rate can be described as
    a. tachycardic.
    b. irregular.
    c. bradycardic.
    d. normal.

Answers to Sidebar Questions

1. During repolarization, positively charged ions, such as potassium, leave the cell, causing the positive charge to lower. Then the other positively charged ions, such as sodium, are removed by special transport systems, such as the sodium-potassium pumps, until the electrical potential inside the cell reaches its original negative charge. **p. 200**

2. The PR segment is the isoelectric line between P wave and QRS complex. **p. 201**

3. Depolarization begins at the endocardial surface and spreads to the epicardium as a positive wave, whereas repolarization begins at the epicardium and spreads to the endocardium but it is restoring the normal balance so takes the same direction as the QRS complex. **p. 204**

What's Online

Go to www.mhhe.com/shadeECG2e to find:

- Presentations on chapter content
- Exercises and chapter quiz
- Fill-in-the-blank exercises and answers

Practice Makes Perfect

For each of the 13 ECG tracings on the following pages, practice the Nine-Step Process for analyzing ECGs. To achieve the greatest learning, you should practice the step immediately after reading the related chapter (i.e., practice determining the heart rate after reading Chapter 4). Below are questions you should consider as you complete each step. All tracings are six seconds in duration.

1. Determine the heart rate. Is it slow? Normal? Fast? What is the ventricular rate? What is the atrial rate?

2. Determine if the rhythm is regular or irregular. If it is irregular, what type of irregularity is it? Occasional or Irregular? Slight? Sudden acceleration or slowing in heart rate? Total? Patterned? Does it have a variable conduction ratio?

3. Determine if P waves are present. If so, how do they appear? Do they have normal height and duration? Are they tall? Notched? Wide? Biphasic? Of differing morphology? Inverted? One for each QRS complex? More than one preceding some or all the QRS complexes? Do they have a sawtooth appearance? An indiscernible chaotic baseline?

4. Determine if QRS complexes are present. If so, how do they appear? Narrow with proper amplitude? Tall? Low amplitude? Delta wave? Notched? Wide? Bizarre? With chaotic waveforms?

5. Determine the presence of PR intervals. If present, how do they appear? Constant? Of normal duration? Shortened? Lengthened? Progressively longer? Varying?

6. Evaluate the ST segments. Do they have normal duration and position? Are they elevated? (If so, are they flat, concave, convex, arched?) Depressed? (If so, are they normal, flat, downsloping or upsloping?)

7. Determine if T waves are present. If so, how do they appear? Of normal height and duration? Tall? Wide? Notched? Inverted?

8. Determine the presence of QT intervals. If present, what is their duration? Normal? Shortened? Prolonged?

9. Determine if U waves are present. If present, how do they appear? Of normal height and duration? Inverted?

1.

ECG Findings:

2.

ECG Findings:

3.

ECG Findings:

4.

ECG Findings:

5.

ECG Findings:

6.

ECG Findings:

7.

ECG Findings:

8.

ECG Findings:

9.

ECG Findings:

10.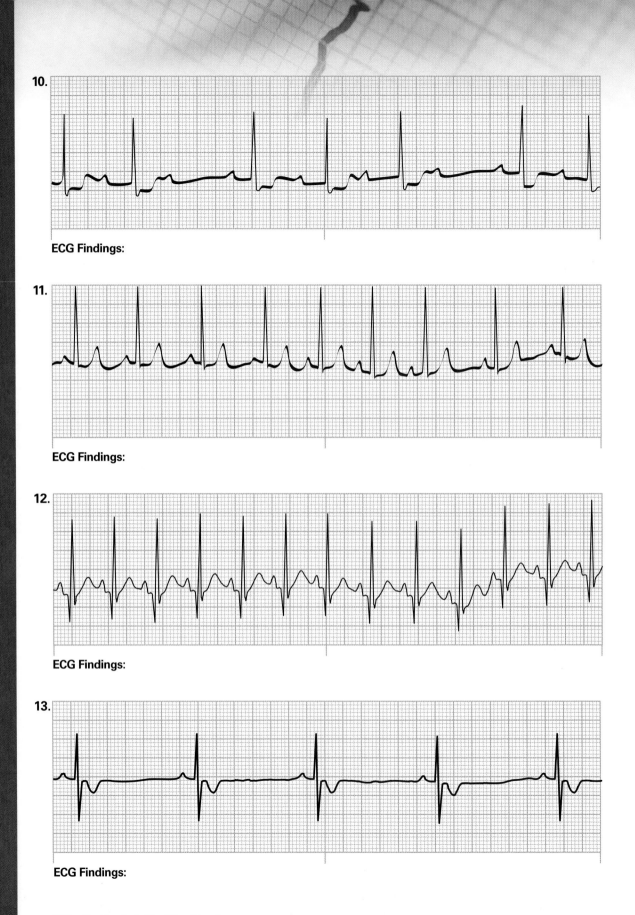

ECG Findings:

11.

ECG Findings:

12.

ECG Findings:

13.

ECG Findings:

section 3

Origin and Clinical Aspects of Dysrhythmias

Chapter 10:   Overview of Dysrhythmias

Chapter 11:   Sinus Dysrhythmias

Chapter 12:   Atrial Dysrhythmias

Chapter 13:   Junctional Dysrhythmias

Chapter 14:   Ventricular Dysrhythmias

Chapter 15:   AV Heart Blocks

Chapter 16:   Pacemakers and Implanted Cardioverter-Defibrillators

10 Overview of Dysrhythmias

Chapter Outline

The Heart's Normal
    Electrical Activity

Dysrhythmias

The Effects of
    Dysrhythmias

Characterizing
    Dysrhythmias

Site of Origin

Leads Used to Identify
    Dysrhythmias

How to Spot
    Dysrhythmias

Treatment of
    Dysrhythmias

Learning Objectives

LO 10.1   Describe the normal electrical activity of the heart.

LO 10.2   Define the term *dysrhythmia*.

LO 10.3   Describe the effects of dysrhythmias.

LO 10.4   Recall the different types of dysrhythmias.

LO 10.5   List and describe the mechanisms and causes of dysrhythmias.

LO 10.6   Categorize dysrhythmias by site of origin.

LO 10.7   Recall which ECG leads are most effective for identifying dysrhythmias.

LO 10.8   Describe how to identify dysrhythmias when analyzing an ECG tracing.

LO 10.9   Describe the treatments used to control or eliminate dysrhythmias.

Case History

A 58-year-old man is at the local grocery store, having just paid for his groceries, when he suddenly feels a pounding in his chest, becomes lightheaded, and then slumps to the floor. Two firefighter/paramedics who are in the store picking up food for dinner quickly come to his side. As the one positions his head into a head/tilt chin/lift position, he wakes up. Feeling embarrassed, he insists on sitting up. The ECG monitor is retrieved from the ambulance, and it is applied while vital signs are obtained, revealing a blood pressure of 90/60, a pulse rate of 220, and a respiratory rate of 22. The cardiac monitor shows a fast, regular rhythm with narrow QRS complexes. Although a T wave follows each QRS complex, P waves cannot be identified.

Within a few minutes the patient's heart rate slows to 82 beats per minute, and he appears more alert. He agrees to be transported to the hospital, where he undergoes evaluation and treatment for episodes of a rapid heart rate.

The Heart's Normal Electrical Activity

Here is a brief review of how the heartbeat originates and is conducted. Each heartbeat arises as an electrical impulse from the SA node. The impulse then spreads across the atria from right to left, depolarizing the tissue and causing both atria to contract. This is seen on the ECG as a P wave. The impulse then activates the AV node, which is normally the only electrical connection between the atria and the ventricles. There, the impulse is delayed slightly, allowing the atria to finish contracting and pushing any remaining blood from their chambers into the ventricles (referred to as the atrial kick). The impulse then spreads through both ventricles via the Bundle of His, right and left bundle branches, and the Purkinje fibers (seen as the QRS complex), causing a synchronized contraction of the primary pumping chambers of the heart, and thus, the pulse (Figure 10-1).

Nerve Impulse Generation in the Heart

In Chapter 1, you may recall that we discussed how nerve impulse generation and muscle contraction occur. In this chapter we get more specific. As previously stated, for any muscle to contract, it must first be electrically stimulated. Myocardial cells, like all other cells in the body, are bathed in electrolyte solution. The primary electrolytes responsible for initiating electrical charges are the positively charged ions (cations) sodium (Na+), potassium (K+), and calcium (Ca++). In the polarized state, cells have a high concentration of negatively charged ions (anions), proteins, and organelles on the inside of the cell. On the outside, there is a high concentration of cations. This difference in electrical charge between the inside and the outside of the cell creates a resting membrane potential (RMP). In the polarized state the RMP is negative,

QUESTION
1. **What is the normal pacemaker of the heart?** *Note:* Answers to sidebar questions can be found at the end of the chapter.

Figure 10-1
Normal electrical activity in heart. (1) Electrical impulse originates in SA node and spreads across atria which contract; (2) impulse conduction slows as it passes through the AV node; (3) the impulse then travels down the bundle of His; (4) the impulse then spreads throughout ventricles with ventricular contraction and pumping of blood.

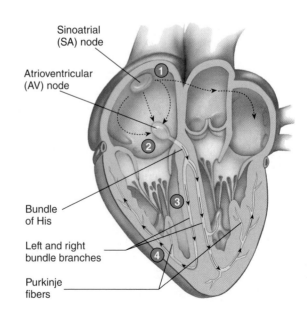

Sinoatrial (SA) node

Atrioventricular (AV) node

Bundle of His

Left and right bundle branches

Purkinje fibers

indicating that the cell is ready to fire or discharge. This negative RMP is sustained by the cell membrane's ability to prevent cations, such as Na+, from entering the cell and the anions from leaving the cell.

After all that is said, it is important to understand that, in order for pacemaker cells to be the self-initiators of the heartbeat, they depolarize differently than the myocardial cells.

Impulse Generation of the SA Node

Through the property of automaticity, the heart's pacemaker, the SA node, fires spontaneously over and over again, normally at a rate of between 60 and 100 times per minute. This occurs because the cells of the SA node have an unstable RMP.

Phase 4

Although the resting potential of the pacemaker cells drops to a minimum negative potential of around −55 to −60 mV between discharges, it is maintained there just for a moment. Then ion channels open, allowing the slow, inward (depolarizing) movement of Na+ currents (called "funny" currents). These currents cause the membrane potential to drift upward (becoming less negatively charged). Once the cell reaches about −50 mV "T," or "transient," Ca++ channels open and Ca++ enters, further neutralizing the intracellular negativity (Figure 10-2). This occurs without a corresponding outflow of K+ (which would otherwise offset the increase in positively charged ions inside the cell). This initial phase of the action potential is called the *prepotential*. Once the pacemaker potential reaches a threshold of −40 mV, the "L," or "long-lasting," voltage-gated Ca++ channels open and Ca++ slowly flows into the cells from the extracellular fluid.

Phase 0

The increased movement of Ca++ through the L-type Ca++ channels produces the depolarizing phase of the action potential, which peaks slightly above 0 mV. Because the movement of Ca++ through the channels into the cell is not rapid, the rate of depolarization (as seen in the slope of Phase 0) is much slower than that found in other cardiac cells. Also, during this phase the "funny" currents and Ca++ ion movement through the T-type channels decline as the channels close.

Phase 3

Repolarization begins when voltage-gated K+ channels open and K+ ions leave the cell. Also, the L-type Ca++ channels close. This makes the inside of the cell increasingly more negative, bringing about repolarization of the cells. When repolarization is complete, the K+ channels close. Polarity is restored to the resting state with the ionic concentrations reversed.

REMINDER
Automaticity is the ability of the cardiac muscles to depolarize spontaneously, i.e., without external electrical stimulation from the nervous system.

KEY CONCEPT
The SA node is the primary pacemaker of the heart.

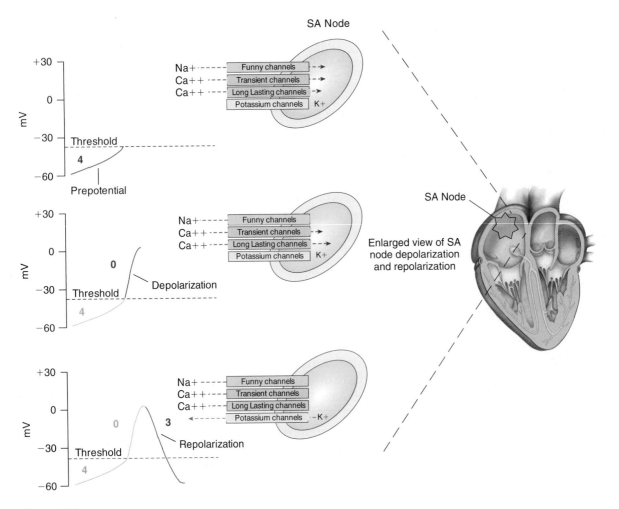

Figure 10-2

SA nodal action potentials occur in three phases. Phase 4 is the spontaneous depolarization that triggers the action potential once the membrane potential reaches threshold between –40 and –30 mV). Phase 0 is the depolarization phase of the action potential. This is followed by phase 3 repolarization. Once the cell is completely repolarized at about –55 to –60 mV, the cycle repeats spontaneously.

The pacemaker potential starts over on its way to producing the next heartbeat. Each depolarization of the SA node initiates one heartbeat. When the SA node fires, it excites the other components in the conduction system which then carry the impulse to the myocytes (the working cells). Normally, the SA node spontaneously depolarizes faster than any other pacemaker site, making it the primary pacemaker for the heart (Figure 10-3).

Depolarization and Repolarization of the Myocytes

In the polarized state, the nonpacemaker myocytes have a very negative resting membrane potential of around −80 to −90 mV. This membrane potential remains stable (the same) until the cell is electrically stimulated, typically via an electric current from an adjacent cell. This electrical stimulus initiates a sequence of events that involve the inflow and outflow of multiple cations and anions that together produce the action potential of the cell and propagate electrical stimulation of the cells that lie next to it. As such, electrical

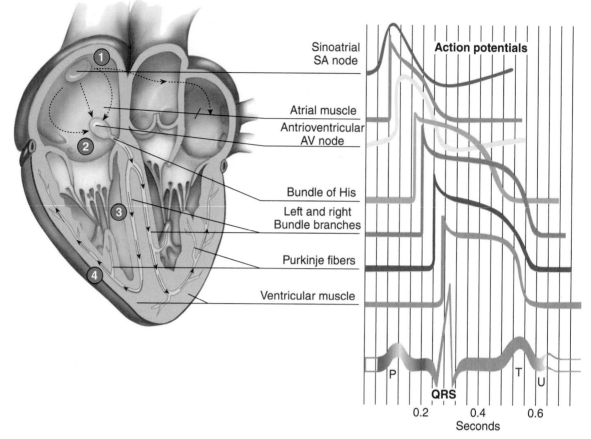

Figure 10-3
This figure shows the action potentials of the heart's pacemaker sites and myocytes from atria and ventricles. Because the SA node depolarizes first, it is the pacemaker of the heart.

stimulation is conducted from one cell to all the cells that are next to it and then to all the cells of the heart.

The action potential of the myocytes consists of five phases; described as follows.

Phase 4

Phase 4 has a role as the termination of the cardiac electrophysiologic cycle, not just the beginning of it. This is the phase that the cell remains in until it is stimulated by an external electrical stimulus. It is the resting membrane potential. This phase of the action potential is associated with atrial and ventricular diastole. During Phase 4 all the fast Na+ and slow Ca++ channels are closed, and special ion-transporting mechanisms within the cell membrane, called *sodium-potassium pumps,* help to restore the original ionic concentrations (and thus maintain a difference in electrical charges between the inside and outside of the cardiac cells) by continually removing Na+ from inside the cell. This process is referred to as *active transport* and requires the expenditure of energy. Further, the K+ channels are open allowing positive K+ ions to enter and leave the cell (Figure 10-4).

Figure 10-4
Myocyte in polarized state with active transport maintaining a difference in electrical charges between the inside and outside of the cardiac cells.

Phase 0

Depolarization begins once the myocyte receives an impulse from a neighboring cell. This is called *Phase 0* (Figure 10-5), or the *rapid depolarization phase*. Na+ quickly enters the cells through voltage-gated channels called *fast Na+ channels* (which are stimulated to open by the electrical impulse). With all this Na+ coming into the cell, it becomes more positively charged. The charge overshoots neutral, rising to about +30 mV. When a certain level is reached, depolarization of the entire cell occurs. The rising phase of the action potential is very brief. Depolarization also causes voltage-gated channels called *slow Ca++ channels* to open and allow some Ca++ to enter

Figure 10-5
Myocyte during Phase 0.

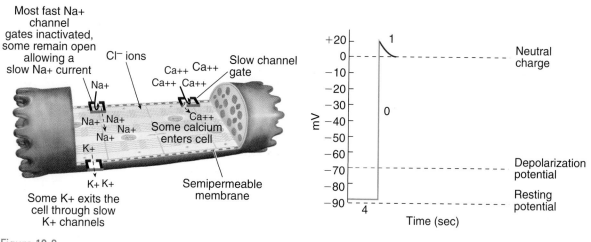

Figure 10-6
Myocyte during Phase 1.

the cell. Compared with Na+ fast channels, the Ca++ slow channels open and close slowly. Also, during this phase the K+ channels close, thereby decreasing the movement of K+ across the cell membrane (causing it to remain inside the cell). Think of the movement of Na+ into the cells at the beginning of depolarization as being like a rush of post-holiday shoppers through the doors of the department store when they first open—it is a mass influx.

Phase 1

Phase 1, also referred to as *early repolarization* (Figure 10-6), occurs next. During this phase voltage-gated Na+ channels close, and a small number of the K+ channels open. This stops the fast inflow of Na+ and allows some K+ to move out of the cell. Also, chloride (Cl−) ions enter the cell. These ion movements lower the positive charge inside the cell somewhat.

Phase 2

Next, during Phase 2, or the *plateau phase* (Figure 10-7), Ca++ enters the cell through voltage-gated L-type Ca++ channels, prolonging the depolarization (thereby creating a plateau). This movement of Ca++ into the cell counteracts the potential change caused by the movement of K+ out of the cell through K+ channels. Ca++ then reacts with myosin and actin causing the cell to contract. This prolonged plateau phase distinguishes cardiac action potentials from the much shorter action potentials found in nerves and skeletal muscle.

As one cell depolarizes, the tendency of the adjacent cell to depolarize increases. This leads to a series of depolarizations down the cells in the heart that are capable of generating, responding to, and/or conducting nerve impulses.

Figure 10-7
Myocyte during Phase 2.

Phase 3

KEY CONCEPT

Repolarization occurs as a result of the rapid outflow of K+ along with Na+ and Ca++ being transported out of the myocyte.

QUESTION

2. How soon can the cell respond to its next electrical stimulus?

Next, Phase 3, or *rapid final repolarization* (Figure 10-8), results when Ca++ channels close and many K+ channels open. This allows a rapid outflow of K+, causing the cell interior to become more negatively charged. During the next phase (Phase 4) K+ is allowed to reenter the cell interior.

Also, during Phase 3, Ca++ and Na+ are pulled out of the cell interior by Na+ and Ca++ pumps. This helps achieve and maintain the very negative resting membrane potential of the myocytes.

Refractory Periods

During what is called the *absolute refractory period*, no stimulus (no matter how strong) will depolarize the cell. This helps assure the rhythmicity of the heartbeat. The absolute refractory period includes Phases 0, 1, 2, and part of

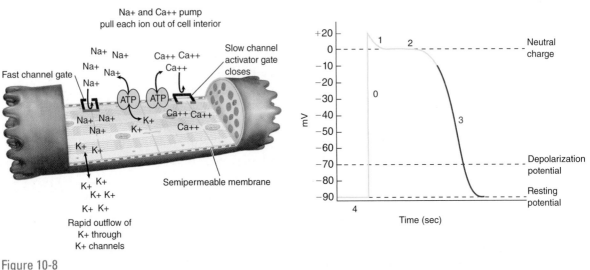

Figure 10-8
Myocyte during Phase 3.

phase 3. It assures that after contraction, relaxation is nearly complete before another action potential can be initiated. This prevents spasm-producing (tetanic) contractions in the cardiac muscle. However, during the later phase of repolarization, called the *relative refractory period,* a sufficiently strong stimulus *will* depolarize the myocardium.

KEY CONCEPT
During what is called the absolute refractory period, no stimulus will depolarize the cell.

Dysrhythmias

LO 10.2

In the previous chapters we talked about the anatomy and physiology of the heart and the machines and leads used to obtain an ECG tracing. We also discussed the nine-step process used to examine the ECG (for a brief review see page 73). We will continue to use this process to evaluate the ECGs throughout the remainder of this book.

One thing we look for when we examine the ECG is the presence of dysrhythmias. In this chapter, as well as the next five, we focus on dysrhythmias—the characteristics associated with them (which allow us to identify them), how they occur, their significance, and how to treat them (if necessary).

First, let's define what we mean by the term *dysrhythmia.* Simply stated, a dysrhythmia is an ECG rhythm that differs from normal sinus rhythm. More specifically, a dysrhythmia is a condition in which there is abnormal electrical activity in the heart. The heartbeat may be slower or faster than normal, it may be irregular, or conduction through the heart may be delayed or blocked. The term *dysrhythmia* covers a large number of electrical abnormalities. Note that although the natural slowing and speeding up of the heart rate differs from the criteria for normal sinus rhythm, many do not consider it a dysrhythmia but, instead, the body's normal response to rest or exertion.

WANT MORE INFORMATION?
Visit the Fast & Easy ECGs Website at www.mhhe.com/shadeECG2e.

While the terms *dysrhythmia* and *arrhythmia* can be used interchangeably, *arrhythmia* suggests there is an absence of a rhythm whereas *dys*rhythmia suggests there is a problem with the rhythm.

The Effects of Dysrhythmias

LO 10.3

Some dysrhythmias are of little consequence and are simply annoying. During the course of their life, most people will occasionally feel their heart skip a beat or give an occasional extra strong beat; neither of these is usually a cause for concern. Other dysrhythmias are life-threatening medical emergencies that can lead to cardiac arrest and sudden death.

Palpitations, an abnormal sensation felt with the heartbeat, are the most common symptom of dysrhythmias. People describe feeling their heart skip a beat or give an occasional extra strong beat; neither of these is usually a cause for alarm. Palpitations may be infrequent, frequent, or continuous.

Figure 10-9
Reduced cardiac output is
caused by a decrease in
heart rate or stroke volume.

KEY CONCEPT

The term symptomatic
refers to patients who
are experiencing signs
and symptoms related to
decreased cardiac output.

Of greater significance are lightheadedness, dizziness, fainting, chest pain, shortness of breath, sweatiness, and/or pallor that may be seen in dysrhythmias which cause a lowering of the blood pressure. We refer to this as being *symptomatic*. When you see the description symptomatic bradycardia, symptomatic tachycardia, or any other that includes the word *symptomatic*, it is referring to a dysrhythmia that produces decreased cardiac output.

When considering the signs and symptoms seen with certain dysrhythmias, let's think back on our discussion in Chapter 1. Remember, heart rate × stroke volume = cardiac output. If either the heart rate or stroke volume is reduced, cardiac output is reduced (Figure 10-9). This can decrease the blood pressure and perfusion of the body's cells, leaving the patient in a perilous condition, and may even become life threatening.

Some dysrhythmias slow the heart rate, and, in that way, decrease cardiac output. Others decrease the stroke volume by making the heart beat too fast (which in turn decreases cardiac output by not allowing the heart to fill properly). Cardiac output can also be decreased when the atria don't contract properly or contract at all (eliminating the atrial kick which normally pushes blood into the ventricles; Figure 10-10). Incomplete contraction of the atria can also lead to clots being formed and passed along to the brain, resulting in the patient experiencing a stroke.

Another adverse effect of dysrhythmias is that they can reduce the oxygen supply to the heart cells by decreasing coronary blood flow or by causing the heart to beat so fast the heart expends its available oxygen due to the rapid heartbeat. The decrease in myocardial oxygen supply can cause chest pain.

Figure 10-10
Decreased cardiac output
due to loss of atrial kick.

↓ **Atrial kick** = ↓ **stroke volume** = ↓ **cardiac output**

The sudden onset of a dysrhythmia in patients with underlying cardiac disease can also precipitate congestive heart failure.

Early beats that arise from the ventricles can also result in a decreased or absent heartbeat. If they occur frequently, cardiac output can be decreased. Dropped beats can also result in decreased cardiac output, particularly if it occurs frequently. Delays or blockage in conduction can lead to a worsening of the blockage or worse, a complete cessation of the heartbeat.

Sometimes the first clinical manifestation of a cardiac dysrhythmia is sudden death. This is particularly true in patients experiencing myocardial infarction. To prevent this, these patients should be hospitalized so that their heart rate and rhythm can be stabilized and monitored.

As we discuss the dysrhythmias throughout this textbook, we will review the effects each may have on the heart and subsequent cardiac output.

Characterizing Dysrhythmias

Dysrhythmias can be categorized many different ways. In this textbook, we describe them by type, causes, mechanisms, and site of origin. Not all dysrhythmias are described in this chapter, as it is meant to serve as an overview. However, all dysrhythmias are discussed in detail in subsequent chapters.

Types of Dysrhythmias   ▐ LO 10.4

Bradycardia

A heart rate less than 60 beats per minute is called *bradycardia*. It can occur for many reasons and may or may not have an adverse affect on cardiac output. In the extreme, it can lead to severe reductions in cardiac output and eventually deteriorate into asystole.

Bradycardia can arise from the SA node. Sometimes this is normal, such as when the patient is at rest or is an athlete with a body that is more efficient and does not require as much oxygen. It can also be caused by increased parasympathetic (vagal) tone or a variety of medical conditions, including intrinsic sinus node disease, hypothermia, hypoxia, drug effects (e.g., digitalis, beta blockers, Ca++ channel blockers), myocardial infarction, and others.

Bradycardia can also be brought about by failure of the SA node, the heart's primary pacemaker. When this occurs, either the SA node will initiate an impulse, or an escape pacemaker from either the AV node or the ventricles should take over and initiate the heartbeat. Remember, the intrinsic rate of the AV node is 40 to 60 beats per minute whereas the ventricle's is 20 to 40 beats per minute (see Chapter 1). Whether the escape pacemaker arises from the AV node (called *junctional escape*) or ventricles (called *ventricular escape* or *idioventricular rhythm*), it is likely to produce bradycardia.

Blockage of the impulse traveling through the AV node can also be a cause of bradycardia. In one type, not all the sinus beats are conducted through to the ventricles; this results in a slower ventricular rate (as such, there are more P waves than QRS complexes). With a more severe form of AV heart block, there is complete blockage of the AV node, resulting in the sinus impulse not reaching the ventricles. An escape pacemaker then arises from somewhere below the AV node, resulting in a slower ventricular rate.

We may also see slower than normal ventricular rates in conditions where the atria repeatedly or chaotically depolarize and bombard the AV node so rapidly that not all the impulses are conducted through to the ventricles. If the number of atrial impulses reaching the ventricles falls to less than normal, it results in a slower than normal ventricular rate, or bradycardia.

Tachycardia

A heart rate greater than 100 beats per minute is called *tachycardia*. Tachycardia has many causes and leads to increased myocardial oxygen consumption, which can have an adverse effect on patients with coronary artery disease and other medical conditions. Extremely fast rates can have an adverse affect on cardiac output. Also, tachycardia that arises from the ventricles may lead to a chaotic quivering of the ventricles called *ventricular fibrillation*.

Sinus tachycardia is a fast rate, greater than 100 beats per minute, that arises from the SA node. Sinus tachycardia can occur with increased sympathetic nervous system stimulation due to exercise, exertion, stress, fear, anxiety, etc. Other common causes of sinus tachycardia include fever, hypoxia, shock, drug effects (such as from amphetamines or cocaine), ingestion of caffeine or alcohol, smoking, and myocardial infarction.

Tachycardia can also be brought about by a pacemaker that arises outside the SA node such as in the atria, AV junction, or ventricles. These tachycardias result from the rapid depolarization of a site that fires before the SA node can. Tachycardia that arises above the ventricles is called *supraventricular tachycardia,* whereas tachycardia that arises in the ventricles is called *ventricular tachycardia.* Atrial tachycardia and junctional tachycardia are supraventricular tachycardias (again, as they arise from above the ventricles). The term *supraventricular* is also used if the origin of the tachycardia cannot be determined as atrial or junctional (often due to the P waves being hidden in the T wave of the preceding beat in faster rates).

We may also see faster than normal ventricular rates in conditions in which the atria repeatedly or chaotically depolarize and bombard the AV node rapidly (see Figure 6-11). In some cases, the number of atrial impulses actually reaching the ventricles is greater.

Typically, tachycardias are referred to as one of five types (Figure 10-11)—narrow QRS complex regular rhythms, wide QRS complex regular rhythms, narrow QRS complex irregular rhythms, wide QRS complex irregular rhythms, and wide QRS complexes of unknown origin. Being able to differentiate between the five types of tachycardia is important because it will help determine what type of treatment should be employed.

Figure 10-11
Five types of tachycardia.

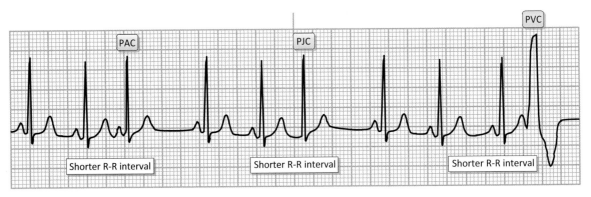

Figure 10-12
Early beats with a shortening of the R-R interval.

Narrow QRS complexes indicate that the site of origin for the tachycardia is above the ventricles (supraventricular) whereas wide QRS complexes typically indicate a ventricular origin. However, some supraventricular tachycardias conduct abnormally through the ventricles, producing wide QRS complexes, and for this reason are referred to as *wide QRS complexes of unknown origin* (until otherwise determined). The tachycardias that are regular come from one site whereas irregular tachycardias originate from more than one site.

Early (Premature) Beats

Another cause of dysrhythmias is an impulse that appears early, called a *premature complex* or *ectopic focus*. As implied by its name, a premature complex fires early, before the SA node has a chance to initiate the impulse. These premature complexes can arise from any of the cells of the heart, including the atria, AV junction, or ventricles. The R-R interval between the normal complex and the premature complex is shorter than the interval between two normal complexes (Figure 10-12). The presence of a premature beat makes the rhythm irregular. The premature beats may occur only a few times a minute, or they can occur often. Frequent premature beats are more likely to progress to very fast atrial, junctional, or ventricular rates (tachycardia). Worse, the rhythm may deteriorate into a quivering of the heart muscle called *ventricular fibrillation*.

KEY CONCEPT
An early beat results in a shorter R-R interval (between the normal complex and the premature complex) causing the rhythm to be irregular.

As described earlier, early beats that originate from above the ventricles (supraventricular) tend to have narrow QRS complexes (unless there is abnormal conduction through the ventricles) whereas those that originate from the ventricles have wide QRS complexes. Premature beats that arise from the atria are called *premature atrial complexes (PACs)*, those that arise from the AV junction are called *premature junctional complexes (PJCs)*, and those that arise from the ventricles are called *premature ventricular complexes (PVCs)*.

Dropped Beats or QRS Complexes

Dropped beats occur when the SA node fails to initiate an impulse. This is seen as a pause in the ECG rhythm (Figure 10-13). Typically, the rhythm leading up to the pause looks normal. Then there is suddenly an absence of a

Figure 10-13
Dropped beats with longer R-R intervals as seen with an intermittent block at the AV junction.

P wave, QRS complex, and T wave. This creates a gap or pause. Usually, with this condition the SA node recovers and fires another impulse. If the SA node fails to fire, then an escape pacemaker from the atria, AV junction, or ventricles initiates an impulse.

Dropped QRS complexes can occur from a partial or intermittent block at the AV junction. In this condition, some impulses that originate from the SA node fail to conduct to the ventricles, resulting in one or more dropped ventricular beats. This causes more P waves than QRS complexes and R-R intervals that are longer wherever there is a dropped ventricular beat (as the QRS complex is absent). Dropped QRS complexes can also occur when a premature beat arises from the atria but fails to conduct to the ventricles. This produces an early beat with a P wave but no QRS complex following it.

Irregularity

An irregular rhythm is caused by some type of dysrhythmia. It includes several we have already discussed, such as early beats and dropped beats or QRS complexes. It also includes dysrhythmias that speed up and slow down in a cyclical manner, those that originate from more than one site (sometimes from many sites), and some types of AV heart block.

Causes and Mechanisms of Dysrhythmias

The primary causes and mechanisms believed to be responsible for dysrhythmias are increased parasympathetic tone, myocardial hypoxia, ischemia or infarction, increased automaticity, triggered activity (afterdepolarization), reentry, and conduction delay or block. Increased automaticity and triggered activity are disorders of impulse formation. Reentry is a problem with impulse conduction.

Increased Parasympathetic Tone

Stimulation of the parasympathetic nervous system causes a slowing of the heart rate and prolongs conduction of impulses through the AV node. This

KEY CONCEPT
Dropped beats result in a longer R-R interval (between the normal complex and the dropped complex) resulting in an irregular rhythm.

LO 10.5

can lead to bradycardia, sinus arrest (a pause in the normal activity of the sinus node) and/or AV heart block (blocking of the electrical impulse on its way from the atria to the ventricles).

Myocardial Hypoxia, Injury, and Infarction

A myocardium deprived of oxygen is extremely susceptible to the development of dysrhythmias. Pulmonary disorders that interfere with the body's ability to bring in adequate supplies of oxygen (e.g., chronic obstructive lung disease, pulmonary embolism) are major causes of dysrhythmias as are myocardial ischemia and infarction. Also, if portions of the heart's conduction system are damaged, impulse formation and/or conduction may be blocked. Sometimes, myocarditis, an inflammation of the heart muscle, can precipitate dysrhythmias.

Increased Automaticity

Automaticity refers to the spontaneous depolarization of myocardial cells, in other words, their ability to fire on their own without an outside stimulus (Figure 10-14). All of the cells of the heart have the ability to initiate an

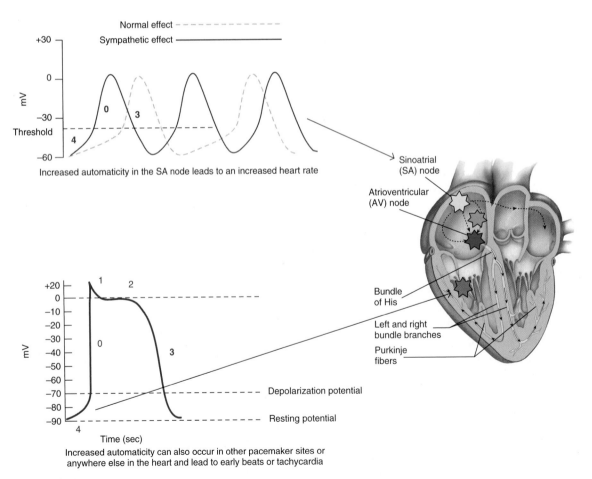

Figure 10-14
Increased automaticity as seen in the SA node as well as in other sites in the heart.

impulse; however, only some are meant to regularly generate the heartbeat. These cells are found in the heart's conduction system and include the SA node, AV junction, Bundle of His, and Purkinje fibers. The SA node is the primary pacemaker, having a higher automaticity (quicker spontaneously depolarization) than the rest of cells, and therefore initiates each heartbeat and sets the heart rate.

Stimulation of the sympathetic nervous system increases automaticity. This causes the cells to spontaneously depolarize more quickly. The resulting heart rhythm depends on where the impulse originates; if it is the SA node, the rhythm remains normal but faster than 100 beats per minute; if it is from a location outside the SA node (called an *ectopic focus*), any number of different dysrhythmias may ensue.

An ectopic focus may cause a single, occasional early beat (also referred to as a *premature beat),* or, if the ectopic focus fires more often than the SA node, it can produce a sustained abnormal rhythm. Sustained rhythms produced by an ectopic focus in the atria or atrioventricular junction are less dangerous than those that arise from the ventricles; however they can still produce a decrease in the pumping efficiency of the heart. This is because depolarization of the atria and ventricles does not occur in the usual manner and myocardial contraction may be poorly coordinated.

The most common causes of increased automaticity include emotional stress or physical exercise, caffeine, amphetamines, ischemia, hypoxia, atrial stretching or dilation (usually due to congestive heart failure, mitral valve disease, increased pulmonary artery pressures, or a combination of these conditions), hyperthyroidism (an overactive thyroid gland), or a myriad of other medical conditions, such as hypovolemia, congestive heart failure, etc.

> **KEY CONCEPT**
> Increased automaticity is a quicker spontaneous depolarization of the myocytes.

Reentry

Reentry occurs when an electrical impulse reenters a conduction pathway (often in a retrograde or reverse manner), rather than moving from one end of the heart to the other and then terminating. To understand this, let's review how impulses normally travel through the heart. Every cardiac cell is able to transmit impulses in every direction but only do so once and just briefly. Normally, the impulse spreads through the heart quickly enough that each cell responds only once. However, if conduction is abnormally slow and/or blocked somewhere along the conductive pathway, part of the impulse arrives late (during myocardial repolarization) and can be responded to as a new impulse.

> **KEY CONCEPT**
> Reentry occurs when an electrical impulse reenters a conduction pathway (often in a retrograde or reverse manner), rather than moving from one end of the heart to the other and then terminating.

Some hearts have an accessory pathway (bundle of connecting tissue) located between either the right atrium and the right ventricle or the left atrium and the left ventricle. These accessory pathways allow electrical impulses to bypass the AV node and depolarize the ventricles. Another abnormality in some people is a dual conduction pathway through the AV node (Figure 10-15). In both accessory pathways and dual conduction pathways through the AV node, under the right circumstances, reentry can occur.

Some people have more than one conduction pathway through the AV node. Under the right conditions, these pathways can form an electrical circuit or loop.

Fast

Slow

Here an early beat from the atria triggers the impulse to indefinitely spin around in the circuit producing a very rapid and regular rhythm.

PAC

PAC

Enlarged view

Figure 10-15
One example of how reentry can occur.

Depending on the timing, this mechanism can generate a sustained abnormal circuit rhythm. Reentry circuits are responsible for a number of dysrhythmias, including atrial flutter, most paroxysmal supraventricular tachycardia, and ventricular tachycardia (to be discussed later).

A unique form of reentry is referred to as *fibrillation*. Fibrillation results when there are multiple micro-reentry circuits in the chambers of the heart and portions or all of it is quivering due to chaotic electrical impulses. Fibrillation that occurs in the atria is called *atrial fibrillation*. Fibrillation that occurs in the ventricles is called *ventricular fibrillation*.

Triggered Beats

Triggered beats occur when problems at the level of the ion channels in individual heart cells lead to partial repolarization. Partial repolarization causes repetitive ectopic firing called *triggered activity*. The depolarization produced by triggered activity is known as *afterdepolarization* and can bring about atrial or ventricular tachycardia. Triggered beats are relatively rare but can result from the action of antidysrhythmic drugs (i.e., digoxin toxicity), cell injury, and other conditions.

Proarrhythmia

The term *proarrhythmia* refers to the development of new or a more frequent occurrence of pre-existing dysrhythmias that are caused by antidysrhythmic therapy or drugs used to treat other conditions. In other words, it is a side effect associated with the use of these medications.

Site of Origin

LO 10.6

It is also appropriate to classify dysrhythmias by site of origin (Figure 10-16). As you will see in the next five chapters, this how we present dysrhythmias in this textbook.

Sinus Dysrhythmias

Dysrhythmias that originate from the SA node are called *sinus dysrhythmias* and include

- Sinus bradycardia
- Sinus tachycardia
- Sinus dysrhythmia
- Sinus arrest
- Sinoatrial exit block
- Sick sinus syndrome

Atrial Dysrhythmias

Dysrhythmias that originate from the atria are called *atrial dysrhythmias* and include

- PACs
- Wandering atrial pacemaker
- Atrial tachycardia
- Supraventricular tachycardia (SVT)

Sinus dysrhythmias
Atrial dysrhythmias
Junctional dysrhythmias
AV heart block
Ventricular dysrhythmias

Figure 10-16
Sites where dysrhythmias originate.

- Multifocal atrial tachycardia
- Atrial flutter
- Atrial fibrillation

Junctional Dysrhythmias

Dysrhythmias that originate from the AV junction are called *junctional dysrhythmias* and include

- PJCs
- Junctional escape
- Accelerated junctional rhythm
- Junctional tachycardia
- AV nodal reentrant tachycardia
- AV reentrant tachycardia

Ventricular Dysrhythmias

Dysrhythmias that originate from the ventricles are called *ventricular dysrhythmias* and include

- PVCs
- Ventricular escape beats
- Idioventricular rhythm
- Accelerated idioventricular rhythm
- Ventricular tachycardia
- Ventricular fibrillation
- Asystole

AV Heart Block

Dysrhythmias that occur due to a delay or blockage in the AV node are called *AV heart blocks* and include

- 1st degree AV block
- 2nd degree AV block, Types I and II
- 3rd degree AV block
- Atrioventricular dissociation

Again, this is how we present dysrhythmias over the next five chapters of this book.

LO 10.7

Leads Used to Identify Dysrhythmias

Typically, dysrhythmias can be identified through the use of one lead, most commonly lead II. This lead has an excellent view of the normal conduction of the impulse through the heart. With lead II the positive electrode is on the left leg (or on the left midclavicular line, below the last palpable rib), resulting in the waveforms appearing upright or positive because depolarization of the heart flows toward the positive electrode. It is particularly helpful in identifying sinus node and atrial dysrhythmias. (Figure 10-17A).

Another lead commonly used to detect dysrhythmias is the modified chest lead (MCL1). With the MCL1, the positive electrode is positioned in the fourth intercostal space in the right sternal border (to the right of the left ventricle). The waveforms take a downward (negative) deflection because depolarization of the heart flows toward the left ventricle (and away from the positive electrode). The lead is effective for monitoring the QRS complexes of dysrhythmias, P wave changes, AV bundle-branch defects, and premature ventricular beats. It is helpful in differentiating between the different types of tachycardia (supraventricular versus ventricular; see Figure 10-17B).

How to Spot Dysrhythmias

LO 10.8

To identify dysrhythmias, you need to look across the ECG tracing and analyze it using a systematic and organized approach. Although six-second tracings are effective for teaching how to analyze and interpret dysrhythmias, they don't give you much information from which to see emerging dysrhythmias. Don't hesitate to print off more of the tracing in order to identify the presence of dysrhythmias. This is particularly important when there are patterns that can be seen only over several seconds.

KEY CONCEPT
Use a systematic, organized approach to analyze each ECG tracing.

An effective way of looking at the tracing is to scan it from left to right, picking out the things that are different than normal and then further analyzing them (Figure 10-18). We look for the presence or absence of key characteristics and then match those up against the characteristics we know to be common with the various dysrhythmias. Unless the findings are extremely subtle, it is usually easy to identify the presence of a dysrhythmia. Determining what the dysrhythmia is, however, can be challenging and hence the reason for using a systematic, organized approach for ECG analysis.

Treatment of Dysrhythmias

LO 10.9

Many dysrhythmias require no treatment as they are either benign or resolve on their own. An example is tachycardia that arises from the SA node in order to resolve a body's increased need for oxygen and nutrients and to remove metabolic waste. Here, there is no need to treat the tachycardia; it will naturally resolve on its own. In other cases, we treat the cause, and that resolves the dysrhythmia. Still at other times, we need to administer a treatment to suppress or eliminate the dysrhythmia. Whenever the dysrhythmia produces a life-threatening condition, it must be corrected promptly if the patient is to survive.

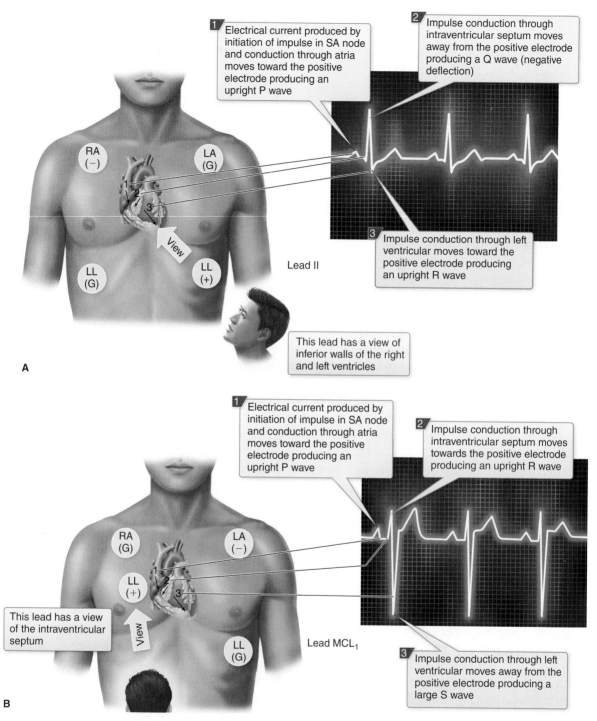

1 Electrical current produced by initiation of impulse in SA node and conduction through atria moves toward the positive electrode producing an upright P wave

2 Impulse conduction through intraventricular septum moves away from the positive electrode producing a Q wave (negative deflection)

3 Impulse conduction through left ventricular moves toward the positive electrode producing an upright R wave

Lead II

This lead has a view of inferior walls of the right and left ventricles

A

1 Electrical current produced by initiation of impulse in SA node and conduction through atria moves toward the positive electrode producing an upright P wave

2 Impulse conduction through intraventricular septum moves towards the positive electrode producing an upright R wave

This lead has a view of the intraventricular septum

Lead MCL₁

3 Impulse conduction through left ventricular moves away from the positive electrode producing a large S wave

B

Figure 10-17
Leads II and MCL1 are commonly used leads for detecting dysrhythmias.

Figure 10-18
Using a systematic, step-by-step process to analyze an ECG tracing.

The method used to manage dysrhythmias depends on whether or not the patient is stable or unstable. Patients who are symptomatic are considered unstable as symptoms indicate decreased cardiac output.

Several options are available to treat dysrhythmias and are employed on the basis of the cause or mechanism of the dysrhythmia. Commonly used treatments include physical maneuvers, electricity therapy, and the administration of certain medications. More advanced treatment of dysrhythmias includes electro- or cryocautery. This procedure is performed in specialized catheter laboratories where cardiologists use very small probes inserted through the blood vessels to map electrical activity from within the heart. This allows abnormal areas of conduction to be located and subsequently eliminated with heat or cold or electrical or laser probes. This can completely resolve some dysrhythmias but not others.

Physical Maneuvers

One way to treat dysrhythmias, specifically tachycardias that arise from above the ventricles, is to employ one of several physical maneuvers. These maneuvers are collectively called *vagal maneuvers* and act to stimulate the parasympathetic nervous system. This slows the rate at which the SA node discharges and how quickly impulses are conducted through the AV node. It is the slowing of AV node conduction that slows the heart rate in supraventricular tachycardias.

Electrical Therapy

Electrical therapy is sometimes used to manage certain dysrhythmias. One type of therapy is the delivery of an electrical shock across the heart—either externally, on the surface of the chest, or internally to the heart via implanted electrodes. It is delivered as either synchronized cardioversion or as defibrillation. Synchronized cardioversion, used to treat patients experiencing symptomatic tachydysrhythmias, is the delivery of the electrical shock timed with the R wave of the QRS complex on the ECG. This helps prevent delivering the shock during the relative refractory period of the cardiac cycle, which could induce ventricular fibrillation. When used electively, the patient is usually sedated or lightly anesthetized for the procedure. Defibrillation differs in that the shock is not synchronized. It is used to treat ventricular fibrillation (a completely chaotic rhythm) and ventricular tachycardia when the patient is pulseless. Often, a higher level of electricity is required for defibrillation than for synchronized cardioversion. With defibrillation, most patients have lost consciousness. Because of this, sedation is not required. Defibrillation or cardioversion may also be accomplished by an implantable cardioverter-defibrillator (ICD).

Electrical treatment of dysrhythmias also includes cardiac pacing. Temporary pacing may be necessary for reversible causes of bradycardia. A permanent pacemaker may be inserted in situations in which the patient is not expected to recover from the bradycardia.

KEY CONCEPT
Defibrillation and synchronized cardioversion act to depolarize all the cardiac cells, thereby allowing the SA node to resume its normal role as the heart's pacemaker.

Medications

Many different medications can be used to treat dysrhythmias.

For slow heart rates, a drug that blocks the effects of the parasympathetic nervous system, such as atropine, may be initially used. These drugs are called **anticholinergic** or **parasympatholytic drugs.** The drug's action allows the heart to resume its inherent rate or sympathetic activity to increase the heart rate. The bradycardic patient may also be treated by directly stimulating the sympathetic nervous system through the use of drugs that have **sympathomimetic** properties, such as epinephrine or dopamine.

Alternatively, medications referred to as *antidysrhythmics* can be used to suppress tachydysrhythmias and ventricular fibrillation. There are many classes of antidysrhythmic medications with different mechanisms of action and many different individual drugs within these classes.

The five main classes of antidysrhythmic agents are Class I through Class V. They are described as follows.

- **Class I** reduce the influx of Na+ ions into the cells during phase 0 of the action potential, minimizing the chance of Na+ reaching its threshold potential and causing depolarization.
- **Class II** block the sympathetic nervous system. Most agents in this class are beta blockers. They depress SA node automaticity and produce increased AV nodal refractoriness (making it resistant to stimulation).
- **Class III** block the efflux of K+ during phase 3 of the action potential and prolong repolarization and the refractory period.

- **Class IV** inhibit the movement of Ca++ ions during phase 2 of the action potential, prolonging conductivity and increasing the refractory period at the AV node.
- **Class V** work by other or unknown mechanisms.

Although drug therapy is used to prevent dysrhythmias, nearly every antidysrhythmic drug has the potential to act as a proarrhythmic (in other words it promotes dysrhythmias), so each must be selected and used carefully.

A number of other drugs can have a role in managing cardiac dysrhythmias. Several groups of drugs slow conduction through the heart, without actually preventing the dysrhythmia. These drugs are used to control the rate of a tachycardia and make it tolerable for the patient.

Some dysrhythmias promote blood clotting within the heart and increased risk of embolus and stroke. Anticoagulant medications and antiplatelet drugs can reduce the risk of clotting.

The treatments used for specific dysrhythmias are listed in the next five chapters.

Key Points

- Each heartbeat arises as an electrical impulse from the SA node and spreads across the atria, depolarizing the tissue, causing both atria to contract. The impulse then activates the AV node where it is delayed slightly. The impulse then spreads through both ventricles via the Bundle of His, right and left bundle branches, and the Purkinje fibers, causing a synchronized contraction of the primary pumping chambers of the heart.
- Through the property of automaticity, the heart's pacemaker cells spontaneously depolarize. Because the SA node reaches it action potential more quickly than the other pacemaker cells, it is the heart's primary pacemaker.
- In the polarized state, the myocytes have a resting membrane potential of −90 mV. In nonpacemaker myocytes, this membrane potential remains stable (the same) until the cell is stimulated.
- The temporary change in electrical potential that occurs between the inside and the outside of a nerve or muscle fiber when a nerve impulse is transmitted is called the *action potential*.
- The action potential of the myocytes consists of five phases labeled 0 to 4.

- One of the things we look for during examination of the ECG is the presence of dysrhythmias.

- A dysrhythmia is an ECG rhythm that differs from normal sinus rhythm. The heartbeat may be slower or faster than normal, it may irregular, or conduction through the heart may be delayed or blocked.

- Some dysrhythmias are of little consequence and simply annoying while others are life-threatening medical emergencies that can lead to cardiac arrest and sudden death.

- The most common symptom of dysrhythmias is palpitations, an abnormal sensation felt with the heartbeat.

- Symptoms such as lightheadedness, dizziness, fainting, chest pain, shortness of breath, sweatiness, and/or pallor may be seen in dysrhythmias that cause decreased cardiac output. We refer to this as being *symptomatic*.

- Sometimes the first clinical manifestation of a cardiac dysrhythmia is sudden death.

- Types of dysrhythmias include bradycardia, tachycardia, early (premature) beats, dropped beats, or QRS complexes and irregular rhythms.

- Causes and mechanisms of dysrhythmias include increased parasympathetic tone, myocardial hypoxia, injury and infarction, increased automaticity, reentry, triggered beats, and proarrhythmia.

- Dysrhythmias can originate from the SA node, atria, AV junction, or ventricles and can occur due to AV heart block.

- Typically, dysrhythmias can be identified through the use of one lead, most commonly lead II. This lead has an excellent view of the normal conduction of the impulse through the heart. Another lead commonly used to detect dysrhythmias is the MCL1. The lead is effective for monitoring the QRS complexes of dysrhythmias, P wave changes, AV bundle-branch defects, and premature ventricular beats. It is helpful in differentiating between the different types of tachycardia (supraventricular versus ventricular).

- Examination of the ECG rhythm on the ECG monitor must be done in a systematic, organized way.

- Many dysrhythmias require no treatment as they are either benign or resolve on their own.

- The method used to manage dysrhythmias depends on whether or not the patient is stable or unstable. Patients who are symptomatic are considered unstable because symptoms indicate decreased cardiac output.

- Several treatment options are available to treat dysrhythmias and are employed on the basis of the mechanism or etiology of the dysrhythmia. Commonly used treatments include physical maneuvers, electricity therapy, and the administration of certain medications.

Assess Your Understanding

The following questions give you a chance to assess your understanding of the material discussed in this chapter. The answers can be found in Appendix A.

1. Which of the following describes the generation and conduction of the normal heartbeat?
   a. The impulse that generates the heartbeat originates from the AV junction.
   b. Impulse conduction is delayed as it passes through the AV node.
   c. Impulses spread through both ventricles by way of accessory pathways.
   d. The impulse that generates the heartbeat progresses through the heart from the ventricles to the atria.

2. SA node depolarization includes
   a. a resting membrane potential that begins at around −55 to −60 mV and becomes less negatively charged until it results in a gradual depolarization called the *pacemaker potential*.
   b. the gradual depolarization of the SA node that occurs because of a slow inflow of Ca++ into the cell without a corresponding outflow of K+.
   c. the pacemaker potential reaching a threshold of −0 mV and voltage-gated Ca++ channels opening and Ca++ flowing into the cells from the extracellular fluid.
   d. the action potential peaking slightly above 40 mV and the voltage-gated K+ channels opening and K+ ions entering the cell.

3. During normal heart activity, the _____ is the primary pacemaker.
   a. bundle of His
   b. SA node
   c. AV node
   d. AV junction

4. Depolarization of nonpacemaker myocytes
   a. occurs spontaneously.
   b. takes over four phases.
   c. occurs during Phase 0.
   d. results from the rapid influx of Ca++ through the fast Ca++ channels.

5. The most common symptom of cardiac dysrhythmias is/are
   a. low blood pressure.
   b. lightheadedness.
   c. shortness of breath.
   d. palpitations.

6. If the patient has a slow heart rate that is producing a low blood pressure, we would describe it as
   a. sinus bradycardia.
   b. symptomatic bradycardia.
   c. bradycardia with low blood pressure.
   d. vagal response.

7. Match the following types of dysrhythmias with the corresponding characteristics.

	Types		Characteristics
a.	Bradycardia	_____	A heart rate greater than 100 beats per minute.
b.	Tachycardia	_____	Impulses that appear early.
c.	Premature complexes	_____	Occur when the SA node fails to initiate an impulse or from a partial or intermittent block at the AV node.
d.	Dropped beats or QRS complexes	_____	A heart rate less than 60 beats per minute.

8. Increased parasympathetic tone causes increased automaticity.
   a. True
   b. False

9. Match the following types of causes or mechanisms with the corresponding characteristics.

	Types		Characteristics
a.	Increased automaticity	_____	A new or more frequent occurrence of preexisting dysrhythmias that are brought about by antidysrhythmic therapy.
b.	Reentry	_____	Occurs with problems at the level of the ion channels in individual heart cells and leads to partial repolarization which can cause repetitive ectopic firing.
c.	Triggered beats	_____	Spontaneous depolarization of the myocytes that occurs more quickly than normal.
d.	Proarrhythmia	_____	Occurs when an electrical impulse goes back into a conduction pathway rather than moving from one end of the heart to the other and then terminating.

10. Dysrhythmias that arise from the atria include
    a. junctional escape.
    b. atrial fibrillation.
    c. sinus arrest.
    d. idioventricular rhythm.

11. AV heart blocks include
    a. 3rd degree AV block.
    b. asystole.
    c. wandering atrial pacemaker.
    d. sinoatrial exit block.

12. The preferred lead for identifying cardiac dysrhythmias is lead
    a. I.
    b. II.
    c. MCL6.
    d. V_3.

13. Physical maneuvers
    a. act to stimulate the sympathetic nervous system.
    b. increase the speed impulses travel through the AV node.
    c. are used to treat AV heart block.
    d. slow the rate at which the SA node fires.

14. Synchronized cardioversion is used to treat
    a. bradycardia.
    b. symptomatic tachydysrhythmias.
    c. ventricular fibrillation.
    d. AV heart block.

15. Drugs that block the effects of the parasympathetic nervous system are used to treat
    a. bradycardia.
    b. rapid heart rates.
    c. ventricular fibrillation.
    d. premature beats.

16. Match the following antidysrhythmic medications with their actions.

Medications	Characteristics
a. Class I	_____ Block the efflux of K+ during Phase 3 of the action potential and prolong repolarization and the refractory period.
b. Class II	_____ Inhibit the movement of Ca++ ions during Phase 2 of the action potential, prolonging conductivity and increasing the refractory period at the AV node.
c. Class III	_____ Block the sympathetic nervous system. Most agents in this class are beta blockers. They depress SA node automaticity and produce increased AV nodal refractoriness (making it resistant to stimulation).
d. Class IV	_____ Reduce the influx of Na+ ions into the cells during phase 0 of the action potential, which minimizes the chance of Na+ reaching its threshold potential and causing depolarization.

Referring to the scenario at the beginning of this chapter, answer the following questions.

17. What type of dysrhythmia did the patient first experience?
    a. Bradycardia
    b. Frequent premature beats
    c. Tachycardia
    d. Fibrillation

18. During the dysrhythmia the patient was
    a. symptomatic.
    b. asymptomatic.
    c. in cardiac arrest.
    d. a and c.

19. Which of the following was the likely cause of this dysrhythmia?
    a. Decreased automaticity
    b. Reentry
    c. Fibrillation
    d. Increased parasympathetic tone

Answers to Sidebar Questions

1. The SA node is the heart's normal pacemaker. It has an inherent rate of 60 to 100 beats per minute. **p. 222**

2. The cell can respond to an electrical stimulus during the relative refractory period (during the later part of Phase 3). **p. 228**

What's Online

Go to www.mhhe.com/shadeECG2e to find:

- Presentations on chapter content
- Exercises and chapter quiz
- Fill-in-the-blank exercises and answers

11 Sinus Dysrhythmias

Chapter Outline

Rhythms Originating from the Sinus Node

Sinus Bradycardia

Sinus Tachycardia

Sinus Dysrhythmia

Sinus Arrest

Sinoatrial Exit Block

Sick Sinus Syndrome

Sinus Rhythm as the Underlying Rhythm

Learning Objectives

LO 11.1   Describe the origin of sinus dysrhythmias.

LO 11.2   Identify the key features of dysrhythmias originating from the sinus node.

LO 11.3   Identify the appearance of normal sinus rhythm.

LO 11.4   Identify the causes, effects, appearance, and treatment of sinus bradycardia.

LO 11.5   Indentify the causes, effects, appearance, and treatment of sinus tachycardia.

LO 11.6   Identify the causes, effects, appearance, and treatment of sinus dysrhythmia.

LO 11.7   Identify the causes, effects, appearance, and treatment of sinus arrest.

LO 11.8   Identify the causes, effects, appearance, and treatment of sinoatrial exit block.

LO 11.9   Identify the causes, effects, appearance, and treatment of sick sinus syndrome.

LO 11.10 Describe sinus rhythm as the underlying rhythm.

Case History

A 26-year-old woman is visiting her dying grandmother in the nursing home when she begins to cry and hyperventilate. She faints and collapses to the floor. The nursing staff brings the code cart to the woman's side while 911 is summoned. The nursing supervisor feels for a pulse and comments that the woman's heart is beating slowly. The cardiac monitor is applied while vital signs are obtained, revealing a blood pressure of 60/30, pulse of 44, and respiratory rate of 16 and unlabored.

The cardiac monitor shows a slow narrow QRS complex rhythm with a normal P wave before every QRS complex and a QRS complex after every P wave and a normal PR interval. The nurses elevate the woman's legs and place a cool cloth on her forehead.

By the time EMS arrives, the patient is awake and alert. Her pulse is now 68 and her blood pressure normal. She refuses transport to the hospital after disclosing that she has not eaten in 24 hours, which she is certain contributed to her fainting episode.

LO 11.1

QUESTION

1. **What is the rate of the heart's three primary pacemaker sites—the SA node, AV junction, and ventricles?** *Note:* Answers to sidebar questions can be found at the end of the chapter.

KEY CONCEPT

Sinus rhythms originate from the SA node and produce a normal P wave that precedes each QRS complex.

Rhythms Originating from the Sinus Node

In the previous chapters we talked about the anatomy and physiology of the heart and the machines and leads used to obtain an ECG tracing. We also discussed the nine-step process (see Figure 3-2) used to examine the ECG. We will continue to use this process to evaluate the ECGs through the rest of this book. One of the things we look for when we examine the ECG is the presence of dysrhythmias. This chapter focuses on sinus dysrhythmias—the characteristics associated with them (which allow us to identify them), how they occur, their significance, and treatments.

Rhythms originating from the SA node are called sinus rhythms (Figure 11-1). These include

- Normal sinus rhythm
- Sinus bradycardia
- Sinus tachycardia
- Sinus dysrhythmia
- Sinus arrest
- Sinoatrial exit block

A condition, called *sick sinus syndrome,* is a group of abnormal rhythms that occur with malfunction of the sinus node. It will also be discussed in this chapter.

LO 11.2

Appearance of Sinus Rhythms

The key characteristics for sinus rhythms include a normal P wave preceding each normal QRS complex and PR intervals within normal duration of 0.12 to 0.20 seconds and constant. The ST segments and T waves should also be normal. The QT intervals may vary depending on the dysrhythmia. U waves may or may not be present.

In any dysrhythmia where P waves or QRS complexes should be normal, such as with sinus bradycardia, they can instead appear different but yet not change what the dysrhythmia is called. For example, the P waves might be notched or wider than normal due to atrial enlargement, or the QRS complexes might be wide or unusual looking if there is intraventricular conduction defect. This does not change what we categorize the dysrhythmia as; instead, we might

WANT MORE INFORMATION?

Visit the Fast & Easy ECGs Website at www.mhhe.com/ shadeECG2e.

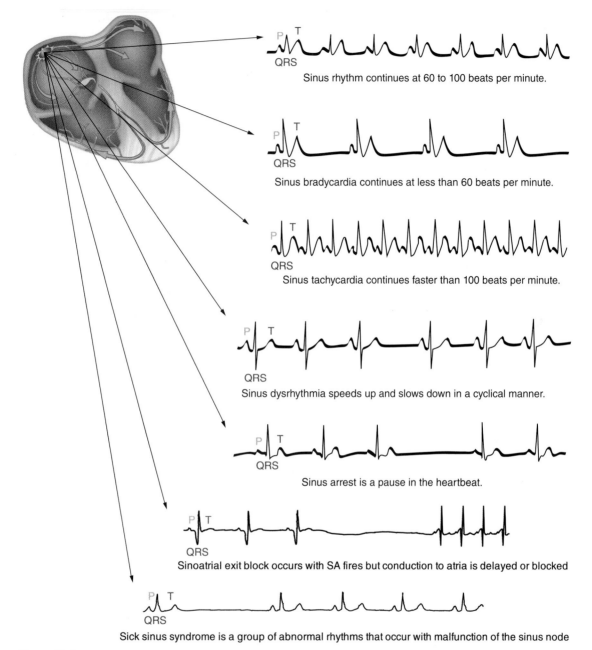

Sinus rhythm continues at 60 to 100 beats per minute.

Sinus bradycardia continues at less than 60 beats per minute.

Sinus tachycardia continues faster than 100 beats per minute.

Sinus dysrhythmia speeds up and slows down in a cyclical manner.

Sinus arrest is a pause in the heartbeat.

Sinoatrial exit block occurs with SA fires but conduction to atria is delayed or blocked

Sick sinus syndrome is a group of abnormal rhythms that occur with malfunction of the sinus node

Figure 11-1
Sinus dysrhythmias originate from the SA node.

refer to it as *sinus bradycardia with wide QRS complexes* (although it would also be correct to call it *sinus bradycardia*).

During normal heart activity, the SA (sinoatrial) node acts as the primary pacemaker. It assumes this role because the rate at which it fires automatically is faster than that of the other pacemakers in the heart. The right coronary artery and the circumflex branch of the left coronary artery supply the SA node with oxygen and nutrients. The vagus nerve and several sympathetic nerves (of the autonomic nervous system) richly innervate the sinus node. Stimulation of the vagus nerve decreases the firing rate of the SA node while stimulation of the sympathetic system increases it.

LO 11.3

> **REMINDER**
>
> Normal sinus rhythm is the rhythm against which we measure dyrhythmias.

> **REMINDER**
>
> Remember, we can use the term supraventricular dysrhythmias to describe dysrhythmias that arise from above the ventricles. This includes dysrhythmias whose origins are the SA node, atria, and AV junction.

Normal Sinus Rhythm

Normal sinus rhythm (NSR) is considered the normal electrical activity of the heart. It is the rhythm with which we compare all other rhythms. Normal sinus rhythm has a heart rate of 60 to 100 beats per minute (in the average adult). It is a regular rhythm with a normal P wave preceding each normal QRS complex. The PR intervals are within the range of 0.12 to 0.20 seconds in duration and are constant (each PR interval is the same). Each normal QRS complex (0.10 seconds or less in duration) is followed by a normal ST segment and T wave (Figure 11-2). The QT interval is within normal limits. U waves may or may not be present.

In some normal sinus rhythms there may be some minor variances, such as a slightly irregular rhythm or an elevated ST segment; you may see these described as regular sinus rhythm or sinus rhythm because they don't fit the textbook description of NSR.

Normal sinus rhythm arises from the SA node. Each impulse travels down through the conduction system in a normal manner.

Figure 11-2
Normal sinus rhythm.

Sinus Bradycardia

LO 11.4

Description

The word part "brady" means slow while "cardia" refers to the heart. Put together, *bradycardia* means slow heart rate. As its name implies, sinus bradycardia is a slower than normal rhythm that arises from the SA node (Figure 11-3). Sinus bradycardia has all the characteristics of normal sinus rhythm, but the heart rate is less than 60 beats per minute (BPM). It looks like a slow NSR. It results from a slowing of the rate at which the heart's pacemaker, the SA node, fires.

Causes

Sinus bradycardia often occurs naturally as the body's way to conserve energy during times of reduced demand for blood flow. In this case, parasympathetic stimulation increases and sympathetic stimulation decreases, resulting in decreased SA node stimulation and the heart rate slowing. This occurs normally during sleep as a result of circadian variations in the heart rate.

KEY CONCEPT
Sinus bradycardia often occurs naturally as a means of conserving energy during times of rest or sleep.

Sinus bradycardia arises from the SA node. Each impulse travels down through the conduction system in a normal manner.

Rate	Rhythm	P waves	QRS complexes	PR intervals
Less than 60 BPM	regular	normal and all look alike, one precedes each QRS complex	of normal duration and all look alike	0.12–0.20 seconds in duration and constant

ST segments	T waves	QT intervals	U waves
normal and isoelectric	normal shape and upright	within normal limits of 0.36 to 0.44 second	may or may not be present

Figure 11-3
Sinus bradycardia.

Sinus bradycardia is considered normal in aerobically conditioned persons or in athletes, whose cardiovascular systems are well-conditioned and whose hearts can maintain a normal stroke volume with less than normal effort. They often have slower heart rates of 40 to 50 beats per minute.

Sinus bradycardia can also occur as a result of various conditions. It is commonly seen in patients who have suffered an inferior-wall MI (this involves the right coronary artery, which supplies blood to the SA node). It is also thought to be one of the body's protective mechanisms in acute myocardial infarction—the heart rate slows to reduce the myocardial oxygen consumption, thereby decreasing the severity of myocardial ischemia and injury (provided that the patient is otherwise well perfused). Sinus bradycardia may also result from a host of other conditions, including noncardiac disorders, conditions involving excessive parasympathetic stimulation or decreased sympathetic stimulation, cardiac diseases, and the use of certain drugs.

Causes of Sinus Bradycardia	
Cause	**Examples**
Cardiac diseases	SA node disease, cardiomyopathy, myocarditis, myocardial ischemia immediately following inferior-wall MI, and heart block
Use of certain drugs	Beta-adrenergic blockers (metoprolol, propranolol), calcium channel blockers (diltiazem, verapamil), antidysrhythmics (amiodarone, propafenone, quinidine, sotalol), lithium, digoxin
Excessive parasympathetic tone or decreased sympathetic stimulation	Carotid sinus massage, Valsalva's maneuver, deep relaxation, sleep, and vomiting
Noncardiac disorders	Hypoxia, hypothermia, hyperkalemia, stroke, increased intracranial pressure, hypothyroidism, and glaucoma

Effects

Often sinus bradycardia is insignificant and the patient is asymptomatic. Typically, most adults are able to tolerate a heart rate of 45 to 59 beats per minute. They are less tolerant of rates less than 45 beats per minute, particularly if they have underlying heart disease that prevents them from compensating for the slow heart rate with an increase in stroke volume or change in vascular resistance.

In some patients the slower rate associated with sinus bradycardia can compromise cardiac output, resulting in hypotension; angina pectoris; cool, clammy skin; crackles; dyspnea; S_3 heart sound (indicating heart failure); and central nervous system symptoms such as lightheadedness, blurred vision, vertigo, and syncope (Stokes-Adams attack). Recall the bradycardic patient in the case history at the beginning of this chapter. She experienced a syncopal episode (she fainted) due to her bradycardia. If a patient is symptomatic (e.g., short of breath, chest pain, dizziness), you should consider the presence of sinus bradycardia to be abnormal and potentially significant. Bradycardia can predispose some patients to more serious dysrhythmias such as ventricular tachycardia and ventricular fibrillation. Also, bradycardia is considered a diagnostic indicator of the seriously ill child because it denotes significant hypoxia and inadequate perfusion.

Appearance

The first thing you will note with sinus bradycardia is the slower than normal heart rate. This causes longer R-R intervals and P-P intervals (making it appear as if there are large spaces between the groups of complexes). The reason for the longer R-R intervals and P-P intervals is because there are fewer R waves and P waves, making the distance between each much greater. Other than that, all the features are essentially the same as what we would expect to see with normal sinus rhythm.

Treatment

Treatment for sinus bradycardia depends on whether or not the patient is symptomatic. Patients who are asymptomatic require no treatment. However, when medical conditions cause the problem, it is essential to observe the heart rhythm for the progression of the bradycardia. Patients who are symptomatic may improve with the administration of atropine (acts to block the effects of parasympathetic nervous system stimulation), IV push, transcutaneous pacing (acts to directly stimulate the heart to beat faster), or the administration of an IV infusion of dopamine or epinephrine (both act to stimulate the sympathetic nervous system).

Sinus Tachycardia

LO 11.5

Description

The opposite of bradycardia is tachycardia. "Tachy" means fast. Tachycardia means a fast heart rate. As its name implies, sinus tachycardia is a faster than normal rhythm that results from an increase in the rate of sinus node discharge (Figure 11-4). It has the same characteristics as normal sinus rhythm but has a rate greater than 100 beats per minute.

It is widely held that the SA node can fire only so fast; generally, it is believed that the upper limit is between 160 and 180 beats per minute. However, each person has a built-in maximum rate so, if in doubt, get a 12-lead ECG to obtain more information.

Causes

We often see sinus tachycardia with physical labor, exercise, pain, fear, excitement, anxiety, and where increased sympathetic stimulation occurs in response to the need for more oxygen and nutrients at the cellular level.

KEY CONCEPT
The most distinguishing characteristic of sinus bradycardia is that it looks like sinus rhythm but instead is slow.

KEY CONCEPT
Sinus bradycardia originates from the SA node and has the same characteristics as normal sinus rhythm except that the rate is slower (less than 60 beats per minute).

Sinus tachycardia arises from the SA node. Each impulse travels down through the conduction system in a normal manner.

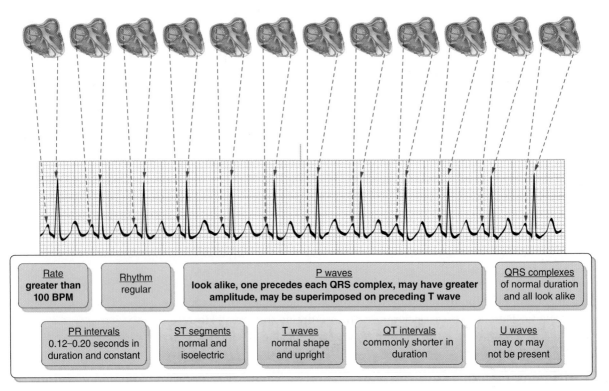

Rate greater than 100 BPM	Rhythm regular	P waves look alike, one precedes each QRS complex, may have greater amplitude, may be superimposed on preceding T wave	QRS complexes of normal duration and all look alike

PR intervals 0.12–0.20 seconds in duration and constant	ST segments normal and isoelectric	T waves normal shape and upright	QT intervals commonly shorter in duration	U waves may or may not be present

Figure 11-4
Sinus tachycardia.

KEY CONCEPT

Sinus tachycardia often occurs naturally as a means of increasing delivery of oxygen and nutrients and removing waste products during times of exertion, exercise, or stress.

QUESTION

2. Sinus tachycardia is produced by stimulation of which branch of the autonomic nervous system?

We also see it with the ingestion of caffeine or alcohol, smoking, or fever, or where there is some type of underlying illness such as hypovolemia, respiratory distress, hyperthyroidism, or anemia. When the stimulus for the tachycardia is removed, the dysrhythmia spontaneously resolves.

Causes of Sinus Tachycardia	
Cause	**Examples**
Cardiac diseases	Congestive heart failure, cardiogenic shock, and pericarditis
Use of certain drugs	Administration of pharmacologic agents that dramatically increase sinus rate, such as sympathomimetic drugs (epinephrine, isoproterenol, dopamine, dobutamine), parasympatholytic drugs (atropine), or other stimulants and amphetamines
Increased sympathetic stimulation	Strenuous exercise, pain, stress, fever, fear, anxiety, hypermetabolism, or as a compensatory mechanism in shock
Other causes	Respiratory distress, hypoxia, pulmonary embolism, anemia, sepsis, hyperthyroidism, alcohol, caffeine, and nicotine

Effects

Although sinus tachycardia may be of no clinical significance, it can reflect an underlying cause that needs to be identified, evaluated, and treated. A significant problem associated with sinus tachycardia is that it increases myocardial oxygen consumption, which can aggravate ischemia (bringing on chest pain) and lead to infarction. It can also predispose the patient to more serious rhythm disturbances, particularly in persons with coronary artery disease (CAD) or obstructive types of heart conditions such as aortic stenosis and hypertrophic cardiomyopathy.

Appearance

The most obvious characteristic you will see with sinus tachycardia is a faster than normal rate. This causes shorter R-R intervals and P-P intervals (making it appear as if there are smaller spaces between the groups of complexes). With the faster rates, the P wave may be **superimposed** on the T wave of the preceding beat, making it harder to identify, and the QT interval is commonly shorter than with normal sinus rhythm. Also, with sinus tachycardia, the P waves may increase in amplitude.

Treatment

No treatment is indicated if the patient is asymptomatic. However, the patient should be encouraged to abstain from triggers such as alcohol, caffeine, and nicotine. Treatment for symptomatic sinus tachycardia is directed at treating the cause. In the presence of an underlying medical or traumatic condition, continued monitoring is indicated.

For patients experiencing myocardial ischemia, consideration may be given to the use of beta-adrenergic blockers (propranolol, atenolol), calcium channel blockers (verapamil, diltiazem) to slow the heart rate, or nitrates to vasodilate the coronary vessels.

> **KEY CONCEPT**
> Sinus tachycardia arises from the SA node and has basically the same characteristics as normal sinus rhythm except that the rate is faster (greater than 100 but rarely more than 160 beats per minute).

Sinus Dysrhythmia

LO 11.6

Description

With the exception of a patterned irregularity, sinus dysrhythmia is characteristically the same as sinus rhythm (normal P waves, QRS complexes, and T waves) (Figure 11-5). It can be described as a repeating cycle of "slowing, then speeding up, then slowing of the heart rate again." The beat-to-beat variation produced by the irregular firing of the pacemaker cells of the SA node corresponds with the respiratory cycle and changes in intrathoracic pressure. The heart rate increases during inspiration (decreased parasympathetic stimulation, increased venous return) and decreases during expiration (increased parasympathetic stimulation, decreased venous return).

There is also evidence to show that sinus dysrhythmia may play an active physiologic role. At the peak of inspiration, the greatest amount of oxygen is present in the alveolar/capillary membrane, so the heart rate speeds up to

Sinus dysrhythmia arises from the SA node. Each impulse travels down through the conduction system in a normal manner.

Rate	Rhythm	P waves	QRS complexes
60 to 100 beats per minute	**Regularly irregular, seems to speed up and then slow in a cyclical fashion**	normal and all look alike, one precedes each QRS complex	of normal duration and all look alike

PR intervals	ST segments	T waves	QT intervals	U waves
0.12–0.20 seconds in duration and constant	normal and isoelectric	normal shape and upright	within normal limits of 0.36 to 0.44 second	may or may not be present

Figure 11-5
Sinus dysrhythmia.

maximize the perfusion to this area. During exhalation, the heart rate drops, thus saving energy expenditure by suppressing unnecessary heartbeats.

Causes

Sinus dysrhythmia can occur naturally in athletes, children, and older adults but is uncommon in infants. It can also occur in patients with heart disease or inferior wall MI, advanced age, or multiple sclerosis; in those receiving certain drugs such as digitalis and morphine; and in conditions where there is increased intracranial pressure. It is usually of no clinical significance and produces no symptoms. However, in some patients and conditions, it may be associated with palpitations, dizziness, and syncope. A marked variation in P-P intervals in the elderly may indicate sick sinus syndrome (a condition we discuss later).

Causes of Sinus Dysrhythmia	
Cause	**Examples**
Cardiac diseases	Inferior-wall MI
Use of certain drugs	Digoxin, morphine, sedatives
Autonomic nervous system stimulation	Inhibition of reflex parasympathetic activity (tone)
Other causes	Increased intracranial pressure, multiple sclerosis

Appearance

As you assess this dysrhythmia, the most distinguishing characteristic is the patterned irregular rhythm. When the rate speeds up, the complexes are closer together; this shortens the P-P and R-R intervals. When the rate slows down, the complexes are farther away, lengthening the P-P and R-R intervals. The other features are essentially the same as normal sinus rhythm, particularly the round normal P wave preceding each QRS complex. The QRS complexes should be normal. The QT interval may vary slightly.

Treatment

Usually, there is no treatment for sinus dysrhythmia provided that the patient is asymptomatic. If unrelated to respirations, consideration may be given to treating the underlying cause.

The next two dysrhythmias we discuss result from either the SA node transiently failing to generate an impulse or an impulse generated by the SA node being delayed or blocked during its conduction through the atria. This produces a pause in the cycle of electrical activity. Remember, sinus node activity is not recorded on the surface ECG. For this reason it is difficult to determine if sinus node automaticity or sinoatrial conduction abnormalities are responsible for the sudden disappearance of sinus P waves for variable intervals. We discuss both types of conditions below.

QUESTION
3. **What method of calculating the heart rate should be used in sinus dysrhythmia?**

KEY CONCEPT
The most distinguishing characteristic of sinus dysrhythmia is that it looks like sinus rhythm but has an irregular rhythm that has a cyclical pattern of speeding up and slowing down and speeding up again.

Sinus Arrest

LO 11.7

Description

Sinus arrest is an abnormality in automaticity. It occurs when the SA node transiently stops firing (Figure 11-6), causing a short period of cardiac standstill until a lower-level pacemaker discharges, creating an escape beat, or the sinus node resumes its normal function. The usual effect of sinus arrest is a brief pause in all electrical activity and cardiac output. The next impulse occurs randomly and not necessarily when the next cardiac cycle would be expected.

This dysrhythmia is referred to as **sinus pause** when one or two beats are not formed and sinus arrest when three or more beats are not formed.

Causes

Sinus arrest is an uncommon rhythm disturbance. It results from a marked depression in SA node automaticity. It is occasionally seen in elderly patients. Causes include an increase in parasympathetic tone on the SA node, hypoxia or ischemia, digitalis or beta-adrenergic blocker toxicity, hyperkalemia, degenerative fibrotic disease, or damage to the SA node such as with MI (particularly with acute inferior or true posterior MI).

Sinus arrest occurs when the SA node fails to initiate an impulse.

SA node fails to
initiate impulse

Rate	Rhythm	P waves	PR intervals	QRS complexes
60 to 100 beats per minute	**Irregular where there is a pause**	normal and all look alike, one precedes each QRS complex*	0.12–0.20 seconds in duration and constant	of normal duration and all look alike*

ST segments	T waves	QT intervals	U waves	
normal and isoelectric*	normal shape and upright*	within normal limits of 0.36 to 0.44 second	may or may not be present	* but absent when there is a pause in rhythm

Figure 11-6
Sinus arrest.

Causes of Sinus Arrest

Cause	Examples
Cardiac diseases	Inferior-wall MI, acute myocarditis, coronary artery disease (CAD), cardiomyopathy, fibrosis, hypertensive heart disease, sinus node disease, sick sinus syndrome
Use of certain drugs	Amiodarone, beta-adrenergic blockers (bisoprolol, metapronol, propranolol), calcium channel blockers (verapamil, diltiazem), digoxin, procainamide, quinidine, salicylates (particularly in toxic doses)
Autonomic nervous system stimulation	Increased parasympathetic tone, carotid sinus sensitivity
Other causes	Acute infection, hyperkalemia, hypoxia

Effects

Sinus arrest becomes clinically significant when there is an extended pause or when there are frequent occurrences of the pause or arrest. This can lead to decreased heart rate and elimination of the atrial contribution to ventricular filling, resulting in a drop in cardiac output and decreased blood pressure and tissue perfusion. There is also a danger that SA node activity will completely cease and an escape pacemaker may not take over pacing (resulting in asystole).

Appearance

The ECG tracing looks like normal sinus rhythm except that there is a pause in the rhythm resulting in an absence of the P, QRS, and T waveforms. This produces an occasional irregularity in the rhythm that is isolated to the event of automaticity failure in the SA node. The rhythm typically resumes its normal appearance after this transient pause unless an escape pacemaker resumes the rhythm.

Depending on how frequently it occurs and how long the sinus arrest lasts, the rate may be normal to slow (less than 60 beats per minute). Again, because the rhythm arises from the SA node, the P waves are normal and each is followed by a QRS complex.

Treatment

If the patient is asymptomatic, no treatment is indicated. If the patient is symptomatic, treatment includes administration of atropine or temporary or permanent ventricular pacing. Reasons to pace sinus arrest include the development of an AV junctional or ectopic ventricular pacemaker that is slow enough to result in such problems as syncope, CHF, angina, or frequent ventricular ectopic beats. As needed, drugs affecting SA node discharge or conduction, such as beta-adrenergic blockers, calcium channel blockers, and digoxin, should be discontinued.

> **KEY CONCEPT**
> Sinus arrest arises from the SA node. It occurs when the SA node transiently stops firing. The SA node then begins to fire again after a brief pause, or a pacemaker lower in the conduction system fires to reinitiate the heartbeat.

Sinoatrial Exit Block

LO 11.8

Description

Sinoatrial exit block occurs when the SA node fires but conduction to the atria is delayed or blocked (Figure 11-7). The mechanism of such blocking is not fully understood. While there are four types of sinoatrial block, only two can be identified by the surface ECG.

Figure 11-7
Example of sinoatrial exit block.

Causes

Sinoatrial exit block results from a block in the conduction of the impulse from SA node to the atria. It is very uncommon. Causes include an increase in parasympathetic tone on the SA node, hypoxia or ischemia, excessive administration of digitalis or propranolol (Inderal), hyperkalemia, and damage to the SA node (such as myocardial infarction [MI] or degenerative fibrotic disease).

Causes of Sinoatrial Exit Block	
Cause	**Examples**
Cardiac diseases	Acute inferior-wall MI, acute myocarditis, CAD, cardiomyopathy, fibrosis, hypertensive heart disease, sinus node disease, sick sinus syndrome
Use of certain drugs	Amiodarone, beta-adrenergic blockers (bisoprolol, metapronol propranolol), calcium channel blockers (verapamil, diltiazem), digoxin, procainamide, quinidine, salicylates (particularly in toxic doses)
Autonomic nervous system stimulation	Increased parasympathetic tone, carotid sinus sensitivity
Other causes	Acute infection, hyperkalemia, hypoxia

Effects

Sinoatrial exit block is usually insignificant. It can become clinically significant when there is an extended pause or when there are frequent occurrences of the dropped P waves (and subsequent QRS complexes). This can lead to decreased heart rate, a drop in cardiac output, and decreased blood pressure and tissue perfusion.

Appearance

KEY CONCEPT

The most prominent characteristic of sinoatrial exit block is a pause in the ECG rhythm.

With one form of SA block, the P-P cycle may progressively shorten until there is a pause. The pause is due to the dropped P wave and measures less than twice the P-P cycle. The cycle is repeated.

Alternatively, in another form of sinoatrial exit block, there is a pause resulting from the absence of a P wave (and associated QRS complex), but then the P wave (and associated QRS complex) reoccurs at the next expected interval. In other words, the cycle of the dropped P wave is exactly equal to two of the basic sinus cycles. If more two or more consecutive sinus impulses are blocked, it creates a considerable pause. However, the P-P intervals have a pattern and are a multiple of the basic sinus cycle.

As a point of information, blocked atrial premature beats (discussed in the next chapter) sometimes mimic sinoatrial exit block.

Depending on how frequently it occurs and how long the sinoatrial exit block lasts, the rate may be normal to slow (less than 60 beats per minute). Again, because the rhythm arises from the SA node, the P waves are normal, and each is followed by a QRS complex.

Treatment

No treatment is indicated provided that the patient is asymptomatic. If the patient is symptomatic, treatment includes administration of atropine or temporary or permanent ventricular pacing. As needed, drugs affecting SA node discharge or conduction, such as beta-adrenergic blockers, calcium channel blockers, and digoxin, should be discontinued.

Sick Sinus Syndrome

LO 11.9

Description

Sick sinus syndrome, also referred to as *sinus node dysfunction,* is a group of abnormal rhythms that occur with malfunction of the sinus node. Bradycardia-tachycardia syndrome is a variant of sick sinus syndrome in which slow dysrhythmias and fast dysrhythmias alternate.

Causes

Sick sinus syndrome is a moderately uncommon disorder. It can result in many abnormal rhythms, including sinus arrest, sinus node exit block, sinus bradycardia, and other types of bradycardia. It can also be associated with tachycardias such as paroxysmal supraventricular tachycardia (PSVT) and atrial fibrillation (which are discussed in the next chapter). Tachycardias that occur with sick sinus syndrome are characterized by a long pause after the tachycardia.

These abnormal rhythms are often caused or worsened by medications such as digitalis, calcium channel blockers, beta-adrenergic blockers, sympatholytic medications, and antidysrhythmic agents. Sick sinus syndrome can also be caused by disorders that produce conduction system scarring, degeneration, or damage. It is more common in elderly adults, in whom the cause is often a nonspecific, scar-like degeneration of the heart's conduction system. In children, cardiac surgery (particularly to the atria) is a common cause of sick sinus syndrome. Coronary artery disease, high blood pressure, and aortic and mitral valve diseases may be associated with sick sinus syndrome, although this association may only be incidental.

Causes of Sick Sinus Syndrome	
Cause	**Examples**
Cardiac diseases	CAD, high blood pressure, and aortic and mitral valve diseases
Scarring of conduction system	Cardiomyopathy, sarcoidosis, and amyloidosis
Use of certain drugs	Digitalis, beta-adrenergic blockers, calcium channel blockers, sympatholytic medications, and antidysrhythmic agents
Others	Cardiac surgery in children

Effects

Although many types of sick sinus syndrome are symptom free, patients may present with Stokes-Adams attacks, fainting, dizziness or lightheadedness, palpitations, chest pain, shortness of breath, fatigue, headache, and nausea.

Appearance

The ECG may show a variety of dysrhythmias, including inappropriate sinus bradycardia, sinus arrest, and sinoatrial exit block, as well as several that are discussed in upcoming chapters, including atrial fibrillation with slow ventricular response, a prolonged period of asystole after a period of tachycardias, atrial flutter, and atrial tachycardia (Figure 11-8).

Figure 11-8
Examples of sick sinus syndrome.

Treatment

Bradydysrhythmias are well controlled with pacemakers whereas tachy-dysrhythmias respond well to medications. However, because both bradydysrhythmias and tachydysrhythmias may be present, drugs to control the rapid heart rates may worsen bradydysrhythmia. For this reason, a pacemaker is implanted before drug therapy is begun for the tachydysrhythmia.

Sinus Rhythm as the Underlying Rhythm

LO 11.10

Sinus rhythm may be what is referred to as an *underlying rhythm*. What that means is the sinus rhythm is seen, but then there is another dysrhythmia or cardiac condition seen as well. For example, if there is a delay in conduction through the AV node (referred to as fir*st degree AV block,* in chapter 15) then we call it *sinus rhythm with first degree AV block* (Figure 11-9A). Similarly, if there are early beats, we call it *sinus rhythm with early beats* (Figure 11-9B). We will cover this in more depth in subsequent chapters.

A.

B.

Figure 11-9
Examples of sinus rhythm as an underlying rhythm.

Practice Makes Perfect

For each of the 57 ECG tracings on the following pages, practice the Nine-Step Process for analyzing ECGs. To achieve the greatest learning, you should practice assessing and interpreting the ECGs immediately after reading this chapter. Below are questions you should consider as you access each tracing. Your answers can be written into the area below each ECG marked "ECG Findings." Your findings can then be compared to the answers provided in Appendix A. All tracings are six seconds in length.

1. Determine the heart rate. Is it slow? Normal? Fast? What is the ventricular rate? What is the atrial rate?

2. Determine if the rhythm is regular or irregular. If it is irregular, what type of irregularity is it? Occasional or frequent? Slight? Sudden acceleration or slowing in heart rate? Total? Patterned? Does it have a variable conduction ratio?

3. Determine if P waves are present. If so, how do they appear? Do they have normal height and duration? Are they tall? Notched? Wide? Biphasic? Of differing morphology? Inverted? One for each QRS complex? More than one preceding some or all the QRS complexes? Do they have a sawtooth appearance? Is there an indiscernible chaotic baseline?

4. Determine if QRS complexes are present. If so, how do they appear? Narrow with proper amplitude? Tall? Low amplitude? Delta wave? Notched? Wide? Bizarre-looking? With chaotic waveforms?

5. Determine the presence of PR intervals. If present, how do they appear? Constant? Of normal duration? Shortened? Lengthened? Progressively longer? Varying?

6. Evaluate the ST segments. Do they have normal duration and position? Are they elevated? (If so, are they flat, concave, convex, arched?) Depressed? (If so, are they normal, flat, downsloping or upsloping?)

7. Determine if T waves are present. If so, how do they appear? Of normal height and duration? Tall? Wide? Notched? Inverted?

8. Determine the presence of QT intervals. If present, what is their duration? Normal? Shortened? Prolonged?

9. Determine if U waves are present. If present, how do they appear? Of normal height and duration? Inverted?

10. Identify the rhythm or dysrhythmia.

1.

ECG Findings:

2.

ECG Findings:

3.

ECG Findings:

4.

ECG Findings:

5.

ECG Findings:

6.

ECG Findings:

7.

ECG Findings:

8.

ECG Findings:

9.

ECG Findings:

10.

ECG Findings:

11.

ECG Findings:

12.

ECG Findings:

13.

ECG Findings:

14.

ECG Findings:

15.

ECG Findings:

16.

ECG Findings:

17.

ECG Findings:

18.

ECG Findings:

19.

ECG Findings:

20.

ECG Findings:

21.

ECG Findings:

22.

ECG Findings:

23.

ECG Findings:

24.

ECG Findings:

25.

ECG Findings:

26.

ECG Findings:

27.

ECG Findings:

28.

ECG Findings:

29.

ECG Findings:

30.

ECG Findings:

31.

ECG Findings:

32.

ECG Findings:

33.

ECG Findings:

34.

ECG Findings:

35.

ECG Findings:

36.

ECG Findings:

37.

ECG Findings:

38.

ECG Findings:

39.

ECG Findings:

40.

ECG Findings:

41.

ECG Findings:

42.

ECG Findings:

43.

ECG Findings:

44.

ECG Findings:

45.

ECG Findings:

46.

ECG Findings:

47.

ECG Findings:

48.

ECG Findings:

49.

ECG Findings:

50.

ECG Findings:

51.

ECG Findings:

52.

ECG Findings:

53.

ECG Findings:

54.

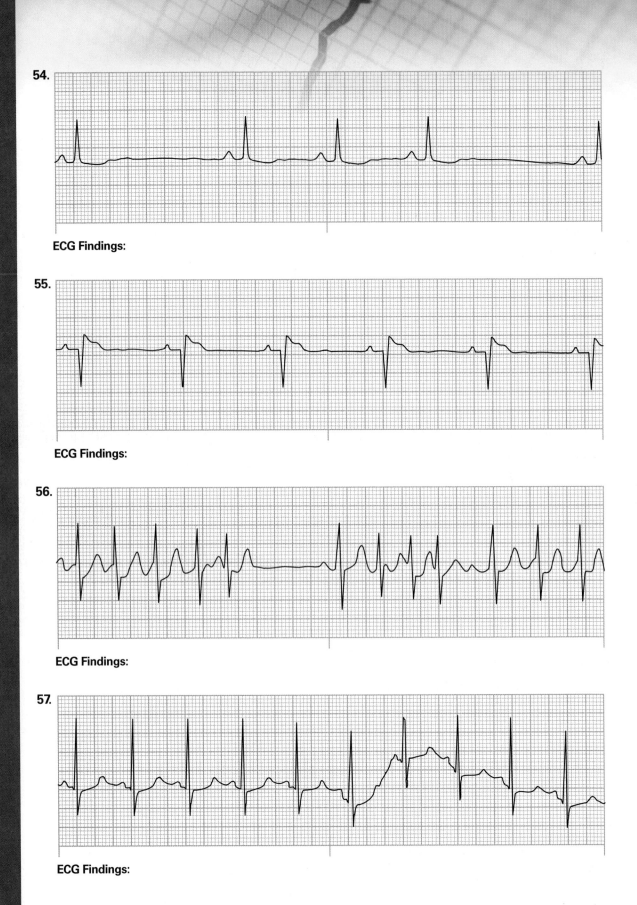

ECG Findings:

55.

ECG Findings:

56.

ECG Findings:

57.

ECG Findings:

Key Points 🔍

- One of the things we look for during examination of the ECG is the presence of dysrhythmias.

- A dysrhythmia is an ECG rhythm that differs from normal sinus rhythm.

- Examination of the ECG rhythm on the ECG monitor must be done in a systematic, organized way.

- Rhythms originating from the SA node are called sinus rhythms.

- Key characteristics for sinus rhythms include a normal P wave preceding each normal QRS complex and PR intervals within normal duration of 0.12 to 0.20 seconds and constant.

- During normal heart activity, the SA (sinoatrial) node acts as the primary pacemaker.

- Normal sinus rhythm has a heart rate of 60 to 100 beats per minute.

- Sinus bradycardia has all the characteristics of normal sinus rhythm but the heart rate is less than 60 beats per minute (BPM). It often occurs naturally as a means of conserving energy during times of rest or sleep.

- Sinus tachycardia has the same characteristics as normal sinus rhythm but has a rate of greater than 100 beats per minute. It often occurs naturally as a means of increasing delivery of oxygen and nutrients and removing waste products during times of exertion, exercise, or stress.

- Sinus dysrhythmia is the same as sinus rhythm except that there is the presence of a patterned irregularity. It can be described as "slowing, then speeding up, then slowing again." This cycle continually repeats.

- With sinus arrest, the ECG rhythm looks like normal sinus rhythm except that there is a pause in the rhythm with an absence of the P, QRS, and T waveforms until a pacemaker site reinitiates the rhythm.

- With sinoatrial exit block, the ECG rhythm looks like normal sinus rhythm except that there is a pause in the rhythm with an absence of the P, QRS, and T waveforms. Then the P wave (and associated QRS complex) reoccurs at the next expected interval.

- Sick sinus syndrome, also referred to as *sinus node dysfunction,* is a group of abnormal rhythms that occur with malfunction of the sinus node.

- Sinus rhythms may be what are referred to as *an underlying rhythm.* What that means is that the sinus rhythm is seen but then another dysrhythmia or cardiac condition is seen as well.

Assess Your Understanding

The following questions give you a chance to assess your understanding of the material discussed in this chapter. The answers can be found in Appendix A.

1. Which of the following is a dysrhythmia that arises from the SA node?
    a. Wandering atrial pacemaker
    b. Sinus arrest
    c. Junctional escape
    d. Ventricular tachycardia

2. Key characteristics of sinus rhythms are
    a. upright and wide QRS complexes.
    b. normal P waves.
    c. PR intervals within normal duration of 0.12 to 0.20 seconds and varying with each beat.
    d. Both b and c.

3. During normal heart activity, the _____ is the primary pacemaker.
    a. bundle of His
    b. SA node
    c. AV node
    d. AV junction

4. Characteristics of normal sinus rhythm include
    a. an irregular rhythm.
    b. a rate of between 60 and 100 beats per minute.
    c. an inverted P wave that follows each QRS complex.
    d. progressively longer PR intervals.

5. The heart rate characteristic of sinus bradycardia is _____ than _____ beats per minute.
    a. less, 80
    b. greater, 100
    c. less, 60
    d. less, 40

6. Sinus bradycardia
    a. often occurs naturally.
    b. is considered abnormal in athletes.
    c. is often seen in Wolff-Parkinson-White syndrome.
    d. is caused by increased sympathetic stimulation.

7. Characteristics of sinus bradycardia include
   a. PR intervals that change.
   b. inverted P waves in lead II.
   c. a regular rhythm.
   d. wide, bizarre QRS complexes.

8. Sinus tachycardia
   a. has mostly the same characteristics as normal sinus rhythm except that it has a rate of greater than 120 beats per minute.
   b. is produced by stimulation of the parasympathetic branch of the autonomic nervous system.
   c. may be caused by ingestion of caffeine or alcohol, smoking, or fever.
   d. continues even after the stimulus causing it is removed.

9. In sinus tachycardia, the P waves, PR intervals, and QRS complexes are
   a. widened.
   b. normal.
   c. shortened.
   d. delayed.

10. The type of irregularity seen with sinus dysrhythmia is called _____ irregularity.
    a. patterned
    b. slight
    c. total
    d. frequent

11. Sinus dysrhythmia
    a. is common in infants.
    b. occurs only in patients who have significant heart disease.
    c. usually produces symptoms.
    d. has round and upright P waves in lead II.

12. Which of the following is true of sinus arrest?
    a. It occurs when there is complete blockage of the SA node.
    b. The rhythm is regular.
    c. It has QRS complexes greater than 0.12 seconds.
    d. It usually results in a brief pause in all electrical activity.

13. With sinus arrest, the escape mechanism that follows the pause in electrical activity may arise from the
    a. SA node.
    b. AV junction.
    c. ventricles.
    d. All of the above.

14. Match the following sinus dysrhythmias with the correct description.

Types		Characteristics
a.	Sinus bradycardia	_____ Has a rate of greater than 100 beats per minute
b.	Sinus dysrhythmia	_____ Occurs when the SA node transiently stops firing
c.	Sinus arrest	_____ Is a dysrhythmia with patterned irregularity.
d.	Sinus tachycardia	_____ Has a rate of less than 60 beats per minute

15. Sinoatrial exit block occurs when the
    a. impulse originating in the SA node is blocked from reaching the atria.
    b. heart rate slows to less than 60 beats per minute.
    c. heart rate speeds up and slows down in a cyclical manner.
    d. heartbeat ceases completely.

16. Treatment for symptomatic bradycardia includes
    a. vagal maneuvers.
    b. atropine with a fluid bolus of 250 cc.
    c. temporary or permanent pacing.
    d. defibrillation.

Referring to the scenario at the beginning of this chapter, answer the following questions.

17. What rhythm is the patient in?
    a. Sinus bradycardia
    b. Junctional
    c. 2nd-degree AV heart block
    d. 3rd-degree AV heart block

18. The stimulation of what nerve causes this rhythm?
    a. Phrenic
    b. Vagus
    c. Carotid
    d. Aortic

19. Which physiologic sensor noted the patient's lowered blood pressure?
    a. Baroreceptor
    b. Cerebral cortex
    c. Vagus nerve
    d. Chemoreceptor

Answers to Sidebar Questions

1. The SA node has an inherent rate of 60 to 100 beats per minute while the AV junction has an inherent rate of 40 to 60 beats per minute. The ventricles have an inherent rate of 20 to 40 beats per minute. **p. 254**

2. Stimulation of the sympathetic branch of the autonomic nervous system produces sinus tachycardia. **p. 260**

3. The 6-second interval × 10 method should be used because of the irregularity of the rhythm. **p. 263**

What's Online

Go to www.mhhe.com/shadeECG2e to find:

- Presentations on chapter content
- Crossword puzzle exercises
- Additional ECG tracings for practicing analyzing sinus dysrhythmias
- Chapter quiz
- Flashcards
- Fill-in-the-blank exercises and answers
- In-depth answers to Practice Makes Perfect ECG tracings and Assess Your Understanding questions

12 Atrial Dysrhythmias

Chapter Outline

Rhythms Originating in the Atria

Premature Atrial Complex

Wandering Atrial Pacemaker

Atrial Tachycardia

Multifocal Atrial Tachycardia

Supraventricular Tachycardia

Atrial Flutter

Atrial Fibrillation

Learning Objectives

LO 12.1 Describe the origin of atrial dysrhythmias.

LO 12.2 Identify the key features of dysrhythmias originating from the atria.

LO 12.3 Identify the causes, effects, appearance, and treatment of premature atrial complexes.

LO 12.4 Identify the causes, effects, appearance, and treatment of wandering atrial pacemaker.

LO 12.5 Identify the causes, effects, appearance, and treatment of atrial tachycardia.

LO 12.6 Identify the causes, effects, appearance, and treatment of multifocal atrial tachycardia.

LO 12.7 Define the term *supraventricular tachycardia*.

LO 12.8 Identify the causes, effects, appearance, and treatment of atrial flutter.

LO 12.9 Identify the causes, effects, appearance, and treatment of atrial fibrillation.

Case History

EMS is called to evaluate an elderly man who passed out in church. The man has a history of chronic obstructive pulmonary disease (COPD) and hypertension. Upon their arrival, the EMS team is met by a physician attending services with the patient. He tells them that the gentleman was sitting in the pew when he arose for prayer and then slumped back down and fell over on his side. The doctor then rushed to the man's side and checked for a pulse, which he says was fast and regular but barely palpable. He says that the patient never stopped breathing or became cyanotic and that once he lay flat he returned to his normal self.

The paramedics introduce themselves and begin their assessment. Oxygen is applied and vital signs are taken, showing a blood pressure of 100/90, pulse 150, respirations of 16 per minute, and oxygen saturation of 92% on room air. They apply the cardiac monitor to the patient and see a fast, regular heart rate with narrow QRS complexes (Figure 12-1). One of the paramedics comments that the rhythm looks like sinus tachycardia. But the physician says, "No, look closely. See the saw-tooth pattern?"

The paramedics nod in agreement after confirming that, indeed, there are no normal P waves and that the QRS complexes are preceded by F waves.

LO 12.1

Rhythms Originating in the Atria

Atrial dysrhythmias originate outside the SA node in the atrial tissue or in the internodal pathways. They are among the most common types of dysrhythmias, particularly in persons older than 60 years of age. Most atrial dysrhythmias are benign, but tachycardias that originate from the atria can be dangerous. The three mechanisms thought to cause atrial dysrhythmias are enhanced automaticity, circus reentry, and afterdepolarization.

LO 12.2

KEY CONCEPT

The P waves associated with dysrhythmias that arise from the atria appear different than the P waves that arise from the SA node.

WANT MORE INFORMATION?

Visit the Fast & Easy ECGs Website at www.mhhe.com/shadeECG2e.

P Wave Appearance

The key characteristics of atrial dysrhythmias include P′ waves (if present) that differ in appearance from normal sinus P waves and normal, abnormal, shortened, or prolonged P′R intervals.

The appearance of the P′ waves will depend on the site where the atrial impulses originate. Typically, the closer the site of origin is to the SA node, the more it looks like a normal P wave. If the ectopic pacemaker arises from the upper- or middle-right atrium, depolarization occurs in a normal direction—from right to left and then downward. If it is initiated from the upper-right atrium, the P′ wave should be upright in lead II, resembling a normal sinus P wave. If it is initiated from the middle of the right atrium, the P′ wave is less positive than one that originates from the upper-right atrium.

If the impulse arises from the lower-right atrium near the AV node or in the left atrium, depolarization occurs in a *retrograde* direction—from left to right and then upward, resulting in the P′ wave being inverted in lead II.

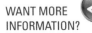

KEY CONCEPT

As with sinus dysrhythmias, the QRS complexes in atrial dysrhythmias appear normal (unless there is an intraventricular conduction defect or aberrancy).

QRS Complex Appearance

As with all dysrhythmias that arise from above the ventricles (sinus, atrial, and junctional dysrhythmias), the QRS complexes should appear narrow (0.06 to 0.10 seconds in duration) and normal (unless there is an intraventricular conduction defect, aberrancy, or ventricular preexcitation).

Effects of Atrial Dysrhythmias

While many atrial dysrhythmias have little effect on cardiac output, others can reduce ventricular filling time and diminish the strength of the atrial "kick," the atrial contraction that normally supplies the ventricles with about 30% of their blood. These effects can lead to decreased cardiac output, decreased blood pressure, and, ultimately, decreased tissue perfusion.

Decreased tissue perfusion can have dire consequences. First, there is not enough oxygen and nutrients for the body to satisfy its energy needs. Second, if the waste products of metabolism are not removed, they accumulate in the tissues and create a toxic environment. If not corrected, both factors can lead to shock and, ultimately, death of the patient.

Atrial dysrhythmias (Figure 12-1) include the following:

- Premature atrial complex (PAC)
- Wandering atrial pacemaker
- Atrial tachycardia
- Multifocal atrial tachycardia (MAT)
- Supraventricular tachycardia (SVT)
- Atrial flutter
- Atrial fibrillation

REMINDER

Dysrhythmias that originate from above the ventricles are called supraventricular dysrhythmias.

QUESTION

1. **What would you expect the appearance of the P waves to be if they originate from one site?** *Note:* Answers to Sidebar Questions can be found at the end of the chapter.

Premature Atrial Complexes

LO 12.3

Description

PACs are early beats that originate outside the SA node (Figure 12-2) somewhere in the atria. The SA node fires an impulse, but then an irritable focus jumps in, firing its own impulse before the SA node can fire again. PACs can originate from a single ectopic site or from multiple sites in the atria. Early beats like PACs aren't really a dysrhythmia. Rather, they are an abnormality that occurs within an underlying rhythm. When referring to early beats, we say, as an example, "we have sinus rhythm with occasional PACs."

Causes

The most common cause of PACs is enhanced automaticity. Patients with healthy hearts can experience PACs due to excessive use of caffeine, nicotine, or alcohol, or in the presence of anxiety, fatigue, or fever. Other common causes of PACs are listed in the table on the next page. In some cases there is no apparent cause.

REMINDER

With premature beats (atrial, junctional, or ventricular), the term complex or contraction may be used. For example, we can call an early ectopic atrial beat a premature atrial complex or a premature atrial contraction. The term contraction is the appropriate term if the premature beat produces a pulse. The term complex may be more fitting though because not all premature beats produce a pulse.

Figure 12-1
Dysrhythmias originating from the atria.

Premature atrial complexes (PACs) are early beats that originate outside the SA node

Atrial flutter is a rapid depolarization of a single focus in the atria at a rate of 250 to 350 BPM

Atrial tachycardia is a rapid dysrhythmia, having a rate of 150 to 250 BPM

In wandering atrial pacemaker site shifts as often as from beat-to-beat between the SA node, atria, and/or AV junction

Multifocal atrial tachycardia (MAT) presents with the same characteristics as wandering atrial pacemaker but has heart rates in the range of 100 to 250 BPM

Atrial fibrillation occurs when there is chaotic, asynchronous firing of multiple areas within the atria

Causes of Premature Atrial Complexes	
Cause	**Examples**
Cardiac diseases	Coronary heart disease, heart failure, valvular heart disease
Use of certain drugs	Digitalis toxicity, drugs that prolong the absolute refractory period of the SA node (procainamide, quinidine)
Increased sympathetic tone	Increased catecholamines
Noncardiac disorders	Acute respiratory failure, alcohol, anxiety, caffeine, certain electrolyte imbalances, nicotine, fatigue, fever, hyperthyroidism, hypoxia, infectious disease, COPD

Premature atrial complexes arise from somewhere in the atrium.

Rate depends on underlying rhythm	Rhythm **irregular due to premature beat**	P' waves **appear different from underlying rhythm, precedes early QRS complex, may be lost in T wave of previous beat**	QRS complexes of normal duration and all look alike*
P'R intervals **normal or shortened**	ST segments normal and isoelectric	T waves normal shape and upright	QT intervals within normal limits of 0.36 to 0.44 second	U waves may or may not be present

* unless aberrantly conducted in which case they may be wide and bizarre-looking

Figure 12-2
Premature atrial complex.

Effects

Isolated PACs seen in patients with healthy hearts are considered insignificant. Commonly they cause no symptoms and can go unrecognized for years. Asymptomatic patients usually require only observation. The patient may perceive PACs as "palpitations" or skipped beats.

However, in patients with heart disease, frequent PACs may predispose the patient to serious atrial dysrhythmias such as atrial tachycardia, atrial flutter, or atrial fibrillation. In a patient experiencing an acute MI, PACs can serve as an early indicator of an electrolyte imbalance or congestive heart failure. PACs with aberrant ventricular conduction may cause wide QRS complexes and be confused with premature ventricular complexes.

QUESTION
2. Why is it important to check for a pulse when there are premature beats in the rhythm?

Appearance

When PACs are present, the first thing you see as you look across the ECG tracing is an irregular rhythm. As you review it more closely, you can see that, wherever there is irregularity, the P'-P and R'-R intervals are shorter than the P-P and R-R intervals of the underlying rhythm. For example, if you look across the ECG tracing at P-P intervals and R-R intervals of three consecutive

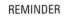
normal beats, the distance should be relatively the same. Where there is an ectopic beat, the P'-P and R'-R interval is shorter. This tells you that the beat(s) producing the irregularity occurred early.

Now that we know there are early beats, it is a matter of identifying from where they are arising. This can be done by looking at the P waves and QRS complexes associated with the early beats. There should be a P' wave (in most leads) preceding the QRS complex, but it will have a different morphology (appearance) than the P waves in the underlying rhythm. Although an upright P' wave is common in PACs, it is dependent upon where in the atria the impulse originates. For example, if the impulse forms near the SA node, the PAC will have a near normal shape and an upright P wave. But if the impulse originates in the atria or near the AV node, the P wave morphology will be very different from the normal P waves and likely be either biphasic or negative in direction. PACs that originate in the atria near the AV node may also have a shortened PR interval in addition to their altered P wave morphology.

Sometimes the P wave will be buried in the T wave of the preceding beat, thus changing its appearance somewhat. The QRS complexes are typically normal (although with aberrant conduction they will look different). Another characteristic that allows us to conclude that early beats are PACs is that they are followed by a noncompensatory pause.

The pause that follows a premature beat is called a **noncompensatory pause** if the beat following the premature complex is normal and occurs before it was expected. In other words, the space between the complex before and after the premature beat is "less than" the sum of two R-R intervals. To determine the presence of a noncompensatory pause, we measure the R-R interval preceding the early beat. We then measure to the R wave of the first normal beat that follows it. If the combined distance is less than the sum of two R-R intervals, the pause is considered a noncompensatory pause (Figure 12-3). The reason a noncompensatory pause occurs is that the electrical activity of the premature atrial beat can enter the sinus node and reset its timing, thus allowing it to fire before its next scheduled beat. This creates an irregularity in the R-R pattern.

In contrast, compensatory pause occurs when there are two full R-R intervals between the R wave of the normal beat that precedes the early beat and the R wave of the first normal beat that follows it. A compensatory pause is characteristically seen with premature beats that arise from the ventricles. These are referred to as *premature ventricular complexes*. The reason a compensatory pause occurs is that the electrical activity of a premature ventricular complex is usually not conducted through the AV node towards the atria; thus the sinus node will not be reset. So the SA node fires as planned and on schedule.

Another way to describe PACs is how they are intermingled among the normal beats. When every other beat is a PAC, it is called *bigeminal PACs* or *atrial bigeminy*. If every third beat is a PAC, it is called *trigeminal PACs* or

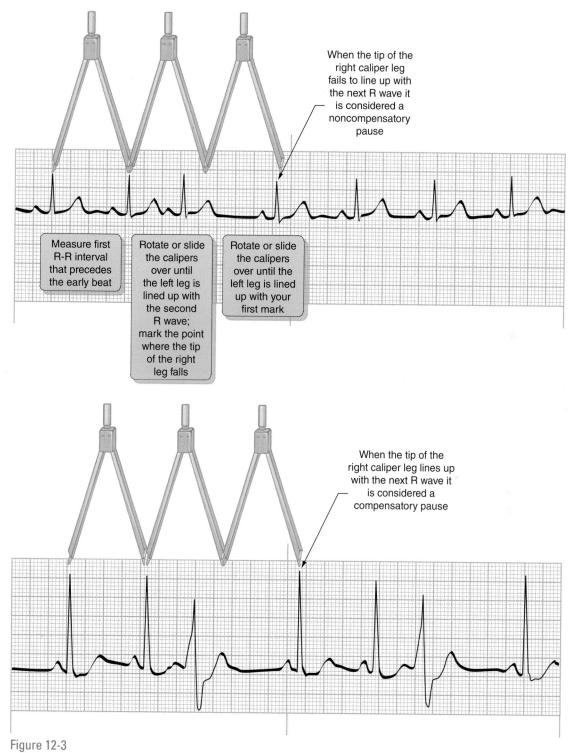

When the tip of the right caliper leg fails to line up with the next R wave it is considered a noncompensatory pause

Measure first R-R interval that precedes the early beat

Rotate or slide the calipers over until the left leg is lined up with the second R wave; mark the point where the tip of the right leg falls

Rotate or slide the calipers over until the left leg is lined up with your first mark

When the tip of the right caliper leg lines up with the next R wave it is considered a compensatory pause

Figure 12-3
Noncompensatory pause and compensatory pause.

atrial trigeminy. Likewise, if PACs occur every fourth beat, they are called *quadrigeminal PACs* or *atrial quadrigeminy.* Regular PACs at greater intervals than every fourth beat have no special name (Figure 12-4).

REMINDER
Remember, bi = 2, tri = 3, and quad = 4.

Figure 12-4
Premature atrial complexes occurring in a (A) bigeminal, (B) trigeminal, and (C) quadrigeminal pattern.

KEY CONCEPT

Premature atrial complexes are early ectopic beats that arise from the atria.

Remember, in PACs with aberrant ventricular conduction, the QRS complexes are preceded by a P′ wave and a constant P′R interval because the pacemaker site is above the ventricles. This is one of the characteristics we can use to differentiate between PACs with aberrancy and premature ventricular complexes.

Nonconducted PACs or **blocked PACs** occur when an atrial impulse arrives too early, before the AV node has a chance to repolarize. As a result, the P′

Premature atrial complex arises from somewhere in the atrium but is blocked before it reaches the ventricles.

Figure 12-5

Blocked PACs are seen as P′ waves not followed by a QRS complex.

wave fails to conduct to the ventricles. You will know this has occurred when you see a premature P′ wave not followed by a QRS complex (Figure 12-5). Sometimes it is necessary to look closely because they can be buried within the T wave of the preceding beat.

Differentiating Blocked PACs from Sinus Arrest

Nonconducted or blocked PACs can sometimes be misinterpreted as sinus arrest. With sinus arrest there should be an absence of P waves following the T wave that precedes the pause. In contrast, with a blocked PAC there should be a nonconducted P wave, which occurs before, during, or just after the T wave preceding the pause. If the P wave is not obviously apparent, compare the T waves that precede the pause with the other T waves in the tracing. A P wave that is buried in the T wave should distort its height or shape. Again, with sinus arrest you shouldn't see the P wave around or buried in the T wave preceding the pause whereas with a blocked PAC you should see a P wave before, during, or just after the T wave that precedes the pause but is not followed by a QRS complex.

Treatment

PACs generally do not require treatment. PACs caused by the use of caffeine, tobacco, or alcohol or by anxiety, fatigue, or fever can be controlled by eliminating the underlying cause. Frequent PACs may be treated with drugs that increase the atrial refractory time. This includes beta-adrenergic blockers and calcium channel blockers.

LO 12.4

Wandering Atrial Pacemaker

Description

Wandering atrial pacemaker is a rhythm in which the pacemaker site shifts location as often as from beat to beat between the SA node, atria, and/or AV junction (Figure 12-6). It is also called *multifocal atrial rhythm.*

Causes

Wandering atrial pacemaker is generally caused by the inhibitory vagal effect of respiration on the SA node and AV junction. With increased vagal stimulation, the SA node slows, allowing faster (briefly) pacemakers in the atria or AV junction to initiate the heartbeat. After the vagal tone decreases, the SA node becomes the dominant pacemaker again.

Causes of Wandering Atrial Pacemaker	
Cause	**Examples**
Cardiac diseases	Organic heart disease (e.g., rheumatic carditis), valvular heart disease
Use of certain drugs	Digoxin toxicity
Vagal stimulation	Inhibitory effect of vagal stimulation of respiration on the SA and AV nodes
Noncardiac disorders	Pulmonary disease with hypoxemia

KEY CONCEPT

The most distinguishing characteristic of wandering atrial pacemaker dysrhythmia is P′ waves of varying size, shape, and direction in any one lead (as often as from beat to beat).

KEY CONCEPT

Wandering atrial pacemaker is a rhythm in which the pacemaker site shifts location from site to site between the SA node and locations throughout the atria. This produces P′ waves that change in appearance and a rhythm that varies slightly.

Effects

Wandering atrial pacemaker is rarely serious, having no effect on cardiac output. It is a normal finding in children, older adults, and well-conditioned athletes and is not usually of any clinical significance.

Appearance

The most characteristic feature of wandering atrial pacemaker is P′ waves that change in appearance, sometimes as often as from beat to beat. Changes in appearance often involve changes in shape (morphology), which may include either positive elements or negative elements of the waveform or both (biphasic). At least three different P wave configurations (seen in the same lead) are needed to diagnose a dysrhythmia as wandering atrial pacemaker. Also, due to the changing pacemaker site, the P′R interval and the regularity of the rhythm often varies. Because the impulse arises above the ventricles, the QRS complexes are normal. The heart rate with this dysrhythmia is within normal rates—60 to 100 beats per minute, but it may also be slow. Wandering atrial pacemaker may be difficult to identify because the dysrhythmia is commonly transient.

Wandering atrial pacemaker arises from different sites in the atria.

Rate usually normal	Rhythm **slightly irregular**	P' waves **Differ in appearance, one precedes each QRS complex**	QRS complexes of normal duration and all look alike	P'R intervals **varies**

ST segments normal and isoelectric	T waves normal shape and upright	QT intervals within normal limits of 0.36 to 0.44 second	U waves may or may not be present

Figure 12-6
Wandering atrial pacemaker.

Treatment

No treatment is necessary for patients experiencing wandering atrial pacemaker. However, chronic dysrhythmias are a sign of heart disease and should be monitored.

Atrial Tachycardia

LO 12.5

Description

Atrial tachycardia is a rapid dysrhythmia, having a rate of 150 to 250 beats per minute (rarely exceeding 250 beats per minute) that arises from the atria (Figure 12-7). It is so fast that it overrides the SA node. Atrial tachycardia can occur at any age.

When the onset of the tachycardia is sudden (and typically witnessed) with a finite duration, it is called **paroxysmal.** Paroxysmal tachycardia may originate in the atria (paroxysmal atrial tachycardia) or AV junction (paroxysmal junctional tachycardia). It is characterized by repeated episodes (paroxysms) of SVT, which often have a sudden onset (lasting minutes to hours) and an abrupt termination. It looks like an extremely fast rate with narrow QRS complexes.

QUESTION
3. What is the heart rate associated with sinus tachycardia?

Atrial tachycardia arises from a single focus in the atria.

Rate between 150 and 250 BPM	**Rhythm** regular unless onset witnessed

| **P' waves** may be upright, differ in appearance from those of underlying rhythm, one precedes each QRS complex | **QRS complexes** of normal duration and all look alike* |

| **P'R intervals** shorter than normal if ectopic impulse arises in lower right atrium or upper part of AV junction | **ST segments** may be normal or distorted | **T waves** usually visible, often distorted by P wave | **QT intervals** usually within normal limits but may be shorted due to fast rate | **U waves** not likely seen |

* unless aberrantly conducted in which case they may be wide and bizarre-looking

Figure 12-7
Atrial tachycardia.

Atrial tachycardia may occur in short bursts or it may be sustained. Short bursts of the tachycardia are well tolerated in otherwise normally healthy people. With sustained rapid ventricular rates, ventricular filling may be decreased during diastole.

Causes

Digitalis toxicity is the most common cause of atrial tachycardia. Also, sudden onset atrial tachycardia is common in patients who have Wolff-Parkinson-White syndrome.

In patients with healthy hearts, excessive use of caffeine or other stimulants, marijuana use, electrolyte imbalances, hypoxia, and physical or psychological stress can cause PACs, which can precipitate atrial tachycardia. Common causes of atrial tachycardia are listed in the box on the next page.

Effects

Symptoms can develop abruptly and may go away without treatment. They may last a few minutes or as long as one to two days, sometimes continuing until treatment is delivered.

With the rapid heartbeat seen with atrial tachycardia, there is less time for the ventricles to fill. This can reduce stroke volume and lead to decreased cardiac

Causes of Atrial Tachycardia	
Cause	**Examples**
Cardiac diseases	MI, cardiomyopathy, congenital anomalies, systemic hypertensive, valvular heart disease, Wolff-Parkinson-White syndrome
Use of certain drugs	Albuterol, cocaine, digitalis toxicity (the most common cause), theophylline
Excessive sympathetic stimulation	Physical or psychological stress
Noncardiac disorders	Alcohol, caffeine, cor pulmonale, hyperthyroidism, electrolyte imbalance, nicotine

output and a drop in blood pressure. Although atrial tachycardia can often be tolerated in healthy persons, it can significantly compromise cardiac output in patients with underlying heart disease. Decreased cardiac output can lead to vertigo (dizziness), lightheadedness, syncope, hypotension, congestive heart failure, and loss of consciousness (in serious cases).

Further, fast heart rates increase oxygen requirements. This can increase myocardial ischemia and the frequency and severity of the patient's chest pain and may lead to MI.

> **KEY CONCEPT**
> Atrial tachycardia is a rapid tachycardia that arises from the atria.

Other symptoms seen with atrial tachycardia include anxiety, nervousness, palpitations, pounding chest, shortness of breath, rapid breathing, and numbness of various body parts.

Appearance

The most striking feature of atrial tachycardia is its rapid rate of 150 to 250 beats per minute. For this reason you should be able to see it almost immediately. It arises from one site, so the rhythm should be regular unless you see the onset or termination, as with paroxysmal atrial tachycardia. Although there is one P′ wave (unless there is a block) preceding each QRS complex, it deviates in appearance from the normal P wave and is typically buried in the T wave of the preceding beat. If present, the P′ waves may be flattened or notched. The P′R intervals are typically indeterminable because the P′ waves tend to be buried. If visible, the P′R interval is often shortened, but it may also be normal. The dysrhythmia arises above the ventricles, so the QRS complexes are normal unless there is aberrant conduction.

With the rapid atrial rates seen with atrial tachycardia, the AV junction is sometimes unable to carry all the impulses, and an atrial tachycardia with block occurs. Most commonly, only one of every two beats (a 2 to 1 block) is conducted to the ventricles. This then results in more than one P′ wave preceding each QRS complex (Figure 12-8). If the block is constant, it will have

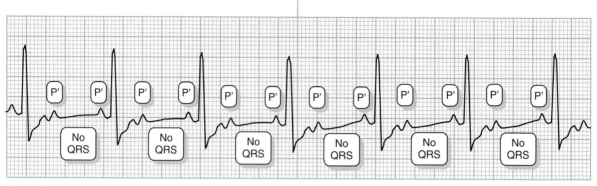

Figure 12-8
Atrial tachycardia with block.

KEY CONCEPT

The hallmark features of atrial tachycardia is a rapid rate with narrow QRS complexes.

the same number of P′ waves preceding each QRS complex, but, if the block is variable, the number of P′ waves will change.

Treatment

Treatment is dependent on the type of tachycardia and symptom severity. It is directed at eliminating the cause and decreasing ventricular rate. Patients who are symptomatic (e.g., chest pain, hypotension) should receive oxygen, an IV infusion of normal saline administered at a keep-open rate, and prompt delivery of synchronized cardioversion, use of vagal maneuvers or medication administration.

Synchronized cardioversion is indicated if the patient is symptomatic. In the conscious patient, consider sedation before cardioversion. However, do not delay cardioversion. If this fails to convert the rhythm, the energy level may be increased.

If the patient is stable, vagal maneuvers and drug therapy (adenosine) may be used. Adenosine can be used in aberrancy. If these treatments fail to resolve the tachycardia, calcium channel blockers (verapamil, diltiazem) and beta-adrenergic blockers (if no contraindications exist) may be considered.

When atrial tachycardia is due to some underlying abnormality (e.g., electrolyte imbalance, drug toxicity), the conversion to a normal rhythm with cardioversion may be temporary because the causative factor has not been eliminated. In such cases, a recurrence of atrial tachycardia soon after successful electrical cardioversion does not warrant additional electrical cardioversion attempts until the underlying problem has been resolved. In the patient with COPD, correction of hypoxia and electrolyte imbalances is indicated.

Atrial overdrive pacing may be employed to stop this dysrhythmia. If the dysrhythmia is related to WPW syndrome, catheter ablation may be indicated. Procainamide, amiodarone, or sotalol may be considered in wide complex tachycardias.

Multifocal Atrial Tachycardia

Description

MAT is a pathological condition that presents with the same characteristics as wandering atrial pacemaker (Figure 12-9) but with heart rates in the range of 100 to 250 beats per minute (usually less than 160 beats per minute).

Causes

MAT is very rare in healthy patients. It is more common in the elderly. It is usually precipitated by acute exacerbation (with resultant hypoxia) of COPD, elevated atrial pressures, or heart failure. Common causes are listed as follows.

Causes of Multifocal Atrial Tachycardia	
Cause	**Examples**
Cardiac diseases	Acute coronary syndromes, elevated atrial pressures, heart failure, rheumatic heart disease
Use of certain drugs	Digitalis, theophylline toxicity
Noncardiac disorders	COPD (most common cause), electrolyte imbalance (hypokalemia, hypomagnesemia), hypoxia

In multifocal atrial tachycardia the pacemaker site shifts between the SA node, atria, and/or the AV junction.

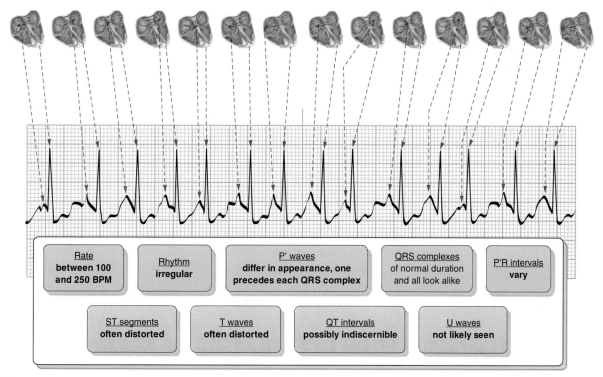

Rate between 100 and 250 BPM	Rhythm irregular	P' waves differ in appearance, one precedes each QRS complex	QRS complexes of normal duration and all look alike	P'R intervals vary

ST segments often distorted	T waves often distorted	QT intervals possibly indiscernible	U waves not likely seen

Figure 12-9
Multifocal atrial tachycardia.

MAT can also occur after MI. It is sometimes associated with digitalis toxicity in patients with heart disease.

Effects

The patient may complain of palpitations. Signs and symptoms of decreased cardiac output, such as hypotension, syncope, and blurred vision, may be seen.

Appearance

KEY CONCEPT
MAT is a fast tachycardia arising from more than one site in the atria. The hallmark features of MAT are a faster than normal rate with changing P waves preceding narrow QRS complexes.

MAT is often misdiagnosed as atrial fibrillation with rapid ventricular response but can be distinguished by looking closely for the clearly visible but changing P′ waves. The P′ waves change in morphology as often as from beat to beat. It results in three or more different-looking P waves. The P waves may be upright, rounded, notched, inverted, biphasic, or buried in the QRS complex. It also results in varying PR intervals and narrow QRS complexes.

Sometimes with SVT we see QRS complexes that appear wide. This is due to an intraventricular conduction defect or other condition such as aberrant conduction. This makes the assessment of SVT difficult as it appears to be ventricular tachycardia. This is called *wide complex tachycardia of unknown origin.*

Treatment

MAT usually represents either severe underlying heart or lung disease; the appropriate therapy is treatment of the underlying condition. In symptomatic patients treatment may include administration of medications such as calcium channel blockers (verapamil, diltiazem). Beta-adrenergic blockers are typically contraindicated because of the presence of severe underlying pulmonary disease.

LO 12.7

Supraventricular Tachycardia

KEY CONCEPT
Supraventricular is a term used to describe a tachycardia that arises from above the ventricles but is so fast that you cannot determine if the site of origin is in the atria or AV junction.

In very fast rates with narrow QRS complexes, it may be difficult to determine whether the tachycardia arises from the atria or AV junction (Figure 12-10) because the P′ waves are often buried in the T wave of the preceding beat. We describe these as **supraventricular tachycardia,** meaning that it is arising from above the ventricles. This group of tachycardias includes paroxysmal SVT (PSVT), nonparoxysmal atrial tachycardia, MAT, AV nodal reentrant tachycardia (AVNRT), atrioventricular reentrant tachycardia, and junctional tachycardia. AVNRT, atrioventricular reentrant tachycardia, and junctional tachycardia are discussed in Chapter 13. Distinguishing among these tachycardias is often difficult as the ventricular rate is so fast it is hard to tell if there are P′ waves or P′R intervals.

Rate extremely fast	**Rhythm** regular unless onset witnessed	**P' waves** cannot be identified	**QRS complexes** of normal duration and all look alike*	**P'R intervals** are absent
ST segments may be normal or distorted	**T waves** usually visible, often distorted by P wave	**QT intervals** usually within normal limits but may be shorted due to fast rate		**U waves** may or may not be present

* unless aberrantly conducted in which case they may be wide and bizzare-looking

Figure 12-10

The term supraventricular tachycardia is used when the rate is so fast you cannot determine whether or not P' waves are present.

Atrial Flutter

LO 12.8

Description

Atrial flutter is a rapid depolarization of a single focus in the atria at a rate of 250 to 350 beats per minute (usually 300; Figure 12-11). It results from circus reentry, a condition during which the impulse from the SA node circles back through the atria, returning to the SA node region and repeatedly restimulating the AV node over and over. Another cause is increased automaticity. On the ECG, the P waves lose their distinction due to the rapid atrial rate. The waves blend together in a saw-tooth or picket fence pattern. They are called flutter waves, or F waves.

KEY CONCEPT

Atrial flutter arises from a single focus in the atria at a rate of 250 to 350 beats per minute.

Causes

Although atrial flutter occasionally occurs in patients with healthy hearts, it is usually caused by conditions that elevate atrial pressures and enlarge the atria. Also, it is commonly seen in patients with severe mitral valve disease, hyperthyroid disease, pericardial disease, and primary myocardial disease. The box on the next page lists causes of atrial flutter.

Effects

Atrial flutter is often well tolerated. However, the number of impulses conducted through the AV node, expressed as the conduction ratio, determines the ventricular rate. Slower ventricular rates (fewer than 40 beats per minute) or faster ventricular rates (greater than 150 beats per minute) can

Atrial flutter arises from rapid depolarization of a single focus in the atria.

Rate	Rhythm	P' waves	QRS complexes
Ventricular rate may be slow, normal or fast; atrial rate is between 250 and 350 BPM	**may regular or irregular**	**absent, instead there are saw-tooth flutter waves**	of normal duration and all look alike

P'R intervals	ST segments	T waves	QT intervals	U waves
not measurable	**not identifiable**	**not identifiable**	**not identifiable because T wave is not identifiable**	**unidentifiable**

Figure 12-11
Atrial flutter.

Causes of Atrial Flutter

Cause	Examples
Cardiac diseases	MI, cardiomyopathy, conditions that enlarge atrial tissue and elevate atrial pressures, following cardiac surgery, mitral or tricuspid valve disease, pericarditis/myocarditis
Use of certain drugs	Digitalis or quinidine toxicity
Noncardiac disorders	COPD, hypoxia, hyperthyroidism, pneumonia, pulmonary embolism, systemic arterial hypoxia, pulmonary hypertension

seriously compromise cardiac output. For example, if the atrial flutter rate is 300 and the ventricular response is at a rate of 150, the conduction ratio is 300:150 or 2:1 (atrial to ventricular beats). This may result in loss of atrial kick, decreased ventricular filling time, and decreased coronary artery perfusion leading to angina, heart failure, pulmonary edema, hypotension, and syncope.

Appearance

The key feature of atrial flutter is the presence of saw-tooth flutter waves. These flutter waves correspond to the rapid atrial rate of 250 to 350 beats per minute. The atrial rhythm is regular, and depending on conduction ratio, the ventricular rhythm may be regular or irregular. The ventricular rate depends on ventricular response; it may be normal, slow, or fast. A 1:1 atrial-ventricular conduction is rare; it is usually 2:1, 3:1, 4:1, or variable. The PR interval is not measurable. QRS complexes are usually normal.

Treatment

Vagal maneuvers may make flutter waves more visible by transiently increasing the degree of the block. In patients experiencing atrial flutter and an associated rapid ventricular rate who are symptomatic but stable, treatment is directed at controlling the rate or converting the rhythm to sinus rhythm. Patients who have serious signs and symptoms (e.g., hypotension, signs of shock, or heart failure) should receive oxygen, an IV infusion of normal saline administered at a keep-open (TKO) rate, and prompt treatment. Synchronized cardioversion should be considered in unstable patients. If necessary, the energy may be increased with subsequent shocks.

Atrial Fibrillation

LO 12.9

Description

Atrial fibrillation occurs when there is chaotic, asynchronous firing of multiple areas within the atria (Figure 12-12). This completely suppresses normal SA node output and causes the atria to quiver instead of contract. This results in an ineffective contraction of the atria and no contribution to filling the ventricles during systole—resulting in a reduction in cardiac output. Atrial fibrillation stems from multiple foci of impulse formation (greater than 350 beats per minute). These impulses bombard the AV node but are only conducted to the ventricles in an irregular and sporadic fashion.

Causes

Atrial fibrillation is more common than atrial tachycardia or atrial flutter. It can occur in healthy persons after excessive caffeine, alcohol, or tobacco ingestion or because of fatigue and acute stress. Atrial fibrillation may also be seen with other conditions, including rheumatic heart disease, CHF (atrial dilation), ischemic heart disease, and pulmonary diseases (COPD). It is rarely caused by digitalis toxicity, but a very slow, regular ventricular response with atrial fibrillation should raise suspicion of digitalis toxicity. Causes of atrial fibrillation are listed in the table on the next page.

Effects

As with atrial flutter, atrial fibrillation leads to a loss of the atrial kick. This decreases ventricular filling by up to 30%. Patients experiencing

KEY CONCEPT
The most prominent characteristic of atrial flutter is the presence of saw-tooth flutter waves.

KEY CONCEPT
Atrial fibrillation occurs when there is rapid, chaotic firing of ectopic impulses (greater than 350 beats per minute) in the atria.

QUESTION
4. Why is the appearance of the atrial waveforms in atrial flutter constant and not in atrial fibrillation?

Figure 12-12
Atrial fibrillation.

Causes of Atrial Fibrillation	
Cause	**Examples**
Cardiac diseases	MI, atrial septal defects, CAD, cardiomyopathy, congestive heart failure, congenital heart disease, ischemic heart disease, mitral regurgitation, mitral stenosis, pericarditis, rheumatic heart disease. May also be caused by cardiac surgery.
Use of certain drugs	Digitalis toxicity, aminophylline
Excessive sympathetic stimulation	Endogenous catecholamines released during exercise
Noncardiac disorders	Advanced age, COPD, diabetes, electrocution, hypoxia, hypokalemia, hypoglycemia, hypertension, hyperthyroidism, pulmonary embolism, WPW syndrome, idiopathic (no clear cause); may also occur in healthy people who use coffee, alcohol, or nicotine to excess or who are fatigued and under stress

atrial fibrillation may develop intraatrial thrombi (clots), as the atria are not contracting and blood stagnates in the atrial chambers. If the thrombi are dislodged from the atria, this predisposes the patient to systemic emboli—particularly stroke. A ventricular response within the normal rate (60 to 100 beats per minute) is often well tolerated whereas a fast ventricular response can result in decreased cardiac output that leads to heart failure, angina, or syncope. Patients who have preexisting heart disease, such as hypertrophic obstructive cardiomyopathy, mitral stenosis, and rheumatic heart disease, or who have mitral prosthetic valves are less tolerant of atrial fibrillation and may experience shock and severe heart failure.

Appearance

The standout feature in atrial fibrillation is a totally (grossly) irregular rhythm (also referred to as *irregularly irregular*). An irregularly irregular supraventricular rhythm is atrial fibrillation until proven otherwise. Another key characteristic is there are no discernible P waves. Instead, a chaotic baseline of fibrillatory waves, or f waves, represents the atrial activity. The absence of discernable P waves occurs because the atria have impulse formations from multiple foci with such high frequency (greater than 350 beats per minute) that no atrial depolarization can occur. The ventricular rate depends on how many impulses bombarding the AV node are conducted through to the ventricles. It may be normal, slow, or fast. There are no PR intervals present because of the absence of P waves. The QRS complexes are usually normal.

KEY CONCEPT
The most prominent characteristics of atrial fibrillation is it a totally irregular rhythm that lacks discernible P waves.

Treatment

If the rate of ventricular response is normal (often seen in patients taking digitalis), the dysrhythmia is usually well tolerated and requires no immediate intervention. In patients experiencing atrial fibrillation and an associated rapid ventricular rate who are symptomatic but stable, treatment is directed at controlling the rate or converting the rhythm to sinus rhythm. Patients who have serious signs and symptoms (e.g., hypotension, signs of shock, or heart failure) should receive oxygen, an IV infusion of normal saline administered at a TKO rate, and prompt synchronized cardioversion. If necessary, the energy level may be increased with subsequent shocks.

Practice Makes Perfect

For each of the 57 ECG tracings on the following pages, practice the Nine-Step Process for analyzing ECGs. To achieve the greatest learning, you should practice assessing and interpreting the ECGs immediately after reading this chapter. Below are questions you should consider as you access each tracing. Your answers can be written into the area below each ECG marked "ECG Findings." Your findings can then be compared to the answers provided in Appendix A. All tracings are six seconds in duration.

1. Determine the heart rate. Is it slow? Normal? Fast? What is the ventricular rate? What is the atrial rate?

2. Determine if the rhythm is regular or irregular. If it is irregular, what type of irregularity is it? Occasional or frequent? Slight? Sudden acceleration or slowing in heart rate? Total? Patterned? Does it have a variable conduction ratio?

3. Determine if P waves are present. If so, how do they appear? Do they have normal height and duration? Are they tall? Notched? Wide? Biphasic? Of differing morphology? Inverted? One for each QRS complex? More than one preceding some or all the QRS complexes? Do they have a sawtooth appearance? Is there an indiscernible chaotic baseline?

4. Determine if QRS complexes are present. If so, how do they appear? Narrow with proper amplitude? Tall? Low amplitude? Delta wave? Notched? Wide? Bizarre-looking? With chaotic waveforms?

5. Determine the presence of PR intervals. If present, how do they appear? Constant? Of normal duration? Shortened? Lengthened? Progressively longer? Varying?

6. Evaluate the ST segments. Do they have normal duration and position? Are they elevated? (If so, are they flat, concave, convex, arched?) Depressed? (If so, are they normal, flat, downsloping or upsloping?)

7. Determine if T waves are present. If so, how do they appear? Of normal height and duration? Tall? Wide? Notched? Inverted?

8. Determine the presence of QT intervals. If present, what is their duration? Normal? Shortened? Prolonged?

9. Determine if U waves are present. If present, how do they appear? Of normal height and duration? Inverted?

10. Identify the rhythm or dysrhythmia.

1.

ECG Findings:

2.

ECG Findings:

3.

ECG Findings:

4.

ECG Findings:

5.

ECG Findings:

6.

ECG Findings:

7.

ECG Findings:

8.

ECG Findings:

9.

ECG Findings:

10.

ECG Findings:

11.

ECG Findings:

12.

ECG Findings:

13.

ECG Findings:

14.

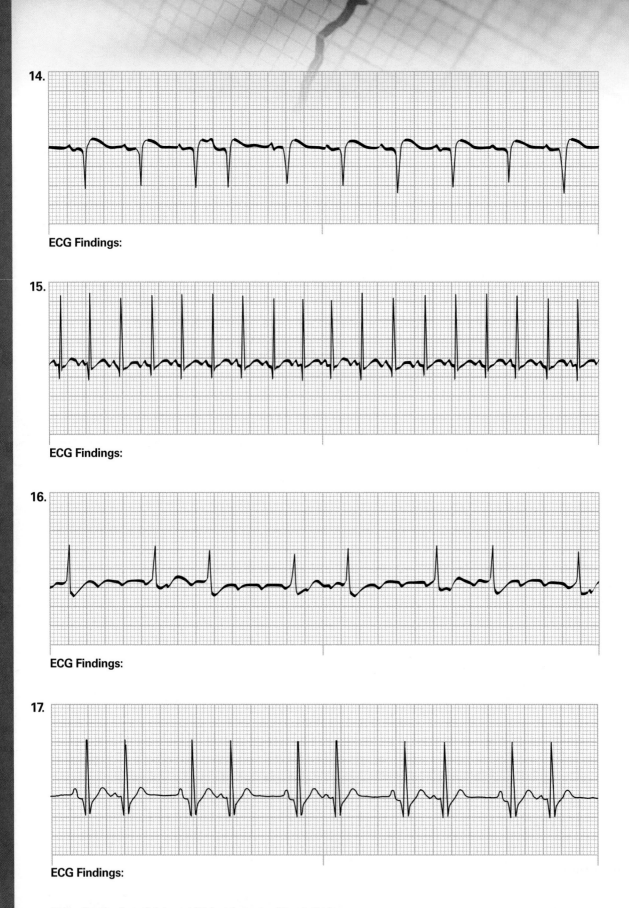

ECG Findings:

15.

ECG Findings:

16.

ECG Findings:

17.

ECG Findings:

18.

ECG Findings:

19.

ECG Findings:

20.

ECG Findings:

21.

ECG Findings:

22.

ECG Findings:

23.

ECG Findings:

24.

ECG Findings:

25.

ECG Findings:

26.

ECG Findings:

27.

ECG Findings:

28.

ECG Findings:

29.

ECG Findings:

30.

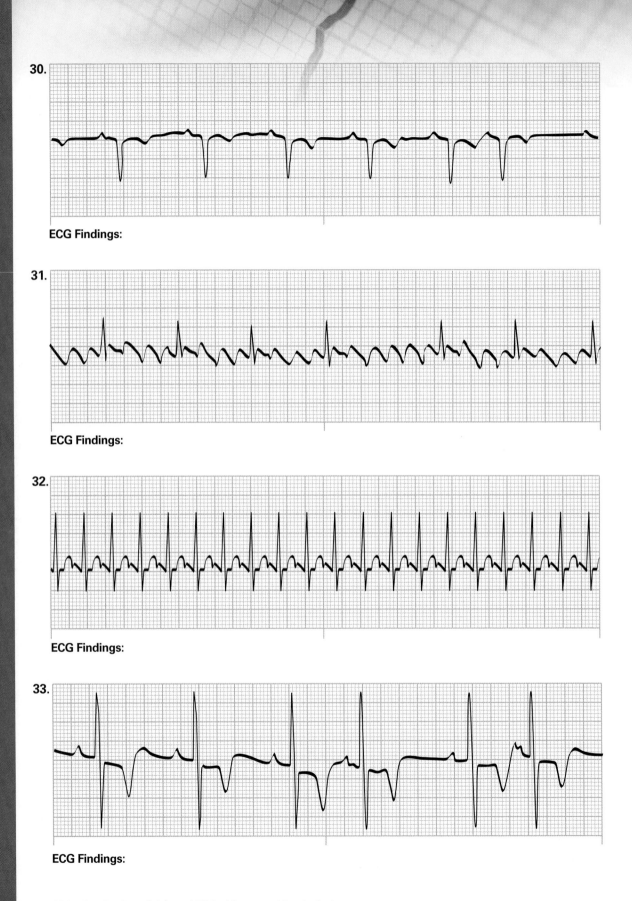

ECG Findings:

31.

ECG Findings:

32.

ECG Findings:

33.

ECG Findings:

34.

ECG Findings:

35.

ECG Findings:

36.

ECG Findings:

37.

ECG Findings:

38.

ECG Findings:

39.

ECG Findings:

40.

ECG Findings:

41.

ECG Findings:

42.

ECG Findings:

43.

ECG Findings:

44.

ECG Findings:

45.

ECG Findings:

46.

ECG Findings:

47.

ECG Findings:

48.

ECG Findings:

49.

ECG Findings:

50.

ECG Findings:

51.

ECG Findings:

52.

ECG Findings:

53.

ECG Findings:

54.

ECG Findings:

55.

ECG Findings:

56.

ECG Findings:

57.

ECG Findings:

Key Points 🔍

- Dysrhythmias originating outside the SA node in the atrial tissue or in the internodal pathways are called *atrial dysrhythmias*.

- Three mechanisms responsible for atrial dysrhythmias are increased automaticity, triggered activity, and reentry.

- Key characteristics for atrial dysrhythmias are P′ waves (if present) that differ in appearance from normal sinus P waves; abnormal, shortened, or prolonged P′R intervals; and QRS complexes that appear narrow and normal (unless there is an intraventricular conduction defect, aberrancy, or preexcitation).

- Wandering atrial pacemaker is a rhythm in which the pacemaker site shifts between the SA node, atria, and/or AV junction producing its most characteristic features, P′ waves that change in appearance and a rhythm that varies slightly.

- PACs are early ectopic beats that originate outside the SA node but above the AV node.

- PACs produce an irregularity in the rhythm where the P′-P and R′-R intervals are shorter than the P-P and R-R intervals of the underlying rhythm. The P′ waves should be an upright (in lead II) preceding the QRS complex but will have a different morphology (appearance) than the P waves in the underlying rhythm.

- Atrial tachycardia is a rapid dysrhythmia (having a rate of 150 to 250 beats per minute) that arises from the atria. It is so fast that it overrides the SA node.

- When the onset of the atrial tachycardia is sudden (and typically witnessed) with a finite duration, it is called *paroxysmal*.

- Atrial tachycardia is regular unless you see the onset or termination, as with paroxysmal atrial tachycardia, and there is one P′ wave preceding each QRS complex, although it is typically buried in the T wave of the preceding beat.

- MAT is a pathological condition that presents with the same characteristics as wandering atrial pacemaker but has heart rates in the 100 to 250 beats per minute range.

- SVT arises from above the ventricles but cannot be definitively identified as atrial or junctional because the P′ waves cannot be seen with any real degree of certainty.

- SVTs include PSVT, nonparoxysmal atrial tachycardia, and MAT.

- Atrial flutter is a rapid depolarization of a single focus in the atria at a rate of 250 to 350 beats per minute.

- Atrial flutter produces atrial waveforms that have a characteristic sawtooth or picket fence appearance. They are called *flutter waves,* or *F waves.*

- Atrial fibrillation occurs when there is chaotic, asynchronous firing of multiple areas within the atria. It stems from the rapid firing of ectopic impulses (greater than 350 beats per minute) in circus reentry pathways.

- Atrial fibrillation is a totally (grossly) irregular rhythm in which there are no discernible P waves. Instead, a chaotic baseline of fibrillatory waves or f waves represents the atrial activity.

Assess Your Understanding

The following questions give you a chance to assess your understanding of the material discussed in this chapter. The answers can be found in Appendix A.

1. With atrial dysrhythmias, the
   a. atrial waveforms differ in appearance from normal sinus P waves.
   b. P′R intervals are almost always prolonged.
   c. QRS complexes are wider than normal.
   d. site of origin is in the bundle of His.

2. In wandering atrial pacemaker, the pacemaker site shifts between the SA node, atria, and/or
   a. Purkinje fibers.
   b. ventricles.
   c. AV junction.
   d. bundle of His.

3. Your patient is a 67-year-old female with a history of cardiac problems. After attaching her to the monitor, you see a slightly irregular rhythm with normal QRS complexes, but each P′ wave is different. This rhythm is
   a. frequent PACs.
   b. sinus arrest.
   c. sinus dysrhythmia.
   d. wandering atrial pacemaker.

4. Premature atrial complexes
   a. are typically preceded by an inverted P′ wave.
   b. are always followed by a compensatory pause.
   c. have a wide and bizarre QRS complex.
   d. may have normal P′R intervals.

5. A PAC arises earlier in the cardiac cycle and will interrupt the regularity of the underlying rhythm.
   a. True
   b. False

6. The heart rate characteristic of atrial tachycardia is _____ beats per minute.
   a. 60 to 100
   b. 100 to 150
   c. 150 to 250
   d. 300 to 350

7. The QRS complexes seen with atrial tachycardia are normally _____ seconds in duration.
   a. 0.06 to 0.10
   b. 0.10 to 0.20
   c. 0.12 to 0.20
   d. 0.20 to 0.24

8. With MAT, the
   a. P′ waves have the same morphology from beat to beat.
   b. heart rate is 100 to 250 beats per minute.
   c. QRS complexes are usually greater than 0.12 seconds.
   d. Both b and c.

9. Which of the following rhythms has a characteristic saw-tooth pattern?
   a. Sinus dysrhythmia
   b. Ventricular flutter
   c. Atrial flutter
   d. Atrial tachycardia

10. Atrial flutter has an atrial rate of _____ beats per minute.
    a. between 40 and 60
    b. between 100 and 150
    c. between 250 and 350
    d. greater than 350

11. Atrial fibrillation typically has
    a. a regular rhythm.
    b. an atrial rate of between 250 and 350 beats per minute.
    c. normal QRS complexes.
    d. a PR intervals of greater than 0.20 seconds.

12. The atrial waveforms associated with atrial fibrillation are _____ and the PR intervals are _____.
    a. referred to as saw toothed; variable
    b. indiscernible; nonexistent
    c. inverted; less than 0.12 seconds
    d. dissociated; between 0.12 and 0.20 seconds

13. Which of the following dysrhythmias is totally irregular?
    a. Sinus bradycardia
    b. 3rd-degree AV heart block
    c. Ventricular tachycardia
    d. Atrial fibrillation

14. Atrial fibrillation has an atrial rate of _____ beats per minute.
    a. between 40 and 60
    b. between 100 and 150
    c. between 250 and 350
    d. greater than 350

Referring to the scenario at the beginning of this chapter, answer the following questions.

15. What rhythm is the patient in?
    a. Accelerated junctional
    b. Atrial fibrillation
    c. Atrial flutter
    d. Ventricular tachycardia

16. The patient passed out because of a decrease in his
    a. diastolic blood pressure.
    b. cardiac output.
    c. epinephrine levels.
    d. heart rate.

17. The formula for cardiac output is
    a. heart rate × systolic blood pressure.
    b. systolic blood pressure/diastolic blood pressure.
    c. stroke volume × heart rate.
    d. heart rate × respiratory rate.

Answers to Sidebar Questions

1. They appear the same from beat to beat. **p. 293**

2. We check for a pulse in rhythms that have premature beats to determine if they are perfusing beats. Typically, PACs produce a pulse, but premature beats that arise from the ventricles may not. You can detect this by watching the ECG in the dynamic mode while simultaneously feeling for a pulse. **p. 295**

3. The heart rate associated with sinus tachycardia is 100 to 160 beats per minute. **p. 301**

4. The origin of the atrial impulse with atrial flutter is constant; thus the appearance of the F waves is consistent. Remember that with atrial fibrillation, the site of the atrial pulse is not consistent, resulting in irregularly shaped f waves and a chaotic baseline. **p. 309**

What's Online

Go to www.mhhe.com/shadeECG2e to find:

- Presentations on chapter content
- Crossword puzzle exercises
- Additional ECG tracings for practicing analyzing sinus dysrhythmias
- Chapter quiz
- Flashcards
- Fill-in-the-blank exercises and answers
- In-depth answers to Practice Makes Perfect ECG tracings and Assess Your Understanding questions

13 Junctional Dysrhythmias

Chapter Outline

Dysrhythmias Originating in the Atrioventricular Junction

Premature Junctional Complex

Junctional Escape Rhythm

Accelerated Junctional Rhythm

Junctional Tachycardia

Atrioventricular Nodal Reentrant Tachycardia

Preexcitation

Atrioventricular Reentrant Tachycardia

Treatment of Supraventricular Tachycardia

Learning Objectives

LO 13.1   Describe the origin of junctional dysrhythmias.

LO 13.2   Recall the key features of dysrhythmias originating from the AV junction.

LO 13.3   Identify the causes, effects, appearance, and treatment of premature junctional complexes.

LO 13.4   Identify the causes, effects, appearance, and treatment of junctional escape rhythm.

LO 13.5   Identify the causes, effects, appearance, and treatment of accelerated junctional rhythm.

LO 13.6   Identify the causes, effects, and appearance of junctional tachycardia.

LO 13.7   Identify the causes, effects, and appearance of AV nodal reentrant tachycardia.

LO 13.8   Identify the causes, effects, and appearance of preexcitation.

LO 13.9   Identify the causes, effects, and appearance of AV reentrant tachycardia.

LO 13.10 Recall the treatments of supraventricular tachycardia.

Case History

A 48-year-old woman presents to the urgent care center complaining of a rapid heart rate. She tells the triage nurse that she has had this before and the condition is called *paroxysmal supraventricular tachycardia* (PSVT). The patient is quickly taken back to the exam room, and the physician is summoned. Her vital signs are normal except for a pulse rate of 180 beats per minute. When the physician enters the exam room, the woman states that she has had this before but usually it goes away if she performs vagal maneuvers such as bearing down and holding her breath. But that it is not working today. The physician orders a 12-lead ECG, which he then examines while the nurse establishes an IV. The physician notes that the patient's heart rate is fast and the rhythm is regular with narrow QRS complexes. He is unable to distinguish discernable P waves because of the fast rate. The nurse administers a medication to slow the heart rate. Within seconds the patient's rhythm converts to normal sinus rhythm.

After further questioning, the physician determines that the woman has not been compliant with her medications and that she continues to smoke and drink a lot of caffeinated beverages, all of which have contributed to the return of her dysrhythmia. He schedules her an appointment with her family physician and refills her medication of beta-blockers. He encourages her to remove nicotine and caffeine from her life.

LO 13.1

Dysrhythmias Originating in the Atrioventricular Junction

KEY CONCEPT
Junctional rhythms originate in the AV junction, the area around the AV node and the bundle of His.

Rhythms that originate in the AV junction, the area around the AV node, and the bundle of His, are called *junctional rhythms* (sometimes referred to as *nodal rhythms*). They can result from suppression or blockage of the SA node, which results in its failure to generate electrical impulses. Without an impulse from the SA node, the next lower pacemaker (the AV junction) should act as a back-up pacemaker and take over. Junctional rhythms may also result from increased automaticity of the AV junction or a reentry mechanism.

LO 13.2

P Wave Appearance

QUESTION
1. What are the characteristics of the normal P wave? *Note:* Answers to Sidebar Questions can be found at the end of the chapter.

The AV junction is located in the middle of the heart; therefore the impulse originating here travels upward and causes backward or retrograde depolarization of the atria (see Figure 6-12), resulting in an inverted P′ wave (when it would otherwise be upright) with a short P′R interval (less than 0.12 seconds in duration). At the same time, the impulse travels down to the ventricles and depolarizes them.

REMINDER
Retrograde depolarization is the backward conveyance of an electrical impulse originating in the AV junction or ventricles. It travels backward to the atria causing atrial depolarization. This is abnormal conduction.

Alternatively, the P′ wave may be absent. This occurs when the electrical impulse, originating in the middle of the heart near the AV node, reaches the atria and ventricles at the same time, resulting in simultaneous depolarization and causing the P′ wave to be buried in the QRS complex (which can change the morphology of the QRS complex). Another reason for an absent P′ wave is that retrograde conduction of the impulse to the atria can be blocked or not conducted at all. As a result, the atrial tissue is not depolarized and a P′ wave is not formed. The impulse can be blocked due to diseased or damaged AV nodal issue or MI, or the AV node is just incapable of retrograde depolarization. Lastly, the P wave may follow the QRS complex. This occurs when retrograde atrial depolarization follows ventricular depolarization.

QRS Complex Appearance

In junctional rhythms, whereas the atria are depolarized in an abnormal way, the ventricles depolarize normally. Electrical impulses travel in a normal pathway from the AV junction through the bundle of His and bundle branches to the Purkinje fibers, ending in the ventricular muscle. This results in the QRS complexes usually being within normal limits of 0.06 to 0.10 seconds. However, in any dysrhythmia where the QRS complexes should be normal, they can instead be wide or unusual looking if there is intraventricular conduction defect, aberrancy, or ventricular preexcitation.

Effects

If the atria are depolarized at the same time or after the ventricles, the atria are forced to pump against the contracting ventricles, which contract with much greater force. This can result in a loss in atrial kick, decreased stroke volume, and, ultimately, decreased cardiac output. Decreased cardiac output can also occur with slow or fast junctional dysrhythmias.

Junctional dysrhythmias include (Figure 13-1):

- Premature junctional complex (PJC)
- Junctional escape complexes or rhythms
- Accelerated junctional rhythm
- Junctional tachycardia
- AV nodal reentrant tachycardia (AVNRT)
- AV reentrant tachycardia

As a reminder, dysrhythmias arising from the SA node, atria, or AV junction can be collectively called *supraventricular dysrhythmias.*

Premature Junctional Complex

Description

A PJC is a single early electrical impulse that originates in the AV junction (Figure 13-2). It occurs before the next expected sinus impulse, interrupting the regularity of the underlying rhythm. Because the impulse arises from the middle of the heart, the atria are depolarized in a retrograde fashion. This causes the P′ wave (if visible) to be inverted. The ventricles are depolarized in the normal manner (measuring 0.06 to 0.10 seconds in duration).

Causes

PJCs are thought to result from enhanced automaticity. Causes are shown in the box on the next page.

WANT MORE INFORMATION?
Visit the Fast & Easy ECGs Website at www.mhhe.com/shadeECG2e.

QUESTION

2. What would you expect the appearance of the P′ waves to be if they originate from the AV junction?

REMINDER

Like atrial dysrhythmias, aberrant conduction may also occur with dysrhythmias that originate from the AV junction.

KEY CONCEPT

As with sinus dysrhythmias and atrial dysrhythmias, the QRS complexes in junctional dysrhythmias typically appear normal.

LO 13.3

Inverted P' wave may precede the QRS complex with a P'R interval shorter than normal

Premature junctional complex (PJC) is a single early electrical impulse that originates in the AV junction

Inverted P' wave may precede each QRS complex with P'R intervals shorter than normal

Junctional escape rhythm arises from a single site in AV junction at a rate of between 40 and 60 beats per minute

P' wave may be buried in the QRS complex

Accelerated junctional rhythm arises from a single site in the AV junction at a rate of between 60 and 100 beats per minute

P' wave may follow each QRS complex

Junctional tachycardia arises from a single site in the AV junction at a rate of between 100 and 180 beats per minute

Figure 13-1
Junctional dysrhythmias originate from the AV junction

Causes of Premature Junctional Complexes	
Cause	**Examples**
Cardiac diseases	Cardiomyopathy, CAD, congestive heart failure, congenital abnormalities, inferior-wall MI, myocardial ischemia, pericarditis, rheumatic heart disease, swelling of the AV node after surgery, valvular heart disease
Use of certain drugs	Digitalis toxicity, cocaine, excessive amphetamine intake
Noncardiac disorders	Acute respiratory failure, alcohol, anxiety, caffeine, certain electrolyte imbalances, COPD, electrolyte imbalance (particularly magnesium and potassium), fatigue, fear or stress, hyperthyroidism, hypoxia, nicotine, vigorous exercise

Premature junctional complex arises from somewhere in the AV junction.

Rate depends on underlying rhythm	Rhythm irregular due to premature beat	P′ waves PJC is inverted; may appear before, during or after QRS complex, may be hidden in QRS complex	QRS complexes of normal duration and all look alike*

P′R intervals shortened if seen	ST segments normal and isoelectric	T waves normal shape and upright	QT intervals within normal limits of 0.36 to 0.44 second	U waves may or may not be present

* unless aberrantly conducted in which case they may be wider than normal and bizarre-looking

Figure 13-2
Premature junctional complex.

Effects

In the healthy heart, isolated PJCs are of little clinical significance. However, frequent PJCs (more than 4 to 6 per minute) warn of more serious conditions.

The patient may be asymptomatic or may experience palpitations. Your assessment will likely reveal the presence of an irregular pulse. Frequent PJCs may cause the patient to experience hypotension due to a transient decrease in cardiac output. Be sure to check for a pulse in rhythms that have premature beats to determine if they are perfusing beats. Typically, PJCs produce a pulse, but premature beats that arise from the ventricles may not. You can detect this by watching the ECG in the dynamic mode while feeling for a pulse.

When looking at the ECG rhythm, PJCs appear as "early beats." This causes the R-R interval to be shorter between the preceding beat and the early beat (as compared with the underlying rhythm).

Appearance

As with any premature beats, you first see an irregular rhythm as the underlying rhythm is disrupted by the presence of early beats. When you look at the area(s) of irregularity you see a shorter R-R interval between the beat of the underlying rhythm and the premature beat. P′ waves may or may not be seen with the PJCs. If P′ waves are present with the premature beats, they will differ from the P waves of the underlying rhythm and are usually inverted. P′R intervals,

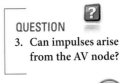

QUESTION
3. Can impulses arise from the AV node?

KEY CONCEPT
The hallmark features of PJCs is an irregular rhythm due to early beats that feature inverted P waves and narrow QRS complexes.

if present with the premature junctional beats, will be less than 0.12 seconds in duration. The impulse arises above the ventricles; therefore the QRS complexes of PJCs are normal and look the same as QRS complexes of the underlying rhythm. The T waves of the premature beats deflect in the same direction as the R waves. PJCs are normally followed by a noncompensatory pause.

PJCs intermingled between normal beats are named depending on how frequent they occur. When every other beat is a PJC, it is called *bigeminal PJCs*, or *junctional bigeminy*. If every third beat is a PJC, it is called *trigeminal PJCs*, or *junctional trigeminy*. Likewise, if a PJC occurs every fourth beat, it is called *quadrigeminal PJCs*, or *junctional quadrigeminy*. Regular PJCs at greater intervals than every fourth beat have no special name.

Treatment

PJCs generally do not require treatment. PJCs caused by the use of caffeine, tobacco, or alcohol, or with anxiety, fatigue, or fever can be controlled by eliminating the underlying cause.

LO 13.4

Junctional Escape Rhythm

Description

Junctional escape rhythm is slow, steady rhythm (40 to 60 beats per minute) with narrow QRS complexes, inverted or absent P′ waves, and shorter than normal P′R intervals (when the P′ wave precedes the QRS complex). It typically occurs when the rate of the primary pacemaker (SA node) falls below that of the AV junctional tissue (Figure 13-3). Remember, if the SA node fails to fire or slows down, the AV junction (or ventricles) in their role as backup pacemakers, should initiate the heartbeat. This serves as a safety mechanism to prevent cardiac standstill. Junctional escape may also be seen as an isolated junctional complex (escape complex) that occurs when the SA node fails to initiate an impulse. This isolated beat is then followed by the SA node resuming the heart beat and sinus rhythm is seen again.

Causes

Junctional escape rhythm is brought about by AV heart block or conditions that interfere with SA node function. Causes of this dysrhythmia are listed in the following box.

Causes of Junctional Escape Rhythm	
Cause	Examples
Cardiac diseases	Cardiomyopathy, disease of the SA node (sick sinus syndrome), heart failure, inferior wall MI, myocarditis, postcardiac surgery, SA node ischemia, rheumatic heart disease, valvular heart disease
Use of certain drugs	Digoxin, quinidine, beta-blockers, calcium channel blockers
Increased autonomic nervous system stimulation	Increased vagal tone on the SA node
Noncardiac disorders	Hypoxia, electrolyte imbalance

Junctional escape rhythm arises from a single site in the AV junction.

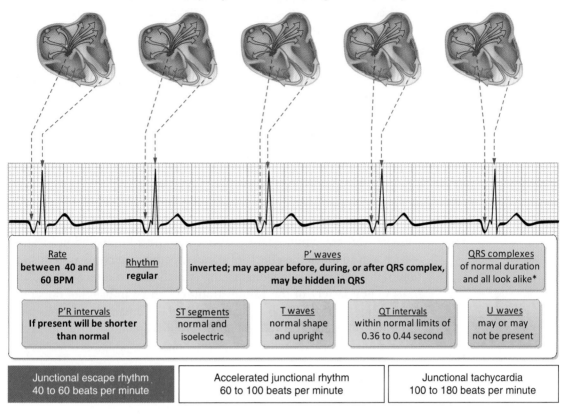

Rate between 40 and 60 BPM	Rhythm regular	P′ waves inverted; may appear before, during, or after QRS complex, may be hidden in QRS		QRS complexes of normal duration and all look alike*
P′R intervals If present will be shorter than normal	ST segments normal and isoelectric	T waves normal shape and upright	QT intervals within normal limits of 0.36 to 0.44 second	U waves may or may not be present

Junctional escape rhythm 40 to 60 beats per minute	Accelerated junctional rhythm 60 to 100 beats per minute	Junctional tachycardia 100 to 180 beats per minute

* unless aberrantly conducted in which case they may be wider than normal and bizarre-looking

Figure 13-3
Junctional escape rhythm.

Effects

The normal firing rate of the AV junction is 40 to 60 beats per minute. Rates of greater than 50 beats per minute are usually well tolerated. Slower rates can cause decreased cardiac output and may lead to symptoms (chest pain or pressure, syncope, altered level of consciousness, hypotension).

Remember from our earlier discussion, decreased cardiac output leads to decreased tissue perfusion. Decreased tissue perfusion can have dire consequences. First, there is insufficient oxygen and nutrients for the body to satisfy its energy needs. Second, if the waste products of metabolism are not removed, they accumulate in the tissues and create a toxic environment. If not corrected, both factors can lead to shock and, ultimately, death of the patient.

Appearance

The key features of this dysrhythmia are a slow heart rate of between 40 and 60 beats per minute; inverted P′ waves that precede, are lost in (buried), or follow the QRS complexes; and, if present, a P′R interval less than 0.12 seconds in duration. The rhythm is regular if it is an escape rhythm but irregular if it is an isolated escape beat. The QRS complexes are normal.

KEY CONCEPT
The most prominent characteristic of junctional escape rhythm is a regular rhythm with a rate of 40 to 60 beats per minute that features inverted or absent P′ waves and narrow QRS complexes.

KEY CONCEPT
Junctional escape rhythm arises from the AV junction at a rate of 40 to 60 beats per minute.

QUESTION
5. What is the inherent rate of the ventricles?

If the junctional escape rhythm has a heart rate of less than 40 beats per minute, it is described as *slow* or *bradycardic junctional escape rhythm or junctional escape rhythm with bradycardia.*

Treatment

When medical conditions cause the problem, it is essential to observe the heart rhythm for a worsening of the bradycardia. Treatment for junctional escape is directed at identifying and correcting the underlying cause and reestablishing the SA node activity at a fast enough rate to prevent the escape rhythm. For example, you should withhold digoxin or correct electrolyte imbalances if serum levels point to inappropriate levels of either. Also, deliver oxygen, place the patient on an ECG monitor, monitor the blood pressure and pulse oximetry, and establish an IV.

Patients who are symptomatic may require the administration of atropine (which acts to block the effects of parasympathetic nervous system stimulation), IV push, transcutaneous pacing (which acts to directly stimulate the heart to beat faster), or the administration of an IV infusion of dopamine or epinephrine (both of which act to stimulate the sympathetic nervous system). A permanent pacemaker may be needed if the patient has little or no chance of regaining a normal rhythm at a normal rate.

LO 13.5

Accelerated Junctional Rhythm

Description

KEY CONCEPT
Accelerated junctional rhythm arises from the AV junction at a rate of 60 to 100 beats per minute.

Accelerated junctional rhythm is a dysrhythmia that arises from the AV junction (Figure 13-4). At a rate of 60 to 100 beats per minute, it speeds up to take over as the heart's pacemaker. Remember that the term *tachycardia* is applied to heart rates above 100 beats per minute. The inherent rate of the AV node/junction is 40 to 60 beats per minute. A heart rate above 60 beats per minute cannot correctly be classified as tachycardia until it reaches a rate of 100 beats per minute, so we use the term *accelerated* to describe this dysrhythmia. The word *accelerated* emphasizes that it is faster than the inherent rate.

Causes

Accelerated junctional rhythm is due to increased automaticity or irritability of the AV junction. The following box lists the causes of accelerated junctional rhythm.

Causes of Accelerated Junctional Rhythm	
Cause	**Examples**
Cardiac diseases	Heart failure, inferior or posterior wall MI, myocardial ischemia, pericarditis, rheumatic heart disease, post open-heart surgery, valvular heart disease
Use of certain drugs	Digitalis (common cause)
Noncardiac disorders	COPD, electrolyte imbalance (hypokalemia)

Accelerated junctional rhythm arises from a single site in the AV junction.

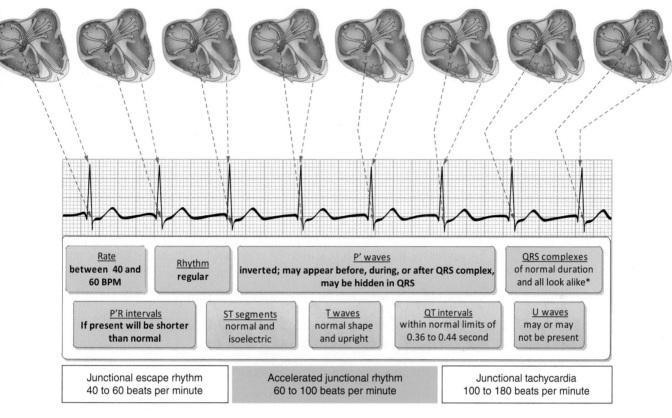

Rate between 40 and 60 BPM	Rhythm regular	P′ waves inverted; may appear before, during, or after QRS complex, may be hidden in QRS		QRS complexes of normal duration and all look alike*
P′R intervals If present will be shorter than normal	ST segments normal and isoelectric	T waves normal shape and upright	QT intervals within normal limits of 0.36 to 0.44 second	U waves may or may not be present

Junctional escape rhythm 40 to 60 beats per minute	Accelerated junctional rhythm 60 to 100 beats per minute	Junctional tachycardia 100 to 180 beats per minute

* unless aberrantly conducted in which case they may be wider than normal and bizarre-looking

Figure 13-4
Accelerated junctional rhythm.

Effects

Accelerated junctional rhythm has the same rate as normal sinus rhythm, so it is usually well tolerated. However, it may predispose patients with myocardial ischemia to more serious dysrhythmias. Also, because the atria are depolarized by way of retrograde conduction and may actually follow ventricular depolarization, blood ejection from the atria into the ventricles (atrial kick) may be prevented. This may cause decreased cardiac output. If cardiac output is low, the patient may exhibit signs of decreased tissue perfusion.

Appearance

The key characteristic of accelerated junctional rhythm is a regular rhythm (as it originates from one site) with P′ waves that precede, are lost in (buried), or follow the QRS complex. When present, the P′ waves are inverted. The P′R intervals, if present, are less than 0.10 seconds. The rate is 60 to 100 beats per minute. Accelerated junctional rhythm arises from above the ventricles, so the QRS complexes are normal.

KEY CONCEPT
The most prominent characteristic of accelerated junctional rhythm is a regular rhythm with a rate of 60 to 100 beats per minute that features inverted or absent P′ waves and narrow QRS complexes.

Treatment

Given the heart rate seen with accelerated junctional rhythm, the patient is typically asymptomatic. Treatment is directed at identifying and correcting the underlying cause. For example, digoxin should be withheld or electrolyte imbalances corrected if serum levels point to inappropriate levels of either. The patient should be continually observed for signs of decreased cardiac output. Temporary pacing may be indicated if the patient is symptomatic.

LO 13.6

Junctional Tachycardia

Description

Junctional tachycardia is a fast ectopic rhythm that originates from an irritable focus (increased automaticity) in the bundle of His and overrides the SA node (Figure 13-5). It is said to be present when there are three or more

Junctional tachycardia arises from a single focus in the AV junction.

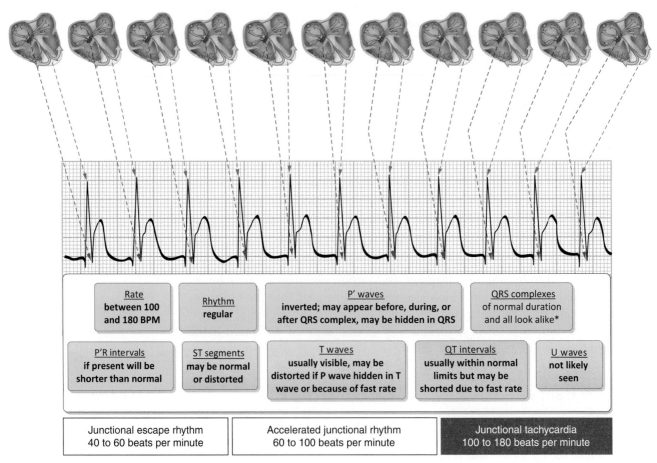

Rate between 100 and 180 BPM	Rhythm regular	P' waves inverted; may appear before, during, or after QRS complex, may be hidden in QRS	QRS complexes of normal duration and all look alike*
P'R intervals if present will be shorter than normal	ST segments may be normal or distorted	T waves usually visible, may be distorted if P wave hidden in T wave or because of fast rate	QT intervals usually within normal limits but may be shorted due to fast rate	U waves not likely seen

Junctional escape rhythm 40 to 60 beats per minute	Accelerated junctional rhythm 60 to 100 beats per minute	Junctional tachycardia 100 to 180 beats per minute

* unless aberrantly conducted in which case they may be wide and bizarre-looking

Figure 13-5
Junctional tachycardia.

premature junctional complexes in a row or there is a junctional rhythm occurring at a rate of between 100 and 180 (and rarely as fast as 200) beats per minute. As with other junctional rhythms, the atria are depolarized by retrograde conduction while conduction through the ventricles occurs in the normal manner.

When the rate in junctional tachycardia exceeds 150 beats per minute, the rhythm becomes hard to distinguish from atrial tachycardia and is often referred to as *supraventricular tachycardia*. The term *paroxysmal* is added to describe junctional tachycardia that starts and ends suddenly. It is frequently precipitated by a premature junctional complex.

Causes

Junctional tachycardia is believed to be caused by enhanced automaticity and is commonly the result of digitalis toxicity. It may also be brought about by myocardial ischemia or infarction and CHF. Other causes of junctional tachycardia are listed in the following box. It can occur at any age without a patient history of underlying heart disease.

Causes of Junctional Tachycardia	
Cause	**Examples**
Cardiac diseases	Swelling of the AV junction after heart surgery, damage to AV junction from inferior or posterior wall MI or rheumatic fever
Use of certain drugs	Digoxin (particularly in the presence of hypokalemia), theophylline
Noncardiac disorders	Excessive catecholamine administration, anxiety, hypoxia, electrolyte imbalance (particularly hypokalemia)

Effects

Palpitations, nervousness, anxiety, vertigo, lightheadedness, and syncope frequently accompany this dysrhythmia. Short bursts of junctional tachycardia are well tolerated in otherwise healthy people. With sustained rapid ventricular rates and retrograde depolarization of the atria, ventricular filling is not as complete during diastole, leading to compromised cardiac output in patients with underlying heart disease. The loss of the atrial kick may cause up to a 30% reduction in cardiac output. Increases in cardiac oxygen requirements may increase myocardial ischemia and the frequency and severity of the patient's chest pain. It can extend the size of MI; cause congestive heart failure, hypotension, and cardiogenic shock; and possibly predispose the patient to ventricular dysrhythmias.

Appearance

The most evident feature of junctional tachycardia is a rapid heart rate with narrow QRS complexes. The rate is 100 to 180 beats per minute. P′ waves may precede, be lost in (buried), or follow the QRS complexes. When present, the P′ waves will be inverted. The P′R intervals, if present, will be less than 0.12 seconds. Junctional tachycardia is coming from one site, so the rhythm is regular (except if there is an onset or termination as seen with PSVT). The QRS complexes are normal.

LO 13.7

Atrioventricular Nodal Reentrant Tachycardia

Description

In Chapter 10, we pointed out that some people have an abnormal extra anatomical pathway (congenital in nature) within or just next to the AV node. Formed from tissue that acts similarly to the AV node, this circuit involves two pathways: a fast pathway and a slow pathway. These pathways conduct impulses at different rates and recover at different speeds. The fast pathway conducts impulses rapidly but recovers more slowly. The slow pathway conducts impulses more slowly but recovers more quickly.

In sinus rhythm, the slow pathway does not transmit impulses as the depolarization wave passes through the fast pathway **anterogradely** (moving downward) and then turns around at the far end and invades the slow pathway **retrogradely** (moving backward), meeting the slow depolarization impulse head on and eliminating it (Figure 13-6).

However, because of its quick recovery period, under the right circumstances, such as the introduction of a PAC, the slow pathway can be stimulated first.

Enlarged view

With an abnormal extra pathway, the impulse travels downward through the fast pathway and then turns around at the far end and invades the slow pathway retrogradely to meet the impulse head on and eliminating it

Fast

Slow

Figure 13-6
Conduction of impulse through an extra AV pathway in sinus rhythm.

Then, at its far end, in addition to stimulating the ventricles, the depolarizing impulse can turn into the fast pathway passing retrogradely. When the impulse reaches the proximal end, in addition to depolarizing the atria retrogradely, it can reenter the slow circuit which has already recovered. The impulse can become trapped within this circuit (of slow and fast pathways), resulting in a continuous circular reentrant pattern that rapidly depolarizes the ventricles and then the atria (Figure 13-7).

This type of supraventricular tachycardia is called *AV nodal reentrant tachycardia* (AVNRT), or *atrioventricular nodal reentrant tachycardia*. AVNRT, the most common regular supraventricular tachycardia, occurs more often in women than men (approximately 75% of cases occurring in females).

Appearance

AVNRT is typically characterized by an abrupt onset and termination. Episodes may last from seconds to minutes to days. Most commonly, because the ventricles are stimulated by the normal route via the AV node, the QRS complexes are narrow. However, the QRS complexes can be broad due to preexisting bundle branch block (discussed in Chapters 7 and 19). The QRS rate is usually 140 to 240 BPM. Because the atria are depolarized retrogradely from the AV node, the P′ wave is often buried in the QRS complex. Sometimes it is seen following the QRS complex. The ST segment depression is common at high heart rates even in the absence of coronary artery disease.

An early beat from the atria can conduct through the slow pathway and then travel back up the fast pathway to reenter the recovering slow pathway, triggering the impulse to indefinitely spin around in the circuit and producing a very rapid and regular rhythm

PAC

PAC

Enlarged view

Figure 13-7
AV nodal reentrant tachycardia.

Effects

In the absence of structural heart disease, AVNRT is usually well tolerated. Common symptoms include palpitations, nervousness, anxiety, lightheadedness, pounding sensation in the neck, chest discomfort, and/or dyspnea. Polyuria can occur after termination of the episode (due to the release of atrial natriuretic factor).

AVNRT may cause or worsen heart failure in patients with poor left ventricular function. It may cause angina or MI in patients with coronary artery disease. Syncope may occur in patients with a rapid ventricular rate or prolonged tachycardia due to poor ventricular filling, decreased cardiac output, hypotension, and reduced cerebral perfusion. Syncope may also occur because of transient asystole when the tachycardia terminates, due to tachycardia-induced depression of the sinus node.

LO 13.8

Preexcitation

In Chapters 8 and 10 we talked about accessory pathways and how they can lead to supraventricular tachycardia. Normally, conduction of the impulse from the atria to the ventricles is delayed in the AV node for about 0.1 seconds. This is long enough for the atria to contract and empty their contents into the ventricles.

Some people have accessory conduction pathways that provide a direct connection between the atria and ventricles, thereby bypassing the AV node and bundle of His. They allow atrial impulses to depolarize the ventricles earlier than usual, a condition called *preexcitation*. The term *bypass tract* is used when one end of an accessory pathway is attached to normal conductive tissue.

Because these accessory pathways do not possess the rate-slowing properties of the AV node, they can conduct electrical activity at a much higher rate than the AV node. For example, if the atrial rate is 300 beats per minute, the accessory bundle may conduct all the electrical impulses from the atria to the ventricles, causing the ventricles to beat up to 300 times per minute. Extremely fast heart rates can be extremely dangerous and cause hemodynamic instability. In some cases, the combination of an accessory pathway and dysrhythmias can trigger ventricular fibrillation (discussed in Chapter 14).

Accessory pathways and bypass tracts are seen in a small percentage of the general population. They sometimes occur in normal healthy hearts as an isolated finding, or may be in conjunction with mitral valve prolapse or hypertrophic cardiomyopathy, as well as various congenital disorders.

The most common preexcitation syndromes are Wolff-Parkinson-White (WPW) syndrome and Lown-Ganong-Levine (LGL) syndrome. Both of these disorders can be diagnosed by the ECG and can present as supraventricular tachycardia.

Another preexcitation syndrome occurs as a result of the Mahaim fibers. Instead of bypassing the AV node, these fibers originate below the AV node and attach into the ventricular wall, circumventing part or all of the bundle of His, bundle branches, and Purkinje fibers.

Wolff-Parkinson-White Syndrome

In WPW syndrome, the bundle of Kent, an accessory pathway, connects the atria to the ventricles, bypassing the AV node (refer to Figure 8-7). It can be left-sided (connecting the left atrium and left ventricle) or right-sided (connecting the right atrium and right ventricle). ECG features include the following:

- Rate is normal
- Rhythm is regular
- P waves are normal
- QRS complexes are widened with slurring of the initial portion (delta wave)
- PR interval is usually shortened (less than 0.12 seconds)

In contrast to bundle branch block, where the QRS complex is widened due to delayed ventricular activation, in WPW it is widened because of premature activation of the ventricles. The QRS complex associated with WPW is a fusion beat. Although most of the ventricular myocardium is stimulated through the normal conduction pathways, a small area is depolarized early via the bundle of Kent. This produces a characteristic slurred initial upstroke, called the *delta wave,* in the QRS complex. Be sure to scan the entire ECG as a true delta wave may be seen in only a few leads.

Lown-Ganong-Levine Syndrome

In LGL syndrome, the accessory pathway, referred to as the *James fibers,* is within the AV node (Figure 13-8). This accessory pathway bypasses the normal delay within the AV node, but unlike WPW there is no small region of ventricular myocardium depolarized independently of the rest of the ventricles. Instead, all ventricular conduction occurs through the usual ventricular conduction pathways. For this reason, there is no delta wave and the QRS complex is not widened. The only indication of LGL on the ECG is shortening of the PR interval as a result of the accessory pathway bypassing the delay within the AV node.

Instead of traveling through the AV node, the impulse is carried to the ventricles by way of an intranodal accessory pathway; the James fibers. The impulse travels down through the atria.

ECG criteria for LGL include the following:

- The PR interval is less than 0.12 seconds
- The QRS complex is not widened
- There is no delta wave

KEY CONCEPT

Preexcitation syndromes occur in some persons because accessory conduction pathways exist between the atria and ventricles that bypass the AV node and bundle of His and allow the atria to depolarize the ventricles earlier than usual.

KEY CONCEPT

WPW syndrome is diagnosed by looking for a short PR interval and a delta wave.

Impulse travels down through the atria

James fibers

Instead of traveling through the AV node, the impulse is carried to the ventricles by way of an intranodal accessory pathway

Figure 13-8
In LGL, the impulse travels through an intranodal accessory pathway, referred to as the *James fibers,* bypassing the normal delay within the AV node. This produces a shortening of the PR interval but no widening of the QRS complex.

Unless tachycardia is present, WPW and LGL are usually of no clinical significance. However, preexcitation (specifically WPW) can predispose the patient to various tachydysrhythmias. The most common tachydysrhythmia is atrioventricular reentrant tachycardia (AVRT), followed by atrial fibrillation and atrial flutter. Atrial fibrillation and atrial flutter seen with WPW are extremely dangerous. As mentioned earlier, very rapid ventricular rates can result from conduction of the atrial impulses directly into the ventricles.

LO 13.9

Atrioventricular Reentrant Tachycardia

Description

AVRT, also known as *circus movement tachycardia* (CMT), results from a reentry circuit that includes the AV node and an accessory pathway from the

a. Impulse travels antegradely through AV node but then retrogradely reenters the atria through accessory pathway. It continues to spin around in the circuit producing a very rapid and regular rhythm

b. Impulse travels antegradely through accessory pathway but then retrogradely reenters the atria through AV node. It continues to spin around in the circuit producing a very rapid and regular rhythm

A

B

Figure 13-9
Atrioventricular reentrant tachycardia: (A) Orthodromic (B) Antedromic.

atria to the ventricle such as the bundle of Kent. This reentry circuit is physically much larger than the one associated with AVNRT.

Appearance

Reentry through an accessory pathway can take one of two directions, orthodromic conduction or antedromic conduction.

Orthodromic AVRT

Most often the AV node serves as the forward portion of the reentry circuit, and the accessory pathway serves as the retrograde portion. What this means is that atrial impulses are conducted down through the AV node and retrogradely reenter the atrium via the accessory pathway (Figure 13.9A). Because of the normal conduction to the ventricles, regular, narrow QRS complexes are seen. Further, a P′ wave may follow each QRS complex due to retrograde conduction.

Antedromic AVRT

When a reentry circuit circulates in the opposite direction, atrial impulses are conducted down through the accessory pathway and reenter the atrium retrogradely via the AV node (Figure 13.9B). Because the accessory pathway initiates conduction in the ventricles outside of the bundle of His, the QRS complex in antidromic AVRT is often wider than usual, with a delta wave.

Effects

Common signs and symptoms associated with a rapid ventricular rate include palpitations, lightheadedness, shortness of breath, anxiety, weakness, dizziness, chest discomfort, and signs of shock.

LO 13.10

Treatment of Supraventricular Tachycardia

As they are the same, the treatment for the three forms of supraventricular tachycardia (SVT) discussed in this chapter (junctional tachycardia, AVNRT, and AVRT) are presented here.

When assessing patients with tachycardia, attempt to determine whether the tachycardia is the primary cause of the presenting symptoms or secondary to an underlying condition that is causing both the presenting symptoms and the faster heart rate.

As with all patients, maintain patent airway and assist breathing as necessary. If oxygenation is inadequate or the patient shows signs of increased breathing effort, provide supplementary oxygen. Attach an ECG monitor to the patient, evaluate blood pressure and oximetry, and establish IV access. If available, obtain a 12-lead ECG to better define the rhythm, but do not delay immediate cardioversion if the patient is unstable.

If the patient demonstrates rate-related decreased cardiac output with signs and symptoms such as acute altered mental status, ischemic chest discomfort, acute heart failure, hypotension, or other signs of shock suspected to be due to the tachydysrhythmia, proceed to immediate synchronized cardioversion. If the patient is conscious, consider establishing IV access before cardioversion and administering sedation. Avoid any delay in cardioversion if the patient is extremely unstable.

If he or she is not hypotensive, the patient with a regular narrow-complex SVT may be treated with adenosine while preparations are made for synchronized cardioversion. Stable patients may await expert consultation because treatment has the potential for harm.

Vagal maneuvers and adenosine are the preferred initial therapeutic choices for the termination of stable supraventricular tachycardia. If stable SVT does not respond to vagal maneuvers, IV adenosine should be administered. A second, higher dose can be administered if the rhythm does not convert within 1 to 2 minutes. Because of the possibility of initiating atrial fibrillation with rapid ventricular rates in a patient with WPW, a defibrillator should be available when adenosine is administered to any patient in whom WPW is suspected. As with vagal maneuvers, the effect of adenosine on other SVTs (such as atrial fibrillation or flutter) is to transiently slow the ventricular rate (which may be useful diagnostically) but not result in their termination or lasting rate control.

If adenosine or vagal maneuvers fail to convert SVT, if it recurs after such treatment, or if these treatments reveal a different form of SVT (such as atrial fibrillation or flutter), the use of longer-acting AV nodal blocking agents, such as the nondihydropyridine calcium channel blockers (verapamil and diltiazem) or beta-blockers, may be considered.

Frequent attacks may require radiofrequency ablation, in which the abnormally conducting tissue in the heart is destroyed. In the clinical setting, patients who have had a recent MI or heart surgery may need a temporary pacemaker to reset the heart's rhythm. A child with a permanent junctional tachycardia may be treated with ablation therapy, followed by permanent pacemaker insertion.

In patients with stable wide-QRS complex tachycardia where it is unclear as to whether it is SVT or ventricular tachycardia (discussed in Chapter 14), a reasonable approach is to try to identify which it is and treat on the basis of the algorithm for that rhythm. If the etiology of the rhythm cannot be determined, the rate is regular, and the QRS is monomorphic, recent evidence suggests that IV adenosine is relatively safe for both treatment and diagnosis.

Practice Makes Perfect

For each of the 53 ECG tracings on the following pages, practice the Nine-Step Process for analyzing ECGs. To achieve the greatest learning, you should practice assessing and interpreting the ECGs immediately after reading this chapter. Below are questions you should consider as you assess each tracing. Your answers can be written into the area below each ECG marked "ECG Findings." Your findings can then be compared to the answers provided in Appendix A. All tracings are six seconds in length.

1. Determine the heart rate. Is it slow? Normal? Fast? What is the ventricular rate? What is the atrial rate?

2. Determine if the rhythm is regular or irregular. If it is irregular, what type of irregularity is it? Occasional or Irregular? Slight? Sudden acceleration or slowing in heart rate? Total? Patterned? Does it have a variable conduction ratio?

3. Determine if P waves are present. If so, how do they appear? Do they have normal height and duration? Are they tall? Notched? Wide? Biphasic? Of differing morphology? Inverted? One for each QRS complex? More than one preceding some or all the QRS complexes? Do they have a sawtooth appearance? An indiscernible chaotic baseline?

4. Determine if QRS complexes are present. If so, how do they appear? Narrow with proper amplitude? Tall? Low amplitude? Delta wave? Notched? Wide? Bizarre? With chaotic waveforms?

5. Determine the presence of PR intervals. If present, how do they appear? Constant? Of normal duration? Shortened? Lengthened? Progressively longer? Varying?

6. Evaluate the ST segments. Do they have normal duration and position? Are they elevated? (If so, are they flat, concave, convex, arched?) Depressed? (If so, are they normal, flat, downsloping or upsloping?)

7. Determine if T waves are present. If so, how do they appear? Of normal height and duration? Tall? Wide? Notched? Inverted?

8. Determine the presence of QT intervals. If present, what is their duration? Normal? Shortened? Prolonged?

9. Determine if U waves are present. If present, how do they appear? Of normal height and duration? Inverted?

10. Identify the rhythm or dysrhythmia.

1.

ECG Findings:

2.

ECG Findings:

3.

ECG Findings:

4.

ECG Findings:

5.

ECG Findings:

6.

ECG Findings:

7.

ECG Findings:

8.

ECG Findings:

9.

ECG Findings:

10.

ECG Findings:

11.

ECG Findings:

12.

ECG Findings:

13.

ECG Findings:

14.

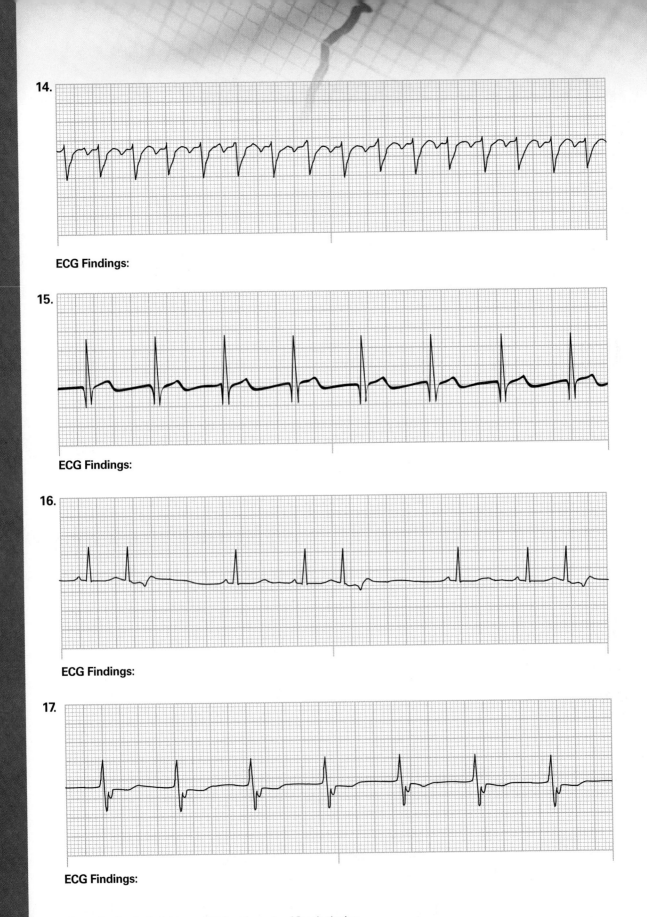

ECG Findings:

15.

ECG Findings:

16.

ECG Findings:

17.

ECG Findings:

18.

ECG Findings:

19.

ECG Findings:

20.

ECG Findings:

21.

ECG Findings:

22.

ECG Findings:

23.

ECG Findings:

24.

ECG Findings:

25.

ECG Findings:

26.

ECG Findings:

27.

ECG Findings:

28.

ECG Findings:

29.

ECG Findings:

30.

ECG Findings:

31.

ECG Findings:

32.

ECG Findings:

33.

ECG Findings:

34.

ECG Findings:

35.

ECG Findings:

36.

ECG Findings:

37.

ECG Findings:

38.

ECG Findings:

39.

ECG Findings:

40.

ECG Findings:

41.

ECG Findings:

42.

ECG Findings:

43.

ECG Findings:

44.

ECG Findings:

45.

ECG Findings:

46.

ECG Findings:

47.

ECG Findings:

48.

ECG Findings:

49.

ECG Findings:

50.

ECG Findings:

51.

ECG Findings:

52.

ECG Findings:

53.

ECG Findings:

Key Points 🔍

- Rhythms that originate in the AV junction, the area around the AV node and the bundle of His, are referred to as *junctional rhythms*.

- Impulses originating in the AV junction travel upward and cause backward or retrograde depolarization of the atria, resulting in inverted P′ waves in lead II with a short P′R interval, absent P′ waves (as they are buried by the QRS complex), or retrograde P′ waves.

- With junctional dysrhythmias, the QRS complexes are usually normal (unless there is an intraventricular conduction defect, aberrancy, or preexcitation).

- A PJC is a single early electrical impulse that arises from the AV junction.

- Junctional escape rhythm arises from the AV junction at a rate of 40 to 60 beats per minute.

- Accelerated junctional rhythm arises from the AV junction at a rate of 60 to 100 beats per minute.

- Junctional tachycardia is a fast, ectopic rhythm that arises from the bundle of His at a rate of between 100 and 180 beats per minute.

- In AVNRT, fast and slow pathways are located within the right atrium in close proximity to or within the AV node and exhibit electrophysiologic properties similar to AV nodal tissue. These pathways can allow for development of SVT.

- Preexcitation syndromes occur when accessory conduction pathways exist between the atria and ventricles that bypass the AV node and bundle of His and allow the atria to depolarize the ventricles earlier than usual.

- Preexcitation is diagnosed by looking for a short PR interval.

- Criteria for WPW include a PR interval less than 0.12 seconds, wide QRS complexes due to a delta wave (seen in some leads). Patients with WPW are vulnerable to PSVT.

- In LGL, there is an intranodal accessory pathway that bypasses the normal delay within the AV node. Criteria for LGL include a PR interval less than 0.12 seconds and a normal QRS complex.

Assess Your Understanding

The following questions give you a chance to assess your understanding of the material discussed in this chapter. The answers can be found in Appendix A.

1. The normal PR interval is _____ seconds.
    a. 0.06 to 0.10
    b. 0.10 to 0.20
    c. 0.12 to 0.20
    d. 0.20 to 0.24

2. PR intervals of less than 0.12 seconds in duration are indicative of a(n)
   a. intermittent blocking of the impulse as it passes through the AV node.
   b. delay in conduction of the impulse between the SA node and the ventricles.
   c. increased rate of impulse discharge from the SA node.
   d. pacemaker site, either in or close to the AV junction.

3. Your patient shows normal sinus rhythm with occasional ectopic beats on the ECG. The ectopic beats appear with absent P waves along with a normal QRS complex. The ectopic beats are premature _____ complexes.
   a. atrial
   b. bundle
   c. junctional
   d. ventricular

4. Which of the following originates from the AV junction?
   a. Atrial tachycardia
   b. Junctional escape rhythm
   c. Premature atrial complex
   d. Sinus bradycardia

5. Match the following junctional rhythms with the appropriate heart rate.

Dysrhythmias	Beats per minute
a. Junctional tachycardia	_____ 40 to 60
b. Junctional escape rhythm	_____ 100 to 180
c. Accelerated junctional rhythm	_____ 60 to 100

6. P′R intervals seen with junctional rhythms will appear
   a. longer than 0.20 seconds in duration.
   b. shorter than 0.12 seconds in duration.
   c. within normal ranges.
   d. varied.

7. Which of the following rhythms may be preceded by an inverted P′ wave?
   a. Atrial flutter
   b. Junctional escape rhythm
   c. Atrial tachycardia
   d. Idioventricular rhythm

8. Match the following types of PJCs with the correct description.

Types	Descriptions
a. Bigeminal	_____ PJCs that occur every third beat
b. Quadrigeminal	_____ PJCs that occur every other beat
c. Trigeminal	_____ PJCs that occur every fourth beat

9. In junctional escape rhythm, the pacemaker site is in the
   a. SA node.
   b. atrial and internodal conduction pathways.
   c. AV junction.
   d. bundle of His.

10. Accelerated junctional rhythm
    a. is regularly irregular.
    b. has upright P′ waves in all leads.
    c. has normal P′R intervals.
    d. has normal QRS complexes.

11. With preexcitation syndromes,
    a. conduction of the impulse from the atria to the ventricles is delayed in the AV node.
    b. the heart is stimulated to beat faster.
    c. wide, bizarre QRS complexes are generated.
    d. impulses are conducted through accessory conduction pathways between the atria and ventricles

12. In WPW,
    a. the T wave is inverted.
    b. impulses bypass the AV node by traveling from the atria to the ventricles via the bundle of Kent.
    c. a small area of myocardium that is depolarized early produces a characteristic slurred initial downstroke in the QRS complex.
    d. the PR interval is prolonged.

Referring to the scenario at the beginning of this chapter, answer the following questions.

13. PSVT stands for
    a. premature ventricular tachycardia.
    b. premature atrial tachycardia.
    c. paroxysmal supraventricular tachycardia.
    d. paradoxical supraventricular tachycardia.

14. The P waves in PSVT are not discernable because
    a. they are not there.
    b. they are hidden in the T wave.
    c. f waves are present instead.
    d. F waves are present instead.

15. PSVT is caused by an electrical impulse circulating in what part of the heart?
    a. Atria
    b. AV node
    c. Bundle of His
    d. Purkinje fibers

Answers to Sidebar Questions

1. When we refer to the P waves as being normal, we mean they appear as an upright and round waveform. There is one P wave preceding each QRS complex. Its amplitude is 0.5 to 2.5 mm in height, and its duration is 0.06 to 0.10 seconds. In leads I, II, aV$_F$, and V$_2$ through V$_6$, the deflection of the P wave is characteristically upright or positive. In leads III, aV$_L$, and V$_1$, the P wave is usually upright but may be negative or biphasic (both positive and negative). In lead aV$_R$, the P wave is negative or inverted. **p. 334**

2. The P′ waves are inverted if they originate from the AV junction. **p. 335**

3. Electrophysiological studies have demonstrated that the AV node does not contain pacemaker cells. The cells nearest the bundle of His in the AV junction are responsible for secondary pacing function. **p. 337**

4. The pause that follows a premature beat is called a *noncompensatory pause* if the beat following the premature complex is normal and occurs before it was expected. In other words, the space between the complex before and after the premature beat is less than two normal R-R intervals. To determine if there is a noncompensatory pause, we measure from the R wave of the normal beat that precedes the PAC or PJC to the R wave of the first normal beat that follows it. If there are fewer than two full R-R intervals between those R waves (with the PAC or PJC in between), it is considered a noncompensatory pause. If, on the other hand, there are two full R-R intervals between those R waves, it is considered a compensatory pause. **p. 338**

5. The inherent rate of the ventricles is 20 to 40 beats per minute. **p. 339**

What's Online

Go to www.mhhe.com/shadeECG2e to find:

- Presentations on chapter content
- Find the P wave exercise
- Crossword puzzle exercises
- Additional ECG tracings for practicing analyzing junctional dysrhythmias
- Chapter quiz
- Flashcards
- Fill-in-the-blank exercises and answers
- In-depth answers to Practice Makes Perfect ECG tracings and Assess Your Understanding questions

14 Ventricular Dysrhythmias

Chapter Outline

Dysrhythmias Originating in the Ventricles

Premature Ventricular Complexes

Ventricular Escape Beats

Idioventricular Rhythm

Accelerated Idioventricular Rhythm

Ventricular Tachycardia

Polymorphic Ventricular Tachycardia

Ventricular Fibrillation

Asystole

Pulseless Electrical Activity

Learning Objectives

LO 14.1   Describe the origin of ventricular dysrhythmias.

LO 14.2   Describe the key features of dysrhythmias originating from the ventricles.

LO 14.3   Identify the causes, effects, and appearance of premature ventricular complexes.

LO 14.4   Identify the causes, effects, and appearance of ventricular escape beats.

LO 14.5   Identify the causes, effects, and appearance of idioventricular rhythm.

LO 14.6   Identify the causes, effects, and appearance of accelerated idioventricular rhythm.

LO 14.7   Identify the causes, effects, and appearance of ventricular tachycardia.

LO 14.8   Identify the causes, effects, and appearance of polymorphic ventricular tachycardia.

LO 14.9   Identify the causes, effects, and appearance of ventricular fibrillation.

LO 14.10 Identify the causes, effects, and appearance of asystole.

LO 14.11 Identify the causes, effects, and appearance of pulseless electrical activity.

Case History

It's two o'clock P.M. when pagers go off, alerting your EMS crew of a male who collapsed outside his home.

Upon arrival you find the patient lying next to the sidewalk. You immediately determine an absence of a pulse and initiate chest compressions. Your partner verifies he can feel a carotid pulse with compressions. She then begins ventilating the patient with a bag-valve-mask (BVM) and 100% oxygen. Shortly afterward a fire department first responder unit arrives on scene to help.

After the defibrillator has been turned on and the pads applied to the patient's chest, you briefly stop CPR and examine the monitor. You see a chaotic and random waveforms with no discernable P waves or QRS complexes. "It's ventricular fibrillation," you say to your team. "Let's charge up and shock." You set the power to 360 joules and push the charge button. The machine makes a characteristic whine as the capacitors prepare the energy for delivery. "I'm clear. You're clear. Everyone is clear," you say while visually confirming that no one is touching the patient. You then push the shock button and the energy is delivered. You watch the monitor as it initially shows a flat line for about 6 seconds, then see ventricular fibrillation (VF) return. With the patient remaining in VF, you direct CPR be continued and have a team member intubate the patient. An IV is established and you administer epinephrine per protocol and defibrillate the patient again, after which the rhythm appears to be a flat line. CPR is continued as you administer epinephrine per protocol. Despite your efforts, the patient is pronounced dead after arrival at the hospital.

LO 14.1

Dysrhythmias Originating in the Ventricles

Ventricular dysrhythmias originate in the ventricles below the bundle of His. This results in the heart being depolarized and contracting much differently than normal. Although some ventricular dysrhythmias may be benign, many ventricular dysrhythmias are potentially life threatening because the ventricles are ultimately responsible for cardiac output and, if they are not pumping effectively, cardiac output is diminished or even ceases.

Ventricular dysrhythmias typically result when the atria, AV junction, or both are unable to initiate an electrical impulse or when there is enhanced automaticity of the ventricular myocardium. Myocardial ischemia is a common cause of enhanced automaticity.

Quick recognition and treatment of ventricular dysrhythmias improves the chance of successful resuscitation. Many respond well to medications, although some medications used to treat ventricular dysrhythmias can actually cause them in certain circumstances. Electrical therapy is the treatment choice for some ventricular dysrhythmias, but in others the condition is lethal despite aggressive treatment.

KEY CONCEPT
Ventricular dysrhythmias originate from the ventricles and occur when the atria, AV junction, or both are unable to initiate an electrical impulse or when there is enhanced excitability of the ventricular myocardium.

REMINDER
A medication with pro-arrhythmic effects can cause dysrhythmias.

LO 14.2

P Wave Appearance

With the impulse originating below the bundle of His, the atria typically do not depolarize. As a result, the P waves are absent. If the impulse does travel backward to depolarize the atria, the P wave is buried in the abnormal QRS complex and is still not visible. If P waves are seen, one of two things is occurring; either the P waves are disassociated from the QRS complexes or the impulse originated from above the ventricles and there is aberrant conduction through the ventricles.

QRS Complex Appearance

Because ventricular dysrhythmias originate in the ventricular tissue and, instead of rapidly moving through the conduction pathways, they travel slowly from cell to cell, producing wide (greater than 0.12 seconds in duration), bizarre-looking QRS complexes. Further, the T waves take an opposite direction to the R wave (see Figure 7-15 in Chapter 7). The ST segment will either be elevated (if the R wave takes a negative deflection) or depressed (if the R wave takes a positive deflection).

Effects

With the loss in atrial kick (as the atria do not depolarize) and decreased stroke volume, ventricular dysrhythmias may produce little or no cardiac output. Some ventricular dysrhythmias fail to provide adequate perfusion because the rate is so slow it does not meet the metabolic needs of the body. In others, such as with ventricular tachycardia (VT), there is insufficient time to allow for ventricular filling. Although some ventricular dysrhythmias may be well tolerated by the patient, many cause symptoms of decreased cardiac output or, even worse, cardiac standstill.

Ventricular dysrhythmias include (Figure 14-1):

- Premature ventricular complex (PVC)
- Idioventricular rhythm
- Accelerated idioventricular rhythm
- VT
- VF
- Asystole

Premature Ventricular Complexes

Description

Premature ventricular complexes (PVCs) are early ectopic beats that interrupt the normal rhythm and originate from an irritable focus in the ventricular conduction system or muscle tissue (Figure 14-2). These beats occur earlier than the next expected sinus beat.

KEY CONCEPT
A stand-out feature of ventricular dysrhythmias are wide (greater than 0.12 seconds in duration), bizarre-looking QRS complexes that have T waves in the opposite direction of the R wave. P waves are not visible.

WANT MORE INFORMATION?
Visit the Fast & Easy ECGs Website at www.mhhe.com/shadeECG2e.

LO 14.3

KEY CONCEPT
PVCs are early ectopic beats originating from the ventricular conduction system or muscle tissue.

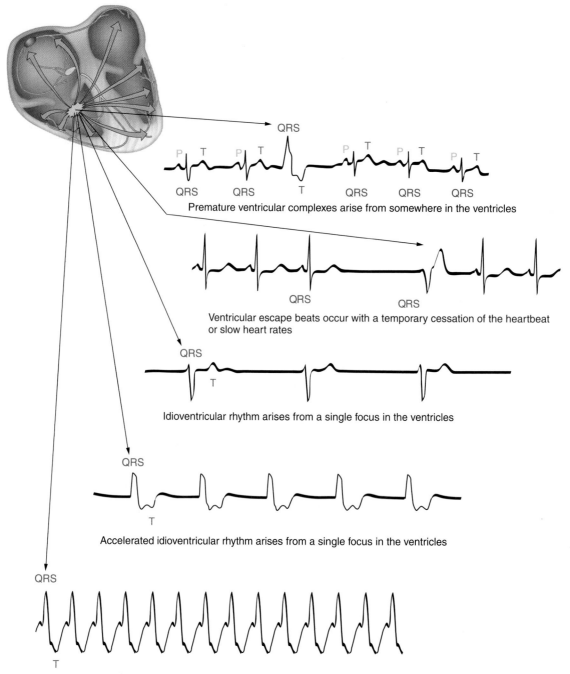

Premature ventricular complexes arise from somewhere in the ventricles

Ventricular escape beats occur with a temporary cessation of the heartbeat or slow heart rates

Idioventricular rhythm arises from a single focus in the ventricles

Accelerated idioventricular rhythm arises from a single focus in the ventricles

Ventricular tachycardia arises from a single focus in the ventricles

Figure 14-1
Ventricular dysrhythmias originate from the ventricles.

Causes

PVCs are caused by enhanced automaticity or reentry, brought about by disruption of the normal electrolyte shifts during cell depolarization and repolarization and other causes listed in the box on the following page.

Figure 14-2
PVC.

Causes of Premature Ventricular Complex	
Cause	**Examples**
Cardiac diseases	Myocardial ischemia and MI, congestive heart failure, irritation of ventricles by pacemaker electrodes or PA catheter, enlargement of the ventricular chambers, mitral valve prolapse, myocarditis
Use of certain drugs	Particularly amphetamine intoxication; cocaine, digoxin, quinidine, phenothiazines, tricyclic antidepressants; sympathomimetic drugs such as aminophylline, dopamine, epinephrine, isoproterenol: thyroid supplements
Autonomic nervous system stimulation	Increased sympathetic stimulation, exercise, emotional stress
Noncardiac disorders	Use of stimulants such as alcohol, caffeine, tobacco; electrolyte imbalance such as hypokalemia, hyperkalemia, hypomagnesemia, and hypocalcemia; hypoxia; metabolic acidosis

PVCs can occur for no apparent reason in individuals who have healthy hearts. They are often of no significance. The incidence of PVCs increases with age and can occur during exercise or at rest.

Effects

PVCs can be significant for two reasons. First, they can precipitate more serious dysrhythmias such as VT or VF. The danger is greater in patients experiencing myocardial ischemia and/or MI. Second, PVCs can result in decreased cardiac output due to reduced diastolic filling time and a loss of atrial kick. This leads to a diminished or nonpalpable pulse. When no pulse is felt during a PVC, it is called a **nonperfusing PVC.** Patients frequently experience the sensation of "skipped beats." Whether PVCs result in decreased cardiac output hinges on how long the abnormal rhythm lasts. Given this information, be sure to count and document how many PVCs are seen each minute.

QUESTION
1. **What type of irregularity does an occasional PVC produce?** *Note:* Answers to Sidebar Questions can be found at the end of the chapter.

With PVCs, it is important to check for a pulse to determine if they are perfusing PVCs. The absence of a pulse may require treatment if the underlying heart rate is slow or there are many PVCs. For example, with a rhythm in which there are PVCs every other beat (bigeminal) and the heart rate is 60 beats per minute, cardiac output will likely be adequate if the PVCs are producing a pulse. Conversely, cardiac output will likely be inadequate if the PVCs are not producing a pulse and the actual heart rate is 30 beats per minute.

Be sure to pay special attention to these rhythm disturbances in persons with acute myocardial ischemia. PVCs that occur with myocardial ischemia may indicate the presence of enhanced automaticity, a reentry mechanism, or both and may trigger lethal ventricular dysrhythmias. If the PVCs are frequent and occur early enough in the cardiac cycle, cardiac output is compromised. PVCs that serve as warning signs of the potential development of serious ventricular dysrhythmias in patients with myocardial ischemia include the following:

- Frequent PVCs
- Multifocal PVCs
- Early PVCs (R-on-T)
- Patterns of grouped PVCs

KEY CONCEPT
The hallmark features of PVCs are an irregular rhythm due to early beats that feature absent P waves and wide, bizarre-looking QRS complexes.

Appearance

Like other early ectopic beats, the first thing you see with PVCs is an irregular rhythm. When you look at the area(s) of irregularity, the PVCs appear earlier in the cycle than the normal set of complexes would be expected to occur. Another characteristic that stands out is a wide (greater than 0.12 seconds), bizarre-looking QRS complex with a T wave that takes an opposite direction to the R wave of the PVC.

The QRS complexes of the PVCs differ from QRS complexes of the underlying rhythm. P waves and PR intervals are typically present with the underlying rhythm but not the premature beats. A pause, called a *compensatory pause,* typically follows the PVC.

Figure 14-3
A compensatory pause is seen with premature ventricular complexes.

As discussed in previous chapters, the pause that follows a premature beat is called a *compensatory pause* if the normal beat following the premature complex occurs when it was expected (Figure 14-3). In other words, the period between the complex before and after the premature beat is the same as two normal R-R intervals. The pause occurs because the ventricle is refractory and cannot respond to the next regularly scheduled P wave from the sinus node. To determine if there is a compensatory pause we measure from the R wave of the beat that precedes the PVC to the R wave of the first beat that follows it. If there are two full R-R intervals between those R waves (with the PVC between), it is considered a compensatory pause.

PVCs may occur as a single beat, in clusters of two or more, or in repeating patterns. Sometimes, PVCs originate from only one location in the ventricle. These beats look the same and are called *uniform* (also referred to as *unifocal*) PVCs. Other times, PVCs arise from different sites in the ventricles. These

QUESTION
2. In which type of premature beats will there be a noncompensatory pause?

Figure 14-4
Multiform PVCs arise from different sites within the ventricles and look different from each other.

beats look different from each other (Figure 14-4) and are called *multiformed (multifocal)* PVCs. Multiform PVCs indicate an irritable myocardium and should prompt you to take corrective action.

QUESTION
3. What type of irregularity do bigeminal, trigeminal, or quadrigeminal PVCs produce?

PVCs may occur as a single, early beat or more frequently (Figure 14-5). PVCs intermingled between normal beats are named depending on their frequency. Bigeminal PVCs are said to be present when every other beat is a PVC, regardless if unifocal or multifocal. If every third beat is a PVC, the condition is called *trigeminal PVCs,* or *ventricular trigeminy*. Similarly, a PVC every fourth beat is called *ventricular quadrigeminy.*

Regular PVCs at greater intervals than every fourth beat have no special name and are referred to as *frequent PVCs.*

PVCs may also occur one after the other. Two PVCs in a row are called a *couplet,* or *pair*. A couplet indicates the ventricles are extremely irritable. Three or more PVCs in a row at a ventricular rate of at least 100 beats per minute constitute an abnormal rhythm known as *ventricular tachycardia.* It may be called a **salvo, run,** or **burst** of VT (Figure 14-6).

Another type of PVC is called an *interpolated PVC* (Figure 14-7). It occurs when a PVC does not disrupt the normal cardiac cycle. It appears as a PVC squeezed between two regular complexes. Another feature is the PR interval of the cardiac cycle that follows the PVC may be longer than normal.

Figure 14-5
Premature ventricular complexes occurring in a (A) bigeminal, (B) trigeminal, and (C) quadrigeminal pattern.

Frequent PVCs, especially if bigeminal, trigeminal, or couplets or runs of VT, may foretell the deterioration of the rhythm into VF.

PVCs occurring on or near the previous T wave also are likely to progress to more life-threatening ventricular dysrhythmias (such as VF) because a portion of the T wave is vulnerable to electrical stimulation during the relative refractory period (Figure 14-8). A PVC occurring during this period of the cardiac cycle may precipitate VT or VF.

Two PVCs in succession are called a couplet

Three or more PVCs in a row are called a run of ventricular tachycardia or a run of PVCs

Figure 14-6
Couplet of PVCs and run of VT.

An interpolated PVC between two normal beats that does not disrupt the R-R interval

Figure 14-7
An interpolated PVC.

KEY CONCEPT
PVCs occurring on or near the previous T wave are called *R-on-T* and are more likely to precipitate VF.

A PVC is not an entire rhythm—it is a single beat. To describe it, refer to the underlying rhythm along with the ectopic beat(s), such as "sinus rhythm at a rate of 70 beats per minute with frequent PVCs."

PVC that occurs on or near the T wave can precipitate ventricular tachycardia or fibrillation

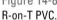

Figure 14-8
R-on-T PVC.

Treatment

Asymptomatic patients seldom require treatment. In patients with myocardial ischemia, treatment of frequent PVCs includes administration of oxygen and placement of an IV line. Care for the patient is focused on identifying and correcting the underlying factor causing the PVCs. In some settings, you may administer lidocaine or other antidysrhythmics (e.g., amiodarone) by IV push and a continued maintenance infusion. Follow your established protocols or consult with the appropriate medical authority.

Other treatments for the patient may include administering potassium chloride intravenously to correct hypokalemia or magnesium sulfate intravenously to correct hypomagnesemia; adjusting drug therapy; or correcting acidosis, hypothermia, and/or hypoxia.

Ventricular Escape Beats

LO 14.4

Description

Ventricular escape beats occur when there is temporary cessation of the heartbeat such as with sinus arrest or when the rate of the underlying rhythm falls to less than that the inherent rate of the ventricles (Figure 14-9). It is a self-generated electrical impulse initiated by and causing contraction of the ventricles. The ventricular escape beat follows a long pause, typically 2 to 3 seconds after an electrical impulse fails to reach the ventricles, and acts to prevent cardiac arrest. As discussed in Chapter 10, the ventricles spontaneously depolarize more slowly than the SA node and AV junction, so one would not expect to see ventricular escape beats unless there is a failure of the heart's electrical conduction system to stimulate the ventricles. A persistent absence of a higher pacemaker causes a continuum of beats, called *idioventricular rhythm,* to arise.

REMINDER
The SA node typically initiates a rate of 60 to 100 beats per minute while the AV node is usually capable only of generating a rhythm at 40 to 60 bpm or less. The inherent rate of the ventricles is 20 to 40 beats per minute.

Figure 14-9
Sinus pause with a ventricular escape beat that acts to initiate a heartbeat.

Causes

Ventricular escape beats are compensatory in nature; in other words, they occur when a higher pacemaker fails to initiate a heartbeat. They are meant to preserve cardiac output. Ventricular escape beats can occur in sinoatrial pause/arrest, by a failure of the conductivity from the SA node to the AV node, or by atrioventricular block (especially 3rd-degree AV block).

Effects

Because of the low heart rate associated with the event that leads up to the appearance of ventricular escape beats, there can be a drop in blood pressure and syncope. Ventricular escape beats should be temporary as the heart should resume its normal electrical activity.

Appearance

Ventricular escape beats appear as only one or two ectopic beats that follow a period of electrical inactivity (cardiac standstill). The ventricular escape beats

Figure 14-10
PVCs result in a shorten R-R interval while ventricular escape beats result in a longer than normal R-R interval.

are wide (greater than 0.12 seconds in duration) and bizarre-looking; there is an absence of a P wave, and the T wave takes a direction opposite of the R wave.

In contrast to PVCs, which occur earlier than normal, resulting in a shortened R-R interval, ventricular escapes come later than normal, resulting in a longer than normal R-R interval (Figure 14-10).

Treatment

Treating patients experiencing ventricular escape beats centers on treating the underlying condition. Support the circulation, airway, and breathing; deliver oxygen; monitor the ECG, blood pressure and pulse oximetry; and establish an IV infusion. Continually reassess the clinical status and correct any reversible conditions. A primary goal of treatment is to maintain a ventricular rate sufficient to produce adequate cardiac output. Atropine (a drug used to speed the heart rate) or transcutaneous pacing can be used to treat the symptomatic patient. Drugs used to suppress ventricular activity such as lidocaine and amiodarone are contraindicated and may be lethal (by suppressing any remaining cardiac activity).

Idioventricular Rhythm

Description

Idioventricular rhythm is a dysrhythmia that occurs when stimuli from higher pacemakers, such as the SA node or AV junction, fail to reach the ventricles (Figure 14-11) or there is a block in the heart's conduction system.

In these instances, the cells of the His-Purkinje system can take over and act as the heart's pacemaker to generate electrical impulses. Idioventricular rhythm normally fires at the inherent rate of the ventricles, 20 to 40 beats per minute. When the event occurs as an escape complex or rhythm, it is considered a safety mechanism to prevent cardiac standstill. Idioventricular rhythm is common during cardiac arrest because it represents the final escape rhythm to be generated in an attempt to perfuse the body. Also, idioventricular rhythm is often the first organized rhythm following defibrillation.

Sometimes idioventricular rhythm is also called *agonal rhythm*. The term *agonal rhythm* usually indicates that the heart rate is less than 10 beats per

> **REMINDER**
> Remember what has been emphasized throughout this text: heart rate × stroke volume = cardiac output. Slow dysrhythmias, because of the slower heart rate, cause decreased cardiac output.

Idioventricular rhythm arises from a single site in the ventricles.

Rate 20 to 40 beats per minute	Rhythm regular	P waves are not visible as they are hidden in QRS complex	QRS complexes are wide (greater than 0.12 seconds in duration) and bizarre in appearance

PR intervals are absent	ST segments depressed or elevated— depends on direction of T wave	T waves take an opposite direction of the R wave	QT intervals usually prolonged	U waves not present

Idioventricular rhythm 20 to 40 beats per minute	Accelerated idioventricular rhythm 40 to 100 beats per minute	Ventricular tachycardia 100 to 250 beats per minute

Figure 14-11
Idioventricular rhythm.

minute. Patients in the final dying stage from a terminal disease often exhibit this rhythm prior to dying. Agonal rhythm has no cardiac output.

Causes

Idioventricular rhythm can be caused by massive myocardial ischemia or MI, digoxin toxicity, pacemaker failure, and metabolic imbalances.

KEY CONCEPT
Idioventricular dysrhythmias are common during cardiac arrest because they represent the final escape rhythm to be generated in an attempt to perfuse the body.

Causes of Idioventricular Rhythm	
Cause	Examples
Cardiac diseases	Myocardial ischemia and MI, failure of all of the heart's higher pacemakers, failure of supraventricular impulses to reach the ventricles due to a block in the conduction system, pacemaker failure, 3rd-degree AV block, sick sinus syndrome
Use of certain drugs	Digoxin beta-adrenergic blockers, calcium channel blockers, tricyclic antidepressants
Autonomic nervous system stimulation	Increased vagal tone
Noncardiac disorders	Metabolic acidosis, hypoxia

Effects

Patient assessment is essential because escape beats and/or idioventricular rhythm may be perfusing or nonperfusing. Ventricular escape beats are usually transient, with a higher pacemaker taking over the heartbeat, in contrast to idioventricular rhythm, which is more likely to continue.

The slow ventricular rate of idioventricular rhythm and the loss of atrial kick can significantly decrease cardiac output. The resultant decreased cardiac output will likely cause the patient to be symptomatic. You can expect to see signs of decreased cardiac output such as disorientation, unconsciousness, hypotension, and/or syncope, and the patient may complain of dizziness, chest pain, and/or shortness of breath. In extreme cases, the patient is pulseless.

Appearance

Wide QRS complexes in a slow regular rhythm are key features of idioventricular rhythm. The heart rate is usually 20 to 40 beats per minute although it may be slower, and the QRS complexes are wide (greater than 0.12 seconds). Also, the T wave typically takes the opposite direction of the R wave. The rhythm is usually regular; however, it becomes irregular as the heart dies. P waves may be present or absent. If present, there is no predictable relationship between P waves and QRS complexes (AV dissociation). This would be called *3rd-degree heart block with an idioventricular escape.* Heart blocks are covered in detail in Chapter 15.

KEY CONCEPT
The hallmark features of idioventricular rhythm is a regular rhythm at a rate of 20 to 40 beats per minute that features absent P waves and wide, bizarre-looking QRS complexes.

Treatment

To treat patients experiencing symptomatic idioventricular rhythm (e.g., chest pain, hypotension), first focus on supporting the airway and breathing. Deliver oxygen, place the patient on an ECG monitor, monitor the blood pressure and pulse oximetry, and place an IV infusion. Continually reassess the clinical status, and correct any reversible conditions. A primary goal of treatment is to maintain a ventricular rate sufficient to produce adequate cardiac output. Atropine or transcutaneous pacing can be used to treat the symptomatic patient. In unresolved idioventricular rhythm, the atropine dose may be repeated. Lidocaine and amiodarone are contraindicated and may be lethal (by suppressing any remaining cardiac activity). If there is no pulse, treat the dysrhythmia as if it is pulseless electrical activity (PEA).

LO 14.6

Accelerated Idioventricular Rhythm

Description

When the rate of the idioventricular rhythm exceeds the inherent rate of the ventricles and is between 40 and 100 beats per minute, it is called *accelerated idioventricular rhythm* (Figure 14-12).

Causes

This dysrhythmia can be caused by the same conditions that lead to idioventricular rhythm. Also, it is very common following acute MI. Further, it is often seen after the administration of thrombolytic medications. For that reason, it is considered a *reperfusion dysrhythmia*.

Effects

While accelerated idioventricular rhythm is usually short lived and because the heart rate is close to normal, no ill effect may be seen. However, with accelerated idioventricular rhythm there may be decreased cardiac output, particularly when the rate is slower.

KEY CONCEPT
The hallmark features of accelerated idioventricular rhythm is a regular rhythm at a rate of 40 to 100 beats per minute that features absent P waves and wide, bizarre-looking QRS complexes.

Appearance

Because it is a rhythm that originates from the ventricles, it has the same characteristics as idioventricular rhythm, except that it is faster.

The key difference that separates this dysrhythmia from idioventricular rhythm and VT is the heart rate.

Treatment

Treatment of the patient depends on whether the rhythm is sustained and whether or not cardiac output is diminished. Transcutaneous pacing or atropine can be used to treat the symptomatic patient. In unresolved idioventricular rhythm, the atropine dose may be repeated. A permanent pacemaker may

Accelerated idioventricular rhythm arises from a single site in the ventricles.

| Rate 40 to 100 beats per minute | Rhythm regular | P waves are not visible as they are hidden in QRS complex | QRS complexes are wide (greater than 0.12 seconds in duration) and bizarre in appearance |

| PR intervals are absent | ST segments depressed or elevated – depends on direction of T wave | T waves take an opposite direction of the R wave | QT intervals usually prolonged | U waves not present |

| Idioventricular rhythm 20 to 40 beats per minute | Accelerated idioventricular rhythm 40 to 100 beats per minute | Ventricular tachycardia 100 to 250 beats per minute |

Figure 14-12
Accelerated idioventricular rhythm.

be required in sustained symptomatic accelerated idioventricular rhythm. Lidocaine and amiodarone are contraindicated and may be lethal (by suppressing any remaining cardiac activity). If there is no pulse, treat the dysrhythmia as if it were pulseless electrical activity (PEA).

Ventricular Tachycardia

LO 14.7

Description

VT is a fast dysrhythmia that arises from the ventricles (Figure 14-13). It is said to be present when there are three or more PVCs in a row. It may come in bursts of 6 to 10 complexes or may persist (sustained VT). It can occur with or without pulses, and the patient may be stable or unstable with this rhythm. Usually this dysrhythmia occurs in the presence of myocardial ischemia or significant cardiac disease. VT often precedes VF and sudden death. It is a common rhythm encountered in out-of-hospital cardiac arrest, and it is commonly called *VT* or *V-Tach*.

KEY CONCEPT
VT is a fast dysrhythmia that arises from the ventricles.

Ventricular tachycardia arises from a single site in the ventricles.

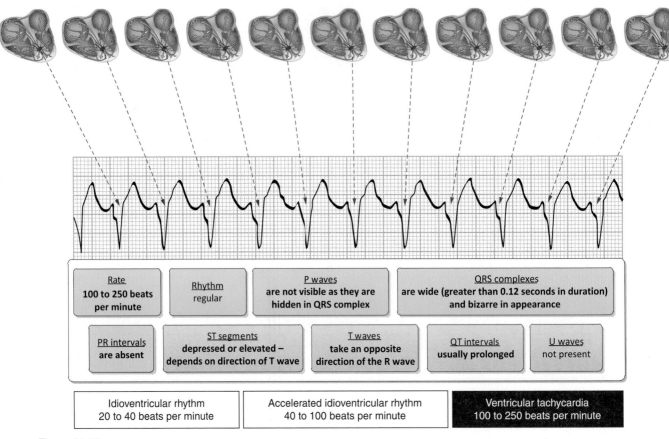

Rate	Rhythm	P waves	QRS complexes
<u>Rate</u> **100 to 250 beats per minute**	<u>Rhythm</u> regular	<u>P waves</u> **are not visible as they are hidden in QRS complex**	<u>QRS complexes</u> **are wide (greater than 0.12 seconds in duration) and bizarre in appearance**

PR intervals	ST segments	T waves	QT intervals	U waves
<u>PR intervals</u> **are absent**	<u>ST segments</u> **depressed or elevated – depends on direction of T wave**	<u>T waves</u> **take an opposite direction of the R wave**	<u>QT intervals</u> **usually prolonged**	<u>U waves</u> not present

Idioventricular rhythm 20 to 40 beats per minute	Accelerated idioventricular rhythm 40 to 100 beats per minute	Ventricular tachycardia 100 to 250 beats per minute

Figure 14-13
Ventricular tachycardia.

Causes

VT is usually caused by increased myocardial irritability that may be triggered by enhanced automaticity, PVCs that occur during the downstroke of the preceding T wave, and reentry in the Purkinje system. Other causes are listed in the following box.

Causes of Ventricular Tachycardia	
Cause	**Examples**
Cardiac diseases	Myocardial ischemia and MI, coronary artery disease, congestive heart failure, cardiomyopathy, valvular heart disease, pulmonary embolism, rheumatic heart disease
Use of certain drugs	Amphetamines, cocaine, digoxin, quinidine, sympathomimetic drugs such as epinephrine, thyroid medications, theophylline drugs
Autonomic nervous system	Increased sympathetic stimulation, exercise, emotional stress
Noncardiac disorders	Electrolyte imbalance, such as hypokalemia, acid-base imbalance, hypoxia, trauma, ingestion of stimulants (alcohol, caffeine, tobacco)

Effects

Clinically, VT is always significant. It may be perfusing or nonperfusing. Even if the rhythm produces a pulse, it should be considered as potentially unstable because patients are likely to develop more life-threatening rhythms which progress into cardiac arrest. Usually VT indicates significant underlying cardiovascular disease. The rapid rate and concurrent loss of atrial kick associated with VT results in compromised cardiac output and decreased coronary artery and cerebral perfusion. The severity of symptoms varies with the rate of the VT and the presence and degree of underlying myocardial dysfunction. Again, the gravest concern is that it may initiate or deteriorate into VF.

Appearance

The most visible characteristics of VT are a rapid rate of between 100 and 250 beats per minute and wide (greater than 0.12 seconds), bizarre-looking QRS complexes. The T waves may or may not be present and typically are of the opposite direction of the R waves. If the rate is between 100 and 150 beats per minute, it is referred to as *slow VT*. Rarely, the rate may be greater than 250 and is then referred to as *ventricular flutter*. Typically, P waves are not discernable (if seen, they are dissociated). The rhythm is usually regular.

Treatment

Treatment of a patient experiencing VT includes maintaining a patent airway, administering oxygen, and placing an IV line.

The stable patient can be treated with antidysrhythmics (such as procainamide, amiodarone, or sotalol).

The patient experiencing decreased level of consciousness, ongoing chest pain, shortness of breath, low blood pressure, or other signs of shock should be considered clinically unstable. Initially these patients are managed with immediate synchronized cardioversion (100 J). Contributing causes should be considered and treated. The initial energy level may be increased if the tachycardia does not convert with initial treatments (100, 200, 300, 360 J or the biphasic equivalent). Patients with pulseless VT should be treated as though they are in VF.

Polymorphic Ventricular Tachycardia

Description

VT may be monomorphic, where the appearance of each QRS complex is similar, or polymorphic, where the appearance varies considerably from complex to complex. Either is potentially life-threatening. A specific, rare variety of **polymorphic ventricular tachycardia** is called **torsades de pointes,** which

REMINDER

Remember what has been emphasized throughout this text: heart rate × stroke volume = cardiac output. Fast dysrhythmias, because of the decreased stroke volume associated with the fast heart rate, cause decreased cardiac output.

KEY CONCEPT

The hallmark feature of VT is a regular rhythm at a rate of 100 to 250 beats per minute that features absent P waves and wide, bizarre-looking QRS complexes.

LO 14.8

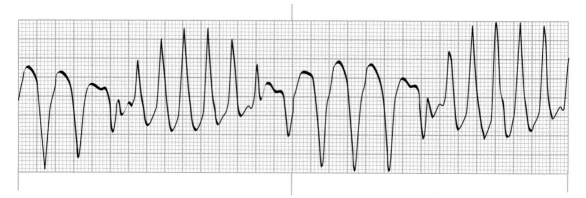

Figure 14-14

Polymorphic VT. Torsades de pointes is characterized by QRS complexes that alternate between upright deflections and downward deflections.

means twisting about the points (Figure 14-14). This form of VT exhibits distinct characteristics on the ECG.

Causes

Torsades de pointes is associated with long QT syndrome, a condition whereby prolonged QT intervals are visible on the ECG. Long QT intervals predispose the patient to an R-on-T phenomenon, where the R wave representing ventricular depolarization occurs simultaneously to the relative refractory period at the end of repolarization (represented by the latter half of the T-wave). Sometimes pathologic T-U waves may be seen in the ECG before the initiation of torsades. Long QT syndrome can either be inherited as congenital mutations of ion channels carrying the cardiac impulse (action potential) or acquired as a result of drugs that block cardiac ion currents. Causes of torsades de pointes are shown in the following box.

Causes of Torsades de Pointes	
Cause	**Examples**
Cardiac diseases	AV heart block, hereditary QT prolongation syndrome, myocardial ischemia, Prinzmetal's angina, SA node disease resulting in severe bradycardia, hypoxia, acidosis, heart failure, left ventricular hypertrophy
Use of certain drugs	Amiodarone, quinidine, procainamide, sotalol toxicity, psychotropic drugs (phenothiazines, tricyclic antidepressants, lithium), chloroquine, clarithromycin (Biaxin) or haloperidol (Haldol) taken concomitantly with a specific cytochrome P450 inhibitor such as fluoxetine (Prozac) or cimetidine (Tagamet), some dietary supplements such as St. John's wort
Noncardiac disorders	Electrolyte imbalance such as hypocalcemia, hypokalemia, hypomagnesemia, diarrhea (commonly seen in malnourished individuals and chronic alcoholics), hypothermia, subarachnoid hemorrhage

Effects

The effects of torsades de pointes depend on the rate and duration of tachycardia and the degree of cerebral hypoperfusion. Findings include rapid pulse, low or normal blood pressure, or syncope or prolonged loss of consciousness. This could be preceded by bradycardia or premature ventricular contractions (PVCs), also called *leading palpitations.* Pallor and diaphoresis may be noted, especially with a sustained episode. It can degenerate into VF, which will lead to sudden death in the absence of medical intervention.

Appearance

Torsades de pointes is characterized by QRS complexes that alternate (usually gradually) between upright deflections and downward deflections. The ventricular rate can range from 150 to 250 bpm.

Treatment

Polymorphic VT cannot be reliably synchronized and should be managed like ventricular fibrillation (VF), with an initial unsynchronized shock. Standard antidysrhythmic drugs (such as procainamide) can worsen the condition, leading to cardiac arrest. Amiodarone may be effective in stable patients with normal QT interval whereas magnesium sulfate should be administered in stable patients with prolonged QT interval. Also, offending drug(s) should be discontinued and electrolyte imbalance corrected. Patients with pulseless VT should be treated as though they are in VF, with the treatment of choice being prompt defibrillation.

Ventricular Fibrillation

Description

VF results from chaotic firing of multiple sites in the ventricles (Figure 14-15). It is the most common cause of prehospital cardiac arrest in adults.

Causes

VF is most commonly associated with significant cardiovascular system disease. Causes are listed below.

LO 14.9

KEY CONCEPT
VF is a chaotic firing of multiple sites in the ventricles. This causes the heart muscle to quiver instead of contract.

Causes of Ventricular Fibrillation	
Cause	**Examples**
Cardiac diseases	Myocardial ischemia/infarction, coronary artery disease, cardiomyopathy, untreated VT, R on T phenomenon
Use of certain drugs	Digoxin [rarely], epinephrine, procainamide, quinidine; drug overdose (cocaine, tricyclics)
Noncardiac disorders	Acid-base imbalance, drowning, electric shock, severe hypothermia, electrolyte imbalances such as hypokalemia, hyperkalemia, hypercalcemia

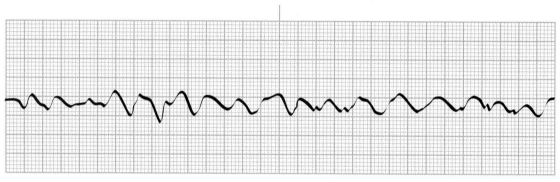

Figure 14-15
VF results from chaotic firing of multiple sites in the ventricles.

Effects

VF causes the heart muscle to quiver, much like a handful of worms, rather than contracting efficiently. It produces ineffective muscular contraction and an absence of cardiac output. Within 10 seconds, the amount of blood pumped by the heart diminishes to zero, causing all life-supporting physiological functions to cease because of lack of circulating blood flow. Death occurs if the patient is not promptly treated (with CPR and defibrillation).

Appearance

KEY CONCEPT
The hallmark feature of VF is a totally chaotic, wavy line that lacks any logic.

VF is generally easy to recognize on the cardiac monitor; it appears like a wavy line, totally chaotic, without any logic. There are no coordinated ventricular complexes present. The unsynchronized ventricular impulses occur at rates from 300 to 500 beats per minute. There are no discernible P waves, QRS complexes, or PR intervals.

Treatment

Treatment includes prompt initiation of CPR and defibrillation. It is critical to provide high-quality CPR (with chest compressions of adequate rate and depth, allowing complete chest recoil after each compression, minimizing interruptions in chest compressions, and avoiding excessive ventilation). Rotate the person delivering chest compressions every 2 minutes. When an out-of-hospital cardiac arrest is not witnessed by healthcare or EMS personnel, you may initiate CPR while checking the rhythm with the AED or on the ECG and preparing for defibrillation. In such instances, 1½ to 3 minutes of CPR may be considered before attempting defibrillation. ACLS actions should be organized around uninterrupted periods of CPR. Securing the airway and placing an IV line should be initiated in the course of treatment. After one shock and a 2-minute period of CPR, administer epinephrine or vasopressin. Amiodarone may be considered when VF/VT is unresponsive to CPR, defibrillation, and vasopressor therapy. If amiodarone is unavailable, lidocaine may be considered if allowed by local protocol. Continue CPR, stopping only to defibrillate and reassess rhythm. Minimize interruptions in chest compressions before and after shock; resume CPR beginning with compressions immediately after each shock. If the rhythm is successfully converted to an effective electromechanical rhythm (with a pulse and good perfusion), assess vital signs, support airway and breathing, and provide medications to support blood pressure, heart rate, and rhythm and to prevent reoccurrence.

> **KEY CONCEPT**
> Defibrillation is considered the true definitive treatment of VF.

Asystole

Description

Asystole is the absence of any cardiac activity (Figure 14-16). It may be the primary event in cardiac arrest, or it may occur in complete heart block when there is an absence of a functional escape pacemaker. It is usually associated with global myocardial ischemia or necrosis and often follows VT, VF, PEA, or an agonal escape rhythm in the dying heart. An ominous dysrhythmia, asystole often represents a predictor of death, as the likelihood of resuscitation from asystole is dismal.

> **KEY CONCEPT**
> Asystole is the absence of electrical activity in the heart.

> **REMINDER**
> Asystole means without contraction of the heart; "a" means without and "systole" means contraction of the heart.

Causes

Some conditions that cause asystole are listed in the following box.

Causes of Asystole	
Cause	**Examples**
Cardiac diseases	MI, cardiac tamponade, massive pulmonary embolism, underlying heart disease, ruptured ventricular aneurysm
Noncardiac disorders	Acute respiratory failure, massive pulmonary embolism, prolonged hypoxemia, severe uncorrected acid-base imbalance (particularly metabolic acidosis), severe electrolyte imbalances (especially hyperkalemia and hypokalemia), tension pneumothorax, hypothermia, drug overdose

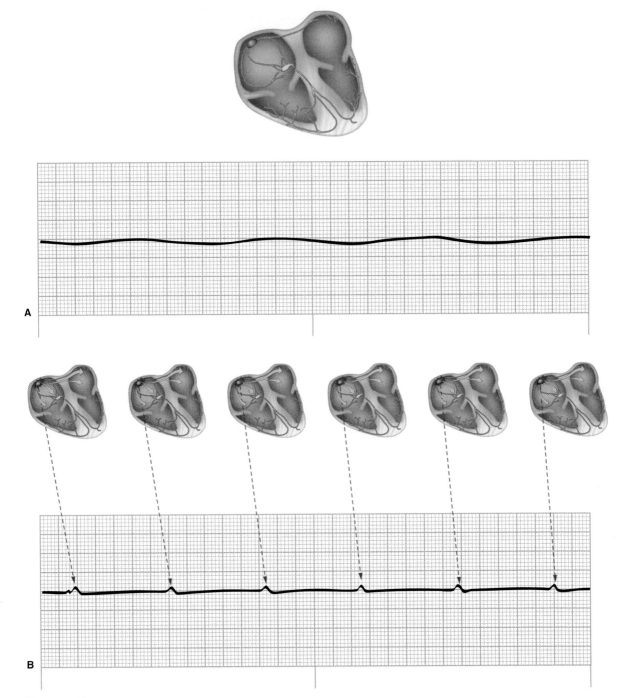

Figure 14-16
Asystole and ventricular standstill. (A) Asystole is a complete absence of cardiac activity. (B) Ventricular standstill occurs when there is electrical activity from the atria but none from the ventricles.

Effects

With asystole, there is no electrical activity. It produces complete cessation of cardiac output. It is a terminal rhythm, and once a person has become asystolic, the chances of recovery are extremely low. Some use the term

ventricular standstill to define a condition where the atria continue to beat but the ventricles have stopped. A rhythm strip of ventricular standstill will have only P waves present without QRS complexes.

Appearance

Asystole appears as a flat (or nearly flat) line on the monitor screen.

Treatment

Treatment of asystole includes prompt initiation of CPR, high-concentration oxygen, placing an IV line, and securing the airway. Administer epinephrine, repeating its administration every 3 to 5 minutes. One dose of vasopressin may replace either the first or second dose of epinephrine. Continue CPR throughout the resuscitation effort, stopping periodically to reassess for a change in the rhythm and to check for the presence of a pulse. Follow local protocols for terminating resuscitation efforts.

Always verify the presence of asystole in two leads prior to initiating treatment. Misplacement of an ECG lead or a loose wire can mimic asystole (or VF) on the monitor. If a patient is in cardiac arrest and appears to be in asystole, be sure to check the following:

- The leads are attached in the proper places to both the machine and the patient.
- The correct lead (e.g., I, II, III) is selected on the monitor.
- The rhythm appears as asystole in more than one lead.
- The monitor batteries are functioning appropriately.

KEY CONCEPT
The hallmark feature of asystole is a flat line, absent of any identifiable electrical activity.

Pulseless Electrical Activity

LO 14.11

Description

Pulseless electrical activity (PEA) is a condition rather than a dysrhythmia. We cover it here for the sake of completeness in our discussion of the various causes of cardiac arrest. With PEA we see an organized electrical rhythm on the ECG monitor that should result in contraction of the heart muscle, but there is no corresponding pulse. This results in the patient being pulseless and apneic. In other words, there is organized electrical activity in the heart that fails to generate effective cardiac contraction (Figure 14-17).

KEY CONCEPT
The primary characteristic associated with PEA is the presence of an organized electrical rhythm without a corresponding pulse.

Causes

This condition is often associated with severe underlying heart disease, but you should always consider reversible causes of PEA, which include acidosis, drug overdose (such as tricyclic antidepressants), hypovolemia (most common), hypoxia, hypothermia, hyperkalemia, hypokalemia, pericardial tamponade, massive MI, and tension pneumothorax.

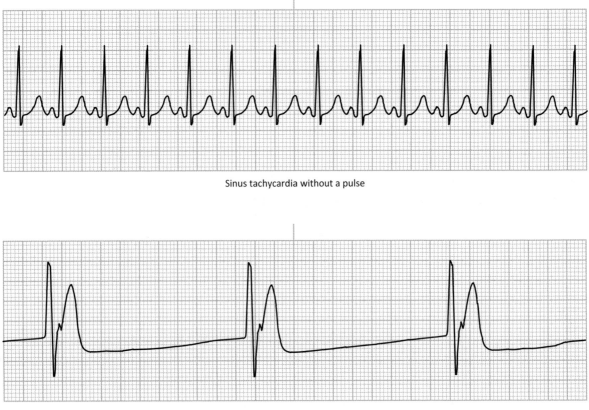

Sinus tachycardia without a pulse

Idioventricular rhythm without a pulse (also called slow PEA)

Figure 14-17
Examples of PEA.

Effects

With PEA there is no cardiac output. The patient will be unconscious, apneic, and pulseless; in other words, they are in cardiac arrest.

Appearance

The electrical activity seen with PEA may be sinus rhythm, sinus tachycardia, idioventricular rhythm, or any rhythm that is generally expected to generate a pulse.

Treatment

Treatment of PEA includes prompt initiation of CPR, high-concentration oxygen, placing an IV line, securing the airway and confirming placement. Administer epinephrine, repeating its administration every 3 to 5 minutes. One dose of vasopressin may replace either the first or second dose of epinephrine. Continue CPR throughout the resuscitation effort, stopping periodically to reassess for a change in the rhythm and to check for the presence of a pulse.

Practice Makes Perfect

For each of the 57 ECG tracings on the following pages, practice the Nine-Step Process for analyzing ECGs. To achieve the greatest learning, you should practice assessing and interpreting the ECGs immediately after reading this chapter. Below are questions you should consider as you assess each tracing. Your answers can be written into the area above each ECG marked "ECG Findings." Your findings can then be compared to the answers provided in Appendix A. All tracings are six seconds in length.

1. Determine the heart rate. Is it slow? Normal? Fast? What is the ventricular rate? What is the atrial rate?

2. Determine if the rhythm is regular or irregular. If it is irregular, what type of irregularity is it? Occasional or Irregular? Slight? Sudden acceleration or slowing in heart rate? Total? Patterned? Does it have a variable conduction ratio?

3. Determine if P waves are present. If so, how do they appear? Do they have normal height and duration? Are they tall? Notched? Wide? Biphasic? Of differing morphology? Inverted? One for each QRS complex? More than one preceding some or all the QRS complexes? Do they have a sawtooth appearance? An indiscernible chaotic baseline?

4. Determine if QRS complexes are present. If so, how do they appear? Narrow with proper amplitude? Tall? Low amplitude? Delta wave? Notched? Wide? Bizarre? With chaotic waveforms?

5. Determine the presence of PR intervals. If present, how do they appear? Constant? Of normal duration? Shortened? Lengthened? Progressively longer? Varying?

6. Evaluate the ST segments. Do they have normal duration and position? Are they elevated? (If so, are they flat, concave, convex, arched?) Depressed? (If so, are they normal, flat, downsloping or upsloping?)

7. Determine if T waves are present. If so, how do they appear? Of normal height and duration? Tall? Wide? Notched? Inverted?

8. Determine the presence of QT intervals. If present, what is their duration? Normal? Shortened? Prolonged?

9. Determine if U waves are present. If present, how do they appear? Of normal height and duration? Inverted?

10. Identify the rhythm or dysrhythmia.

1.

ECG Findings:

2.

ECG Findings:

3.

ECG Findings:

4.

ECG Findings:

5.

ECG Findings:

6.

ECG Findings:

7.

ECG Findings:

8.

ECG Findings:

9.

ECG Findings:

10.

ECG Findings:

11.

ECG Findings:

12.

ECG Findings:

13.

ECG Findings:

14.

ECG Findings:

15.

ECG Findings:

16.

ECG Findings:

17.

ECG Findings:

18.

ECG Findings:

19.

ECG Findings:

20.

ECG Findings:

21.

ECG Findings:

22.

ECG Findings:

23.

ECG Findings:

24.

ECG Findings:

25.

ECG Findings:

26.

ECG Findings:

27.

ECG Findings:

28.

ECG Findings:

29.

ECG Findings:

30.

ECG Findings:

31.

ECG Findings:

32.

ECG Findings:

33.

ECG Findings:

34.

ECG Findings:

35.

ECG Findings:

36.

ECG Findings:

37.

ECG Findings:

38.

ECG Findings:

39.

ECG Findings:

40.

ECG Findings:

41.

ECG Findings:

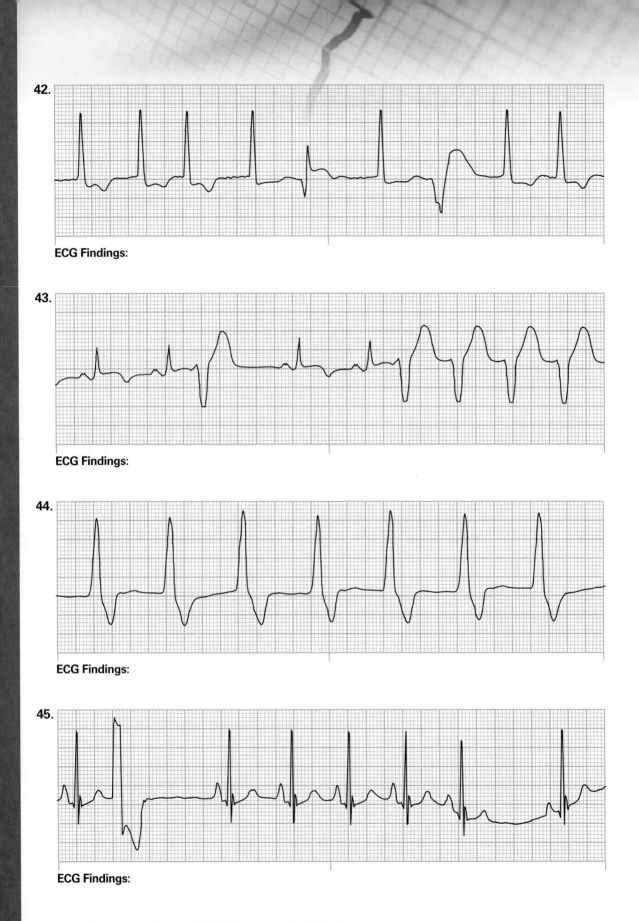

42.

ECG Findings:

43.

ECG Findings:

44.

ECG Findings:

45.

ECG Findings:

46.

ECG Findings:

47.

ECG Findings:

48.

ECG Findings:

49.

ECG Findings:

50.

ECG Findings:

51.

ECG Findings:

52.

ECG Findings:

53.

ECG Findings:

54.

ECG Findings:

55.

ECG Findings:

56.

ECG Findings:

57.

ECG Findings:

Key Points 🔍

- Ventricular dysrhythmias occur when the atria, AV junction, or both are unable to initiate an electrical impulse or when there is enhanced automaticity of the ventricular myocardium.

- A key feature of ventricular dysrhythmias are wide (greater than 0.12 seconds in duration), bizarre-looking QRS complexes that have T waves in the opposite direction of the R wave and an absence of P waves.

- Ventricular dysrhythmias include PVC, ventricular escape complexes or rhythm, VT, VF, and asystole.

- PVCs are early ectopic beats that interrupt the normal rhythm and originate from an irritable focus in the ventricular conduction system or muscle tissue.

- PVCs that look the same are called *uniform (unifocal),* whereas PVCs that look different from each other are called *multiform (multifocal).*

- PVCs occurring every other beat are called *bigeminal PVCs,* whereas PVCs occurring every third beat are called *trigeminal PVCs* and a PVC seen every fourth beat is called *ventricular quadrigeminy.*

- Two PVCs in a row are called a *couplet* and indicate extremely irritable ventricles.

- An interpolated PVC occurs but does not disrupt the normal cardiac cycle. It appears as a PVC squeezed between two regular complexes.

- Ventricular escape beats occur when there is temporary cessation of the heartbeat, such as with sinus arrest or when the rate of the underlying rhythm falls to less than that the inherent rate of the ventricles. They are compensatory in nature.

- Idioventricular rhythm is a slow dysrhythmia with wide QRS complexes that arise from the ventricles at a rate of 20 to 40 beats per minute.

- VT is a fast dysrhythmia, between 100 and 250 beats per minute, that arises from the ventricles. It is said to be present when there are three or more PVCs in a row. It may come in bursts of 6 to 10 complexes or may persist (sustained VT).

- VT can occur with or without pulses, and the patient may be stable or unstable with this rhythm.

- VT may be monomorphic, where the appearance of each QRS complex is similar, or polymorphic, where the appearance varies considerably from complex to complex.

- Torsades de pointes, which means twisting about the points, is form of VT that exhibits distinct characteristics on the ECG.

- VF results from chaotic firing of multiple sites in the ventricles. This causes the heart muscle to quiver rather than contract efficiently, producing no effective muscular contraction and an absence of cardiac output.

- On the cardiac monitor, VF appears like a wavy line, totally chaotic, without any logic.

- Asystole is the absence of any cardiac activity. It appears as a flat (or nearly flat) line on the monitor screen and produces a complete cessation of cardiac output.
- The presence of asystole should always be verified in two leads.
- PEA is a condition in which there is an organized electrical rhythm on the ECG monitor (which should produce a pulse) but the patient is pulseless and apneic. Sinus rhythm, sinus tachycardia, idioventricular rhythm, or any rhythm that is generally expected to generate a pulse may be the electrical activity seen with PEA.

Assess Your Understanding

The following questions give you a chance to assess your understanding of the material discussed in this chapter. The answers can be found in Appendix A.

1. Ventricular dysrhythmias
   a. originate above the bundle of His.
   b. are seldom life threatening.
   c. have QRS complexes greater than 0.12 seconds in duration.
   d. have notched P waves that precede each QRS complex.

2. The presence of PVCs is an indication of which of the following?
   a. Irritability of the myocardium
   b. Possible hypoxia
   c. Drug toxicity
   d. All of the above

3. Premature ventricular complexes (PVCs)
   a. arise from the AV node.
   b. have a QRS complex that appears narrow and normal in configuration.
   c. have T waves in the same direction as the R waves of complexes.
   d. are followed by a compensatory pause.

4. Match the following types of PVCs with the correct description.

Descriptions	Types of PVCs
a. PVCs that occur every other beat	_____ R-on-T phenomenon
b. PVCs that appear different from one another	_____ Multiform
c. Occurs when the PVC wave falls on the T wave	_____ Bigeminal
d. PVCs that occur every 4th beat	_____ Quadrigeminal

5. Two PVCs in a row are called
   a. a run of PVCs.
   b. polymorphic.
   c. a couplet.
   d. interpolated.

6. Three PVCs in succession are referred to as a _____ of VT.
   a. couplet
   b. run
   c. trigeminy
   d. succession

7. Idioventricular rhythm has a rate of _____ beats per minute.
   a. 20 to 40
   b. 30 to 60
   c. 50 to 75
   d. 100 to 150

8. Idioventricular rhythm
   a. is regularly irregular.
   b. has wide, bizarre-looking QRS complexes.
   c. has upright P waves preceding each QRS complex.
   d. arises from the AV junction.

9. VT has
   a. inverted T waves.
   b. a rate of between 60 and 100 beats per minute.
   c. an irregular rhythm.
   d. QRS complexes greater than 0.12 seconds in duration.

10. Polymorphic VT
    a. arises from one location in the ventricles.
    b. has narrow QRS complexes.
    c. has an appearance that varies considerably from complex to complex.
    d. results from chaotic firing of multiple sites in the ventricles.

11. VF appears on the ECG monitor as having
    a. an overall pattern that appears irregularly shaped, chaotic, and lacks any regular repeating features.
    b. narrow QRS complexes.
    c. electrical signals that are the same height.
    d. P waves interspersed between bizarre-looking QRS complexes.

12. With asystole
    a. the heart quivers.
    b. there is a flat line on the ECG monitor.
    c. there are QRS complexes but no P waves.
    d. there is an organized rhythm but no corresponding mechanical contraction of the heart.

Referring to the scenario at the beginning of this chapter answer the following questions.

13. There is no pulse with VF because the
    a. heart is contracting too fast.
    b. heart is contracting too slow.
    c. heart is not contracting at all.
    d. stroke volume is too high.

14. The flat line rhythm that occurred after defibrillation is called
    a. asystole.
    b. sinus arrest.
    c. ventricular arrest.
    d. agonal.

15. The goal of defibrillation is to create _____ and hope that a pacemaker will awaken and stimulate ventricular contraction.
    a. sinus rhythm
    b. sinus tachycardia
    c. asystole
    d. VT

Answers to Sidebar Questions

1. PVCs produce occasional irregularity unless there are many PVCs. **p. 376**

2. Noncompensatory pauses are seen with premature atrial complexes and premature junctional complexes. **p. 377**

3. Bigeminal, trigeminal, or quadrigeminal PVCs produce regularly or patterned irregularity. This is where the irregularity repeats over and over in a cycle. **p. 378**

What's Online

Go to www.mhhe.com/shadeECG2e to find:

- Presentations on chapter content
- Types of PVCs exercise
- Crossword puzzle exercises
- Additional ECG tracings for practicing analyzing ventricular dysrhythmias
- Chapter quiz
- Flashcards
- Fill-in-the-blank exercises and answers
- In-depth answers to Practice Makes Perfect ECG tracings and Assess Your Understanding questions

15 AV Heart Blocks

Chapter Outline

Block of the Atrioventricular Node

1st-Degree Atrioventricular Heart Block

2nd-Degree Atrioventricular Heart Block, Type I

2nd-Degree Atrioventricular Heart Block, Type II

3rd-Degree Atrioventricular Heart Block

Atrioventricular Dissociation

Learning Objectives

LO 15.1 Describe the origin and key features of block of the AV node.

LO 15.2 Identify the causes, effects, and appearance of 1st-degree AV heart block.

LO 15.3 Identify the causes, effects, and appearance of 2nd-degree AV heart block, type I.

LO 15.4 Identify the causes, effects, and appearance of 2nd-degree AV heart block, type II.

LO 15.5 Identify the causes, effects, and appearance of 3rd-degree AV heart block.

LO 15.6 Identify the causes, effects, and appearance of atrioventricular dissociation.

Case History

A 65-year-old man presents to the emergency department complaining of palpitations. He denies chest pain, shortness of breath, or light headedness. He had a heart attack five years ago and has hypertension controlled by medication.

After obtaining his vital signs, normal except for a slow pulse, the charge nurse attaches the ECG leads and turns on the monitor. The emergency room (ER) physician enters the room and examines the tracing while the nurse starts an IV. The physician calls the paramedic student into the exam room and hands her the ECG strip and asks her to interpret it. The student indicates that the rate is slow, but the rhythm is regular. She also notices that the PR interval is normal but that there are more P waves than QRS complexes.

Block of the Atrioventricular Node

AV heart blocks are partial delays or complete interruptions in the cardiac conduction pathway between the atria and ventricles (Figure 15-1). The block can occur at the AV node, the bundle of His, or the bundle branches.

With AV heart block, cardiac output can be negatively affected if the ventricular rate slows. This can occur either due to electrical impulses from the

Figure 15-1
AV heart blocks.

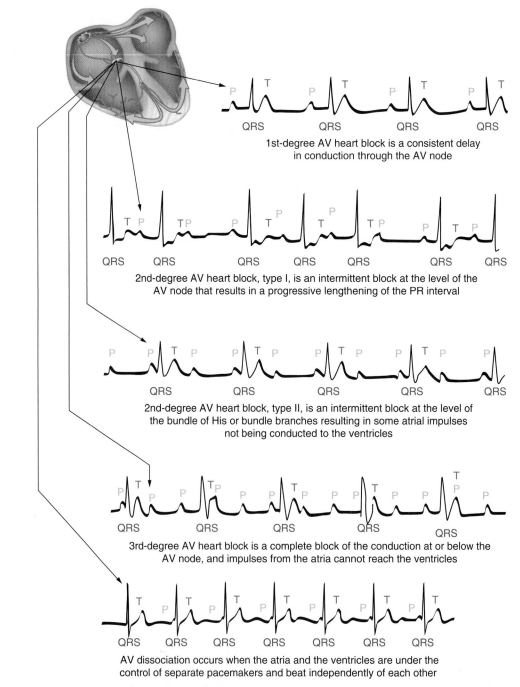

1st-degree AV heart block is a consistent delay in conduction through the AV node

2nd-degree AV heart block, type I, is an intermittent block at the level of the AV node that results in a progressive lengthening of the PR interval

2nd-degree AV heart block, type II, is an intermittent block at the level of the bundle of His or bundle branches resulting in some atrial impulses not being conducted to the ventricles

3rd-degree AV heart block is a complete block of the conduction at or below the AV node, and impulses from the atria cannot reach the ventricles

AV dissociation occurs when the atria and the ventricles are under the control of separate pacemakers and beat independently of each other atria being blocked from entering the ventricles, or, as what can occur with complete AV heart block, the ventricular escape beats arise from a site that is lower in the ventricles (producing a slower rate).

The most common causes of heart block are ischemia, MI, degenerative disease of the conduction system, congenital anomalies, and medications (especially digitalis preparations). Dysrhythmias resulting from AV heart blocks include the following:

- 1st-degree AV heart block
- 2nd-degree AV heart block, type I (Wenckebach)
- 2nd-degree AV heart block, type II
- 3rd-degree AV heart block

REMINDER
The initial electrical impulse begins high in the right atrium, in the SA node. It travels through the atria via intraatrial and intranodal pathways to the AV node.

KEY CONCEPT
Heart blocks are partial delays or complete inter-ruptions in the cardiac conduction pathway between the atria and ventricles.

1st-Degree Atrioventricular Heart Block

Description

1st-degree AV heart block is not a true block because all impulses are con-ducted from the atria to the ventricles, but rather it is a consistent delay of conduction at the level of the AV node (Figure 15-2). It results in prolonga-tion of the PR interval that remains the same duration from beat to beat.

WANT MORE INFORMATION?
Visit the Fast & Easy ECGs Website at www.mhhe.com/shadeECG2e

Causes

LO 15.2

While 1st-degree AV heart block may occur in healthy persons for no apparent reason (particularly athletes), it is sometimes associated with other conditions such as myocardial ischemia, acute MI, increased vagal (parasympathetic) tone, and digitalis toxicity. Other causes of 1st-degree AV heart block are shown in the following box.

Causes of 1st-Degree Heart Block	
Cause	**Examples**
Cardiac diseases	Myocardial ischemia or infarction (often inferior wall MI), injury or ischemia to the AV node or junction, myocarditis, degenerative changes (age related) in the heart
Use of certain drugs	Beta-adrenergic blockers (i.e., propranolol), calcium channel blockers (i.e., verapamil), digoxin, antidysrhythmics (i.e., amiodarone, quinidine, procainamide)
Autonomic nervous system stimulation	Increased vagal tone
Noncardiac disorders	Hypokalemia and hyperkalemia, hypothermia, hypothyroidism

In 1st-degree AV heart block impulses arise from the SA node but their passage through the AV node is delayed.

Rate	Rhythm	P waves	QRS complexes
underlying rhythm may be slow, normal, or fast	underlying rhythm is usually regular	normal and all look alike; one precedes each QRS complex	of normal duration and all look alike

PR intervals	ST segments	T waves	QT intervals	U waves
longer than 0.20 seconds in duration and constant	normal and isoelectric	normal shape and upright, but may be abnormal if QRS complex is prolonged	within normal limits of 0.36 to 0.44 second	may or may not be present

Figure 15-2
1st-degree AV heart block.

QUESTION

1. **What is the normal duration for the PR interval?** *Note:* Answers to the Sidebar Questions can be found at the end of the chapter.

KEY CONCEPT
The most prominent characteristic of 1st-degree AV heart block is a PR interval that is greater than 0.20 seconds in duration.

Effects

1st-degree AV heart block is of little or no clinical significance because all impulses are conducted to the ventricles. The patient experiencing this condition is usually asymptomatic. 1st-degree AV heart block may be temporary, particularly if it stems from ischemia early in the course of MI or certain medications. Conversely, it may also progress to higher degree block, especially in the presence of inferior wall MI.

Appearance

The most obvious characteristic of 1st-degree AV heart block is PR intervals greater than 0.20 seconds in duration and constant. The underlying rhythm is usually regular whereas the rate is that of the underlying rhythm. It can occur in bradycardic, normal rate, and tachycardic rhythms. The P waves are normal; one precedes each QRS complex, and the QRS complexes are within normal limits.

1st-degree AV block is more of a condition than a dysrhythmia. For this reason we typically describe it as part of the underlying rhythm (e.g., sinus rhythm, sinus tachycardia, or sinus bradycardia with 1st-degree AV block).

Treatment

As cardiac output is not affected, no specific treatment is indicated for 1st-degree AV heart block. However, efforts are directed toward identifying and treating the cause.

2nd-Degree Atrioventricular Heart Block, Type I

LO 15.3

Description

2nd-degree AV heart block, type I, also called **Wenckebach** or **Mobitz Type I**, is an intermittent block at the level of the AV node (Figure 15-3). The PR interval (representing AV conduction time) increases until a QRS complex is not generated (dropped). By then, AV conduction recovers and the sequence repeats.

Some describe the pathophysiology of this dysrhythmia as a weakened AV junction that grows more tired with each heartbeat (thus producing

In 2nd-degree AV heart block, type I (Wenckebach), impulses arise from the SA node but their passage through the AV node is progressively delayed until the impulse is blocked.

Rate	Rhythm	P waves	QRS complexes
underlying rhythm may be slow, normal, or fast	patterned irregularity	normal and all look alike, but not all followed by QRS complex	usually of normal duration and all look alike, periodically one is absent

PR intervals	ST segments	T waves	QT intervals	U waves
progressively longer in duration until a QRS complex is dropped, then cycle begins again	normal and isoelectric	normal size and configuration	within normal limits of 0.36 to 0.44 second	may or may not be present

Figure 15-3
2nd-degree AV heart block, type I (Wenckebach).

a progressively longer PR interval following each P wave). Finally, the AV junction is too tired to carry the impulse, and a QRS complex is dropped (only a P wave appears). The lack of conduction through the AV junction allows it to rest; thus the next PR interval is shorter. Then as each subsequent impulse is generated and transmitted through the AV junction, there is a progressively longer PR interval until, again, a QRS complex is dropped. This cycle repeats.

The number of beats in which the P wave is followed by a QRS complex before a QRS complex is finally dropped can vary among individuals. For example, one patient may have a dropped beat after every third beat, and another patient may drop the QRS complex after every fifth complex.

Causes

2nd-degree AV heart block, type I, often occurs in acute MI or acute myocarditis. Common causes are shown in the following box.

Causes of 2nd-Degree AV Heart Block, Type I	
Cause	**Examples**
Cardiac diseases	AV nodal ischemia secondary to right coronary artery occlusion, myocardial ischemia or MI (inferior wall MI), cardiac surgery, myocarditis, rheumatic fever
Use of certain drugs	Beta-adrenergic blockers, calcium channel blockers, digitalis, quinidine, procainamide
Autonomic nervous system stimulation	Increased vagal tone
Noncardiac disorders	Electrolyte imbalance (hyperkalemia)

Effects

2nd-degree AV heart block, type I, may occur in otherwise healthy persons. By itself, it is usually transient and reversible, resolving when the underlying condition is corrected. However, particularly if it occurs early in MI, it may progress to more serious blocks. If dropped beats occur frequently, the patient may show signs and symptoms of decreased cardiac output. Those types of heart block that result in dropped QRS complexes or a slower ventricular rate can lead to a decrease in cardiac output (decreased heart rate × stroke volume = decreased cardiac output).

Appearance

QUESTION
2. **What type of irregularity does 2nd-degree AV heart block, type I, produce?**

The characteristics that stand out in 2nd-degree AV heart block, type I, are a patterned, irregular rhythm; cycles of progressively longer PR intervals; and more P waves than QRS complexes. The irregularity appears as a pattern (the cycle seems to occur over and over); it is often described as *grouped beating*. The PR intervals become progressively longer until a P wave fails to conduct, resulting in a "dropped" QRS complex. After the blocked beat, the cycle starts again. The P waves are upright and uniform, but there are more P waves than QRS complexes as some of the QRS complexes are blocked.

The atrial rate is that of the underlying rhythm whereas the ventricular rate is slightly less than the atrial rate (slower than normal). The QRS complexes are within normal limits unless the block is infranodal, in which case the QRS complexes will be wide. Infranodal refers to a block caused by an abnormality below the AV node, either in the bundle of His or in both bundle branches. An infranodal block has more serious clinical implications than a block at the level of the AV node. It most often occurs in older persons. Symptoms include frequent episodes of fainting and a pulse rate of 20 to 40 bpm. The P-P interval is constant while the R-R interval increases until a QRS complex is dropped.

Treatment

If patient is asymptomatic, no specific treatment is needed. Patients who are symptomatic (e.g., chest pain, hypotension) should receive oxygen, an IV lifeline, and administration of atropine and transcutaneous pacing should be considered.

KEY CONCEPT
With 2nd-degree AV heart block, type I, the key feature that helps identify it are PR intervals that become progressively longer until a QRS complex is dropped. There are also more P waves than QRS complexes, and the QRS complexes are normal.

2nd-Degree Atrioventricular Heart Block, Type II

LO 15.4

Description

2nd-degree AV heart block, type II, is an intermittent block at the level of the AV node, bundle of His, or bundle branches resulting in atrial impulses that are not conducted to the ventricles (Figure 15-4). It is less common than type I, but it is more serious as it may progress to complete AV heart block. It differs from type I in that the PR interval is *constant* prior to a beat being "dropped."

Causes

Type II block is usually associated with anterior-wall MI, degenerative changes in the conduction system, or severe coronary artery disease. Common causes of type II block are shown in the following box.

Common Causes of 2nd-Degree AV Heart Block, Type II

Cause	Examples
Cardiac diseases	Anterior wall MI, severe coronary artery disease, organic heart disease, degenerative changes in the conduction system, cardiac surgery, myocarditis, rheumatic fever
Use of certain drugs	Beta-adrenergic blockers, calcium channel blockers, digitalis, quinidine, procainamide
Autonomic nervous system stimulation	Increased vagal tone
Noncardiac disorders	Electrolyte imbalance (hyperkalemia)

In 2nd-degree AV heart block, type II, impulses arise from the SA node but some are blocked in the AV node.

Rate	Rhythm	P waves	QRS complexes
ventricular rate may be slow, normal, or fast; atrial rate is within normal range	may be regular or irregular (depends or whether conduction ratio remains the same)	normal and all look alike; not all followed by a QRS complex	usually of normal duration and all look alike; periodically one is absent

PR intervals	ST segments	T waves	QT intervals	U waves
are of constant duration for conducted beats	normal and isoelectric	normal size and configuration	within normal limits of 0.36 to 0.44 second	may or may not be present

Figure 15-4
2nd-degree AV heart block, type II.

Effects

Type II is a serious dysrhythmia, usually considered malignant in the emergency setting when it is symptomatic. Slow ventricular rates result in decreased cardiac output and may produce signs and symptoms of hypoperfusion (low blood pressure, shortness of breath, congestive heart failure, pulmonary congestion, and decreased level of consciousness). It may progress to a more severe heart block and even to ventricular asystole.

Appearance

The feature that stands out in 2nd-degree AV heart block, type II, is the presence of more P waves than QRS complexes. The number of P waves for each QRS complex (e.g., 2:1, 3:1, or 4:1), may be fixed or it may vary (e.g., 2:1, then 3:1, or 4:1, or vice versa). The PR interval may be normal or prolonged, but it is constant for each conducted complex. The QRS complexes are usually within normal limits, but they may also be wide (if the block is infranodal). The rhythm is typically regular. It will be irregular if the conduction ratio (number of P waves to each QRS complex) varies. The atrial rate is that of underlying rhythm whereas the ventricular rate is less than the atrial rate.

QUESTION
3. How can you distinguish between a nonconducted PAC and 2nd-degree AV heart block?

The key characteristic that helps you differentiate between the two types of 2nd-degree AV block is whether the PR interval changes or remains constant.

Treatment

Patients who are symptomatic (e.g., chest pain, hypotension) should receive supplemental oxygen, an IV lifeline, and you should consider transcutaneous pacing. Atropine may be used in type II AV block with new wide QRS complexes while setting up the transcutaneous pacemaker.

KEY CONCEPT
The key feature that helps identify 2nd-degree AV heart block, type II, is more P waves than QRS complexes and constant PR intervals for the conducted beats.

3rd-Degree Atrioventricular Heart Block   ■ LO 15.5

Description

3rd-degree AV heart block is a complete block of the conduction at or below the AV node so that impulses from the atria cannot reach the ventricles (Figure 15-5). It is also called **complete AV heart block.** The SA node serves as

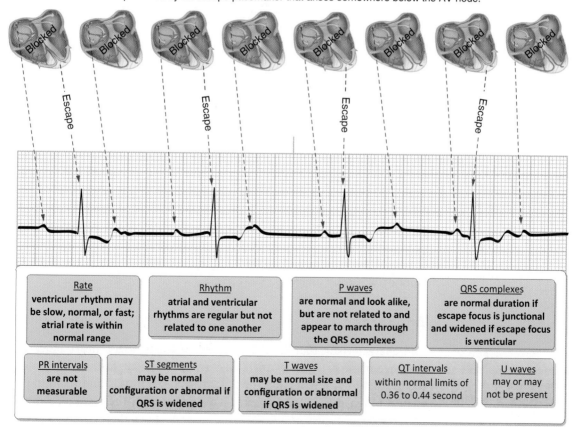

Figure 15-5
3rd-degree AV heart block.

QUESTION
4. **What is the inherent rate of the AV junction and the ventricles?**

the pacemaker for the atria, typically maintaining a regular rate of 60 to 100 beats per minute. The pacemaker for the ventricles arises as an escape rhythm from the AV junction at a rate of 40 to 60 beats per minute or from the ventricles at a rate of 20 to 40 beats per minute. P waves and QRS complexes occur rhythmically, but the rhythms are unrelated to each other.

Causes

3rd-degree AV heart block occurring at the AV node is most commonly caused by a congenital condition. It may also occur in older adults because of chronic degenerative changes in the conduction system. Common causes are listed in the following box.

Common Causes of 3rd-Degree AV Heart Block	
Cause	**Examples**
Cardiac diseases	Anterior or inferior wall MI, AV node damage, cardiac surgery injury, severe coronary artery disease, degenerative changes in the conduction system, myocarditis, rheumatic fever, septal necrosis
Use of certain drugs	Beta-adrenergic blockers, calcium channel blockers, digitalis, quinidine, procainamide
Autonomic nervous system stimulation	Increased vagal tone
Noncardiac disorders	Hyperkalemia

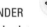

REMINDER
Going back to our discussion in Chapter 14, an escape pacemaker that fails to originate from below the AV node results in the atria continuing to beat but the ventricles being silent. It appears on the ECG as a rhythm that has only P waves; there are no QRS complexes. This condition is called ventricular standstill.

Effects

Most occurrences of 3rd-degree AV heart block are well tolerated as long as the escape rhythm is fast enough to generate a sufficient cardiac output to maintain adequate perfusion. However, severe bradycardia and decreased cardiac output may occur with 3rd-degree AV heart block because of the slow ventricular rate and asynchronous action of the atria and ventricles. If it occurs with wide QRS complexes, it is considered an ominous sign. This type of heart block is potentially lethal, as patients with this dysrhythmia are often hemodynamically unstable.

Appearance

KEY CONCEPT
With 3rd-degree AV heart block, the key feature that helps identify it are P waves that march through the QRS complexes.

The characteristic that stands out with 3rd-degree AV heart block is the presence of more P waves than QRS complexes. But further assessment of the dysrhythmia reveals that the P waves appear normal and seem to march right through the QRS complexes. This reveals that there is no relationship between the P waves and QRS complexes. As such, the PR intervals can be described as being "absent." The atrial rate is that of the underlying rhythm. The ventricular rate depends on the escape focus—40 to 60 beats per minute

	Rhythm	P Waves	QRS Complexes	PR Intervals
1st-degree	Underlying rhythm is usually regular	Present and normal; all the P waves are followed by a QRS complex	Normal	Longer than 0.20 seconds and is constant
2nd-degree, type I	Patterned irregularity	Present and normal; not all the P waves are followed by a QRS complex	Normal or can be widened	Progressively longer until a QRS complex is dropped; the cycle then begins again
2nd-degree, type II	May be regular or irregular (depends on whether conduction ratio remains the same)	Present and normal; not all the P waves are followed by a QRS complex	Normal or can be widened	Constant for all conducted beats
3rd-degree	Atrial rhythm and ventricular rhythms are regular but not related to one another	Present and normal; not related to the QRS complexes; appear to march through the QRS complexes	Normal if escape QRS focus is junctional and widened if escape focus is ventricular	Not measurable

Table 15-1
Types of AV Heart Blocks

if it is junctional and 20 to 40 beats per minute if it is ventricular. The atrial and ventricular rhythms are regular but independent of each other. The QRS complexes are normal if the escape focus is junctional and widened if the escape focus is ventricular.

Treatment

Patients who are symptomatic (e.g., chest pain, hypotension) should receive oxygen, an IV lifeline, and transcutaneous pacing. Atropine may be used in 3rd-degree block with new wide QRS complexes while you are setting up the transcutaneous pacemaker.

Learning AV heart blocks can be challenging. Table 15-1 shows the key differences between the four types of AV heart block.

> **QUESTION**
> 5. In which of the AV heart blocks are there more P waves than QRS complexes?

Atrioventricular Dissociation

LO 15.6

Description

AV dissociation occurs when the atria and the ventricles are under the control of separate pacemakers and beat independently of each other. AV dissociation is not a dysrhythmia but instead is a result of some mechanism that causes independent beating of atria and ventricles. With AV dissociation, the ventricular rate is the same or faster than the atrial rate (Figure 15-6).

AV dissociation occurs when the atria and the ventricles are under the control of separate pacemakers and beat independently of each other.

Rate	Rhythm	P waves	QRS complexes
ventricular and atrial rates the same	atrial and ventricular rhythms are regular but not related to one another	are normal size and configuration; can be distorted if P wave overlaps other waveforms	are normal duration if escape focus is junctional and widened if escape focus is ventricular

PR intervals	ST segments	T waves	QT intervals	U waves
are not measurable	may be normal configuration or abnormal if QRS is widened	may be normal size and configuration or abnormal if QRS is widened	within normal limits of 0.36 to 0.44 second	may or may not be present

Figure 15-6
AV dissociation.

Causes

Four causes of AV dissociation include slowing of the primary pacemaker, acceleration of a pacemaker lower in the heart, AV block, and interference.

- With slowed or impaired sinus impulse formation or SA nodal conduction, such as sinus bradycardia or sinus arrest, a junctional or ventricular pacemaker emerges to take control of the ventricles, resulting in AV dissociation.

- Impulse formation in the AV junction or ventricles that is faster than the firing rate of the sinus node allows the lower pacemaker to take over control of the ventricles while the sinus node still controls the atria.

- Complete AV block results in the SA node and ventricles firing independently of each. However, AV block and AV dissociation is not necessarily the same thing: *All 3rd-degree block is AV dissociation but not all AV dissociation is 3rd-degree block.*

- Anything that interferes with the ability of an atrial impulse to conduct to the ventricles, such as pauses produced by premature beats, presents an opportunity for a pacemaker lower in the heart to emerge and take charge of the ventricles. Drug toxicity from digitalis, calcium channel blockers, disopyramide, and amiodarone also can result in interference.

KEY CONCEPT
In AV dissociation, the SA node loses control of the ventricular rate, leading to the atria and ventricles beating independent of each other, usually at about the same rate.

Effects

Signs and symptoms vary depending on the underlying cause. Signs of decreased cardiac output may be present if the heart rate is reduced.

Appearance

With AV dissociation, the atrial and ventricular rhythms are regular. The atrial rate usually equals the ventricular rate. The P waves are of normal size and configuration. However, they can be distorted if the P wave overlaps other waveforms. The PR interval is absent or unidentifiable because the atria and ventricles are firing independently of each other. The QRS complex depends on the origin of the ventricular beat. A pacemaker high in the AV junction produces a narrow QRS complex whereas a pacemaker lower in the bundle of His produces a wide QRS complex. The T wave may be altered or inverted depending on the underlying cause.

Treatment

No treatment is needed if the condition causing AV dissociation is clinically insignificant. If the condition causing the AV dissociation reduces cardiac output, treatment is directed at managing the underlying problem. Specific measures include delivering atropine and other rate-accelerating agents and/or pacemaker insertion. If drug toxicity caused the original disturbance, the drug should be discontinued.

Practice Makes Perfect.

For each of the 53 ECG tracings on the following pages, practice the Nine-Step Process for analyzing ECGs. To achieve the greatest learning, you should practice assessing and interpreting the ECGs immediately after reading this chapter. Below are questions you should consider as you assess each tracing. Your answers can be written into the area above each ECG marked "ECG Findings." Your findings can then be compared to the answers provided in Appendix A. All tracings are six seconds in length.

1. Determine the heart rate. Is it slow? Normal? Fast? What is the ventricular rate? What is the atrial rate?

2. Determine if the rhythm is regular or irregular. If it is irregular, what type of irregularity is it? Occasional or frequent? Slight? Sudden acceleration or slowing in heart rate? Total? Patterned? Does it have a variable conduction ratio?

3. Determine if P waves are present. If so, how do they appear? Do they have normal height and duration? Are they tall? Notched? Wide? Biphasic? Of differing morphology? Inverted? One for each QRS complex? More than one preceding some or all the QRS complexes? Do they have a sawtooth appearance? An indiscernible chaotic baseline?

4. Determine if QRS complexes are present. If so, how do they appear? Narrow with proper amplitude? Tall? Low amplitude? Delta wave? Notched? Wide? Bizarre-looking? With chaotic waveforms?

5. Determine the presence of PR intervals. If present, how do they appear? Constant? Of normal duration? Shortened? Lengthened? Progressively longer? Varying?

6. Evaluate the ST segments. Do they have normal duration and position? Are they elevated? (If so, are they flat, concave, convex, arched?) Depressed? (If so, are they normal, flat, downsloping or upsloping?)

7. Determine if T waves are present. If so, how do they appear? Of normal height and duration? Tall? Wide? Notched? Inverted?

8. Determine the presence of QT intervals. If present, what is their duration? Normal? Shortened? Prolonged?

9. Determine if U waves are present. If present, how do they appear? Of normal height and duration? Inverted?

10. Identify the rhythm or dysrhythmia.

1.

ECG Findings:

2.

ECG Findings:

3.

ECG Findings:

4.

ECG Findings:

5.

ECG Findings:

6.

ECG Findings:

7.

ECG Findings:

8.

ECG Findings:

9.

ECG Findings:

10.

ECG Findings:

11.

ECG Findings:

12.

ECG Findings:

13.

ECG Findings:

14.

ECG Findings:

15.

ECG Findings:

16.

ECG Findings:

17.

ECG Findings:

18.

ECG Findings:

19.

ECG Findings:

20.

ECG Findings:

21.

ECG Findings:

22.

ECG Findings:

23.

ECG Findings:

24.

ECG Findings:

25.

ECG Findings:

26.

ECG Findings:

27.

ECG Findings:

28.

ECG Findings:

29.

ECG Findings:

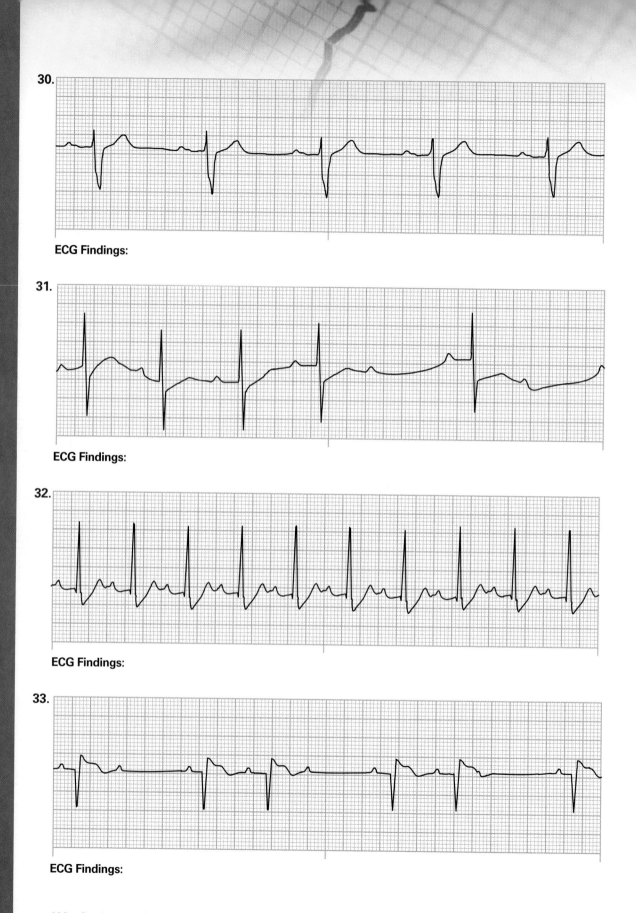

30.

ECG Findings:

31.

ECG Findings:

32.

ECG Findings:

33.

ECG Findings:

34.

ECG Findings:

35.

ECG Findings:

36.

ECG Findings:

37.

ECG Findings:

38.

ECG Findings:

39.

ECG Findings:

40.

ECG Findings:

41.

ECG Findings:

42.

ECG Findings:

43.

ECG Findings:

44.

ECG Findings:

45.

ECG Findings:

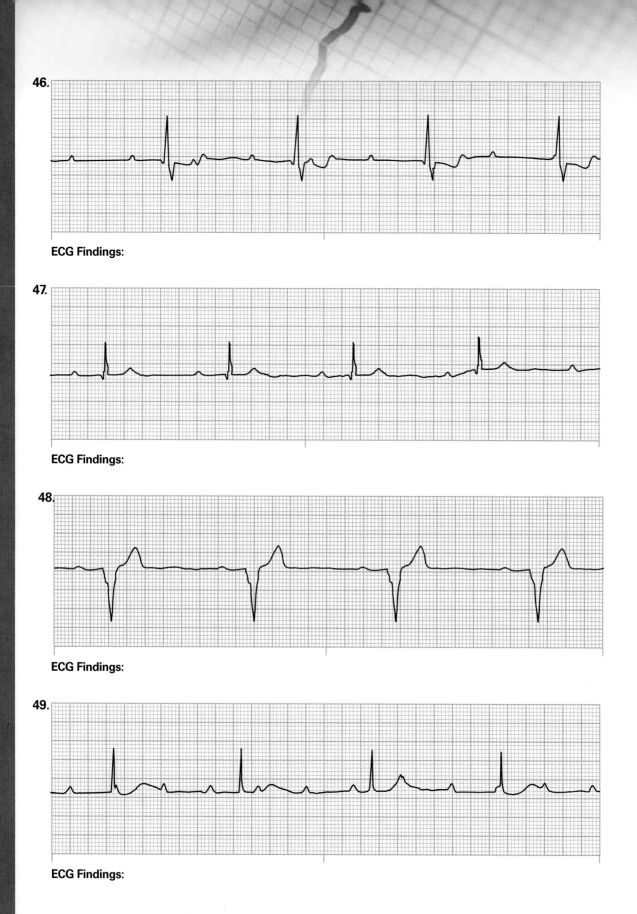

46.

ECG Findings:

47.

ECG Findings:

48.

ECG Findings:

49.

ECG Findings:

50.

ECG Findings:

51.

ECG Findings:

52.

ECG Findings:

53.

ECG Findings:

Key Points

- Heart blocks are partial delays or complete interruptions in the cardiac conduction pathway between the atria and ventricles. A block can occur at the AV node, the bundle of His, or the bundle branches.

- 1st-degree AV heart block is not a true block. Instead, it is a consistent delay of conduction at the level of the AV node that results in a PR interval greater than 0.20 seconds in duration.

- 2nd-degree AV heart block, type I, is also referred to as *Wenckebach*. It is an intermittent block at the level of the AV junction.

- With 2nd-degree AV heart block, type I, the PR interval increases until a QRS complex is dropped. After the dropped beat, the next PR interval is shorter. Then, as each subsequent impulse is generated and transmitted through the AV junction, there is a progressively longer PR interval until, again, a QRS complex is dropped. This cycle can repeat over and over.

- With 2nd-degree AV heart block, type I, there are more P waves than QRS complexes, and the rhythm is regularly irregular. This is also called a *patterned irregularity*.

- 2nd-degree AV heart block, type II, is an intermittent block at the level of the bundle of His or bundle branches resulting in atrial impulses that are not conducted to the ventricles.

- With 2nd-degree AV heart block, type II, there are more P waves than QRS complexes, and the duration of PR interval of the conducted beats remains the same (is constant).

- 3rd-degree AV heart block is a complete block of the conduction at or below the AV junction so that impulses from the atria cannot reach the ventricles.

- In 3rd-degree AV heart block, the pacemaker for the atria arises from the SA node whereas the pacemaker for the ventricles arises as an escape rhythm from the AV junction at a rate of 40 to 60 beats per minute or from the ventricles at a rate of 20 to 40 beats per minute.

- With 3rd-degree AV heart block, the upright and round P waves seem to march right through the QRS complexes. This reveals that there is no relationship between the P waves and QRS complexes.

- 2nd- and 3rd-degree AV heart block can lead to decreased cardiac output.

- In AV dissociation, the SA node loses control of the ventricular rate, leading to the atria and ventricles beating independently of each other, usually at about the same rate.

Assess Your Understanding

The following questions give you a chance to assess your understanding of the material discussed in this chapter. The answers can be found in Appendix A.

1. Heart blocks are
   a. partial delays or complete interruptions in the cardiac conduction pathway between the atria and ventricles.
   b. early ectopic beats that originate outside the SA node.
   c. a shifting of the pacemaker site between the SA node, atria, and/or AV junction.
   d. the result of accessory conduction pathways between the atria and ventricles.

2. In 1st-degree AV heart block,
   a. the PR intervals are greater than 0.20 seconds in duration.
   b. not all the P waves are followed by QRS complexes.
   c. the P waves are inverted.
   d. the underlying rhythm is slow.

3. 1st-degree AV heart block is considered a/an
   a. intermittent block.
   b. complete block.
   c. consistent delay in conduction.
   d. partial block.

4. In 2nd-degree AV heart block, type I,
   a. the PR intervals get progressively shorter.
   b. not all the P waves are followed by a QRS complex.
   c. the P waves are inverted.
   d. the rhythm appears to be irregularly irregular.

5. In 2nd-degree AV heart block, type II,
   a. the P waves are all the same.
   b. a QRS complex follows each P wave.
   c. the pacemaker site is in the AV junction.
   d. the ventricular rate is less than 40 beats per minute.

6. Which of the following rhythms has a constant PR interval for all conducted beats?
   a. 2nd-degree AV heart block, type I
   b. 3rd-degree AV heart block
   c. 2nd-degree AV heart block, type II
   d. All of the above

7. The difference between 2nd-degree AV heart block, type I, and type II is that
   a. in type II, the PR intervals are constant.
   b. the ventricular rate in type II is usually greater than 60 beats per minute.
   c. in type II, the P waves appear to march right through the QRS complexes.
   d. in type II, there appears to be a pattern to the irregularity.

8. An ECG rhythm that has no correlation between P waves and QRS complexes is known as
   a. 1st-degree AV heart block.
   b. 2nd-degree AV heart block, type II.
   c. 2nd-degree AV heart block, type I.
   d. 3rd-degree AV heart block.

9. Which of the following dysrhythmias has P waves that seem to march through the QRS complexes?
   a. 2nd-degree AV heart block, type I
   b. 2nd-degree AV heart block, type II
   c. 3rd-degree AV heart block
   d. 1st-degree AV heart block

10. Which of the following heart blocks is irregular?
    a. 1st-degree AV heart block
    b. 2nd-degree AV heart block, type I
    c. 3rd-degree AV heart block
    d. All of the above

11. Match the following heart blocks with the correct characteristics.

Heart Blocks	Characteristics
a. 1st-degree AV heart block	_____ The PR interval gets progressively longer until a P wave fails to conduct, resulting in a dropped QRS complex. After the blocked beat, the cycle starts again.
b. 2nd-degree AV heart block, type I	_____ There is a complete block at or below the AV node; there is no relationship between the P waves and QRS complexes.
c. 2nd-degree AV heart block, type II	_____ Some beats are conducted while others are blocked.
d. 3rd-degree AV heart block	_____ This is not a true block; there is a delay at the AV node; each impulse is eventually conducted.

Referring to the scenario at the beginning of this chapter, answer the following questions.

12. What rhythm is the patient in?
    a. 1st-degree AV heart block.
    b. 2nd-degree AV heart block, type I.
    c. 2nd-degree AV heart block, type II.
    d. 3rd-degree AV heart block.

13. The most common cause of this condition is
    a. medication.
    b. MI.
    c. atherosclerotic heart disease.
    d. a malfunctioning artificial pacemaker.

14. The treatment of this condition usually requires which of the following?
    a. An artificial pacemaker
    b. An implanted defibrillator
    c. A heart transplant
    d. Cardiac stimulant medication

Answers to Sidebar Questions

1. There are more P waves than QRS complexes in both types of 2nd-degree AV heart block and in 3rd-degree AV heart block. **p. 420**

2. The normal PR interval is 0.12 to 0.20 seconds in duration. **p. 422**

3. 2nd-degree AV heart block, type I, produces regularly or patterned irregularity. This is where the irregularity repeats over and over in a cyclic fashion. **p. 424**

4. With nonconducted PACs (or blocked PACs), the P-P interval, including the extra P wave, isn't constant, whereas with 2nd-degree AV heart block, the P-P interval, including the extra P wave, is constant. **p. 426**

5. The inherent rate of the AV junction is 40 to 60 beats per minute, whereas the inherent rate of the ventricles is 20 to 40 beats per minute. **p. 427**

What's Online

Go to www.mhhe.com/shadeECG2e to find:

- Presentations on chapter content
- Types of heart blocks exercise
- Crossword puzzle exercise
- Additional ECG tracings for practicing analyzing AV heart blocks
- Chapter quiz
- Flashcards
- Fill-in-the-blank exercises and answers
- In-depth answers to Practice Makes Perfect ECG tracings and Assess Your Understanding questions

16 Pacemakers and Implanted Cardioverter-Defibrillators

Chapter Outline

Pacemakers and Implantable Defibrillators

Temporary Pacemakers

Permanent Pacemakers

Appearance of the Paced ECG

Pacemaker Failure

Complications of Pacemakers

Implantable Cardioverter-Defibrillator

Learning Objectives

LO 16.1 Describe the purpose and use of artificial pacemakers and implantable defibrillators.

LO 16.2 Differentiate between temporary and permanent pacemakers.

LO 16.3 Identify the common location where permanent pacemakers are implanted.

LO 16.4 Identify the uses for permanent pacemakers.

LO 16.5 List the different components of the permanent pacemaker and describe the function of each.

LO 16.6 Describe the different operating modes of the permanent pacemaker.

LO 16.7 Recall the characteristics associated with various paced rhythms seen on the ECG.

LO 16.8 Identify the different causes of pacemaker failure.

LO 16.9 Identify the uses for the implantable defibrillator.

LO 16.10 Describe the operation of the implantable defibrillator.

Case History

A 45-year-old man experienced syncope, which prompted his family to call for an ambulance. The paramedics arrive to find the patient sitting upright but feeling lightheaded. Assessment reveals the patient is confused and has a blood pressure of 80/60 mmHg, a pulse rate of 40 beats per minute, and a respiratory rate of 14 breaths per minute. The ECG is attached to reveal the presence of 3rd-degree AV block with wide QRS complexes. The paramedics administer oxygen, place an IV line, position two electrode pads on the patient's chest, and begin pacing him. Within a few minutes the patient's heart rate increases to 70 beats per minute, and he appears more alert. He agrees to be transported to the hospital, where he undergoes evaluation and treatment. The treating physician then consults with the on-call cardiologist, who orders implantation of an internal pacemaker. Following successful insertion of the pacemaker, the patient is discharged to recover at home.

LO 16.1

Pacemakers and Implantable Defibrillators

In this chapter, we discuss artificial pacemakers and implanted defibrillators. Artificial pacemakers are medical devices that deliver electrical impulses to the heart to stimulate a normal heartbeat. They are used to maintain an adequate heart rate when the heart's own pacemaker cannot or when there is a block in its electrical conduction system that slows the heart rate. Some pacemakers are external to the body and used to provide temporary treatment whereas others are permanently implanted in the chest. An implantable defibrillator is a device that delivers electrical shocks to the heart in the presence of life-threatening ventricular tachycardia or ventricular fibrillation. Some modern implantable devices have both a pacemaker and defibrillator combined into one unit.

LO 16.2

WANT MORE INFORMATION?
Visit the Fast & Easy ECGs Website at www.mhhe.com/shadeECG2e.

KEY CONCEPT
A pacemaker is an artificial device that produces an impulse and conveys it to the myocardium.

Temporary Pacemakers

In Chapter 10, we discussed the use of the transcutaneous pacemaker, a temporary pacemaker in which the electrode pads are applied to the surface of the patient's chest. Two other temporary pacemakers can be used: the epicardial pacemaker and the transvenous pacemaker.

Epicardial Pacing

Epicardial pacing is employed during open heart surgery when the surgical procedure causes atrioventricular block and bradycardia. The electrode is placed in contact with the ventricular epicardium, and small electrical charges are delivered to maintain satisfactory cardiac output until a temporary transvenous electrode can be inserted.

Transvenous Pacing

With transvenous pacing, an electrode is fed through a vein and into either the right atrium or right ventricle. This is done using sterile technique. The pacing electrode is then connected to a pacemaker, the location of which is external to the body, to deliver emergency pacing. Transvenous pacing is used until a permanent pacemaker can be implanted or there is no longer a need for a pacemaker and the pacing electrode is removed.

LO 16.3

Permanent Pacemakers

A permanent pacemaker is a medical device that is implanted in a surgically created pocket beneath the skin in the patient's chest wall just below the clavicle. It is often called an *internal pacemaker*. Pacemakers work because of two main things:

- Electrical current flow results in cardiac activity and can be identified.
- An intrinsic property of the heart is that an action potential, firing in a few cells, spreads as a self-propagating wave throughout the chamber.

First developed in the 1960s, pacemakers originally sent a steady flow of electrical impulses to the heart. Modern pacemakers can monitor the heart and activate only when necessary.

The basic function of pacemakers is to sense for normal heart activity, and if it does not occur, induce action potentials by passing depolarizing currents into a heart chamber, triggering a self-propagating wave. This restores electrical stimulation of the chamber and, ideally, mechanical pumping of the heart. The more complex permanent pacemakers have the ability to sense and/or stimulate both the atrial and ventricular chambers.

Uses

LO 16.4

Pacemakers can be of tremendous clinical benefit in various circumstances including

- Symptomatic bradycardia.
- Sick sinus syndrome.
- Atrial fibrillation with bradycardia.
- 3rd-degree (complete) AV heart block.
- Symptomatic 2nd-degree AV heart block, particularly type II.
- The sudden development of various combinations of AV heart block and bundle branch block in patients experiencing acute MI.
- Recurrent tachycardias that can be overdriven and thereby terminated by pacemaker activity.
- Synchronization of the heart beat in heart failure (cardiac resynchronization therapy)

Most often, implantation of a permanent pacemaker does not change a person's activities or lifestyle. Typically, only a small bump is seen in the skin over the site where the pacemaker has been placed. Whereas most people who receive pacemakers are 60 years or older, pacemakers can be implanted in persons of any age, even in children.

The pacemaker consists of a generator and one or more lead wires that connect the device to the heart (Figure 16-1).

Generator

LO 16.5

The pacemaker generator is a small device (about the size of a man's wristwatch), weighing less than 13 grams (under half an ounce). It consists of

QUESTION

1. **What does the term self-propagating mean?** *Note:* Answer to the sidebar questions can be found at the end of the chapter.

Electrodes inserted into vein leading to heart

Pacemaker generator

Electrode in right ventricle

Electrode

Stimulation of heart muscle

Pacemaker spike

Figure 16-1
Pacemakers are used to provide electrical stimuli for hearts with an impaired ability to initiate or conduct an electrical impulse. The two primary components of the implanted pacemaker are the generator and the lead wire(s).

a power source, a sensing amplifier that processes the electrical activity of the heart as detected by the pacemaker electrodes, the computer logic for the pacemaker, and the output circuitry, which delivers the pacing impulse to the lead wire(s) to stimulate the heart to beat at the desired rate. The casing of the pacemaker is made of titanium or a titanium alloy and is hermetically sealed to prevent diffusion of water vapor from the body fluids into the electronic circuitry and rejection by the body's immune system (as titanium is very inert in the body). The power source, usually a lithium battery, is extremely durable. Depending on how many leads the pacemaker is configured with and how much energy the device uses, the battery can be expected to last an average of 7 to 15 years. Alternatively, cadmium/nickel oxide or nuclear batteries may be used. When a new battery is needed, the unit can be exchanged in a simple outpatient procedure.

Lead Wire(s)

The lead wires are tiny, thin wires composed of a coiled metal conductor that is insulated with plastic. The only exposed part of the electrode is the distal end, which has a bare metal tip that is affixed against the wall of the heart chamber with soft plastic hooks, a short metal screw, or a screw-in tip. The tip has either one electrode (unipolar) or two electrodes (bipolar). The proximal end of the lead wire is attached to the pacemaker. Because the heartbeat is constantly flexing the lead wire, it must be resistant to fracture.

To insert the lead wire, the surgeon, with the assistance of a physician or cardiologist, makes an incision in a suitable vein and feeds the lead wire(s) along, until it eventually passes into the atrial chamber or through the heart valve and into the ventricular chamber. The procedure is facilitated by fluoroscopy, which enables the viewing of the passage of the lead wire lead. Once in place, the lead wire(s) pass electricity from the spontaneous cardiac activity into the generator and from the pacemaker into the heart.

Function

LO 16.6

Today's pacemakers can be externally programmed, receiving and transmitting data/programming through the skin via electromagnetic waves. They can be adjusted according to pacing mode, output, sensitivity, refractory period, and rate adaption. This allows the cardiologist to select the optimum pacing modes for individual patients. Further, the ECG can be used to find if a patient's pacemaker is properly working. You need to be familiar with the pacemaker modes, capabilities, and coding in order to compare the intended versus actual pacemaker function.

KEY CONCEPT
The demand pacemaker is the most widely used pacemaker.

Pacing Modes

Permanent pacemakers are categorized by how many chambers they stimulate and how they operate. They include the following:

- *Single-chamber.* One pacing lead is inserted into either the right atrium or right ventricle but not both.
- *Dual-chamber.* Electrodes are placed into two chambers of the heart. One lead paces the atrium while the other paces the ventricle. By assisting the heart in coordinating the function between the atria and ventricles, this type of pacemaker acts similarly to how the heart naturally paces itself and may also be referred to as an AV sequential pacemaker. Most dual-chamber systems can be programmed to a single chamber mode, which can be useful if the atrial lead wire fails.
- *Fixed-rate.* This pacemaker paces the heart at a single, preset rate.
- *Demand.* This pacemaker senses the heart's native electrical impulses and, if no electrical activity is detected within a certain period of time, delivers a short low-voltage pulse to the chamber to stimulate the heartbeat. This sensing and stimulating activity continues on a beat-by-beat basis. It is the most widely used pacemaker.

- *Rate-responsive.* This pacemaker has sensors that identify increases or decreases in the patient's physical activity and automatically adjusts the base pacing rate to meet the body's metabolic needs. It can boost the heart rate in response to motion or increased respirations for those patients whose body, because of either disease of the sinus node or the effects of medications, cannot appropriately increase the heart rate during activity.

Output

The energy delivered to the lead wires can be adjusted. Using a lower energy level conserves power and increases battery life whereas using a higher energy level makes certain pacing occur when necessary. The voltage output is usually set to 50% above the capture threshold. The threshold is the pacemaker output that just captures the chamber. The pulse duration can also be altered.

Sensitivity

A pacemaker should detect the presence of appropriate cardiac electrical activity (and not pace) whereas at the same time it needs to ignore nonrelevant electrical activity. For atrial pacemakers the relevant activity is the P wave; for ventricular systems it is the R wave. Pacemaker sensitivity is the level of current the generator recognizes or ignores as coming from a cardiac chamber. The pectoral muscle generates 2 to 3 mV currents while the heart generates 5 to15 mV currents. Most often, sensitivity is set at around 4 to 5 mV, thus excluding pectoral muscle as well as electrical activity occurring in distant chambers. If the lead wire starts to fail, the amount of electricity passed up the lead wire may decrease, leading to failure to sense and inappropriate pacing. Altering the sensitivity can deal with this problem.

Refractory Period

It is important that pacemakers not misinterpret electrical activity from one chamber as coming from another. As an example, an atrial lead wire can sense ventricular activity, label it as atrial, and inappropriately inhibit pacing when it might be needed. Programming the generator not to detect electrical activity at certain times of the cardiac cycle (e.g., inhibiting the atrial lead wire from detecting electrical activity during the time period when normal ventricular activity occurs) can prevent this.

Rate Adaptation

Rate-responsive pacemakers detect physical activity (using motion detectors or QT interval sensors), and react by increasing the pacing rate. These are useful in mimicking the physiological effects of exercise on the heart rate.

Coding System

In order to be standardized, the pacemaker mode and function are described by a coding system that uses five letters. In practice however, only three to four are commonly used.

The first letter (Position I) represents the heart chamber being paced. This letter may be

- O = none
- A = atrium
- V = ventricle
- D = dual (ventricle and atrium)

The second letter (Position II) represents the chamber of the heart being sensed by the pacemaker. This letter may be

- O = none
- A = atrium
- V = ventricle
- D = dual (ventricle and atrium)

The third letter (Position III) indicates how the pacemaker generator responds to sensing. This letter may be

- O = none
- T = triggers pacing
- I = inhibits pacing
- D = dual (triggers and inhibits pacing)

The fourth letter (Position IV) has to do with adjustment of the pacing rate in response to exercise. If the pacemaker is rate responsive, it is denoted with the letter R. These pacemakers have extra sensors that can detect a patient's physical activity and respond by increasing heart rate to a set limit. If there is none, it is denoted as "O". A common pacemaker is a VVI-R. This has a single lead that senses and paces the ventricle, and if the patient exercises, increases the paced heart rate.

The fifth letter indicates multisite pacing. This letter may be

- O = none
- A = atrium
- V = ventricle
- D = dual (ventricle and atrium).

Thus, the coding system for the pacemaker might be

- VOO. In this mode, the ventricle is paced and there is no sensing function. This is a temporary mode used to check pacing threshold.
- AAI. In this mode, the pacemaker paces and senses in the atrium. When it senses atrial activity, pacing is inhibited.

- VVI. In this mode the ventricle is paced and sensed. If spontaneous cardiac output is detected, then the device is inhibited.
- VDD. Here the pacemaker paces the ventricle and senses both the atrium and ventricle. On sensing intrinsic atrial activity, the pacemaker triggers ventricular pacing; on sensing ventricular activity, the pacemaker inhibits pacing. It is also known as a *P-synchronous pacer*.
- DVI. In this mode, the pacemaker can pace in the atrium, the ventricle, or both. Sensing takes place only in the ventricle. When the pacemaker senses intrinsic ventricular activity, it inhibits pacing.
- DDD. In this mode, the pacemaker paces and senses in the atrium, the ventricle, or both. On sensing activity in either chamber, the pacemaker inhibits pacing in that chamber. Or, on sensing atrial activity, the pacemaker may trigger ventricular pacing.

Cardiac Resynchronization Therapy

Another type of pacemaker is the biventricular pacemaker. Also called *cardiac resynchronization therapy* (CRT), this pacemaker paces both the right and left ventricles. It is used to resynchronize a heart that does not beat in synchrony, a common problem in patients with heart failure.

Asynchronous contractions lead to blood being moved within, rather than out of the ventricle. This results in reduced cardiac output. Further, these patients experience greater mitral regurgitation and reduced diastolic filling time.

The biventricular pacemaker employs three leads: one is placed in the right atrium, one is located in the right ventricle, and the last one is inserted through the coronary sinus to pace the free wall of the left ventricle. These three wires are connected to a CRT generator and programmed so that the two ventricular wires are activated simultaneously.

Simultaneous contraction of the right and left ventricles results in less blood being shunted within the ventricle and more blood being propelled into the aorta. These devices relieve symptoms of heart failure, improve prognosis, and lessen the chance of ventricular dysrhythmias.

LO 16.7

Appearance of the Paced ECG

On the ECG, the firing of the pacemaker and its movement down the lead wire appears as a narrow vertical line referred to as a *pacing spike* or *pacing artifact*. What the waveforms of the chamber being depolarized look like depends on which chamber(s) is (are) being paced (Figure 16-2).

A lead wire that is positioned in the atria produces a pacing spike and a P wave of normal duration and shape. The reason for this is that the atrial lead

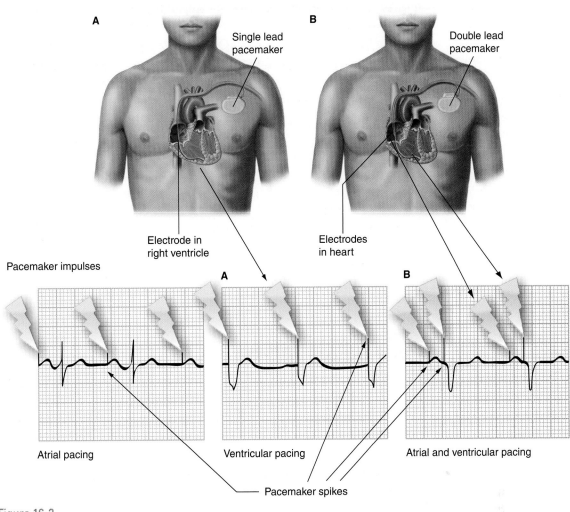

Figure 16-2
Pacing spikes.

wire is close to the sinus node, resulting in the wave of depolarization spreading across the atria in a normal manner.

With a ventricular pacemaker, the pacing spike is followed by a broad QRS complex. This occurs because the electrode sits at the apex of the right ventricle. After the pacemaker fires, the wave of depolarization slowly spreads from myocyte to myocyte across the right ventricle. The left ventricle is then depolarized. Because the left ventricle is the last to depolarize, it produces a pattern identical to left bundle branch block. A retrograde P wave may or may not be seen.

With a dual-chamber pacemaker, there will be an initial pacing spike followed by a P wave and a second pacing spike followed by a broad QRS complex.

Simultaneous stimulation of both ventricles (biventricular pacing) produces a QRS that is not as wide as is typically associated with right ventricular pacing.

It is important to note that pacemaker spikes do not appear in every lead. For this reason, you should check more than one lead to identify their presence. Because lead aV_R produces small QRS complexes, the pacemaker spikes are less likely to be obstructed and may be easier to see.

Unipolar vs. Bipolar Systems

In a unipolar system, the positive electrode is positioned in the heart tissue and the negative electrode is connected to the pulse generator. Because the two poles are so far apart, a unipolar system produces tall pacing spikes on the ECG. In a bipolar system, the electrodes are only millimeters apart in the cardiac tissue. This produces short pacemaker spikes.

In some patients, pacemaker spikes are not easy to see on an ECG because their amplitude is less than 1 mV. If the patient is able to communicate and is appropriately oriented, asking the question "Do you have a pacemaker?" may be of use when broad QRS complexes and left axis deviation are seen on the ECG.

LO 16.8

Pacemaker Failure

Pacemakers may not work properly for a number of reasons, including the following: failure to capture, failure to pace, failure to sense, oversensing, and pacemaker-mediated tachycardia. Regardless of why a pacemaker does not work, you should always focus on treating the patient first and not the device.

Failure to Capture

Failure to capture occurs when the pacemaker fires but does not trigger an atrial or ventricular depolarization.

Identifying It

Failure to capture can be recognized by the presence of pacemaker spikes which are not followed by P waves (if an atrial electrode is used) or by broad QRS complexes (if a ventricular electrode is used) (Figure 16-3). Other signs and symptoms that may be seen include bradycardia, fatigue, and hypotension.

Causes

Failure of the pacemaker to capture can be caused by an electrode tip that is out of place, the pacemaker voltage being set too low, a dead battery, a broken lead wire, the presence of edema or scar tissue at the electrode tip, perforation of the myocardium by the lead, or MI at the electrode tip.

Interventions

Correcting the problem depends on the cause. Interventions used to correct failure to capture include repositioning the electrode tip, increasing

Pacemaker fires but does fails to capture ventricular depolarization

Figure 16-3
Example of failure to capture.

the voltage, replacing the battery, repositioning or replacing the lead wire, and/or surgical intervention.

Failure to Pace

Failure to pace occurs when the pacemaker fails to send a signal to depolarize one or both chambers.

Identifying It

The absence of apparent pacemaker activity on the ECG is the primary way of identifying a failure to pace (Figure 16-4). Depending on the underlying heart rate, the patient may present with bradycardia and hypotension. Another indicator has to do with a magnet being applied over the pacemaker. Normally, a magnet will cause a synchronous pacemaker to be converted to an asynchronous pacemaker. With failure to pace, the application of a magnet produces no response.

Failure to pace results in an absence of pacemaker spikes and electrical activity

Figure 16-4
Failure to pace is seen as an absence of pacemaker spikes when they should be present.

Causes

Possible causes of failure to pace include a battery or circuit failure, a displaced or broken lead, or a loose lead-generator connection.

Interventions

Interventions used to correct failure to pace include replacing the battery, generator, or lead; repairing the connection; or tightening the terminal (if it is a temporary pacemaker).

Failure to Sense

With correct sensing, when an atrial or ventricular beat occurs, there should be no paced beat within the time period determined by the minimum paced rate. If there is, then the pacemaker has failed to sense.

Identifying It

Failure of the pacemaker to sense is seen as ECG pacemaker spikes that fall where they should not. For example, the pacemaker spikes may be seen falling on T waves (Figure 16-5). Also, the patient may complain of palpitations or skipped beats and may even develop ventricular tachycardia.

Causes

Possible causes of a failure to sense include a dead battery, an electrode tip that is out of position, a broken lead wire, the presence of edema or fibrosis at the electrode tip causing decreased R or P wave amplitude, or the "sensitivity" being set too high (this is a programmable function, and can be adjusted).

Interventions

Interventions used to resolve failure to sense include replacing the battery or lead, repositioning the electrode, positioning the patient on his or her left side, or making sure the sensitivity setting is correct.

Pacemaker fails to sense impulse and fires unnecessarily

Figure 16-5
Failure to sense is seen as pacemaker spikes occurring when they should not be present.

Oversensing

Oversensing occurs when the pacemaker misinterprets certain types of electrical activity as being cardiac activity and does not fire when it should. This leaves the patient vulnerable to a slow heart rate.

Identifying It

The main identifying feature of oversensing is an absence of pacemaker spikes in the presence of a heart rate that is slower than the rate set for the pacemaker (which is normally faster than the patient's spontaneous rate). The patient may also be symptomatic (i.e., fatigue and hypotension) due to decreased cardiac output that may coincide with the slow heart rate.

Causes

One cause of oversensing is the pacemaker sensitivity's being set too low. Another is the pacemaker's detection of nonrelevant electrical activity and its perception that the atria have depolarized when they haven't. This results in the pacemaker not firing when it should. Examples include skeletal muscle contractions (in unipolar lead systems) or distant cardiac chamber electrical activity (T waves or atrial impulses). Electromagnetic interference can also result in pacemaker oversensing.

Interventions

Interventions used to correct oversensing include inserting a bipolar lead, testing with a magnet, increasing the sensitivity setting (if the pacemaker is temporary), and, lastly, reprogramming the internal pacemaker.

Pacemaker-Mediated Tachycardia

In dual-chamber pacemakers, the electrodes and generator can sometimes act as an accessory pathway leading to tachydysrhythmias.

Identifying It

Pacemaker-mediated tachycardia is seen as a fast heart rate with a pacemaker spike preceding each QRS complex on EGG (Figure 16-6).

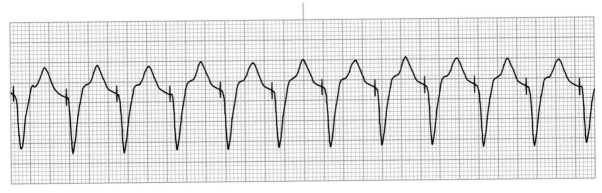

Figure 16-6
Pacemaker-mediated tachycardia is seen as a tachycardia with a pacemaker spike preceding each QRS complex on the EGG.

Causes

Pacemaker-mediated tachycardia occurs due to retrograde conduction through the AV node (from dual-chamber pacing), which depolarizes the atria and triggers the rapid heart rate.

Interventions

Due to the rapid heart rate, the patient must be monitored for ventricular tachycardia and ventricular fibrillation. Interventions include reprogramming the pacemaker to an atrial nonsensing mode or prolonging the postventricular atrial refractory period of the pacemaker so that it will no longer sense retrograde P waves. In an emergency, the heart rate can be decreased by holding a magnet over the pulse generator. This acts to convert the pacemaker from synchronous to asynchronous until it can be reprogrammed.

Complications of Pacemakers

Aside from the pacemaker's failing to properly function there are two complications that deserve discussion: infection and pacemaker syndrome.

Infection

Infection should be suspected in anyone with an implanted pacemaker presenting with an inflammatory illness. Signs and symptoms might include fever, weight loss, anemia, raised erythrocyte sedimentation rate (ESR), and C-reactive protein (CRP), and/or positive blood cultures. Treatment includes antibiotic administration, complete pacemaker system removal, and, when sterility is achieved, inserting a new system.

Pacemaker Syndrome

Patients who have a VVI pacemaker (ventricle paced and sensed device inhibited if spontaneous cardiac output detected) and intact AV conduction can develop retrograde ventricular atrial conduction. As such, shortly after ventricular systole, the atria fire, contracting on a closed AV valve. This results in atrial distension, brain natriuretic peptide release, and reflexes that lower blood pressure, causing faintness or syncope. This problem can be corrected by lowering the rate at which pacing starts (less pacing occurs) or upgrading to a DDD system.

LO 16.9

Implantable Cardioverter-Defibrillators

An implantable cardioverter-defibrillator (ICD) is an electronic device that is positioned in the left pectoral region similarly to how pacemakers are implanted. It can perform several functions including pacing to treat bradycardia, overdrive pacing, or cardioversion to treat ventricular tachycardia and delivering internal defibrillation to the ventricle to treat ventricular fibrillation. Generally, ICDs are used in cases where drug therapy, surgery, or catheter ablation have failed to prevent the dysrhythmia(s) for which the ICDs are being implanted. The ICD consists of a programmable pulse generator and one or more lead wires.

Pulse Generator

The pulse generator is a small (weight of only 70 grams and thickness of about 12.9 mm), fully programmable, battery-powered computer (Figure 16-7). It monitors the heart's electrical activity and delivers electrical therapy when an abnormal rhythm is identified. The device has a solid-state memory that allows it to store information about the heart's activity before, during, and after the dysrhythmia, along with tracking delivered treatments and outcomes. Many devices also store electrograms (which are similar to ECGs). Using an interrogation device, this information can be retrieved and used to evaluate ICD function and battery status as well as to adjust the ICD settings. Because of all the functions performed by the ICD,

LO 16.10

KEY CONCEPT
An ICD is implanted in patients who are at risk of ventricular fibrillation and ventricular tachycardia. It is programmed to detect and correct cardiac dysrhythmias by delivering paced beats, cardioversion, or defibrillation.

Figure 16-7
The ICD implanted in a patient's chest.

it is equipped with a battery that stores substantial energy and charges the capacitor rapidly.

Electrode Wires

The ICD includes an electrode wire that is passed through a vein to the right chambers of the heart and lodged in the right ventricular apex. When the ICD discharges, energy is delivered to the heart via this electrode wire.

Recognition of Ventricular Dysrhythmias

ICDs continually monitor the heart rate and rhythm and can deliver electrical therapy when the heart's electrical activity exceeds the preset number. They can distinguish between ventricular tachycardia and ventricular fibrillation. These devices use a number of methods to determine if a fast rhythm is normal, ventricular tachycardia, or ventricular fibrillation. This includes rate discrimination, rhythm discrimination, and morphology discrimination.

Rate Discrimination

The ICD evaluates the ventricular rate and compares it with the atrial rate. If the atrial rate is faster than or equal to the ventricular rate, then the rhythm is not likely of ventricular origin. Instead it is usually something benign; in this case, the ICD will not deliver any therapy. The following are problems that can occur when using the heart rate to diagnose ventricular tachycardia or fibrillation.

- If the heart rate increases from supraventricular dysrhythmias such as atrial fibrillation, the rhythm may be interpreted as not having P waves.
- Occasionally, prominent T waves are counted as R waves, leading to double counting.

Incorrect diagnosis can result in the ICD identifying ventricular tachycardia as being present, thus leading to the inappropriate delivery of antitachycardia therapy.

Rhythm Discrimination

The ICD determines the regularity of ventricular tachycardia. Generally, ventricular tachycardia is regular. If the rhythm is irregular, it is usually due to the presence of an irregular rhythm that originates in the atria, such as atrial fibrillation.

Morphology Discrimination

The ICD assesses the morphology of every ventricular beat and compares it with what the ICD believes to be a normally conducted ventricular impulse for the patient. This normal ventricular impulse is often an average of a multiple of beats of the patient taken in the recent past.

Therapies Provided by the ICD

The ICD can treat several conditions including bradycardia (pacing), ventricular tachycardia (overdrive pacing or cardioversion), and ventricular fibrillation (internal defibrillation). Each of these therapies is described in Table 16-1.

Antitachydysrhythmia pacing is also known as *fast pacing* or *overdrive pacing*. It is only effective if the underlying rhythm is monomorphic ventricular tachycardia; it is never effective if the rhythm is ventricular fibrillation or polymorphic ventricular tachycardia. Occasionally, this type of pacing results in the ventricular tachycardia speeding up and becoming hemodynamically unstable or progressing to ventricular fibrillation, in which case defibrillation is delivered. This treatment is not used for all patients; instead it may be ordered after appropriate evaluation of electrophysiologic studies.

Dysrhythmia definitions are programmed into the ICD and altered according to the clinical situation. For example, the device may be programmed to identify the following heart rates and deliver an appropriate therapy:

- Normal heart rhythm: 60 to 150 beats per minute; no action taken
- Slow ventricular tachycardia: 150 to 200 beats per minute. Leads to antitachydysrhythmia pacing
- Fast ventricular tachycardia: 200 to 250 beats per minute; leads to several attempts of antitachydysrhythmia pacing followed by cardioversion/defibrillation
- Ventricular fibrillation: greater than 250 beats per minute; leads to immediate defibrillation.

Table 16-1
Types of ICD Therapy

Therapy	Description
Antibradycardia pacing	As described earlier, electrical pacing is used to increase the heart rate when it is too slow. Most ICDs can pace one chamber at a preset rate. Some devices sense and pace both chambers.
Antitachydysrhythmia pacing	This mode generates a series of small, rapid electrical pacing pulses to interrupt ventricular tachycardia (by "capturing" the ventricle and breaking the reentry circuit) and return the heart to its normal rhythm.
Cardioversion	This mode uses a low- or high-energy shock (up to 35 joules), which is timed to the R wave (which is detected by the right ventricular electrode) to terminate VT and return the heart to its normal rhythm.
Defibrillation	This mode delivers a high-energy shock (up to 35 joules) to the heart to terminate ventricular fibrillation and return the heart to its normal rhythm.

Provider Safety

A patient who has an ICD should be treated as if they did not have a device. If the ICD discharges while you are in contact with the patient, you may feel the shock; however, it is not likely to be dangerous. Providers shocked by an ICD report sensations similar to contact with an electrical current. If the patient has an ICD that is delivering shocks as demonstrated by the patient's muscles contracting in a manner similar to that observed during external defibrillation, you should allow 30 to 60 seconds for the ICD to complete the treatment cycle before attaching an AED or defibrillator pads. Occasionally, the analysis and shock cycles of automatic ICDs and AEDs will conflict. There is the potential for pacemaker or ICD malfunction after defibrillation when the pads are in close proximity to the device. For this reason, avoid placing the pads or paddles over the device. Pacemaker spikes with unipolar pacing may confuse AED software and may prevent VF detection. The anteroposterior and anterolateral locations are acceptable in patients with these devices. In patients with ICDs or pacemakers, pad/paddle placement should not delay defibrillation.

Practice Makes Perfect

For the following tracings, identify if a pacemaker is present and what type it is. Then determine if there is a pacemaker failure. Record your answers on a separate sheet of paper or directly on these pages. Your findings can then be compared to the answers provided in Appendix A.

1.

ECG Findings:

2.

ECG Findings:

3.

ECG Findings:

4.

ECG Findings:

5.

ECG Findings:

6.

ECG Findings:

7.

ECG Findings:

8.

ECG Findings:

9.

ECG Findings:

10.

ECG Findings:

11.

ECG Findings:

12.

ECG Findings:

13.

ECG Findings:

14.

ECG Findings:

15.

ECG Findings:

16.

ECG Findings:

17.

ECG Findings:

18.

ECG Findings:

19.

ECG Findings:

Key Points 🔍

- Artificial pacemakers are medical devices used to deliver electrical impulses to the heart to stimulate a normal heartbeat. Some pacemakers are external to the body and provide temporary treatment whereas others are permanently implanted in the chest.

- One type of temporary pacemaker is the transcutaneous pacemaker. It delivers electrical impulses through lead wires to electrode pads that are applied to the surface of the patient's chest.

- Permanent pacemakers are implanted in a surgically created pocket beneath the skin in the patient's chest wall just below the clavicle. They may be used to increase the heart rate when it is slow (antibradycardia devices), slow the heart rate when it is fast (antitachycardia devices), and synchronize the heart beat in heart failure (CRT).

- A pacemaker consists of a generator and one or more lead wires. The generator has a power source (often a lithium battery) and logic circuits that detect cardiac electrical activity and determine the appropriate response.

- Pacemaker electrodes are either positioned in the atrium or ventricle alone (single-chamber pacemakers) or, more often, in both chambers (dual-chamber pacemakers or AV sequential pacemakers).

- Pacemakers are programmable; they receive and transmit data/programming instructions through the skin using electromagnetic waves.

- The demand pacemaker is most commonly used. It fires only when the patient's intrinsic heart rate falls below a given threshold level. For example, if the pacemaker is set at 60 beats per minute, it remains inactive until there is a pause between beats that translates into a rate below 60. The pacemaker then fires.

- Depending on how many chambers are paced, the firing of a pacemaker produces one or two narrow pacemaker spikes on the ECG.

- A paced ECG complex shows two features: (a) a narrow "pacing spike," which reflects the impulse depolarizing the paced chamber and (b) a P wave or QRS complex that immediately follows the pacing spike.

- Pacemakers may not work properly for a number of reasons, including a failure to capture, a failure to pace, a failure to sense, oversensing, and pacemaker-mediated tachycardia.

- Failure to capture is seen as the presence of pacemaker spikes that are not followed by a P wave or broad QRS complex. Failure of the pacemaker to sense is seen as the presence of ECG pacemaker spikes that fall where they shouldn't. Oversensing is seen as an absence of pacemaker spikes in the presence of a heart rate that is slower than the rate set for the pacemaker. Pacemaker-mediated tachycardia is seen as a fast heart rate with a pacemaker spike preceding each QRS complex on EGG.

- An ICD is implanted in patients who are at risk of sudden cardiac death due to ventricular fibrillation and ventricular tachycardia. The device is programmed to detect cardiac dysrhythmias and correct them by delivering paced beats, cardioversion, or defibrillation.

Assess Your Understanding

The following questions give you a chance to assess your understanding of the material discussed in this chapter. The answers can be found in Appendix A.

1. A cardiac pacemaker is used to deliver electrical:
   a. impulses to the heart to stimulate a normal heartbeat.
   b. shocks to the heart in the presence of life-threatening ventricular fibrillation.
   c. currents to the autonomic nervous system to stimulate myocardial contraction.
   d. signals to the SA node to initiate the heartbeat through the normal conductive pathways.

2. A pacemaker that is permanently implanted into a patient is called a/an _____ pacemaker.
   a. transcutaneous
   b. transvenous
   c. internal
   d. epicardial

3. A permanent pacemaker is implanted in a surgically created pocket beneath the skin in the patient's
   a. abdomen.
   b. chest.
   c. neck.
   d. upper thigh.

4. Permanent pacemakers can be used to treat all of the following conditions EXCEPT
   a. symptomatic bradycardia.
   b. 3rd-degree AV heart block.
   c. recurrent tachycardia.
   d. premature ventricular complexes.

5. The pacemaker generator
   a. consists of a power source, sensing amplifier, computer logic for the pacemaker, and output circuitry.
   b. is powered by two or three AAA rechargeable batteries.

c. is susceptible to damage from body water vapor diffusing into the computer circuitry and rejection by the immune system.

d. is typically replaced after every 5 years of use.

6. The lead wires of the permanent pacemaker
   a. are inflexible to prevent dislodgement of the electrode from the chamber wall.
   b. are composed of a coiled metal conductor that is insulated with a fine linen mesh.
   c. consist of two electrodes implanted in the outside myocardial wall (epicardium).
   d. are passed through a suitable vein into one or both of the heart's chambers.

7. A pacemaker that senses the heart's native electrical impulses and, if no electrical activity is detected within a certain period of time, delivers a short low voltage pulse to the chamber to stimulate the heartbeat is referred to as a _____ pacemaker.
   a. fixed-rate
   b. demand
   c. rate-responsive
   d. dual-chamber

8. In the following mode the ventricle is paced and sensed. If spontaneous cardiac output is detected, then the device is inhibited.
   a. VDD
   b. DVI
   c. VVI
   d. DDD

9. On the ECG, the firing of the pacemaker and its movement down the lead wire appears as a
   a. narrow vertical line.
   b. square box.
   c. jagged biphasic wave.
   d. flat line.

10. With a ventricular pacemaker, the pacing spike is followed by a
    a. normal P wave.
    b. broad P wave and normal QRS complex.
    c. broad QRS complex.
    d. narrow QRS complex.

11. In a unipolar system, the positive electrode
    a. produces short pacemaker spikes.
    b. is positioned in the heart tissue while the negative electrode is connected to the pulse generator.
    c. has two electrodes that are only millimeters apart in the cardiac tissue.
    d. is attached to myocardial epicardium.

12. Pacemaker spikes appear in every lead and can be easily seen.
    a. True
    b. False

13. Failure to capture can be recognized by
    a. the presence of pacemaker spikes that are not followed by P waves or by broad QRS complexes.
    b. an absence of pacemaker spikes in the presence of a heart rate that is slower than the rate set for the pacemaker.
    c. ECG pacemaker spikes that fall where they shouldn't.
    d. a tachycardia with a pacemaker spike preceding each QRS complex on the EGG.

14. An ICD can perform all of the following functions EXCEPT
    a. pacing to treat bradycardia.
    b. overdrive pacing or cardioversion to treat ventricular tachycardia.
    c. delivering internal defibrillation to the ventricle to treat ventricular fibrillation.
    d. pacing both the right and left ventricles to resynchronize an asynchronous heartbeat.

These questions refer to the case history at the beginning of the chapter.

15. The paramedics used what type of pacemaker to increase the patient's heart rate?
    a. Transcutaneous
    b. Transvenous
    c. Internal
    d. Epicardial

16. The cardiologist has ordered the implantation of a(n)
    a. implantable cardioverter-defibrillator.
    b. biventricular pacemaker.
    c. transvenous pacemaker.
    d. permanent pacemaker.

Answer to Sidebar Question

1. Self-propagation is the spreading movement of a depolarization wave from myocyte to myocyte across the heart. **p. 451**

What's Online

Go to www.mhhe.com/shadeECG2e to find:

- Presentations on chapter content
- Chapter quiz
- Fill-in-the-blank exercises and answers
- In-depth answers to Practice Makes Perfect ECG tracings and Assess Your Understanding questions

Section 4
12-Lead ECGs

Chapter 17: Overview of 12-Lead ECGs and Electrical Axis

Chapter 18: Atrial Enlargement and Ventricular Hypertrophy

Chapter 19: Bundle Branch Block

Chapter 20: Myocardial Ischemia, Injury, and Infarction

Chapter 21: Other Cardiac Conditions and the ECG

17

Overview of 12-Lead ECGs and Electrical Axis

Chapter Outline

Heart's Normal
    Electrical Activity

The 12-Lead ECG

Planes of the Heart

Putting the Views
    Together

15- and 18-Lead
    ECGs

Analyzing the 12-Lead
    ECG

Electrical Axis and
    the ECG

Calculating the
    Electrical Axis

Altered QRS Axis

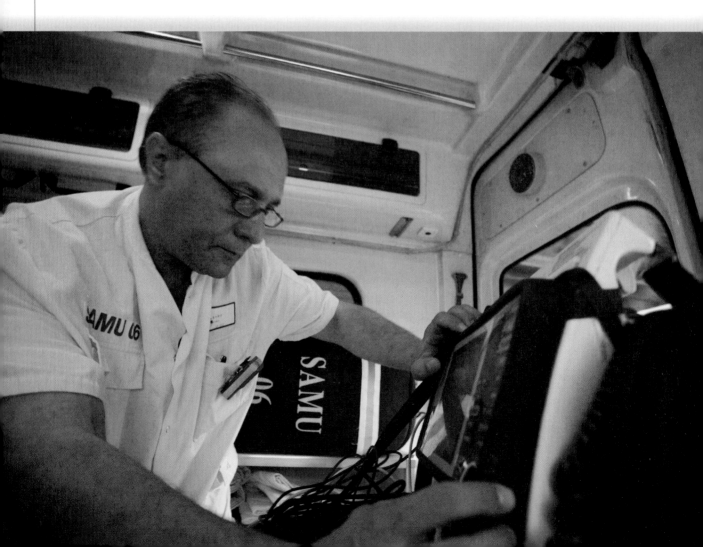

Learning Objectives

LO 17.1 Relate the normal electrical activity of the heart to waveform generation.

LO 17.2 Discuss the benefits and use of a 12-lead ECG.

LO 17.3 Differentiate between the frontal and horizontal planes of the heart.

LO 17.4 Recall the ECG electrodes that view the frontal plane and where they are placed.

LO 17.5 Identify the view each limb lead has of the heart and the deflection each ECG waveform takes in that lead.

LO 17.6 Recall the ECG leads that view the horizontal plane.

LO 17.7 Identify the view each precordial lead has of the heart and the deflection each ECG waveform takes in that lead.

LO 17.8 Describe the proper positioning for each precordial lead.

LO 17.9 Identify the ECG leads that make up the inferior, lateral, septal, and anterior ECGs leads.

LO 17.10 Define the term *contiguous leads*.

LO 17.11 Identify the electrodes locations for 15- and 18-lead ECGs.

LO 17.12 Describe how to analyze the printout of a 12-lead ECG.

LO 17.13 Define the terms *instantaneous vectors, electrical axis,* and *mean QRS axis.*

LO 17.14 Identify the plane and ECG leads used to determine the electrical axis.

LO 17.15 Describe the hexaxial reference system.

LO 17.16 Recall how to use the four-quadrant and degree methods.

LO 17.17 Define the terms *right axis deviation, left axis deviation,* and *extreme axis deviation* and describe when each is seen.

LO 17.18 Identify factors that influence electrical axis.

Case History

Paramedics are called to the home of an 83-year-old man complaining of shortness of breath. After obtaining a set of vital signs that reveal the patient to be hypertensive, one of the paramedics auscultates the lungs and discovers rales throughout both lung fields. They place the patient on supplemental oxygen, administer furosemide, and take a 12-lead ECG. The 12-lead ECG indicates that the patient has an enlarged heart but does not show evidence of a heart attack.

LO 17.1

Heart's Normal Electrical Activity

Let's briefly review how the heartbeat originates and is conducted. Each heartbeat arises as an electrical impulse from the SA node. The impulse then spreads across the atria, depolarizing the tissue and causing them both to contract. The initial wave of depolarization spreads anteriorly through the right atrium and toward the AV node. It then travels posteriorly and toward the left atrium. This is seen on the ECG as a P wave. The impulse then activates the AV node, which is normally the only electrical connection between the atria and the ventricles. There, the impulse is delayed slightly, allowing the atria to finish contracting and pushing any remaining blood from their chambers into the ventricles (referred to as the *atrial kick*). The impulse then spreads through both ventricles via the bundle of His, right and left bundle branches, and the Purkinje fibers (seen as the QRS complex), causing a synchronized contraction of the primary pumping chambers of the heart and, thus, the pulse.

We can divide ventricular depolarization into three main phases. In the first phase, ventricular activation begins in the septum as it is depolarized from left to right. Early depolarization of the right ventricle also occurs. In the second phase, the right and left ventricular apex are depolarized, and the depolarization of the right ventricle is completed. In the third phase, the remainder of the left ventricle is depolarized toward the lateral wall. Because the right ventricle has already been depolarized at this point, the left ventricle will depolarize unopposed by the right, so large voltages will be displayed on the ECG at this time. As we describe the view of each lead as follows, we will review how the electrical events occurring in the heart will be displayed.

KEY CONCEPT
The location where the electrodes are placed determines the view of the heart or lead. Electrodes can be placed on the arms, legs, and chest (or upper torso).

LO 17.2

The 12-Lead ECG

The 12-lead ECG is a device that can be used to identify various cardiac conditions as well as to differentiate between dysrhythmias where the origin is uncertain (i.e., supraventricular vs. ventricular).

Views

KEY CONCEPT
The ECG shows a positive deflection as the impulse travels toward the positive electrode but a negative deflection as it travels away from it.

As mentioned before, a 12-lead ECG is just that; instead of looking at just one view of the heart, you can see 12 different views. Each lead provides a view that the other leads cannot. This gives you a more complete picture of the heart's electrical activity as well as specific diagnostic information.

These views are obtained by placing electrodes on the patient's extremities and chest (or upper torso). The location or sites where the electrodes are placed vary depending on which view of the heart's activity is being assessed. Although we say there are 12 leads, there are actually only 10 lead wires.

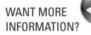
WANT MORE INFORMATION?
Visit the Fast & Easy ECGs Website at www.mhhe.com/ shadeECG2e.

Depending on which lead is used and where the positive electrode is placed, the waveforms generated by the electrical activity of the heart can be seen as upright deflections or downward deflections, or they can be biphasic.

Planes of the Heart

LO 17.3

With the 12-lead ECG, electrodes are placed at specific spots on the patient's extremities and/or torso and chest wall to view the heart's electrical activity from two distinct planes, the frontal and horizontal. These planes provide a cross-sectional view of the heart.

Frontal Plane

LO 17.4

The frontal plane is a vertical cut through the middle of the heart providing viewing of the heart from top to bottom. Electrical activity is recorded from an anterior to posterior axis. Leads arranged on this plane view the superior (above), lateral (side) and inferior (below) aspects of the heart (see Figure 2.9).

To obtain the heart's electrical activity along the frontal plane, four electrodes are positioned as follows (Figure 17-1):

- The right arm electrode, labeled RA, is positioned on the right arm
- The left arm electrode, labeled LA, is positioned on the left arm
- The left leg electrode, labeled LL, is positioned on the left leg
- The right leg electrode, labeled RL, is positioned on the left leg

These electrodes can be placed far down on the limbs or close to the hips and shoulders, but they must be even (right vs. left). Alternatively, these electrodes can be placed on the chest or upper torso. The leads that view the heart along this plane include I, II, III and aV_R, aV_L, and aV_F. They are referred to as *limb leads*.

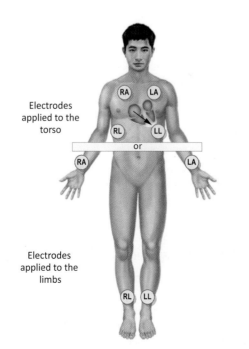

Electrodes applied to the torso

Electrodes applied to the limbs

Figure 17-1
Position of limb-lead electrodes.

REMINDER

There are four limb lead wires for 12 lead ECGs but there may only be three lead wires for ECG machines which monitor just a single lead.

LO 17.5

Leads I, II, and III

Leads I, II and III are referred to as the *standard* limb leads (based on the use of the first ECG). All three are bipolar leads.

With lead I, the LA lead is the positive electrode, the RA lead is the negative electrode, and the LL and RL leads are the ground and there to complete the circuit. Lead I views the high lateral surface of the left atria and left ventricle and detects the dominant electrical activity of the heart as it moves from right to left. The waveforms in lead I are mostly upright because the wave of depolarization is moving toward the positive electrode (Figure 17-2). This includes the P wave, the R wave, and the T wave. The Q wave (if seen) will take an opposite direction as it represents the brief

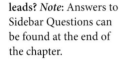

QUESTION

1. **What are bipolar leads?** *Note:* Answers to Sidebar Questions can be found at the end of the chapter.

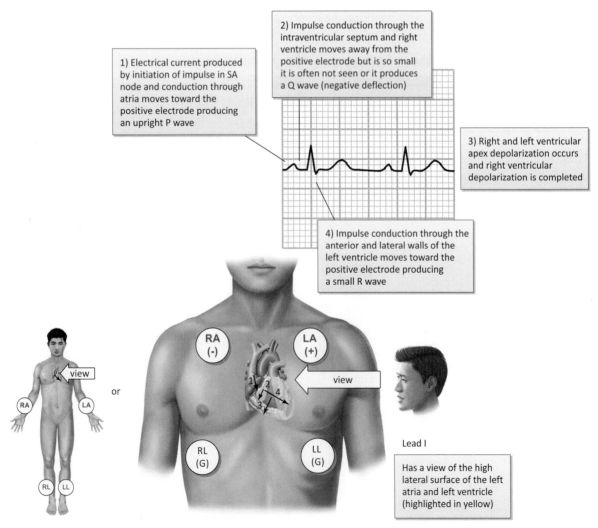

1) Electrical current produced by initiation of impulse in SA node and conduction through atria moves toward the positive electrode producing an upright P wave

2) Impulse conduction through the intraventricular septum and right ventricle moves away from the positive electrode but is so small it is often not seen or it produces a Q wave (negative deflection)

3) Right and left ventricular apex depolarization occurs and right ventricular depolarization is completed

4) Impulse conduction through the anterior and lateral walls of the left ventricle moves toward the positive electrode producing a small R wave

RA (-)   LA (+)

view   or   view

RL (G)   LL (G)

Lead I

Has a view of the high lateral surface of the left atria and left ventricle (highlighted in yellow)

Figure 17-2
Electrode placement, view of the heart, and waveform direction in lead I.

depolarization of the interventricular septum, which is moving away from the positive lead.

With lead II, the LL lead is the positive electrode, the RA lead is the negative electrode, and the LA and RL leads are ground and there to complete the circuit. Lead II views the inferior surface of the right and left ventricles. It detects the dominant electrical activity of the heart as it moves in a right superior to a left inferior direction. The waveforms in lead II are mostly upright because the wave of depolarization is moving toward the positive electrode (Figure 17-3). This includes the P wave, R wave, and T wave. The Q wave (if seen) will take an opposite direction, as it represents the brief depolarization of the interventricular septum, which is moving away from the positive lead.

1) Electrical current produced by initiation of impulse in SA node and conduction through atria moves toward the positive electrode producing an upright P wave

2) Impulse conduction through the intraventricular septum and right ventricle moves away from the positive electrode but is so small it is often not seen or it produces a Q wave (negative deflection)

3) Right and left ventricular apex depolarization occurs and right ventricular depolarization is completed

4) Impulse conduction through the anterior and lateral walls of the left ventricle moves toward the positive electrode producing a tall R wave

Lead II

Views the inferior wall of the right and left ventricles (highlighted in yellow)

Figure 17-3
Electrode placement, view of the heart, and waveform direction in lead II.

With lead III, the LL lead is the positive electrode, the LA lead is the nega-tive electrode, and the RA and RL leads are ground. Lead III views the infe-rior wall of the right and left ventricles and detects the dominant electrical activity of the heart as it moves in a right superior to a left inferior direction. The P and T waves should be upright while the QRS complex may be mostly positive, although the R wave is not as tall as in lead II. Alternatively, the QRS complex may be biphasic as depolarization of the ventricles intersects the negative to positive layout of the ECG electrodes (Figure 17-4). The Q wave is typically not seen in this lead.

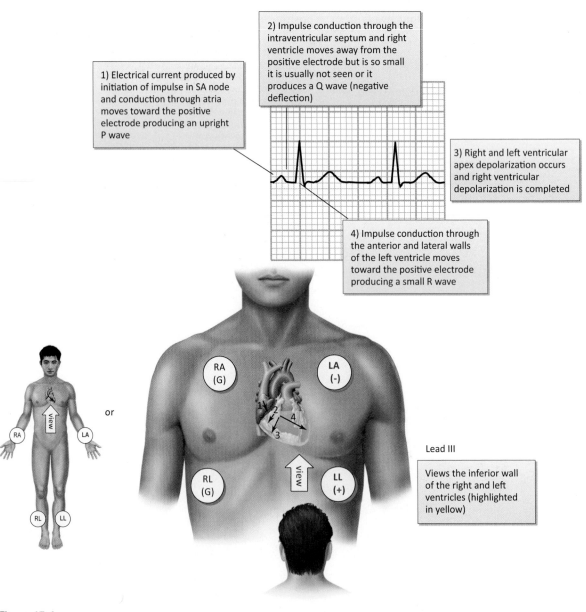

Figure 17-4
Electrode placement, view of the heart, and waveform direction in lead III.

Einthoven's Triangle

Leads I, II, and III form what is known as Einthoven's triangle (Figure 17-5), which is an electrically equilateral triangle based on these three limb leads' positions relative to one another. These leads intersect at angles of 60 degrees. The axis of lead I extends from shoulder to shoulder with the right-arm electrode being the negative electrode and the positive electrode being the left-arm electrode. The axis of lead II extends from the negative right-arm electrode to the positive left-leg electrode. The axis of lead III extends from the negative left-arm electrode to the positive left-leg electrode. This information will be helpful later in the chapter as we discuss determining electrical axis.

> **QUESTION**
> 2. **Which leads are referred to as the standard limb leads?**

Leads aV$_R$, aV$_L$, and aV$_F$

The other three leads that view the frontal plane are the augmented limb leads, aV$_R$, aV$_L$, and aV$_F$ ("a" means augmented, "V" means voltage, "R" means right, "L" means left, and "F" means foot). The ECG waveforms produced by these leads are small, and for this reason the ECG machine enhances or augments them by 50%. This results in their amplitude being comparable to other leads. The augmented leads are unipolar. Each uses only one positive electrode on the body surface, and the heart is the negative pole. All other lead wires are made negative, with their average essentially serving as the negative electrode (common ground).

Figure 17-5
Einthoven's triangle.

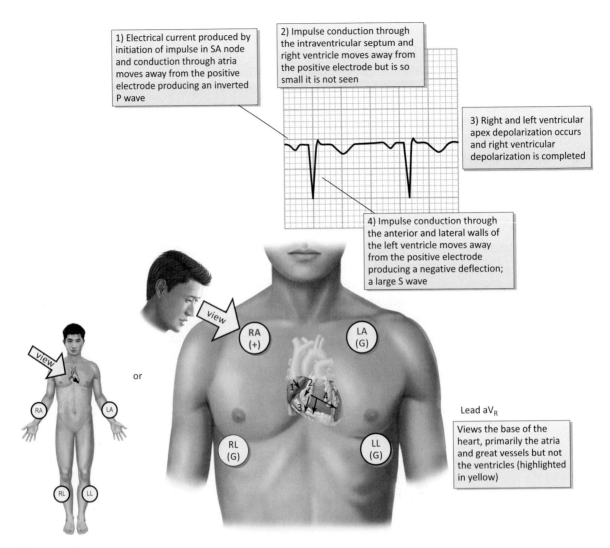

Figure 17-6
Electrode placement, view of the heart, and waveform direction in lead aV_R.

In lead aV_R the RA lead is the positive electrode. This lead views the base of the heart, primarily the atria and great vessels, but doesn't view any part of the ventricles. Because the heart's electrical activity moves away from the positive electrode, the waveforms take a negative deflection. (Figure 17-6). This includes the P wave, R wave, and T wave.

In lead aV_L the LA lead serves as the positive electrode. This lead views the lateral wall of the left ventricle. Because the heart's electrical activity moves toward the positive electrode (or perpendicular to it), the waveforms take a positive (or biphasic) deflection (Figure 17-7). This includes the P wave, R wave, and T wave. The Q wave (if seen) will take an opposite direction because it represents the brief depolarization of the interventricular septum, which is moving away from the positive lead.

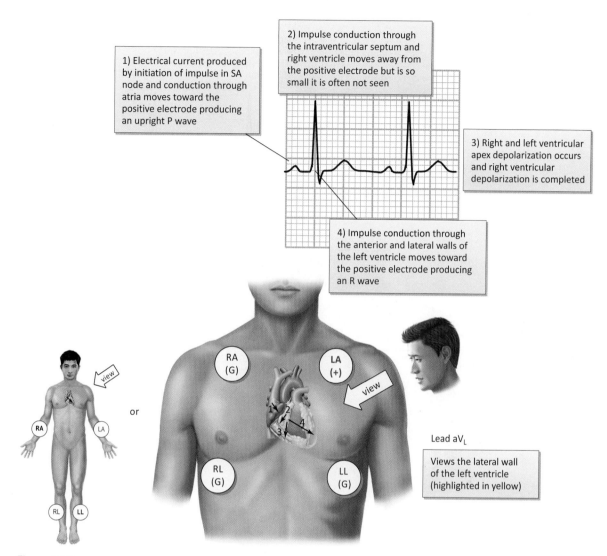

1) Electrical current produced by initiation of impulse in SA node and conduction through atria moves toward the positive electrode producing an upright P wave

2) Impulse conduction through the intraventricular septum and right ventricle moves away from the positive electrode but is so small it is often not seen

3) Right and left ventricular apex depolarization occurs and right ventricular depolarization is completed

4) Impulse conduction through the anterior and lateral walls of the left ventricle moves toward the positive electrode producing an R wave

or

Lead aV_L

Views the lateral wall of the left ventricle (highlighted in yellow)

Figure 17-7
Electrode placement, view of the heart, and waveform direction in lead aV_L.

Lastly, in lead aV_F the LL lead is the positive electrode. This lead views the inferior wall of the left ventricle. The waveforms take a positive deflection because the heart's electrical activity moves toward the positive electrode (Figure 17-8). This includes the P wave, R wave, and T wave. The Q wave is typically not seen in this lead.

QUESTION
3. What does the term *augmented* mean?

Horizontal Plane

LO 17.6

The horizontal plane is a transverse (upper and lower, also referred to as a *superior and inferior*) cut through the middle of the heart. The leads arranged along this plane give us an anterior, lateral, and posterior (back) view of the heart and are called *precordial leads, V leads,* or *chest leads.*

The precordial leads are unipolar, requiring only a single positive electrode. The opposing pole of those leads is the center of the heart as calculated by

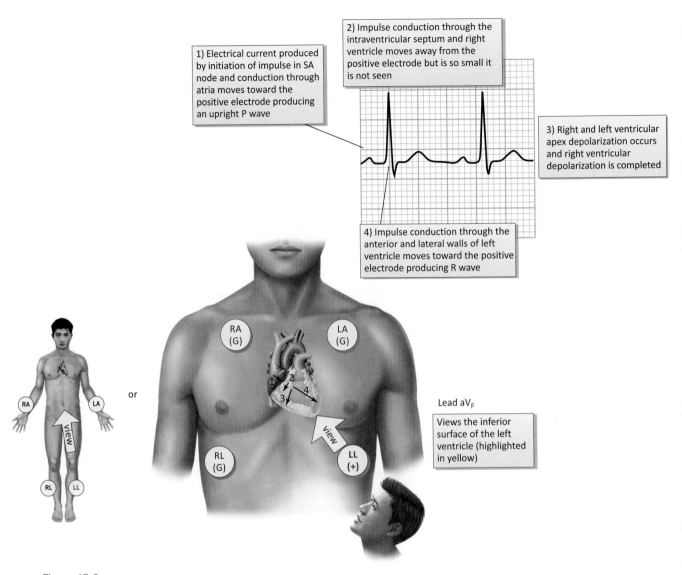

1) Electrical current produced by initiation of impulse in SA node and conduction through atria moves toward the positive electrode producing an upright P wave

2) Impulse conduction through the intraventricular septum and right ventricle moves away from the positive electrode but is so small it is not seen

3) Right and left ventricular apex depolarization occurs and right ventricular depolarization is completed

4) Impulse conduction through the anterior and lateral walls of left ventricle moves toward the positive electrode producing R wave

Lead aV_F

Views the inferior surface of the left ventricle (highlighted in yellow)

Figure 17-8
Electrode placement, view of the heart, and waveform direction in lead aV$_F$.

the ECG. The six precordial leads are positioned in order across the chest and include $V_1, V_2, V_3, V_4, V_5,$ and V_6. Because of their close proximity to the heart, they do not require augmentation.

With the SA node being above the positive electrode and with the electrical flow moving toward it, the direction of the P waves in the precordial leads is upright. The T waves should also be upright. As discussed in Chapter 1, the septum depolarizes from left to right and the ventricles from right to left. For this reason, the QRS complexes start out in a downward direction, then go through a transitional zone where they become half upright and half downward, and then become upright (Figure 17-9). If the transition occurs in V_1 or V_2, it is considered early transition, and if it occurs in V_5 or V_6, it is considered

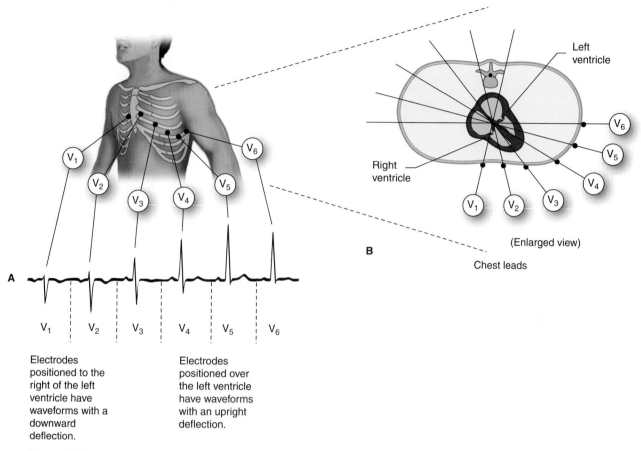

Figure 17-9
Direction of waveforms in the precordial leads.

late transition. Both early and late transition can indicate the presence of various cardiac conditions.

As you will see from our discussion throughout the text, the leads we discuss cannot view all areas of the heart. Later, as we talk about how to locate ischemia and infarction in the right ventricle and posterior surface of the heart, we will describe ways to accommodate for this and other types of ECG leads that can be selected.

Lead V₁

The first precordial lead is V_1. Its electrode is positioned in the fourth intercostal space (between the fourth and fifth ribs) just to the right of the sternum. It faces and is close to the right ventricle. It also has a view of the ventricular septum. Since septal and right ventricular depolarization send the current toward the positive electrode, there is a small initial upright deflection (the R wave). Then, as the current travels toward the left ventricle and away from the positive electrode, it produces a negative deflection, a deep S wave (Figure 17-10).

Lead V_1 is particularly effective at showing the P wave, QRS complex, and the ST segment. It is helpful in identifying ventricular dysrhythmias, ST segment changes, and bundle branch blocks.

LO 17.7

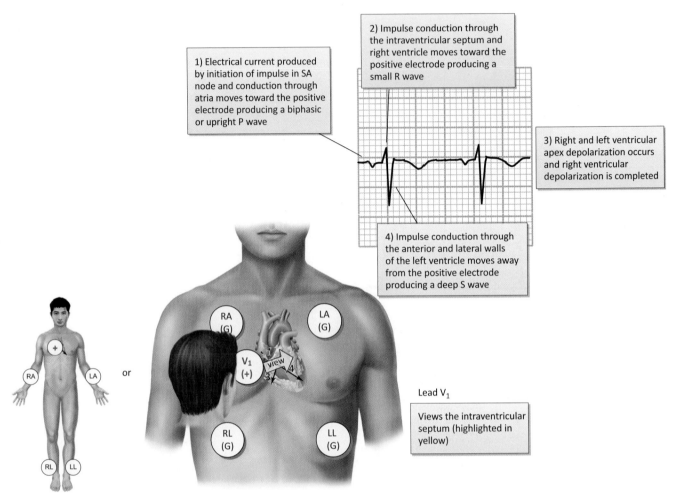

1) Electrical current produced by initiation of impulse in SA node and conduction through atria moves toward the positive electrode producing a biphasic or upright P wave

2) Impulse conduction through the intraventricular septum and right ventricle moves toward the positive electrode producing a small R wave

3) Right and left ventricular apex depolarization occurs and right ventricular depolarization is completed

4) Impulse conduction through the anterior and lateral walls of the left ventricle moves away from the positive electrode producing a deep S wave

Lead V₁

Views the intraventricular septum (highlighted in yellow)

Figure 17-10
Position of positive electrode and direction of electrical current flow, area of heart it views, and direction of waveforms in lead V₁.

LO 17.8

Placing the V₁ Electrode   To find the position for the V₁ electrode, gently place your fingers centrally at the base of the patient's throat and move them down until you can feel the top of the sternum (or rib cage). From there, continue moving your fingers down until you feel a bony lump. This is the angle of Louis (also called the *sternal angle*). The angle of Louis is most easily found when the patient is in a supine position, as the surrounding tissue is tighter against the rib cage. From the angle of Louis, move your fingers to the right, and you will feel a gap between the ribs. This gap is the 2nd intercostal space. From this position, move your fingers down across the next rib, and then the next. This space is the 4th intercostal space (Figure 17-11). Where the fourth intercostal space meets the sternum is the location you place the V₁ electrode.

A Locate the base of the patient's throat.

B Palpate for the angle of Louis.

C Move your fingers to the patient's right.

D Locate the second intercostal space (immediately below the second rib).

E Move your fingers down two intercostal spaces to the fourth intercostal space.

F Lead V_1 positioned in the fourth intercostal space just to the right of the sternum.

Figure 17-11
Steps used to place the V_1 electrode.

Lead V_2

Lead V_2 is positioned in the 4th intercostal space (between the fourth and fifth ribs) just to the left of the sternum. Horizontally, it is at the same level as lead V_1 but on the opposite side the sternum. Just like lead V_1, V_2 faces and is close to the right ventricle. Although it has a view of the right ventricle and anterior wall of the heart, it is more recognized for its view of the ventricular septum (Figure 17-12), particularly when locating myocardial injury. Because it views both the septum and the heart's anterior wall, it is said to have an

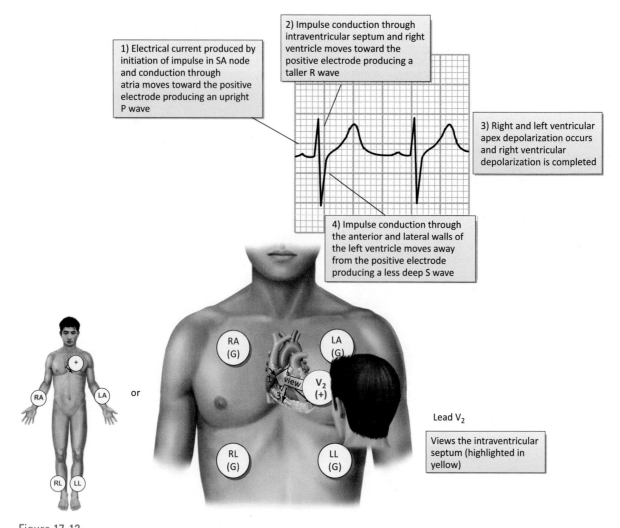

Figure 17-12
Position of positive electrode and direction of electrical current flow, area of heart it views, and direction of waveforms in lead V₂.

anteroseptal view. Similar to what we see with lead V_1, in lead V_2 the depolarization initially moves toward the positive electrode, producing a R wave. Then, as depolarization moves away from the positive electrode, it produces a less deep S wave.

Placing the V₂ Electrode   There are two quick ways to position the lead V_2 electrode. The easiest is to draw an imaginary line horizontally from the V_1 electrode to the 4th intercostal space on the opposite side of the sternum. Alternatively, you can go back to the angle of Louis, slide your finger into the 2nd intercostal space on the left side, and then move down over the next two ribs. You are now at the 4th intercostal space. Where this space meets the sternum is where you place the V_2 electrode (Figure 17-13). Note that

A From the V_1 position, find the corresponding intercostal space on the left side of the sternum.

B Place the V_1 electrode in the fourth intercostal to the left of the sternum.

Figure 17-13
Steps for placing the V_2 electrode.

leads V_1 and V_2 are essentially in the same location on opposite sides of the chest.

Lead V_3

Lead V_3 is located midway between leads V_2 and V_4. For this reason you need to locate the position for lead V_4 before you apply the electrode for lead V_3. Lead V_3 views the anterior wall of the left ventricle. Depolarization of the septum and right ventricle produces such a small electrical force that it is not seen whereas the current depolarization of the left ventricle moves perpendicular to the positive electrode, resulting in a biphasic waveform that has an R wave and S wave that are relatively the same amplitude in lead V_3 (Figure 17-14).

Lead V_4

Lead V_4 is placed at the 5th intercostal space (between the fifth and sixth ribs) in the midclavicular line (the imaginary line that extends down from the midpoint of the clavicle). V_4 views the anterior wall of the left ventricle and is close to the heart's apex. Depolarization of the septum and right ventricle produces such a small electrical force that it is not seen while the current depolarization of the left ventricle moves perpendicular to the positive electrode, resulting in a biphasic waveform that has an R wave larger than the S wave in lead V_4 (Figure 17-15).

Placing the V_3 and V_4 Electrodes   To locate this spot, position your fingers at the lead V_2 position. Then, slide your fingers down and below the next rib; you are now in the 5th intercostal space. Next, look at the chest and identify the left clavicle. Find the middle of the clavicle and draw an imaginary line (called the *midclavicular line*) down to the 5th intercostal space. Position

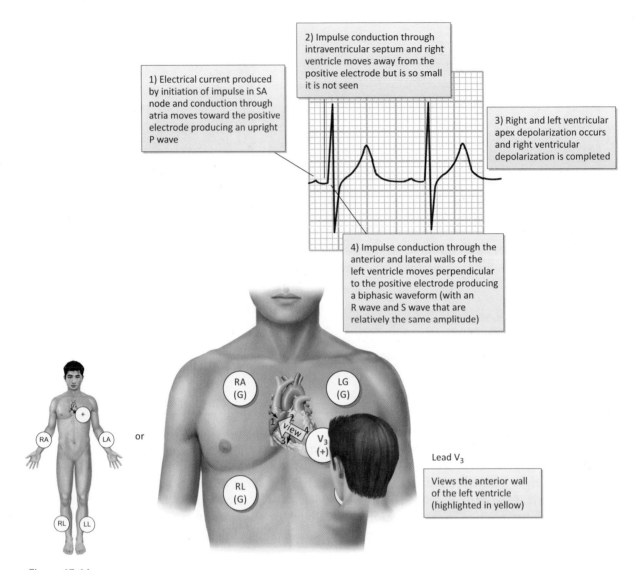

1) Electrical current produced by initiation of impulse in SA node and conduction through atria moves toward the positive electrode producing an upright P wave

2) Impulse conduction through intraventricular septum and right ventricle moves away from the positive electrode but is so small it is not seen

3) Right and left ventricular apex depolarization occurs and right ventricular depolarization is completed

4) Impulse conduction through the anterior and lateral walls of the left ventricle moves perpendicular to the positive electrode producing a biphasic waveform (with an R wave and S wave that are relatively the same amplitude)

Lead V$_3$

Views the anterior wall of the left ventricle (highlighted in yellow)

Figure 17-14
Position of positive electrode and direction of electrical current flow, area of heart it views, and direction of waveforms in lead V$_3$.

the lead V$_4$ electrode there. The lead V$_3$ electrode is then placed in the intercostal space midway between leads V$_2$ and V$_4$ (Figure 17-16).

Lead V$_5$

Lead V$_5$ is placed in the 5th intercostal space at the anterior axillary line. Horizontally, it is even with V$_4$ but in the anterior axillary line. Lead V$_5$ views the lateral wall of the left ventricle. As the impulse conducts through the septum and right ventricle, it moves away from the positive lead, producing a small Q wave in lead V$_5$. Then, as the impulse conducts through the left ventricle, it moves toward the positive electrode, producing a tall R wave (Figure 17-17). Because of its location closest to the left ventricle, it will have the tallest R waves of the precordial leads. Then depolarization of the posterobasal right and left ventricular free walls and basal right septal mass produces a small S wave.

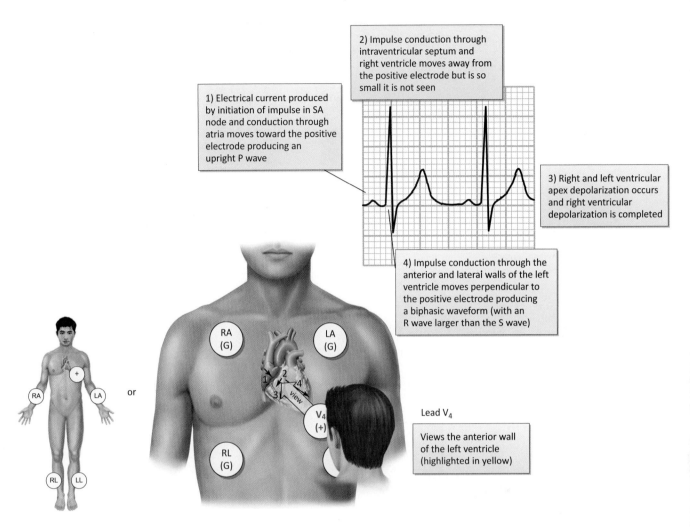

1) Electrical current produced by initiation of impulse in SA node and conduction through atria moves toward the positive electrode producing an upright P wave

2) Impulse conduction through intraventricular septum and right ventricle moves away from the positive electrode but is so small it is not seen

3) Right and left ventricular apex depolarization occurs and right ventricular depolarization is completed

4) Impulse conduction through the anterior and lateral walls of the left ventricle moves perpendicular to the positive electrode producing a biphasic waveform (with an R wave larger than the S wave)

Lead V₄

Views the anterior wall of the left ventricle (highlighted in yellow)

Figure 17-15
Position of positive electrode and direction of electrical current flow, area of heart it views, and direction of waveforms in lead V_4.

Placing the V_5 Electrode To locate the position for the V_5 electrode, while remaining horizontally level with V_4, follow the 5th intercostal space to the left until your fingers are just below the beginning of the axilla (armpit area). This is the anterior axillary line (the imaginary line that runs down from the point midway between the middle of the clavicle and the lateral end of the clavicle; the lateral end of the collarbone is the end closer to the arm). Place the electrode there (Figure 17-18).

Lead V_6

Lead V_6 is located horizontally level with V_4 and V_5 at the midaxillary line (middle of the armpit). Just like V_5, this lead views the lateral wall of the left ventricle. As the impulse conducts through the septum and right ventricle,

A From the V₂ position, locate the fifth intercostal space and follow it to the midclavicular line.

B Position the V₄ electrode in the fifth intercostal the midclavicular line.

C Lead V₃ positioned halfway between V₂ and V₄.

Figure 17-16
Steps for placing leads V₃ and V₄.

it moves away from the positive lead, producing a small Q wave in lead V_5. Then, as the impulse conducts through the left ventricle, it moves toward the positive electrode, producing a tall R wave (Figure 17-19). Because it is not as close to the left ventricle, the R wave in lead V_6 is smaller than that found in Lead V_5. Lastly, depolarization of the posterobasal right and left ventricular free walls and basal right septal mass produce a small S wave.

Placing the V₆ Electrode   Follow the line of the 5th intercostal space from the lead V_5 electrode until you are horizontally level with leads 4 and 5 (Figure 17-20) at the midaxillary line (center point of the axilla). This is where you place the lead V_6 electrode.

An important thing to remember is that if you have placed leads V_4 through V_6 correctly, they should line up horizontally.

Each view provides different information. When assessing the 12 lead ECG we look for characteristic normalcy and changes in all leads. Figure 17-21

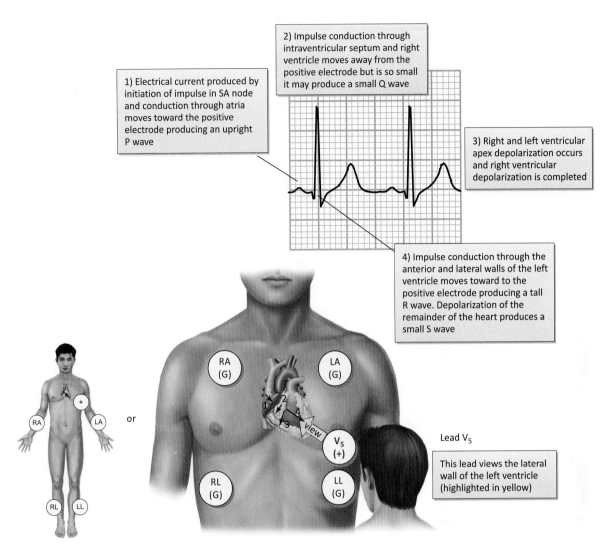

2) Impulse conduction through intraventricular septum and right ventricle moves away from the positive electrode but is so small it may produce a small Q wave

1) Electrical current produced by initiation of impulse in SA node and conduction through atria moves toward the positive electrode producing an upright P wave

3) Right and left ventricular apex depolarization occurs and right ventricular depolarization is completed

4) Impulse conduction through the anterior and lateral walls of the left ventricle moves toward to the positive electrode producing a tall R wave. Depolarization of the remainder of the heart produces a small S wave

RA (G)

LA (G)

RA   or   LA

RL   LL

V₅ (+)

RL (G)

LL (G)

Lead V₅

This lead views the lateral wall of the left ventricle (highlighted in yellow)

Figure 17-17
Position of positive electrode and direction of electrical current flow, area of heart it views, and direction of waveforms in lead V₅.

Figure 17-18
Steps for placing the V₅ electrode.

To locate the position for the V₅ electrode, follow the 5th intercostal space across to where it intersects with the anterior axillary line.

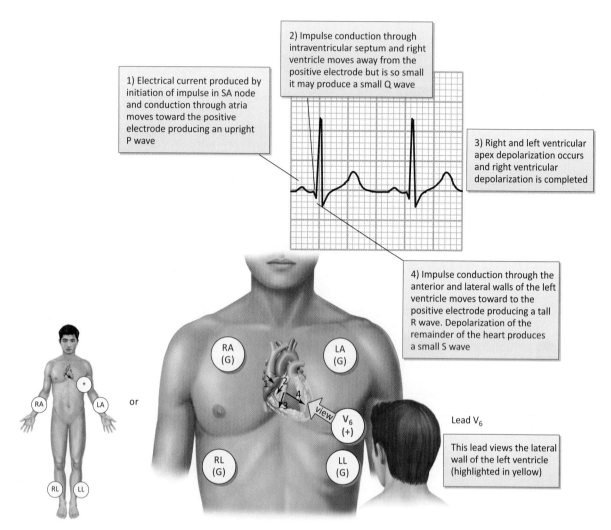

1) Electrical current produced by initiation of impulse in SA node and conduction through atria moves toward the positive electrode producing an upright P wave

2) Impulse conduction through intraventricular septum and right ventricle moves away from the positive electrode but is so small it may produce a small Q wave

3) Right and left ventricular apex depolarization occurs and right ventricular depolarization is completed

4) Impulse conduction through the anterior and lateral walls of the left ventricle moves toward to the positive electrode producing a tall R wave. Depolarization of the remainder of the heart produces a small S wave

RA (G)   LA (G)

RL (G)   LL (G)

V_6 (+)

or

RA   LA   +

RL   LL

Lead V_6

This lead views the lateral wall of the left ventricle (highlighted in yellow)

Figure 17-19
Position of positive electrode and direction of electrical current flow, area of heart it views, and direction of waveforms in lead V_6.

Figure 17-20
Steps for placing lead V_6.

To locate the position for the V_6 electrode, follow the 5th intercostal space across to where it intersects with the mid axillary line.

Figure 17-21
Normal appearance of ECG complexes in
12 lead ECG

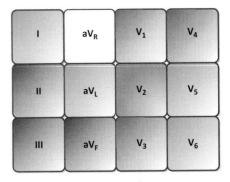

Figure 17-22
Matrix of the ECG leads
showing which leads view
what area of the heart.

shows the normal appearance of the 12 lead ECG. Memorizing what view(s) of the heart each lead provides will help you decide which lead to use to gain the information you need to make a proper assessment or diagnosis.

Putting the Views Together

Now, let's look at the collective view of the heart. This is important as it will help us to identify the location of myocardial ischemia and/or MI and other cardiac conditions (Figure 17-22).

Specific Leads and Associated Views

LO 17.9

The 12 ECG leads each record the electrical activity of the heart from a different perspective, which also correlates to different anatomical areas of the heart.

In leads II, III, and aV_F, the positive electrode is positioned below the heart, so these leads have a view of the inferior (or diaphragmatic) surface. For this reason they are called the *inferior leads*.

In leads I, aV_L, V_5, and V_6, the positive electrode is positioned to the left of the heart, so they have a view of the lateral wall. For this reason they are called the *lateral leads*. Similarly, the positive electrode for leads I and aV_L is located on the left arm or upper torso, these leads are sometimes referred to as the *high lateral leads*. Similarly, due to the positive electrodes for leads V_5 and V_6 being on the patient's chest, they are sometimes referred to as the *low lateral leads*.

In leads V_1 and V_2, the positive electrode is positioned in front but slightly to the left of the heart, so they have a view of the septal wall of the ventricles and are called the *septal leads*.

In leads V_3 and V_4, the positive electrode is positioned in front of the heart, so they have a view of the anterior wall and are called the *anterior leads*. They also have an apical view of the heart. Lead V_2 can also be considered an anterior lead as it, too, has a view of the anterior wall. The combination of leads V_1, V_2, V_3, and V_4 are referred to as *anteroseptal leads*.

LO 17.10

Contiguous Leads

Two leads that look at neighboring anatomical areas of the heart are said to be contiguous. As an example, V_4 and V_5 are contiguous (as they are next to each other on the patient's chest), even though V_4 is an anterior lead and V_5 is a lateral lead. The following lists the contiguous leads:

Contiguous Inferior Leads

- Lead II is contiguous with lead III
- Lead III is contiguous with leads II and aV_F
- Lead aV_F is contiguous with lead III

Contiguous Septal, Anterior and Lateral Leads

- V_1 is contiguous with V_2
- V_2 is contiguous with V_1 and V_3
- V_3 is contiguous with V_2 and V_4
- V_4 is contiguous with V_3 and V_5
- V_5 is contiguous with V_4 and V_6
- V_6 is contiguous with V_5 and lead I
- Lead I is contiguous with V_6 and aV_L
- aV_L is contiguous with lead I

The relevance of this is it helps in determining whether an abnormality on the ECG is likely to represent true disease such as acute coronary ischemia or injury or just a false finding.

LO 17.11

15- and 18-Lead ECGs

While the 12-lead ECG is useful in the detection of MI of the inferior, anterior, and lateral walls of the left ventricle, it is not as effective in revealing an MI involving the right ventricle and/or the posterior wall of the left ventricle.

Nonstandard ECG leads can be used to increase the detection of right ventricle and posterior wall infarction. These nonstandard leads are commonly identified as *right precordial leads* (V_4R, V_5R, V_6R) and *posterior leads* (V_7, V_8, V_9). By combining these leads, a 15- or 18-lead ECG can be created. Although specialized equipment is available to obtain 15- and 18-lead ECGs, it is not absolutely required. The data can be obtained from these additional leads

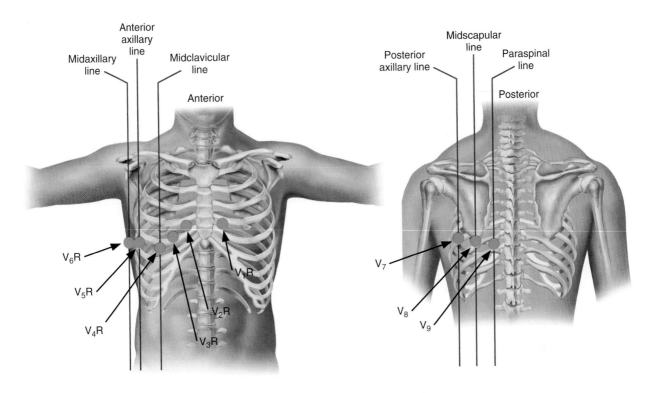

Figure 17-23
15- and 18-lead locations

with the standard 12-lead ECG machine by moving electrodes to specified locations and running the "12-lead" a second time.

To attain the additional leads for a 15-lead ECG, move the lead wires from the precordial electrode positions to the following locations (Figure 17-23):

Right Side Leads

- V_1R is placed in the 4th intercostal space to the left of the patient's sternum (use V_1 lead)
- V_2R is placed in the 4th intercostal space to the right of the patient's sternum (use V_2 lead)
- V_3R is placed in the 5th intercostal space between V_2R and V_4R
- V_4R is placed in the 5th intercostal space even with right midclavicular line (use the V_4 lead)
- V_5R is placed horizontally (straight across) with V_4R even with the right anterior axillary line (use V_5 lead)
- V_6R is placed horizontally with V_5R even with the right midaxillary line (use V_6 lead)

Posterior Leads

- V_7 is placed horizontally with V_6 in the left posterior axillary line (use V_4 lead)
- V_8 is placed horizontally with V_7 in the left midscapular line (use V_5 lead)
- V_9 is placed horizontally with V_8 in the left paraspinal line (use V_6 lead)

Two alternatives to moving all the leads to create the V_R leads is to move just the V_4 lead to the V_4R position or to move just the V_4, V_5, and V_6 to the V_4R, V_5R, and the V_6R positions. Be sure to follow your local protocol.

Then press the 12-lead ECG button to obtain the recording. Label the second 12-lead recording with the label of the new leads (V_1R, V_2R, etc.), as the ECG machine does not know where the electrodes are located. Also, be sure to have the patient lie as still as possible to avoid artifact in the posterior leads.

Indications for using additional leads include patients who have clinical findings highly suggestive of acute coronary ischemia but whose ECG findings are either normal or nondiagnostic. Further, additional leads are recommended for patients in whom changes are seen in the inferior leads or where there are reciprocal changes in leads V_1 and V_2 (ST segment depression indicating a posterior infarction).

Because ST-segment elevation in V_4R to V_6R may resolve within 12 to 18 hours, the 15- or 18-lead ECG should be done soon after presentation of symptoms. In addition, the presence of anterior wall infarction obscures the changes in the right precordial leads.

Increasing the detection of right ventricular and posterior wall infarction will lead to more aggressive treatment with reperfusion therapies, as well as avoiding inappropriate treatments that may cause undue harm to the patient. These ECGs can be obtained with a minimal increase in time and cost of care and can result in increasingly positive outcomes.

LO 17.12

Analyzing the 12-Lead ECG

To analyze a 12-lead ECG printout, we begin by looking at the left column from top to bottom, the middle from top to bottom, and the right from top to bottom. That doesn't mean you can't do it differently; it is just one approach. Now, much the same as what we do when analyzing an ECG tracing for characteristics that help to identify the presence of dysrhythmias, we do the same by looking for certain characteristics that tell us the presence of given cardiac conditions.

In Table 17-1 that follows, we list the conditions we cover in this text. Although there are more that can be identified through the use of a 12-lead ECG, the ones listed are the more common conditions we see.

Because we have 12 views, and each sees different areas of the heart, we can use them to help us identify certain conditions. So, in addition to remembering characteristics of given conditions, you also need to remember in which lead you can expect to find those characteristics. For example, the better view of the ventricles is seen in leads V_1, V_2 (right ventricle), V_5, and V_6 (left ventricle) as well as in leads I and aV_F. Thus, to identify abnormal conduction

Condition	Description
Hypertrophy	Hypertrophy is a condition in which the muscular wall of the ventricle(s) becomes thicker than normal. It results from the ventricle having to pump against increased resistance within the cardiovascular system. Conditions that cause hypertrophy include systemic hypertension and aortic stenosis.
Chamber Enlargement	An enlarged chamber occurs as the result of volume overload—the chamber dilates to accommodate the increased blood volume. It is therefore bigger and can hold more blood than normal. Unlike hypertrophy, the muscular wall of the dilated chamber typically does not become thicker. Enlargement is most often seen with certain types of valvular disease. For example, left atrial enlargement can result from mitral valve insufficiency.
Bundle Branch Block	Bundle branch block is a disorder that leads to one or both of the bundle branches failing to properly conduct impulses. This produces a delay in the depolarization of the ventricle it supplies. Right bundle branch block occurs with anterior wall MI, coronary artery disease, and pulmonary embolism. It may also be caused, as can any type of heart block, by drug toxicity. Left bundle branch block can be caused by anterior wall MI, hypertensive heart disease, aortic stenosis, or degenerative changes of the conduction system.
Myocardial Ischemia	Myocardial ischemia is a deprivation of oxygen and nutrients to the myocardium. It typically occurs when the heart has a greater need for oxygen than the narrowed coronary arteries can deliver or when there is a loss of blood supply to the myocardium. Causes of myocardial ischemia include atherosclerosis, vasospasm, thrombosis, embolism, decreased ventricular filling time (such as that produced by tachycardia), and decreased filling pressure in the coronary arteries (such as that caused by severe hypotension or aortic valve disease).
Myocardial Injury	If the myocardial oxygen demand fails to lower, the coronary artery blockage worsens, or the ischemia is allowed to progress untreated, myocardial injury will occur. Myocardial injury reflects a degree of cellular damage beyond ischemia. It occurs if the blood flow is not restored (and ischemia reversed) within a few minutes. If blood flow is not restored to the affected area, tissue death will occur.
Myocardial Infarction	MI is the death of injured myocardial cells. It occurs when there is a sudden decrease or total cessation of blood flow through a coronary artery to an area of the myocardium. MI commonly occurs when the intima of a coronary artery ruptures, exposing the atherosclerotic plaque to the blood within the artery. This initiates the abrupt development of a clot (thrombus). The vessel, already narrowed by the plaque, becomes completely blocked by the thrombus. The area of the heart normally supplied by the blocked artery goes through a characteristic sequence of events described as zones of ischemia, injury, and infarction.
Pericarditis	Pericarditis is inflammation of the pericardium. The most common causes of pericarditis are viral and bacterial infections. Other causes include uremia, renal failure, rheumatic fever, posttraumatic pericarditis, connective tissue disease, and cancer. Sometimes pericarditis can accompany an acute MI. When pericarditis occurs in conjunction with MI, it develops several days after the infarction.
Pericardial Effusion	Pericardial effusion is a buildup of an abnormal amount of fluid and/or a change in the character of the fluid in the pericardial space. The pericardial space is the space between the heart and the pericardial sac. Formation of a substantial pericardial effusion dampens the electrical output of the heart, resulting in low voltage QRS complex in all leads.

Continued

Pulmonary Embolism	A pulmonary embolism is an acute blockage of one of the pulmonary arteries by a blood clot or other foreign matter. This leads to obstruction of blood flow to the lung segment supplied by the artery. The larger the artery occluded, the more massive the pulmonary embolus and, therefore, the larger the effect the embolus has on the heart. Due to the increased pressure in the pulmonary artery caused by the embolus, the right atrium and ventricle become distended and unable to function properly, leading to right-sided heart failure.
Electrolyte Imbalances	Changes in potassium and calcium serum levels can profoundly affect the ECG. Those involving potassium are the most immediately life threatening. Levels that are too high (hyperkalemia) or too low (hypokalemia) can quickly result in serious cardiac dysrhythmias. The presence of ECG changes may be a better measure of clinically significant potassium toxicity than is the serum potassium level.
Medication Use and Toxicity	Some medications can have striking effects on ECG waveforms by altering the way the cells depolarize, repolarize, and innervate surrounding tissues. These changes may indicate expected and, therefore benign effects of certain medications, as well as provide evidence of medication toxicity.

Table 17.1
Common Cardiac Conditions

through the ventricles such as with bundle branch block or hypertrophy of one or both ventricles, we need to look at those leads.

Seems complicated, doesn't it? Well, once you start doing it, it really isn't all that bad.

LO 17.13

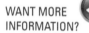

WANT MORE INFORMATION?

For a quick reference source to help you recall normal and abnormal electrical axis while in the field or clinical setting, refer to the ECG Pocket Guide.

Electrical Axis and the ECG

Changes in the size or condition of the heart muscle and/or conduction system will affect how electrical impulses are conducted through the tissue and, subsequently, the appearance of the ECG waveforms. What we discuss next will help you to understand why given waveforms change in direction, duration, or appearance. Further, it will help you identify the presence of certain cardiac conditions when using the 12-lead ECG.

Vectors

The wave of depolarization and repolarization of the cardiac cells produces many small electrical currents or impulses called *instantaneous vectors*. Remember, depolarization is the advancing wave of ionic exchange. If you think about the millions of cells in the ventricles alone, that is a lot of electrical current. These currents vary in intensity and direction and can be visually represented by arrows (Figure 17-24). While these tiny swirls of current are moving simultaneously in many different directions, the ECG only records the sum or average of the current flow or instantaneous vectors at any given moment. The sum of these vectors is called the *mean instantaneous vector*. The instantaneous vectors are represented by each part of the QRS complex. The mean vector or electrical axis is derived by looking at the QRS complex asa whole and deciding whether it is more positive or negative. This is what clinically determines the axis.

QUESTION
4. A 12-lead ECG includes what two general types of leads?

Figure 17-24
Depolarization and repolarization of the heart produces many small electrical currents or impulses. The overall direction and force of the current flow through the heart is called the heart's *electrical axis*.

Mean Instantaneous Vector

Whereas the sum of the small vectors is called the *mean instantaneous vector*, its direction and magnitude as it travels through the heart is called the heart's *electrical axis*. The heart's electrical axis reveals important information about the movement of electrical impulses through the heart. The axis is depicted as a single large arrow. The angle of orientation represents the direction of current flow whereas its length represents its voltage (amperage). Axis is defined in the frontal plane only. The mean instantaneous vector generated during the depolarization of the atria and its direction and amplitude is called the *P axis*. It is rarely determined. The mean instantaneous vector generated during the depolarization of the ventricles and its direction and amplitude is referred to as the *mean QRS axis*. The mean QRS axis is the most clinically important and therefore the axis we measure (Figure 17-24). Normally, the QRS axis points to the left and downward, reflecting the dominance of the left ventricle over the right ventricle.

Waveform Direction

Remember from our earlier discussion that when the electrical current traveling through the heart is moving toward a positive electrode, the ECG machine records it as a positive or upright waveform. When the impulse is traveling away from a positive electrode and toward a negative electrode, the ECG machine records it as a negative or downward deflection (Figure 17-25).

Ventricular Depolarization and Mean QRS Axis

In a healthy heart, waves of depolarization originate in the SA node and travel through the atria, the AV node, and on to the ventricles. The ventricular conduction system quickly conducts the stimulus to the ventricles (Figure 17-26).

KEY CONCEPT
The mean vector is the average of all the instantaneous vectors that the ECG detects. Its direction is called the electrical axis and is depicted as a single large arrow.

QUESTION
5. What direction will the ECG waveform deflection take when depolarization is moving toward a positive electrode?

KEY CONCEPT
The ECG machine records current traveling through the heart and moving toward a positive ECG electrode as a positive or upright waveform.

Impulses traveling away from a positive electrode and/or toward a negative electrode produce downward deflections

Negative electrode

Impulses traveling toward a positive electrode produce an upward deflection

Positive electrode

Figure 17-25
Direction of ECG waveforms when the electrical current is traveling toward a positive ECG electrode or away from it.

Figure 17-26
The ventricular conduction system quickly conducts the impulse to the ventricles.

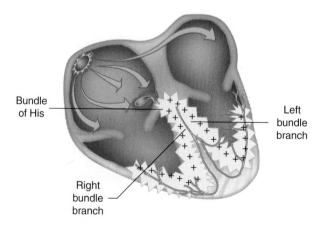

Bundle of His

Left bundle branch

Right bundle branch

The Purkinje fibers carry the impulse from the endocardial lining of the right and left ventricles in the apical region of the heart near the septum through the full thickness of the ventricular wall toward the outside surface (or epicardium). The impulse continues through the ventricles in all areas at once and ends in the lateral and posterior aspect of the left ventricle near its base.

Even though the impulse arrives at the subendocardial lining of both ventricles at about the same time, completion of right ventricle depolarization occurs first. This is because the thinner wall of the right ventricle transmits the impulse in a fraction of the time that it takes the impulse to travel through the thick lateral wall of the left ventricle.

As identified earlier, the QRS complex represents the simultaneous depolarization of both ventricles (Figure 17-27).

The vectors arising in the right ventricle are directed mostly to the right when viewed in the frontal plane; those in the left ventricle are directed mostly to the left (Figure 17-28). The left ventricular vectors are larger and persist longer than those of the smaller right ventricle, primarily because of the greater thickness of the left ventricular wall.

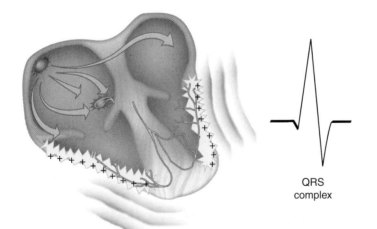

QRS
complex

Figure 17-27
Ventricular depolarization and the QRS complex.

Figure 17-28
The vectors of the left ventricle are larger and persist longer than those of the right ventricle.

Figure 17-29
The mean QRS axis points
downward and toward the
patient's left side.

KEY CONCEPT
The vectors of the left ventricle are larger and persist longer because the muscular wall of the left ventricle is thicker than that of the right ventricle.

Again, we call the sum of all the small vectors of ventricular depolarization the *mean QRS vector*. The mean QRS axis represents both its direction and magnitude. The small depolarization vectors of the thicker left ventricle are larger, resulting in greater magnitude, so the mean QRS axis points more to the left (Figure 17-29). The ventricles are in the left side of the chest and angle downward to the left. For this reason the mean QRS axis points downward and toward the patient's left side.

LO 17.14

Calculating the Electrical Axis

As described earlier, the electrical axis is the average direction of the heart's electrical activity during ventricular depolarization. ECG leads positioned on the body sense the sum of the heart's electrical activity and record it as waveforms. The patient's electrical axis can be identified by assessing the waveforms recorded by the six leads that view the frontal plane. This includes leads I, II, III, aV_R, aV_L, and aV_F. Imaginary lines drawn from the location of each of the leads intersect in the center of the heart and form a diagram referred to as the *hexaxial reference system*.

LO 17.15

Hexaxial Reference System

To better explain the hexaxial reference system, think of an imaginary circle drawn over the patient's chest (Figure 17-30). This circle lies in the frontal plane. The center of the circle is the AV node. The limb leads view electrical forces moving up and down and left and right through this circle. Within the

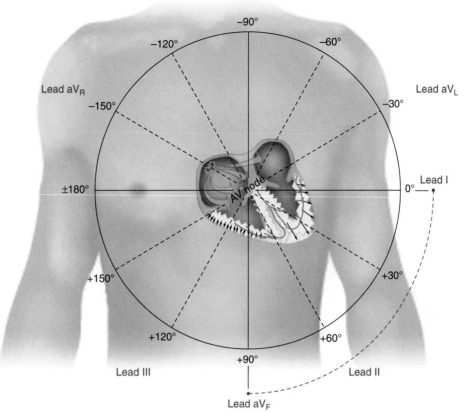

Figure 17-30
The imaginary circle used to determine the heart's axis is divided into equal 30-degree segments with lead I at the 3 o'clock position and lead aV_F located at the 6 o'clock position.

circle are six bisecting lines, each representing one of the six limb leads. The intersection of all lines divides the circle into equal, 30-degree segments. Lead I starts at 0 degrees and is located at the 3 o'clock position. Lead aV_F starts at 90 degrees and is located at the 6 o'clock position. Remember though, that the starting point of each lead is the position of the positive electrode.

As you can see moving from the 3 o'clock position counterclockwise, the degrees are more and more negative, until you reach the 9 o'clock position, where it is ±180 degrees. Moving clockwise from the 3 o'clock position each segment represents positive-degree positions; however, it doesn't necessarily mean that pole is positive.

A normal axis is one that falls between 0 and +90 degrees. An axis that falls between +90 degrees and +180 degrees is considered right axis deviation. One that falls between 0 and −90 degrees indicates left axis deviation, and one that falls and between −90 and ±180 degrees is considered extreme axis deviation (also referred to as *indeterminate axis*).

To determine the electrical axis we can use one of two methods: the four-quadrant method and the degree method.

QUESTION
6. Can you list the six limb leads and identify which are augmented?

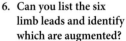

KEY CONCEPT
The mean QRS magnitude normally points downward and to the patient's left because this is the general direction of ventricular depolarization.

Figure 17-31
The mean QRS axis normally points downward and to the patient's left between 0 and +90 degrees.

LO 17.16   Four-Quadrant Method

With the four-quadrant method the axis is determined by examining the QRS complex in leads I and aV_F.

The mean QRS axis normally points downward and to the patient's left, between 0 and 90 degrees (Figure 17-31). As long as it remains within this range, it is considered normal. If it is outside this range, it is considered abnormal.

Any lead records a positive deflection if the wave of depolarization is moving toward it. Lead I is oriented at 0 degrees. If the mean QRS axis is directed anywhere between –90 degrees and +90 degrees, the right half of the circle, you can expect lead I to record a positive QRS complex (Figure 17-32). Lead I is created by making the left arm positive and the right arm negative, so the left half of the circle is positive while the right half is negative.

Lead aV_F is oriented at +90 degrees. If the mean QRS axis is directed anywhere between 0 degrees and ±180 degrees, the bottom half of our circle, you can expect lead aV_F to record a positive QRS complex (Figure 17-33). Lead aV_F is created by making the legs positive and the other limbs negative, so the bottom half of the circle is positive while the upper half is negative.

Figure 17-32
If the mean QRS axis is directed anywhere between −90 degrees and +90 degrees (the left half of our circle), a positive QRS complex is seen in lead I.

With lead I we can see whether the impulses are moving to the right or to the left whereas lead aV_F tells us whether they are moving up or down.

If the main deflection of the QRS complex points up (positive) in lead I, then the electrical impulses are moving from right to left in a normal manner. Conversely, if the deflection points down (negative), then the impulses are moving abnormally from left to right (Figure 17-34).

If the deflection of the QRS complex is positive in lead aV_F, the electrical impulses are traveling downward in a normal manner. If the deflection is negative, the impulses are traveling upward; this would be considered abnormal (Figure 17-35).

An easy way to remember the direction of the deflection of the QRS complexes in leads I and aV_F is to think of your thumbs pointing up or down. Two thumbs up indicates normal axis; anything else is considered abnormal.

To determine whether the QRS complex is positive or negative, you examine it and decide whether the average deflection is positive or negative. Often, this

Figure 17-33
If the mean QRS axis is directed anywhere between 0 and ±180 degrees (the bottom half of our circle), a positive QRS complex is seen in lead aV_F.

Figure 17-34
If the mean QRS axis is directed anywhere between −90 degrees and +90 degrees (the right half of our circle), a negative QRS complex is seen in lead I.

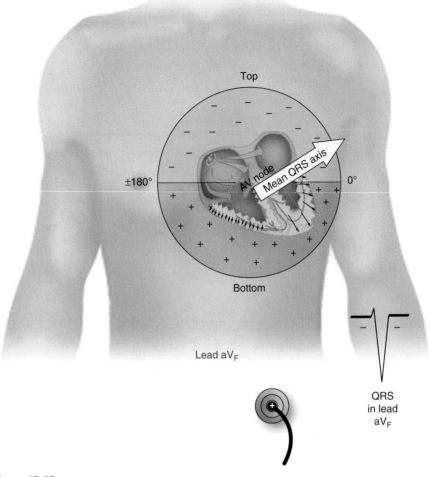

Figure 17-35
If the mean QRS axis is directed anywhere between 0 and 180 degrees (the top half of our circle), a negative QRS complex is seen in lead aV_F.

is easy to estimate by merely looking at the QRS complex and deciding what the overall complex looks like. More accuracy can be obtained by measuring the number of small squares on the ECG paper grid of negative and positive deflection. If there are more small squares on the negative side, the QRS complex is referred to as negative. If there are more small squares on the positive side, the QRS complex is referred to as positive.

Degree Method

Although the quadrant method is easier, a more accurate axis calculation is the degree method. Aside from being more accurate, it also allows you to determine the axis even when the QRS complex is not clearly positive or negative in leads I and aV_F.

There are three easy ways to employ the degree method. In the six limb leads of the ECG tracing:

1. Identify the lead with tallest (most positive deflection) QRS. It points directly toward the ECG axis.

2. Alternatively, identify the lead with the most negative QRS. It points directly away from the ECG axis.

3. Alternatively, identify the lead with an equiphasic QRS (which has an equal deflection above and below the baseline) or the smallest QRS complex. This lead is at right angles (or perpendicular) to the QRS axis. For example, if lead III has the smallest QRS complex, then the lead perpendicular to the line representing lead III would be lead aV_R. After you have identified the perpendicular lead, examine its QRS complex. If the electrical activity is moving toward the positive pole of a lead, the QRS complex deflects upward. If it is moving away from the positive pole of a lead, the QRS complex deflects downward. Plot this information on the hexaxial diagram to determine the direction of the electrical axis.

Let's look at some examples to see these three ways to determine axis in use (Figure 17-36).

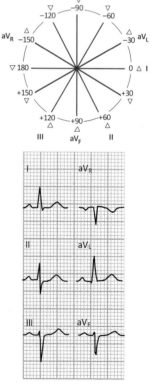

a. The QRS in lead II has the most voltage. It is positive so the mean QRS vector is pointing directly at lead II or +60°. For this example the axis is +60°.

b. The QRS in lead III has the most voltage. It is negative so the mean QRS vector is pointing directly away from lead III. For this example the axis is –60°.

c. aVL is perpendicular to the equiphasic QRS in lead II so it is either ±150° or –30°. Since the deflection in lead aV_L is positive it indicates the mean QRS vector is traveling toward the electrode. The axis for this example is –30°.

Figure 17-36
Shown above are three examples using the degree method to determine QRS axis.

Altered QRS Axis

As was mentioned earlier, the mean QRS axis normally points downward and to the patient's left, between 0 and +90 degrees. An axis between +90 and ±180 degrees indicates right axis deviation, and one between 0 and −90 degrees indicates left axis deviation. An axis deviation between ±180 and −90 degrees indicates extreme axis deviation and is called an *indeterminate axis* (Figure 17-37).

Again, if the QRS complex deflection is positive in both leads I and aVF, the electrical axis is normal. If the QRS complex in lead I is upright and the QRS complex in lead aVF has a negative deflection, then left axis deviation exists. If the QRS complex in lead I is negative and lead aVF has a QRS complex

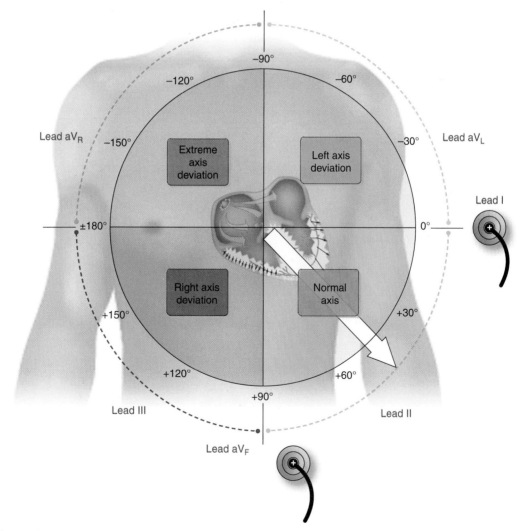

Figure 17-37
Normal axis, right axis deviation, extreme axis deviation, and left axis deviation.

with a positive deflection, then right axis deviation exists. If the QRS complex is negative in both leads, extreme axis deviation exists (Figure 17-38).

LO 17.18   Causes of Altered Electrical Axis

If the heart is displaced, the mean QRS axis is also displaced in the same direction. For example, in tall, slender individuals the heart may be rotated toward the patient's right side. This is referred to as a *vertical heart*. This causes the

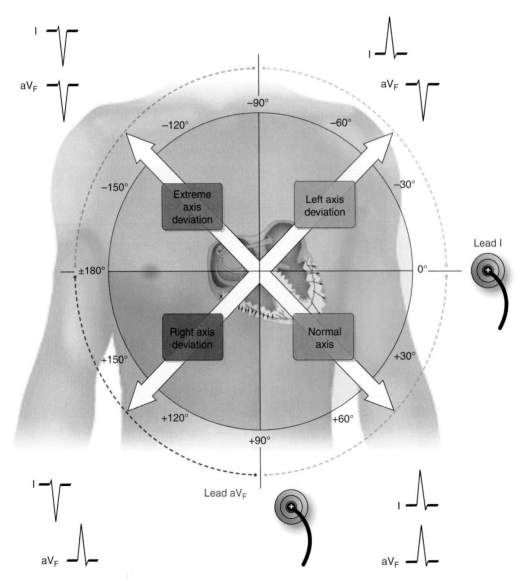

Figure 17-38
Positive QRS complexes in leads I and aV$_F$ indicate a normal QRS axis. A negative QRS complex in lead I and an upright QRS complex in lead aV$_F$ indicate right axis deviation. Negative QRS complexes in both lead I and lead aV$_F$ indicate extreme axis deviation, and an upright QRS complex in lead I and a negative QRS complex in lead aV$_F$ indicate left axis deviation.

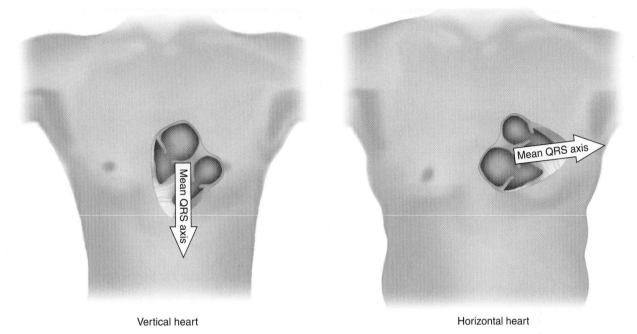

Vertical heart   Horizontal heart

Figure 17-39
In thin individuals the apex of the heart can be directed vertically whereas with very obese individuals and in pregnancy the apex can be directed horizontally. As the apex of the heart shifts, so does the mean QRS axis.

mean QRS axis to shift toward the right. With obesity and in pregnancy, the diaphragm (and the heart) is pushed up by the increased abdominal pressure so that the mean QRS axis will likely point directly to the patient's left. This is referred to as a *horizontal heart* (Figure 17-39).

Another condition that causes the axis to shift is enlargement or *hypertrophy*, of one or both of the heart's chambers (Figure 17-40). The resultant greater depolarization activity displaces the mean P or QRS axis toward the enlarged, or hypertrophied, region. This is because an enlarged, or hypertrophied, chamber has more (and larger) vectors, which draws the mean P or QRS axis in that direction.

MI is another condition that causes the mean QRS axis to point in a different direction than normal (Figure 17-41). With MI, a branch of the coronary arteries supplying an area of the heart with blood becomes occluded and the tissue becomes necrotic. This infarcted tissue cannot depolarize and therefore has no vectors. The vectors from the other side are unopposed vectors because of this, so the mean QRS vector tends to point away from the infarct.

Finding a patient's electrical axis can help confirm a diagnosis or narrow a range of possible diagnoses. Factors that influence the location of the axis include the heart's position in the chest, the heart's size, the patient's body

Figure 17-40
With enlargement or
hypertrophy, of one or both
of the heart's chambers, the
mean QRS axis shifts toward
the enlarged or hypertrophied
side.

AV node

Mean QRS axis

Mean QRS axis

Hypertrophy of
left ventricle

Figure 17-41
The infarcted tissue seen
with MI cannot depolarize
and therefore has no vectors.
The vectors from the other
side are unopposed vectors
because of this, so the mean
QRS vector tends to point
away from the infarct.

Mean QRS axis

Mean QRS axis

Area of
infarction
(infarct)

Vector points
away from
infarction

size or type, the conduction pathways, and the force of the electrical impulses being generated. Remember that electrical activity in the heart swings away from areas of damage or necrosis, so the damaged part of the heart will be the last area to be depolarized.

Axis deviation isn't always a cause for alarm, and it isn't always cardiac in origin. For example, infants and children normally have right axis deviation whereas pregnant women normally have left axis deviation.

Practice Makes Perfect

For each of the following *Practice Makes Perfect* exercises, the waves recorded by the six leads of the frontal plane are shown. Determine if the mean QRS axis is normal or if there is axis deviation. Answers to these exercises can be found in Appendix A.

1.

2.

3.

4.

Key Points 🔍

- Because the electrodes positioned on the patient's skin detect the heart's electrical activity, placing them in a different location changes the lead or view.

- The shape of the waveform is described from the perspective of the positive electrode of the selected lead.

- Bipolar leads include leads I, II, and III.

- Unipolar leads include leads aV_R, aV_L, and aV_F and the precordial leads V_1, V_2, V_3, V_4, V_5, and V_6.

- The limb leads are produced by placing electrodes on the right arm (RA), left arm (LA), left leg (LL), and right leg (RL). The limb leads include leads I, II, and III; augmented voltage right (aV_R); augmented voltage left (aV_L); and augmented voltage foot (aV_F). They provide a view of the electrical activity along the heart's frontal plane.

- The precordial leads include leads V_1, V_2, V_3, V_4, V_5, and V_6. They provide information about the electrical activity along the horizontal plane of the heart.

- Depolarization and repolarization of the cardiac cells produce many small electrical currents or impulses that vary in intensity and direction. These currents are called *instantaneous vectors*.

- The mean or average of all the instantaneous vectors the ECG detects is called the *mean vector*. The direction of the mean vector is called the *electrical axis*.

- When the electrical current traveling through the heart is moving toward a positive electrode, the ECG machine records it as a positive or upright waveform.

- When the impulse is traveling away from a positive electrode and toward a negative electrode, the ECG machine records it as a negative or downward deflection.

- The mean of all vectors that result from ventricular depolarization is called the *QRS axis*. It is the most important and also the most frequently determined axis.

- A sequence of vectors is produced as the Purkinje fibers carry the impulse from the endocardial lining of the right and left ventricles through the full thickness of the ventricular wall toward the epicardium.

- Completion of right ventricular depolarization occurs first because the thinner wall of the right ventricle transmits the impulse in a fraction of the time it takes the impulse to travel through the thick lateral wall of the left ventricle.

- The sum of all the small vectors of ventricular depolarization is called the *mean QRS vector*. The mean QRS axis points more to the left because the instantaneous vectors of the thicker left ventricle are larger.

- The limb leads provide information about the frontal plane and are used to determine the position of the mean QRS axis, described in degrees within an imaginary circle drawn over the patient's chest. The center of the circle is the AV node.

- Leads I and aV_F can be used to quickly determine whether the mean QRS axis on any ECG is normal.

- The intersection of all lines divides the circle into equal 30-degree segments. Lead I starts at 0 degrees and is located at the 3 o'clock position. The mean QRS axis normally points downward and to the patient's left, between 0 and +90 degrees.

- An axis between −90 and ±180 degrees indicates right axis deviation, and one between 0 and −90 degrees indicates left axis deviation. An axis deviation between ±180 and −90 degrees indicates extreme axis deviation and is called an *indeterminate axis*.

- If the QRS complex is positive in leads I and aV_F, the QRS axis is normal.

- If the QRS complex is upright in lead I and negative in lead aV_F, then left axis deviation exists. If the QRS complex is negative in lead I and positive in lead aV_F, then right axis deviation exists. If the QRS complex is negative in both leads, extreme right axis deviation exists.

- Factors that influence the location of the axis include the heart's position in the chest, the heart's size, the patient's body size or type, the conduction pathways, and the force of the electrical impulses being generated.

Assess Your Understanding

The following questions give you a chance to assess your understanding of the material discussed in this chapter. The answers can be found in Appendix A.

1. With lead I, the ____ lead wire is the positive electrode.
   a. LL
   b. RA
   c. LA
   d. RL

2. With the aV_F lead, the positive electrode is positioned in/on the
   a. right arm.
   b. left leg.
   c. 4th intercostal space in the right sternal border.
   d. 5th intercostal space in the left midaxillary border.

3. Bipolar leads
   a. record the flow of the electrical impulse between the three selected electrodes.
   b. include leads aV_R, aV_L, and aV_F.
   c. require two electrodes of opposite polarity.
   d. use only one positive electrode and a reference point calculated by the ECG machine.

4.   The horizontal plane gives us a/an _____ view of the heart's electrical activity.

   a.   anterior and posterior
   b.   superior and inferior
   c.   anterior and superior
   d.   lateral and inferior

5.   Which of the following leads views the heart on the horizontal plane?

   a. $V_1, V_2, V_3, V_4, V_5,$ and V_6
   b. $aV_R, aV_L,$ and aV_F
   c. MCL_1 and MCL_6
   d.   I, II, and III

6.   The limb leads are obtained by placing electrodes on the

   a.   right arm, left arm, left leg and right leg.
   b.   chest and back.
   c.   right arm, left leg, and right leg.
   d.   left arm and left leg.

7.   Leads _____ are referred to as the standard limb leads.

   a.   I, II, and III
   b. $aV_R, aV_L,$ and aV_F
   c. $V_1, V_2, V_3, V_4, V_5,$ and V_6
   d. MCL_1 and MCL_6

8.   Leads _____ are referred to as the precordial leads.

   a. MCL_1 and MCL_6
   b. $aV_R, aV_L,$ and aV_F
   c.   I and II
   d. $V_1, V_2, V_3, V_4, V_5,$ and V_6

9.   Match the following ECG leads with the correct description.

Leads	Referred to as
a. V_1 and V_2	_____ inferior leads
b. V_3 and V_4	_____ lateral leads
c. II, III, and aV_F	_____ septal leads
d. $V_1, V_2, V_3,$ and V_4	_____ anterior leads
e. I, $aV_L, V_5,$ and V_6	_____ anteroseptal leads

10. Contiguous ECG leads
    a. include any two standard limb leads.
    b. include any two leads that are anatomically next to one another.
    c. are also called anteroseptal leads.
    d. are those that view the heart from a superior direction.

11. The currents produced by depolarization and repolarization of the cardiac cells are called
    a. mean vectors.
    b. instantaneous vectors.
    c. the mean electrical axis.
    d. positive deflections.

12. The electrical axis is depicted as a
    a. large circle.
    b. negative deflection.
    c. positive deflection.
    d. single large arrow.

13. Axis is defined
    a. in the frontal plane only.
    b. immediately upon attaching the ECG leads.
    c. as a waveform that has a negative deflection.
    d. as the amperage of a waveform.

14. The QRS axis
    a. is rarely determined.
    b. is the mean of all vectors generated during the depolarization of the atria.
    c. is the most important and also the most frequently determined axis.
    d. normally points up and to the right.

15. Completion of right ventricular depolarization occurs _____ completion of left ventricular depolarization.
    a. before
    b. after
    c. during
    d. both a and b

16. The right ventricular vectors are larger and persist longer than those of the left ventricle.
    a. True
    b. False

17. The sum of all the small vectors of ventricular depolarization is called the mean
    a. P wave vector.
    b. QRS axis.
    c. T axis.
    d. ST axis.

18. The center(s) of the circle used to determine the axis of the mean QRS vector is (are) the
    a. AV node.
    b. SA node.
    c. Purkinje fibers.
    d. apical region of the ventricle.

19. The circle used to determine the axis of the mean QRS vector is divided into equal _____-degree segments.
    a. 10
    b. 15
    c. 30
    d. 60

20. On the circle used to determine the axis of the mean QRS vector, lead I starts at _____ degrees and is located at the _____ o'clock position.
    a. −90, 6
    b. ±180, 9
    c. −120, 11
    d. 0, 3

21. The mean QRS axis normally points _____ and to the patient's _____, between _____ degrees.
    a. downward, right, −90 and ±180
    b. upward, left, 0 and −90
    c. downward, left, 0 and +90
    d. upward, right, ±180 and −90

22. Match the following axis deviations with the correct degrees.

Deviation Degrees	
a. Right axis deviation	_____ 0 and 90 degrees
b. Left axis deviation	_____ 180 and 90 degrees
c. Extreme axis deviation	_____ 90 and 180 degrees

23. Fill in the following table of QRS deflections

Direction of QRS in lead I	Direction of QRS in lead aV$_F$	Electrical axis
a. Positive	Positive	
b. Positive	Negative	
c. Negative	Positive	
d. Negative	Negative	

24. What direction will the ECG waveform take (negative, positive, or biphasic) in this example?

Positive electrode

25. In this illustration showing lead I, identify with + or – signs which half of the circle will be positive and which half will be negative.

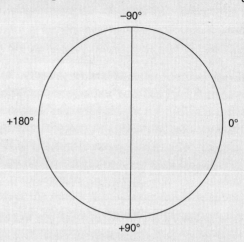

26. In this illustration showing lead aVF, identify with + or – signs which half of the circle will be positive and which half will be negative.

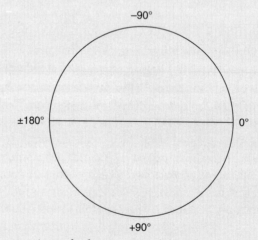

Referring to the scenario at the beginning of this chapter, answer the following questions.

27. When the left ventricle is enlarged, the axis of the heart moves
   a. leftward.
   b. rightward.
   c. upward.
   d. lower.

28. The axis shifts because the sum of the electrical impulses in the enlarged ventricle is
   a. equal on both sides of the heart.
   b. greater on the left than the right.
   c. lesser on the left than the right.
   d. greater on the bottom than the top.

29. Infarcted tissue cannot depolarize and therefore has no vectors.
   a. True
   b. False

Answers to Sidebar Questions

1. A bipolar lead requires two electrodes of opposite polarity (positive and negative). **p. 482**

2. Leads I, II, and III are referred to as the *standard limb leads*. **p. 485**

3. In the context of the ECG, waveforms produced by the aV_R, aV_L, and aV_F leads are normally small. The ECG machine enhances or augments the leads to make them easier to see because of this. It magnifies the leads by 50%. **p. 487**

4. A 12-lead ECG includes extremity leads, called limb leads, and chest, or precordial, leads. **p. 504**

5. Depolarization moving toward a positive electrode produces a positive or upright deflection on the ECG machine. **p. 505**

6. The six limb leads are I, II, III, aV_R, aV_L, and aV_F. Leads aV_R, aV_L, and aV_F are considered augmented leads. **p. 509**

What's Online

Go to www.mhhe.com/shadeECG2e to find:

- Presentations on chapter content
- Chapter quiz
- Additional practice tracings
- Fill-in-the-blank exercises and answers
- In-depth answers to Practice Makes Perfect ECG tracings and Assess Your Understanding questions

18 Atrial Enlargement and Ventricular Hypertrophy

Chapter Outline

Hypertrophy and Enlargement

Atrial Enlargement

Ventricular Hypertrophy

Learning Objectives

LO 18.1 Define the terms *hypertrophy* and *enlargement*.

LO 18.2 Recall the electrical waveforms that can change with enlargement and hypertrophy.

LO 18.3 List the conditions that can lead to right atrial enlargement, and describe the ECG changes that can be used to identify it.

LO 18.4 List the conditions that can lead to left atrial enlargement, and describe the ECG changes that can be used to identify it.

LO 18.5 List the conditions that can lead to right ventricular hypertrophy, and describe the ECG changes that can be used to identify it.

LO 18.6 List the conditions that can lead to left ventricular hypertrophy, and describe the ECG changes that can be used to identify it.

LO 18.7 Identify the ST segment and T wave changes that may be seen with severe hypertrophy.

Case History

You are a member of the EMS squad who responds to the local high school for a 16-year-old boy complaining of chest pain. You enter the nurse's station where the school nurse is kneeling over a thin, pale young man lying on a cot. He is awake and alert but is holding his chest. After introducing yourself, you ask him how he feels. The patient indicates that he gets chest pain when he overexerts himself in physical education class. The nurse hands you a card with the patient's medical history. It indicates that he has an enlarged heart as a result of a viral infection that attacked his heart, resulting in cardiomyopathy.

You apply oxygen to the patient and establish an IV line. After obtaining a 12-lead ECG, you hand it to your partner who comments on the unusually tall R waves in V_1 and V_2. You also note a down-sloping ST segment depression and T wave inversion in those leads.

LO 18.1

Hypertrophy and Enlargement

KEY CONCEPT
A hypertrophied ventricle has a thick muscular wall. An enlarged chamber is bigger and can hold more blood than normal but does not necessarily have a thicker muscular wall.

QUESTION
1. **What do the heart's ventricles do?** *Note:* Answers to Sidebar Questions can be found at the end of the chapter.

Hypertrophy means an increase in muscle mass. As it relates to this textbook, it is a condition in which the muscular wall of the ventricle(s) becomes thicker than normal (Figure 18-1). It results from the ventricle having to pump against increased resistance within the cardiovascular system. A number of conditions cause hypertrophy, including systemic hypertension and aortic stenosis.

Another condition we discuss is **dilation** or **enlargement** of a chamber (Figure 18-2). An enlarged chamber occurs as the result of volume overload—the chamber dilates to accommodate the increased blood volume. It is therefore bigger and can hold more blood than normal. Unlike hypertrophy, the muscular wall of the dilated chamber typically does not become thicker. Enlargement is most often seen with certain types of valvular disease. For example, left atrial enlargement can result from mitral valve insufficiency.

Enlargement and hypertrophy often exist together as both are ways in which the heart tries to increase its cardiac output. It is common to associate enlargement with the atria (as they dilate more than they hypertrophy) and hypertrophy with the ventricles. We look at the P wave to assess for atrial

Figure 18-1
Hypertrophy is a condition in which the muscular wall of the ventricle becomes thicker.

Left ventricular hypertrophy

Left atrial
enlargement

Figure 18-2
Enlargement of a heart
chamber occurs to
accommodate increased
blood volume

enlargement because the P wave represents atrial depolarization. Similarly, we examine the QRS complex to help us identify ventricular hypertrophy.

Changes on the ECG

Changes that we see in the ECG that indicate the presence of enlargement or hypertrophy include

- An increase in duration of the waveform
- An increase in the amplitude of the waveform
- Axis deviation
- T wave changes

As a point of information, the ECG is not all that effective at identifying hypertrophy. In about 50% of cases where hypertrophy is shown to exist, the ECG will be normal. Other diagnostic tools, such as x-ray and echocardiography, are much more effective at revealing hypertrophy. However, when the electrocardiographic indicators are present, the ECG is (about 90%) accurate.

Atrial Enlargement

The duration of a normal P wave is no more than 0.10 seconds whereas its amplitude, whether a positive or negative deflection, should not exceed 2.5 mm. The first portion of the P wave represents right atrial depolarization whereas the terminal part represents left atrial depolarization (Figure 18-3).

KEY CONCEPT
Chamber enlargement is associated with the atria whereas hypertrophy is associated with the ventricles.

LO 18.2

QUESTION
2. Which of the heart's atria depolarizes first?

QUESTION
3. How many small squares on the ECG paper represent 0.10 seconds in duration? How many represent an amplitude of 2.5 mm?

Figure 18-3
Atrial conduction and the
normal P wave. Leads II
and V_1 provide the best
information regarding atrial
conduction.

Leads II and V_1 provide the necessary information to assess atrial enlargement. Lead II is nearly parallel to the flow of current through the atria (the
mean P wave vector). For this reason it records the largest deflections and
can reveal abnormalities in atrial depolarization. Lead V_1 is placed just to the
right of the sternum in the 4th intercostal space. This positions it directly
over the atria and gives the most accurate information about atrial enlargement, which allows easy separation of the right and left atrial components
of the P wave. A P wave that has both positive and negative deflections is
termed *biphasic*. A biphasic P wave in lead V_1 is normal. A biphasic P wave
will have two components, the initial component from the right atrium and

the terminal component from the left atrium. Note that a biphasic P wave has deflections above and below the baseline.

Right Atrial Enlargement

Right atrial enlargement results in the right atrium's electrical dominance over the left atrium. The diagnosis of right atrial enlargement is made when you see an increase in the amplitude or peaking of the first part of the P wave (Figure 18-4). Remember, the first part of the P wave represents depolarization of the right atrium.

The width of the P wave, however, stays within normal limits because its terminal part originates from the left atrium, which depolarizes normally if left atrial enlargement is absent.

Characteristics of Right Atrial Enlargement

- The P wave is taller than 2.5 mm in lead II (as well as in the other inferior leads III and aV$_F$)

- The initial component of the P wave is taller than the terminal component (if it is biphasic)

KEY CONCEPT
We use leads II and V$_1$ to diagnose atrial enlargement.

LO 18.3

KEY CONCEPT
Right atrial enlargement is diagnosed by the P waves exceeding 2.5 mm in amplitude in the inferior leads II, III, and aV$_F$ and the first part of the biphasic P wave being taller than normal in lead V$_1$.

Figure 18-4
Right atrial enlargement leads to an increase in the amplitude of the first part of the P wave.

Right atrial enlargement is often secondary to pulmonary hypertension related to emphysema. Therefore, the P wave changes in right atrial enlargement are termed *P pulmonale.*

Left Atrial Enlargement

With left atrial enlargement, the amplitude of the terminal portion of the P wave may increase in V_1 (Figure 18-5). Diagnostically we say left atrial enlargement is present when the terminal (left atrial) portion of the P wave drops more than 1 mm below the isoelectric line (in lead V_1).

However, a more telling indicator of left atrial enlargement is an increase in the duration or width of the terminal portion of the P wave. This occurs because depolarization of the left atrium is the latter part of atrial depolarization. The diagnosis of left atrial enlargement requires that the terminal portion of the P wave be greater than one small square (0.04 seconds) in duration.

Often the presence of ECG evidence of left atrial enlargement reflects only a nonspecific conduction irregularity. For this reason, you must carefully weigh the interpretation of atrial enlargement on the ECG with the patient's clinical presentation. However, the presence of ECG evidence of left atrial enlargement may also be the result of mitral valve stenosis causing the left atrium to

Figure 18-5
Left atrial enlargement leads to an increase in the amplitude and width of the terminal portion of the P wave.

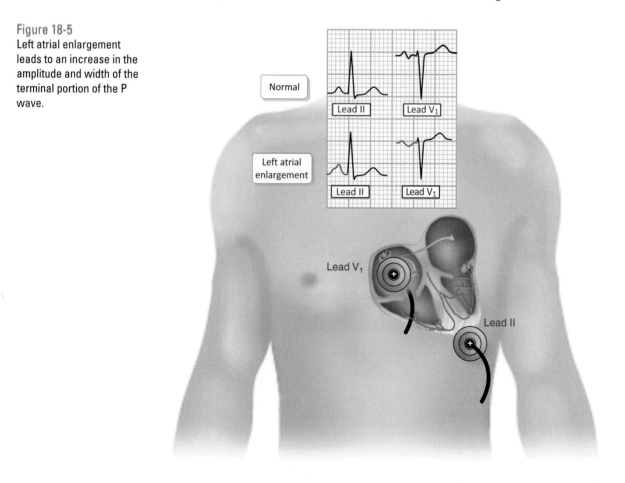

enlarge to force blood across the stenotic (tight) mitral valve. The presence of left atrial enlargement from mitral stenosis is termed *P mitrale*.

Characteristics of Left Atrial Enlargement

- The amplitude of the terminal (negative) portion of the P wave increases, descending more than 1 mm below the isoelectric line in lead V_1

- The duration of the P wave is increased to greater than 0.12 seconds in duration, or the terminal (negative) portion of the P wave is greater than 1 small square (0.04 seconds) in width

Ventricular Hypertrophy

Using the ECG to diagnose ventricular hypertrophy requires careful assessment of the QRS complex in many leads (Figure 18-6). Let's begin by quickly reviewing how the QRS complex should appear in lead V_1. Ventricular depolarization will move downward to the left side and posteriorly because the thicker left ventricle is located mostly posteriorly. The V_1 electrode is positive; therefore, the wave of depolarization moving through the left ventricle will be mostly moving away from it, producing a mainly negative QRS complex. For this reason, the R wave is usually very short whereas the S wave is much larger than the R wave in this lead.

Right Ventricular Hypertrophy

Right ventricular hypertrophy is far less common than left ventricular hypertrophy. It is often the result of severe pulmonary stenosis or primary pulmonary hypertension.

KEY CONCEPT

Left atrial enlargement is diagnosed by the terminal (left atrial) portion of the P wave dropping more than 1 mm below the isoelectric line in V_1 and an increase in the duration of the P wave.

QUESTION

4. How would you describe to someone the degrees where the QRS axis in the normal heart lies?

REMINDER

Remember that, normally, the R waves are more positive in the leads closer to the left ventricle.

LO 18.5

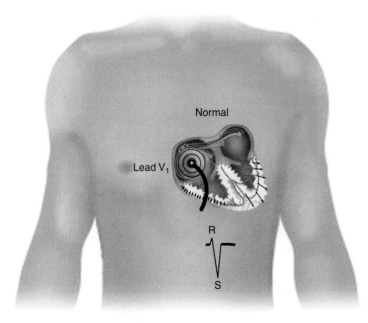

Figure 18-6

In lead V_1 the QRS complex normally has a short R wave and a deeper S wave.

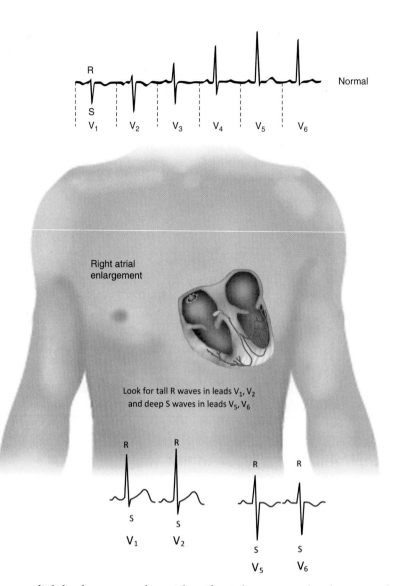

Figure 18-7
The thick wall of the enlarged right ventricle causes tall R waves in lead V_1 (and leads that lie close to it) and deep S waves in V_6.

The precordial leads are used to identify right ventricular hypertrophy (Figure 18-7). The thick wall of the enlarged right ventricle causes the R waves to be more positive in the leads that lie closer to lead V_1 (the electrode located directly over the right ventricle). Thus, moving from the right to the left chest leads (from V_1 to V_6), the R waves go from being larger to being smaller. This is a progressive but gradual change. As such, the S waves are smaller in lead V_1 and become larger as you move from V_1 to V_6. This produces the following:

- Leads V_1, V_2—the R waves are equal to or larger than the S waves
- Leads V_5, V_6—the S waves are larger than the R waves

Additionally, in the limb leads, right axis deviation is the most common characteristic seen with right ventricular hypertrophy (Figure 18-8). Instead of falling within the normal range of 0 degrees to +90 degrees, the QRS axis now falls between + 90 degrees and ±180 degrees. This causes the QRS complex to be slightly more negative than positive in lead I and positive in lead aV_F. However, it takes a significant increase in right ventricular wall thickness to overcome the

Figure 18-8
In right ventricular hypertrophy the QRS axis moves to between +90 and ±180 degrees. The QRS complexes in right ventricular hypertrophy are slightly more negative in lead I and positive in lead aV$_F$.

aV$_F$

electrical forces that naturally allow the left ventricle to be dominant. In other words, to see it, there has to be significant right ventricular hypertrophy.

Characteristics of Right Ventricular Hypertrophy

- The R waves are larger than or equal to S waves in leads V$_1$, V$_2$ and the S waves are larger or equal to the R waves in leads V$_5$, V$_6$

- The R waves in V$_1$ and S waves in lead V$_6$ are equal to or greater than 11 mm

- The presence of right axis deviation (with the QRS axis exceeding 100 degrees)

KEY CONCEPT
The most common attribute seen with right ventricular hypertrophy is right axis deviation in the limb leads.

Left Ventricular Hypertrophy

LO 18.6

Frequent causes of left ventricular hypertrophy are systemic hypertension and valvular heart disease.

Diagnosing left ventricular hypertrophy is more complicated than diagnosing right ventricular hypertrophy (Figure 18-9). An axis deviation of 15 degrees is often seen but is not a very helpful diagnostic tool.

The precordial leads are more sensitive than the limb leads in the diagnosis of left ventricular hypertrophy. Therefore, increased R wave amplitude in those leads overlying the left ventricle forms the basis for the ECG diagnosis of left ventricular hypertrophy. Also, the S waves are smaller in the leads overlying the left ventricle (leads V$_5$, V$_6$) but deeper in the leads overlying the right ventricle (leads V$_1$, V$_2$).

Figure 18-9
The thick wall of the enlarged left ventricle causes the R waves to be more positive in the leads that lie closer to leads V_5, V_6 and the S waves to be deeper in the leads that are closer to V_1, V_2.

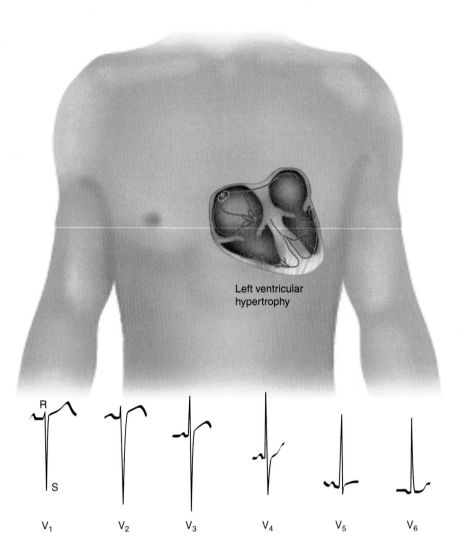

Left ventricular hypertrophy

V_1 V_2 V_3 V_4 V_5 V_6

The most useful criteria for identifying left ventricular hypertrophy in the precordial leads are the following:

- The amplitude of S waves in V_1, V_2 + the amplitude of R waves in leads V_5, V_6 exceed 35 mm
- R wave amplitude in lead V_5 or V_6 exceeds 27 mm
- R wave amplitude in lead V_6 exceeds the R wave amplitude in lead V_5

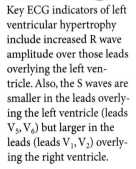

KEY CONCEPT
Key ECG indicators of left ventricular hypertrophy include increased R wave amplitude over those leads overlying the left ventricle. Also, the S waves are smaller in the leads overlying the left ventricle (leads V_5, V_6) but larger in the leads (leads V_1, V_2) overlying the right ventricle.

Characteristics of Left Ventricular Hypertrophy

- There is increased R wave amplitude over those leads overlying the left ventricle

- The S, waves are smaller in the leads overlying the left ventricle but deeper in the leads overlying the right ventricle

The more criteria present, the more likely the patient has left ventricular hypertrophy.

The limb leads can also provide evidence of left ventricular hypertrophy. The limb-lead criteria for left ventricular hypertrophy include the R wave amplitude in

- Lead aV_L exceeds 11 mm
- Lead aV_F exceeds 21 mm
- Lead I exceeds 14 mm
- Lead I plus the S wave amplitude in lead III exceeds 25 mm

It is possible for both the right and left ventricles to be hypertrophied. This produces a combination of features such as left ventricular hypertrophy in the precordial leads and right axis deviation in the limb leads. However, most often the indicators of left ventricular hypertrophy hide those of right ventricular hypertrophy. The criteria listed are of little value in persons younger than 35 years of age because they frequently have increased voltage due to a relatively thin chest wall.

ST Segment and T Wave Changes

LO 18.7

In severe hypertrophy, you may also see changes in the ST segment and T waves. This is called *secondary repolarization abnormalities* and includes the following (Figure 18-10):

1. Down-sloping ST segment depression
2. T wave inversion (which takes an opposite direction to the R wave)

The depressed ST segment and the inverted T wave appear to blend together, forming a single asymmetric wave. The downward slope is gradual whereas the upslope is abrupt.

Repolarization abnormalities are not uncommon. They are easier to see in those leads with tall R waves because the electrical forces of the hypertrophied ventricle are greater. For this reason, right ventricular repolarization abnormalities are seen in leads V_1 and V_2. Left ventricular repolarization abnormalities are seen in leads I, aV_L, V_5, and V_6.

Figure 18-10
Down-sloping ST segment depression and T wave inversion seen with ventricular hypertrophy.

Practice Makes Perfect

For the following 12-lead ECGs, identify if atrial enlargement or hypertrophy are present and the type.

1.

2.

3.

4.

5.

6.

Key Points 🔍

- Hypertrophy is a condition in which the muscular wall of the ventricle(s) becomes thicker than normal.

- Dilation or enlargement of a chamber occurs as the result of volume overload, where the chamber dilates to accommodate the increased blood volume.

- Chamber enlargement is associated with the atria (as they dilate more than they hypertrophy) whereas hypertrophy is associated with the ventricles.

- We look at the P wave to assess for atrial enlargement. Similarly, we examine the QRS complex to help us identify ventricular hypertrophy. Indicators of enlargement or hypertrophy include an increase in the duration of the waveform, an increase in the amplitude of the waveform, and axis deviation.

- The duration of the normal P wave is less than 0.10 seconds whereas its amplitude should not exceed 2.5 mm.

- The first portion of the P wave represents right atrial depolarization whereas the terminal portion represents left atrial depolarization.

- Leads II and V_1 provide the necessary information to assess atrial enlargement.

- Key characteristics of right atrial enlargement include the following: The first part of the P wave will be taller than normal in lead V_1, P waves have an amplitude that exceeds 2.5 mm in the inferior leads, and there is no change in the duration of the P wave. The duration of the P wave does not appear longer in right atrial enlargement because it is hidden by the portion of the P wave that represents left atrial depolarization.

- Two indicators of left atrial enlargement are increased amplitude in the terminal portion of the P wave in V_1 and increased duration or width of the P wave.

- Normally, since the V_1 electrode is positive, the wave of depolarization moving through the left ventricle will be moving away from it, producing QRS complexes that are negative (very short R waves with much larger S waves).

- In the limb leads, right axis deviation is the most common characteristic seen with right ventricular hypertrophy.

- In the precordial leads, right ventricular hypertrophy causes the R waves to be more positive in the leads that lie closer to lead V_1.

- Left ventricular hypertrophy is identified by increased R wave amplitude over those precordial leads overlying the left ventricle and S waves that are smaller in the leads overlying the left ventricle (lead V_6) but larger in the leads (lead V_1) overlying the right ventricle.

- The duration of the QRS complex may be slightly prolonged in both right and left ventricular hypertrophy. However, it is rarely greater than 0.12 seconds.

- In severe hypertrophy, you may also see changes in the ST segment and T waves. This is called *secondary repolarization abnormalities* and includes ST segment depression and T wave inversion.

Assess Your Understanding

The following questions give you a chance to assess your understanding of the material discussed in this chapter. The answers can be found in Appendix A.

1. Hypertrophy is a condition in which the
   a. muscular wall of the ventricle becomes thicker than normal.
   b. ventricular chamber dilates to accommodate increased blood volume.
   c. heart tries to decrease its cardiac output.
   d. ECG always accurately reflects the change in muscle thickness.

2. Hypertrophy is identified by changes in the
   a. P waves.
   b. QRS complexes.
   c. T waves.
   d. PR intervals.

3. Which of the following are changes seen in the ECG that can indicate the presence of enlargement or hypertrophy?
   a. An increase in duration of the waveform
   b. A biphasic waveform
   c. Axis deviation
   d. All of the above

4. The P wave
   a. is normally 5 mm in amplitude.
   b. normally has a duration of less than 0.10 seconds.
   c. represents left atrial depolarization.
   d. is normally upright in lead V_1.

5. Which leads provide the necessary information to assess atrial enlargement?
   a. V_1 through V_6
   b. All the limb leads
   c. I and aV_F
   d. II and V_1

6. Characteristics of right atrial enlargement include
   a. the P wave appearing tallest in lead II instead of lead aV_F.
   b. an increase in the amplitude of the first part of the P wave in V_1.
   c. increased amplitude of the terminal portion of the P in V_1.
   d. the terminal portion of the P wave being at least 0.04 seconds in width.

7. With left atrial enlargement,
   a. the P wave vector swings to the right.
   b. the initial part of the P wave is enlarged.
   c. there is an increase in the duration of the terminal portion of the P wave.
   d. the P wave is taller than 2.5 mm in lead V_1.

8. The ECG evidence of atrial enlargement
   a. almost always correlates with pathological changes in the atrium.
   b. is seen in only 10 to 20% of the patients diagnosed using other procedures.
   c. should be tempered with the patient's clinical presentation.
   d. requires careful assessment of the QRS complex in many leads.

9. To diagnose ventricular hypertrophy, we assess the
   a. P waves.
   b. T waves.
   c. QRS complexes.
   d. P wave axis.

10. Normally, in lead V_1, the QRS complex will appear
    a. mainly negative.
    b. positive, with a large R wave and a short S wave.
    c. biphasic, with an R wave and an S wave of equal height.
    d. mainly positive.

11. The most common characteristic(s) seen with right ventricular hypertrophy
    a. are R waves that are more positive in the leads that lie closer to lead V_6.
    b. are S waves that are larger in lead V_1.
    c. are QRS complexes that are slightly more positive than negative in lead I and negative in lead aV_F.
    d. is right axis deviation.

12. The most common characteristic(s) seen with left ventricular hypertrophy
    a. are R waves that are more positive in the leads that lie closer to lead V_6.
    b. are S waves that are smaller in lead V_1.
    c. are R waves in lead V_2 that have an amplitude that exceeds 26 mm.
    d. is left axis deviation.

13. Left ventricular repolarization abnormalities can be identified by down-sloping ST segment depression and T wave inversion in leads
    a. I, II, and III.
    b. V_1 and V_2.
    c. V_5 and V_6.
    d. I, aV_L, V_5, V_6.

14. The patient in this case is likely experiencing:
    a. right atrial enlargement.
    b. left atrial enlargement.
    c. left ventricular hypertrophy.
    d. right ventricular hypertrophy.

Answers to Sidebar Questions

1. The ventricles are responsible for pumping blood through the circulatory system. The right ventricle pumps blood to the pulmonary circulation whereas the left ventricle pumps blood to the systemic circulation. **p. 534**

2. The right atrium depolarizes first because the SA node in which the impulse normally arises is located in the upper-right atrium. **p. 535**

3. Two and a half small squares represent 0.10 seconds in duration while 2½ small squares represent 2.5 mm in amplitude. **p. 535**

4. The QRS axis in the normal heart lies between 0 degrees and +90 degrees. This reflects the electrical dominance of the larger left ventricle over the right ventricle. **p. 539**

What's Online

Go to www.mhhe.com/shadeECG2e to find:

- Presentations on chapter content
- Chapter quiz
- Fill-in-the-blank exercises and answers
- In-depth answers to Practice Makes Perfect ECG tracings and Assess Your Understanding questions

19 Bundle Branch Block

Chapter Outline

Ventricular Conduction Disturbances

The Bundle Branches

Bundle Branch Block

Learning Objectives

LO 19.1 Define the term *ventricular conduction disturbance.*

LO 19.2 Recall how impulses are conducted through right and left bundle branches.

LO 19.3 Describe how bundle branch block occurs and list the possible sites of block within the ventricular conduction system.

LO 19.4 Describe the ECG changes that can be used to identify right bundle branch block and list the conditions that can lead to right bundle branch block.

LO 19.5 Describe the ECG changes that can be used to identify left bundle branch block and list the conditions that can lead to left bundle branch block.

LO 19.6 Describe the T wave changes seen in bundle branch block.

LO 19.7 Define the term *incomplete bundle branch block.*

LO 19.8 Define the term *hemiblock* and describe the mechanism by which it occurs.

LO 19.9 Describe the ECG changes that can be used to identify left anterior and left posterior hemiblock.

LO 19.10 Be familiar with the terms *bifascicular* and *trifascicular block.*

LO 19.11 Recall treatments for bundle branch block.

Case History

Your patient is a 60-year-old male who is complaining of chest pain. He was brought into the emergency department by the local fire department. They tell you he was picked up at work after a brisk walk at lunch time. You find a pale, sweating man lying on a cot. He is awake and alert but is holding his chest. After introducing yourself, you ask him how he feels. The patient indicates that he experienced a sudden onset of chest pain and shortness of breath. The paramedic hands you a card with the patient's medical history. It indicates that he has a history of hypertension and high cholesterol.

Oxygen is being administered to the patient and an intravenous line has been established. After obtaining a 12-lead ECG, you hand it to the doctor who has just entered the treatment room. He comments on the pattern of the QRS complex in V_1. You note that it looks like rabbit ears. The QRS complex is also much wider than normal, indicating that the patient's heart has a conduction defect.

LO 19.1

QUESTION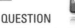

1. How is the impulse that brings about the heartbeat conducted from the SA node to the AV node? *Note:* Answers to sidebar questions can be found at the end of the chapter.

LO 19.2

Ventricular Conduction Disturbances

Ventricular conduction disturbances involve delays in electrical conduction through either the AV node, the bundle branches (right or left), the fascicles (anterior, posterior), or a combination of these. Each of these conduction delays is referred to as a *heart block.*

The Bundle Branches

The normal electrical impulse begins in the SA node and quickly moves across the atria, depolarizing them. It then slows as it passes through the AV node and progresses rapidly into the bundle of His. From there it moves into the right and left **bundle branches** (Figure 19-1). As it progresses, it activates the intraventricular septum from left to right. The right bundle branch continues in the direction of the apex, spreading throughout the right ventricle. The left bundle branch divides further into three divisions—the septal fascicle, the anterior fascicle, and the posterior fascicle. The septal fascicle carries the impulse to the interventricular septum in a right-to-left direction. The anterior fascicle carries the impulse to the anterior (superior) portions of the left ventricle. The posterior fascicle carries the impulse to the posterior (inferior) portions of the left ventricle. The very small Purkinje fibers take the current from the bundle branches to the individual myocardial cells. The right bundle branch does not divide into separate fascicles (or at least they have not yet been identified anatomically).

QUESTION

2. Which side of the interventricular septum is the first to be depolarized?

The normal QRS begins with activation of the septum from left to right, which produces a small R wave in leads V_1 and V_2 (as the impulse travels toward the positive electrode) and a small Q wave in leads V_5 and V_6 (as the impulse travels away from the positive electrode). Then, as the impulse moves through the left ventricle, it produces a deep S wave in V_1 and V_2 (as it is moving away from the positive electrode) and a tall R wave in V_5 and V_6 (as the impulse is traveling toward the positive electrode). The deep S wave and tall R wave represent the electrical dominance of the left ventricle.

1. Electrical impulses originate in the SA node and travel across the wall of the atrium (*arrows*) from the SA node to the AV node

2. Electrical impulses pass through the AV node and along the bundle of His, which extends from the AV node, through the fibrous skeleton, into the interventricular septum

3. The bundle of His divides into right and left bundle branches and electrical impulses descend to the apex of each ventricle along the bundle branches

4. Electrical impulses are carried by the Purkinje fibers from the bundle branches to the ventricular walls

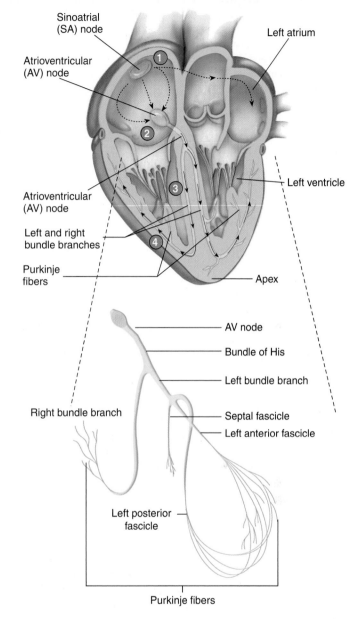

Sinoatrial (SA) node
Left atrium
Atrioventricular (AV) node
Left ventricle
Atrioventricular (AV) node
Left and right bundle branches
Purkinje fibers
Apex

AV node
Bundle of His
Left bundle branch
Septal fascicle
Left anterior fascicle

Enlarged section of the His-Purkinje system
Right bundle branch

Left posterior fascicle

Purkinje fibers

Figure 19-1
The heart's conduction system with enlarged section showing the His-Purkinje system and the three divisions of the left bundle branch.

The right and left ventricles are quickly and simultaneously stimulated so that the QRS complex is narrow—0.10 seconds in duration or less (Figure 19-2). Although depolarization of both ventricles is simultaneous, the electrical forces of the left ventricle dominate those of the right because the mass of the left ventricle is so much larger than that of the right. This results in the electrical axis being drawn leftward, lying between 0 degrees and +90 degrees. Thus, with normal ventricular depolarization, the QRS complex is narrow and the electrical axis is between 0 degrees and +90 degrees.

KEY CONCEPT
With normal ventricular depolarization, the QRS complex is narrow—0.10 seconds or less in duration—and the electrical axis lies between 0 degrees and +90 degrees.

Figure 19-2
The QRS complex represents
ventricular depolarization
from beginning to end and is
narrow—0.10 seconds or less
in duration.

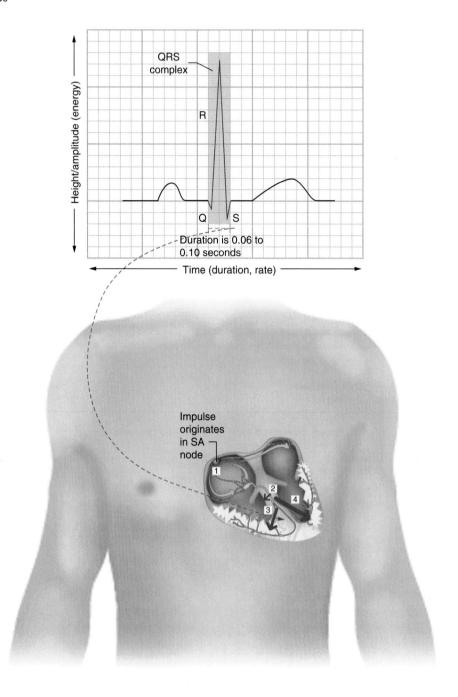

LO 19.3

Bundle Branch Block

A **bundle branch block** leads to one or both of the bundle branches failing
to conduct impulses (Figure 19-3). This produces a delay in the depolarization of the ventricle it supplies because the impulse must travel through the
surrounding muscle (which conducts more slowly than the specialized tissue
of the bundle branch) to stimulate the ventricle below the block. Depolarization of the individual ventricles is still of normal duration; however, the

Impulse originates in SA node

Figure 19-3
In bundle branch block, conduction of the electrical impulse is partially or completely blocked in one of the bundle branches while conduction (1) continues uninterrupted through the unaffected bundle branch. Then the impulse activates the intraventricular septum (2). Finally, the impulse activates the other ventricle (3).

unblocked ventricle will depolarize out of synch with the blocked ventricle, thus producing wider than normal QRS complexes.

Bundle branch block occurs only in supraventricular rhythms (sinus, atrial, and junctional) because the impulse originates above the ventricles and travels down through the bundle branches in these rhythms. Conversely, ventricular rhythms originate from the ventricular tissue and therefore do not conduct through the bundle branches to stimulate the ventricles.

The most telling sign of bundle branch block is a wide QRS complex, at least 0.12 seconds (three small squares) or more in duration. As such, bundle branch block is diagnosed by first analyzing the width of the QRS complexes.

Then we look at the morphology. Because of the nonsimultaneous depolarization of the ventricles (one depolarizes normally while the other is delayed), it produces what looks like two QRS complexes (Figure 19-4) superimposed

KEY CONCEPT
Bundle branch block is a disorder that leads to one or both of the bundle branches failing to conduct impulses. This produces a delay in the depolarization of the ventricle it supplies.

QUESTION
3. What is the normal duration of the QRS complex?

Figure 19-4
QRS complex changes in bundle branch block are due to depolarization of the ventricles being out of sync with one another.

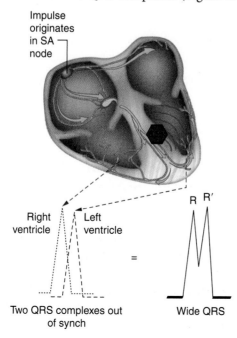

Impulse originates in SA node

Right ventricle   Left ventricle

=

R R'

Two QRS complexes out of synch

Wide QRS

Figure 19-5
QRS complexes seen with bundle branch block are wider than normal and may appear as two complexes joined together.

The two R waves are named in sequential order—R and R′

The QRS complex is at least 0.12 seconds (three small squares) or greater

on one another. The ECG records this combined electrical activity as notched or slurred QRS complexes or QRS complexes having two peaks (sometimes referred to as an *M like* or a *rabbit ears* appearance).

When we see two R waves, we name them in sequential order, the R and R′. The R′ is referred to as *R prime* and represents delayed depolarization of the blocked ventricle (Figure 19-5).

If only a portion of the left bundle branch is blocked, this is called a *fascicular block*.

Possible sites of block within the ventricular conduction system include

- The right bundle branch—right bundle branch block
- The left bundle branch—left bundle branch block
- The left anterior fascicle—left anterior fascicular block (LAFB), also called left *anterior hemiblock* (LAHB)
- The left posterior fascicle—left posterior fascicular block (LPFB), also called left posterior hemiblock (LPHB)
- Any combination of these or along with prolongation of the PR interval (first degree AV block)

LO 19.4

Right Bundle Branch Block

With **right bundle branch block (RBBB)**, conduction through the right bundle branch is blocked, causing depolarization of the right ventricle to be delayed; conduction does not start until the left ventricle is almost fully depolarized (Figure 19-6).

The impulse starts off normally. It is initiated in the SA node and travels through the atria, depolarizing them. It and then transverses the AV node and passes through the bundle of His. It then moves down the left bundle, initiates septal depolarization, and at the same time attempts to travel down the right bundle branch. Because the right bundle is blocked, the impulse travels

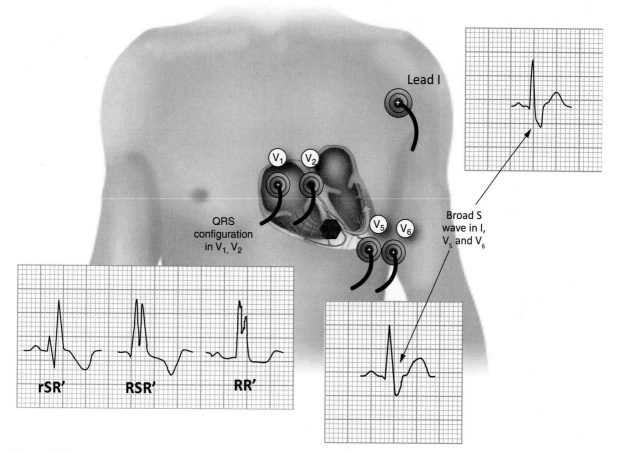

Figure 19-6
In RBBB, conduction through the right bundle is blocked, causing depolarization of the right ventricle to be delayed; conduction does not start until the left ventricle is almost fully depolarized.

through the anterior and posterior fascicles and into the Purkinje fibers of the left ventricle. The impulse then travels from the left ventricle across the septum and depolarizes the right ventricle. Its movement across the ventricles is slower than normal because it is moving cell by cell instead of via the faster conduction pathways.

RBBB occurs with anterior wall MI, coronary artery disease, hypertension, scar tissue that develops after heart surgery, viral or bacterial infection of the heart muscle (myocarditis), and pulmonary embolism. It may also be caused, as can any type of heart block, by drug toxicity. Further, it can also be due to a heart abnormality that's present at birth (congenital), such as atrial septal defect (a hole in the wall separating the upper chambers of the heart).

RBBB causes the QRS complex to have a unique shape. This occurs because of late depolarization of the right ventricle.

In RBBB the QRS begins normally with activation of the septum from left to right, which produces a small R wave in leads V_1 and V_2 (as the impulse

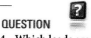

QUESTION
4. **Which leads are best for assessing the electrical activity in the right ventricle?**

travels toward the positive electrode) and a small Q wave in leads V_5 and V_6 (as the impulse travels away from the positive electrode). Then, as the impulse moves through the left ventricle, it produces an S wave in V_1 and V_2 (as it is moving away from the positive electrode) and an R wave in V_5 and V_6 (as it is traveling toward the positive electrode). Then, the delayed depolarization of the right ventricle produces a tall R' wave in leads V_1 and V_2 (as it is moving toward the positive electrode) and a broad S wave in lead V_5 and V_6 (as it is moving away from the positive electrode), as well as the other leads overlying the left ventricle (I and aV_L). This produces a wide QRS complex that appears in one of several different shapes (see Figure 19-6); an rSR' complex with a wide S and R' wave, an rsR' complex with a wide R' wave, or a wide R wave with an M-shaped appearance. Some liken its appearance to rabbit ears. Also, in most leads, the T waves deflect opposite that of the QRS deflection.

In the left lateral leads, late right ventricular depolarization produces reciprocal late broad S waves.

KEY CONCEPT

To diagnose RBBB, check for an R, R' wave in leads V_1 or V_2. The appearance of right bundle block has been likened to the letter M.

Characteristics of RBBB
• Tall, wide QRS complexes in leads V_1 and V_2 that appear in one of several different shapes:
—an rSR' complex with a wide S and R' wave
—an rsR' complex with a wide R' wave
—a wide R wave with an M-shaped appearance
• Reciprocal late broad S waves in I, aV_L, V_5, and V_6
• A T wave that deflects opposite of the QRS complex in most leads

LO 19.5

Left Bundle Branch Block

In **left bundle branch block (LBBB),** depolarization of the left ventricle is delayed (Figure 19-7). Again, the impulse starts off normally. It is initiated in the SA node and travels through the atria, depolarizing them. It then transverses the AV node, passes through the bundle of His, and attempts to move down the right and left bundle branches. It passes through the right bundle normally but is blocked from passing through the left bundle. Following right ventricular depolarization, the impulse travels across the septum and depolarizes the left ventricle. Its movement across the ventricle is slower than normal because depolarization is moving cell by cell instead of via the faster conduction pathways of the anterior and posterior fascicles and Purkinje fibers.

LBBB can be caused by anterior wall MI; hypertensive heart disease; aortic stenosis; degenerative changes of the conduction system; or thickened, stiffened, or weakened heart muscle (cardiomyopathy).

Activation of the ventricles in the left bundle branch is greatly different than what occurs in the normal heart. This leads to a much different-looking QRS complex.

Figure 19-7
In LBBB, conduction through the left bundle is blocked, causing depolarization of the left ventricle to be delayed; it does not start until the right ventricle is almost fully depolarized.

In leads V_1 and V_2 (which overlie the right ventricle), the initial movement of the impulse from right to left instead of left to right through the septum can produce a small Q wave (which is often not seen) as the impulse is traveling away from the positive electrode. Then as the right ventricle depolarizes, it can appear as a very small R wave (or it may even be absent) as the impulse is now moving toward the positive electrode. The abnormal depolarization of the left ventricle produces a wide, largely negative S wave as the current is moving away from the positive electrode. This is referred to as a wide rS complex. If the R wave is absent, it is an entirely negative and wide QS complex.

Normally, in leads V_5, V_6, I, and aV_L (which overlie the left ventricle), the QRS complexes are seen as a Q wave and tall R wave. In LBBB, because the impulse moves from right to left through the septum by way of the right ventricle (instead of from left to right), there is an absence of a Q wave in these leads. Then, as the impulse is traveling toward the positive electrode, the slow left ventricular depolarization produces a wide, tall, slurred R wave (see Figure 19-7). The R waves can also be flattened on top or notched (with two tiny points). However, the M-shaped appearance is less likely to be seen than in RBBB.

Also, in most leads, the T wave deflection is opposite that of the QRS deflection, without a Q or S wave.

Characteristics of LBBB
• Tall, wide, slurred R waves in I, aV$_L$, V$_5$, and V$_6$, (the R waves can also be flattened on top or notched)
• Wide, largely negative rS complexes or entirely negative QS complexes in V$_1$ and V$_2$
• A T wave that deflects opposite of the QRS complex in most leads

LO 19.6

Bundle Branch Block and Repolarization

Similar to repolarization changes seen in hypertrophy, repolarization abnormalities may occur in both RBBB and LBBB. These changes mimic those seen with myocardial ischemia/injury, such as ST segment depression and T-wave inversion.

In RBBB, ST segment depression and T-wave inversion (see Figure 19-6) is seen in the right precordial leads (V$_1$ and V$_2$). Likewise, in LBBB, ST segment depression and T-wave inversion (Figure 19-7) may be seen in most leads, particularly the left precordial leads (V$_5$ and V$_6$).

LO 19.7

Incomplete Bundle Branch Block

At times either the right or the left bundle branch conducts the electrical impulse more slowly than normal, but is not totally blocked. When this happens on the side of the slow conduction, the electrical impulse reaches the ventricle slightly later than normal. As a result, the QRS complex may have a similar appearance to bundle branch block and is slightly wider than normal (Figure 19-8), but it is not as wide as with complete bundle branch block (having a duration of no greater 0.11 seconds). This slight widening of the QRS is often referred to as **incomplete bundle branch block.** It may also be called an *intraventricular conduction defect* (or an IVCD).

Whereas incomplete bundle branch block may indicate underlying heart disease, incomplete bundle branch block is often of no significance, especially when it occurs on the right side (i.e., incomplete RBBB).

LO 19.8

Hemiblock

As previously described, the left bundle branch consists of three separate branches or fascicles. A block in conduction through one of the fascicles is called **hemiblock.** There are many fascicles in the heart's conduction system,

Figure 19-8
Incomplete bundle branch block.

0.11 seconds or less in duration

but the anterior and posterior fascicles of the left bundle branch are the most clinically significant. Whereas the ECG appearance of anterior and posterior hemiblocks differs from that of bundle branch blocks, the mechanism is essentially the same—the normal conduction pathway is blocked, and the affected myocardium receives its electrical stimulation via cell-to-cell depolarization and retrograde conduction from the remaining intact parts of the conduction system. Whereas there is minimal prolongation with hemiblock, it is not enough to widen the QRS complex to any appreciable degree. However, the morphology of the QRS complex does change.

Axis deviation is the key ECG characteristic of hemiblocks. It occurs because, when one fascicle is blocked, the electrical current travels down the other to stimulate the heart. This causes the axis to shift accordingly. When diagnosing hemiblock, be sure to rule out other causes of axis deviation, such as ventricular hypertrophy.

KEY CONCEPT
Hemiblocks cause axis deviation.

The anterior fascicle is longer and thinner and has a more fragile blood supply than the posterior fascicle, so LAHB is far more common than LPHB. While LAHB can be seen in both normal and diseased hearts, LPHB almost always is associated with heart disease.

QUESTION
5. What ECG changes tell us left axis deviation is present?

Left Anterior Hemiblock

LO 19.9

With LAHB, conduction down the left anterior fascicle is blocked (Figure 19-9). For this reason, the electrical impulse rushes down the left posterior fascicle to the inferior surface of the heart. Depolarization of the left ventricle occurs, progressing in an inferior-to-superior and right-to-left direction. The axis of ventricular depolarization is therefore redirected upward and slightly to the left, producing tall positive R waves in the left lateral leads and deep S waves inferiorly. This results in left axis deviation.

Left Posterior Hemiblock

KEY CONCEPT
LAHB results in left axis deviation.

In LPHB, the electrical impulse rushes down the left anterior fascicle, resulting in ventricular myocardial depolarization occurring in a superior-to-inferior

Figure 19-9
With LAHB, conduction down the left anterior fascicle is blocked, resulting in all the current rushing down the left posterior fascicle to the inferior surface of the heart. There are tall positive R waves in the left lateral leads (lead I), deep S waves inferiorly (lead aV$_F$), and left axis deviation.

KEY CONCEPT
LPHB results in right axis deviation.

and left-to-right direction (Figure 19-10). Therefore, the main electrical axis is directed downward and to the right, producing tall R waves inferiorly and deep S waves in the left lateral leads. This results in right axis deviation.

In contrast to complete LBBB and RBBB, the QRS complex in hemiblock S is not prolonged.

Patients with any type of ventricular conduction block and especially those with a combination of blocks are at high risk of developing complete heart block.

LO 19.10

Bifascicular and Trifascicular Blocks

Although a 2009 American Heart Association Electrocardiography and Arrhythmias Committee, Council on Clinical Cardiology; the American College of Cardiology Foundation; and the Heart Rhythm Society (AHA/ACCF/HRS) scientific statement on the standardization and interpretation of the electrocardiogram recommended against using the terms *bifascicular* and *trifascicular block*

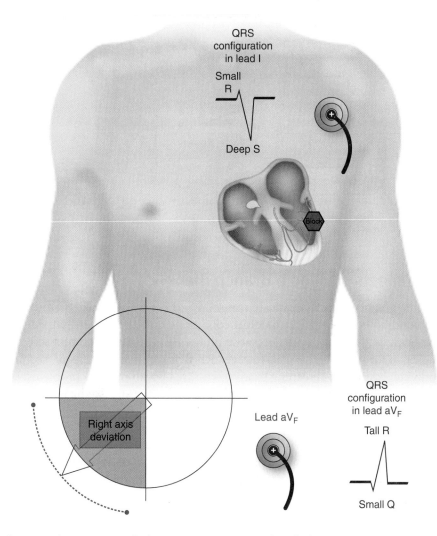

QRS
configuration
in lead I

Small
R

Deep S

Right axis
deviation

Lead aV_F

QRS
configuration
in lead aV_F

Tall R

Small Q

because these patterns lack unique anatomic and pathologic substrates, we have included coverage of these terms because they are still widely used.

Bifascicular block is a conduction disturbance in which two of the three main fascicles of the His/Purkinje system are blocked. Most often, it refers to a combination of RBBB and either LAHB (more commonly) or LPHB.

Some authors include LBBB in the definition of bifascicular block because the block occurs above the bifurcation of the left anterior and left posterior fascicles of the left bundle branch.

Trifascicular block is a conduction disturbance in which there are three features seen on the ECG (Figure 19-11):

- Prolongation of the PR interval (first degree AV block)
- RBBB
- Either LAFB or LPFB

Trifascicular block is uncommon.

Figure 19-11
Trifascicular block

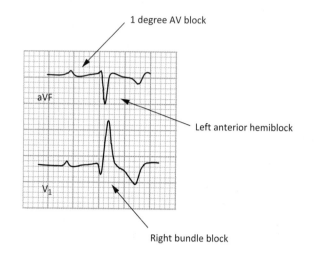

1 degree AV block

aVF

Left anterior hemiblock

V₁

Right bundle block

LO 19.11

Treatments of Bundle Branch Block

Bundle branch block is relatively common and occurs in a variety of medical conditions. It is seen in medical conditions that affect the right side of the heart or the lungs, so its presence on the ECG should prompt a screening exam for such conditions. However, RBBB is common in normal, healthy individuals, and the screening exam often turns up no medical problems. In such cases, RBBB has no apparent medical significance and can be written off as a "normal variant" and safely ignored.

In contrast, LBBB usually indicates underlying cardiac pathology. Whereas, occasionally, LBBB occurs in apparently healthy people, its appearance should prompt a thorough assessment for underlying cardiac problems.

Fortunately, in general it is quite uncommon for stable bundle branch block to progress to complete heart block. For this reason, despite the fact that bundle branch block is a common ECG finding, it does not require pacemaker implantation. Often patients can be monitored to determine if they progress to a more complete block.

However, a few conditions in which people with bundle branch block require implantation of a pacemaker include:

1. RBBB along with LAHB, which is associated with acute MI. Here, the conduction system disease tends to be unstable and can progress to complete heart block. These patients often need pacemakers.

2. When bundle branch block is associated with syncope. Generally speaking, an electrophysiology study should be considered to test for impending complete heart block. A permanent pacemaker can then be used to eliminate the problem.

3. In certain patients with dilated cardiomyopathy and either complete or incomplete bundle branch block. Here a new form of pacing—called *CRT*—has been shown to improve symptoms and prolong life. CRT can be considered in any patient with heart failure and bundle branch block.

Practice Makes Perfect

For the following 12-lead ECGs, identify if bundle branch block or hemiblock are present and the type.

1.

2.

3.

4.

5.

6.

Key Points 🔍

- Ventricular conduction disturbances involve delays in electrical conduction through either the AV node, the bundle branches (right or left), the fascicles (anterior, posterior), or a combination of these.

- The bundle of His divides to form the right and left bundle branches. The left bundle branch then divides to form the septal, anterior, and posterior fascicles.

- The QRS complex is normally narrow—less than 0.10 seconds in duration—and the electrical axis lies between 0 degrees and +90 degrees.

- Bundle branch block is a disorder that leads to one or both of the bundle branches failing to conduct impulses. This produces a delay in the depolarization of the ventricle it supplies.

- In bundle branch block you will see widened QRS complexes in the leads that view the right and left ventricles. You may also see an R, R′ configuration.

- To diagnose RBBB, check for widened QRS complexes (and R, R′) in leads V_1 or V_2.

- To diagnose LBBB, check for widened QRS complexes (and R, R′) in leads V_5 or V_6.

- Sometimes an R, R′ wave is seen in a QRS complex of normal duration. This is called *incomplete bundle branch block*.

- Similar to the repolarization abnormalities seen in hypertrophy, so too can these changes be seen in both RBBB and LBBB.

- If only a portion of the left bundle branch is blocked, it is called a *fascicular block*.

- Hemiblocks cause axis deviation. LAHB results in left axis deviation. LPHB results in right axis deviation.

- Bundle branch block often does not require treatment.

Assess Your Understanding

The following questions give you a chance to assess your understanding of the material discussed in this chapter. The answers can be found in Appendix A.

1. The QRS complex
   a. is normally narrow.
   b. is greater than 0.5 seconds in direction.
   c. begins just as the impulse enters the AV node.
   d. represents ventricular repolarization.

2. With normal ventricular depolarization, the electrical axis is drawn
   a. rightward, between 0 degrees and 90 degrees.
   b. leftward, between 0 degrees and 90 degrees.
   c. upward, at 45 degrees.
   d. downward, between 0 degrees and 30 degrees.

3. Bundle branch block
   a. causes narrowed QRS complexes to appear on the ECG.
   b. is a disorder in which one or both of the bundle branches fails to conduct impulses.
   c. accelerates depolarization of the ventricle it supplies.
   d. is diagnosed by analyzing only the width of the QRS complexes.

4. To diagnose RBBB, you check for an R R′ in leads
   a. aV_F and aV_L.
   b. I and II.
   c. V_1 or V_2.
   d. V_3 or V_4.

5. Hemiblocks
   a. cause axis deviation.
   b. result from accessory pathways between the atria and ventricles.
   c. result in R waves being superimposed on the other.
   d. lead to a complete absence in conduction below the level of block.

Referring to the scenario at the beginning of this chapter, answer the following questions.

6. The appearance of the QRS complex in this case indicates the presence of a(n)
   a. complete AV heart block.
   b. RBBB.
   c. incomplete heart block.
   d. 1st-degree AV heart block.

7. The rabbit ear appearance of the QRS complex is technically referred to as
   a. QR′S.
   b. Q′R′S′.
   c. RR′.
   d. R′SR.

Answers to Sidebar Questions

1. The initial electrical impulse begins high in the right atrium, in the SA node. It travels through the atria via intraatrial and intranodal pathways to the AV node. **p. 552**

2. Normally, the left side of the interventricular septum is the first part of the ventricle to be depolarized. The impulse passes through the septum to the other side. **p. 552**

3. The normal duration of the QRS complex is less than 0.10 seconds (2 ½ small squares or less). **p. 555**

4. The leads overlying the right ventricle are V_1 and V_2 so they are best for assessing the electrical activity of that ventricle. **p. 557**

5. If the QRS complex deflection is positive in both leads I and aV_F, the electrical axis is normal. If the QRS complex in lead I is upright and the QRS complex in lead aV_F has a negative deflection, then left axis deviation exists. **p. 561**

What's Online

Go to www.mhhe.com/shadeECG2e to find:

- Presentations on chapter content
- Additional practice tracings for identifying bundle branch block
- Chapter quiz
- Fill-in-the-blank exercises and answers
- In-depth answers to Practice Makes Perfect ECG tracings and Assess Your Understanding questions

20 Myocardial Ischemia, Injury, and Infarction

Chapter Outline

Coronary Circulation

The ECG Waveforms

Coronary Artery Disease

ECG Indicators of Ischemia, Injury, and Infarction

Criteria for Diagnosing Myocardial Infarction

Identifying the Myocardial Infarction Location

Treatment of Myocardial Infarction

Learning Objectives

LO 20.1 Describe how the myocardium is perfused by the coronary vasculature.

LO 20.2 Recall the normal morphology of the Q wave, ST segment, and T wave.

LO 20.3 Define the terms *coronary artery disease, myocardial ischemia, myocardial injury,* and *myocardial infarction.*

LO 20.4 Describe the ECG changes that occur with myocardial ischemia, injury, and infarction.

LO 20.5 List the criteria for diagnosing MI.

LO 20.6 Describe the ECG changes that can be used to identify MI.

LO 20.7 State how the location of myocardial ischemia, injury, and infarction can be identified.

LO 20.8 Recall the ECG leads that can be used to identify myocardial ischemia, injury, and infarction in various areas of the heart.

LO 20.9 Describe how a posterior MI can be identified.

Case History

EMS is called to a local office building to evaluate a 46-year-old man complaining of chest pain. Upon entering the man's office, the paramedics see an ashen, grey, and diaphoretic middle-aged man sitting at his desk. They notice an overflowing ashtray on the desk as they move to his side.

The paramedics perform a rapid assessment and find the patient to be hypertensive with labored respirations. Oxygen is applied and an IV established. Following their cardiac protocol, the paramedics give the patient an aspirin, start him on nitroglycerin, and obtain a 12-lead ECG.

The 12-lead ECG shows 5 mm of ST elevation in leads II, III, and aV_F indicating that the chest pain may be from a heart attack. The patient gives the paramedics permission to transport him to the nearest cardiac center.

The paramedics call the cardiac center and speak to the emergency medicine physician on duty. They have a diagnostic 12-lead ECG, so the physician mobilizes the cardiac team, and the patient is taken immediately for emergent angioplasty. Three days later, the cardiologist tells the patient that because of the rapid care of the paramedics, combined with their ability to obtain and interpret a 12-lead ECG, he did not sustain any permanent damage to his heart and should fully recover.

LO 20.1

KEY CONCEPT

The oxygen and nutrient demand of the heart is extremely high. The coronary arteries deliver the needed blood supply to the myocardial cells.

Coronary Circulation

The heart constantly pumps blood to the body. Because of this, its oxygen consumption is proportionately greater than that of any other single organ. With the oxygen demand in the myocardial cells being so high, the heart must have its own blood supply. The coronary arteries provide a continuous supply of oxygen and nutrients to the myocardial cells.

Arising from the aorta just above the aortic valve, the right and left coronary arteries lie on the heart's surface and have many branches that penetrate into all parts of the heart. The terminal branches of the arteries have many interconnections, forming an extensive vascular network—each perfusing a particular portion of the myocardium.

Right Main Coronary Artery

The **right main coronary artery** originates from the right side of the aorta and passes along the atrioventricular sulcus between the right atrium and right ventricle (Figure 20-1A). It then divides into two branches, the marginal artery and the posterior interventricular artery. The portion of the myocardium supplied by the right coronary artery includes the right atrium, right ventricle, inferior and posterior walls of the left ventricle, and posterior one-third of the interventricular septum. The right coronary artery also supplies blood to the SA node (in about 50% to 60% of the population), to the AV node (in about 80% to 95% of the population), and to the posterior-inferior fascicle of the left bundle branch.

Left Main Coronary Artery

The **left main coronary artery** originates from the left side of the aorta. It divides into the anterior descending and circumflex branches (Figure 20-1B). The anterior descending artery perfuses the anterior surface and part of the lateral surface of the left ventricle and the anterior two-thirds of the interventricular septum. Branches of the anterior descending artery, the diagonal artery, and the septal perforators help supply blood to the lateral walls of the left ventricle. The circumflex artery supplies the left atrium and the anterolateral, posterolateral, and the posterior wall of the left ventricle.

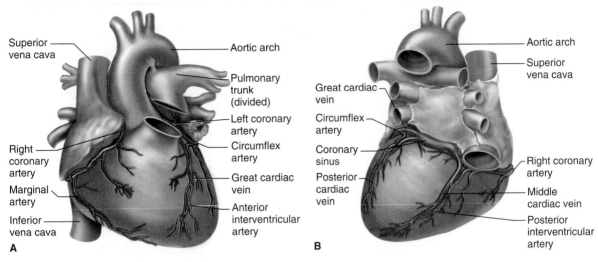

Figure 20-1
The coronary blood vessels. (A) Anterior aspect. (B) Posterior aspect.

The anterior descending artery supplies blood to the majority of the right bundle branch. It also supplies blood to both the anterior and posterior fascicles of the left bundle branch. The circumflex artery supplies blood to the SA node (in about 40% to 50% of the population) and the AV node (in about 10% to 15% of the population).

Between the coronary arterioles are anatomic connections called *anastomoses*. These anastomoses allow the development of alternative routes for blood to flow in the event of blockage. This is referred to as *collateral circulation*.

Coronary Veins

Deoxygenated venous blood from the heart drains into five different coronary veins that empty into the right atrium via the coronary sinus. This blood then mixes with the systemic venous return.

KEY CONCEPT
The coronary veins return deoxygenated venous blood from the heart to the right atrium via the coronary sinus.

Increased Oxygen Needs

The resting heart extracts most of the oxygen from the coronary blood as it flows through the coronary arteries surrounding the heart muscle. Coronary perfusion occurs during diastole, when the heart is relaxed. Increased oxygen demands of the myocardium that result from exercise or emotional stress can only be satisfied by increases in coronary blood flow, mostly through vasodilation.

The need for oxygen in local heart tissue causes the arteries to dilate, which increases blood flow. Stimulation of the sympathetic nervous system also affects coronary blood flow. The coronary blood vessels are innervated by both alpha and beta receptors. Stimulation of the alpha receptors leads to vasoconstriction whereas stimulation of certain beta receptors causes vasodilation.

KEY CONCEPT
Increased myocardial oxygen demands can be satisfied only by increases in coronary blood flow, mostly through vasodilation.

LO 20.2

The ECG Waveforms

As discussed in earlier chapters, the electrical impulse that initiates the heart-beat normally arises from the SA node. From there it travels through the atria to the AV node, where there is a delay in the conduction of the impulse before it is sent to the ventricles. This delay in conduction is represented by a flat line, called the *PR segment* (Figure 20-2). The PR segment can be used as a baseline from which to evaluate depression or elevation of the ST segment. Alternatively, the flat line between the T wave and the P wave of the following beat (called the *TP segment*) can also be used to evaluate depression or elevation of the ST segment.

The impulse then travels through the bundle of His, the right and left bundle branches, and the Purkinje fibers. The spread of impulse through the ventricles produces the QRS complex.

KEY CONCEPT

ST segment depression or elevation can be evaluated by comparing the ST segment with the PR segment.

Q Waves

Remember, the interventricular septum is the wall of muscle separating the right and left ventricles. A tiny septal branch (fascicle) of the left bundle branch conducts the wave of depolarization to the interventricular septum. It happens so quickly that septal depolarization is not always visible on the ECG, but when it is, this small left-to-right depolarization produces a tiny, negative deflection from the baseline called the *Q wave* (Figure 20-3). It may be seen in leads I, aV_L, V_5, V_6, and sometimes in the inferior leads and in V_3 and V_4. When it is present, the normal, and clinically insignificant, Q wave should have a duration of less than 0.04 seconds (1 mm or 1 small square) and be less than 25% the amplitude of the R wave in that lead.

KEY CONCEPT

The Q wave is the first part of the QRS complex. It is the first downward, or negative, deflection from the baseline and is not always present.

Figure 20-2
The PR segment or TP segment can be used as a baseline to evaluate changes in the ST segment, such as depression or elevation.

Figure 20-3
The Q wave is the first part of the QRS complex; it is a tiny negative deflection from the baseline.

Characteristics of a Normal Q Wave

- Small negative deflection from the baseline

- Duration of less than 0.04 seconds (1 mm or 1 small square)

- Less than 25% the amplitude of the R wave in that lead

Normal ST Segments

The ST segment is the line that follows the QRS complex and connects it to the T wave (Figure 20-4). The term *ST segment* is used regardless of whether the final wave of the QRS complex is an R or an S wave. It begins at the isoelectric line extending from the S wave until it gradually curves upward to the T wave. During the period of the ST segment, the ventricles are beginning to repolarize. Under normal circumstances, the ST segment appears as a flat line

Figure 20-4
The ST segment is the line that follows the QRS complex and connects it to the T wave.

QUESTION
1. Why are T waves larger in the precordial leads than the limb leads?
Note: Answers to Sidebar Questions can be found at the end of the chapter.

REMINDER
Remember, atrial repolarization occurs during the QRS complex and is not visible on the regular ECG.

QUESTION
2. Why is the direction of the T wave the same as the QRS complex?

(neither positive nor negative), although it may vary by 0.5 to 1.0 mm in some precordial leads. The point that marks the end of the QRS and the beginning of the ST segment is known as the *J point.*

Again, the PR segment is used as the baseline from which to evaluate the degree of displacement of the ST segment from the isoelectric line. To determine this, measure at a point 0.04 seconds (one small box) after the J point. The ST segment is considered elevated if it is above the baseline and considered depressed if it is below it.

Characteristics of a Normal ST Segment

- Flat line
- Follows the QRS complex and connects it to the T wave
- Can vary by 0.5 to 1.0 mm in some precordial leads

Normal T Waves

Next, we should see the T wave (Figure 20-5). The T wave represents the completion of ventricular repolarization. It is larger than the P wave and slightly asymmetrical. The peak of the T wave is closer to the end than the beginning, and the first half has a more gradual slope than the second half. Normally, the T wave is not more than 5 mm to 6 mm in height in the limb leads or 10 mm to 12 mm in height in any precordial lead. The T wave is normally oriented in the same direction as its associated QRS complex. T waves are normally positive in leads I and II and V_2 to V_6 and negative in lead aV_R. They are also positive in aV_L and aV_F but may be negative if the QRS complex is less than 6 mm in height. In leads III and V_1, the T wave may be positive or negative.

Figure 20-5
The T wave follows the ST segment and represents ventricular repolarization.

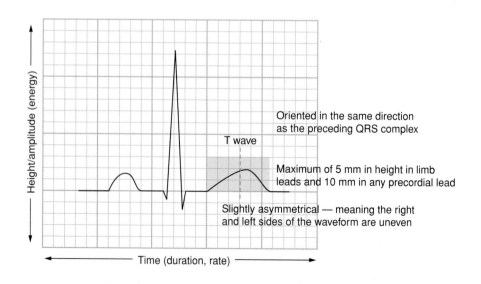

Oriented in the same direction as the preceding QRS complex

T wave

Maximum of 5 mm in height in limb leads and 10 mm in any precordial lead

Slightly asymmetrical — meaning the right and left sides of the waveform are uneven

Time (duration, rate)

Height/amplitude (energy)

Characteristics of a Normal T Wave
• Slightly asymmetrical
• Maximum of 5 mm in height in the limb leads
• Maximum of 10 mm in height in any precordial lead
• Oriented in the same direction as the preceding QRS complex

Coronary Artery Disease

LO 20.3

Any major interruption of blood flow through the coronary arteries can cause ischemia, injury, and infarction of the heart muscle. This can lead to impairment of myocardial function and sudden death.

Coronary artery disease is an umbrella term for the various diseases that reduce or stop blood flow through the coronary arteries. **Atherosclerosis** accounts for over 90% of the cases of coronary artery disease.

Atherosclerosis is a gradual, progressive process involving obstruction and hardening of the arterial wall. It begins with small deposits of fatty material, particularly cholesterol, invading the intima, the inner lining, of the arteries (Figure 20-6). This produces a nonobstructive lesion called a *fatty streak*. Later, these areas of deposit become invaded by fibrous tissue, including lipoprotein-filled smooth muscle cells, collagen, and muscle fibers that become calcified and harden into plaque. Eventually, the plaque infiltrates the arterial wall, and the intima becomes thickened, hardened, and inelastic. This leads to narrowing of these vessels and a reduction of blood flow through them. If narrowing of the artery reaches the stage where blood flow is insufficient to meet the oxygen demands of the myocardium, coronary artery disease is said to exist.

KEY CONCEPT
Interruption of coronary artery blood flow can lead to myocardial ischemia, injury, and infarction.

We use the term **acute coronary syndrome** to denote any group of clinical symptoms compatible with acute myocardial ischemia. Acute myocardial ischemia is chest pain due to insufficient blood supply to the heart muscle that results from coronary artery disease (also called *coronary heart disease*).

Myocardial Ischemia

Myocardial ischemia is a lack of oxygen and nutrients to the myocardium (Figure 20-7). It typically occurs when the heart has a greater need for oxygen than the narrowed coronary arteries can deliver or when there is a loss of blood supply to the myocardium. Causes of myocardial ischemia include atherosclerosis, vasospasm, thrombosis, embolism, decreased ventricular filling time (such as that produced by tachycardia), and decreased filling pressure in the coronary arteries (such as that caused by severe hypotension or aortic valve disease).

WANT MORE INFORMATION?
Visit the Fast & Easy ECGs Website at www.mhhe.com/ shadeECG2e. Also, for a quick reference source to help you recall the indicators of myocardial ischemia, injury, and infarction while in the field or clinical setting, refer to the ECG Pocket Guide.

Normal coronary artery

Enlarged view

Artery

Cholesterol particles circulating in blood stream

Cholesterol deposited in lining of artery

Buildup of fibrous tissue begins

Plaques form

Development and progression

Atherosclerosis

Figure 20-6
Development and progression of coronary artery disease.

Figure 20-7
Myocardial ischemia is a lack of nutrients and oxygen to the myocardium.

Ischemia

Angina

When ischemia occurs due to an intermittent shortage of oxygen to the myocardium brought on by exertion, emotional stress, or even the stress of cold weather, it produces chest pain, also known as **angina** or **angina pectoris.** The ischemia is usually relieved within 2 to 10 minutes of rest or by administration of a medicine such as nitroglycerin that dilates the coronary arteries and allows the needed blood (and oxygen) to flow to the myocardium. A patient who has angina may remain stable for many years or may go on to experience an infarction. Angina is considered unstable if it is more easily provoked, becomes less predictable, and/or worsens over time.

KEY CONCEPT
Decreased delivery of oxygen and other nutrients to the myocardium can result in ischemia. Ischemia can be reversed if the supply of oxygen and nutrients is restored or increased to a level that satisfies the myocardial oxygen demand.

Ischemia as the First Phase of Myocardial Infarction

Ischemia may also be the onset of MI. As a point of information though, permanent damage can often be avoided if the blood supply is quickly restored to the ischemic tissue.

Myocardial Injury

If the myocardial oxygen demand fails to lower, the coronary artery blockage worsens, or the ischemia is allowed to progress untreated, myocardial injury will occur (Figure 20-8). **Myocardial injury** reflects a degree of cellular damage beyond ischemia. It occurs if the blood flow is not restored (and ischemia reversed) within a few minutes. The degree of injury depends on if and how quickly the blood supply is restored as well as how much myocardium is involved. If blood flow is not restored to the affected area, tissue death will occur. Treatments used to restore blood flow include administration of fibrinolytic agents, coronary angioplasty, and coronary artery bypass graft.

KEY CONCEPT
Myocardial injury will likely occur if ischemia brought about by increased myocardial oxygen demands is not resolved or if the ischemia is allowed to progress untreated.

Myocardial Infarction

Myocardial infarction (MI) is the death of injured myocardial cells (Figure 20-9). It occurs when there is a sudden decrease or total cessation of blood flow through a coronary artery to an area of the myocardium. MI commonly occurs when the intima of a coronary artery ruptures, exposing

Figure 20-8
Myocardial injury is a degree of cellular damage beyond ischemia.

Figure 20-9
Myocardial infarction is the death of injured myocardial cells.

Ischemia

Injury

Infarction

the atherosclerotic plaque to the blood within the artery. This initiates the abrupt development of a clot (thrombus). The vessel, already narrowed by the plaque, becomes completely blocked by the thrombus. The area of the heart normally supplied by the blocked artery goes through a characteristic sequence of events described as zones of ischemia, injury, and infarction. Each zone is associated with characteristic ECG changes. There is ischemic and injured myocardial tissue surrounding the infarcted area so the size of the infarction can increase if coronary perfusion is not restored. If the patient survives the acute MI, the infarcted tissue is replaced with scar tissue.

When blockage occurs in the left anterior descending artery, it is particularly dangerous because this vessel supplies a much larger portion of the total myocardial mass than the right coronary and left circumflex arteries. Even more serious is obstruction of the left main coronary artery. Significant narrowing of this short vessel causes reduction in blood flow through both the left anterior descending and circumflex arteries. This compromises the blood supply of almost the entire left ventricle. Fortunately, obstruction of the left main coronary artery occurs in only 5% to 10% of patients with symptoms of coronary artery disease.

LO 20.4

ECG Indicators of Ischemia, Injury, and Infarction

The ECG can help identify the presence of ischemia, injury, and/or MI. It can also help identify which coronary artery or branch is occluded.

Key ECG indicators of ischemia, injury, and/or MI are (Figure 20-10):

1. Changes in the T wave (peaking or inversion)
2. Changes in the ST segment (depression or elevation)
3. Enlarged Q waves or appearance of new Q waves
4. A new or presumably new bundle branch block
5. Reciprocal changes in leads facing the affected area from opposing angles

Figure 20-10
Key ECG changes with myocardial ischemia, injury, or infarction.

Although the ECG usually progresses through these three indicators during an MI, any one of these changes may be present without any of the others. For this reason, it is not unusual to see ST segment depression without T wave inversion. As we discuss ischemia, remember that it can be transient, such as in angina, or it can be related to MI.

KEY CONCEPT
The ECG can help identify the presence of ischemia, injury, and/or infarction of the heart muscle.

T Wave Changes

Inverted T Waves

Inverted T waves are a characteristic sign of myocardial ischemia (Figure 20-11) and indicate that ischemia is present through the full thickness of the myocardium. T waves invert because the lack of oxygen results in leaking of potassium from the ischemic tissue. This delays the process of repolarization.

KEY CONCEPT
With myocardial ischemia, the appearance of T waves may change.

T wave inversion may be present with angina but may also be seen during an MI due to the ischemic tissue surrounding the infarct. In transient ischemia, the ECG must be obtained as closely as possible to the onset of chest pain; otherwise, the ECG changes may disappear. The inverted T wave from

Figure 20-11
Inverted T waves are a
characteristic of myocardial
ischemia.

Ischemia

Delay in ventricular
repolarization

Inverted T wave

ischemia is symmetrical, meaning that the right and left sides of the T wave
are mirror images. T waves inverted in the leads where they should be positive are referred to as *"flipped" T waves.*

Inverted T waves will be present in the leads facing the affected area of the
myocardium. The chest leads (V_1 through V_6) are closest to the ventricles, so
they are the best for checking for T wave inversion (Figure 20-12). Also, be
sure to check the limb leads.

Aside from myocardial ischemia, there are many other causes of T wave
inversion, including pericarditis, ventricular hypertrophy, bundle branch
block, shock, electrolyte imbalance, and subarachnoid hemorrhage (Figure
20-13). Asymmetrical T waves with a gentle downslope and rapid upslope
are an indicator of inverted T waves associated with other causes rather than
inverted T waves associated with ischemia.

Inverted T waves will revert to normal if the ischemia subsides, as with angina.
T-wave inversion may persist from months to years after an MI because of the
damage done to the myocardium, which affects its ability to repolarize normally. Therefore, T-wave inversion by itself is only indicative of ischemia if it
is consistent with the patient's clinical findings and is not diagnostic of MI.

Hyperacute T Waves

Sometimes hyperacute T waves are the first sign of MI. These are abnormally tall and narrow (Figure 20-14) and can also be referred to as *peaked
T waves.* Hyperacute T waves are often not seen because they are present only

Figure 20-12
The precordial (chest) leads
are best for detecting T-wave
inversion.

Endocardium
Myocardium
Epicardium

Enlarged
view

Ischemia—
through full
thickness of
myocardium

V_2 V_3 V_4

T wave is symmetrical — meaning the right and left sides
of the waveform are the same size

Asymmetric T wave
inversion with a gentle
downward slope and
rapid upslope may be
seen in right ventricular
hypertrophy.

Deeply inverted,
wide T waves may
be seen in
subarachnoid
bleeding.

Depressed ST
segments with a very
gradual downslope is
seen with digitalis use.

Figure 20-13
Examples of T wave inversion
due to other causes.

for 2 to 30 minutes following the onset of infarction. After a period of time, these T waves invert. In general, the T wave should not be more than 6 mm high in the limb leads and 12 mm high in the precordial leads. A helpful rule to follow is this: if the T wave is more than two-thirds the height of the R wave, it is abnormal.

Peaked T waves can also been seen with hyperkalemia, so be sure to distinguish between the two conditions (early onset MI and hyperkalemia).

Figure 20-14
Abnormally tall and narrow
T waves are another sign of
MI.

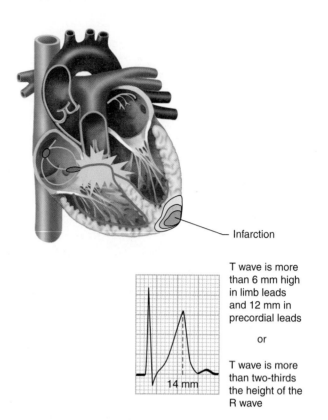

— Infarction

T wave is more
than 6 mm high
in limb leads
and 12 mm in
precordial leads

or

T wave is more
than two-thirds
the height of the
R wave

14 mm

ST Segment Changes

As with differences in the T wave appearance, changes we see in the ST segment can be due to injured myocardium delaying the process of repolarization. To measure for ST segment deviation, we draw a baseline from either the PR segment to the ST segment or the end of the T wave to the beginning of the P wave.

KEY CONCEPT

Two characteristic signs of myocardial ischemia are inverted T waves and ST segment depression.

ST Segment Depression

ST segment depression is another characteristic sign of myocardial ischemia (Figure 20-15). ST segment changes are considered significant when the ST segment falls more than 1 mm below the baseline at a point one small square (0.04 seconds) to the right of the J point and is seen in two or more leads facing the same anatomic area of the heart.

ST segments may be depressed and may or may not include T wave inversion (Figure 20-16).

Flat ST Segment Depression

KEY CONCEPT

Subendocardial infarction produces a flat depression of the ST segment.

A flat depression of the ST segment occurs with subendocardial infarction (often referred to as *subendocardial injury*) (Figure 20-17). It may be either horizontal or downsloping in leads where the QRS complex is upright. Subendocardial infarction is an infarct that does not extend through the full surface of the ventricular wall; it involves only a small area of myocardium just below the endocardial lining.

Figure 20-15
ST segment depression is another sign of myocardial ischemia.

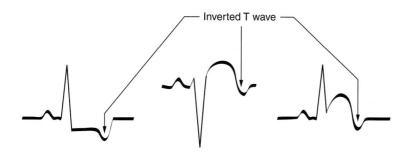

Figure 20-16
Examples of inverted T waves with ST segment depression and elevation.

ST Segment Elevation

As described earlier, myocardial injury reflects a degree of cellular damage beyond ischemia. Myocardial injury produces ST segment elevation in the leads facing the affected area (Figure 20-18). This occurs because depolarization of the injured myocardium is incomplete, with the tissue remaining electrically more positive than the uninjured areas surrounding it.

Figure 20-17
The ST segment is flat (or downsloping) in subendocardial infarction.

Myocardial injury produces a distinctive ST segment that bows upward and tends to merge imperceptibly with the T wave. The ST segment may be only slightly elevated or it may be elevated as much as 10 mm above the baseline. It is said to be significant when the ST segment is raised more than 1 mm above the baseline at a point one small square (or 0.04 seconds) to the right of the J point in the limb leads or more than 2 mm in the precordial leads, with these changes being seen in two or more leads facing the same anatomic area of the heart. ST segment depression may be seen in the leads opposite the affected area.

ST segment elevation is the earliest reliable sign that MI has occurred. It tells us that the MI is acute.

KEY CONCEPT
ST segment elevation occurs with myocardial injury. It is the earliest reliable sign that MI has occurred and tells us the MI is acute.

Figure 20-18
ST segment elevation is a sign of myocardial injury.

STEMI and NSTEMI   The ECG findings allow us to distinguish between ST elevation MI (STEMI) and non-ST elevation MI (NSTEMI). The reason this is important is that most cases of STEMI can be treated with reperfusion therapy such as thrombolysis (the use of thrombolytic drugs) or, if possible, with percutaneous coronary intervention (PCI) that includes angioplasty and stent insertion, in the hospitals that have facilities for coronary angiography. NSTEMI is managed through the use of medication, although PCI is often performed in the course of hospital admission. In patients suffering from multiple blockages and whose conditions are relatively stable, or in some extraordinary emergency cases, bypass surgery may be used as a treatment for the blocked coronary artery.

ST Elevation from Other Causes   Other than in myocardial injury, ST segment elevation may be a normal variant (so-called male pattern, which is seen in approximately 90% healthy young men) or seen in early repolarization, left ventricular hypertrophy, old left bundle branch block, pulmonary embolism, spontaneous pneumothorax, intracranial hemorrhage, hyperkalemia, and acute pericarditis (Figure 20-19). With pericarditis, an inflammation of the heart, the ST segment elevation is usually flat or concave (the middle

With pericarditis   Elevated ST segment is flat or concave

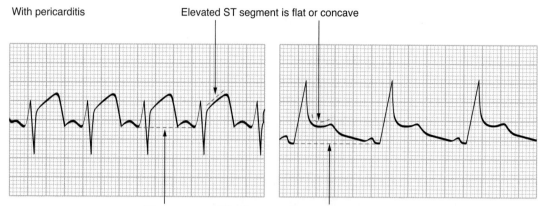

ST segments and T waves are off the baseline,
gradually angling back down to the next QRS complex

Figure 20-19
ST segment elevation may be caused by a variety of other conditions, including pericarditis.

sags downward) and is seen in all leads except aV$_R$. This resolves with time. It also seems to elevate the entire T wave off the baseline, with the baseline gradually slanting back downward all the way to the next QRS complex. The P wave is often a part of this downward slanting of the baseline.

A ventricular aneurysm, a weakening and bulging of the ventricular wall, should be suspected if ST segment elevation following an MI persists.

Q Wave Changes

The presence of pathologic (also called *significant*) Q waves indicates that irreversible myocardial damage has occurred (Figure 20-20). As the Q wave develops, the R wave disappears. Although we can expect to see the Q waves within several hours of the onset of infarction, in some patients they may take several days to appear. Further, by the time the Q waves appear, the ST segment usually has returned to the baseline. Q waves often persist for the lifetime of the patient.

For the Q waves to be considered pathologic, they must

- Be greater than 0.04 seconds in duration or;
- Have a depth at least one-third the height of the R wave in the same QRS complex and;
- Be present in two or more contiguous leads (leads that look at the same area of the heart)

Q waves develop because the infarcted areas of the heart fail to depolarize, producing an electrical void (Figure 20-21). As a result, the electrical forces of the heart are directed away from the area of infarction. An electrode overlying the infarction therefore records a deep negative deflection, a Q wave. The electrical activity of the heart moves away from aV$_R$, so a Q wave is commonly seen here and therefore is not considered significant.

Figure 20-20
Pathological Q waves are a sign of MI.

In the past, Q-wave infarcts were referred to as *transmural,* meaning that the infarct extended completely through the myocardial wall. However, recent discoveries indicate that this is not the case and confirms that the development of Q waves has more to do with the resulting electrical void than it does the amount of tissue injured.

MI can occur without Q waves developing. The only changes in the ECG with non-Q-wave infarctions are T wave inversion and ST segment elevation.

Bundle Branch Block

A new or presumably new bundle branch block can be another indicator of MI. However, you must have access to the patient's old ECGs to confirm this. A challenge with left bundle branch block (as well as pacing) is that it interferes with your ability to identify acute MI by making it difficult to accurately interpret the ST segment.

Reciprocal changes seen on the 12-lead ECG may assist you in distinguishing between MI and conditions that mimic it. Further, closely scrutinizing

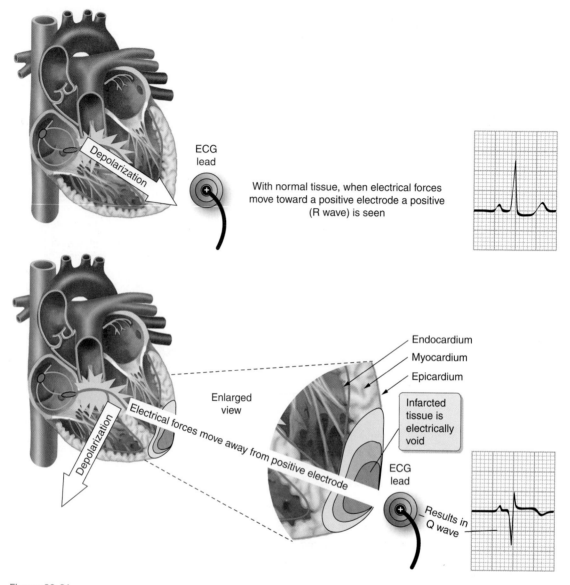

With normal tissue, when electrical forces move toward a positive electrode a positive (R wave) is seen

ECG lead

Endocardium
Myocardium
Epicardium

Infarcted tissue is electrically void

Enlarged view

Electrical forces move away from positive electrode

Depolarization

ECG lead

Results in Q wave

Figure 20-21
Q waves occur because infarcted tissue is electrically silent, allowing the wave of depolarization moving away from the positive electrode to be seen.

the contour of the ST segment may also be helpful. With MI the ST segment tends to be straight or upwardly convex (nonconcave).

Reciprocal Changes

The simplest explanation of reciprocal changes is that they are a mirror image that occurs when you have two leads viewing the same MI from opposite angles (Figure 20-22).

An example is when you have a lead located over the infarcted area and a lead on the direct opposite side of the heart. The infarcted zone is electrically

Figure 20-22
Reciprocal changes are a mirror image (opposite image) that occurs when two leads view the same infarction from opposite angles.

neutral, so the lead directly over the heart registers only an unopposed vector moving away from it. This causes the waveform to be negative, thus producing a Q wave. Next, the lead registers the other vectors contributing to the QRS and the injured tissue that causes ST elevation. The T wave is flipped because of repolarization abnormalities generated by the areas of ischemia and injury. The electrode opposite of the infarction sees an unopposed vector coming at it, giving rise to a high R wave. This lead registers the zones of ischemia as a pattern of ST depression and the injury as an upright T wave. The second lead essentially sees the mirror image of what the first electrode saw. The recording made by the lead on the wall opposite the MI is registering the reciprocal change of that MI. This concept is particularly important as it relates to looking for ECG changes in areas of the heart (posterior and the right ventricle) where there is not a lead directly over that area.

ECG Evolution during Myocardial Infarction

During MI the ECG often evolves through three stages (Figure 20-23). First, with the acute onset of ischemia, there is the appearance of hyperacute T waves (peaking) followed by T-wave inversion. In the presence of actual MI, the T wave can remain inverted for months to years. Next, as the infarction progresses from ischemia to actual injury of the myocardium, ST segment elevation occurs. Acutely, the ST segment elevates and merges with the T wave. If myocardial injury progresses to infarction, the ST segment often returns to baseline within a few hours. Later, if perfusion is not restored, there may be loss of R wave height, and new Q waves appear, usually within hours to days. Q waves signify MI and the formation of scar tissue. Usually, the T wave recovers, leaving a pathologic Q wave as the only lasting sign that an MI has occurred.

Whereas during MI the ECG characteristically evolves through these three stages, any of these changes may be present without the others. For example, it is not unusual to see ST segment elevation without T-wave inversion. In addition, as mentioned earlier, MI does not always generate Q waves.

Figure 20-23
ECG changes associated with evolution of MI.

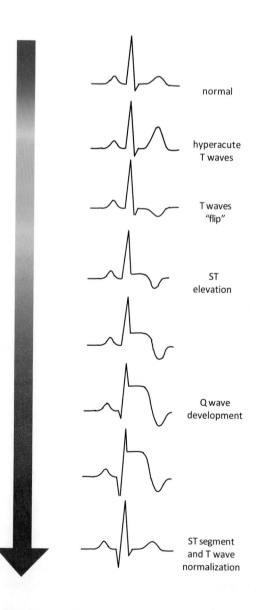

normal

hyperacute
T waves

T waves
"flip"

ST
elevation

Q wave
development

ST segment
and T wave
normalization

Criteria for Diagnosing Myocardial Infarction

The diagnosis of MI is based on the presence of at least two of the following three criteria:

1. Clinical history of ischemic-type chest discomfort/pain
2. Rise and fall in serum cardiac markers
3. Changes on serially obtained ECG tracings

Clinical History

Symptoms characteristic of MI includes gradual (over several minutes) onset chest pain, shortness of breath, nausea, vomiting, palpitations, diaphoresis, and anxiety (often expressed as a sense of impending doom). The patient may describe the pain as tightness, pressure, squeezing, crushing, or vice-like. Some patients tell of it feeling like there is an elephant standing on their chest. The pain often radiates to the left arm or left side of the neck but may also radiate to the lower jaw, neck, right arm, back, and epigastrium, where it may mimic heartburn. Women often have fewer typical symptoms than men, most commonly shortness of breath, weakness, a feeling of indigestion, and fatigue. Approximately 25 percent of MIs are silent, in other words, occurring without characteristic chest pain or other symptoms. This is often seen in the elderly and diabetics.

Serum Cardiac Markers

The cell membranes of dying myocardial cells break and leak substances into the blood. Blood tests can be used to determine the presence of these substances in the blood. These substances (called *cardiac markers* or *serum cardiac markers*) include creatine kinase MB isoforms, troponin, and myoglobin. Troponin-T and troponin-I are two tests that may be ordered for a patient with a suspected MI. Elevated levels (positive test) indicate that MI has occurred. The troponin-I test may have better specificity than troponin-T.

ECG Findings

Often, characteristic ECG changes accompany MI. The earliest changes occur almost immediately following the onset of compromised myocardial perfusion. As a matter of practice, a 12-lead ECG should be immediately performed on anyone even remotely suspected of experiencing MI. However, early ECGs do not always reveal MI because the progression of electrocardiographic changes varies between individuals and because unstable ischemic syndromes have rapidly changing supply versus demand characteristics. For this reason, it is important to obtain serial 12-lead ECGs throughout patient assessment and treatment. This is particularly true if the first ECG is obtained during a pain-free episode.

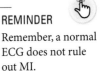

REMINDER
Remember, a normal ECG does not rule out MI.

■ **LO 20.7**

Identifying the Myocardial Infarction Location

As we discussed earlier, the ECG can help identify which coronary artery or branch is occluded in the presence of myocardial ischemia, injury, and/or infarction. Leads II, III, and aV_F provide a view of the tissue supplied by the right coronary artery, whereas leads I, aV_L, V_1, V_2, V_3, V_4, V_5, and V_6 view the tissue supplied by the left coronary artery.

REMINDER

Coronary artery anatomy can vary between given individuals, so the precise vessel involved is not always predictable from the ECG.

When evaluating the extent of infarction produced by a left coronary artery occlusion, it is important to determine how many of these leads show changes consistent with an acute infarction. The more of these eight leads demonstrating acute changes, the larger the infarction.

■ **LO 20.8**

Septal Wall Infarction

Leads V_1 and V_2 overlie the ventricular septum, so ischemic changes seen in these leads, and possibly in the adjacent precordial leads, are considered to be septal wall infarctions (Figure 20-24). The suspected culprit artery in septal wall infarctions is the left anterior descending artery. Reciprocal changes are not seen in the other leads.

KEY CONCEPT

Leads V_3 and V_4 provide the best view for identifying anterior left ventricular infarction.

Anterior Wall Infarction

Anterior infarction involves the anterior surface of the left ventricle (Figure 20-25). It may occur as a result of left anterior descending artery occlusion. Leads V_3, and V_4 are immediately over the anterior surface of the heart; therefore, they provide the best view for identifying anterior MI. ST segment elevation, T wave inversion, and the development of significant Q waves in these leads indicate MI involving the anterior surface of the heart. Reciprocal changes are not seen in the other leads.

If the ECG changes are seen in leads V_1, V_2, V_3, and V_4, we call it an *anteroseptal wall infarction*.

KEY CONCEPT

ECG changes in leads I, aV_L, V_5, and V_6, such as ST segment elevation, T wave inversion, and the development of significant Q waves, indicate left lateral wall infarction.

Lateral Wall Infarction

Infarction of the left lateral wall of the heart is referred to as a *lateral wall infarction*. It is often due to occlusion of the left circumflex artery. With lateral wall infarction you should see ECG changes such as ST segment elevation, T wave inversion, and the development of significant Q waves in leads I, aV_L, V_5, and V_6 (Figure 20-26). Reciprocal changes are seen in leads II, III, and aV_F.

Anterolateral Wall Infarction

If the ECG changes are seen in leads V_3, V_4, V_5, V_6, I, and aV_L we call it an *anterolateral wall infarction* (Figure 20-27). Reciprocal changes are seen in leads II, III and aV_F. The suspected culprit artery in anterolateral wall infarctions is the left anterior descending artery.

Septal infarction

Figure 20-24
Leads V$_1$ and V$_2$ are used to identify septal wall MI.

Extensive Anterior Wall Infarction

The term *extensive anterior wall infarction* (sometimes called *anteroseptal with lateral extension*) is used if we see ECG changes in leads V$_1$, V$_2$, V$_3$, V$_4$, V$_5$, V$_6$, I, and aV$_L$ (Figure 20-28). Reciprocal changes are seen in leads II, III, and aV$_F$. The suspected culprit artery in extensive anterior wall infarction is the left main coronary artery.

Inferior Infarction

Inferior infarction involves the inferior or diaphragmatic surface of the heart. It is frequently caused by occlusion of the right coronary artery or circumflex artery. ST segment elevation, T-wave inversion, and the development of significant Q waves in leads II, III, and aV$_F$ indicate MI involving the inferior

KEY CONCEPT
ECG changes consistent with MI in leads II, III, and aV$_F$ indicate MI involving the inferior surface of the heart.

Figure 20-25
Leads V_3 and V_4 are used to identify anterior MI.

surface of the heart (Figure 20-29). Reciprocal changes are seen in leads I and aV_L. *It is important to know that sinus bradycardia is common in inferior-wall MI.*

LO 20.9

Posterior Wall Infarction

Posterior infarctions are usually caused by occlusion of the posterior descending branch of the right coronary artery (RCA) or circumflex artery and involve the posterior surface of the heart. They are usually associated with inferior or lateral wall infarctions but can be isolated. Since there are no ECG leads over the posterior surface of the heart (unless posterior leads are used), posterior infarctions can be diagnosed by looking for reciprocal changes in leads V_1 and V_2 (the anterior leads). Normally, the R waves in leads V_1 and V_2 are mostly negative. An unusually large R wave in leads V_1 or V_2 can be the reciprocal of a posterior Q wave (Figure 20-30). Likewise, an upright T wave in these leads is reciprocal of posterior T-wave inversion.

KEY CONCEPT

Posterior infarctions can be diagnosed by looking for reciprocal changes in leads V_1 and V_2 (the anterior leads).

Figure 20-26
Leads I, aV$_L$, V$_5$, and V$_6$ are used to identify lateral MI.

Figure 20-27
Leads V$_3$, V$_4$, V$_5$, V$_6$, I, and aV$_L$ are used to identify anterolateral MI.

Figure 20-28
Leads V_1, V_2, V_3, V_4, V_5, V_6, I, and aV_L are used to identify extensive anterior MI. Note in this example, lead V_6 is not highlighted as changes are not seen but leads III and aV_F are highlighted as reciprocal changes are present.

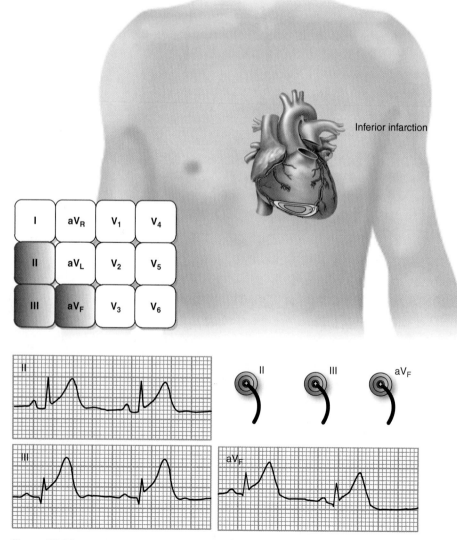

Figure 20-29
Leads II, III, and aV_F are used to identify inferior wall MI.

Figure 20-30
Leads V_1 and V_2 are used to identify posterior MI.

Use of Additional ECG Leads

The use of additional ECG leads such as the posterior leads V_7, V_8, and V_9 may improve your ability to detect posterior MI (Figure 20-31). The reason for this is the standard 12-lead ECG does not directly view the posterior basal

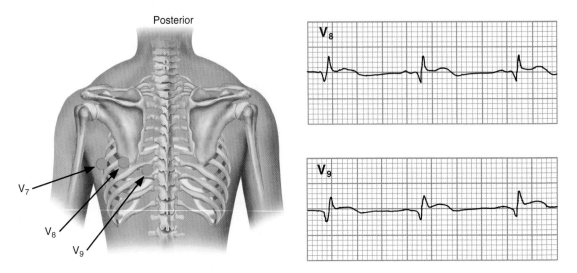

Figure 20-31
Posterior leads V_7, V_8, and V_9 can be used to identify posterior MI.

and lateral walls of the left ventricle. In particular, MI resulting from block-age of the circumflex artery may produce a nondiagnostic ECG. For these reasons, the use of these additional leads should be considered. An additional point of information is inferior wall MI may reveal the presence of right ventricular MI. For this reason the VR leads should be applied.

Right Ventricular Infarction

Between 30 to 50% of patients experiencing inferior wall (of the left ventricle) MI also have right ventricular involvement. For this reason, a patient showing signs of inferior wall MI should receive a right-sided ECG analysis in addition to application of the standard 12 lead. Right ventricular MI usually occurs due to an obstruction of the right coronary artery. The proximal segment of this vessel supplies the SA node and the right atrial wall; the middle segment supplies the lateral and inferior right ventricle; and the distal segment supplies the posterior portion of the left ventricle, the inferior septum, inferior left ventricular wall and AV node. A few patients may have a right ventricle that is supplied by the circumflex artery. It is important to recognize the signs of a right ventricular MI because treatment differs significantly between patients with an RVI and those with other infarction sites.

A 12-lead tracing that shows ST segment elevation in leads II, III or aV_F (the inferior leads), or relative ST segment depression in V_2 or V_3 compared with lead V_1, should immediately trigger acquisition of a right-sided 12-lead. With right ventricular infarction (RVI), the ECG may also show an acute anterior Q wave pattern in leads V_1 through V_3. The right-sided ECG should be done

Figure 20-32
Leads V_1R through V_6R can be used to identify right ventricular infarction.

just the same as a left-sided ECG with the exception of where the electrodes are placed. ST segment elevation in V_4R is diagnostic of right ventricular infarction (Figure 20-32); however, any ST elevation in the leads V_2R through V_6R should raise suspicion that a RVI may be present. Further, in RV_1, the T wave in V_4R usually has a convex or "domed" shape when injury is occurring. Pathological Q waves reflect a completed MI. When the tracing is printed, write "R" beside the V leads to mark that they are right leads, not left.

Although this is useful information, remember that these guidelines are generalized as each person's ECG tracings will vary due to variances in body structure, underlying heart and lung disease, and other factors. Thus, abnormal findings may overlap somewhat in the various leads.

Treatment of Myocardial Infarction

Initial treatment of MI includes the administration of aspirin, oxygen, and sublingual nitroglycerin. Additionally, serial 12-lead ECGs should be taken, along with the placement of an IV line.

Early recognition of an evolving MI is essential. The reason is that therapy delivered within the first few hours after the onset of MI can, in effect, prevent the completion of the infarct and improve chances for patient survival. Among these treatments are thrombolytic agents and direct plasminogen activators that act to lyse (disintegrate) clots that are occluding the coronary arteries and return blood flow to the heart muscle before actual myocardial death occurs. Further, many hospitals are equipped to deliver catheterization and angioplasty. Emergency angioplasty, performed within the initial six hours of infarction onset, offers greater survival than thrombolysis alone. Upon successful completion of angioplasty, stents coated with cytotoxic drugs are placed to prevent reocclusion at the site of the original vascular injury. To further improve patient outcome, oral and intravenous platelet inhibiting agents are administered.

Regardless of which treatment is employed, the key to success is timing. You must act quickly to prevent lasting myocardial damage. Being able to recognize the acute changes of an MI on the ECG is a critical diagnostic skill that can make a difference between life and death.

Right Ventricular Infarction Treatment

Treatment for RVI differs from treatment used for other infarction sites. Since the right ventricle is dependent on preload for adequate stroke volume, left ventricular stroke volume and cardiac output, treatments that produce vasodilation can have a deleterious effect on the heart. In RVI, or inferior wall MI with right ventricular involvement, the administration of nitroglycerin and morphine could cause an abrupt drop in blood pressure and thus should be avoided. For these patients a careful fluid infusion is the mainstay of treatment.

If adequate blood pressure and cardiac output cannot be maintained with fluids alone, dobutamine infusion is the preferred agent in RVI patients with systolic BP of 70–100 mmHg and no signs of shock. Other inotropic agents that can be employed include milrinone, norepinephrine, and possibly low-dose vasopressin. Symptomatic bradycardias can be treated with atropine and AV blocks may require external pacing.

Further, these patients presenting within 6 hours of the onset of inferior wall infarction with right ventricular involvement benefit from thrombolytic therapy or coronary angioplasty.

Practice Makes Perfect

For the following 12-lead ECGs, identify if myocardial ischemia, injury and/or infarction are present and the location.

1.

2.

3.

4.

5.

6.

7.

8.

9.

10.

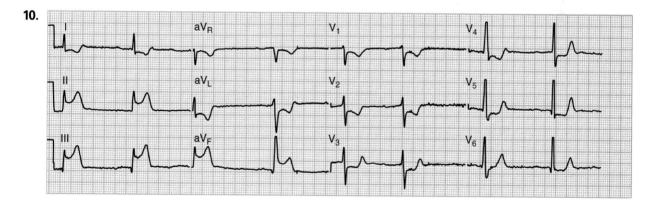

Key Points 🔍

- The oxygen and nutrient demand of the heart is extremely high; therefore, it requires its own continuous blood supply. The coronary arteries deliver the needed blood supply to the myocardial cells.

- The coronary veins return deoxygenated venous blood to the right atrium via the coronary sinus.

- By increasing coronary blood flow through vasodilation, the coronary arteries satisfy increased myocardial oxygen demands.

- The ST segment is the flat line that follows the QRS complex and connects it to the T wave.

- The ST segment can be compared with the PR segment to evaluate ST segment depression or elevation.

- The T wave is slightly asymmetrical and oriented in the same direction as the preceding QRS complex.

- The Q wave is the first part of the QRS complex. It is the first downward deflection from the baseline. It is not always present.

- Myocardial ischemia, injury, and death can occur with the interruption of coronary artery blood.

- Ischemia results from decreased oxygen delivery to the myocardium. It can be reversed if the supply of oxygen is restored or increased to a level that satisfies the myocardial oxygen demand.

- Myocardial injury results if ischemia is allowed to progress untreated.

- MI is the death of myocardial cells.

- The ECG can help identify the presence of ischemia, injury, and/or infarction of the heart muscle.

- Inverted T waves and ST segment depression are considered two characteristic signs of myocardial ischemia.

- Subendocardial infarction results in a flat depression of the ST segment.

- ST segment elevation occurs with myocardial injury. It is the earliest reliable sign that MI has occurred and tells us that the MI is acute.

- Pathologic Q waves indicate the presence of irreversible myocardial damage or a past MI.

- MI can occur without the development of Q waves.

- Septal wall MI can be identified by ECG changes seen in leads V_1 and V_2.

- Leads, V_3, and V_4 provide the best view for identifying anterior MI. Leads V_5 and V_6, while located more laterally, may also help identify anterior infarction.

- Lateral infarction is identified by ECG changes such as ST segment elevation; T wave inversion; and the development of significant Q waves in leads I, aV_L, V_5, and V_6.

- Inferior infarction is determined by ECG changes such as ST segment elevation; T wave inversion; and the development of significant Q waves in leads II, III, and aV_F.

- Posterior infarctions can be diagnosed by looking for reciprocal changes in leads V_1 and V_2.

Assess Your Understanding

The following questions give you a chance to assess your understanding of the material discussed in this chapter. The answers can be found in Appendix A.

1. The blood vessels that supply the myocardial cells with a continuous supply of oxygen and nutrients are referred to as the
   a. coronary veins.
   b. cerebral arteries.
   c. coronary arteries.
   d. carotid arteries.

2. The heart requires its own blood supply because the demand for oxygen of the myocardial cells is extremely high.
   a. True
   b. False

3. ST segment depression or elevation can be evaluated by comparing the ST segment with the
   a. Q wave.
   b. PR segment.
   c. position of the T wave.
   d. QT interval.

4. Which is true regarding the normal Q wave?
   a. It is always present.
   b. It is a small positive deflection from the baseline.
   c. It has a duration of less than 0.04 seconds.
   d. It is greater than 25% the amplitude of the R wave in that lead.

5. The ST segment
   a. contains at least two waves.
   b. begins at the peak of the R wave and gradually curves downward to the T wave.
   c. represents right and left ventricular depolarization.
   d. is the line that follows the QRS complex and connects it to the T wave.

6. The normal T wave is
   a. perfectly round.
   b. not more than 5 mm tall in the limb leads.
   c. oriented in the opposite direction of the preceding QRS complex.
   d. normally inverted in lead II.

7. MI
    a. is caused by coronary artery vasodilation.
    b. is also known as *angina* or *angina pectoris*.
    c. is the death of injured myocardial cells.
    d. can be reversed if the supply of oxygen and nutrients can be increased to a level that meets the myocardial oxygen demand.

8. Myocardial _____ is the most severe result of an interruption of coronary artery blood flow.
    a. ischemia
    b. infarction
    c. injury
    d. interruption

9. The ECG can help identify the presence of ischemia, injury, and/or infarction of the heart muscle.
    a. True
    b. False

10. All of the following are key ECG indicators of myocardial ischemia, injury, and/or infarction EXCEPT
    a. inversion of the T wave.
    b. absence of Q waves in the limb leads.
    c. elevation of the ST segment.
    d. peaking of the T wave.

11. All the characteristic ECG indicators must be present to diagnose myocardial ischemia, injury, or infarction.
    a. True
    b. False

12. Match the following ECG changes with the cardiac condition in which they are seen.

ECG Change Myocardial Condition	
a. Enlarged Q waves or presence of new Q waves ___	___ ischemia
b. ST segment depression ___	___ injury
c. ST segment elevation ___	___ infarction

13. ST segment depression is considered significant when the
    a. ST segment falls more than 1 mm below the baseline at a point one small square to the right of the J point.
    b. changes are seen in at least one or more leads facing the opposite anatomic area of the heart.

c. associated T wave is inverted.

  d. All of the above.

14. On the following illustrations, draw examples of each of the items listed beneath the figures.

  a. Inverted T wave

  b. Depressed ST segment

  c. Elevated ST segment

  d. Enlarged Q wave

15. Inverted T waves associated with myocardial ischemia

  a. indicate the ischemia is present through the full thickness of the myocardium.

  b. occur just at the start of the ischemia.

  c. are asymmetrical.

  d. are observed best in the limb leads.

16. Of the following three examples of inverted T waves, circle those that are symmetrical.

17. Two characteristic signs of myocardial ischemia are inverted T waves and ST segment elevation.
    a. True
    b. False

18. ST segment elevation associated with myocardial injury
    a. is usually only slight.
    b. produces a distinctive ST segment that has a sharp inclination upward and tends to merge abruptly with the T wave.
    c. occurs because there is rapid depolarization of the injured myocardium.
    d. is seen in the leads facing the affected area.

19. ST segment elevation is the earliest reliable ECG indication that myocardial injury/MI has occurred.
    a. True
    b. False

20. The appearance of Q waves
    a. indicates that irreversible myocardial damage has occurred.
    b. usually disappears after the MI ends.
    c. always occurs in conjunction with ST segment elevation.
    d. is considered pathologic if they are less than 0.04 seconds in duration.

21. Match the following leads where ECG changes will be seen with type of infarction.

Infarction Location Affected Leads	
a. Anterior ___	___ V_1 and V_2 (for reciprocal changes)
b. Inferior ___	___ II, III, and aV_F
c. Lateral ___	___ V_3 and V_4
d. Posterior ___	___ I, aV_L, V_5, and V_6

Referring to the scenario at the beginning of this chapter, answer the following questions.

22. What part of the heart was affected by the MI?
    a. Anterior
    b. Anteroseptal
    c. Posterior
    d. Inferior

23. What is the minimum amount of ST elevation required to make the diagnosis of myocardial injury
   a. 1 mm
   b. 1.5–2 mm
   c. 2.5–3 mm
   d. 3.5–5 mm

24. The most important intervention the paramedics can perform to improve the patient's outcome is to
   a. apply oxygen.
   b. administer nitroglycerin.
   c. administer aspirin.
   d. rapidly transport to an appropriate facility.

Answers to Sidebar Questions

1. The T waves are larger in the precordial leads than the limb leads because the precordial leads are closer to the ventricles than the limb leads. **p. 576**

2. The epicardial cells repolarize earlier than the endocardial cells so the wave of repolarization spreads in the direction opposite of depolarization and either toward or away from the positive electrode. This results in the T wave being deflected in the same direction as the QRS complex. **p. 576**

What's Online

Go to www.mhhe.com/shadeECG2e to find:
- Presentations on chapter content
- Chapter quiz
- Animation quiz
- Fill-in-the-blank exercises and answers
- In-depth answers to Practice Makes Perfect ECG tracings and Assess Your Understanding questions

21 Other Cardiac Conditions and the ECG

Chapter Outline

Pericarditis

Pericardial Effusion

Pulmonary Embolism

Electrolyte Imbalance

Drug Effects and Toxicity

Learning Objectives

LO 21.1 Recall how pericarditis occurs and the signs and symptoms a patient will likely experience when suffering from it.

LO 21.2 List the ECG changes that are seen with pericarditis.

LO 21.3 Define the term *pericardial effusion* and describe when it occurs.

LO 21.4 Describe the ECG changes that occur with pericardial effusion.

LO 21.5 Recall how pulmonary embolism occurs and the signs and symptoms a patient will likely experience when suffering from it.

LO 21.6 Describe the ECG changes that can be used to identify pulmonary embolism.

LO 21.7 Describe the effects changes in potassium and calcium serum levels can have on the ECG.

LO 21.8 Recall the ECG changes that occur with hyperkalemia.

LO 21.9 Recall the ECG changes that occur with hypokalemia.

LO 21.10 List the effects calcium disorders may have on the ECG.

LO 21.11 State the ECG characteristics seen in the patient who takes digoxin.

LO 21.12 Describe the effects of antidysrhythmic drugs on the ECG.

Case History

A 72-year-old man with renal failure presents to the emergency department by ambulance for evaluation of weakness and palpitations. The physician enters the exam room and introduces himself to the patient. While doing so, he notices that the patient is in sinus rhythm on the monitor, with frequent PVCs.

The patient indicates he is feeling very weak. He missed his last two dialysis appointments, and he can't seem to catch his breath. The physician examines the patient and determines that he has frothy pulmonary edema. The ECG shows runs of ventricular tachycardia and tall, peaked T-waves with a prolonged QT interval. The physician immediately summons the nurse and tells her that the patient is volume overloaded and he suspects the patient's potassium is critically elevated because he missed his dialysis appointments.

WANT MORE INFORMATION?
Visit the Fast & Easy ECGs Website at www.mhhe.com/shadeECG2e. Also, for a quick reference source to help you recall the indicators of the conditions discussed in this chapter while in the field or clinical setting, refer to the ECG Pocket Guide.

The nurse places the patient on supplemental oxygen, and the physician orders blood work and one ampule of calcium gluconate, two ampules of D_{50}, 20 units of insulin, and a dose of sodium bicarbonate to be administered in fairly rapid succession.

Follow-up ECGs indicate normal T waves and diminished ectopy. The patient is taken to dialysis, where the excess fluid in his system is removed.

LO 21.1

Pericarditis

Pericarditis is another condition that can lead to changes in the ECG (Figure 21-1). Pericarditis is inflammation of the pericardium that can produce sharp, substernal chest pain. The pericardium is a double-layered membrane that surrounds the heart. The potential space between the two layers holds 15 to 25 mL of serous, lubricating fluid. The pain has an abrupt onset that worsens on inspiration or by movement, particularly when the individual is lying down. The pain lessens when sitting up and leaning forward. The most common causes of pericarditis are viral and bacterial infections. Other causes include uremia, renal failure, rheumatic fever, connective tissue disease, and cancer. Sometimes pericarditis can accompany an MI. When pericarditis occurs in conjunction with MI, it develops several days after the infarction.

KEY CONCEPT

Pericarditis is inflammation of the pericardium. It can produce sharp substernal chest pain.

LO 21.2

QUESTION

1. What are the two layers of the pericardium?
Note: Answers to Sidebar Questions can be found at the end of the chapter.

ECG Changes

Initially with pericarditis, the T wave is upright and may be elevated. During the recovery phase it inverts. This may take several weeks to develop. The ST segments demonstrate a diffuse, upward-concave elevation (not convex as in MI) in all leads except aV_R and V_1. It is sometimes described as a saggy appearance. If the ST segment is elevated, it appears off the baseline, gradually sloping back down to the next QRS complex (and may include the P wave). Given that the signs and symptoms are similar, it is easy to mistake these changes for a developing MI. Certain features of the ECG can be helpful in differentiating pericarditis from MI:

KEY CONCEPT

In pericarditis the T wave is initially upright and may be elevated. During the recovery phase it inverts. Also in pericarditis, the ST segment is elevated and usually flat or concave. If it is elevated, it appears off the baseline, gradually sloping back down to the next QRS complex.

Characteristics of Pericarditis

- Because pericarditis involves the whole heart, the ST segment and T wave changes in pericarditis are diffuse. Therefore, the ECG changes will be present in all leads while those of MI are localized to the affected area.

- In pericarditis, T wave inversion usually occurs only after the ST segments have returned to baseline. In MI, T wave inversion is usually seen before ST segment normalization.

- In pericarditis, development of a Q wave does not occur.

- In pericarditis, there is sometimes depression of the PR segment in virtually any lead except aV_R.

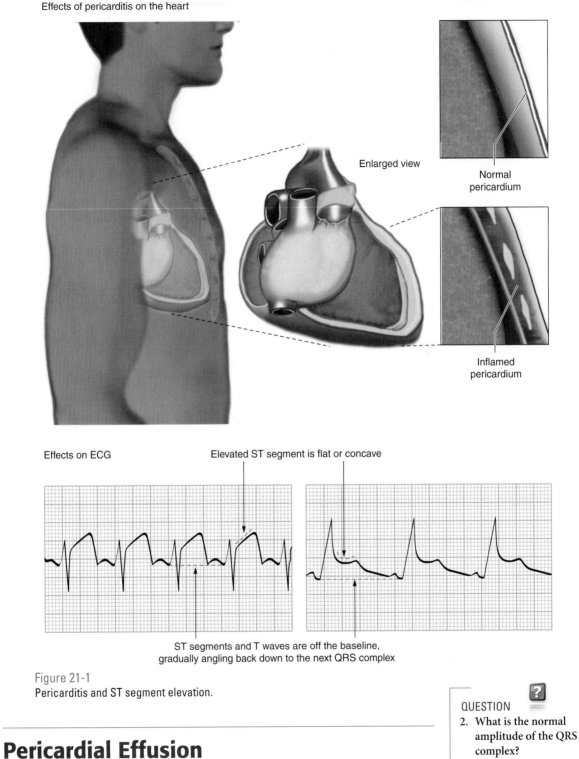

Figure 21-1
Pericarditis and ST segment elevation.

QUESTION
2. What is the normal amplitude of the QRS complex?

LO 21.3

Pericardial Effusion

The inflammatory process associated with pericarditis can stimulate the body's immune response, resulting in white cells or serous, fibrous, purulent, and hemorrhagic exudates being send to the injured area. This can lead to pericardial effusion (Figure 21-2). Pericardial effusion is a buildup of an

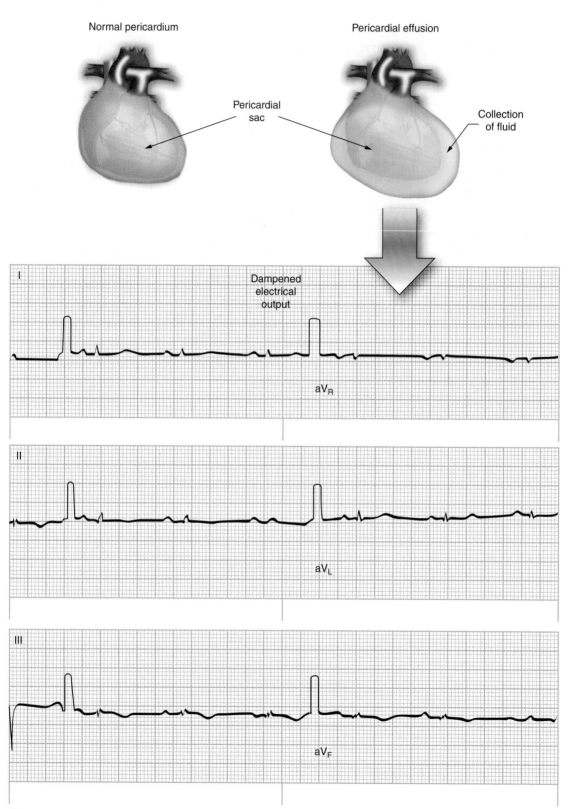

Figure 21-2
Large pericardial effusion with low-voltage QRS complexes.

abnormal amount of fluid and/or a change in the character of the fluid in the pericardial space. The pericardial space is the space between the heart and the pericardial sac.

ECG Changes

Formation of a substantial pericardial effusion dampens the electrical output of the heart, resulting in low-voltage QRS complexes in all leads. However, the ST segment and T wave changes of pericarditis may still be seen.

If an effusion is large enough, the heart may rotate freely within the fluid-filled sac. This can cause electrical alternans, a condition in which the electrical axis of the heart varies with each beat (Figure 21-3). A varying axis is most easily recognized on the ECG by the presence of QRS complexes that change in height with each successive beat. This condition can also affect the P and T waves.

LO 21.4

KEY CONCEPT
In pericarditis, formation of a substantial pericardial effusion causes low-voltage QRS complexes in all leads.

KEY CONCEPT
A large effusion seen with pericarditis may cause electrical alternans. This is seen on the ECG as QRS complexes that change in height with each successive beat.

Figure 21-3
Large pericardial effusion with electrical alternans.

The accumulation of fluid or exudate in the pericardial sac can lead to the development of cardiac tamponade—a condition in which the heart is compressed. Cardiac tamponade can lead to compromised cardiac output.

LO 21.5

KEY CONCEPT
A pulmonary embolism is an acute blockage of one of the pulmonary arteries that leads to obstruction of blood flow to the lung segment supplied by the artery.

Pulmonary Embolism

A pulmonary embolism is an acute blockage of one of the pulmonary arteries by a blood clot or other foreign matter (Figure 21-4). This leads to obstruction of blood flow to the lung segment supplied by the artery. The larger the artery occluded, the more massive the pulmonary embolus and therefore the larger the effect the embolus has on the lungs and heart. Due to the increased pressure in the pulmonary artery caused by the embolus, the right atrium and ventricle become distended and unable to function properly, leading to right heart failure. This condition is referred to as *acute cor pulmonale.*

Massive pulmonary embolism impairs oxygenation of the blood, and death may result. The most common source of the clot is in one of the large pelvic or leg veins. The pain that accompanies a pulmonary embolus is pleuritic, and shortness of breath is often present.

LO 21.6

ECG Changes

ECG changes that suggest the development of a massive pulmonary embolus are shown in the box below.

Characteristics of Pulmonary Embolism
• Tall, symmetrically peaked P waves in leads II, III, and aV$_F$ and sharply peaked biphasic P waves in leads V$_1$ and V$_2$. These changes are indicative of right atrial enlargement.
• A large S wave in lead I, a deep Q wave in lead III, and an inverted T wave in lead III. This is called the *S1 Q3 T3 pattern* (see Figure 21–4).
• ST segment depression in lead II.
• Right bundle branch block (which usually subsides after the patient improves).
• A QRS axis greater than 90° (right axis deviation).
• Inversion of the T waves in leads V$_1$–V$_4$.
• Q waves generally limited to lead III.

KEY CONCEPT
The characteristic ECG changes seen with massive pulmonary embolus include a large S wave in lead I, a deep Q wave in lead III, and an inverted T wave in lead III. This is called the *S1 Q3 T3 pattern.*

A number of dysrhythmias may be seen with massive pulmonary embolism, most commonly sinus tachycardia and atrial fibrillation. In the case of a minimal or small pulmonary embolism, the ECG is usually normal, or it may show a sinus tachycardia.

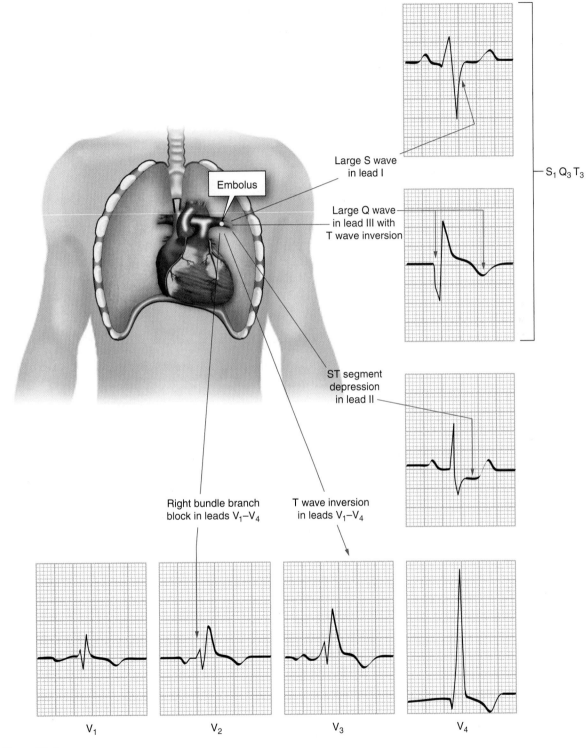

Figure 21-4
ECG changes seen with pulmonary embolism.

Electrolyte Imbalance

Changes in potassium and calcium serum levels can profoundly affect the ECG. Those involving potassium are the most immediately life threatening. Levels that are too high (hyperkalemia) or too low (hypokalemia) can quickly result in serious cardiac dysrhythmias. The presence of ECG changes may be a better measure of clinically significant potassium toxicity than the serum potassium level.

Hyperkalemia

Hyperkalemia is an abnormally elevated level of potassium in the blood. The normal potassium level in the blood is 3.5–5.0 milliequivalents per liter (mEq/L). Potassium levels between 5.1 mEq/L and 6.0 mEq/L reflect mild hyperkalemia. Potassium levels of 6.1 mEq/L to 7.0 mEq/L reflect moderate hyperkalemia, and levels above 7 mEq/L reflect severe hyperkalemia. Signs and symptoms of hyperkalemia include weakness, paralysis, and respiratory failure.

Hyperkalemia can generate a rapid progression of changes in the ECG that can end in ventricular fibrillation and death (Figure 21-5). For this reason you should take immediate corrective action with any changes you see on the ECG that are due to hyperkalemia.

T wave peaking begins as the potassium level starts to rise. You may remember, from Chapter 21, peaked T waves can also be seen in MI. The distinction between the two is that the changes in MI are limited to those leads overlying the infarcted area whereas, with hyperkalemia, the changes are seen in all leads. Another distinctive feature of the hyperkalemic T wave is that both the up and down slopes are concave, giving the appearance of a tent. As the serum potassium increases more, the PR interval becomes prolonged, and the P wave eventually flattens and then disappears. Finally, the QRS complex widens until it blends with the T wave, forming what is called a *sine-wave pattern*. Idioventricular rhythm or ventricular fibrillation may ultimately develop.

ECG changes seen with hyperkalemia are shown in the box below.

Characteristics of Hyperkalemia
• Peaked T waves (tenting)
• Flattened P waves
• Prolonged PR interval (1st-degree AV heart block)
• Widened QRS complex
• Deepened S waves and merging of S and T waves
• Concave up and down slope of the T wave
• Sine-wave pattern

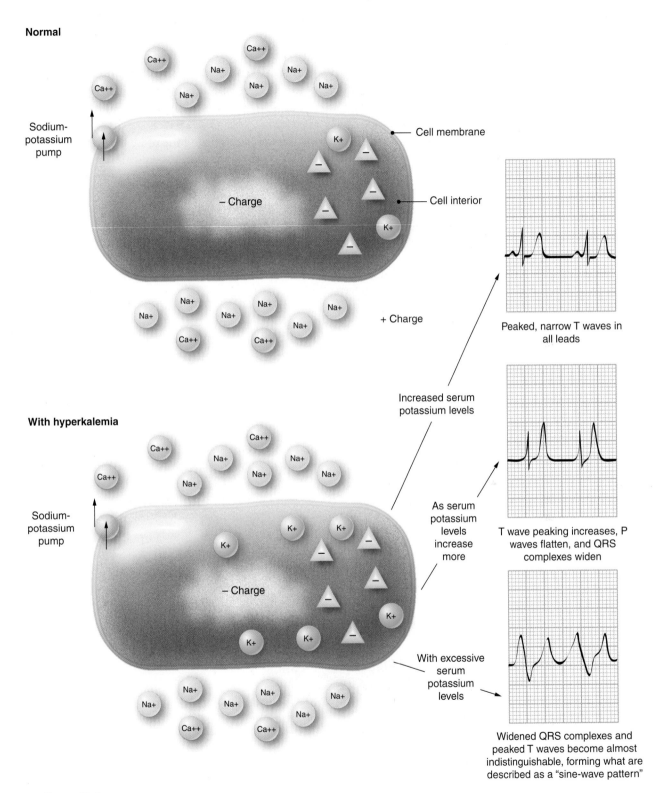

Normal

Sodium-potassium pump

− Charge

+ Charge

Cell membrane

Cell interior

Increased serum potassium levels

Peaked, narrow T waves in all leads

With hyperkalemia

Sodium-potassium pump

− Charge

As serum potassium levels increase more

T wave peaking increases, P waves flatten, and QRS complexes widen

With excessive serum potassium levels

Widened QRS complexes and peaked T waves become almost indistinguishable, forming what are described as a "sine-wave pattern"

Figure 21-5
ECG changes seen with hyperkalemia.

Hypokalemia

Hypokalemia is a lower-than-normal amount of potassium in the blood. Symptoms of hypokalemia include weakness, fatigue, paralysis, respiratory difficulty, constipation, and leg cramps. Severe hypokalemia can lead to dysrhythmias and pulseless electrical activity (PEA) or asystole.

The ECG is also an effective means of determining the presence of hypokalemia (Figure 21-6). The four key changes in the ECG seen with serious hypokalemia are shown in the box below.

Characteristics of Hypokalemia

- ST segment depression
- Flattening of the T wave
- Appearance of U waves
- Prolongation of the QT interval

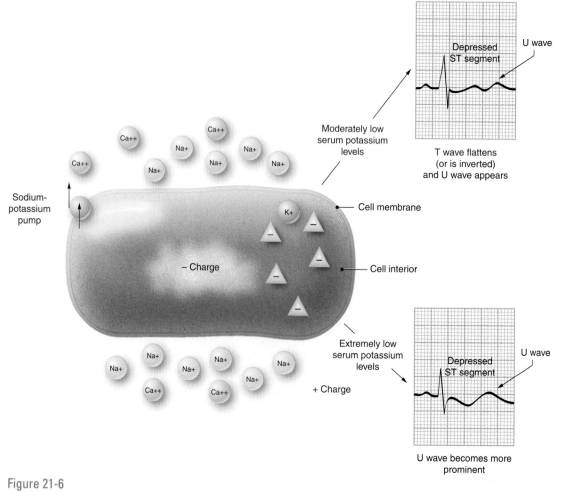

Figure 21-6
ECG changes seen with hypokalemia.

A wave that occurs after the T wave in the cardiac cycle is called a *U wave*. Although U waves are the most distinguishing characteristic of hypokalemia, by themselves they are not diagnostic. U waves are seen in other conditions and can sometimes be seen in patients with normal hearts and normal serum potassium levels.

Calcium Disorders

Calcium is needed by the myocardial cells to contract. Alterations in serum calcium levels mainly affect the QT interval (Figure 21-7). Hypocalcemia prolongs the QT interval while hypercalcemia shortens it. Torsades de pointes, a variant of ventricular tachycardia, is seen in patients with prolonged QT intervals. Hypocalcemia also results in decreased cardiac contraction.

Drug Effects and Toxicity

Some medications can have striking effects on ECG waveforms by altering the way the cells depolarize, repolarize, and innervate surrounding tissues. These changes may indicate expected, and, therefore, benign effects of certain medications as well as provide evidence of medication toxicity.

Digoxin

Digoxin is in a class of drugs referred to as *cardiac glycosides*. Digitalis preparations have been used to treat people since the 13th century. In certain circumstances or in high concentrations, digitalis can induce deadly dysrhythmias. These drugs slow the influx of sodium while allowing a greater influx of calcium during both depolarization and repolarization. This increases myocardial contractility and improves the heart's pumping ability. Digoxin can be used in heart failure to improve cardiac output.

Two types of ECG changes are seen with digoxin: those associated with therapeutic blood levels of the drug and those associated with toxic blood levels.

In therapeutic doses, digoxin has a parasympathetic effect that slows the pacing rate of the SA node and conduction through the AV node. The slowing of the heart rate is called a *negative chronotropic effect* while the slowing of the conduction rate is called a *negative dromotropic effect*. These effects can slow the rates associated with fast dysrhythmias. It also inhibits the receptiveness of the AV node to multiple stimuli, allowing fewer stimuli to reach the ventricles. This can be particularly helpful in the treatment of dysrhythmias such as atrial fibrillation and flutter. However, if the heart rate slows too much, decreased cardiac output can result.

Therapeutic Blood Levels—ECG Changes

Digoxin produces a characteristic gradual downward curve of the ST segment (it looks like a ladle) (Figure 21–8). The R wave slurs into the ST segment. Sometimes the T wave is lost in this scooping effect. The lowest portion

LO 21.10

QUESTION
4. What is torsades de pointes?

KEY CONCEPT
In hypocalcemia the QT interval is slightly prolonged.

LO 21.11

KEY CONCEPT
Digoxin increases myocardial contractility and improves the heart's pumping ability. It also slows the heart rate and AV conduction, making it useful in the treatment of fast atrial dysrhythmias.

KEY CONCEPT
A characteristic gradual downward curve of the ST segment is seen with digoxin. Further, the downward slope of the R wave gradually slurs as it curves downward into the ST segment.

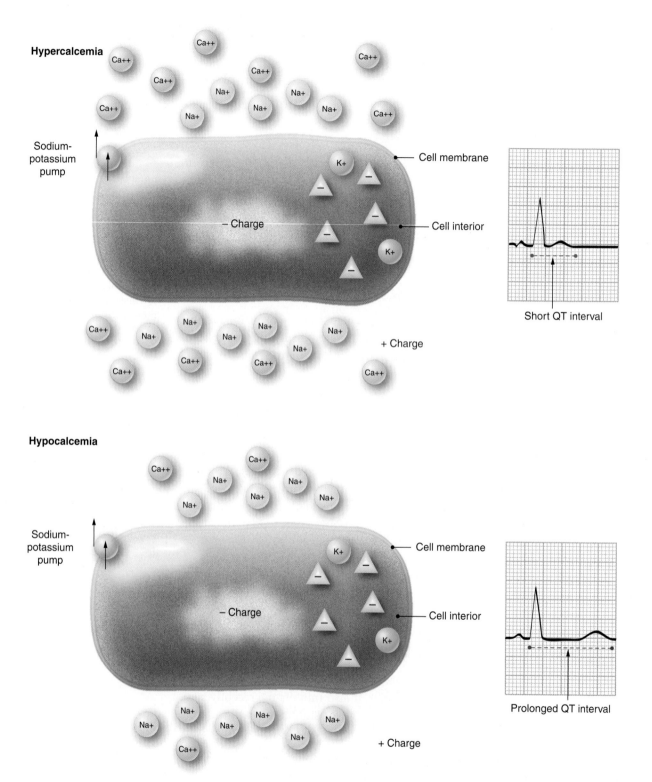

Figure 21-7
With hypercalcemia, the QT interval shortens, and with hypocalcemia, the QT interval is prolonged.

Figure 21-8
Effects of digoxin on the ECG.

Gradual downward curve of the ST segment

of the ST segment is depressed below the baseline. When seen, the T waves have shorter amplitude and can be biphasic. The QT interval is usually shorter than anticipated, and the U waves are more visible. Also, the PR interval may be prolonged.

Digoxin has a very narrow therapeutic margin of 0.5 to 1.5 mg/dL, and it is excreted from the body slowly. Toxic levels can occur and cause life-threatening dysrhythmias. The chance of developing toxicity is increased in hypokalemia, hypercalcemia, renal impairment, advanced age, acute hypoxia, and hypothyroidism.

Toxic Blood Levels—ECG Changes

Digoxin levels greater than the therapeutic range can cause any dysrhythmia because they increase the automatic behavior of all cardiac conducting cells, causing them to act more like pacemakers. The most common dysrhythmia seen with digoxin toxicity is paroxysmal atrial tachycardia (PAT) with 2nd-degree AV heart block. The conduction block is usually 2:1 but may vary unpredictably. Other abnormal heart rhythms that may be seen include those with slower rates (junctional rhythms, heart blocks), those with faster rates (atrial, junctional, and ventricular tachycardia), and premature complexes (PACs, PJCs, and PVCs). Atrial flutter and fibrillation are least commonly seen with digoxin toxicity.

Other Medications

LO 21.12

Class I (specifically type IA) antidysrhythmics are a group of drugs that include procainamide, quinidine, and disopyramide. These antidysrhythmic drugs slow both atrial and ventricular rates. They do not affect rhythm but prolong AV conduction. When patients receive these antidysrhythmic drugs, the ECG may show a slight widening of the QRS complex and a lengthening of the QT interval. The increase of the QT interval is concerning as it can increase the risk of ventricular tachydysrhythmias. The QT interval must be carefully monitored in all patients taking these medications and the drug withheld if significant—usually more than 25%—prolongation occurs. Class I antidysrhythmics can also produce AV blocks, a slowed or completely blocked SA node, and other dysrhythmias.

KEY CONCEPT
Digoxin has a very narrow therapeutic margin and is excreted from the body slowly. Excessive digitalis levels can cause slower heart rates, faster heart rates, and PVCs.

REMINDER
The effect seen with digoxin is also referred to as a slurring of the ST segment.

Quinidine

ECG indicators of quinidine use include a wide, notched P wave; widening of the QRS complex; and, often, ST depression with a prolonged QT interval. The presence of U waves is typical as well. U waves represent delayed repolarization of the ventricular conduction system. These do not require any adjustment in drug dosage.

Hypotension; tachycardia; widening of the QRS complex, QT interval, and PR interval; heart block; and heart failure can develop with quinidine toxicity. Episodes of torsades de pointes can also result.

Procainamide

Adverse cardiovascular effects of procainamide include bradycardia, tachycardia, hypotension, worsening heart failure, AV heart block, torsades de pointes, ventricular fibrillation, and asystole.

Calcium Channel and Beta Blockers

Calcium channel blockers primarily block the AV node, but the extent of block varies significantly within different drugs in this class. Beta blockers slow automaticity of the SA node and the Purkinje system and block the AV node. They can have a number of effects on the cardiovascular system, including bradycardia, hypotension, heart failure, chest pain, and palpitations.

Additional drugs that can increase the QT interval are other antidysrhythmic agents (e.g., amiodarone and dofetilide), the tricyclic antidepressants, the phenothiazines, erythromycin, and various antifungal medications.

Practice Makes Perfect

You can practice identifying the various conditions detailed in this chapter in the following *Practice Makes Perfect* exercises. Identify if pulmonary embolism, low-amplitude waveforms, electrical alternans, electrolyte imbalance, or digitalis use are present. Answers to these exercises can be found in Appendix A.

1.

ECG Findings:

2.

ECG Findings:

3.

ECG Findings:

4.

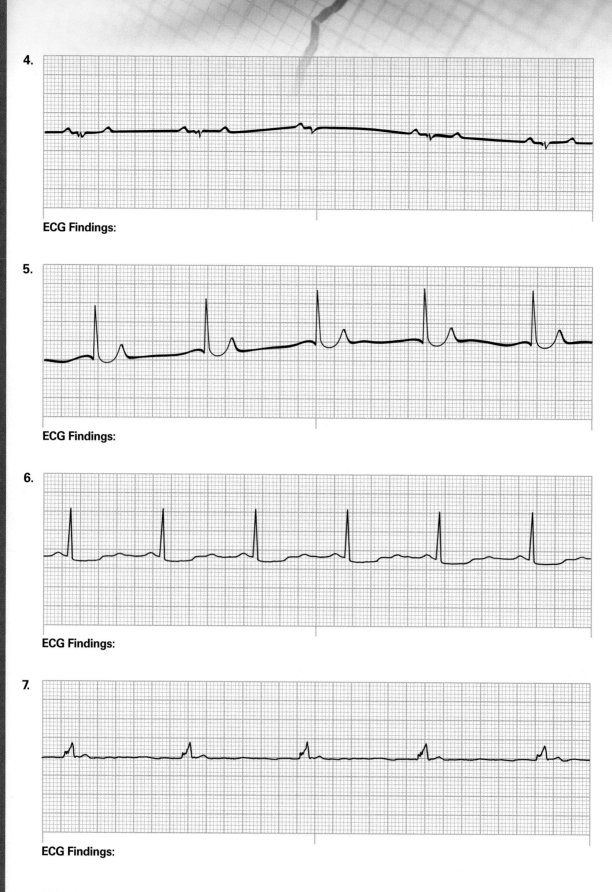

ECG Findings:

5.

ECG Findings:

6.

ECG Findings:

7.

ECG Findings:

8.

ECG Findings:

9.

ECG Findings:

10.

ECG Findings:

11.

ECG Findings:

Key Points 🔍

- Inflammation of the pericardium is called *pericarditis*. It can produce sharp substernal chest pain that worsens with inspiration and movement, particularly when the individual is lying down.

- In pericarditis the T wave is initially upright and elevated, but then during the recovery phase it inverts. The ST segment is elevated and usually flat or concave.

- A substantial pericardial effusion can occur with pericarditis. This can cause ECG changes, including low-voltage QRS complexes in all leads and electrical alternans, a condition in which the QRS complexes change in height with each successive beat.

- An acute blockage of one of the pulmonary arteries that leads to obstruction of blood flow to the lung segment supplied by the artery is called a *pulmonary embolism*.

- The characteristic ECG changes seen with massive pulmonary embolus include a large S wave in lead I, a deep Q wave in lead III, and an inverted T wave in lead III. This is called the *S1 Q3 T3 pattern*.

- Increases or decreases in the potassium and calcium serum levels can have a profound effect on the ECG.

- Key characteristics of hyperkalemia include T wave peaking, flattened P waves, 1st-degree AV heart block, widened QRS complexes, deepened S waves, merging of S and T waves, and sine waves.

- Key ECG characteristics of hypokalemia include ST segment depression, flattening of the T wave, and appearance of U waves.

- In hypocalcemia the QT interval is slightly prolonged.

- Digoxin slows the influx of sodium while allowing a greater influx of calcium. This increases myocardial contractility and improves the heart's pumping ability. It also slows the heart rate and AV conduction, making it useful in the treatment of fast atrial dysrhythmias.

- A characteristic gradual downward curve of the ST segment is seen with digoxin. Further, the downward slope of the R wave gradually slurs as it curves downward into the ST segment.

- Digoxin has a very narrow therapeutic margin and is excreted from the body slowly. Excessive digitalis levels can cause slower heart rates, faster heart rates, and PVCs.

Assess Your Understanding

The following questions give you a chance to assess your understanding of the material discussed in this chapter. The answers can be found in Appendix A.

1. Inflammation of the pericardium is called
    a. preexcitation syndrome.
    b. myocardial ischemia.
    c. pericarditis.
    d. pulmonary embolism.

2. ECG changes seen with pericarditis include
    a. a large Q wave.
    b. an elevated ST segment, usually flat or concave.
    c. right bundle branch block.
    d. a large S wave in lead I.

3. In comparison to MI, the ECG changes seen with pericarditis include
    a. diffuse ST segment and T wave changes.
    b. T wave inversion that usually occurs at the onset of the chest pain.
    c. development of a Q wave.
    d. the S1 Q3 T3 pattern.

4. Electrical alternans
    a. occurs with a small pericardial effusion.
    b. is a condition in which the electrical axis of the heart varies with each beat.
    c. is recognized on the ECG by QRS complexes, which change height every fifth or sixth beat.
    d. is diagnosed by analyzing just the width of the QRS complexes.

5. A pulmonary embolism
    a. is most commonly caused by a thrombus in one of the large neck veins.
    b. is an acute blockage of one of the coronary arteries.
    c. often produces chest pain unaffected by breathing efforts.
    d. can lead to acute cor pulmonale.

6. ECG changes seen with pulmonary embolism include
    a. right bundle branch block.
    b. the S1 Q3 T3 pattern.
    c. tall, symmetrically peaked P waves in leads II, III, and aV_F.
    d. All of the above.

7. Match the following ECG changes with the cardiac condition with which they are seen.

ECG Change	Condition
Peaked T waves, widened QRS complexes, and sine waves ____	a. Hypocalcemia
Appearance of U waves, prolongation of the QT interval ____	b. Hyperkalemia
Slightly prolonged QT interval ____	c. Hypokalemia
	d. Hypercalcemia

8. Increases or decreases in the potassium and calcium serum levels can have a profound effect on the ECG.
   a. True
   b. False

9. Prolonged QT intervals are associated with
   a. atrial fibrillation.
   b. complete AV heart block.
   c. sinus bradycardia.
   d. torsades de pointes.

10. ECG changes associated with digoxin use include a(n)
    a. longer QT interval.
    b. elevated ST segment.
    c. gradual downward curve of the ST segment.
    d. shorter than normal PR interval.

11. The most common dysrhythmia seen with digoxin toxicity is
    a. 3rd-degree AV heart block.
    b. paroxysmal atrial tachycardia with 2nd-degree AV heart block.
    c. junctional tachycardia.
    d. torsades de pointes.

12. On the following illustrations draw an example of
    a. tall T waves.
    b. sine waves.
    c. U waves.

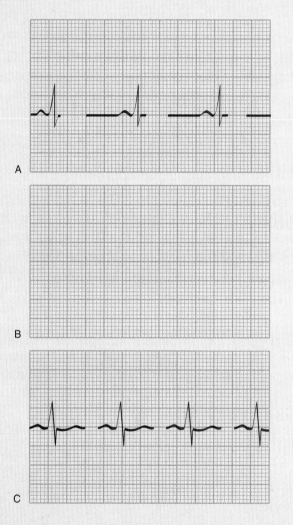

A

B

C

Referring to the scenario at the beginning of this chapter, answer the following questions.

13. What electrolyte abnormality is responsible for the patient's cardiac irregularity?
    a. Hyponatremia
    b. Hypercalcemia
    c. Hyperkalemia
    d. Hypoglycemia

14. What is characteristic of the T-wave configuration in this condition?
    a. Shaped like a tent
    b. Shaped like a mound
    c. Notched
    d. Round and wide

15. What other changes to the ECG can be expected with this condition?
    a. Prolonged PR interval and widening of the QRS complex
    b. Shortened PR interval and widening of the QRS complex
    c. Prolonged P wave and inverted T waves
    d. Prolonged PR interval and notching of the T waves

Answers to Sidebar Questions

1. The pericardium, a double-walled closed sac, has two layers. The tough, fibrous outer layer is called the *fibrous pericardium,* and the inner, thin transparent lining is called the *serous pericardium.* **p. 614**

2. The amplitude of the normal QRS complex is 5- to 30-mm high. **p. 615**

3. Potassium plays a key role in repolarization of the nerve cells. **p. 620**

4. Torsades de pointes is a unique variant of polymorphic ventricular tachycardia. It is characterized by QRS complexes that alternate (usually gradually) between upright deflections and downward deflections. **p. 623**

What's Online

Go to www.mhhe.com/shadeECG2e to find:

- Presentations on chapter content
- Chapter quiz
- Fill-in-the-blank exercises and answers
- In-depth answers to Practice Makes Perfect ECG tracings and Assess Your Understanding questions

section 5

Review and Assessment

Chapter 22:   Putting It All Together

Final Assessment: Practice Makes Perfect

22 Putting It All Together

Chapter Outline

Using the Nine-
  Step Process and
  Deductive Analysis

Step 1: Heart Rate

Step 2: Regularity

Step 3: P Waves

Step 4: QRS Complexes

Step 5: PR Intervals

Step 6: ST Segments

Step 7: T Waves

Step 8: QT Intervals

Step 9: U Waves

So Why Do It?

Practice Ruling Out
  Dysrhythmias and
  Conditions

Learning Objectives

LO 22.1 List those dysrhythmias that have a slow, normal, or fast heart rate.

LO 22.2 List those dysrhythmias that are regular or irregular. For those that are irregular, identify the types of irregularity with which they are associated.

LO 22.3 Identify the presence or absence of P waves, as well as how they appear with each dysrhythmia.

LO 22.4 Identify the presence or absence of QRS complexes, as well as how they appear with each dysrhythmia.

LO 22.5 Identify the presence or absence of PR intervals, as well as how they appear with each dysrhythmia.

LO 22.6 Recall the normal appearance of the ST segments and T waves and identify the conditions in which they can look different.

LO 22.7 Recall the normal duration of the QT intervals and identify the conditions in which they may be different.

LO 22.8 Identify when U waves may be present.

LO 22.9 Demonstrate how to analyze ECG tracings using the deductive analysis process.

Case History

Paramedics are dispatched to a nursing home where a middle-aged man is complaining of chest pain. The man has a history of heart disease and hypertension. Upon their arrival, the EMS team is met by a nurse who has been talking with the patient. She tells you that the man was visiting his mother when he became pale and diaphoretic. When she asked if he was okay, he grasped his chest and said "I think I am having a heart attack." The nurse then checked for a pulse, which she says was of a normal rate but irregular. She reports the patient never stopped breathing or became cyanotic.

The paramedics introduce themselves and begin their assessment. Oxygen is applied and vital signs are taken, showing a blood pressure of 170/96, pulse of 120, irregular respirations of 16 per minute, and oxygen saturation of 94% on room air. They apply the cardiac monitor to the patient and see a rhythm that has a faster than normal rate, is irregular, and has narrow QRS complexes which are each preceded by different looking P wave. One of the paramedics comments, "This looks like an interesting rhythm." His partner remarks, "It won't take long to figure this out; let's just rule out those things it can't be and that will tell us what it is."

The paramedics nod in agreement and begin analyzing the rhythm.

Using the Nine-Step Process and Deductive Analysis

As described throughout this book, each dysrhythmia and/or condition has certain characteristics. If you remember the characteristics that are associated with each and can identify which characteristics are present, you can identify what dysrhythmia and/or condition (if any) is present. That's why learning about normal and abnormal characteristics is so important for ECG analysis and interpretation.

In this chapter, following the nine-step process, we group dysrhythmias and conditions with similar characteristics together (Figure 22-1). Then we show how to apply the principles of deductive analysis to eliminate those that do not fit the characteristics we see. Then last, we provide you with some examples of how to "put it all together."

LO 22.1

KEY CONCEPT
Dysrhythmias can be categorized by their heart rate.

Step 1: Heart Rate

Based on their heart rate, dysrhythmias can be grouped into one of three categories (Figure 22-2): they are either slow, normal, or fast. Some dysrhythmias may produce more than one heart rate or even all three.

Slow Rate

Slow heart rates are those that are less than 60 beats per minute. Dysrhythmias with slow heart rate include sinus bradycardia, junctional escape, and

Figure 22-1
The Nine-Step Process.

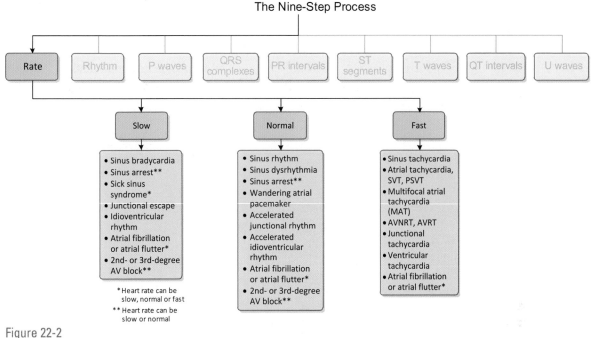

Figure 22-2
Heart rate algorithm.

idioventricular rhythm. Several others may have also have a slow heart rate including sinus arrest, sick sinus syndrome, 2nd-degree AV heart block, and 3rd-degree AV heart block. Whereas the atrial heart in atrial flutter and fibrillation is faster than normal, the ventricular rate can be slow.

Normal Rate

Dysrhythmias having a normal heart rate (between 60 and 100 beats per minute) include normal sinus rhythm, sinus dysrhythmia, wandering atrial pacemaker, accelerated junctional rhythm, and accelerated idioventricular rhythm. Note that accelerated idioventricular rhythm spans both slow and normal heart rates, with a rate of 40 to 100 beats per minute. Also, 2nd- and 3rd-degree AV heart blocks, sick sinus syndrome and sinus arrest can be slow, but they can also have a normal heart rate. Atrial flutter and atrial fibrillation can also have a normal ventricular rate.

Fast Rate

Dysrhythmias having a fast heart rate (greater than 100 beats per minute) include sinus tachycardia, atrial tachycardia, multifocal atrial tachycardia, junctional tachycardia, AVNRT, AVRT and ventricular tachycardia. Atrial flutter or fibrillation can also be fast.

Step 2: Regularity   LO 22.2

Dysrhythmias will either be regular or irregular (Figure 22-3). As we have discussed, you can further characterize irregularity into the following groups:

Figure 22-3
Irregularity algorithm.

occasional or very, slight, sudden acceleration or slowing, patterned, total, or variable conduction ratio irregularity.

Regular Rhythms

Dysrhythmias having a regular rhythm include sinus rhythm, sinus bradycardia, sinus tachycardia, junctional escape, accelerated junctional rhythm, junctional tachycardia, idioventricular rhythm and accelerated idioventricular rhythm. Atrial flutter and 2nd-degree AV heart block, type II, can also be regular. This occurs if the conduction ratio remains constant. In 3rd-degree AV heart block, the atrial rhythm is regular, as is the ventricular rhythm; however, the two are not related.

Irregular Rhythms

Irregular rhythms are rhythms in which the distance between the P waves and/or the QRS complexes change. They can be identified by how they appear and as described as follows.

Occasional or Very Irregularity

Sinus arrest and premature beats arising from the atria, AV junction, or ventricles (such as premature atrial complexes, premature junctional complexes, and premature ventricular complexes) can produce an occasional irregularity in the rhythm. Frequently occurring early beats produce a very irregular rhythm.

Slight Irregularity

Wandering atrial pacemaker is characteristically slightly irregular. Multifocal atrial tachycardia, a fast form of wandering atrial pacemaker, can be slightly irregular, but it can also be very irregular.

Sudden Acceleration or Slowing Irregularity

This type of irregularity is characteristically seen with either sinus arrest or paroxysmal tachycardia. You don't always see the sudden slowing or acceleration in the heart rate. When you do see a sudden onset of tachycardia, it is referred to as *paroxysmal.*

Patterned Irregularity

Sinus dysrhythmia, premature beats that occur in a bigeminal, trigeminal, or quadrigeminal pattern, and 2nd-degree AV block, Type I all produce a patterned irregularity. Sometimes it takes a longer tracing in order to effectively identify this type of irregularity.

Total Irregularity

Only one dysrhythmia, atrial fibrillation, is characterized as totally irregular. It is considered one of the key features of this dysrhythmia.

Variable Conduction Ratio Irregularity

Atrial flutter and 2nd-degree AV heart block, Type II can produce irregularity due to variable conduction ratio. It occurs when the number of impulses arising from the atria and reaching the ventricles changes.

Step 3: P Waves

LO 22.3

Depending on where each dysrhythmia originates, P waves are either present or not present (Figure 22-4). If P waves are present, they are either normal or abnormal. Sometimes there are more P waves than QRS complexes. Also, with certain dysrhythmias, flutter or fibrillatory waveforms are present instead of P waves.

KEY CONCEPT
Dysrhythmias can be categorized by the presence, morphology, number, or absence of P waves.

Normal P Waves

Normal P waves seen preceding each QRS complex occur with normal sinus rhythm, sinus bradycardia, sinus tachycardia, sinus dysrhythmia, and sinus arrest.

Abnormal P Waves

Abnormal P waves are those that look different; are inverted, absent, or follow the QRS complex; or are not followed by a QRS complex. Also, there may be a pacemaker spike that precedes or appears instead of P waves.

The Nine-Step Process

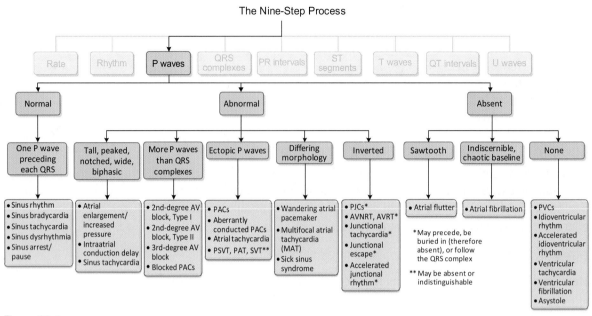

Figure 22-4
P wave algorithm.

Different-Looking Sinus P Waves

P waves that are tall and symmetrically peaked may be seen with increased right atrial pressure and right atrial dilation as well as with sinus tachycardia. Notched or wide (prolonged) P waves may be seen in increased left atrial pressure and left atrial dilation, as well as when there is a conduction delay or block in the interatrial conduction tract. Biphasic P waves may occur with both right and left atrial dilation.

Ectopic P′ Waves

The P wave also appears different when the pacemaker site originates from a site other than the SA node. Ectopic P′ waves are seen with premature atrial complexes, aberrantly conducted beats, and atrial tachycardia. With atrial ectopy, the P′ waves may be obscured or buried in the T wave of the preceding beat (resulting in a short P′-P interval). This causes the T wave to appear different than those following the other beats. The T wave may look peaked, notched, or larger than normal.

You may see an atrial P′ wave that is not followed by a QRS complex. This occurs with a nonconducted or blocked premature atrial complex and with atrial tachycardia with block. The appearance of either type of ectopy can be confused with AV heart block.

P Waves of Differing Morphology

P′waves of differing morphology occur with wandering atrial pacemaker and multifocal atrial tachycardia. In these dysrhythmias, the pacemaker site shifts transiently from beat to beat from the SA node to other latent (hidden) pacemaker sites in the atria and AV junction.

Inverted P Waves

Inverted P′ waves occur when the electrical impulse travels upward through the AV junction into the atria, causing retrograde (backward) atrial depolarization. The four dysrhythmias in which inverted P′ waves are seen are premature junctional complexes (PJCs), junctional escape rhythm, accelerated junctional rhythm, and junctional tachycardia.

More P Waves than QRS Complexes

More P waves than QRS complexes indicate that the impulse was initiated in the SA node or other ectopic sites in the atria but was blocked and did not reach the ventricles. More P waves than QRS complexes are seen with both types of 2nd-degree AV heart block, with 3rd-degree AV heart block, with blocked PACs, and with atrial tachycardia with block.

Sawtooth Waveforms

Sawtooth waveforms or flutter waves (F waves) that appear instead of P waves are seen with atrial flutter.

Indiscernible P Waves

A chaotic-looking baseline with no discernable P waves (in other words an absence of P waves) is seen with atrial fibrillation. Instead of P waves, we see uneven baseline of f waves.

Absent P Waves

With ventricular dysrhythmias, P waves are absent. They can also be absent with junctional rhythms (when the atrial and ventricular depolarization occur simultaneously). Absent P waves may also occur with supraventricular tachycardia (a fast heart rate with narrow QRS complexes).

Step 4: QRS Complexes

LO 22.4

Depending on where each dysrhythmia originates, QRS complexes are either normal or abnormal (Figure 22-5). In certain conditions, they are absent.

KEY CONCEPT
Dysrhythmias can be categorized by the presence, morphology, or absence of QRS complexes.

Normal QRS Complexes

Depending the lead viewed, QRS complexes should appear normal (upright and narrow) in sinus rhythm, sinus bradycardia, sinus tachycardia, sinus dysrhythmia, sinus arrest/block, wandering atrial pacemaker, premature atrial complexes, atrial tachycardia, atrial fibrillation, atrial flutter, junctional escape, accelerated junctional rhythm, premature atrial complexes, and junctional tachycardia.

Abnormal QRS Complexes

The morphology of the abnormal QRS complex can vary from being only slightly abnormal to being extremely wide, notched, or slurred. We refer to these extremely abnormal configurations as bizarre-looking because they deviate so far from

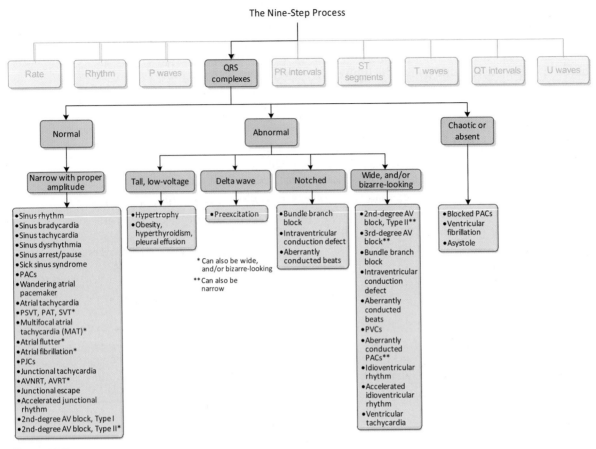

Figure 22-5
QRS complex algorithm.

normal. Abnormal QRS complexes can occur when the pacemaker is initiated from above the ventricles as well as when it is initiated from within the ventricles.

Tall and Low Amplitude QRS Complexes

Very tall QRS complexes are usually caused by hypertrophy of one or both ventricles or by an abnormal pacemaker or aberrantly conducted beat. Low-voltage or abnormally small QRS complexes may be seen in obese patients, hyperthyroid patients, and patients with pleural effusion.

Wide and/or Abnormal QRS Complexes of Supraventricular Origin

Wide, bizarre QRS complexes seen in supraventricular rhythms are often the result of an intraventricular conduction defect, usually caused by RBBB or LBBB. With 2nd-degree AV block, type II the QRS complexes may be wide if the block is infranodal.

Other causes of wide QRS complexes include MI; fibrosis; hypertrophy; electrolyte imbalance, such as hypokalemia and hyperkalemia; and excessive administration of cardiac drugs such as quinidine, procainamide, and flecainide. Aberrant conduction, ventricular preexcitation, and pacemaker-induced rhythms can also produce wide and/or abnormal QRS complexes.

KEY CONCEPT

Tall QRS complexes suggest hypertrophy of one or both ventricles, an abnormal pacemaker, or aberrantly conducted beat.

Wide, Bizarre QRS Complexes of Ventricular Origin

Dysrhythmias that originate from the ventricular tissue produce wide and bizarre QRS complexes. This includes PVCs, idioventricular rhythm, and ventricular tachycardia. Wide, bizarre-looking QRS complexes may also be produced by an escape ventricular pacemaker in 3rd-degree AV block.

Absent QRS Complexes

Absent QRS complexes result from ventricular standstill and asystole. A chaotic wavy line, rising and falling without any logic, instead of the normal ECG waveforms is seen with ventricular fibrillation.

Step 5: PR Intervals

The PR interval is either present or absent (Figure 22-6). When the PR interval is present, it can be either normal or abnormal.

Normal PR Intervals

The PR interval is usually normal and constant with normal sinus rhythm, sinus bradycardia, sinus tachycardia, sinus dysrhythmia, sinus arrest and 2nd-degree AV block. A PR interval within 0.12 to 0.20 seconds can also be present

LO 22.5

KEY CONCEPT
Dysrhythmias can be categorized by the presence or absence of PR intervals, their duration, and their constancy or variance in duration.

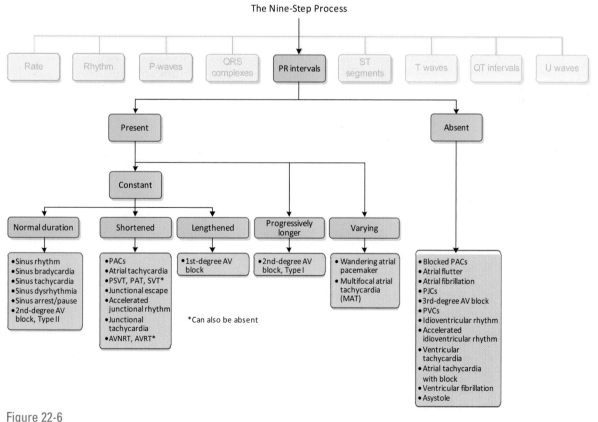

Figure 22-6
PR interval algorithm.

with some dysrhythmias that arise from the atria, provided the ectopic site is located in the upper-atrial wall.

Abnormal PR Intervals

Abnormal PR intervals are those that are shorter than 0.12 seconds, are longer than 0.20 seconds, are absent, or vary in duration.

Shorter PR Intervals

Shorter-than-normal PR intervals occur with premature beats that arise from the atria (PACs) or junction (PJCs), atrial or junctional tachycardia, and preexcitation.

Longer PR Intervals

Longer-than-normal PR intervals occur in 1st-degree AV heart block. The PR intervals seen in 1st-degree AV block are constant in duration.

Varying PR Intervals

The PR interval varies or changes in two dysrhythmias; wandering atrial pacemaker and 2nd-degree AV heart block, type I.

Absent or Not Measurable PR Intervals

The PR interval is absent or not measurable in blocked PACs, atrial flutter, atrial fibrillation, PVCs, idioventricular rhythm, ventricular tachycardia, atrial tachycardia with blocks, and 3rd-degree AV block. It may also be absent or not measurable in PJCs, accelerated junctional rhythm, and junctional tachycardia.

LO 22.6

KEY CONCEPT
Dysrhythmias can be categorized by the presence, appearance, or absence of ST segments.

Step 6: ST Segments

ST segments are either present or not present (Figure 23-7). If they are present, they are either normal or abnormal.

Normal ST Segments

Usually, normal ST segments are seen in sinus bradycardia, sinus rhythm, sinus tachycardia, sinus dysrhythmia, sinus arrest (for the conducted beats), wandering atrial pacemaker, PACs, PJCs, atrial tachycardia, multifocal atrial tachycardia PSVT, PAT, SVT, junctional escape, accelerated junctional rhythm, junctional tachycardia, 2nd-degree AV heart block, 3rd-degree AV heart block AVNRT and AVRT.

Abnormal ST Segments

Abnormal ST segments are categorized as either elevated or depressed ST segments. Also, the ST segments may be indistinguishable in certain dysrhythmias.

The Nine-Step Process

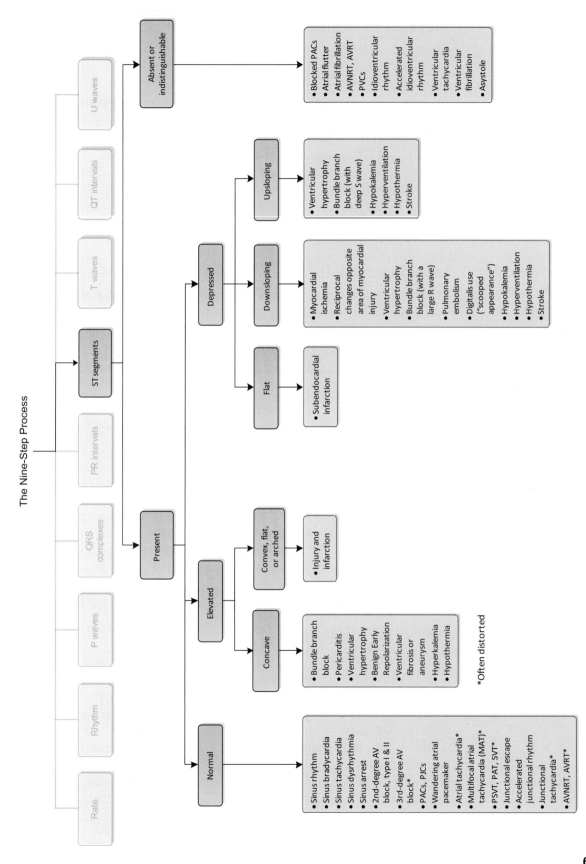

Figure 22-7
ST segment algorithm.

Elevated ST Segments

Elevated ST segments are seen in marked myocardial injury and may be an early indicator of MI. Other causes of elevated ST segment include bundle branch block, pericarditis, Benigh Early Repolarization ventricular hypertrophy, ventricular fibrosis or aneurysm, hyperkalemia, and hypothermia.

Depressed ST Segments

A depressed ST segment is seen with myocardial ischemia or reciprocal changes opposite the area of myocardial injury. ST segment depression may also occur with right and left ventricular hypertrophy (strain pattern), right and left bundle branch block, pulmonary embolism, digitalis use, hypokalemia, hyperventilation, hypothermia, and stroke. ST segment depression that appears flat is seen in subendocardial infarction.

Indistinguishable ST Segments

The ST segment is typically indistinguishable in blocked PACs, atrial fibrillation, atrial flutter, AVNRT, AVRT PVCs, idioventricular rhythm, accelerated idioventricular rhythm, ventricular tachycardia ventricular fibrillation and asystole. It may also be indistinguishable in PSVT.

Step 7: T Waves

KEY CONCEPT
Dysrhythmias can be categorized by the presence, appearance, deflection, or absence of T waves.

T waves are either present or not present (Figure 22-8). If they are present, they are either normal or abnormal.

Normal T Waves

Usually, normal T waves are seen in sinus bradycardia, sinus rhythm, sinus tachycardia, sinus dysrhythmia, sinus arrest (for the conducted beats), wandering atrial pacemaker, PACs, PJCs, atrial tachycardia, multifocal atrial tachycardia, PSVT, PAT, SVT, junctional escape, accelerated junctional rhythm, junctional tachycardia, 2nd-degree AV heart block, and 3rd-degree AV heart block. With atrial dysrhythmias, junctional dysrhythmias, and 3rd-degree AV block, the T wave may be distorted if the P wave is buried in the T wave.

Abnormal T Waves

Tall or peaked T waves, also known as *tented T waves*, are seen in myocardial ischemia, ventricular hypertrophy, and hyperkalemia. Heavily notched or pointed T waves in an adult may indicate pericarditis. Inverted T waves in leads where they are characteristically upright may be seen with myocardial ischemia. Deeply inverted T waves are seen with significant cerebral disease such as subarachnoid hemorrhage. Flat T waves are seen with certain electrolyte imbalances. T waves with bumps may be seen when P waves are buried in the T waves. This occurs with early beats that arise from the atria or AV junctional tissue or in certain types of AV heart block.

Also, T waves seen with impulses that arise from the ventricles take a direction opposite of their associated QRS complexes.

The Nine-Step Process

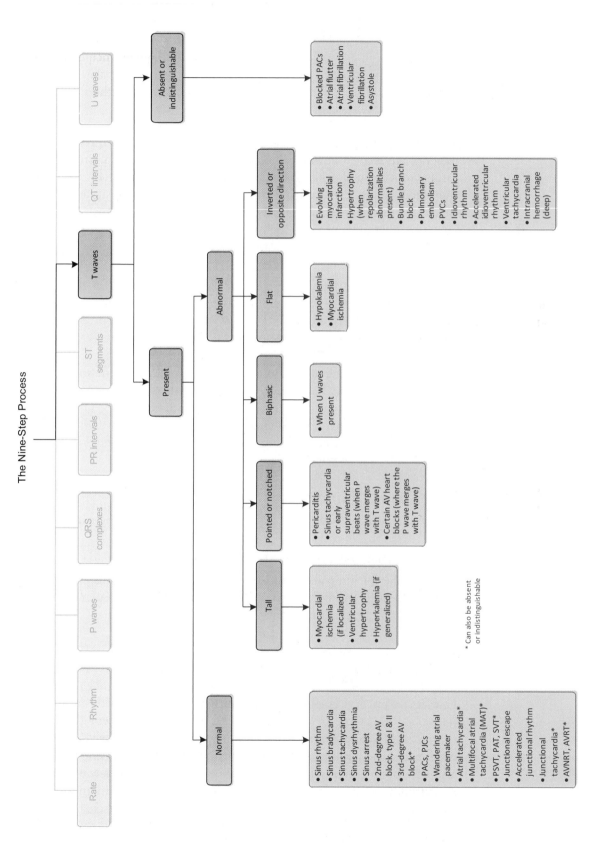

Figure 22-8
T wave algorithm.

649

Step 8: QT Intervals

Unless there are no Q waves and/or T waves, the QT interval is present (Figure 22-9). It may be normal or abnormal.

Normal QT Intervals

The normal QT interval is 0.36 to 0.44 seconds in duration. Normal QT intervals are seen in normal sinus rhythm, sinus dysrhythmia, sinus bradycardia (which can also be prolonged), sinus tachycardia (which can also be shortened), sinus arrest (during conducted beats), PACs, atrial tachycardia, wandering atrial pacemaker, PJCs, junctional escape rhythm, accelerated junctional rhythm, junctional tachycardia, 1st-degree AV block, types I & II, 2nd-degree AV block, and 3rd-degree AV block.

Abnormal QT Intervals

Abnormal QT intervals are either prolonged, shortened, or indiscernible.

Prolonged QT Intervals

One cause of prolonged QT intervals is congenital conduction system defect. Drugs such as haloperidol and methadone and Class IA antidysrhythmic drugs like amiodarone or sotalol can also produce QT interval prolongation. Moreover, prolonged QT intervals can be present in idioventricular rhythm, accelerated idioventricular rhythm, torsades de points, hypokalemia, and hypocalcemia.

Shortened QT Intervals

A shortened QT interval can be caused by hypercalcemia or digoxin toxicity.

Indiscernible or Not Measurable QT Intervals

Indiscernible QT intervals occur in multifocal atrial tachycardia, paroxysmal atrial tachycardia, atrial flutter, atrial fibrillation, PVCs, ventricular tachycardia, ventricular fibrillation, and asystole.

Step 9: U Waves

U waves are either present or not present (Figure 22-10).

Prominent U waves are most often seen in hypokalemia but may be present in hypercalcemia, thyrotoxicosis, digitalis toxicity, use of epinephrine and Class 1A and Class 3 antidysrhythmics, mitral valve prolapse, and left ventricular hypertrophy, as well as in congenital long QT syndrome and with intracranial hemorrhage. An inverted U wave may represent myocardial ischemia or left ventricular volume overload.

The Nine-Step Process

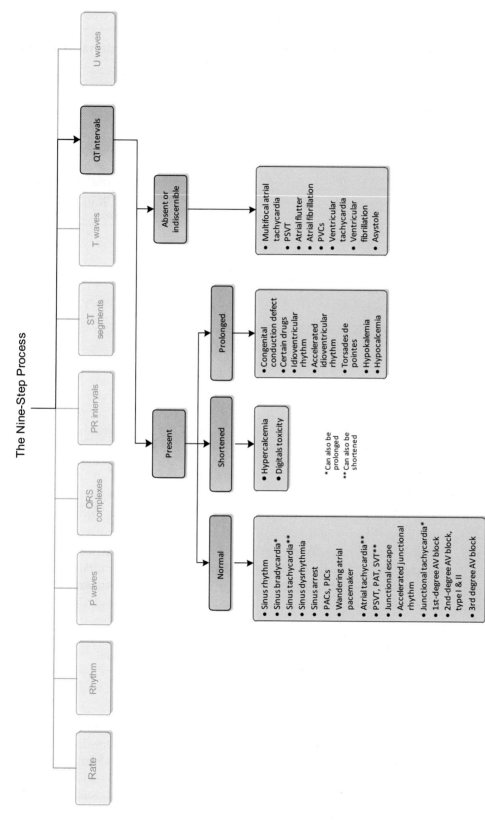

Figure 22-9
QT interval algorithm.

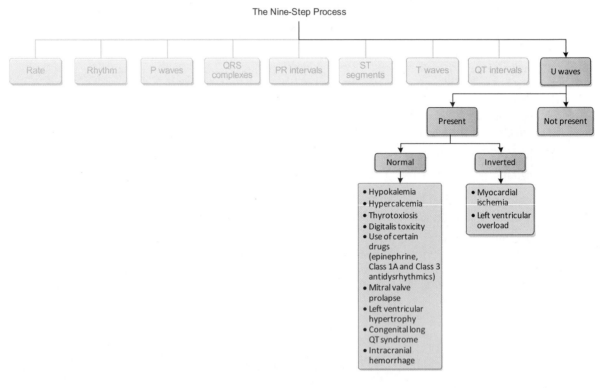

Figure 22-10
U wave algorithm.

So Why Do It?

From the practice tracings that follow you can see how we are able to narrow down the possibilities when we identify what each problem might be. We start with the heart rate. Just putting it into a slow, normal, or fast group narrows down the field considerably. Then we are able to eliminate other possibilities when we identify the regularity of the tracing. This continues as we move through each step of the analysis process. Sometimes we can quickly identify the dysrhythmia or cardiac condition; at other times it requires us to go through all nine steps to reach a conclusion. Although it is not required that you use this process, you will find that it actually makes it easier to identify cardiac dysrhythmias and conditions.

Practice Ruling Out Dysrhythmias and Conditions

Okay, let's analyze 10 ECG tracings. Be sure to apply the principles we learned throughout this book as well as what is described earlier in this chapter. For the dysrhythmias, The Five-Step Process is often sufficient. However, for the 12-lead ECGs, The Nine-Step Process as listed below is needed. Following each practice tracing is an analysis to which you can compare your findings.

1. Is the rate of this dysrhythmia slow, normal or fast?

2. Is this rhythm regular or irregular? If it is irregular, what type of irregularity is it?

3. Are there P waves? What do they look like? Is each followed by a QRS complex?

4. Are the QRS complexes present? If so, what do they look like?

5. Are the PR intervals present? If so, what is their duration and is it constant?

6. Are the ST segments present? If so, are they normal or abnormal?

7. Are the T waves present? If so, are they normal or abnormal?

8. Are the QT intervals measurable? If so, are they normal or abnormal?

9. Are U waves present?

1.

ECG Findings:

Analysis

If you said this rhythm is slow, you are correct. As such, it must be sinus bradycardia, junctional escape, idioventricular rhythm, sinus arrest, sick sinus syndrome, 2nd-degree AV heart block, 3rd-degree AV heart block, atrial flutter, or atrial fibrillation. Next, if you said this rhythm is regular, you are correct again. Of the dysrhythmias listed above, only sinus bradycardia, junctional escape, idioventricular rhythm, and 3rd-degree AV block are regular. Atrial flutter can be regular if the conduction ratio remains constant. Because the rhythm is regular, it cannot be sinus arrest or atrial fibrillation. Next, if you said the dysrhythmia has a normal P wave preceding each QRS complex, you are correct. Of the remaining dysrhythmias, only sinus bradycardia has a normal P wave preceding each QRS complex. Thus, we can say with reasonable certainty that this is sinus bradycardia. To make sure, we evaluate the QRS complexes, which are normal, and the PR intervals, which are normal. Further, the ST segments are normal, the T waves are biphasic, and the QT intervals are normal. Lastly, there are no U waves. Therefore, we can conclude this is sinus bradycardia.

2.

ECG Findings:

Analysis

If you said this dysrhythmia is fast, you are correct. As such, it must be sinus tachycardia, sick sinus syndrome, atrial tachycardia, multifocal atrial tachycardia, junctional tachycardia, SVT, AVRT, AVNRT, ventricular tachycardia, atrial flutter, or atrial fibrillation. Next, if you said the rhythm was regular, you are correct. Sinus tachycardia, junctional tachycardia, and ventricular tachycardia are regular. Atrial flutter can also be regular. Next, we look at the P waves; none are identifiable. Only junctional tachycardia and ventricular tachycardia have no P wave preceding each QRS complex, so this must be one of the two. Next, we evaluate the QRS complexes, which are normal. Of the two dysrhythmias it could be, only junctional tachycardia has narrow QRS complexes. Therefore, it is most likely junctional tachycardia. To further review our findings, we evaluate the PR interval and find none. Also, the ST segments, T waves, and QT intervals are normal, and there are no U waves. This confirms this rhythm is junctional tachycardia. Now, we also recognize that atrial tachycardia can display all the same characteristics, so we can also call this *supraventricular tachycardia.*

3.

ECG Findings:

Analysis

Your answer is right if you said that this rhythm is slow. As such, it can only be sinus bradycardia, junctional escape, idioventricular rhythm, sinus arrest, sick sinus syndrome, 2nd-degree AV heart block, 3rd-degree AV heart block, atrial flutter, or atrial fibrillation. Next, if you identified this rhythm as irregular, you are correct. Of the remaining dysrhythmias, we need to rule out those that are regular. Sinus node arrest, 2nd-degree AV heart block, and atrial fibrillation are irregular. Atrial flutter can also be irregular. However, this rhythm has patterned irregularity. Only one of the remaining dysrhythmias, type I, 2nd-degree AV block, has patterned irregularity, so on the basis of that information, it is most likely that dysrhythmia. Next, we look at the P waves. Only one of the remaining dysrhythmias has upright, normal P waves that are not all followed by a QRS complex. Next, we evaluate the QRS complexes, which are normal. Last, we review the PR intervals. Here we see the characteristic that occurs with just one dysrhythmia, a progressively longer PR interval that leads to a dropped QRS complex. This cycle repeats itself over and over again. Further, the ST segments, T waves, and QT intervals are normal, and there are no U waves present. Therefore, this dysrhythmia can only be type I, 2nd-degree AV block.

4.

ECG Findings:

Analysis

If you said this dysrhythmia is fast, you are correct. As such, it must be sinus tachycardia, atrial tachycardia, multifocal atrial tachycardia, junctional tachycardia, ventricular tachycardia, atrial flutter, or atrial fibrillation. This rhythm is irregular, specifically a totally irregular rhythm. Of the dysrhythmias listed earlier, only atrial fibrillation is totally irregular. Next, look for the P waves to find that none are identifiable. Instead there is a chaotic baseline preceding each QRS complex. This is characteristic of only one dysrhythmia, atrial fibrillation. Next, evaluate the QRS complexes. These are normal. Again, this is more evidence this dysrhythmia is atrial fibrillation. Lastly, we look for PR intervals; we find they are absent. Also, the ST segments, T waves, and QT intervals are indiscernible, and there are no U waves. There is sufficient evidence to call this dysrhythmia *atrial fibrillation* (with a rapid ventricular response).

5.

ECG Findings:

Analysis

You are correct if you said this rhythm is slow. As such, it can only be one of the following dysrhythmias: sinus bradycardia, junctional escape, idioventricular rhythm, sinus arrest, sick sinus syndrome, 2nd-degree AV heart block, 3rd-degree AV heart block, atrial flutter, or atrial fibrillation. If you said this rhythm is regular, you are also correct. Of the listed dysrhythmias, those that are regular include sinus bradycardia, junctional escape, idioventricular rhythm, and 3rd-degree AV block (although, there is no correlation between the P waves and QRS complexes). Atrial flutter can also be regular. Next, if you said there is an absence of P waves, you are correct. Only two of the listed dysrhythmias have an absence of P wave preceding each QRS complex: junctional escape and idioventricular rhythm. Next, you are correct if you identified this dysrhythmia as having narrow QRS complexes. Of the remaining two dysrhythmias, only junctional escape has narrow QRS complexes. Thus, this dysrhythmia must be junctional escape. To make sure, we evaluate the PR intervals, which are absent. Further, the ST segments, T waves, and QT intervals are normal, and no U waves are present. Therefore, we can conclude this is junctional escape.

6.

ECG Findings:

Analysis

If you said this rhythm is fast, you are correct. As such, it can only be sinus tachycardia, sick sinus syndrome, atrial tachycardia, multifocal atrial tachycardia, junctional tachycardia, ventricular tachycardia, atrial flutter, or atrial fibrillation. Also, this rhythm is regular. Of the listed dysrhythmias, only sinus tachycardia, junctional tachycardia, and idioventricular tachycardia are regular. Atrial flutter can also be regular. Next, we can see there are no identifiable P waves. Only junctional tachycardia and ventricular tachycardia have no identifiable P. Next, we evaluate the QRS complexes, which are wide and bizarre in appearance. Of the two dysrhythmias listed earlier, only ventricular tachycardia has wide, bizarre-looking QRS complexes. Therefore, this dysrhythmia is most likely ventricular tachycardia. A further review of our findings shows that there is no PR interval. Further, the ST segments and QT intervals are indistinguishable, the T waves take the opposite direction of the QRS complexes, and there are no U waves present. This rhythm then is ventricular tachycardia.

7.

ECG Findings:

Analysis

If you said that this rhythm has a normal rate, you are correct. As such, it can only be sinus rhythm, sinus dysrhythmia, wandering atrial pacemaker, accelerated junctional rhythm, accelerated ventricular rhythm, sinus arrest, 2nd-degree AV heart block, 3rd-degree AV heart block, atrial flutter, atrial fibrillation, or a paced rhythm. (These rhythms may or may not include ectopic beats.) Next, we can see this rhythm is irregular. More specifically, it is occasionally irregular. In looking at the irregularity, it is apparent there are two premature beats. Therefore, we need to identify the underlying rhythm and then the origin of the premature beats, in others words, dissect it a bit to see what we have. First, let's look closely at the underlying rhythm. There is one normal-looking P wave preceding each of the normal beats, and the QRS complexes and PR intervals are normal. Further, the distance between the normal beats is the same. Only one of the rhythms listed above has these characteristics. Our underlying rhythm is sinus rhythm. Next, let's look at our early beats. If you said there is an absence of P waves, the QRS complexes are wide and bizarre-looking, and there are no PR intervals with the early beats, you are correct. Remember what we learned earlier, if the QRS complexes are wide, it typically means they have arisen from the ventricles. The exception to this rule is if the impulse arises from the SA node, atria, or AV junction but conduction through the ventricles is abnormal (preexcitation, aberrant conduction, bundle branch block, etc.). Then the QRS complexes can appear wide and bizarre. In looking closer at the early beats, we see there are no P waves or PR intervals, so they can only be PVC. Thus, our dysrhythmia is sinus rhythm with two PVCs. Further, the ST segments, T waves, and QT intervals in the underlying rhythm are normal, and no U waves are present.

8.

ECG Findings:

Analysis

The rate is 100 BPM, so it can be considered fast. Dysrhythmias having a fast rate include sinus tachycardia, sick sinus syndrome, atrial tachycardia, multifocal junctional tachycardia, ventricular tachycardia, atrial flutter, and atrial fibrillation. Whereas atrial tachycardia is also fast, we rule it out as atrial tachycardia normally has a rate of at least 160 BPM. The rhythm is regular. Of the listed dysrhythmias, those having a regular rhythm include sinus tachycardia, atrial tachycardia, junctional tachycardia, ventricular tachycardia, and atrial flutter (if the conduction ratio remains constant). There are sinus P waves preceding each QRS complex. However, the P waves are wide and notched in leads III, V_4, V_5, and V_6 and normal in the others. Of the dysrhythmias listed earlier, only one has a P wave: sinus tachycardia. However, the morphology of the P waves indicates left atrial enlargement. The QRS complexes are wider than normal with an rsR′ pattern in lead V_1 and a broad slurred S wave in leads I, aV_L, and V_6. This is characteristic of just one condition, RBBB. The PR intervals are within normal duration (0.14 seconds). The ST segments are normal, and the T waves are inverted in III and V_1 and flattened in lead aV_F. This patient has sinus tachycardia with left atrial enlargement and RBBB.

9.

ECG Findings:

Analysis

At 135 BPM, this heart rate is fast. Dysrhythmias having a fast rate include sinus tachycardia, sick sinus syndrome, atrial tachycardia, multifocal junctional tachycardia, ventricular tachycardia, atrial flutter, and atrial fibrillation. Whereas atrial tachycardia is also fast, we rule it out because atrial tachycardia normally has a rate of at least 160 BPM. This rhythm is regular. Of the listed dysrhythmias, those having a regular rhythm include sinus tachycardia, atrial tachycardia, junctional tachycardia, ventricular tachycardia, and atrial flutter (if the conduction ratio remains constant). There are sinus P waves preceding each QRS complex. They are normal in most leads but biphasic in lead I. Of the dysrhythmias listed earlier, just sinus tachycardia has a sinus P wave preceding each QRS complex. The QRS complexes are narrow with elevated R waves in leads V_2 and V_3. This further supports this dysrhythmia being sinus tachycardia. The PR intervals are 0.18 seconds in duration. This allows us to rule out the presence of 1st-degree AV heart block. The ST segments are elevated (upsloping) in leads I, aV_L, and V_1 through V_6 and depressed in leads III and aV_F. There are Q waves forming in leads V_4 and V_5. The extensive anterior lateral ST segment elevation with reciprocal changes in inferior leads is characteristic of just one cardiac condition, acute MI. Further, no U waves are present. This patient has sinus tachycardia with acute anterolateral myocardial injury.

10.

ECG Findings:

Analysis

The heart rate is 88 BPM, so it is normal. As such, it can only be sinus rhythm, sinus dysrhythmia, wandering atrial pacemaker, accelerated junctional rhythm, accelerated ventricular rhythm, sinus arrest, 2nd-degree AV heart block, 3rd-degree AV heart block, atrial flutter, atrial fibrillation, or a paced rhythm. The rhythm is regular, so we can eliminate a couple of dysrhythmias from consideration. Whereas there are P waves, a more telling characteristic is the small narrow spike preceding each wide QRS complex. The only rhythm having this characteristic is a paced rhythm. Evaluating this rhythm further, we see the PR intervals are within normal duration (0.16 seconds). However, the PR interval is inconsequential because the ventricles are being stimulated to beat by the pacemaker. Along with the wide and bizarre-looking QRS complexes are T waves that take the opposite direction of the QRS complex. The ST segments and QT intervals cannot be identified, and there are no U waves. This patient has sinus rhythm with an AV sequential pacemaker with atrial sensing and ventricular pacing.

Key Points 🔍

- The dysrhythmias that will or are likely to have slow heart rates are sinus bradycardia, junctional escape rhythm, idioventricular rhythm, AV heart block, and atrial flutter, or fibrillation with slow ventricular response. Sinus arrest and sick sinus syndrome may also have a slow rate.

- Dysrhythmias having a normal heart rate include normal sinus rhythm, sinus dysrhythmia, wandering atrial pacemaker, accelerated junctional rhythm, and accelerated idioventricular rhythm (which spans across both slow and normal heart rates). Also, 2nd- and 3rd-degree AV heart blocks, sinus arrest, sick sinus syndrome, atrial flutter, and atrial fibrillation can have a normal (ventricular) heart rate.

- The dysrhythmias that will or are likely to have fast heart rates are sinus tachycardia, atrial tachycardia, SVT, PSVT, junctional tachycardia, AVNRT, AVRT, ventricular tachycardia, and atrial flutter, or fibrillation with rapid ventricular response.

- Dysrhythmias having a regular rhythm include sinus rhythm, sinus bradycardia, sinus tachycardia, junctional escape, accelerated junctional rhythm, junctional tachycardia, idioventricular rhythm, and accelerated idioventricular rhythm. Atrial flutter, 2nd-degree AV heart block, type II, and 3rd-degree AV block can also be regular.

- The only dysrhythmia characterized as being totally irregular is atrial fibrillation.

- Normal P waves preceding each QRS complex are seen in normal sinus rhythm, sinus bradycardia, sinus tachycardia, sinus dysrhythmia, and sinus arrest.

- In atrial fibrillation, there are no discernable P waves. Instead, there is a chaotic-looking baseline of *f waves* preceding the QRS complexes.

- Impulses that arise from the AV junction produce an inverted P′ wave that may immediately precede, or occur during or following, the QRS complex.

- Tall and symmetrically peaked P waves may be seen with increased right atrial pressure and right atrial dilation.

- Notched or wide (enlarged) P waves may be seen in increased left atrial pressure and left atrial dilation.

- In wandering atrial pacemaker, the P′ waves appear different, and the P′R intervals appear to vary.

- More P waves than QRS complexes are characteristic of 2nd-degree AV heart block (types I and II) 3rd-degree AV heart block, and blocked PACs.

- Normal sinus rhythm and dysrhythmias that arise from above the ventricles will usually (unless there is a conduction delay through the ventricles or other type of abnormality as described earlier in the text) have normal QRS complexes.

- Very tall QRS complexes are usually caused by hypertrophy of one or both ventricles or by an abnormal pacemaker or aberrantly conducted beat.

- Low-voltage or abnormally small QRS complexes may be seen in obese patients, hyperthyroid patients, and patients with pleural effusion.

- Wide, bizarre-looking QRS complexes with T waves that deflect in an opposite direction to the R waves are key characteristics seen with PVCs, idioventricular rhythm, accelerated idioventricular rhythm, and ventricular tachycardia.

- 3rd-degree AV heart block is another dysrhythmia where there may be abnormal QRS complexes.

- With type I, 2nd-degree AV heart block, PR intervals are progressively longer until a QRS complex is dropped and then the cycle starts over.

- There will be an absence of PR intervals in atrial flutter and fibrillation and in ventricular dysrhythmias.

- In 3rd-degree AV heart block, the PR interval is not measurable.

- In type II, 2nd-degree AV heart block, the PR intervals associated with the P waves conducted through to the ventricles are constant.

Assess Your Understanding

The following questions give you a chance to assess your understanding of the material discussed in this chapter. The answers can be found in Appendix A.

1. A rhythm that arises from the SA node and has a heart rate of less than 60 beats per minute is called
    a. junctional escape.
    b. idioventricular rhythm.
    c. sinus bradycardia.
    d. normal sinus rhythm.

2. Which of the following dysrhythmias has a normal heart rate?
    a. Accelerated junctional rhythm
    b. Sinus tachycardia
    c. Idioventricular rhythm
    d. Junctional tachycardia

3. Sinus bradycardia has a/an _____ rhythm.
    a. patterned irregular
    b. regular
    c. occasionally irregular
    d. variable conduction ratio

4. Which of the following produces a totally irregular rhythm?
    a. Paroxysmal atrial tachycardia
    b. Wenckebach
    c. Atrial fibrillation
    d. Atrial flutter with varying conduction ratio

5. A patterned irregular rhythm is seen when
    a. the heart rate suddenly accelerates.
    b. there are many early beats.
    c. initiation of the heartbeat changes from site to site with each heartbeat.
    d. premature complexes occur every other (second) complex, every third complex, or every fourth complex.

6. Which of the following has more P waves than QRS complexes?
    a. A dysrhythmia in which the pacemaker changes from site to site with each beat
    b. Premature complexes that arise from the atria
    c. AV heart block
    d. Dysrhythmias that arise from the AV junction

7. Which of the following will produce P waves that look different than sinus P waves?
    a. Enlarged or damaged atria
    b. 2nd-degree AV heart block
    c. Sinus dysrhythmia
    d. 3rd-degree AV heart block

8. Which of the following dysrhythmias will likely have narrow QRS complexes?
    a. Bundle branch block
    b. Idioventricular rhythm
    c. Paced rhythm
    d. Sinus tachycardia

9. Low-voltage or abnormally small QRS complexes are seen in
    a. hypertrophy.
    b. obese patients.
    c. premature ventricular complexes.
    d. sinus bradycardia.

10. Premature ventricular complexes
    a. arise from the atria.
    b. always have an inverted QRS complex.
    c. produce QRS complexes that look different than those that arise above or at the AV junction.
    d. have narrow, upright QRS complexes.

11. With 3rd-degree AV block, the QRS complexes
    a. are always wide and bizarre-looking.
    b. are associated with irregular and frequent PVCs.
    c. follow each P wave but at a slower rate.
    d. are slower than the P wave rate because there is complete blockage of the AV node.

12. Which of the following is characteristic of 1st-degree AV heart block?
    a. Varying PR intervals
    b. PR intervals of less than 0.12 seconds
    c. More P waves than QRS complexes
    d. Constant PR intervals of greater than 0.20 seconds

13. With wandering atrial pacemaker, the P'R intervals
    a. are constant.
    b. vary.
    c. are longer in duration than 0.20 seconds.
    d. become progressively longer.

14. The PR intervals with 2nd-degree AV heart block, type I
    a. are constant.
    b. are absent.
    c. are shorter in duration than 0.12 seconds.
    d. become progressively longer.

15. There will be an absence of PR intervals in
    a. premature atrial complexes.
    b. 1st-degree AV heart block.
    c. 3rd-degree AV heart block.
    d. wandering atrial pacemaker.

16. Type II 2nd-degree AV heart block has PR intervals that
    a. continually change in duration.
    b. are constant.
    c. have no relationship.
    d. are less than 0.12 seconds in duration.

17. With atrial dysrhythmias, the
    a. atrial waveforms differ in appearance from normal sinus P waves.
    b. P'R intervals are almost always prolonged.
    c. QRS complexes are wider than normal.
    d. site of origin is in the bundle of His.

18. Your patient is a 67-year-old female with a history of cardiac problems. After attaching her to the monitor, you see a slightly irregular rhythm with normal QRS complexes, but each P′ wave is different. This rhythm is

    a. frequent PACs.

    b. sinus arrest.

    c. sinus dysrhythmia.

    d. wandering atrial pacemaker

Referring to the scenario at the beginning of this chapter answer the following questions.

19. What is the origin of the narrow QRS complexes?

    a. Supraventricular

    b. Ventricular

20. The underlying rhythm is most likely

    a. Multifocal atrial tachycardia

    b. Atrial flutter

    c. Idioventricular rhythm

    d. Sinus rhythm

What's Online

Go to www.mhhe.com/shadeECG2e to find:

- Presentations on chapter content
- Chapter quiz
- Fill-in-the-blank exercises and answers
- In-depth answers to Practice Makes Perfect ECG tracings and Assess Your Understanding questions

Practice Makes Perfect

For each of the tracings on the following pages, practice the Nine-Step Process for analyzing ECGs. To achieve the greatest learning, you should practice assessing and interpretating the ECGs immediately after reading Chapter 22. Below are questions you should consider as you assess each tracing. Your answers can be written into the area below each ECG marked "ECG Findings." Your findings can be compared to the answers provided in Appendix A. All tracings are six seconds in length.

1. Determine the heart rate. Is it slow? Normal? Fast? What is the ventricular rate? What is the atrial rate?

2. Determine if the rhythm is regular or irregular. If it is irregular, what type of irregularity is it? Occasional or frequent? Slight? Sudden acceleration or slowing in heart rate? Total? Patterned? Does it have a variable conduction ratio?

3. Determine if P waves are present. If so, how do they appear? Do they have normal height and duration? Are they tall? Notched? Wide? Biphasic? Of differing morphology? Inverted? One for each QRS complex? More than one preceding some or all the QRS complexes? Do they have a sawtooth appearance? An indiscernible chaotic baseline?

4. Determine if QRS complexes are present. If so, how do they appear? Narrow with proper amplitude? Tall? Low amplitude? Delta wave? Notched? Wide? Bizarre-looking? With chaotic waveforms?

5. Determine the presence of PR intervals. If present, how do they appear? Constant? Of normal duration? Shortened? Lengthened? Progressively longer? Varying?

6. Evaluate the ST segments. Do they have normal duration and position? Are they elevated? (If so, are they flat, concave, convex, arched?) Depressed? (If so, are they normal, flat, downsloping, or upsloping?)

7. Determine if T waves are present. If so, how do they appear? Of normal height and duration? Tall? Wide? Notched? Inverted?

8. Determine the presence of QT intervals. If present, what is their duration? Normal? Shortened? Prolonged?

9. Determine if U waves are present. If present, how do they appear? Of normal height and duration? Inverted?

10. Identify the rhythm or dysrhythmia.

1.

ECG Findings:

2.

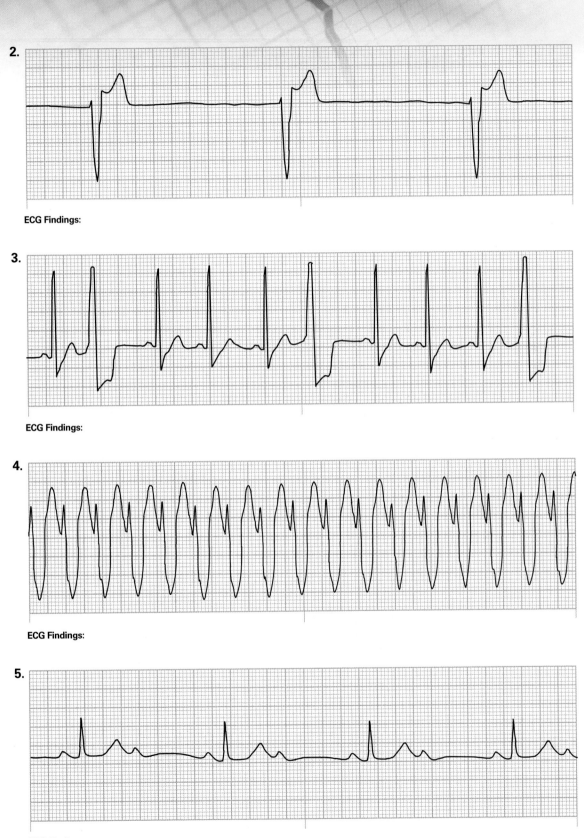

ECG Findings:

3.

ECG Findings:

4.

ECG Findings:

5.

ECG Findings:

6.

ECG Findings:

7.

ECG Findings:

8.

ECG Findings:

9.

ECG Findings:

10.

ECG Findings:

11.

ECG Findings:

12.

ECG Findings:

13.

ECG Findings:

14.

ECG Findings:

15.

ECG Findings:

16.

ECG Findings:

17.

ECG Findings:

18.

ECG Findings:

19.

ECG Findings:

20.

ECG Findings:

21.

ECG Findings:

22.

ECG Findings:

23.

ECG Findings:

24.

ECG Findings:

25.

ECG Findings:

26.

ECG Findings:

27.

ECG Findings:

28.

ECG Findings:

29.

ECG Findings:

30.

ECG Findings:

31.

ECG Findings:

32.

ECG Findings:

33.

ECG Findings:

34.

ECG Findings:

35.

ECG Findings:

36.

ECG Findings:

37.

ECG Findings:

38.

ECG Findings:

39.

ECG Findings:

40.

ECG Findings:

41.

ECG Findings:

Answers

Assess Your Understanding

The following are answers to the **Assess Your Understanding** sections at the end of each chapter. More in-depth answers for each can be found at the Fast & Easy ECGs Website at www.mhhe.com/shadeECG2e.

Chapter 1

1. d
2. b
3. b
4. b
5. c
6. d
7. a
8. b
9. a
10. b
11. d
12. b
13. b
14. a
15. d
16. b
17. a
18. c
19. b
20. b
21. d
22. b
23. d
24. c
25. c
26. a
27. b
28. d

Chapter 2

1. a
2. b
3. a
4. d
5. d
6. a
7. c
8. a
9. a
10. c
11. b
12. c
13. b
14. a
15. a
16. a
17. c
18. b
19. d
20. c

Chapter 3

1. c
2. d
3. c
4. a
5. a
6. b
7. c
8. c
9. a
10. a
11. c
12. a
13. b
14. c
15. b

Chapter 4

1. d
2. a
3. c
4. a

5. d

6. a

7. c

8. b

9. d

10. d

11. d

12. a

Chapter 5

1. d

2. c

3. a

4. d

5. c

6. d

7. a

8. c

9. a

10. b

11. d

12. a

13. d

14. a

15. a

Chapter 6

1. b

2. b

3. d

4. d

5. c

6. b

7. a

8. c

9. c

10. b

11. a

12. a

13. b

14. d

15. c

16. d

17. d

Chapter 7

1. b

2. b

3. c

4. a

5. d

6. a

7. c

8. c

9. c

10. b

11. c

12. a

13. d

14. c

15. a

16. b

17. d

18. b

19. d

20. a

21. c

Chapter 8

1. b

2. b

3. b

4. d

5. a

6. c

7. d

8. b

9. c

10. b

11. d

12. a

13. c

14. d

Chapter 9

1. c

2. a

3. d

4. d

5. a

6. c

7. b

8. c

9. b

10. d

11. b

12. c

13. a

14. d

15. c

16. a

17 a

18. c

19 d

20. c

Chapter 10

1. b
2. b
3. b
4. c
5. d
6. b
7. b, c, d, a
8. b
9. d, c, a, b
10. b
11. a
12. b
13. d
14. b
15. a
16. c, d, b, a
17 c
18. a
19 b

Chapter 11

1. b
2. b
3. b
4. b
5. c
6. a
7. c
8. c
9. a
10. a
11. d
12. d
13. d

14. d, c, b, a
15. a
16. c
17 a
18. b
19 a

Chapter 12

1. a
2. c
3. d
4. d
5. a
6. c
7. a
8. b
9. c
10. c
11. c
12. b
13. d
14. d
15. c
16. b
17. c

Chapter 13

1. c
2. d
3. c
4. b
5. b, a, c
6. b
7. b

8. c, a, b
9. c
10. d
11. d
12. c
13. c
14. b
15. b

Chapter 14

1. c
2. d
3. d
4. c, b, a, d
5. c
6. b
7. a
8. b
9. d
10. c
11. a
12. b
13. c
14. a
15. c

Chapter 15

1. a
2. a
3. c
4. b
5. a
6. c
7. a
8. d

9. c

10. b

11. b, d, c, a

12. c

13. b

14. a

Chapter 16

1. a
2. c
3. b
4. d
5. a
6. d
7. b
8. c
9. a
10. c
11. b
12. b
13. a
14. d
15. a
16. d

Chapter 17

1. c
2. b
3. c
4. b
5. a
6. a
7. a

8. d

9. c, e, a, b, d

10. b

11. b

12. d

13. a

14. c

15. a

16. b

17. b

18. a

19. c

20. d

21. c

22. b, c, a

23. a. normal; b. left axis deviation; c. right axis deviation; d. extreme axis deviation

24. Positive

25. Right is negative, left is positive

26. Top is negative, bottom is positive

27. a

28. b

29. a

Chapter 18

1. a
2. b
3. d
4. b
5. d

6. b

7. c

8. c

9. c

10. a

11. d

12. a

13. d

14. d

Chapter 19

1. a
2. b
3. b
4. c
5. a
6. b
7. d

Chapter 20

1. c
2. a
3. b
4. c
5. d
6. b
7. c
8. b
9. a
10. b
11. b
12. b, c, a
13. a

14.

15. a
16. c
17. b
18. d
19. a
20. a
21. d, b, a, c
22. d
23. a
24. d

Chapter 21

1. a
2. b
3. a
4. b
5. d
6. d
7. b, c, a
8. a
9. d
10. c
11. b

12.

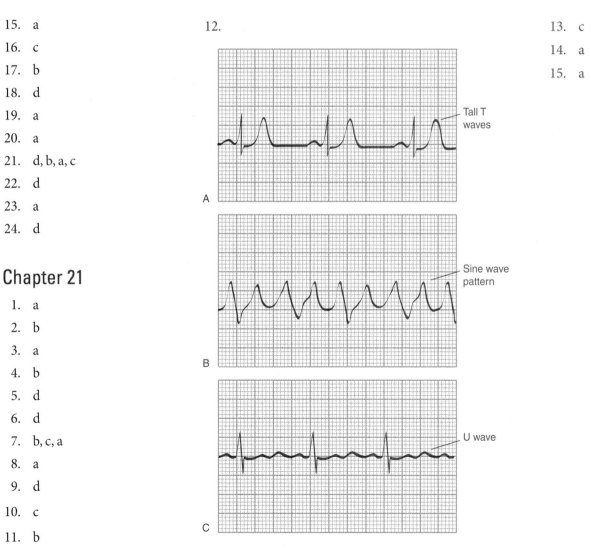

13. c
14. a
15. a

Chapter 22

1. c
2. a
3. b
4. c
5. d
6. c
7. a
8. d
9. b
10. c
11. d
12. d
13. b
14. d
15. c
16. b
17. a
18. d
19. a
20. a

Practice Makes Perfect

Answers to the **Practice Makes Perfect** exercises. More in-depth answers for each can be found at the Fast & Easy ECGs Website at www.mhhe.com/shadeECG2e.

Section 2

1. 39 BPM, regular, normal P waves, normal QRS complexes, normal PR intervals, ST segment depression, biphasic T waves, prolonged QT interval.

2. Underlying rhythm, 94 BPM, patterned irregularity, normal P waves, normal QRS complexes, normal PR intervals, ST segment depression, normal T waves, and normal QT interval. Early beats wide and bizarre-looking QRS complexes not preceded by a P wave and T waves deflect opposite of QRS complexes.

3. Underlying rhythm, 60 BPM, irregular due to sudden onset of tachycardic rhythm, P waves present in underlying rhythm but not the tachycardia, QRS complexes normal throughout, normal PR intervals in underlying ST segment, depression in tachycardia, T waves normal in underlying but indiscernible in tachycardia. QT intervals normal in underlying, indeterminable in tachycardia.

4. 120 BPM, regular, normal P waves, normal QRS complexes, borderline PR intervals (at 0.20 seconds in duration), normal ST segment, normal T waves, short QT interval.

5. 140 BPM, totally irregular, no discernible P waves, narrow but abnormal QRS complexes, absent PR intervals, depressed ST segments and biphasic T waves where they can be seen, indiscernible QT intervals.

6. 48 BPM, regular, normal P waves marching through wide bizarre-looking QRS complexes, absent PR intervals, elevated ST segment and T wave, normal QT intervals.

7. 160 BPM, regular, absent P waves, narrow but abnormal QRS complexes, absent PR intervals, normal ST segment, normal T waves, short QT interval.

8. Underlying rhythm, 56 BPM, occasionally irregular, normal P waves, normal QRS complexes, normal PR intervals, ST segment depression, biphasic T waves, and normal QT interval. Two early beats have wide and bizarre-looking QRS complexes not preceded by a P wave and T waves deflect opposite of QRS complexes.

9. 130 BPM, regular, absent P waves, wide bizarre-looking QRS complexes, absent PR intervals, indiscernible ST segments, T waves deflect opposite QRS complexes, indiscernible QT intervals.

10. 70 BPM, patterned irregularity, upright normal P waves but not all are followed by a QRS complex, normal QRS complexes but some are dropped, cyclical progressively longer PR intervals, depressed ST segments, biphasic T waves, normal QT intervals.

11. 90 BPM, patterned irregularity, normal P waves, normal QRS complexes, normal PR intervals, normal ST segments, normal T waves, normal QT intervals.

12. 130 BPM, regular, tall P waves, QRS complexes have deep Q wave, normal PR intervals, normal ST segments, normal T waves, and short QT intervals.

13. 45 BPM, regular, normal P waves, biphasic QRS complexes, normal PR intervals, normal ST segment, inverted T waves, short QT intervals.

Chapter 11

1. Sinus rhythm
2. Sinus arrest with sinus escape
3. Sinus bradycardia
4. Sinus dysrhythmia
5. Sinus tachycardia
6. Sinus rhythm with intraventricular conduction defect (IVD)
7. Sinus dysrhythmia
8. Sinus bradycardia
9. Sinus rhythm
10. Sinus rhythm with IVD
11. Sinus dysrhythmia
12. Sinus bradycardia
13. Sinus rhythm/borderline sinus tachycardia
14. Sinus tachycardia
15. Sinus dysrhythmia
16. Sinus tachycardia
17. Sinus bradycardia (severe)
18. Sinus tachycardia with IVD
19. Sinus bradycardia with IVD
20. Sinus rhythm/borderline sinus bradycardia
21. Sinus dysrhythmia
22. Sinus rhythm
23. Sinus bradycardia
24. Sinus tachycardia
25. Sinus tachycardia with IVD
26. Sinus pause with sinus escape
27. Sick sinus syndrome
28. Sinus tachycardia with IVD
29. Sinus rhythm with IVD
30. Sinus tachycardia
31. Sinus pause with sinus escape
32. Sinus tachycardia with elevated ST segments
33. Sinus rhythm/borderline sinus tachycardia
34. Sinus bradycardia
35. Sinus rhythm
36. Sinus bradycardia
37. Sinus tachycardia
38. Sinus bradycardia
39. Sinus bradycardia
40. Sinus arrest with sinus escape
41. Sinus dysrhythmia
42. Sinus rhythm with ST elevation
43. Sinus tachycardia
44. Sinus arrest with junctional escape
45. Sinus tachycardia with IVD
46. Sinus dysrhythmia
47. Sinus bradycardia
48. Sinus tachycardia
49. Sinus arrest with junctional escape
50. Sinus rhythm
51. Sick sinus syndrome
52. Sick sinus syndrome
53. Sinus tachycardia
54. Sinus pause (2 episodes)
55. Sinus bradycardia
56. Sick sinus syndrome
57. Sinus tachycardia with artifact

Chapter 12

1. Sinus rhythm with one PAC
2. Wandering atrial pacemaker
3. Atrial fibrillation
4. Atrial flutter (2 to 1 conduction ratio)
5. Atrial tachycardia
6. Sinus rhythm with two PACs

7. Atrial fibrillation with rapid ventricular response (uncontrolled)

8. Atrial flutter

9. Sinus rhythm with two PACs

10. Sinus rhythm with PSVT (sustained)

11. Sinus rhythm with two PACs

12. Supraventricular tachycardia

13. Atrial fibrillation with rapid ventricular response (uncontrolled)

14. Sinus tachycardia with one PAC

15. Atrial tachycardia

16. Atrial flutter (with variable conduction ratio)

17. Sinus rhythm with bigeminal PACs

18. Atrial fibrillation/flutter

19. Wandering atrial pacemaker

20. Sinus rhythm with trigeminal aberrantly conducted PACs

21. Multifocal atrial tachycardia

22. Atrial fibrillation

23. Sinus tachycardia with two PACs

24. Atrial fibrillation

25. Sinus rhythm with one PAC

26. Bradycardic wandering atrial pacemaker

27. Atrial fibrillation with rapid ventricular response (uncontrolled)

28. Sinus rhythm with bigeminal PACs

29. Atrial fibrillation

30. Sinus rhythm with one PAC

31. Atrial flutter

32. Atrial tachycardia

33. Sinus rhythm with two PACs (it is bigeminal if it continues in this pattern)

34. Atrial flutter (with variable conduction ratio)

35. Sinus dysrhythmia with two PACs

36. Multifocal atrial tachycardia

37. Atrial flutter (with variable conduction ratio)

38. Multifocal atrial tachycardia

39. Sinus rhythm with bigeminal PACs

40. Sinus rhythm with two PACs (one blocked and one conducted)

41. Atrial fibrillation with rapid ventricular response (uncontrolled)

42. Atrial flutter (with variable conduction ratio)

43. Sinus rhythm with two blocked PACs

44. Wandering atrial pacemaker

45. Multifocal atrial tachycardia

46. Atrial flutter (with variable conduction ratio)

47. Atrial fibrillation with rapid ventricular response (uncontrolled)

48. Sinus tachycardia with two PACs

49. Atrial fibrillation

50. Atrial flutter (with variable conduction ratio)

51. Atrial fibrillation with rapid ventricular response (uncontrolled)

52. Sinus rhythm with two PACs

53. Multifocal atrial tachycardia

54. Sinus rhythm with paroxysmal atrial tachycardia

55. Sinus rhythm with trigeminal aberrantly conducted PACs

56. Sinus rhythm with one blocked PAC

57. Atrial tachycardia with areas of 2 to 1 block

Chapter 13

1. Sinus rhythm with bigeminal PJCs

2. Supraventricular tachycardia

3. Junctional escape rhythm

4. Accelerated junctional rhythm

5. Junctional tachycardia

6. Sinus rhythm with two PJCs

7. Bradycardic junctional escape

8. Junctional tachycardia

9. Junctional escape rhythm

10. Sinus rhythm with one PJC

11. Junctional tachycardia

12. Accelerated junctional rhythm
13. Accelerated junctional rhythm
14. Junctional tachycardia
15. Accelerated junctional rhythm
16. Sinus rhythm with trigeminal PJCs
17. Accelerated junctional rhythm
18. Junctional escape rhythm
19. Sinus rhythm with two PJCs
20. Junctional escape rhythm
21. Junctional tachycardia
22. Accelerated junctional rhythm
23. Junctional tachycardia
24. Sinus tachycardia with two PJCs
25. Accelerated junctional rhythm
26. Sinus rhythm with trigeminal PJCs
27. Accelerated junctional rhythm
28. Sinus rhythm with bigeminal PJCs
29. Junctional tachycardia
30. Sinus tachycardia with two PJCs
31. Sinus rhythm with trigeminal PJCs
32. Junctional escape rhythm
33. Sinus rhythm with a couplet of PJCs
34. Sinus rhythm with WPW and run of paroxysmal junctional tachycardia

35. Junctional escape rhythm
36. Junctional tachycardia
37. Sinus rhythm with two PJCs (may be trigeminal PJCs if it continues in this pattern)
38. Accelerated junctional rhythm
39. Sinus rhythm with one PJC
40. Antedromic AV reentrant tachycardia
41. Sinus tachycardia with quadrigeminal PJCs
42. Sinus pause with junctional escape rhythm
43. Sinus rhythm with bigeminal PJCs
44. Junctional escape rhythm
45. Junctional tachycardia
46. Accelerated junctional rhythm
47. Sinus rhythm with two PJCs
48. Junctional escape rhythm
49. Antedromic AV reentrant tachycardia
50. Sinus rhythm with bigeminal PJCs
51. Accelerated junctional rhythm
52. Sinus rhythm with two PJCs
53. Accelerated junctional rhythm

Chapter 14

1. Sinus rhythm with two PVCs
2. Ventricular tachycardia

3. Idioventricular rhythm
4. Sinus rhythm with bigeminal PVCs
5. Sinus tachycardia with multiform PVCs
6. Ventricular fibrillation
7. Sinus tachycardia with trigeminal PVCs
8. Accelerated idioventricular rhythm
9. Sinus rhythm with trigeminal PVCs
10. Ventricular tachycardia
11. Sinus rhythm with bigeminal PVCs
12. Ventricular tachycardia
13. Sinus rhythm with one PVC
14. Idioventricular rhythm
15. Sinus tachycardia with trigeminal PVCs
16. Sinus bradycardia with trigeminal PVCs
17. Asystole
18. Sinus bradycardia with a couplet of PVCs
19. Ventricular fibrillation
20. Sinus rhythm with one PVC
21. Ventricular tachycardia
22. Idioventricular rhythm
23. Sinus tachycardia with quadrigeminal PVCs
24. Sinus rhythm with two interpolated PVCs
25. Sinus rhythm with two multiform PVCs
26. Sinus rhythm with four PVCs (there is a couplet of PVCs among the four)

27. Ventricular tachycardia

28. Sinus rhythm with trigeminal PVCs

29. Ventricular tachycardia

30. Sinus rhythm with multiform PVCs

31. Idioventricular rhythm

32. Sinus rhythm with quadrigeminal PVCs

33. Sinus rhythm with quadrigeminal PVCs

34. Sinus rhythm with bigeminal PVCs

35. Sinus tachycardia with two PVCs

36. Idioventricular rhythm

37. Accelerated idioventricular rhythm

38. Sinus rhythm with four multiform PVCs (two of which occur as a couplet)

39. Idioventricular rhythm

40. Sinus rhythm with ventricular escape

41. Sinus rhythm with two couplets of PVCs

42. Atrial fibrillation with 2 multiform PVCs

43. Sinus rhythm with one PVC and a run of ventricular tachycardia

44. Accelerated idioventricular rhythm

45. Sinus dysrhythmia with one PVC

46. Sinus tachycardia with two runs of ventricular tachycardia

47. Junctional tachycardia with three multiform PVCs

48. Sinus rhythm with trigeminal PVCs

49. Ventricular tachycardia

50. Sinus bradycardia with one PVC

51. Sinus tachycardia with two uniform PVCs

52. Ventricular tachycardia

53. Sinus tachycardia with three multiform PVCs

54. Accelerated idioventricular rhythm

55. Sinus rhythm (borderline sinus bradycardia) with trigeminal PVCs

56. Multiform ventricular tachycardia—Torsades de pointes

57. Sinus pause with ventricular escape rhythm

Chapter 15

1. 2nd-degree AV heart block, type I

2. Sinus bradycardia with 1st-degree AV block

3. 2nd-degree AV heart block, type II

4. 3rd-degree AV block

5. Sinus bradycardia with 1st-degree AV block

6. 2nd-degree AV heart block, type I

7. 3rd-degree AV heart block

8. 2nd-degree AV heart block, type II

9. 3rd-degree AV heart block

10. Sinus tachycardia with 1st-degree AV block

11. 2nd-degree AV block, type I

12. 3rd-degree AV block

13. 2nd-degree AV block, type I

14. Sinus bradycardia with 1st-degree AV block (and IVD)

15. 2nd-degree AV block, type I

16. 2nd-degree AV block, type I

17. 2nd-degree AV block, type II

18. AV dissociation

19. Sinus bradycardia with 1st-degree AV block

20. 2nd-degree AV block, type II

21. 3rd-degree AV block

22. 2nd-degree AV block, type I

23. 2nd-degree AV block, type II

24. Sinus bradycardia with 1st-degree AV block

25. 2nd-degree AV block, type I

26. 3rd-degree AV block

27. 2nd-degree AV block, type II (with variable conduction ratio)

28. 2nd-degree AV block, type I

29. 3rd-degree AV block

30. Sinus bradycardia with 1st-degree AV block

31. 2nd-degree AV block, type II

32. Sinus tachycardia with 1st-degree AV block

33. 2nd-degree AV block, type I

34. 2nd-degree AV block, type II

35. 2nd-degree AV block, type I

36. 2nd-degree AV block, type I

37. 2nd-degree AV block, type II

38. 3rd-degree AV block

39. 2nd-degree AV block, type I

40. 3rd-degree AV block

41. Sinus tachycardia with 1st-degree AV block

42. 2nd-degree AV block, type II

43. Sinus bradycardia with 1st-degree AV block
44. 3rd-degree AV block
45. 2nd-degree AV block, type II
46. 3rd-degree AV block
47. Sinus bradycardia with 1st-degree AV block
48. Sinus bradycardia with IVD and 1st-degree AV block
49. 3rd-degree AV block
50. 2nd-degree AV block, type II
51. Sinus rhythm with 1st AV block and 2nd-degree AV block, type II
52. AV dissociation
53. Sinus rhythm with 1st AV degree and 2nd-degree AV block, type II

Chapter 16

1. Pacemaker failure to pace
2. Ventricular pacemaker
3. Atrioventricular pacemaker
4. Ventricular pacemaker
5. Demand pacemaker
6. Pacemaker failure to capture
7. Pacemaker failure to sense
8. Pacemaker failure to pace
9. Pacemaker failure to capture
10. Pacemaker mediated tachycardia
11. Pacemaker failure to pace
12. Pacemaker failure to capture
13. Pacemaker failure to pace
14. Sinus rhythm with demand pacemaker
15. Ventricular pacemaker

16. Pacemaker failure to capture
17. Accelerated junctional rhythm with demand pacemaker
18. Pacemaker mediated tachycardia
19. Pacemaker failure to pace with ventricular escape and resumption of sinus rhythm

Chapter 17

1. Left axis deviation
2. Normal axis
3. Left axis deviation
4. Extreme left axis deviation

Chapter 18

1. Sinus rhythm, left atrial enlargement, left ventricular hypertrophy
2. Sinus tachycardia, right atrial enlargement, right ventricular hypertrophy
3. 2nd-degree AV block, type I, right ventricular hypertrophy
4. Sinus rhythm, left ventricular hypertrophy
5. Sinus rhythm, right atrial enlargement, right ventricular hypertrophy
6. Atrial fibrillation, rSR' pattern in V1 suggests right ventricular conduction delay, voltage criteria for left ventricular hypertrophy, marked ST abnormality suggestive of possible inferolateral subendocardial injury

Chapter 19

1. Atrial fibrillation, right bundle branch block
2. Sinus tachycardia, left atrial enlargement, right axis deviation, incomplete right bundle branch block
3. Sinus rhythm, left bundle branch block
4. Sinus rhythm, left axis deviation indicating left anterior (fascicular) hemiblock, voltage criteria for left ventricular hypertrophy, cannot rule out Septal infarct (age undetermined)
5. Sinus tachycardia with occasional PVCs, incomplete left bundle branch block, ST & T wave abnormality suggestive of inferolateral ischemia
6. Sinus rhythm, right bundle branch block, left axis deviation indicating left anterior (fascicular) hemiblock

Chapter 20

1. Junctional escape rhythm, acute inferior wall injury or MI, anterolateral injury pattern
2. Sinus bradycardia, acute inferior wall injury or MI
3. Atrial fibrillation, Septal infarct (age undetermined), ST & T wave abnormality— lateral wall ischemia
4. Sinus rhythm with PVCs, acute anteroseptal MI
5. Sinus rhythm, left axis deviation, marked ST

abnormality, possible lateral wall subendocardial injury

6. Sinus bradycardia with 1st-degree AV block, acute inferior wall injury/MI

7. Atrial fibrillation with rapid ventricular response, left axis deviation, low voltage QRS complexes, cannot rule out anterior infarct (age undetermined), inferior infarct (age undetermined), marked ST abnormality, possible lateral subendocardial injury

8. Sinus rhythm with anterior lateral wall MI

9. Sinus bradycardia, acute inferior wall injury/MI

10. Sinus bradycardia, acute inferior wall injury/MI, lateral wall injury pattern

Chapter 21

1. Sinus tachycardia, electrical alternans
2. Sinus tachycardia, pericarditis
3. Sinus bradycardia, hypocalcemia
4. Sinus bradycardia, low amplitude QRS complexes
5. Sinus bradycardia, digitalis effect
6. Sinus rhythm, hypokalemia
7. Junctional escape rhythm, hypercalcemia
8. Sinus tachycardia, hyperkalemia

9. Sinus rhythm, hypocalcemia
10. Sinus bradycardia, hyperkalemia
11. Sinus tachycardia, low amplitude QRS complexes

Section 5

1. Sinus dysrhythmia
2. Idioventricular rhythm
3. Sinus tachycardia with quadrigeminal PVCs
4. Ventricular tachycardia
5. 2nd-degree AV block, type II
6. Pacemaker rhythm
7. Ventricular tachycardia
8. Atrial flutter (2 to 1 conduction)
9. Sinus pause with sinus escape
10. Sinus rhythm with 2nd-degree AV block, type II.
11. Atrial fibrillation
12. Sinus dysrhythmia
13. Sinus tachycardia with two multiform PVCs
14. Antedromic atrioventricular reentrant tachcyardia
15. Sinus rhythm with a run of ventricular tachycardia and multiform PVCs
16. Atrial flutter (with 2 to 1 conduction ratio)
17. Sinus tachycardia with two PVCs
18. Sinus bradycardia

19. Ventricular tachycardia
20. Sinus rhythm with 1st degree AV block and paroxysmal junctional tachycardia
21. 3rd-degree AV heart block
22. Atrioventricular dissociation
23. Sinus dysrhythmia
24. Sinus tachycardia with two PACs
25. 3rd-degree AV block
26. Sinus tachycardia
27. Sinus dysrhythmia
28. Atrial fibrillation
29. 2nd-degree AV heart block, type I
30. Sinus tachycardia
31. Sinus rhythm with two PACs
32. Sinus tachycardia with 1st-degree AV block
33. Sinus rhythm with one aberrantly conducted PAC
34. Accelerated junctional rhythm
35. Sinus dysrhythmia
36. Atrial flutter
37. Ventricular standstill (asystole) with a ventricular escape beat
38. 2nd-degree AV block, type I
39. 3rd-degree AV heart block (with sinus tachycardia)
40. Sinus bradycardia
41. Junctional escape with one PJC

Glossary

1st-degree AV heart block A delay in conduction of the impulse arising from the SA node as it passes through the AV node to the ventricles. This delay produces a longer-than-normal PR interval. Because all the impulses are conducted, each P wave will be followed by a QRS complex.

2nd-degree AV heart block, type I A dysrhythmia in which there is a progressively longer delay in conduction of the impulse from the SA node through the AV node until finally the impulse fails to conduct and a ventricular beat is dropped. This results in progressively longer PR intervals until a QRS complex is absent. This occurs in a cyclical manner. It is considered an incomplete block. It is also referred to as *Wenckebach* and sometimes Mobitz Type I.

2nd-degree AV heart block, type II A dysrhythmia in which not all the impulses arising from the SA node are conducted through the AV node to the ventricles, resulting in more P waves than QRS complexes. It is considered an incomplete block.

3rd-degree AV heart block A dysrhythmia in which none of the impulses arising from the SA node are conducted through the AV node to the ventricles. The ventricles are stimulated to beat by an escape pacemaker that arises below the level of the AV node. This results in the P waves having no relationship to the QRS complexes because each is beating independently of each other. This is a complete block.

A

Absolute refractory period The portion of repolarization during which no stimulus, no matter how strong, will depolarize the cell.

Accelerated junctional rhythm A dysrhythmia that arises from the AV junction and produces a heart rate of 60 to 100 BPM

Action potential The measure over time of the change in electrical charge of the cell. The action potential reflects the ability of the cell to depolarize.

Actin One of the two components of the contractile filaments involved in muscular contraction.

Accessory pathway A conduction pathway from the SA node to the ventricles that does not pass through the normal AV node pathway.

Acute Sudden and recent onset of a condition, sign, or symptom.

Acute coronary syndrome The condition of ischemic chest pain consisting of the following conditions: unstable angina, non-ST segment elevation MI, and ST segment elevation MI.

Adrenalin A natural catecholamine that causes bronchodilation and increased AV conduction, muscular contractility, heart rate, and vasoconstriction; also called *epinephrine*.

Adrenergic Nerves that release epinephrine or epinephrine-like substances.

Afterload The pressure against which the left ventricle must pump blood during contraction.

Alpha adrenergic receptors Any of the adrenergic receptor tissues that respond to norepinephrine.

Amplitude The height and depth, or waveform size, of an ECG complex.

Anemia A deficiency in the oxygen-carrying hemoglobin molecule contained in blood.

Aneurysm A pathological blood-filled dilation of a blood vessel.

Angina See angina pectoris.

Angina pectoris Chest pain resulting when the supply of oxygen and coronary perfusion is insufficient to that demanded by the heart muscle.

Antegrade Occurring or performed in the normal or forward direction of conduction or flow.

Artery A vessel that carries blood away from the heart. Arteries generally carry oxygenated blood. The exception is the pulmonary artery, which carries deoxygenated blood to the lungs.

Aorta The major vessel that carries oxygenated blood from the heart to the body.

Aortic valve The valve that separates the left ventricle from the aorta.

Apex The tip of a structure that may be either at the top or bottom. The apex of the heart is the bottom of the heart.

Arrhythmia Technically speaking, the absence of a rhythm, but this term is used synonymously with the term *dysrhythmia.*

Artifact Extraneous spikes and waves produced by anything other than the physiological activity of the heart. Common causes include electrical or mechanical factors such as muscle tremor, alternating current interference, loose leads, chest compressions, and patient movement. Also called *electrical interference* or *noise.*

Asymmetrical Not identical on both sides of a central line; lacking symmetry.

Asystole Absence of cardiac electrical activity; seen on the ECG as an absence of upward or downward deflection on the isoelectric line of the ECG.

Atherosclerosis An accumulation of fat-containing deposits within the arterial wall.

Atria The chamber of the heart that collects blood returning from the rest of the body. The right atrium collects deoxygenated blood from the body and passes it to the right ventricle. The left atrium collects oxygenated blood from the lungs and passes it to the left ventricle.

Atrial kick The additional volume of blood pushed into the ventricle by the contraction of the atria.

Atrial tachycardia with block Tachycardia that arises from the atria at a rate of between 150 and 250 BPM. However, the AV node fails to carry some of the impulses through to the ventricles. This results in a faster-than-normal rate with more P' waves that QRS complexes.

Atrioventricular dissociation (AV dissociation) Any rhythm characterized by the atria and ventricles beating independently but at the same rate per minute.

Atrioventricular junction (AV junction) The area of conductive tissue that includes the AV node, its atrial pathways, and the bundle of His.

Atrioventricular node (AV node) Specialized tissue at the base of the wall between the two upper heart chambers (atria). Electrical impulses pass from the SA node to the AV node, then on to the bundle of His.

Augmented limb leads The limb leads aV$_R$, aV$_L$, and aV$_F$. The ECG waveforms produced by these leads is so small that the ECG machine enhances, or augments, them by 50% so their amplitude is comparable to other leads.

Automaticity The ability of cardiac cells to initiate spontaneous electrical impulses.

Autonomic nervous system The involuntary portion of the peripheral nervous system that regulates vital body functions. It is separated into the parasympathetic and sympathetic divisions. The autonomic nervous system controls cardiac, smooth muscle, and glandular activity.

Axis The sum of all the vectors of electrical activity associated with conduction of the action potential through the heart.

Axis deviation An abnormal shift of the normal axis of the cardiac muscle action potential, often associated with ventricular hypertrophy and certain conduction defects.

B

Baroreceptors Pressure-sensitive nerve endings in the walls of the atria of the heart and in some larger blood vessels such as the carotid artery. Baroreceptors stimulate reflex mechanisms that allow the body to adapt to changes in blood pressure by dilating or constricting blood vessels.

Beta receptors Adrenergic receptors of the nervous system that respond to adrenaline. Activation causes relaxation of smooth muscles and increases in cardiac rate and contractility.

Bifascicular block Conduction abnormality in the heart where two of the three main fascicles of the His-Purkinje system are blocked.

Bicuspid valve See mitral valve.

Bigeminy Cardiac electrical activity characterized by a pattern of one ectopic beat followed by one normal beat. These ectopic beats can be either atrial or ventricular in origin and indicate cardiac irritability.

Bipolar limb lead An ECG lead with both a positive and negative electrode. Leads I, II, and III are bipolar limb leads.

Biphasic A waveform having both a positive and negative deflection.

Blocked PACs Premature beats that arise from the atria but are not conducted through the AV node to the ventricles. This lack of conduction results in a P wave that is seen earlier than normal in the cardiac cycle and is not followed by a QRS complex.

Blood pressure The pressure exerted by circulating blood upon the walls of blood vessels. It is one of the key patient vital signs.

Bradycardia A heart rate below 60 beats per minute, when related to atrial or sinus rhythms.

Bradycardic junctional escape rhythm A dysrhythmia that arises from the AV junction as an escape mechanism but is slower than the inherent rate of the AV junction, which is normally 40 to 60 BPM. Also known as junctional escape rhythm with bradycardia.

Bundle branch Either of the parts of the bundle of His passing respectively to the right and left ventricles.

Bundle branch block Disorder that leads to one or both of the bundle branches failing to conduct impulses. This produces a delay in depolarization of the ventricle it supplies.

Bundle of His Specialized muscle fibers in the intraventricular septum that carry the electric impulses to the ventricles.

Burst See Salvo.

C

Calibration Is the process of determining that the settings on the ECG match the proper standards. The internal regulation of the ECG machine is such that a 1-mV electrical signal results in a 10-mm deflection.

Cardiac cycle The sequence of events that occur when the heart beats. The cycle has two main phases: diastole, when the heart ventricles are relaxed, and systole, when the ventricles contract. One cardiac cycle is defined as the contraction of the two atria followed by contraction of the two ventricles.

Cardiac output The volume of blood pumped by the heart, usually measured in milliliters per minute. Cardiac output is calculated by multiplying the heart rate by the stroke volume.

Cardiac tamponade See pericardial tamponade.

Catecholamine Sympathetic nervous system neurotransmitter such as epinephrine, norepinephrine, and dopamine.

Cardiomyopathy Any structural or functional disease of heart muscle that is marked especially by hypertrophy of cardiac muscle, enlargement of the heart, rigidity and loss of flexibility of the heart walls, or narrowing of the ventricles.

Chemoreceptor A sensory nerve cell that is activated by chemicals such as the carbon dioxide detectors in the brainstem.

Cholinergic Nerve fibers that release acetylcholine.

Chordae tendineae Thin, strong strings of connective tissue that anchor the papillary muscles to the floor of the heart.

Chronotropic Affecting the rate of the heartbeat. A positive chronotropic effect increases the heart rate whereas a negative chronotropic effect decreases the heart rate.

Circadian rhythm The biological clock in humans based on a 24-hour cycle. At regular intervals each day, the body becomes active or tired. Some medications affect the body more at certain times during the day than at others.

Compensatory pause The pause following a premature complex that allows the original rhythm to begin again at its normal rate. The compensatory pause will be exactly twice the R-R interval of the normally conducted beat, as seen following a PVC.

Complete AV heart block See 3rd-degree AV heart block.

Contractility Ability of the cardiac muscle to contract in response to electrical stimulation.

Conductive pathway Route followed by nerve impulses as they pass through the heart. A pathway is made of two nodes (special conduction cells) and a series of conduction fibers or bundles.

Conductivity The ability of the cardiac muscle to transmit an electrical stimulus from cell to cell.

Coronary arteries A pair of arteries that branch from the ascending aorta and supply oxygenated blood to the myocardium.

Coronary artery disease The gradual narrowing and hardening of the coronary arteries. Coronary artery disease is usually the result of atherosclerosis.

Coronary veins Vessels that transport deoxygenated blood from the capillaries of the heart to the right atrium.

Couplet Two consecutive complexes.

Cyanosis A condition in which a person's skin is discolored to a bluish hue because of inadequate oxygenation of the blood.

D

Delta wave A slurred or widened upstroke at the beginning of the cardiac QRS complex causing prolongation of the complex. It indicates anomalous impulse conduction and is diagnostic of Wolff-Parkinson-White syndrome.

Depolarization Loss of the difference in charge between the inside and outside of the plasma membrane of a muscle or nerve cell due to a change in permeability and migration of positively charged ions into the cell.

Desemones A specialized local thickening of the plasma membrane of myocytes that serves to anchor contiguous cells together and prevent them from pulling apart during contraction.

Diastole The period of relaxation during the cardiac cycle when the cardiac muscle fibers lengthen, causing the heart to dilate and fill with blood. Coronary perfusion occurs during this phase.

Dilation Expansion or widening of an organ, opening, or vessel.

Dynamic ECGs ECGs which are displayed on an ECG oscilloscope. They reflect what is currently occurring in the heart.

Dysrhythmia Any abnormality in the otherwise normal rhythmic pattern of the heartbeat.

Dyspnea Difficulty in breathing.

E

Early beats Premature beats that arise from somewhere in the heart other the SA node before the SA node has a chance to initiate the heartbeat.

Ectopic A cardiac complex originating from somewhere other than the SA node. It may be early (premature) or late (escape) in nature.

ECG tracings Electrocardiogram printouts. Also referred to as static ECGs.

Einthovan's Triangle An electrical triangle formed by the patients' right arm, left arm, and left leg, used to position electrodes for ECG monitoring. This positioning is used to determine the direction of cardiac vectors to various leads.

Electrical axis See axis.

Electrocardiogram The tracing made by an electrocardiograph; also known as *ECG* or *EKG*.

Electrocardiograph Device used to record electrical variation within cardiac tissue.

Electrode The electrical sensor applied to the body to record the ECG.

Electrolyte Element or compound that, when melted or dissolved in water or other solvent, dissociates into ions (atoms able to carry an electric charge). Sodium, potassium, and calcium are the primary electrolytes involved in myocardial activity.

Electromechanical dissociation (EMD) A condition characterized by seemingly normal electrical heart activity without discernible mechanical activity. This term is no longer used and has been replaced by the term *Pulseless Electrical Activity* (PEA).

Endocardium The serous membrane that lines the inner aspect of the four chambers of the heart and its valves.

Enlargement An increase in size.

Epinephrine See adrenalin.

Epicardium A thick serous membrane that constitutes the smooth outer surface of the heart.

Escape complex A beat that occurs after the normal pacemaker fails to fire.

Excitability The degree to which a myocardial cell is reactive to external stimuli.

Extrasystole A premature complex.

F

f waves Waves associated with atrial fibrillation. They occur with an atrial rate of greater than 350 times per minute.

F waves Saw-toothed waves associated with atrial flutter. They occur with atrial rate of 250 to 350 times per minute.

Fascicle A small bundle of conducting fibers.

Fibrillation Quivering of the muscle fibers of the heart, resulting in a lack of heartbeat and pulse.

Fibrillatory waves Chaotic baseline that lacks any semblance of organized electrical waveforms. Also know as f waves.

Flutter An abnormal rapid spasmodic and usually rhythmic motion or contraction of the atria or ventricles.

Flutter waves Waveforms seen in atrial flutter where the atria are firing at a rate of 250–350 BPM. They are sometimes described as having a *picket fence* or *sawtooth* appearance.

Fusion beat A beat that occurs when two complexes originating from different pacemakers fuse to form one complex as seen with some types of PVCs.

G

Ganglia A group of nerve cells forming a nerve center along the thoracic and sacral spine associated with the parasympathetic nervous system.

Gap junctions An area of the conducting cell that improves the rate of electrical conduction.

H

Hemiblock Failure of conduction of the muscular excitatory impulse in either of the two fascicles of the left branch bundle branch.

Hyperkalemia An abnormally high level of potassium in the blood.

Hypertrophy Increase in bulk (as by thickening of muscle fibers) without multiplication of parts.

Hypertension A condition in which a person's blood pressure is abnormally high. For normal adults, the blood pressure should be less than 130 mm Hg systolic and less than 85 mm Hg diastolic. Pressures above 140/90 indicate a mild form of hypertension; above 180/110 is considered severe.

Hypokalemia An abnormally low level of potassium in the blood.

I

Idioventricular rhythm Relating to, or arising in the ventricles of the heart independent of the atria.

Incomplete bundle branch block A partial block of the bundle branch in which the QRS complexes are less than 0.12 seconds in duration

Infarction Irreversible cell death caused by prolonged obstruction of arterial blood supply to an area of the body.

Innervated A part of the body supplied with nerves.

Inotropic Something that increases the force of contraction of the heart.

Intercalated disks The specialized regions of the cardiac muscle cells that comprise the longitudinal and end-to-end junctions between adjacent cells and that function to connect them mechanically and electrically.

Interpolated A beat that occurs between normal heartbeats without disturbing the succeeding beat or the basic rhythm of the heart.

Intraatrial pathway Electrical pathways that travel through the atria from the SA node to the AV node.

Intranodal pathway The conduction pathways through the AV node.

Ion An atom or group of atoms that carries a positive or negative electric charge as a result of having lost or gained one or more electrons.

Ischemia Local tissue hypoxia caused by a reduction in arterial blood supply and/or oxygen to an area of the body.

Isoelectric A condition of the cell that is neither negatively nor positively charged in relation to its neighboring cells. This also refers to the baseline on the ECG that indicates neither a positive or negative deflection.

J

J point The point at which the QRS complex meets the ST segment; also called the *junction*.

Junctional A cardiac rhythm resulting from impulses coming from a locus of tissue in the area of the AV junction.

Junctional escape rhythm with bradycardia See Bradycardic junctional escape rhythm.

L

Latent Present but not visible, apparent, or actualized; existing as potential.

Left bundle branch The portion of the heart's conduction system that supplies the left ventricle. It is composed of two fascicles: the left anterior fascicle and the left posterior fascicle.

Left bundle branch block In this condition, activation of the left ventricle is delayed, which results in the left ventricle contracting later than the right ventricle.

Left main coronary artery Abbreviated as LCA and also known as the left coronary artery. It arises from the aorta above the left cusp of the aortic valve. It then divides into the left anterior descending artery and the circumflex branch both of which supply blood to the left ventricle and left atrium.

M

Mediastinum The space in the chest between the pleural sacs of the lungs that contains all the viscera of the chest except the lungs and includes the heart, aorta, and vena cava.

Mitral valve A valve in the heart between the left atrium and the left ventricle. It prevents the blood in the ventricle from returning to the atrium during systole and consists of two triangular flaps; also called *bicuspid valve* or *left atrioventricular valve*.

Mobitz Type I See 2nd-degree AV heart block, type I

Morphology The configuration or shape of a wave or complex on the ECG.

Multifocal Impulses that arise from different sites within the heart.

Myocardial infarction Irreversible cell death caused by prolonged obstruction of arterial blood supply to an area of the myocardium.

Myocardial injury A degree of cellular damage beyond ischemia.

Myocardial ischemia Local tissue hypoxia caused by a reduction in arterial blood supply and/or oxygen to an area of the myocardium.

Myocardium The muscular layer of the heart.

Myocytes The individual muscle cells of the heart.

Myosin One of the two components of the contractile filaments involved in the muscular contraction.

N

Neurotransmitter A substance, such as norepinephrine or acetylcholine, used to transmit a nerve impulse across the synapse between nerve cells or to the organ being stimulated (innervated).

Noise See Artifact.

Noncompensatory pause The pause following a premature complex that resets the rate of the original rhythm. The R-R interval following a noncompensatory pause is less than two preceding R-R intervals; seen following a PAC.

Nonconducted PACs See blocked PAC.

Nonperfusing PVC A premature ventricular complex that fails to produce a pulse.

Norepinephrine The chemical compound used to transmit impulses by the sympathetic nervous system. A precursor to epinephrine and referred to as *noradrenaline*.

Normal sinus rhythm (NSR) Normal beating of the heart, as measured by an ECG. It has certain generic features that serve as hallmarks for comparison with normal ECGs. The rate is between 60 and 100 beats per minute, and the beats are synchronized.

O

Osborn wave A narrow, positive deflection wave at the junction of the QRS complex and the ST segment associated with hypothermia.

Oscilloscope An instrument that displays the fluctuating electrical quantity as a visible waveform on the fluorescent screen of a cathode-ray tube.

P

P wave The electrical representation of atrial contraction. It precedes the QRS complex.

P mitrale Right atrial enlargement associated with severe lung disease such as COPD and pulmonary hypertension.

P pulmonale Hypertrophy of the right ventricle associated with severe lung disease such as emphysema.

Palpitations Heartbeat sensations that feel as if the heart is pounding or racing. It may present as an unpleasant awareness of a person's own heartbeat or feel like a skipped beat. Palpitations can be felt in the chest, throat, or neck.

Papillary muscles The thin muscles that connect to the cusps of the mitral and tricuspid valves and contract to facilitate their ability to resist prolapsing during systole.

Parasympathetic The part of the autonomic nervous system that chiefly contains cholinergic fibers. The nerves of this system tend to induce secretion, to increase the tone and contractility of smooth muscle, and to slow the heart rate.

Parietal pericardium The tough thickened membranous outer layer of the pericardium that is attached to the central part of the diaphragm and the posterior part of the sternum.

Paroxysmal An abrupt beginning and ending of an event such as a different cardiac rhythm.

PEA See Pulseless Electrical Activity.

Pericardial tamponade A condition characterized by a collection of fluid within the pericardial sac that constricts the heart and inhibits its ability to fill during diastole; also called *cardiac tamponade*.

Pericarditis Inflammation of the pericardium.

Pericardium The conical sac of serous membranes that encloses the heart and the roots of the aorta, pulmonary artery, and vena cava. It is composed of one layer that is closely adherent to the heart while the other lines the inner surface of the outer coat, with the intervening space being filled with pericardial fluid.

Polarization Refers to the cell returning to its resting state during which no electrical activity occurs and its intracellular fluid is negatively charged relative to the extra-cellular fluid.

Polarized In a resting state during which no electrical activity takes place.

Polymorphic ventricular tachycardia A type of ventricular tachycardia that is irregular in rate and rhythm and has varying shapes or morphologies on the ECG.

PR intervals Is the distance from the beginning of the P wave to the beginning of the Q wave (or R wave if the Q wave is absent).

PR segment The flat isoelectric line that represents the electrical impulse traveling through the His-Purkinje system.

Precordial Situated in front of the heart.

Preload The stretched condition of the heart muscle at the end of diastole just before contraction.

Premature ventricular complexes (PVCs) Early beats that arise from the ventricles before the SA node has a chance to initiate a heartbeat.

Pulmonic valve The heart valve that separates the right ventricle from the pulmonary artery; also called the *semilunar valve*.

Pulseless Electrical Activity (PEA) A condition characterized by seemingly normal electrical heart activity without discernible mechanical activity.

Purkinje fibers Specialized heart cells capable of conducting electrical impulses and directly stimulating myocardial cells to contract.

Q

Q wave The first negative deflection of the QRS complex not following an R wave.

QRS complex The waveform that represents electrical conduction through the ventricles. It is associated with ventricular contraction.

QT interval Period of time measured from the beginning of the Q wave to the end of the T wave, representing the time required to depolarize and repolarize the ventricles.

Quadrigeminal Cardiac electrical activity characterized by a pattern of one ectopic beat followed by three normal beats. These ectopic beats can be either atrial or ventricular in origin and indicate cardiac instability.

R

R wave The positive deflection in the QRS complex.

Reentry A cardiac mechanism that explains certain abnormal heart actions (such as tachycardia) and that involves the transmission of a wave of depolarization along an alternate pathway when the original pathway is blocked, with return of the impulse along the blocked pathway resulting in a reinitiation of the impulse.

Refractory period The phase during repolarization during which a stimulus may or may not cause the cell to depolarize; also see relative and absolute refractory period.

Regular sinus rhythm See normal sinus rhythm.

Relative refractory period A later phase of repolarization during which a sufficiently strong stimulus will depolarize the cell.

Repolarization Restoration of the difference in charge between the inside and outside of the plasma membrane of a muscle fiber or cell following depolarization.

Resting membrane potential (RMP) The relative difference between the electrical charge of the inside as compared with the outside of the cell.

Retrograde Occurring or performed in a direction opposite to the normal or forward direction of conduction or flow.

Right bundle branch The portion of the heart's conduction system that supplies the right ventricle.

Right bundle branch block Occurs when transmission of the electrical impulse is delayed or not conducted along the right bundle branch. This leads to the right ventricle depolarizing by means of cell-to-cell conduction that spreads from the interventricular septum and left ventricle to the right ventricle.

Right main coronary artery (RCA) One of the two main coronary arteries. It divides into the right posterior descending and acute marginal arteries and supplies blood to the right ventricle, right atrium, sinoatrial node, and atrioventricular node.

R-R interval The interval of time between consecutive R waves.

Run Three or more premature beats presenting in a row.

S

SA node See sinoatrial node.

S wave First negative deflection that *extends below* the baseline in the QRS complex following the R wave

Salvo A series of three or more consecutive and identical beats, as in a salvo of ventricular tachycardia.

Sarcolemma The plasma membrane surrounding the myocytes of the heart.

Sarcoplasmic reticulum The specialized area of the myocyte for storage of calcium required to trigger contraction of the actin and myosin filaments.

Septal necrosis Infarction of an area of the septum.

Semilunar valve See pulmonic valve.

Septum The curved slanting wall that separates the right and left ventricles of the heart and is composed of a muscular lower part and a thinner more membranous upper part.

Sick sinus syndrome A collection of heart rhythm disorders that include persistent sinus bradycardia, tachycardias, bradycardia-tachycardia (alternating slow and fast heart rhythms), atrial fibrillation and atrial flutter.

Sinoatrial node A small mass of tissue made up of nerve fibers that is embedded in the musculature of the right atrium. It initiates the impulses stimulating the heartbeat and is the primary pacemaker of the heart; also called *SA node, sinus node.*

Sinus arrest A pause in the normal cardiac rhythm, due to a momentary failure of the sinus node to initiate an impulse, that lasts three or more intervals. The pause is not an exact multiple of the normal cardiac cycle.

Sinus pause A pause in the normal cardiac rhythm, due to a momentary failure of the sinus node to initiate an impulse, that lasts for one to two intervals. The pause is not an exact multiple of the normal cardiac cycle.

Sodium-potassium pump The energy-requiring process by which the cellular membrane actively moves sodium out of the cell and potassium into the cell.

ST segment The phase following ventricular depolarization before repolarization begins. It is helpful in assessing the presence of cardiac ischemia.

Static ECGs An ECG tracing that is printed.

Stroke volume The volume of blood pumped from a ventricle of the heart in one beat.

Superimposed (waveform) An ECG waveform that forms over another waveform, distorting the appearance of both. It is commonly seen as a P wave superimposed on the T wave of the preceding beat.

Supraventricular Relating to or being a rhythmic abnormality of the heart caused by impulses originating above the ventricles.

Supraventricular tachycardia (SVT) Tachycardia that arises from a site above the ventricles.

Sustained Continuous; failing to cease spontaneously.

Sympathetic The part of the autonomic nervous system that contains chiefly adrenergic fibers. It tends to decrease glandular secretion and to speed the heart rate.

Syncytium The network of anastomoses (connections) between adjoining myocytes.

Systole The contraction of the ventricles during which blood is ejected from the ventricles into the aorta and pulmonary artery.

T

T wave A wave representing ventricular repolarization.

Tachycardia A heart rate greater than 100 when referring to sinus rhythms or a rate greater than is normally expected with any rhythm.

Thrombolytics Medications that attack and accelerate the body's ability to break up or lyse a blood clot (thrombus).

Torsades de pointes Ventricular tachycardia characterized by fluctuation of the QRS complexes around the electrocardiographic baseline. It is typically caused by a long QT interval.

Tricuspid valve Heart valve situated between the right atrium and the right ventricle. It resembles the mitral valve in structure but consists of three triangular membranous flaps; also called the *right atrioventricular valve.*

Trifascicular block Is a combination of bifascicular block and prolongation of the PR interval.

Trigeminal Cardiac electrical activity characterized by a pattern of one ectopic beat followed by two normal beats. These ectopic beats can be either atrial or ventricular in origin and indicate cardiac instability.

U

U wave A positive wave that may follow the T wave, representing the final repolarization phase of the ventricles.

Unifocal Complexes originating from the same location (focus).

V

Vagus nerve Either of the pair of 10th cranial nerves that arise from the medulla and chiefly supply the heart with autonomic sensory and motor fibers.

Vector The geometric direction of travel of an electrical impulse in the heart.

Vein A vessel that carries blood toward the heart.

Ventricles The chambers of the heart that receive blood from a corresponding atrium and from which blood is forced into the arteries.

Ventricular conduction disturbances Delayed intraventricular conduction that results in abnormal-appearing QRS complexes.

Ventricular standstill A condition in which the atria continue to beat but the ventricles have stopped.

Visceral pleura The fibrous connective tissue adhering to the outer surface of an organ.

W

Wenckebach Mobitz type I See 2nd-degree AV block, type I.

Wide complex tachycardia of unknown origin Tachycardia with wide and bizarre-looking QRS complexes but with an unknown site of origin.

Wide complex regular tachycardia Tachycardia with wide and bizarre-looking QRS complexes but with a regular rhythm. Indicates rhythm is arising from one site.

Wide complex irregular tachycardia Tachycardia with wide and bizarre-looking QRS complexes but with an irregular rhythm. Indicates rhythm is arising from more than one site.

Photo Credits

Front Matter: Courtesy Bruce Shade

Chapter 1

Opener: © McGraw-Hill Higher Education, Inc./Rick Brady, photographer; 1.1: All Photos Courtesy Philips Healthcare; 1.2: Courtesy Physio-Control; 1.9: Courtesy Bruce Shade.

Chapter 2

Opener: © McGraw-Hill Higher Education, Inc./Rick Brady, photographer; 2.2a–c: Photo Courtesy Philips Healthcare; 2.3: Courtesy Physio-Control; 2.4: Courtesy Bruce Shade; 2.11a–b: © McGraw-Hill Higher Education, Inc./Rick Brady, photographer; 2.13: Courtesy Physio-Control.

Chapter 3

Opener: © McGraw-Hill Higher Education, Inc./Rick Brady, photographer; 3.3–3.10: Courtesy Bruce Shade; 3.13: Courtesy Bruce Shade.

Chapter 4

Opener: © Image Source/Getty Images/RF; 4.4: Courtesy Bruce Shade.

Chapter 5

Opener: Courtesy Physio-Control.

Chapter 6

Opener: Courtesy Physio-Control.

Chapter 7

Opener: Courtesy Physio-Control.

Chapter 8

Opener: © Photodisc Collection/Getty Images/RF.

Chapter 9

Opener: Photo Courtesy Philips Healthcare.

Chapter 10

Opener: Courtesy Physio-Control.

Chapter 11

Opener: Courtesy Physio-Control.

Chapter 12

Opener: Courtesy Physio-Control.

Chapter 13

Opener: Courtesy Physio-Control.

Chapter 14

Opener: Courtesy Physio-Control.

Chapter 15

Opener: Courtesy Physio-Control.

Chapter 16

Opener: Photo Courtesy Philips Healthcare.

Chapter 17

Opener: Courtesy Physio-Control.

Chapter 18

Opener: Courtesy Physio-Control.

Chapter 19

Opener: Photo Courtesy Philips Healthcare.

Chapter 20

Opener: Courtesy Physio-Control.

Chapter 21

Opener: Courtesy Physio-Control.

Chapter 22

Opener: Courtesy Physio-Control.

Index

A

Aberrant conduction, QRS complex and, 161–162
Absent P wave, 140, 643
Absent QRS complex, 169–171, 645
Absolute refractory period, 17–18, 228–229
Accelerated idioventricular rhythm, 386–387
Accelerated junctional rhythm
  appearance of, 341
  causes of, 340
  description, 340
  effects of, 341
  treatment of, 342
Accessory pathways, 184
Acetylcholine, 33
Actin, 12
Action potential, 16
Active transport, 225–226
Acute coronary syndrome, 577
Acute cor pulmonale, 618
Adrenalin, 32
Adrenergic system, 32
Afterdepolarization, 238
Afterload, 24
Agonal rhythm, 384
Alpha receptors, 32
Amiodarone, 207
Angina, 579
  inverted T wave and, 581–582
Angina pectoris, 579
Angioplasty, 601
Angle of Louis, 490, 491
Antedromic AVRT, 349–350
Anterior leads, 499
Anterior wall infarction, 594
Anterolateral wall, 594
Anteroseptal leads, 499
Anteroseptal wall infarction, 594
Anteroseptal with lateral extension, 595
Antibradycardia pacing, 465
Anticholinergic drugs, 244
Antidysrhythmic agents, 244–245, 625–626

Antitachydysrhythmia pacing, 465
Aortic valve, 11
Apex, of heart, 7
Arrhythmia, vs. dysrhythmia, 229
Artifact, ECG machine, 62–64
  defined, 62
  differentiating from waveforms, 64
  muscle artifact, 62–63
  preparing electrode site and, 49
  wandering baseline, 63
Asystole, 393–395
  absent QRS complex, 169–171
  appearance of, 395
  causes of, 393
  defined, 169
  description of, 393
  effects of, 394–395
  treatment of, 395
Atherosclerosis
  defined, 577
  development and progression of, 577, 578
Atria
  absent PR interval with impulses from, 188–189
  accessory pathways, 184
  anatomy of, 10–11
  blood flow through, 25–26
  depolarization and contraction, 27
  dysrhythmias originating from, 29, 293–311
  regularity and P-P interval, 111–112
  repolarization, 30
  retrograde atrial depolarization, 136, 292
  rhythms originating in, 292–293
  short PR interval arising from, 183–184
Atrial bigeminy, 296, 298
Atrial diastole, Phase 4, 225
Atrial dysrhythmias, 290–311
  atrial kick and, 293
  defined, 239
  effects of, 293
  P waves, 292
  QRS complex, 292

  retrograde atrial depolarization, 136, 292
  short PR interval and, 183–184
  types of, 239–240
    atrial fibrillation, 309–311
    atrial flutter, 307–309
    atrial tachycardia, 301–304
    multifocal atrial tachycardia, 305–306
    premature atrial complexes (PACs), 293–299
    supraventricular tachycardia, 306–307
    wandering atrial pacemaker, 300–301
Atrial enlargement, 535–539
  biphasic P wave, 536
  causes of, 534
  changes on ECG and, 535
  defined, 534
  left, 538–539
  P mitrale, 536
  P pulmonale, 538
  P wave and, 535–537
  right, 537–538
Atrial fibrillation, 309–311
  appearance of, 311
  causes of, 309
  characteristics of, 82
  compared to normal sinus rhythm, 81–82
  description of, 309
  effects of, 309–310, 309–311
  as form of reentry, 238
  irregularly irregular, 311
  treatment of, 311
Atrial flutter, 307–309
  appearance of, 308–309
  causes of, 307
  description of, 307
  effects of, 307–308
  treatment of, 309
Atrial kick, 27, 480
  atrial dysrhythmias and, 293
  loss of, and decreased cardiac output, 230–231
Atrial muscle, action potential of, 225
Atrial overdrive pacing, 304

Atrial P wave, 135–142
Atrial quadrigeminy, 297–298
Atrial rate, counting, 103–104
Atrial tachycardia, 301–304
    appearance of, 303–304
    with block, 303–304
    causes of, 302
    description of, 301–302
    effects of, 302–303
    paroxysmal, 301
    sustained, 302
    treatment for, 304
Atrial trigeminy, 297–298
Atrioventricular dissociation, 427–429
    appearance of, 429
    causes of, 428
    description of, 427
    effects of, 429
    treatment of, 429
Atrioventricular (AV) node. See AV node
Atrioventricular (AV) valves, 11
Atropine, to treat dysrhythmias, 244
Automaticity
    increased, as cause of dysrhythmia,
        236–237
    of myocardial cells, 14, 18, 20, 26
    premature atrial complexes, 293
Autonomic nervous system, influence
    on heart, 31
AV bundle, in conductive pathway, 20
AV dissociation, 427–429
    causes of, 428
    description of, 427
    effects and appearance of, 429
    treatment of, 429
AV heart block, 77, 416–429
    AV dissociation, 427–429
    comparison of types of, 427
    complete, 425
    constant PR intervals with more P
        waves, 192
    defined, 240, 418
    1st-degree, 419–421, 427
    flat T waves and, 206
    grouped beating, 422
    irregularity and, 123–124
    longer PR interval and, 184–187
    Mobitz Type I, 421
    overview of, 418–419
    PR interval non-measurable, 191
    P wave with, 142–143
    QRS complex, 168–169
    2nd-degree, type I, 421–423, 427
    2nd-degree, type II, 423–425, 427
    3rd-degree, 425–427
    types of, 240
    varying PR interval, 187–188
    Wenckebach, 421

AV junction. See also Junctional
    dysrhythmias
    blockage of, 184–187
    dysrhythmias originating from, 334–335
    as latent pacemaker site, 187
    P wave appearance, 334
    QRS complex, 335
    short PR interval and, 184
AV nodal reentrant tachycardia (AVNRT)
    appearance of, 345
    description of, 344–345
    effects of, 346
    treatment for, 350–351
AV node. See also AV heart block
    action potential of, 225
    bradycardia arising from, 232
    conduction through, 27–28
    in conductive pathway, 20
    depolarization, 16
    pacemaker cells in, 20, 21
    structure and function, 20
AV reentrant tachycardia
    antedromic, 349–350
    appearance of, 349–350
    description of, 348–349
    effects of, 350
    orthodromic, 349
    treatment for, 350–351

B

Bachmann's bundles, 18
Baroreceptors, 30–31
Beta receptors, 32
Biatrial enlargement, 135
Bicuspid valve, 11
Bifascicular block, 562–563
Bigeminal PACs, 296, 298
Bigeminal PJCs, 338
Bigeminy, 122
Biphasic P wave, 536–537
Biphasic waveform, 51
Bipolar leads, 53, 54
Biventricular pacemaker, 456
Bizarre-looking QRS complex
    AV heart block, 168–169
    defined, 158
    early beats from ventricles, 164, 166
    escape rhythm from ventricle, 164,
        166–167
    tachycardia that arises from
        ventricles, 167–168
Blocked PACs, 298–299
    differentiating from sinus arrest, 299
Blood
    blood flow through circulatory
        system, 23–30
    cardiac cycle, 23–24

    flow through heart, 25–30
    heart's blood supply, 22–23
Blood pressure
    defined, 25
    diastole and systole, 23–24
Bradycardia
    causes of, 232
    defined, 104, 231, 257
    sinus bradycardia, 257–259
    as type of dysrhythmia, 231–232
Bradycardia junctional escape rhythm, 340
Bundle branch
    aberrant conduction and, 161–162
    normal electrical conduction, 552–554
Bundle branch block
    bifascicular and trifascicular block,
        562–563
    defined, 554
    description of, 503
    fascicular block, 556
    hemiblock, 560–562
    incomplete bundle branch block, 560
    as indicator of myocardial infarction,
        589–590
    as intraventricular conduction defect,
        160–161
    left bundle branch block, 558–560
    possible sites of, 556
    QRS complex, 160–161
    repolarization and, 560
    right bundle branch block (RBBB),
        556–558
    ST segment depression, 203
    ST segment elevation, 203
    treatment of, 564
    12-lead tracing, 554–564
    wide QRS complex, 555–556
Bundle of His
    action potential of, 225
    in conductive pathway, 20
    normal electrical conduction, 552–553
Bundle of Kent, 347
Burst of VT, 378
Bypass tract, 346

C

Calcium channel blockers, 626
Calcium channels, 223, 225, 226–227
Calcium disorders, 623–624
Calibrating ECG machine, 61–62
Caliper method, 114–115
Cardiac cycle, 23–24
    atrial and ventricular repolarization, 30
    atrial depolarization and contraction,
        26–27
    blood flow through atria, 25–26
    conduction through AV node, 27–28

conduction through His-Purkinje system, 28
  initiation of impulse in SA node, 26
  ventricular depolarization and contraction, 29
Cardiac glycosides, 623
Cardiac markers, 593
Cardiac output
  defined, 24
  formula for, 24
  reduced, as effect of dysrhythmias, 230–231
Cardiac pacing, 244
Cardiac resynchronization therapy, 456
Cardiac tamponade, 618
Cardioversion, implantable cardioverter-defibrillator (ICD) and, 465
Chamber enlargement, 503
Chaotically irregular rhythm, 121–122
Chaotic-looking baseline waves, 140–141
Chemoreceptors, 30–31
Chest leads, 56–57, 487–499
Cholinergic system, 33
Chordae tendineae, 11
Circulatory system
  blood flow through, 23–30
  cardiac cycle, 23–24
  function and components of, 21–23
  influences on, 30–34
Circus movement tachycardia (CMT), 348
Compensatory pause, 164
  appearance of PVC and, 376–377
Complete AV heart block, 425
Conduction ratio
  defined, 125
  irregularity caused by varying, 125
Conductive pathway, heart's, 18–21
Conductivity, of myocardial cells, 14–15, 27
Contiguous leads, 500
Contractility, of myocardial cells, 14
Coronary arteries
  left main, 23, 572–573
  right main, 23, 572
Coronary artery disease, 577–580
  defined, 577
  various diseases of, 577–580
Coronary circulation, 572–573
Coronary collateral vessels, 23
Coronary heart disease, 577
Coronary veins, 23, 573
Countdown method, 98–101
Counting small square method, 115

D

Defibrillation, 244
  implantable cardioverter-defibrillator (ICD) and, 465

Degree method, 513–514
Delta wave, 163, 347
Depolarization, 16–17
  of atria, 27
  of myocytes, 224–228
  rapid depolarization phase, 226–227
  SA node, 223
  ventricular, 29
Depolarizing phase, 223
Desmosomes, 14
Diagnostic mode, 58
Diastole blood pressure, 23–24
Digitalis
  ST segment depression, 203
  toxicity, 302
    U waves and, 210
Digoxin
  defined, 623
  therapeutic blood levels and ECG changes, 623, 625
  toxicity and ECG changes, 209, 625
Dilation, 534
Dopamine, to treat dysrhythmias, 244
Double R prime (R″), 157
Double S prime (S″), 157
Dropped beats, as type of dysrhythmia, 234–235
Dynamic ECGs, 58, 82–83
Dysrhythmias, 4, 229–245. *See also specific dysrhythmias*
  vs. arrhythmia, 229
  causes and mechanisms of
    increased automaticity, 236–237
    increased parasympathetic tone, 235–236
    myocardial hypoxia, injury and infarction, 236
    proarrhythmia, 239
    reentry, 237–238
    triggered beats, 238
  defined, 44, 229
  effects of, 229–231
    decreased/absent heartbeat, 231
    palpitations, 229
    reduced cardiac output, 230–231
    reduced oxygen, 230–231
  identifying, 241
  leads used to identify, 240–241
  originating from atria, 29
  originating from ventricles, 29
  site of origin
    atrial dysrhythmias, 239–240, 290–311
    AV heart block, 240, 416–429
    junctional dysrhythmias, 240, 332–351
    sinus dysrhythmias, 239, 252–269

ventricular dysrhythmias, 240, 370–396
  treatment of, 241–245
    defibrillation, 244
    electrical therapy, 243–244
    medications, 244–245
    pacing, 244
    physical maneuvers, 243
    synchronized cardioversion, 244
    vagal maneuvers, 243
  types of
    bradycardia, 231–232
    dropped beats or QRS complexes, 234–235
    early (premature) beats, 234
    irregularity, 235
    tachycardia, 232–234

E

Early beats, 117–118
  aberrant conduction, 162
  from atria, and PR interval, 183–184
  as cause of dysrhythmia, 234
  compensatory pause, 164
  flat T waves and, 206
  premature atrial complexes, 234, 293, 296
  premature junctional complexes (PJCs), 234, 338
  premature ventricular complexes, 234
  P′ waves with, 136–138
  at regular intervals, 122
  that arise from ventricles and wide, bizarre-looking QRS complex, 164, 166
  as type of dysrhythmia, 234
  ventricular fibrillation, 118
Early repolarization, 227
ECG (electrocardiogram)
  artifact, 62–64
  characteristics of normal, 72
  defined, 4
  dynamic, 58, 82–83
  normal sinus rhythm, 72
  static, 58
  uses of, 4–5
ECG leads, 50–57
  bipolar/unipolar leads, 53, 54
  chest leads, 56–57
  concept of, 52–53
  frontal plane of heart, 54–55
  horizontal plane of heart, 56
  limb leads, 54–55
  precordial, 56–57
  purpose of multiple leads, 51–52
  V leads, 56–57
ECG lead wires and cables, 47–49

ECG machine. *See* Electrocardiograph
ECG monitor, 82–83
ECG paper
  characteristics of, 59
  horizontal lines, 59–60
  recording tracings, 60–61
  vertical lines, 60
ECG tracings, 58
  characteristics of normal ECG, 72
  defined, 58
  horizontal lines, 59–60
  isoelectric line, 60
  Nine-Step Process overview, 73–79
  of paced ECG, 456–458
  paper for, 59
  reading, 59–61
  recording tracings, 60–61
  vertical lines, 60
Ectopic focus, 234, 237
Ectopic P′ waves, 642
Ectopy, 117
18-lead ECGs, 500–502
Einthoven, Willem, 44
Einthoven's Triangle, 44, 483–485
Electrical alternans, 617
Electrical axis, 502–518
  altered QRS axis, 515–516
  calculating, 508–518
    degree method, 513–514
    four-quadrant method, 509–513
    hexaxial reference system, 508–509
  causes of altered electrical axis, 516–518
  defined, 504
  mean instantaneous vector, 504–505
  vectors, 504
  ventricular depolarization and mean QRS axis, 505–507
  waveform direction, 505
Electrical conducting cells, 14–15
Electrocardiograph
  artifact, 62–64
  calibrating, 61–62
  defined, 4
  displays, 58
  ECG monitor, 58
  electrode, 49–51
  electromagnetic interference, 63–64
  historical perspective, 44–45
  how does it work, 5–6
  input, 47–57
  lead wires and cables, 47–49
  output, 57–61
  printouts, 58–61
  terms for, 44
  types of, 45–46
  uses of, 44–45

Electrodes, ECG
  characteristics of, 49
  ground, 53
  limb lead placement, 55
  placing, 50–51
  preparing site, 49
Electrolyte imbalance
  calcium disorder, 623
  description of, 504, 620
  flat T waves and, 206
  hyperkalemia, 620–621
  hypokalemia, 622–623
Electromagnetic interference, 63–64
Endocardium, 9
Enlargement
  atrial enlargement, 535–539
  causes of, 535
  changes on ECG and, 535
  defined, 534
Epicardial pacemaker, 450
Epicardium, 10
Epinephrine, 32
  to treat dysrhythmias, 244
  U waves, 210
Escape beats, ventricular escape beats, 381–383
Escape pacemaker, 263
  bradycardia and, 232
  dropped beats and, 235
Escape rhythm
  bradycardia junctional escape rhythm, 340
  junctional escape rhythm, 338–340
    with bradycardia, 340
  that arise from ventricles and wide, bizarre-looking QRS complex, 164, 166–167
  3rd-degree AV heart block, 426
Excitability, of myocardial cells, 14–15, 27
Extensive anterior wall infarction, 595

F

Fascicular block, 556
Fast pacing, 465
Fast sodium channels, 226
Fatty streak, 577
Fibrillation
  as reentry, 238
  ventricular fibrillation (VF), 391–393
Fibrillatory waves, 140–141, 311
15-lead ECGs, 500–502
1500 method, 101–102
Fight-or-flight response, 32
1st-degree AV heart block, 419–421
  appearance of, 420
  causes of, 419

  compared to other AV heart blocks, 427
  description of, 419
  effects of, 420
  treatment, 421
Flat T wave, 206
Flipped T waves, 582
Flutter waves, 138, 140, 307, 308, 643
Four-quadrant method, 509–513
Frontal plane
  Einthoven's Triangle, 483–484
  Lead I, 481–483
  Lead II, 481–483
  Lead III, 481–483
  Lead VF, 484–487
  Lead VL, 484–487
  Lead VR, 484–487
  overview of, 481
Frontal plane of heart, 54–55, 481–487
Funny currents, 223
f waves (fibrillatory waves), 311
F waves (flutter waves), 138, 140, 307, 308, 643

G

Gap junctions, 14
Generator, pacemaker, 451–452
Grossly irregular rhythm, 121–122
Ground electrode, 53
Grouped beating, 422

H

Haloperidol, 207
Heart
  blood flow through, 21–22, 25–30
  blood supply for, 22–23
  cardiac cycle, 23–24
  cardiac output, 24
  cells of, 12–15
  conductive pathway, 18–21
  coronary arteries, 572–573
  coronary circulation, 572–573
  coronary veins, 573
  frontal plane of, 54–55, 481–487
  functional pumps of, 10–11
  horizontal plane of, 56, 487–499
  increased oxygen needs of, 572, 573
  internal, 10–12
  nerve impulse generation, 15–18, 222–223
  nervous system influences on, 30–34
  normal electrical activity of, 222–229, 480
  pericardial sac, 7–9
  shape and position of, 7
  skeleton of, 11–12

structure of, 6–12
valves of, 11
wall of, 9–10
Heart block. *See also* AV heart block;
    Bundle branch block
    3rd-degree heart block with
        idioventricular escape, 385
    ventricular conduction disturbances,
        552
Heart rate, 92–107
    average, 73
    bradycardia, 104
    conditions of, and deductive
        reasoning algorithm for, 639
    countdown, sequence or triplicate
        method, 98–101
    counting atrial and ventricular rates,
        103–104
    fast rates, 104, 639
    1500 method, 101–102
    importance of determining, 94
    irregularity caused by sudden
        changes in, 120–121
    methods of determining, 95–103
    in Nine-Step Process, 73, 638–639
    normal, 639
    paroxysmal, 120–121
    quick check of, 94–95
    rate calculators, 103
    6-second interval x 10 method, 96–98
    slow rates, 104, 638–639
    tachycardia, 104
    300, 150, 100, 75, 60, 50 method,
        98–101
Hemiblock, 560–562
Hexaxial reference system, 508–509
High lateral leads, 499
His-Purkinje system, 20
    conduction through, 28
Horizontal heart, 516
Horizontal lines on ECG paper, 59–60
Horizontal plane
    Lead V1, 489–490
    Lead V2, 491–492
    Lead V3, 493
    Lead V4, 493–494
    Lead V5, 494–495
    Lead V6, 495–499
    overview, 487–489
Horizontal plane of heart, 56, 487–499
Hyperacute T waves, 582–583
Hypercalcemia, 623–624
    shortened QT interval, 209
    U waves, 210
Hyperkalemia, 135
    characteristics of, 620
    description of, 620

ECG changes, 620–621
ST segment elevation, 203
tall T waves, 205
U waves, 210
Hyperthyroid, low amplitude QRS
    complex, 159
Hypertrophy, 503
    altered electrical axis and, 516
    causes of, 534
    changes on ECG and, 535
    defined, 534
    ventricular hypertrophy, 159, 203,
        539–543
Hyperventilation, ST segment
    depression, 203
Hypocalcemia, 623–624
Hypokalemia, 135
    characteristics of, 622
    description of, 622
    ECG changes, 622–623
    ST segment depression, 203
Hypothermia, ST segment
    elevation, 203

I

Idioventricular rhythm, 232, 381,
    384–386
    accelerated, 386–387
    as agonal rhythm, 384
    appearance of, 385
    causes of, 385
    description of, 384
    effects of, 385
    3rd-degree heart block with
        idioventricular escape, 385
    treatment of, 386
Implantable cardioverter-defibrillator
    (ICD), 462–466
    electrode wires, 464
    function of, 463
    provider safety, 466
    pulse generator, 463–464
    recognition of ventricular
        dysrhythmias
        morphology discrimination, 464
        rate discrimination, 464
        rhythm discrimination, 464
    therapies provided by, 465
    to treat dysrhythmias, 244
Incomplete bundle branch block, 560
Indeterminate axis, 509, 515
Inferior infarction, 595–596
Inferior leads, 499
Inferior-wall MI, sinus bradycardia
    and, 258
Input for ECG machine, 47–57

Instantaneous vectors, 504
Intercalated disks, 14
Internal pacemaker, 451. *See also*
    Pacemaker device, permanent
Interpolated PVC, 378
Intra cranial hemorrhage,
    U waves, 210
Intraventricular conduction defect
    bundle branch block, 160–161, 560
    causes of, 161
    QRS complex, 160–161
Inverted P wave, 140–142, 643
Irregularity
    conditions of, and deductive
        reasoning algorithm for, 640
    as type of dysrhythmia, 235
    types of, 116–125
        caused by sudden changes in heart
            rate, 120–121
        early beats, 117–118
        irregularly irregular, 121–22
        occasionally or very irregular,
            116–119, 640–641
        patterned irregularity, 122–124, 641
        pause or arrest of sinus node,
            118–119
        slightly irregular, 119–120, 641
        slowing irregularity, 641
        sudden acceleration, 641
        total irregularity, 641
        varying conduction ratios, 125, 641
Irregularly irregular, 121–122, 311
Isoelectric line, 60

J

James fibers, 347, 348
J point, 154, 576
Junction, 154
Junctional bigeminy, 338
Junctional dysrhythmias, 332–351
    defined, 240
    P wave, 334
    QRS complex, 335
    types of, 240
        accelerated junctional rhythm,
            340–342
        AV nodal reentrant tachycardia,
            344–346
        AV reentrant tachycardia, 348–350
        defined, 334
        junctional escape rhythm, 338–340
        junctional tachycardia, 342–344
        preexcitation, 346–348
        premature junctional complex,
            335–338
Junctional escape, 232

Junctional escape rhythm
appearance of, 339–340
with bradycardia, 340
causes of, 338
description of, 338
effects of, 339
treatment for, 340
Junctional tachycardia
appearance of, 343–344
causes of, 343
description of, 342–343
effects of, 343
treatment for, 350–351
Junctional trigeminy, 338

L

Lateral leads, 499
Lateral wall infarction, 594
Lead I
Einthoven's Triangle, 483–485
QRS complex in, 157
as standard limb lead, 481–483
Lead II
characteristics of, 56
defined, 56
Einthoven's Triangle, 483–485
to identify dysrhythmias, 240–242
P wave configuration in, 133–134
QRS complex in, 157
as standard limb lead, 481–483
Lead III
Einthoven's Triangle, 483–485
QRS complex in, 157
as standard limb lead, 481–483
Leading palpitations, 391
Lead V1, 489–492
Lead V2, 491–493
Lead V3, 493–494
Lead V4, 493–494
Lead V5, 494–495
Lead V6, 495–499
Lead VF, 484–487
Lead VL, 484–487
Lead VR, 484–487
Lead wires, pacemaker, 453
Lead wires and cables, ECG, 47–49
Left anterior fascicular block
(LAFB), 556
Left anterior hemiblock (LAHB), 556, 561
Left atrial enlargement, 538–539
Left bundle branch, 20, 28
Left bundle branch block, 558–560
Left main coronary artery, 23, 572–573
Left posterior fascicular block (LPFB), 556
Left posterior hemiblock (LPHB), 556,
561–562

Left ventricular hypertrophy, 541–543
U waves, 210
Left ventricular volume overload,
inverted U wave, 210
Limb leads, 54–55, 481–487
augmented, 484
standard, 481
Long QT syndrome, 390
Low lateral leads, 499
Lown-Ganong-Levine syndrome, 347–348

M

MCL1 lead, to identify dysrhythmias,
241–242
Mean instantaneous vector, 504–505
Mean QRS axis, 505, 507
Mean QRS vector, 507
Mediastinum, 7
Methadone, 207
Midclavicular line, 493
Mitral valve, 11
Mitral valve prolapse, U waves, 210
M like, 556
Mobitz Type I, 421
Monitor mode, 58
Monitor screen, analyzing ECG on, 82–83
Morphology
defined, 74
P wave, 133–134
QRS complex, 153
Multifocal atrial rhythm, 300
wide complex tachycardia of
unknown origin, 306
Multifocal atrial tachycardia (MAT)
appearance of, 306
causes of, 305–306
description of, 305
effects of, 306
treatment of, 306
Multiformed (multifocal) PVC, 378
Muscle artifact, 62–63
Muscles, cardiac, nerve impulse generation
and contraction of, 15–18
Myocardial hypoxia
as cause of dysrhythmia, 236
ECG indicators of, bundle branch
block, 589–590
Myocardial infarction
altered electrical axis and, 516–518
as cause of dysrhythmia, 236
criteria for diagnosing
clinical history, 593
ECG findings, 593
serum cardiac markers, 593
defined, 579
description of, 503, 579–580

ECG indicators of, 580–592
evolution of ECG during MI,
590–591
hyperacute T waves, 582
Q wave, 588–589
reciprocal changes, 592
identifying location of
anterior wall infarction, 594
anterolateral wall, 594
extensive anterior wall
infarction, 595
inferior infarction, 595–596
lateral wall infarction, 594
posterior wall infarction, 596
septal wall infarction, 594
use of additional ECG leads,
599–600
prolonged QT interval, 207
sinus bradycardia and, 258
ST segment elevated as early
indicator, 202
treatment of, 601
Myocardial injury
defined, 579
description of, 503, 579
ECG indicators of
reciprocal changes, 592
ST segment changes, 584–588
ST segment elevated, 202
treatment of, 579
Myocardial ischemia
as cause of dysrhythmia, 236
causes of, 577
defined, 577
description of, 503, 577
ECG indicators of
inverted T waves, 581–582
reciprocal changes, 592
inverted U wave, 210
prolonged QT interval, 207
ST segment depression, 203
tall T waves, 205
Myocardium, 9–10
Myocytes, 12–15
depolarization and repolarization
of, 224–228
Phase 0, 226–227
Phase 1, 227
Phase 2, 227
Phase 3, 227
Phase 4, 225
Myosin, 12

N

Narrow complex-irregular
tachycardia, 233

Narrow complex-regular
    tachycardia, 233
Negative chronotropic effect, 623
Negative dromotropic effect, 623
Nerve impulses
    depolarized state, 16–17
    generation in heart, 222–223
    polarized state, 15–16
    refractory period, 17–18
    repolarization, 17
Nervous system, influences on heart
    and circulatory system, 30–34
Neurotransmitters, 30–31
Nine-Step Process. *See also specific step*
    flexibility in, 79
    heart rate, 73, 638–639
    overview of, 73–79
    PR interval, 75–77, 645–646
    P waves, 74, 641–643
    QRS complex, 75, 643–645
    QT interval, 78, 650–651
    regularity, 73–74, 639–641
    ST segment, 77, 646–648
    T waves, 77, 648–649
    U waves, 79, 650–652
Nitroglycerin, 579
Nodal rhythms, 334
Noise, 62. *See also* Artifact, ECG
    machine
Noncompensatory pause, 296
Nonconducted PACs, 298–299
    differentiating from sinus arrest, 299
Nonpacemaker cells, depolarization, 16
Nonperfusing PVC, 376
Norepinephrine, 32
Normal ECG, 72
Normal sinus rhythm (NSR)
    characteristics of, 256
    defined, 256
Notched P wave, 135
NSTEMI, 587

O

Occasionally irregular, 116–119,
    640–641
Orthodromic AVRT, 349
Oscilloscope, 5
Output for ECG machine, 57–61
Overdrive pacing, 465

P

Pacemaker
    escape, 232, 235
    to treat dysrhythmias, 244
    wandering atrial pacemaker, 300–301

Pacemaker cells
    alternate sites for, 21
    in AV node, 20
    in conductive pathway, 18
    function of, 14–15
    in Purkinje fibers, 21
    in SA node, 18
Pacemaker device, permanent, 450–462
    appearance of paced ECG, 456–458
    biventricular pacemaker, 456
    cardiac resynchronization
        therapy, 456
    clinical uses of, 451
    coding system for, 454–456
    complications
        infection, 462
        pacemaker syndrome, 462
    failure of
        failure to capture, 458–459
        failure to pace, 459–460
        failure to sense, 460
        oversensing, 461
        pacemaker-mediated tachycardia,
            461–462
    function of, 451
    generator of, 451–452
    lead wires, 453
    output, 454
    pacing modes of, 453–454
        demand, 453
        dual-chamber, 453
        fixed-rate, 453
        rate-responsive, 454
        single-chamber, 453
    pacing spike, 456–458
    rate adaptation of, 454
    refractory period, 454
    sensitivity of, 454
    unipolar vs. bipolar systems pacing
        spikes, 458
Pacemaker device, temporary
    epicardial pacing, 450
    transcutaneous pacemaker, 450
    transvenous pacing, 244, 450
Pacemaker-induced QRS complex,
    163, 164
Pacemaker site
    AV heart block and, 168–169
    changing, and PR interval,
        187–188
    latent sites, 187
Pacemaker spike, 163, 164
Pacemaker syndrome, 462
Pacing artifact, 456–457
Pacing spike, 456–457
Palpitations, as symptom of
    dysrhythmias, 229

Paper and pen method, determining
    regularity of, 113
Papillary muscles, 11
Parasympathetic nervous system
    effect on heart, 33–34
    increased parasympathetic tone as
        cause of dysrhythmia, 235–236
Parasympatholytic drugs, 244
Paroxysmal, in heart rate rhythm,
    120–121, 301
Paroxysmal atrial tachycardia, 301
Paroxysmal junctional tachycardia, 301
Paroxysmal supraventricular
    tachycardia (PSVT), 267
Patterned irregularity, 122–124, 641
P axis, 505
Peaked P wave, 134–135
Peaked T wave, 205, 582
Perfusion, 7
Pericardial effusion
    description of, 503, 615–617
    ECG changes, 617–618
Pericardial tamponade, 9
Pericarditis
    characteristics of, 614
    defined, 614
    description of, 503, 614
    ECG changes, 614–615
    ST segment elevation, 203
    tall T waves, 205
Pericardium, 7–8
Phase 0
    impulse generation in SA node,
        223, 224
    myocytes depolarization and
        repolarization, 226–227
Phase 1, myocytes depolarization and
    repolarization, 227
Phase 2, myocytes depolarization and
    repolarization, 227
Phase 3
    impulse generation in SA node,
        223–224
    myocytes depolarization and
        repolarization, 228
Phase 4
    impulse generation in SA node,
        223, 224
    myocytes depolarization and
        repolarization, 225
Plasminogen activators, 601
Plateau phase, 227
Pleural effusion, low amplitude QRS
    complex, 159
P mitrale, 135, 536
Polarized state, cardiac muscles, 15–16,
    222–223

Polymorphic ventricular tachycardia, 389–391
appearance of, 391
causes of, 390
description of, 389–390
effects of, 391
treatment of, 391
Posterior leads, 500
Posterior wall infarction, 596
Potassium channels, 223, 225–226, 228
P-P interval
to determine regularity, 111–112, 115
premature atrial complexes, 295–296
sinoatrial exit block, 266
sinus bradycardia, 259
sinus dysrhythmia, 263
sinus tachycardia, 261
slightly irregular, 119–120
sudden changes in heart rate, 120–121
P pulmonale, 135, 538
Precordial leads, 56–57, 487–499
Preexcitation
description of, 346–347
Lown-Ganong-Levine syndrome, 347–348
Wolff-Parkinson-White syndrome, 347
Preload, 24
Premature atrial complexes (PACs), 234, 293–299
appearance of, 295–299
bigeminal, trigeminal, quadrigeminal, 296–298
blocked, 298–299
causes of, 293–294
description of, 293
differentiating blocked PACs from sinus arrest, 299
effects of, 295
noncompensatory pause, 296
nonconducted, 298–299
nonperfusing PVC, 376
treatment, 299
Premature beats, 117
as cause of dysrhythmia, 234
ectopic focus and, 237
Premature complex, 234
Premature junctional complexes (PJCs), 234
appearance of, 337–338
causes of, 335–336
description of, 335
effects of, 337
∼mes for, 338
∼ment for, 338

Premature ventricular complexes (PVCs), 234, 296, 373–381
appearance of, 376–380
causes of, 374–375
compensatory pause, 376–377
couplet or pair, 378
description of, 373–374
effects of, 376
interpolated PVC, 378
multiformed (multifocal), 378
R-on-T, 380–381
salvo run or burst of VT, 378
treatment for, 381
trigeminal and quadrigeminy, 378
uniform (unifocal), 377–378
Prepotential, 223
PR interval (PRI), 179–192
absent, 646
with impulses from atria, 188–189
AV heart block, 184–187, 187–188, 191, 192
1st-degree, 419–420
2nd-degree, type I, 421–422
2nd-degree, type II, 423–425
changing pacemaker site, 187–188
conditions of, and deductive reasoning algorithm for, 645
constant PR intervals with more P waves, 192
defined, 75
early beat from atria, 183–184
importance of determining, 180
longer, 184–187, 646
measuring, 181–182
in Nine-Step Process, 73, 75–77, 645–646
non measurable, 191–192
normal ECG, 72, 76, 180–181, 645–646
quick check of, 180
short PR interval, 646
with accessory pathways, 184
with dysrhythmias from atria, 183–184
with dysrhythmias from AV junction, 183–184
varying, 187–188, 646
ventricular dysrhythmias and non-measurable, 191
ventricular preexcitation, 184
Printouts
characteristics of normal ECG, 72
defined, 58
horizontal lines, 59–60
isoelectric line, 60
Nine-Step Process overview, 73–79
normal sinus rhythm, 72

paper for, 59
recording tracings, 60–61
vertical lines, 60
Proarrhythmia, 239
Procainamide, 626
Prolonged QT interval syndrome, 207, 210, 650
PR segment
as baseline to evaluate ST segment, 574, 576
defined, 28, 76
Pulmonary circulation, 22
Pulmonary embolism
characteristics of, 618
description of, 504, 618
ECG changes, 618–619
Pulmonic valve, 11
Pulseless electrical activity (PEA), 395–396
appearance of, 396
causes of, 395
description of, 395
effects of, 396
treatment of, 396
Purkinje fibers, 209
action potential of, 225
in conductive pathway, 20–21
normal electrical conduction, 552–553
pacemaker cells in, 21
P wave, 130–148
absent wave, 140, 643
atrial dysrhythmias, 292
atrial enlargement, 535–539
atrial fibrillation and, 311
atrial rate and counting, 103–104
AV heart block, 142–143
constant PR intervals with more P waves, 192
biphasic, 536–537
caliper method, 114–115
chaotic-looking baseline waves, 140–141
conditions of, and deductive reasoning algorithm for, 642
defined, 27
early beats arising from atria, 136–138
ectopic P′ waves, 642
fibrillatory waves, 140–141
flutter waves, 138, 140
importance of determining, 132
indiscernible, 643
inverted wave, 140–142, 643
junctional dysrhythmias, 334
more P waves than QRS complexes, 142–143, 643
morphology, 133–134

multifocal atrial tachycardia, 306
in Nine-Step Process, 73, 74, 641–643
normal ECG, 72, 74–75, 133–134, 641
paper and pen method of regularity, 113
peaked, notched, or enlarged sinus, 134–135
preceding QRS complex and bundle branch block, 161
premature atrial complexes, 296
quick check of, 132
retrograde depolarization and, 292
saw-toothed waveforms, 138, 140, 643
2nd-degree AV heart block, type II, 424
sinoatrial exit block, 266
tachycardia arising from atria, 136, 139
3rd-degree AV heart block, 426
varying atrial, 136, 139
ventricular dysrhythmias, 372–373
wandering atrial pacemaker, 300–301

Q

QRS complex
    aberrant conduction, 161–162
    abnormal, 158–171
    absent, 169–171, 645
    asystole, 169–171
    atrial dysrhythmias, 292
    AV heart block, 168–169
    bizarre-looking, 158, 163–168
    bundle branch block, 160–161, 555–556
    conditions causing abnormal, 158–159
    conditions of, and deductive reasoning algorithm for, 644
    defined, 29
    in different leads, 157
    dropped, 234–235
        as type of dysrhythmia, 234–235
    early beats that arise from ventricles, 164, 166
    escape rhythm that arises from ventricles, 164, 166–167
    importance of determining, 152
    intraventricular conduction defect, 160–161
    junctional dysrhythmias, 335
    measuring, 154–155
    M-like, 556
    more P waves than, 142–143
    narrow complex-irregular, 233
    narrow complex-regular, 233
    in Nine-Step Process, 73, 75, 643–645
    normal ECG, 72, 75–76, 153–154, 157–158, 643

pacemaker-induced, 163, 164
quick check of, 152
Q wave, normal, 153–154
rabbit ears, 556
R wave
    more than one, 157
    normal, 154
6-second interval x 10 method, 96–98
spindle-shaped rhythm, 168
S wave
    more than one, 157
    normal, 154
tachycardia
    that arises from ventricles, 167–168
    types of, 233–234
tall and low amplitude, 159, 644
3rd-degree AV heart block, 426
300, 150, 100, 75, 60, 50 method, 98–101
variations in, 155–157
ventricular dysrhythmias, 373
ventricular fibrillation, 169–170
ventricular hypertrophy, 539–543
ventricular preexcitation, 162–163
wide, bizarre-looking QRS complex of ventricular origin, 163–168, 645
wide complex-irregular, 233
wide complex-regular, 233
wide complex-unknown origin, 233
wide QRS complex of supraventricular origin, 159–163, 644
QS complex, 155, 156
QT interval (QTI)
    abnormal, 207–209, 650
    conditions of, and deductive reasoning algorithm for, 651
    defined, 78
    indiscernible, 650
    long QT syndrome, 390
    measuring, 206–207
    in Nine-Step Process, 73, 78, 650–651
    normal ECG, 72, 78, 206, 650
    prolonged, 207, 650
    prolonged QT interval syndrome, 207
    shortened, 209, 650
Quadrigeminal PACs, 297–298
Quadrigeminal PJCs, 338
Quadrigeminy, 122
Quinidine, 626
Q wave
    characteristics of normal, 574–575
    defined, 574–575
    as indicator of myocardial infarction, 588–589
    in QRS complex, 153–154

R

Rabbit ears, 556
Rapid depolarization phase, 226–227
Rapid final repolarization, 228
Rate calculators, 103, 115
Reciprocal changes, 592
Reentry
    as cause of dysrhythmia, 237–238
    circus reentry, 307
Refractory period, 17–18
    absolute, 17, 228–229
    relative, 17, 229
Regularity, 108–129
    caliper method, 114–115
    conditions of, and deductive reasoning algorithm for, 640
    counting small square method, 115
    importance of, 110
    methods for determining, 111–115
    in Nine-Step Process, 73–74, 639–641
    paper and pen method, 112–113
    quick check of, 110–111
    rate calculator, 115
    types of irregularity, 116–125
    using P-P and R-R intervals to determine, 111–112
Regularly irregular, 122–124
Regular sinus rhythm, 256
Relative refractory period, 17–18, 229
Reperfusion dysrhythmia, 386
Repolarization, 17, 223–224
    atrial and ventricular, 30
    bundle branch block and, 560
    early repolarization, 227
    of myocytes, 224–228
    rapid final repolarization, 228
    SA node, 223–224
Resting membrane potential (RMP), 15–16, 222–223
Resting state, cardiac muscles, 15–16
Retrograde atrial depolarization, 136, 292
Rhythm strips
    analyzing, 83–84
    characteristics of normal ECG, 72
    defined, 58
    horizontal lines, 59–60
    isoelectric line, 60
    Nine-Step Process overview, 73–79
    normal sinus rhythm, 72
    paper for, 59
    reading, 59–61
    recording tracings, 60–61
    vertical lines, 60
Right atrial enlargement, 537–538
Right bundle branch, 20, 28

Right bundle branch block (RBBB), 556–558
Right main coronary artery, 23, 572
Right precordial leads, 500
Right ventricular hypertrophy, 539–541
R-on-T PVC, 380–381
R prime (R'), 157
R-R interval
    to determine regularity, 111–112, 115
    early beats, 118
    noncompensatory pause, 296
    patterned irregularity, 122–124
    pause or arrest of SA node, 119
    premature atrial complexes, 295–296
    for premature complex, 234
    sinus bradycardia, 259
    sinus dysrhythmia, 263
    sinus tachycardia, 261
    slightly irregular, 119–120
    sudden changes in heart rate, 120–121
    totally irregular rhythm, 121–122
    ventricular escape beats, 383
RS complex, 155, 156
R wave
    caliper method, 114–115
    1500 method, 101–102
    more than one, 157
    paper and pen method of regularity, 113
    in QRS complex, 154
    300, 150, 100, 75, 60, 50 method, 98–101

S

Salvo run, 378
SA node
    action potential of, 225
    appearance of sinus rhythm, 254–256
    bradycardia arising from, 232
    in conductive pathway, 18–19
    depolarization, 16
    as heart's primary pacemaker, 18–19, 223–224
    impulse generation in, 223–224
    initiation of nerve impulse in, 18–19, 26
    pacemaker cells in, 18, 21
    pause or arrest of, 118–119
    Phase 0, 223, 224
    Phase 3, 223–224
    Phase 4, 223, 224
    rhythms originating from, 254–269
    structure and function, 18–19
    mma, 12
    ed waveforms, 138, 140, 643

Secondary repolarization abnormalities, 543
2nd-degree AV heart block
    type I, 421–423
        appearance of, 422–423
        causes of, 422
        compared to other AV heart blocks, 427
        description of, 421–422
        effects of, 422
        grouped beating, 422
        treatment of, 423
    type II, 423–425
        appearance of, 424–425
        causes of, 423
        compared to other AV heart blocks, 427
        description of, 423
        effects of, 424
        treatment of, 425
Semilunar valve, 11
Septal leads, 499
Septal wall infarction, 594
Septum, 10–11
Sequence method, 98–101
Serum cardiac markers, 593
Sick sinus syndrome, 254
    appearance of, 268–269
    causes of, 267
    defined, 267
    effects of, 268
    treatment of, 269
Sinoatrial exit block
    appearance of, 265, 266–267
    causes of, 266
    defined, 265
    effects of, 266
    treatment of, 267
Sinus arrest
    appearance of, 264, 265
    causes of, 263–264
    defined, 263
    differentiating from blocked PACs, 299
    effects of, 264
    treatment of, 265
Sinus bradycardia
    appearance of, 257, 259
    causes of, 257–258
    compared to normal sinus rhythm, 80–81
    defined, 257
    effects of, 258–259
    inferior wall infarction, 596
    treatment for, 259
Sinus dysrhythmias, 252–269
    appearance of, 262, 263
    causes of, 262

defined, 239, 261–262
    treatment for, 263
    types of, 239
        sick sinus syndrome, 267–269
        sinoatrial exit block, 265–267
        sinus arrest, 263–265
        sinus bradycardia, 257–259
        sinus dysrhythmia, 261–263
        sinus tachycardia, 259–261
Sinus node dysfunction, 267
Sinus pause, 265
Sinus rhythm
    appearance of, 254–256
    characteristics of normal, 72, 256
    defined, 72
    normal sinus rhythm (NSR), 256
    regular sinus rhythm, 256
    as underlying rhythm, 269
Sinus tachycardia, 232
    appearance of, 260, 261
    causes of, 259–260
    defined, 259
    effects of, 260–261
    treatment for, 261
6-second interval x 10 method, 96–98
Skeleton of heart, 11–12
Slightly irregular, 119–120, 641
Slow calcium channels, 226–227
Slowing irregularity, 641
Slow VT, 389
Sodium-potassium pumps, 17
    in Phase 4, 225
Sotalol, 207
Spindle-shaped rhythm, 168
S prime (S'), 157
Static ECGs, 58
STEMI, 587
Sternal angle, 490, 491
Stroke volume, cardiac output and, 24
ST segment
    characteristics of normal, 200–201, 575–576
    conditions of, and deductive reasoning algorithm for, 647
    defined, 30, 77, 575
    depressions in, 203, 584–585, 648
    elevations in, 202–203, 584–588, 648
    as indicator of myocardial injury, 584–588
    indistinguishable, 648
    measuring, 201–202
    in Nine-Step Process, 73, 77, 646–648
    normal, 646
    normal ECG, 72
    normal variant, 203
    STEMI, 587
    ventricular hypertrophy and, 543

Subarachnoid hemorrhage, inverted T waves, 205
Subendocardial injury, 584
Sudden acceleration, 641
Supraventricular dysrhythmias
    aberrant conduction, 161–162
    intraventricular conduction defect, 160–161
    pacemaker-induced QRS complex, 163
    ventricular preexcitation, 162–163
    wide QRS complex, 159–163
Supraventricular tachycardia, 142, 306–307
    defined, 343
    treatment for, 350–351
Supraventricular tachycardias, 233
S wave
    more than one, 157
    in QRS complex, 154
Sympathetic nervous system
    characteristics of, 32
    effect on heart, 33
    stimulation of, and increased automaticity, 237
Sympathomimetic properties, 244
Synchronized cardioversion, 244, 304
Syncytium, 13
Systemic circulation, 22
Systole blood pressure, 23–24

T

Tachycardia
    aberrant conduction, 162
    atrial tachycardia, 301–304
    AV nodal reentrant tachycardia, 344–346
    AV reentrant tachycardia, 348–350
    causes of, 232–234
    circus movement tachycardia (CMT), 348
    defined, 104, 232, 259
    junctional tachycardia, 342–344
    multifocal atrial tachycardia, 305–306
    pacemaker-mediated tachycardia, 461–462
    polymorphic ventricular tachycardia, 389–391
    P′ waves with, 136, 139
    sinus tachycardia, 232, 259–261
    supraventricular tachycardia, 142, 306–307, 343, 350–351
    supraventricular tachycardias, 233
    as type of dysrhythmia, 232–234
    types of
        narrow complex-irregular, 233
        narrow complex-regular, 233
        wide complex-irregular, 233

wide complex-regular, 233
        wide complex-unknown origin, 233
    ventricular tachycardia, 167–168, 233, 378, 387–389
Tall T wave, 205
Tented T wave, 205, 648
3rd-degree heart block with idioventricular escape, 385
3rd-degree AV heart block, 425–427
    appearance of, 426–427
    causes of, 426
    compared to other AV heart blocks, 427
    description of, 425–426
    effects of, 426
    treatment of, 427
300, 150, 100, 75, 60, 50 method, 98–101
Thrombolytic agents, 601
Thyrotoxicosis, U waves, 210
Torsades de pointes, 389–391
    prolonged QT interval, 207
Totally irregular rhythm, 121–122
TP interval, 201, 584
TP segment, 574
Transcutaneous pacemaker, 244, 450
Transvenous pacemaker, 450
Tricuspid valve, 11
Trifascicular block, 562–563
Trigeminal PACs, 296–298
Trigeminal PJCs, 338
Trigeminal PVCs, 378
Trigeminy, 122
Triggered activity, 238
Triggered beats, 238
Triplicate methods, 98–101
T wave
    abnormal, 205–206, 649
    angina and, 581–582
    characteristics of normal, 77–78, 203–204, 576–577
    conditions of, and deductive reasoning algorithm for, 649
    defined, 30, 77
    flat, 206
    flipped T waves, 582
    hyperacute, 582–583
    as indicator of myocardial infarction, 582–583
    as indicator of myocardial ischemia, 581–582
    measuring, 204–205
    in Nine-Step Process, 73, 77–78, 648–649
    normal, 648
    peaked T waves, 582
    tall or peaked, 205
    tented, 205, 648
    ventricular hypertrophy and, 543
12-lead tracing, 480–518

analyzing, 83–86, 502–504
    atrial enlargement, 535–539
    bundle branch block, 554–564
    common cardiac conditions to identify with, 503–504
    drug effects and toxicity, 623–626
    electrical axis and, 502–518
        altered QRS axis, 515–516
        calculating, 508–518
        causes of altered electrical axis, 516–518
        degree method, 513–514
        four-quadrant method, 509–513
        hexaxial reference system, 508–509
        mean instantaneous vector, 504–505
        vectors, 504
        ventricular depolarization and mean QRS axis, 505–507
        waveform direction, 505
    electrolyte imbalance, 620–623
    frontal plane
        Einthoven's Triangle, 483–484
        Lead I, 481–483
        Lead II, 481–483
        Lead III, 481–483
        Lead V_F, 484–487
        Lead V_L, 484–487
        Lead V_R, 484–487
        overview of, 481
    horizontal plane
        Lead V_1, 489–490
        Lead V_2, 491–492
        Lead V_3, 493
        Lead V_4, 493–494
        Lead V_5, 494–495
        Lead V_6, 495–499
        overview, 487–489
    identifying myocardial infarction location, 594–600
    myocardial ischemia, injury and infarction, 577–600
    pericardial effusion, 615–618
    pericarditis, 614–615
    pulmonary embolism, 618–619
    putting views together
        contiguous leads, 500
        15- and 18-lead ECGs, 500–502
        specific leads and associated views, 499
    uses of, 480
    ventricular hypertrophy, 539–543

U

Underlying rhythm, 269
Uniform (unifocal) PVC, 377–378
Unipolar leads, 53, 54

U waves
abnormal, 210, 650
conditions of, and deductive
reasoning algorithm for, 652
defined, 79
inverted, 210, 650
in Nine-Step Process, 73, 79, 650–652
normal characteristics of, 209

V

Vagal maneuvers, 243
Vagus nerve, 31, 32, 33
Valves, heart, 11
Vectors, 504
Ventricles
accessory pathways, 184
anatomy of, 10–11
cardiac output, 24
depolarization and contraction, 29
dysrhythmias originating from, 29,
372–373
regularity and R-R interval, 111–112
repolarization, 30
stroke volume, 24
Ventricular conduction disturbances,
552. See also Bundle branch block
Ventricular diastole, Phase 4, 225
Ventricular dysrhythmias, 370–396
defined, 240
early beats, 164, 166
effects of, 373
escape rhythm, 164, 166–167
non-measurable PR interval and, 191
P wave appearance, 372–373
QRS complex, 373
types of, 240
accelerated idioventricular rhythm,
386–387
asystole, 393–395
idioventricular rhythm, 384–386
polymorphic ventricular
tachycardia, 389–391
premature ventricular complexes
(PVCs), 373–381

pulseless electrical activity, 395–396
ventricular escape beats, 381–383
ventricular fibrillation (VF), 391–393
ventricular tachycardia (VT),
387–389
wide, bizarre-looking QRS complex
of ventricular origin, 163–168
Ventricular escape, 232
Ventricular escape beats, 381–383
appearance of, 382–383
causes of, 382
description of, 381
effects of, 382
treatment of, 383
Ventricular fibrillation, 104
absent QRS complex, 169–170
appearance of, 392
causes of, 391
characteristics of, 169
description of, 391
early beats and, 118, 234
effects of, 392
as form of reentry, 238
tachycardia and, 232
treatment of, 392–393
Ventricular fibrosis, ST segment
elevation, 203
Ventricular flutter, 389
Ventricular hypertrophy, 539–543
causes of, 534
changes on ECG and, 535
defined, 534
QRS complex, 539–541
right, 539–541
secondary repolarization
abnormalities, 543
ST segment, 543
ST segment depression, 203
ST segment elevation, 203
tall and low amplitude QRS complex
and, 159
T wave changes, 543
using ECG to diagnose, 535, 539
Ventricular muscle, action
potential of, 225

Ventricular preexcitation, 184
QRS complex, 162–163
Ventricular quadrigeminy, 378
Ventricular rates, counting, 103–104
Ventricular repolarization, prolonged
QT interval, 207
Ventricular standstill, 395
Ventricular tachycardia (VT), 233, 378,
387–389
appearance of, 389
causes of, 388
description of, 387
effects of, 389
polymorphic, 389–391
QRS complex, 167–168
slow VT, 389
spindle-shaped rhythm, 168
torsades de pointes, 389–390
treatment for, 389
ventricular flutter, 389
Ventricular trigeminy, 378
Vertical heart, 516
Vertical lines on ECG paper, 60
V leads, 56–57, 487–499
Voltage-gated channel, 17

W

Wandering atrial pacemaker
appearance of, 300–301
causes of, 300
description of, 300
effects of, 300
treatment for, 301
Wandering baseline, 63
Wenckebach, 421
Wide complex-irregular tachycardia,
233
Wide complex-regular tachycardia, 233
Wide complex tachycardia of unknown
origin, 306
Wide complex-unknown origin
tachycardia, 233
Wolff-Parkinson-White syndrome,
302, 347